A Handbook of

HUMAN RESOURCE MANAGEMENT PRACTICE

A Handbook of

HUMAN RESOURCE MANAGEMENT PRACTICE

8th edition

Michael Armstrong

KOGAN
PAGE

First published as *A Handbook of Personnel Management Practice* in 1977
Second edition 1984
Third edition 1988
Fourth edition 1991
Fifth edition 1995
Reprinted in 1997
Sixth edition 1996
Reprinted 1997
Reprinted 1998 (twice)
Seventh edition published as *A Handbook of Human Resource Management Practice* in 1999
Reprinted 1999
Reprinted 2000
Eighth edition 2001

Kogan Page Limited
120 Pentonville Road
London N1 9JN
UK

Kogan Page US
22 Broad Street
Milford CT 06460
USA

British Library Cataloguing in Publication Data

A CIP record for this book is available from the British Library.

ISBN 0 7494 3393 0

Typeset by Jean Cussons Typesetting, Diss, Norfolk
Printed and bound in Great Britain by The Bath Press, Bath

Contents

PART I   THE FOUNDATIONS OF HUMAN RESOURCE MANAGEMENT

PART VI   HUMAN RESOURCE MANAGEMENT PROCESSES

PART VII   EMPLOYEE RESOURCING

PART VIII   PERFORMANCE MANAGEMENT

PART IX   HUMAN RESOURCE DEVELOPMENT

APPENDICES

List of figures

List of tables

About the author

Michael Armstrong is an honours graduate in economics from the London School of Economics, a Companion of the Chartered Institute of Personnel and Development and a Fellow of the Institute of Management Consultancy.

This book is largely based on Michael Armstrong's hands-on experience as a personnel practitioner, initially in the engineering industry, specializing in industrial relations, and then in the engineering and food industries as an employee development specialist.

For 12 years he was an executive director with responsibility for HR in a large publishing firm and for a further 10 years he headed up the HR consultancy division of Coopers & Lybrand. He now practises as an independent consultant. This experience has been supplemented recently by a number of research projects carried out on behalf of the Chartered Institute of Personnel and Development. These covered the personnel function's contribution to the bottom line, strategic HRM, incentive pay, job evaluation, team rewards, broad-banded pay structures, and performance management.

His publications for Kogan Page include *Reward Management*, *Performance Management*, *How to Be an Even Better Manager*, *A Handbook of Management Techniques* and *Managing People*.

Foreword

This new edition incorporates the considerable amount of new thinking and research that has taken place in the field of human resource management. This includes:

- the concept of HRM itself;
- the concept of strategic HRM;
- the theory of intellectual capital and its practical implications;
- the contribution made by HR to organizational performance;
- knowledge management practices;
- the concepts of organizational learning and the learning organization;
- new developments in reward management, especially in pay structures;
- the changing industrial relations scene.

The handbook is divided into the following parts:

1. An overview of the foundations of human resource management, covering the concepts of HRM, strategic HRM and intellectual capital theory.
2. An examination of the practice of HR management with particular reference to the roles of HR practitioners and the HR function, the contribution made by the function to organizational success, methods of evaluating that contribution and a survey of international HRM.

3. A review of the theoretical framework which provides the basis for good people management practices including the factors affecting individual behaviour, motivation theory, the significance of commitment, how organizations function and the important area of organizational culture.

4. An examination of the main considerations affecting work and employment, including a description of the nature of work, the factors affecting the employment relationship, and the key concept of the psychological contract.

5. A description of the processes used in organization design and development and job and role design.

6. A description of the major HR processes that affect most people management practices, namely, HR policies, competence-related HR management, knowledge management and job and role analysis.

7. An examination of the major aspects of resourcing, starting with an overview of human resource planning and then exploring techniques of recruitment and selection and approaches to dealing with matters concerning introduction to and release from the organization.

8. A review of the main features of performance management processes, including 360-degree feedback.

9. A survey of the wide field of human resource development, starting with an overview of strategic HRD and continuing with an analysis of organizational and individual learning processes, training, management development and career management.

10. A description of each of the major aspects of reward systems covering job evaluation, market rate analysis, pay structures, contingent pay, rewarding special groups (directors, expatriates and sales staff), pensions and benefits, and managing the system.

11. A review of the employee relations scene covering the framework, processes, negotiating skills, involvement and participation and communications.

12. A description of health and safety and welfare management processes.

13. A final section covering employment practices, HR procedures and HR information systems.

Part I

The foundations of human resource management

The first two chapters of this part contain general analyses of the concepts of human resource management (HRM) and strategic human resource management (SHRM) as a foundation for the more detailed descriptions of HRM policies, processes and practice contained in other parts of this handbook. A review of intellectual capital theory and its practical implications is given in the third chapter, as this theory underpins many of the approaches to HRM discussed later.

1

Human resource management

The concept of human resource management is described in this chapter under the following headings:

- definition of HRM;
- aims of HRM;
- versions of HRM;
- the initial development of the HRM concept;
- further developments to the HRM concept;
- reservations about HRM;
- HRM and personnel management;
- reactions to HRM;
- key HRM activities;
- key requirements of HRM;
- the HRM context;
- conclusions.

HUMAN RESOURCE MANAGEMENT DEFINED

Human resource management (HRM) can be defined as a strategic and coherent approach to the management of an organization's most valued assets: the people working there who individually and collectively contribute to the achievement of its objectives. The main characteristics of the HRM approach are:

● It meets the need for a strategic approach to human resource management which achieves 'fit' between the business and the HR strategy.
● A comprehensive and coherent approach to the provision of mutually supporting employment policies and practices is adopted, through the development of integrated HR policies and practices (configuration or bundling).
● The importance of gaining commitment to the organization's mission and values is stressed – it is 'commitment-orientated'.
● Employees are seen as assets or human capital to be invested in through the provision of learning opportunities and the development of a 'learning organization'.
● Human resources are viewed as a source of competitive advantage in line with the concept of resource-based strategy (see Chapter 2).
● The approach to employee relations is unitarist not pluralist: it is believed that employees share the same interests as employers, rather than that these interests will not necessarily coincide.
● The performance and delivery of HRM is a line management responsibility.

The early advocates of HRM believed that organizations should move away from 'the bureaucracy of personnel management to the apparent flexibility and responsiveness of HRM' (Hope-Hailey *et al*, 1998).

AIMS OF HRM

The overall purpose of human resource management is to ensure that the organization is able to achieve success through people. As Ulrich and Lake (1990) have remarked, 'HRM systems can be the source of organizational capabilities that allow firms to learn and capitalize on new opportunities'. Specifically, HRM is concerned with achieving objectives in the areas summarized below.

Resourcing and development

Ensure that the organization obtains and retains the skilled, committed and well-motivated workforce it needs. This means taking steps to assess and satisfy future people needs and to enhance and develop the inherent capacities of people – their contributions, potential and employability – by providing learning and continuous development opportunities. It can also involve the development of high performance work systems which enhance flexibility and include 'rigorous recruitment and selection procedures, performance-contingent incentive compensation systems, and management development and training activities linked to the needs of the business' (Becker *et al*, 1997).

Valuing employees

Enhance motivation and commitment by introducing policies and processes which ensure that people are valued and rewarded for what they do and achieve and for the levels of skill and competence they reach.

Relationships

Create a climate in which productive and harmonious relationships can be maintained through partnerships between management and employees and where teamwork can flourish. Introduce high commitment management practices which recognize that employees are valued stakeholders in the organization and help to develop a climate of cooperation and mutual trust. Help the organization to balance and adapt to the needs of its stakeholders (owners, government bodies or trustees, management, employees, customers, suppliers and the public at large). Manage a diverse workforce, taking into account individual and group differences in employment needs, work style and aspirations. Take steps to ensure that equal opportunities are available to all and that an ethical approach to managing employees is adopted based on concern for people, fairness and transparency.

These aims are ambitious and could be regarded as mere rhetoric. The research conducted by Gratton *et al* (1999) found that there was generally a wide gap between this sort of rhetoric and reality. Managements may start with good intentions to do some or all of these things but the realization of them – 'theory in use' – is often very difficult. This arises because of contextual and process problems: other business priorities, short-termism, lack of support from line managers, an inadequate infrastructure of supporting processes, lack of resources, resistance to change and a climate in which employees do not trust management, whatever the latter say.

VERSIONS OF HRM

As described above, the concept of HRM could be regarded as a philosophy governing how employees should be treated *in the interests of the organization*. But this philosophy can be applied in many different ways and there is no single model which can be used to describe HRM. Storey (1989) distinguished between the hard and soft versions.

Hard HRM

The hard approach to human resource management emphasizes the quantitative, calculative and business-strategic aspects of managing the headcount resource in as 'rational' a way as for any other economic factor. It adopts a business-orientated philosophy which focuses on the need to manage people in ways which will obtain added value from them and thus achieve competitive advantage. It regards people as human capital from which a return can be obtained by investing judicially in their development. Fombrun, Tichy and Devanna (1984) quite explicitly presented workers as another key resource which managers use to achieve competitive advantage for their companies. The concept of intellectual capital as described in Chapter 3 provides theoretical underpinning for this belief. Guest (1999a) comments that 'The drive to adopt HRM is…based on the business case of a need to respond to an external threat from increasing competition. It is a philosophy that appeals to managements who are striving to increase competitive advantage and appreciate that to do this they must invest in human resources as well as new technology.' He also remarked that HRM 'reflects a long-standing capitalist tradition in which the worker is regarded as a commodity'.

Soft HRM

The soft model of HRM traces its roots to the human-relations school; it emphasizes communication, motivation and leadership. As described by Storey (1989) it involves 'treating employees as valued assets, a source of competitive advantage through their commitment, adaptability and high quality (of skills, performance and so on)'. It therefore views employees, in the words of Guest (1999a), as means rather than objects. The soft approach to HRM emphasizes the need to gain the commitment – the 'hearts and minds' – of employees through involvement, communications and other methods of developing a high-commitment, high-trust organization. Attention is also drawn to the key role of organizational culture.

The focus is on 'mutuality': a belief that the interests of management and employees can, indeed should, coincide. It is therefore a unitarist approach. In the words of Gennard and Judge (1997), organizations are assumed to be 'harmonious and integrated, all employees sharing the organizational goals and working as members of one team'.

It has, however, been observed by Truss (1999) that 'even if the rhetoric of HRM is soft, the reality is often hard, with the interests of the organization prevailing over those of the individual'. And research carried out by Gratton *et al* (1999) identified a mixture of hard and soft HRM approaches in the eight organizations they studied. This suggested to the researchers that the distinction between hard and soft HRM was not as precise as some commentators have implied.

THE DEVELOPMENT OF THE HRM CONCEPT

Some aspects of the basic philosophy of 'soft HRM' can be traced back to the writings of Douglas McGregor (1960) who, as mentioned by Truss (1999), even used the terminology 'hard' and 'soft' to characterize forms of management control. McGregor's theory X essentially describes the 'control' model of management referred to by Walton (1985b), while McGregor's theory Y emphasises the importance of integrating the needs of the organization and those of the individual – the principle of mutual commitment, again expressed by Walton. The full concept of HRM emerged in the mid-1980s in company with the efforts of the popularist writers on management in that decade, including Pascale and Athos (1981) and Peters and Waterman (1982), who produced lists of the attributes which they claimed characterized successful companies. These 'school of excellence' writers may have exerted some influence on management thinking about the need for strong cultures and commitment (two features of the HRM philosophy) but, as Guest (1993) has commented, they were 'right enough to be dangerously wrong'.

It was during the 1980s that the first models of HRM were produced (christened by Boxall, 1992, as the matching model and the Harvard framework). Best practice (outcomes) and contingency (strategic fit) models have also been identified by Hope-Hailey *et al* (1998).

MODELS OF HRM

The matching model of HRM

One of the first explicit statements of the HRM concept was made by the Michigan School (Fombrun *et al*, 1984). They held that HR systems and the organization structure should be managed in a way which is congruent with organizational strategy (hence the name 'matching model'). They further explained that there is a human resource cycle (an adaptation of which is illustrated in Figure 1.1) which consists of four generic processes or functions that are performed in all organizations. These are:

- *selection* – matching available human resources to jobs;
- *appraisal* – (performance management);
- *rewards* – 'the reward system is one of the most under-utilized and mishandled managerial tools for driving organizational performance'; it must reward short as well as long-term achievements, bearing in mind that 'business must perform in the present to succeed in the future';
- *development* – developing high quality employees.

Figure 1.1 The HR cycle
(Adapted from Fombrun *et al*, 1984)

The Harvard framework

The other founding fathers of HRM were the Harvard School of Beer *et al* (1984) who developed what Boxall (1992) calls the 'Harvard framework'. This framework is based on the belief that the problems of historical personnel management can only be solved:

> … when general managers develop a viewpoint of how they wish to see employees involved in and developed by the enterprise, and of what HRM policies and practices may achieve those goals. Without either a central philosophy or a strategic vision – which can be provided *only* by general managers – HRM is likely to remain a set of independent activities, each guided by its own practice tradition.

Beer and his colleagues believed that 'Today, many pressures are demanding a broader, more comprehensive and more strategic perspective with regard to the organization's human resources'. These pressures have created a need for 'A longer-term perspective in managing people and consideration of people as potential assets rather than merely a variable cost'. They were the first to underline the HRM tenet that it belongs to line managers. They also stated that 'Human resource management involves all management decisions and action that affect the nature of the relationship between the organization and its employees – its human resources.'

The Harvard school suggested that HRM had two characteristic features:

● line managers accept more responsibility for ensuring the alignment of competitive strategy and personnel policies;
● personnel has the mission of setting policies that govern how personnel activities are developed and implemented in ways that make them more mutually reinforcing.

Figure 1.2 The Harvard framework for HRM
(Source: M Beer, B Spector, P Lawrence, D Quinn Mills and R Walton, *Managing Human Assets*, Free Press, New York, 1984)

The Harvard framework as modelled by Beer *et al* is shown in Figure 1.2. According to Boxall (1992) the advantages of this model are that it:

● incorporates recognition of a range of stakeholder interests;
● recognizes the importance of 'trade-offs', either explicitly or implicitly, between the interests of owners and those of employees as well as between various interest groups;
● widens the context of HRM to include 'employee influence', the organization of work and the associated question of supervisory style;
● acknowledges a broad range of contextual influences on management's choice of strategy, suggesting a meshing of both product-market and socio-cultural logics;
● emphasizes strategic choice – it is not driven by situational or environmental determinism.

The Harvard model has exerted considerable influence over the theory and practice of HRM, particularly in its emphasis on the fact that HRM is the concern of management in general rather than the personnel function in particular.

Walton (1985b), also of Harvard, expanded the concept by emphasizing the importance of commitment and mutuality as follows:

> The new HRM model is composed of policies that promote mutuality – mutual goals, mutual influence, mutual respect, mutual rewards, mutual responsibility. The theory is that policies of mutuality will elicit commitment which in turn will yield both better economic performance and greater human development.

This commitment model of human resource management is associated with the concept of soft HRM referred to earlier.

The best practice model

The best practice or 'outcome' model, echoing Walton, emphasizes commitment rather than compliance and advocates processes of culture management to achieve cultural control.

The contingency model

The contingency model concentrates on the achievement of fit between business and HR strategies.

FURTHER DEVELOPMENTS IN THE CONCEPT OF HRM

A number of academic commentators in the UK have developed the original American concept of HRM as described below.

David Guest

David Guest (1987, 1989a, 1989b, 1991) has taken the Harvard model and expanded it by defining four policy goals which he believes can be used as testable propositions:

1. *Strategic integration* – the ability of the organization to integrate HRM issues into its strategic plans, ensure that the various aspects of HRM cohere, and provide for line managers to incorporate an HRM perspective into their decision-making.
2. *High commitment* – behavioural commitment to pursue agreed goals, and attitudinal commitment reflected in a strong identification with the enterprise.
3. *High quality* – this refers to all aspects of managerial behaviour which bear directly on the quality of goods and services provided, including the management of employees and investment in high-quality employees.
4. *Flexibility* – functional flexibility and the existence of an adaptable organization structure with the capacity to manage innovation.

Guest believes that the driving force behind HRM is 'the pursuit of competitive advantage in the market place through provision of high-quality goods and services, through competitive pricing linked to high productivity and through the capacity swiftly to innovate and manage change in response to changes in the market place or to breakthroughs in research and development'. He considers that HRM values are:

- *unitarist* to the extent that they assume no underlying and inevitable differences of interest between management and workers;
- *individualistic* in that they emphasize the individual-organization linkage in preference to operating through group and representative systems.

Guest has also asserted that HRM has been 'talked up' and its impact has been on attitudes rather than behaviour.

Karen Legge

Karen Legge (1989) considers that the common themes of the typical definitions of HRM are that:

> Human resource policies should be integrated with strategic business planning and used to reinforce an appropriate (or change an inappropriate) organizational culture, that human resources are valuable and a source of competitive advantage, that they may be tapped most effectively by mutually consistent policies that promote commitment and which, as a consequence, foster a willingness in employees to act flexibly in the interests of the 'adaptive organization's' pursuit of excellence.

In 1995 she noted that HRM policies are adapted to drive business values and are modified in the light of changing business objectives and conditions. She describes this process as 'thinking pragmatism' and suggests that evidence indicates more support for the hard versions of HRM than the soft version.

In 1998, Karen Legge defined the 'hard' model of HRM as a process emphasizing 'the close integration of human resource policies with business strategy which regards employees as a resource to be managed in the same rational way as any other resource being exploited for maximum return'. In contrast, the soft version of HRM sees employees as 'valued assets and as a source of competitive advantage through their commitment, adaptability and high level of skills and performance'. She regards the three key features of HRM as first, various forms of flexibility, second, team-building, empowerment and involvement, and third, cultural management.

Chris Hendry and Andrew Pettigrew

Hendry and Pettigrew (1990) play down the prescriptive element of the Harvard model and extend the analytical elements. As pointed out by Boxall (1992), such an approach rightly avoids labelling HRM as a single form and advances more slowly by proceeding more analytically. It is argued by Hendry and Pettigrew that 'better descriptions of structures and strategy-making in complex organizations, and of frameworks for understanding them, are an essential underpinning for HRM'. They believe that as a movement, HRM expressed a mission, to achieve a turnaround in industry: 'HRM was thus in a real sense heavily normative from the outset: it provided a diagnosis and proposed solutions'. They also suggested that 'What HRM did at this point was to provide a label to wrap around some of the observable changes, while providing a focus for challenging deficiencies – in attitudes, scope, coherence, and direction – of existing personnel management'.

John Purcell

John Purcell (1993) thinks that 'the adoption of HRM is both a product of and a cause of a significant concentration of power in the hands of management', while the widespread use 'of the language of HRM, if not its practice, is a combination of its intuitive appeal to managers and, more importantly, a response to the turbulence of product and financial markets'. He asserts that HRM is about the rediscovery of management prerogative.

Purcell considers that HRM policies and practices, when applied within a firm as a break from the past, are often associated with words such as commitment, competence, empowerment, flexibility, culture, performance, assessment, reward, teamwork, involvement, cooperation, harmonization, quality and learning. But 'the danger of descriptions of HRM as modern best-management practice is that they stereotype the past and idealize the future'.

Keith Sisson

Keith Sisson (1990) suggests that there are four main features increasingly associated with HRM:

1. There is a stress on the integration of personnel policies both with one another and with business planning more generally.
2. The locus of responsibility for personnel management no longer resides with (or is 'relegated to') specialist managers.
3. The focus shifts from manager–trade union relations to management–employee relations, from collectivism to individualism.
4. There is a stress on commitment and the exercise of initiative, with managers now donning the role of 'enabler', 'empowerer' and 'facilitator'.

John Storey

John Storey (1989) believes that HRM can be regarded as a 'set of interrelated policies with an ideological and philosophical underpinning'. He suggests four aspects which constitute the *meaningful* version of HRM:

● a particular constellation of beliefs and assumptions;
● a strategic thrust informing decisions about people management;
● the central involvement of line managers;
● reliance upon a set of 'levers' to shape the employment relationship: these are different from those used under proceduralist and joint regulative regimes typical of classical industrial relations systems.

He has written that: 'In stereotyped form it (HRM) appears capable of making good each of the main shortcomings of personnel management'. The HR function becomes recognized as a central business concern, and training and development assumes a higher profile: 'Its performance and delivery are integrated into line management: the aim shifts from merely securing compliance to the more ambitious one of winning commitment.'

The concept locates HRM policy formulation firmly at the strategic level and insists that a characteristic of HRM is its internally coherent approach.

ASSIMILATION OF HRM

Personnel managers are increasingly being called human resource managers. This may often mean that it is only the name that has changed, but by a process of osmosis, much of the philosophy of HRM seems to be spreading into the day-to-day thinking and practice of personnel professionals. The debate that raged during the second phase of development referred to above no longer seems relevant to these practitioners. They simply get on with doing it; often imperfectly because of organizational constraints, but many are trying hard.

RESERVATIONS ABOUT HRM

On the face of it, HRM has much to offer, at least to management. But strong reservations have been expressed about it by many academics and one practitioner, Alan Fowler (1987). These reservations can be summed up as follows:

- HRM does not pass muster either as a reputable theory or as an alternative and better form of personnel management.
- HRM is, in David Guest's (1991) words, an 'optimistic but ambiguous concept', it is all hype and hope.
- Even if HRM does exist as a distinct process, which many doubt, it is full of contradictions, manipulative, and, according to the Cardiff school (Blyton and Turnbull, 1992), downright pernicious.
- The 'prized goals' of HRM remain unproven at best, and unfulfilled at worst (Mabey *et al*, 1998).

HRM as a theory

Noon (1992) has commented that HRM has serious deficiencies as a theory:

> It is built with concepts and propositions, but the associated variables and hypotheses are not made explicit. It is too comprehensive... If HRM is labelled a 'theory' it raises expectations about its ability to describe and predict.

HRM is simplistic

As Alan Fowler (1987) has written:

> The HRM message to top management tends to be beguilingly simple. Don't bother too much about the content or techniques of personnel management, it says. Just manage the context. Get out from behind your desk, bypass the hierarchy, and go and talk to people. That way you will unlock an enormous potential for improved performance.

HRM as rhetoric

The HRM rhetoric presents it as an all or nothing process which is ideal for all organizations, despite the evidence that different business environments require different approaches. This produces the gap between rhetoric and reality referred to (frequently) by Gratton *et al* (1999).

HRM is over-ambitious and impractical

HRM can be accused of promising more than it can deliver. As Mabey *et al* (1998) comment, 'the heralded outcomes (of HRM) are almost without exception unrealistically high'. They imply that management has either been conned by consultants offering quick fix solutions or is indulging in rhetoric influenced by 'extra-organizational values' such as excellence, flexibility, quality and customer focus.

To put the concept of HRM into practice involves strategic integration, developing a coherent and consistent set of employment policies, and gaining commitment. This requires high levels of determination and competence at all levels of management and a strong and effective HR function staffed by business-orientated people. It may be difficult to meet these criteria, especially when the proposed HRM culture conflicts with the established corporate culture and traditional managerial attitudes and behaviour.

It is claimed by some commentators that the development of integrated HR strategies, a central feature of HRM, is difficult if not impossible in companies which lack any real sense of strategic direction. Business strategies, they say, where they *are* formulated, tend to be dominated by product-market imperatives, leading to product and systems developments. To support these, priority is given, understandably enough, to obtaining financial resources and maintaining a sound financial base. Human resource considerations often come off a poor second.

HRM and industrial relations

As Fowler (1987) has stated:

> At the heart of the concept is the complete identification of employees with the aims and values of the business – employee involvement but on the company's terms. Power in the HRM system remains very firmly in the hands of the employer. Is it really possible to claim full mutuality when at the end of the day the employer can decide unilaterally to close the company or sell it to someone else?

The morality of HRM

In spite of all their protestations to the contrary, the academics who have advocated HRM could be seen to be introducing alternative and more insidious forms of 'control by compliance' when they emphasize the need for employees to be committed to doing what the organization wants them to do. As Legge (1989) pointed out:

> In its emphasis on 'strong culture', in theory HRM is able to achieve a cohesive work-force, but without the attendant dilemma of creating potentially dysfunctional solidarity. For a 'strong culture' is aimed at uniting employees through a shared set of managerially sanctioned values ('quality', 'service', 'innovation' etc) that assume an identification of employee and employer interests. Such co-optation – through cultural management of course – reinforces the intention that autonomy will be exercised 'responsibly', ie in management's interests.

Legge (1998) summed up her reservations about the morality of HRM as follows:

> Sadly, in a world of intensified competition and scarce resources, it seems inevitable that, as employees are used as means to an end, there will be some who will lose out. They may even be in the majority. For these people, the soft version of HRM may be an irrelevancy, while the hard version is likely to be an uncomfortable experience.

She contends that managements only go in for HRM out of self-interest.

HRM is accused by many academics of being manipulative. Willmott (1993) remarks that HRM operates as a form of insidious control. It preaches mutuality but the reality is that behind the rhetoric it exploits workers. It is, they say, a wolf in sheep's clothing (Keenoy, 1990a). They note that chief executives with a mission for HRM tend to adapt the principle of 'what is good for General Motors is good for America' to that of 'what is good for the business must be good for everyone in it' – in other words, like an apple a day, HRM is good for you. Such executives could be right, but not always, and the forces of internal persuasion and propaganda may have to be deployed to get people to accept values with which they may not be in accord and which in any case may be against their interests.

Essentially, the accusation as formulated by Legge (1998) is that HRM treats employees as means to an end. However, it could be argued that if organizations exist to achieve ends, which they clearly do, and if those ends can only be achieved through people, which is clearly the case, the concern of managements for commitment and performance from those people is not unnatural and is not attributable to the concept of HRM – it existed in the good old days of personnel management before HRM was invented. What matters is *how* managements treat people as ends and *what* managements provide in return. And the philosophy of HRM can provide positive guidance on approaches to managing people in, for example, the concept of mutual commitment. It could also be argued that changes that have been taking place over the last decade or so in managing people have taken place because of changes in the environment in which organizations have been operating, not because managements seized upon the HRM concept as a rationalization for exploiting workers. Many employers have been doing this for years – they did not need to invoke HRM as their justification, even if they had heard of it.

Contradictions in HRM

Karen Legge (1989) believes that the concept of HRM contains the following internal contradictions:

- the complementarity and consistency of 'mutuality' policies designed to generate commitment, flexibility, quality etc;
- problems over commitment: as Guest (1987) asked, 'commitment to what?';
- HRM appears torn between preaching the virtues of individualism (concentration on the individual) and collectivism (team work etc);
- there is a potential tension between the development of a strong corporate culture and employees' ability to respond flexibly and adaptively.

Guest (1999a) has suggested that there are two contradictory concerns about HRM. The first as formulated by Legge (1995, 1998) is that while management rhetoric may express concern for workers, the reality is harsher. And Keenoy (1997) complains that 'The real puzzle about HRMism is how, in the face of such apparently overwhelming critical "refutation", it has secured such influence and institutional presence.'

Other writers, however, simply claim that HRM does not work. Scott (1994) for example, finds that both management and workers are captives of their history and find it very difficult to let go of their traditional adversarial orientations.

But these contentions are contradictory. Guest (1999a) remarks that 'It is difficult to treat HRM as a major threat (though what it is a threat to is not always made explicit) deserving of serious critical analysis while at the same time claiming that it is not practised or is ineffective'.

HRM AND PERSONNEL MANAGEMENT

In the words of David Guest (1989b), 'Personnel and HRM: can you tell the difference?' An earlier answer to this question was made by Armstrong (1987):

> HRM is regarded by some personnel managers as just a set of initials or old wine in new bottles. It could indeed be no more and no less than another name for personnel management, but as usually perceived, at least it has the virtue of emphasizing the virtue of treating people as a key resource, the management of which is the direct concern of top management as part of the strategic planning processes of the enterprise. Although there is nothing new in the idea, insufficient attention has been paid to it in many organizations. The new bottle or label can help to overcome that deficiency.

Similarities

It can be argued that the similarities between personnel management and HRM are as follows:

- Personnel management strategies, like HRM strategies, flow from the business strategy.
- Personnel management, like HRM, recognizes that line managers are responsible for managing people. The personnel function provides the necessary advice and support services to enable managers to carry out their responsibilities.
- The values of personnel management and at least the 'soft' version of HRM are identical with regard to 'respect for the individual', balancing organizational and individual needs, and developing people to achieve their maximum level of competence both for their own satisfaction and to facilitate the achievement of organizational objectives.
- Both personnel management and HRM recognize that one of their most essential functions is that of matching people to ever-changing organizational requirements: placing and developing the right people in and for the right jobs.
- The same range of selection, competence analysis, performance management, training, management development and reward management techniques are used both in HRM and personnel management.

● Personnel management, like the 'soft' version of HRM, attaches importance to the processes of communication and participation within an employee relations system.

Differences

The differences between personnel management and human resource management can be seen as a matter of emphasis and approach rather than one of substance. Or, as Hendry and Pettigrew (1990) put it, HRM can be perceived as a 'perspective on personnel management and not personnel management itself'.

From her review of the literature, Legge (1989) has identified three features which seem to distinguish HRM and personnel management:

1. Personnel management is an activity aimed primarily at non-managers whereas HRM is less clearly focused but is certainly more concerned with managerial staff.
2. HRM is much more of an integrated line management activity whereas personnel management seeks to influence line management.
3. HRM emphasizes the importance of senior management being involved in the management of culture whereas personnel management has always been rather suspicious of organization development and related unitarist, social-psychologically orientated ideas.

The strategic nature of HRM is another difference commented on by a number of people who, in effect, dismiss the idea that traditional personnel management was ever really involved in the strategic areas of business. Hendry and Pettigrew (1990), for example, believe that the strategic character of HRM is distinctive.

Perhaps the most significant difference is that the concept of HRM is based on a management and business orientated philosophy. It is claimed to be a central, senior management-driven strategic activity which is developed, owned and delivered by management as a whole to promote the interests of the organization which it serves. It purports to be a holistic approach concerned with the total interests of the organization: the interests of the members of the organization are recognized but subordinated to those of the enterprise. Hence the importance attached to strategic integration and strong cultures, which flow from top management's vision and leadership, and which require people who will be committed to the strategy, who will be adaptable to change, and who will fit the culture. By implication, as Guest (1991) says: 'HRM is too important to be left to personnel managers'.

HRM could be described as an approach to rather than as an alternative to traditional personnel management. When comparing HRM and personnel management more similarities emerge than differences. However, concepts such as strategic integration, culture management, commitment, total quality, and investing in human capital, together with a unitary philosophy (the interests of management and employees coincide), are essential parts of the HRM model. And this model fits the way in which organizations have to do business and manage their resources in the environments in which they now exist. This is why, in spite of the reservations expressed about HRM by academics, the term HR is increasingly being used in businesses as an alternative to personnel management. This is because more and more people feel that it is in tune with the realities of organizational life.

Human resource management has been described as 'high-concept personnel management' (Armstrong, 1996). Some commentators (Legge, 1989, 1995; Keenoy, 1990a; Sisson, 1990; Storey, 1993; Hope-Hailey *et al*, 1998) have highlighted the revolutionary nature of HRM. The latter mention the 'rhetoric' of HR practitioners, but should more accurately have referred to the rhetoric of the HR academics who have been debating what HRM means, how different it is, whether or not it is a good thing, indeed whether or not it exists, endlessly and unproductively. Practitioners have pressed on regardless, in the justified belief that what the academics were writing about had little relevance to their day to day lives as they wrestled with the realities of organizational life. They did not suddenly see the light in the 1980s and change their ways, for better or for worse. The true personnel or HR professionals just kept on doing what they had always done but tried to do it better. They took note of the much wider range of publications about personnel practices and the information on so-called 'best practice' provided by management consultants and conference organizers, and they learned from the case studies emanating from the research conducted by the burgeoning academic institutions. They also recognized that to succeed in an increasingly competitive world they had to become more professional, and they were encouraged to do so by bodies such as the then Institute of Personnel Management. They took account of new ideas and implemented new practices because they were persuaded that they were appropriate, not because they fitted into any sort of HRM philosophy. As Armstrong (2000b) pointed out, 'HRM cannot be blamed or given credit for changes that were taking place anyway. For example, it is often alleged to have inspired a move from pluralism to unitarism in industrial relations. But newspaper production was moved from Fleet Street to Wapping by Murdoch, not because he had read a book about HRM but as a means of breaking the print unions' control.'

Conclusions?

A number of commentators have denied that there is any significant difference between the concepts of personnel management and HRM. Torrington (1989) commented that 'Personnel management has grown through assimilating a number of additional emphases to produce an even richer combination of experience… HRM is no revolution but a further dimension to a multi-faceted role.'

The conclusion based on interviews with HR and personnel directors reached by Gennard and Kelly (1994) on this issue was that 'it is six of one and half a dozen of the other and it is a sterile debate'. All that seems to have emerged from this debate is a distinction without a difference. As Lowry (1990) remarked when he was President of the Institute of Personnel Management:

> Personnel work has always included strategic matters and the present emphasis on strategic issues merely represents another change in the environment to which the personnel manager adapts by strengthening the competence required for the new situation. Human resource management is just the continuing process of personnel management – it is not different.

Lowry's point is significant. It is the context within which people are managed that is changing, and personnel management has had to re-position itself in the ever-changing environment of global competition, new technology, and new methods of working and organizing work. In the private sector the mantras are sustainable competitive advantage, added value, core competencies and strategic capability. In the public sector the driving force is 'best value', while in the voluntary sector, charities are saying, 'we may not be businesses but we have to be business-like'. In this situation personnel management has had to become more strategic, but this is simply building on what effective personnel directors were already doing in the 1970s and 1980s. As Don Beattie commented in 1998 when he was Personnel Director of STC plc (cited by Armstrong, 1989): 'Personnel directors are paid to know what business they are in, to know where it is going, and to ensure that the input to get there is available from a human resourcing and organizational capability point of view.'

REACTIONS TO HRM

Much of the hostility to HRM expressed by a number of academics is based on the belief that it is hostile to the interests of workers, ie, that it is managerialist. Research conducted by Guest and Conway (1997) covering a stratified random sample of 1,000 workers established that a notably high level of HRM was found to be in place. This contradicts the view that management has tended to 'talk up' the adoption of HRM practices. The HRM characteristics covered by the survey included the opportunity to express grievances and raise personal concerns on such matters as opportunities for training and development, communications about business issues, single status, effective systems for dealing with bullying and harassment at work, making jobs interesting and varied, promotion from within, involvement programmes, no compulsory redundancies, performance-related pay, profit sharing and the use of attitude surveys. The reports of workers on outcomes showed that a higher number of HR practices was associated with higher ratings of fairness, trust and management's delivery of their promises. Those experiencing more HR activities also felt more secure in and more satisfied with their jobs. Motivation was significantly higher for those working in organizations where more HR practices were in place. In summary, as commented by Guest (1999b), it appears that workers like their experience of HRM. These findings appear to contradict the 'radical critique' view produced by academics such as Mabey *et al* (1998) that HRM has been ineffectual, pernicious (ie managerialist) or both. Some of those who adopt this stance tend to dismiss favourable reports from workers about HRM on the grounds that they have been brainwashed by management. But there is no evidence to support this view.

However, Gratton *et al* (1999) are convinced on the basis of their research that there is 'a disjunction between rhetoric and reality in the area of human resource management between HRM theory and HRM practice, between what the HR function says it is doing and that practice as perceived by employers, and between what senior management believes to be the role of the HR function, and the role it actually plays'. In their conclusions they refer to the 'hyperbole and rhetoric of human resource management'. The incessant use of the word 'rhetoric' by these and other academics suggests that there is a deeply held and cynical belief amongst them that managements never mean what they say, or if they do mean it, they don't do anything about it.

KEY HRM ACTIVITIES

The key activities of HRM carried out by both line managers and HR professionals are:

Organization

● *Organization design* – developing an organization which caters for all the activities required, groups them together in a way which encourages integration and cooperation, operates flexibly in response to change, and provides for effective communication and decision making.

- *Job and role design* – deciding on the content and accountabilities of jobs or roles in order to maximize intrinsic motivation and job satisfaction.
- *Organizational development* – stimulating, planning and implementing programmes designed to improve the effectiveness with which the organization functions and adapts to change.

The employment relationship

Improving the quality of the employment relationship by creating a climate of trust, developing a more positive psychological contract.

Knowledge management

Developing processes for capturing and sharing knowledge to enhance organizational learning and performance.

Resourcing

- *Human resource planning* – assessing future people requirements in terms both of numbers and of levels of skill and competence, and formulating and implementing plans to meet those requirements.
- *Recruitment and selection* – obtaining the number and type of people the organization needs.

Performance management

Getting better results from the organization, teams and individuals by measuring and managing performance within agreed frameworks of objectives and competence requirements; assessing and improving performance; identifying and satisfying learning and development needs.

Human resource development

- *Organizational and individual learning* – systematically developing organizational and individual learning processes; providing employees with learning opportunities to develop their capabilities, realize their potential and enhance employability.

- *Management development* – providing learning and development opportunities which will increase the capacity of managers to make a significant contribution to achieving organizational goals.
- *Career management* – planning and developing the careers of people with potential.

Reward management

- *Pay systems* – developing pay structures and systems which are equitable, fair and transparent.
- *Contingent pay* – relating financial rewards to results, competence, contribution, skill and effort.
- *Non-financial rewards* – providing employees with non-financial rewards such as recognition, increased responsibility and the opportunity to achieve and grow.

Employee relations

- *Industrial relations* – managing and maintaining formal and informal relationships with trade unions and their members.
- *Employee involvement and participation* – giving them a voice, sharing information with employees and consulting them on matters of mutual interest.
- *Communications* – creating and transmitting information of interest to employees.

HRM IN CONTEXT

Human resource management processes take place within the context of the internal and external environment of the organization. They will be largely contingent on the environmental factors that affect them.

Contingency theory

Contingency theory tells us that definitions of aims, policies and strategies; lists of activities; and analyses of the role of the HR department are valid only if they are related to the circumstances of the organization. Descriptions in textbooks such as this can be only generalizations which suggest approaches and provide guidelines for action; they cannot be prescriptive in the sense of laying down what should be done.

Contingency theory is essentially about the need to achieve *fit* between what the organization is and wants to become (its strategy, culture, goals, technology, the people it employs and its external environment) and what the organization does (how it is structured, and the processes, procedures, and practices it puts into effect).

Contextual factors

The main contextual factors which influence HR policies and practices are:

Technology

The technology of the business exerts a major influence on the internal environment – how work is organized, managed and carried out. The introduction of new technology may result in considerable changes to systems and processes. Different skills are required, new methods of working are developed. The result may be an extension of the skills base of the organization and its employees, including multiskilling (ensuring that people have a range of skills which enable them to work flexibly on a variety of tasks, often within a team-working environment). But it could result in de-skilling and a reduction in the number of jobs (downsizing).

New technology can therefore present a considerable threat to employees. The world of work has changed in many ways. Knowledge workers are employed in largely computerized offices and laboratories, and technicians work in computer integrated manufacturing systems. They may have to be managed differently from the clerks or machine operators they displace.

The service industries have become predominant and manufacturing is in decline. New work environments such as call centres have become common and teleworking (working from home with a networked computer) is increasing.

Competitive pressures

Global competition in mature production and service sectors is increasing. This is assisted by easily transferable technology and reductions in international trade barriers. Customers are demanding more as new standards are reached through international competition. Organizations are reacting to this competition by becoming 'customer focused', speeding up response times, emphasizing quality and continuous improvement, accelerating the introduction of new technology, operating more flexibly and 'losing cost'.

The pressure has been for businesses to become 'lean and mean', downsizing and cutting out layers of management and supervision. They are reducing permanent staff to a core of essential workers and increasing the use of peripheral workers (sub-contractors, temporary staff) and 'outsourcing' work to external service providers, thus reducing employment costs and enabling the enterprise easily to increase or reduce the numbers available for work in response to fluctuations in the level of business activity. They become the so-called 'flexible firms'. The ultimate development of this process is the 'virtual' firm or corporation, where through the extensive use of information technology a high proportion of marketing and professional staff mainly work from home, only coming into the office on special occasions to occupy their 'hot desks', and spending more time with their customers or clients.

Another popular response to competitive pressures is business process re-engineering (BPR) which examines the process that contains and links those functions together from initiation to completion. It looks at processes in organizations horizontally to establish how they can be integrated more effectively as well as streamlined. It can therefore form the basis for an organizational re-design exercise. From an HR point of view, the outcome of a BPR exercise may well be the need to attract or develop people with new skills as well as pressure for the improvement of teamworking. It also emphasizes the importance of an integrated – a coherent – approach to the development and implementation of HR policies and employment practices. Re-engineering often promises more than it achieves and the human aspects have often been neglected, insufficient attention having been given to the management of change and re-training staff.

Responses affecting people

The responses to the increased use of technology and to economic and competitive pressures have significantly changed the nature of people management in the 1980s and 1990s. The term 'human resource management' simply encapsulates those changes and is not a new approach.

In *People Make the Difference* the Institute of Personnel and Development (1994) suggested that the driving forces of competition were affecting the way in which people are organized and managed as follows:

● decentralization and devolvement of decision-making;
● slimmer and flatter organization structures;
● total quality and lean organization initiatives;
● fewer specialists directly employed;
● the development of a flexible workforce;
● more project-based and cross-functional initiatives and team working;
● empowered rather than command structures;
● greater self-management and responsibility for individuals and teams;
● openness, fairness and partnership in employment relations;

● greater need for managers to develop their interpersonal, team leadership and motivational skills when carrying out their facilitating and co-ordinating roles;
● pressure for everyone to become more customer-orientated;
● emphasis on continuous development to achieve competitive advantage through people.

However, the Employment in Britain Survey as described by Gallie *et al* (1998) provided a different perspective in many respects. The main findings were as follows:

● a rising demand for skills and qualifications which was particularly marked for managerial and professional workers, technical and office staff and skilled manual workers;
● a growth in job insecurity, more so for men than for women;
● an increase in the number of part-time and female workers; the expansion of women's work has been almost entirely an expansion of part-time work (the number of female part-time jobs rose from 3.3 million in 1971 to 5 million in 1995);
● the emergence of human resource management as a philosophy of managing people which emphasized investment in training, the development of commitment; communications and paying for performance;
● a greater emphasis on flexible working to provide for rapid response;
● an associated increase in the number of workers on non-standard contracts (part-time, short-term and the use of self-employed sub-contract workers);
● a reduction in career prospects through promotion as a result of the rise of the flatter organization;
● a reduction in the power of the trade unions, partly because of legislation, but more significantly in numerical terms for structural reasons, ie the decline of large scale manufacturing and the rise of the service industries;
● associated with the decline in the significance of the trade unions, a move towards individualizing the employment relationship with less reliance on collective bargaining;
● little evidence that participation in industry increased with the re-structuring of employment in the last decade;
● a widely prevalent view that the level of strain (tension and fatigue) had increased as a result of the greater intensity of work and long working hours.

The challenge to HRM

Ulrich (1998) points out that, environmental and contextual changes present a number of competitive challenges to organizations which mean that HR has to be involved in helping to build new capabilities. These are set out below.

Globalization requires organizations to move people, ideas, products and information around the world to meet local needs. New and important ingredients must be added to the mix when making strategy: volatile political situations, contentious global trade issues, fluctuating exchange rates and unfamiliar cultures.

Profitability through growth – the drive for revenue growth means that companies must be creative and innovative, and this means encouraging the free flow of information and shared learning among employees.

Technology – the challenge is to make technology a viable, productive part of the work setting.

Intellectual capital – this is the source of competitive advantage for organizations. The challenge is to ensure that firms have the capability to find, assimilate, compensate and retain human capital in the shape of the talented individuals they need who can drive a global organization that is both responsive to its customers and 'the burgeoning opportunities of technology'. They have also to consider how the social capital of the organization – the ways in which people interact – can be developed. Importantly, organizations have to focus on organizational capital – the knowledge they own and how it should be managed.

Change, change and more change – the greatest challenge companies face is adjusting to – indeed, embracing – non-stop change. They must be able to 'learn rapidly and continuously, and take on new strategic imperatives faster and more comfortably'.

CONCLUSIONS

The range of contextual factors mentioned above, the lessons from contingency theory and the information available on the considerable variations between HR practices in organizations indicate that there is no such thing as a universal model of HRM. When comparing the concepts of HRM and personnel management all that happens is the production of distinctions without differences. As David Guest (1989a) has written, 'The HRM model is just one among a variety of forms of personnel management, and for some companies it may not be the most viable'. It can be argued, however, that one of the defining aspects of HRM is its strategic focus and, as expressed in the concept of strategic HRM, this is discussed in the next chapter.

HRM is something that managements tend to believe in, and it could therefore be regarded as simply a notion of how people can best be managed to achieve organizational goals. If this is the case, then concepts such as strategic integration, culture management, commitment and total quality management, and a unitary philosophy (the interests of management and employees coincide) fit in well with the HRM model. Certainly, these notions have entered into the vocabulary of managers and support the idea that something which could be broadly described as strategic HRM (although they may not use this phrase) will help them to improve organizational performance in the longer-term. However, their expectations of what HRM can achieve by the use of various simplistic mechanisms, eg performance-related pay, may be unrealistic as Mabey *et al* (1998) and Gratton *et al* (1999) have demonstrated.

There can be no doubt that there is something, whether people like it or not, which can be described as an HRM philosophy, even if it does no more than capture the changes in methods of managing people that were happening anyhow. But HRM can be put into practice by people who are described as personnel directors just as well as those who have been re-titled human resource directors.

Notions of HRM have been influenced by contextual developments, as described above, so that definitions of HRM have simply expressed how these developments influence people management policies. HRM is an evolving concept. It is not a new approach. Unitarist personnel approaches existed long before it was invented. Some employers have always exploited their workers, as explained by labour process theory (Braverman, 1974), and do not need to invoke the HRM philosophy to justify doing so. Similarly, some managements have always treated workers in effect as machines (Taylorism) without dubbing this approach HRM. However, it is much to be regretted that some managements still invoke the rhetoric of HRM and then in reality continue to exploit their workers, treating them simply as factors of production to be acquired and disposed of as management pleases. Issues concerning the conversion of rhetoric to reality within a strategic framework are considered in the next chapter.

2

Strategic human resource management

Strategic human resource management (HRM) is a term describing an integrated approach to the development of HR strategies which will enable the organization to achieve its goals. It is linked to the concept of strategy which, as defined by Johnson and Scholes (1993) is 'The direction and scope of an organization over the longer term, which ideally matches its resources to its changing environment, and in particular, to its markets, customers and clients to meet stakeholder expectations'.

The concept of strategic HRM and its practical implications are considered in this chapter under the following headings:

- strategic HRM defined;
- aims of strategic HRM;
- the rationale for strategic HRM;
- resource-based strategic HRM;
- approaches to strategic HRM;
- limitations to the concept of strategic HRM;
- formulating and implementing HR strategies.

STRATEGIC HRM DEFINED

Strategic HRM is an approach to making decisions on the intentions and plans of the organization concerning the employment relationship and the organization's recruitment, training, development, performance management, reward and employee relations strategies, policies and practices. The defining characteristic of strategic HRM is that it is integrated – HR strategies are generally integrated vertically with the business strategy and horizontally with one another. The HR strategies developed by a strategic HRM approach are essential components of the organization's business strategy.

Concerns of strategic HRM

Strategic HRM is concerned with the relationship between human resource management and strategic management in the firm. Strategic HRM refers to the overall direction the organization wishes to pursue in achieving its objectives through people. It is argued that, because intellectual capital is a major source of competitive advantage, and in the last analysis it is people who implement the strategic plan, top management must take these key considerations fully into account in developing its corporate strategies. Strategic HRM is an integral part of those strategies.

Strategic HRM addresses broad organizational issues relating to changes in structure and culture, organizational effectiveness and performance, matching resources to future requirements, the development of distinctive capabilities, knowledge management and the management of change. It is concerned with both meeting human capital requirements and the development of process capabilities, ie the ability to get things done effectively. Overall, it will consider any major people issues which affect or are affected by the strategic plan of the organization. As Boxall (1996) remarks: 'The critical concerns of HRM such as choice of executive leadership and formation of positive patterns of labour relations, are strategic in any firm'.

The focus of strategic HRM

Strategic HRM focuses on actions that differentiate the firm from its competitors (Purcell, 1999). It develops declarations of intent which define means to achieve ends, and it is concerned with the long-term allocation of significant company resources and with matching those resources and capabilities to the external environment. Strategy is a perspective on the way in which critical issues or success factors can be addressed, and strategic decisions aim to make a major and long-term impact on the behaviour and success of the organization.

The meaning of strategic HRM

According to Hendry and Pettigrew (1986), strategic HRM has four meanings:

- the use of planning;
- a coherent approach to the design and management of personnel systems based on an employment policy and manpower strategy and often underpinned by a 'philosophy';
- matching HRM activities and policies to some explicit business strategy;
- seeing the people of the organization as a 'strategic resource' for the achievement of 'competitive advantage'.

AIMS OF STRATEGIC HRM

The fundamental aim of strategic HRM is to generate strategic capability by ensuring that the organization has the skilled, committed and well-motivated employees it needs to achieve sustained competitive advantage. Its objective is to provide a sense of direction in an often turbulent environment so that the business needs of the organization, and the individual and collective needs of its employees, can be met by the development and implementation of coherent and practical HR policies and programmes. As Dyer and Holder (1998) remark, strategic HRM should provide 'unifying frameworks which are at once broad, contingency based and integrative'.

When considering the aims of strategic HRM it is necessary to address the extent to which HR strategy should take into account the interests of all the stakeholders in the organization, employees in general as well as owners and management. In Storey's (1989) terms 'soft strategic HRM' will place greater emphasis on the human relations aspect of people management, stressing security of employment, continuous development, communication, involvement, the quality of working life and work-life balance. Ethical considerations will be important. 'Hard strategic HRM' on the other hand will emphasize the yield to be obtained by investing in human resources in the interests of the business.

Ideally, strategic HRM should attempt to achieve a proper balance between the hard and soft elements. All organizations exist to achieve a purpose and they must ensure that they have the resources required to do so, and that they use them effectively. But they should also take into account the human considerations contained in the concept of soft strategic HRM. In the words of Quinn Mills (1983) they should plan with people in mind, taking into account the needs and aspirations of all the members of the organization. The problem is that hard considerations in many businesses will come first, leaving soft ones some way behind.

THE RATIONALE FOR STRATEGIC HRM

The rationale for strategic HRM is the perceived advantage of having an agreed and understood basis for developing approaches to people management in the longer term. It has been suggested by Lengnick-Hall and Lengnick-Hall (1990) that underlying this rationale in a business is the concept of achieving competitive advantage through HRM: 'Competitive advantage is the essence of competitive strategy. It encompasses those capabilities, resources, relationships and decisions which permit an organization to capitalize on opportunities in the marketplace and to avoid threats to its desired position.' Increasingly, they claim, it is being acknowledged that a resource-based approach to strategic HRM as described below is the key to generating a competitive edge.

RESOURCE-BASED STRATEGIC HRM

The concept of resource-based strategic HRM is founded on the belief expressed by Hamel and Prahalad (1989) that competitive advantage is obtained if a firm can obtain and develop human resources which enable it to learn faster and apply its learning more effectively than its rivals. Barney (1991) contends that sustained competitive advantage stems from the acquisition and effective use of bundles of distinctive resources that competitors cannot imitate.

Unique talents among employees, including superior performance, productivity, flexibility, innovation, and the ability to deliver high levels of personal customer service are ways in which people provide a critical ingredient in developing an organization's competitive position. People also provide the key to managing the pivotal interdependencies across functional activities and the important external relationships. It can be argued that one of the clear benefits arising from competitive advantage based on the effective management of people is that such an advantage is hard to imitate. An organization's HR strategies, policies and practices are a unique blend of processes, procedures, personalities, styles, capabilities and organizational culture. One of the keys to competitive advantage is the ability to differentiate what the business supplies to its customers from those supplied by its competitors. Such differentiation can be achieved by having HR strategies which ensure that:

- the firm has higher quality people than its competitors;
- the unique intellectual capital possessed by the business is developed and nurtured;
- a culture is developed which encourages organizational learning.

The aim of a resource-based approach is to improve resource capability – achieving strategic fit between resources and opportunities and obtaining added value from the effective deployment of resources. In line with intellectual capital theory, resource-based theory emphasizes that investment in people adds to their value to the firm. Resource-based strategy, as Barney (1991) indicates, can develop strategic capability. The strategic goal will be to 'create firms which are more intelligent and flexible than their competitors' (Boxall, 1996) by hiring and developing more talented staff and by extending their skills base.

Resource-based strategy is therefore concerned with the enhancement of the intellectual capital of the firm. As Ulrich (1998) comments: 'Knowledge has become a direct competitive advantage for companies selling ideas and relationships. The challenge to organizations is to ensure that they have the capability to find, assimilate, compensate and retain the talented individuals they need'. A convincing rationale for resource-based strategy has been produced by Grant (1991):

> When the external environment is in a state of flux, the firm's own resources and capabilities may be a much more stable basis on which to define its identity. Hence, a definition of a business in terms of what it is capable of doing may offer a more durable basis for strategy than a definition based upon the needs (eg markets) which the business seeks to satisfy.

APPROACHES TO STRATEGIC HRM

A resource-based approach to strategic HRM focuses on meeting the intellectual capital requirements of the organization. To this end, strategic HRM is concerned generally with developing resource capability and achieving strategic fit as described below, and particularly with assessing the relative merits of approaches based on best practice, best fit or configurational considerations as discussed later in this section.

Resource capability

A resource-capability approach is concerned with the acquisition, development and retention of intellectual capital. Human resources are seen as a major source of competitive advantage. As expressed by Kamoche (1996), the basis of this approach to HR strategy is the acknowledgement of the 'stock of know-how' in the firm. He claims that the resource-capability view of the firm is one that 'builds on and provides a unifying framework for the field of strategic human resource management'. As Schuler and Jackson (1987) note: 'Within this framework, firms attempt to gain competitive advantage using human resources through developing distinctive capabilities (competencies) that arise from the nature of the firm's relationships with its suppliers, customers and employees'.

Strategic fit

The key feature of strategic HRM is the concept of fit or integration. This is sometimes known as the 'matching model'. Walker (1992) defines strategic HRM as 'the means of aligning the management of human resources with the strategic content of the business'.

The HR strategy should be aligned to the business strategy (vertical fit). Better still, HR strategy should be an integral part of the business strategy, contributing to the business planning process as it happens. Vertical integration is necessary to provide congruence between business and human resource strategy so that the latter supports the accomplishment of the former and, indeed, helps to define it. Horizontal integration with other aspects of the HR strategy is required so that its different elements fit together. The aim is to achieve a coherent approach to managing people in which the various practices are mutually supportive.

Guest (1989b) has suggested that strategic human resource management is largely about integration and that one of the key policy goals of HRM is to ensure that it 'is fully integrated into strategic planning so that HRM policies cohere both across policy areas and across hierarchies, and HRM practices are used by line managers as part of their everyday work'. Walker (1992) has pointed out that HR strategies are functional strategies like marketing, production or IT strategies, but they are different in the sense that they are intertwined with all other strategies. The management of people is not a distinct function but the means by which all business strategies are implemented. HR planning should be an integral part of all other strategy formulations. Where it is separate, it needs to be closely aligned.

The three main approaches

The three main approaches to the development of HR strategies have been defined by Richardson and Thompson (1999) as follows:

1. The *'best practice'* approach, which is based on the belief that there is a set of superior HRM practices which, if adopted, will lead to better organizational performance.

2. The 'best fit' approach, which is based on the belief that there can be no universal prescriptions for HRM policies and practices. It is all contingent on the organization's context and culture and its business strategy.

3. The 'configurational' approach, which focuses on the search for distinctive configurations – arrangements of 'joined-up' HR practices which combined together will function more effectively than if they existed as unrelated entities. This concept is commonly referred to as 'bundling'.

Best practice

This approach is based on the belief that there is a set of best HRM practices and that adopting them will lead to superior organizational performance as illustrated in Table 2.1.

These could all be regarded as 'good practice' but in accordance with contingency theory, it is difficult to accept that they universally constitute 'best practice'. What works well in one organization will not necessarily work well in another because it may not fit its strategy, culture, management style, technology or working practices. Becker *et al* (1997) remark that: 'Organizational high-performance work systems are highly idiosyncratic and must be tailored carefully to each firm's individual situation to achieve optimum results'. Purcell (1999) has also criticized the best practice or universalist view by pointing out the inconsistency between a belief in best practice and the resource-based view which focuses on the intangible assets, including HR, that allow the firm to do better than its competitors. He asks how can 'the universalism of best practice be squared with the view that only some resources and routines are important and valuable by being rare and imperfectly imitable?' The danger, as Legge (1995) points out, is that of 'mechanistically matching strategy with HRM policies and practices'.

Best fit

For the reasons given above, it is accepted by many commentators that 'best fit' is more important than 'best practice'. There can be no universal prescriptions for HRM policies and practices. It all depends. Of course, this is not to say that 'good practice', ie practice that does well in one environment, should be ignored. Benchmarking has its uses as a means of identifying areas for innovation or development which are practised to good effect elsewhere. But having learned about what works and, ideally, what does not work in comparable organizations, it is up to the firm to decide what may be relevant in general terms and what lessons can be learned which can be adapted to fit its particular strategic and operational requirements. The starting point

Table 2.1 HRM best practices

Guest (1999a)	Patterson et al (1997)	Pfeffer (1994)	US Department of Labor (1993)
• Selection and the careful use of selection tests to identify those with potential to make a contribution • Training, and in particular a recognition that training is an ongoing activity • Job design to ensure flexibility, commitment and motivation, including steps to ensure that employees have the responsibility and autonomy to use their knowledge and skills to the full • Communication to ensure that a two-way process keeps everyone fully informed • Employee share-ownership programmes (ESOPS) to keep employees aware of the implications of their actions, including absence and labour turnover, for the financial performance of the firm	• Sophisticated selection and recruitment processes • Sophisticated induction programmes • Sophisticated training • Coherent appraisal systems • Flexibility of workforce skills • Job variety on shop floor • Use of formal teams • Frequent and comprehensive communication to workforce • Use of quality improvement teams • Harmonized terms and conditions • Basic pay higher than competition • Use of incentive schemes	• Employment security • Selective hiring • Self-managed teams • High compensation contingent on performance • Training to provide a skilled and motivated workforce • Reduction of status differentials • Sharing information	• Careful and extensive systems for recruitment, selection and training • Formal systems for sharing information with employees • Clear job design • High-level participation processes • Monitoring of attitudes • Performance appraisals • Properly functioning grievance procedures • Promotion and compensation schemes that provide for the recognition and reward of high-performing employees

should be an analysis of the business needs of the firm within its context (culture, structure, technology and processes). This may indicate clearly what has to be done. Thereafter, it may be useful to pick and mix various 'best practice' ingredients, and develop an approach which applies those that are appropriate in a way which is aligned to the identified business needs.

But there are problems with the best fit approach, as pointed out by Purcell (1999) who, having rubbished the concept of best practice, proceeded to do the same for the notion of best fit: 'Meanwhile, the search for a contingency or matching model of HRM is also limited by the impossibility of modelling all the contingent variables, the difficulty of showing their interconnection, and the way in which changes in one variable have an impact on others.' In Purcell's view, organizations should be less concerned with best fit and best practice and much more sensitive to processes of organizational change so that they can 'avoid being trapped in the logic of rational choice'.

Bundling (configuration)

'Bundling' is the development and implementation of several HR practices together so that they are inter-related and therefore complement and support one another.

The process is sometimes referred to as the adoption of a 'configurational mode' (Delery and Doty, 1996) or the use of 'complementarities' (MacDuffie, 1995). MacDuffie states that: 'Implicit in the notion of a "bundle" is the idea that practices within bundles are interrelated and internally consistent, and that "more is better" with respect to the impact on performance, because of the overlapping and mutually reinforcing effect of multiple practices.'

Dyer and Reeves (1995) define human resource strategies as 'internally consistent bundles of human resource practices'. MacDuffie (1995), Arthur (1992) and Ichniowski *et al* (1997) have explored the extent to which combinations of practices can be determined and whether organizational performance is related to the adoption of such 'bundles'. Their conclusion was that a firm with bundles of HR practices should have a higher level of performance, providing it also achieves high levels of fit with its competitive strategy. Dyer and Reeves note that: 'The logic in favour of bundling is straightforward... Since employee performance is a function of both ability and motivation, it makes sense to have practices aimed at enhancing both.' Thus there are several ways in which employees can acquire needed skills (such as careful selection and training) and multiple incentives to enhance motivation (different forms of financial and non-financial rewards). A study by Dyer and Reeves of various models listing HR practices for analysing the link between HRM and business performance found that the activities appearing in most of the models were involvement, careful selection, extensive training and contingent compensation.

The problem with the bundling approach is to decide which is the best way to relate different practices. There is no evidence that one bundle is generally better than another. Delaney and Huselid (1996) failed to find any positive impact for specific combinations of practices as opposed to the total number of HR practices although, as noted by Guest (1997), a number of researchers have shown that simply using a larger number of high performance practices will produce better results.

In one sense, strategic HRM is holistic; it is concerned with the organization as a total entity and addresses what needs to be done across the organization as a whole in order to enable it to achieve its corporate strategic objectives. It is not interested in isolated programmes and techniques, or in the ad hoc development of HR programmes.

Guest (1989b) includes in his set of propositions about HRM the point that strategic integration is about, *inter alia*, the ability of the organization to ensure that the various aspects of HRM cohere. One way of looking at the concept is to say that some measure of coherence will be achieved if first, there is an overriding strategic imperative or driving force such as quality, performance or the need to develop skills and competencies, and secondly, this initiates various processes and policies which are designed to link together and operate in concert to deliver certain defined results. For example, if the driving force were to improve performance, competence profiling techniques could be used to specify recruitment standards, identify learning and development needs and indicate the standards of behaviour or performance required. The competence frameworks could be used as the basis for human resource planning and in development centres. They could also be incorporated into performance management processes in which the aims are primarily developmental and competencies are used as criteria for reviewing behaviour and assessing learning and development needs. Job evaluation could be based on levels of competence, and competence-based pay systems could be introduced. This ideal may be difficult to achieve as a 'grand design' which can be put into immediate effect, and may have to be developed progressively.

LIMITATIONS TO THE CONCEPT OF STRATEGIC HRM

The concept of strategic HRM appears to be based on the belief that the formulation of strategy is a rational and linear process as modelled in Figure 2.1. This indicates that the overall HR strategy flows from the business strategy and generates specific HR strategies in key areas. All this takes place by reference to systematic reviews of

Figure 2.1   A linear strategic HRM model

the internal and external environment of the organization which identify the business, organizational and HR issues that need to be addressed.

But strategic HRM in reality is not usually a formal, well-articulated and linear process which flows logically from the business strategy. Mintzberg (1987) has emphasized that strategies emerge over time in response to evolving situations. And Tyson (1997) points out that:

- strategy is emergent and flexible – it is always 'about to be', it never exists at the present time;
- strategy is not only realized by formal statements but also comes about by actions and reactions;
- strategy is a description of a future-orientated action which is always directed towards change;
- the management process itself conditions the strategies that emerge.

Business strategies may be formulated as they are used; they are in a constant state of evolution and they may be obscure. How, in these circumstances, can 'strategic fit' be achieved?.

The research conducted by Gratton *et al* (1999) in eight British organizations established that there was little evidence of a comprehensive and successful attempt to achieve internal fit: 'In no case was there a clearly developed and articulated strategy that was translated into a mutually supportive set of human resource initiatives or practices.'

Problems of achieving internal fit may arise for the following reasons:

- the sheer complexity of the organization and its strategies, which might make it hard to achieve any coherence across a diverse range of activities and plans;
- senior managers who want quick fixes which lead to innovations that are isolated from complementary HR activities – the most common example of this is the introduction of performance-related pay without the existence of embedded performance management processes;
- incremental approaches to the development of HR practices, possibly arising from management pressures or the existence of financial constraints;
- difficulty in deciding which 'bundles' are likely to be most appropriate in the circumstances;
- lack of understanding amongst HR practitioners of the need actively to achieve integration;
- implementation difficulties where even when there is a 'grand design' and much rhetoric, the reality is different – the links are difficult to maintain, line managers are indifferent or incapable of playing their part, and employees are suspicious or hostile to the newly linked initiatives.

FORMULATING HR STRATEGIES

The concept of strategic HRM can be somewhat nebulous and, as Gratton *et al* found, it may be difficult to convert rhetoric into reality. It is relatively easy to produce broad statements of strategic intent, but the development and articulation of specific long-term strategies may be much harder. However, although it may be difficult to develop and successfully implement HR strategies, a strategic approach is desirable in order to give a sense of direction and purpose and as a basis for the development of relevant and coherent HR policies and practices. Achieving strategic fit may not be easy but it is well worth trying.

Approach to the formulation of HR strategies

It has been suggested by Richardson and Thompson (1999) that strategy, whether it is an HR strategy or any other kind of management strategy, must have two key elements: there must be strategic objectives, ie things the strategy is supposed to achieve; and there must be a plan of action, ie the means by which it is proposed that the objectives will be met. The objectives need to be defined in general terms of what needs to be done to satisfy the business needs of the organization and the individual needs of employees. Against this background, more specific HR strategies can be formulated and plans made to implement them.

It is, however, necessary to remember that strategic HRM is largely an attitude of mind: a belief in the benefits of clarifying intentions, and of ensuring that what is planned fits the business strategy and that the various components of the HR strategy are integrated with one another. It is not a process that can be reduced to a sequence of logical steps. It is usually a much less orderly affair than models such as that shown in Figure 2.1 suggest. This is entirely understandable if it is remembered that strategic HRM is as much about the management of change in conditions of uncertainty as about the rigorous development and implementation of a logical plan.

Perhaps the best way to look at the reality of strategic HRM is to remember Mintzberg *et al's* (1988) statement that strategy formulation is about 'preferences, choices, and matches' rather than an exercise 'in applied logic'. It is also desirable to follow Mintzberg's analysis and treat HR strategy as a perspective rather than a rigorous procedure for mapping the future.

Strategic planning questions

The two basic strategic planning questions are 'Where are we going?' and 'What do we need to do to get there?' Answers to the 'Where are we going?' question are provided by finding out what the organization intends to do (its strategic plan, if one exists) and the business needs that need to be satisfied if these intentions are to be realized. The human resource implications of the plans can then be assessed in terms of organization design and development, resourcing, human resource development, performance management, reward and employee relations. Answers to the 'What do we need to do?' question will be based on an initial assessment of the current situation, possibly in the form of a 'SWOT' analysis – strengths, weaknesses, opportunities and threats. From this analysis, specific proposals for HR innovations and programmes can be developed and the resources required to implement them can be determined. It is essential to define objectives in terms of how these proposals will meet business needs, and to establish success criteria.

In carrying out this strategic planning process it may be useful to bear in mind the various models which describe approaches to strategic HRM, namely high performance management, high-commitment management and high-involvement management as described below. These are not prescriptive – there will be a choice of which model or parts of various models might be adopted, although the extent to which there is real choice will be contingent upon factors such as the business strategy, the resources available and the environment in which the firm operates. It is also necessary to consider how vertical and horizontal fit will be achieved and the extent to which 'bundling' is possible and desirable.

High-performance management

High-performance management (called in the United States high-performance work systems or practices) aims to make an impact on the performance of the firm through its people in such areas as productivity, quality, levels of customer service, growth, profits, and ultimately the delivery of increased shareholder value. High-performance management practices include rigorous recruitment and selection procedures, extensive and relevant training and management development activities, incentive pay systems and performance management processes. The characteristics of high-performance management as defined by the US Department of Labor (1993) are set out in Table 2.1 (see page 38).

The high-commitment management model

One of the defining characteristics of HRM is its emphasis on the importance of enhancing mutual commitment (Walton, 1985b). High-commitment management has been described by Wood (1996) as: 'A form of management which is aimed at eliciting a commitment so that behaviour is primarily self-regulated rather than controlled by sanctions and pressures external to the individual, and relations within the organization are based on high levels of trust.'

The approaches to creating a high-commitment organization as described by Beer *et al* (1984) and Walton (1985b) are:

- the development of career ladders and emphasis on trainability and commitment as highly valued characteristics of employees at all levels in the organization;
- a high level of functional flexibility with the abandonment of potentially rigid job descriptions;
- the reduction of hierarchies and the ending of status differentials;
- a heavy reliance on team structure for disseminating information (team briefing), structuring work (team working) and problem solving (quality circles).

Wood and Albanese (1995) added to this list:

● job design as something management consciously does in order to provide jobs which have a considerable level of intrinsic satisfaction;

● a policy of no compulsory lay-offs or redundancies and permanent employment guarantees with the possible use of temporary workers to cushion fluctuations in the demand for labour;

● new forms of assessment and payment systems and, more specifically, merit pay and profit sharing;

● a high involvement of employees in the management of quality.

Approaches to achieving commitment are described in Chapter 11.

High-involvement management

This approach involves treating employees as partners in the enterprise whose interests are respected and who have a voice on matters that affect them. It is concerned with communication and involvement. The aim is to create a climate in which a continuing dialogue takes place between managers and the members of their teams, in order to define expectations and share information on the organization's mission, values and objectives. This establishes mutual understanding of what *is* to be achieved and a framework for managing and developing people to ensure that it *will* be achieved.

Achieving vertical fit – integrating business and HR strategies

When considering how to integrate business and HR strategies, managers should remember that business and HR issues influence each other and in turn influence corporate and business unit strategies. It is also necessary to note that in establishing these links, account must be taken of the fact that strategies for change have also to be integrated with changes in the external and internal environments. Fit may exist at a point in time but circumstances will change and the fit may no longer exist. An excessive pursuit of 'fit' with the status quo will inhibit the flexibility of approach which is essential in turbulent conditions. This is the 'temporal' factor in achieving fit identified by Gratton *et al* (1999). An additional factor which will make the achievement of good vertical fit difficult is that the business strategy may not be clearly defined – it could be in an emergent or evolutionary state. This would mean that there could be nothing with which to fit the HR strategy.

But an attempt can be made to understand the direction in which the organization is going, even if this is not expressed in a formal strategic plan. All businesses have strategies in the form of intentions, although these may be ill-formed and subject to change. The ideal of achieving a link in rigorous terms may be difficult to attain.

Table 2.2 Linking HR and competitive strategies

Competitive strategy	HR strategy		
	Resourcing	HR development	Reward
Achieve competitive advantage through innovation	Recruit and retain high quality people with innovative skills and a good track record in innovation	Develop strategic capability and provide encouragement and facilities for enhancing innovative skills and enhancing the intellectual capital of the organization	Provide financial incentives and rewards and recognition for successful innovations
Achieve competitive advantage through quality	Use sophisticated selection procedures to recruit people who are likely to deliver quality and high levels of customer service	Encourage the development of a learning organization, develop and implement knowledge management processes, support total quality and customer care initiatives with focused training	Link rewards to quality performance and the achievement of high standards of customer service
Achieve competitive advantage through cost-leadership	Develop core/periphery employment structures; recruit people who are likely to add value; if unavoidable, plan and manage downsizing humanely	Provide training designed to improve productivity; inaugurate just-in-time training which is closely linked to immediate business needs and can generate measurable improvements in cost-effectiveness	Review all reward practices to ensure that they provide value for money and do not lead to unnecessary expenditure
Achieve competitive advantage by employing people who are better than those employed by competitors	Use sophisticated recruitment and selection procedures based on a rigorous analysis of the special capabilities required by the organization	Develop organizational learning processes; encourage self-managed learning through the use of personal development plans as part of a performance management process	Develop performance management processes which enable both financial and non-financial rewards to be related to competence and skills; ensure that pay levels are competitive

A possible approach to linking business and HR strategies is to relate the latter to the firm's competitive strategies, including those listed by Porter (1980). An illustration of how this might be expressed is given in Table 2.2.

As suggested by Wright and Snell (1998), the achievement of vertical fit requires:

● knowledge of the skills and behaviour necessary to implement the strategy;
● knowledge of the HRM practices necessary to elicit those skills and behaviours;
● the ability to quickly implement the desired system of HRM practices.

Achieving horizontal fit

Horizontal fit is achieved when the various HR strategies cohere and are mutually supporting. This can be attained by the process of 'bundling' or 'configuration'. If a deliberate attempt to 'bundle' is made, this process will be driven by the needs and characteristics of the business. The steps required are:

1. Analyse what the needs of the business and its characteristics are.
2. Assess how HR strategy can help to meet the business needs and also be congruent with the characteristics of the business.
3. Identify the capabilities and behaviours required of employees if they are to make a full contribution to the achievement of strategic goals.
4. Assess the effectiveness of existing HR practices and the need for change.
5. Analyse the scope for linking the various practices together as a 'bundle' so that they become mutually reinforcing and therefore coherent. This may mean identifying integrating practices such as the use of competency-based HR processes which impacts on recruitment, training, performance management and reward, and performance management which affects personal development and reward.
6. Formulate programmes for the development of these practices, paying particular attention to the links between them.

The aim is to achieve coherence and this means adopting a holistic approach – no innovation should be considered in isolation. It is necessary to seek opportunities to create synergy by looking for ways in which one practice can support another practice, and to identify common requirements which can be met by initiatives in different areas of HR practice, as long as they are deliberately linked. Examples of how this may happen are given in Table 2.3.

Table 2.3 Common elements in HR strategy areas

Overall HR strategy	HR strategy area – common elements		
	Resourcing	HR development	Reward
Improve performance	Competence-based recruiting; assessment centres	Competence-based training; development centres	Competence-related pay
Extend skills base	Identify skills development needs of recruits	Skills analysis; focused training in identified needs; accreditation of skills	Skills-based pay
Provide for competence and career development	Develop competency frameworks and profiles; identify competence levels and potential through performance management processes	Use performance management and personal development plans as a basis for defining and meeting learning needs; establish broad 'career development' bands for mapping lateral development paths; identify career ladders in job families defined in competence terms	Develop broad-banded or job family structures defined in competence terms and which indicate clearly 'aiming points' (competence requirements in different roles within or outside a job family); institute systems of career development pay for lateral progression through bands
Provide for employability	Develop a positive psychological contract based on an undertaking to identify and develop transferable skills; provide scope for job enlargement/ enrichment and opportunities to move into new roles	Identify skills development needs through personal development planning; institute programmes for developing transferable skills	Develop broad-banded/job family structures which identify competence levels for roles or job families and provide a basis for identifying learning needs

Increase commitment	Analyse characteristics of committed employees; use sophisticated selection methods to identify candidates who have these characteristics and are likely to be committed to the organization; define and communicate organizational core values	On the basis of the analysis of the characteristics of committed employees, provide learning experiences which enhance understanding and acceptance of organizational core values and encourage value-driven behaviour	Reinforce value-driven behaviour by providing rewards which are based on evidence that core values are being upheld
Increase motivation	Analyse characteristics of well-motivated employees and structure selection interviews to obtain evidence of the extent to which candidates are likely to be well-motivated	Provide learning opportunities which reinforce characteristics of well-motivated employees	Use performance management processes as a basis for providing non-financial rewards related to opportunities for development and growth

IMPLEMENTING HR STRATEGIES

Because strategies tend to be expressed as abstractions, they must be translated into programmes with clearly stated objectives and deliverables. But getting strategies into action is not easy. The term 'strategic HRM' has been devalued in some quarters; sometimes to mean no more than a few generalized ideas about HR policies, at other times to describe a short term plan, for example, to increase the retention rate of graduates. It must be emphasized that HR strategies are not just programmes, policies, or plans concerning HR issues which the HR department happens to feel are important. Piecemeal initiatives do not constitute strategy.

The problem with strategic HRM as noted by Gratton *et al* (1999) is that, too often, strategic intentions are not achieved in practice. As they put it:

> One principal strand that has run through this entire book is the disjunction between rhetoric and reality in the area of human resource management, between HRM theory

and HRM practice, between what the HR function says it is doing and how that practice is perceived by employees, and between what senior management believes to be the role of the HR function, and the role it actually plays.

The factors identified by Gratton *et al* which contribute to creating this gap included:

- the tendency of employees in diverse organizations only to accept initiatives they perceive to be relevant to their own areas;
- the tendency of long-serving employees to cling to the status quo;
- complex or ambiguous initiatives may not be understood by employees or will be perceived differently by them, especially in large, diverse organizations;
- it is more difficult to gain acceptance of non-routine initiatives;
- employees will be hostile to initiatives if they are believed to be in conflict with the organization's identity, eg downsizing in a culture of 'job-for-life';
- the initiative is seen as a threat;
- inconsistencies between corporate strategies and values;
- the extent to which senior management is trusted;
- the perceived fairness of the initiative;
- the extent to which existing processes could help to embed the initiative;
- a bureaucratic culture which leads to inertia.

Barriers to the implementation of HR strategies

The barriers which can be met by HR strategists when attempting to implement strategic initiatives are often concerned with a failure to understand the strategic needs of the business, with the result that HR strategic initiatives are seen as irrelevant, even counter-productive. This problem is compounded if there has not been an adequate assessment of the environmental and cultural factors which affect the content of the strategies. Initiatives which are ill-conceived and irrelevant, possibly because they are current fads or because there has been a badly digested analysis of best practice which does not fit the organization's requirements, will not help.

Implementation will also be difficult if one initiative is pursued in isolation without considering its implications on other areas of HR practice or trying to ensure that a coherent, holistic approach is adopted. It will be very hard to implement anything if the practical problems of getting the initiative accepted by all concerned, including, importantly, top management, have not been addressed. Inability to achieve ownership amongst line managers or to develop the skills they require to play their part in implementation will be a major obstacle. (The key role of line managers in making HR initiatives work is often underestimated.) It is also necessary to ensure that supporting processes for the initiative (eg performance management to support performance pay) and the financial and people resources required are available.

Overcoming the barriers

To overcome these barriers it is necessary to:

1. *Conduct a rigorous initial analysis.* The initial analysis should cover business needs, corporate culture and internal and external environmental factors. The framework could be a SWOT analysis of strengths, weaknesses, opportunities and threats facing the organization, or a PESTLE analysis (the political, economic, social, technological, legal and environmental contexts within which the organization operates).

2. *Formulate strategy.* The formulation should set out the rationale for the strategy and spell out its aims, cost and benefits.

3. *Gain support.* Particular care needs to be taken to obtain the support of top managers (for whom a business case must be prepared), line managers, employees generally and trade unions. This means communication of intentions and their rationale and the involvement of interested parties in the formulation of strategic plans.

4. *Assess barriers.* An assessment is required of potential barriers to implementation, especially those relating to indifference, hostility (resistance to change) and lack of supporting processes or resources. Unless and until a confident declaration can be made that the initiative will receive a reasonable degree of support (it could be too much to expect universal acclamation) and that the resources will be available, it is better not to plunge too quickly into implementation.

5. *Prepare action plans.* These should spell out what is to be done, who does it and when it should be completed. A project plan is desirable which indicates the stages of the implementation programme, the resources required at each stage, and the stage and final completion dates. The action plan should indicate the consultation, involvement, communication and training programmes that will be required. It should also state how progress will be monitored and the criteria for measuring success against objectives.

6. *Project-manage implementation.* This should be conducted by reference to the action or project plan, and involves monitoring progress and dealing with problems as they arise.

7. *Follow up and evaluate.* Nothing can be taken for granted. It is essential to follow up and evaluate the results of the initiative. Follow-up can take place through interviews, focus groups, and, desirably, attitude surveys. The evaluation should

point the way to action in the form of amendments to the original proposals, the provision of supporting processes, additional support to line managers, intensified communication and training, and the need for more resources.

Setting out the strategy

The following is an example of the headings under which a strategy and the plans for implementing could be set out.

1. *Basis:*
   - business needs in terms of the key elements of the business strategy;
   - environmental factors and analysis (SWOT/PESTLE);
   - cultural factors – possible helps or hindrances to implementation.
2. *Content* – details of the proposed HR strategy.
3. *Rationale* – the business case for the strategy against the background of business needs and environmental/cultural factors.
4. *Implementation plan:*
   - action programme;
   - responsibility for each stage;
   - resources required;
   - proposed arrangements for communication, consultation, involvement and training;
   - project management arrangements.
5. *Costs and benefits analysis* – an assessment of the resource implications of the plan (costs, people and facilities) and the benefits that will accrue, for the organization as a whole, for line managers and for individual employees. (As far as possible these benefits should be quantified in terms of value added.)

3

Intellectual capital: the theory and its practical implications

INTELLECTUAL CAPITAL DEFINED

Intellectual capital consists of the stocks and flows of knowledge available to an organization. These can be regarded as intangible resources which, together with tangible resources (money and physical assets), comprise the market or total value of a business. Bontis (1996; 1998), defines intangible resources as the factors other than financial and physical assets that contribute to the value-generating processes of a firm and are under its control. As described by Edvinson and Malone (1997), these comprise the value of all relationships inside and outside the organization including those with customers and suppliers. They also cover the values attached to such intangibles as goodwill, corporate image and brands.

The three elements of intellectual capital are:

1. *Human capital* - the knowledge, skills and abilities of the employees in an organization.
2. *Social capital* – the stocks and flows of knowledge derived from networks of relationships within and outside the organization.
3. *Organizational capital* – Youndt (2000) defines this as the institutionalized knowl-

edge possessed by an organization which is stored in databases, manuals etc. It is often called *structural capital* (Edvinson and Malone, 1997), but the term organizational capital is preferred by Youndt because, he argues, it conveys more clearly that this is the knowledge that the organization actually *owns*.

THE SIGNIFICANCE OF INTELLECTUAL CAPITAL

This tripartite concept of intellectual capital indicates that, while it is individuals who generate, retain and use knowledge (human capital), this knowledge is enhanced by the interactions between them (social capital) to generate the institutionalized knowledge possessed by an organization (organizational capital). Clearly, it is the knowledge, skills and abilities of individuals that create value, which is why the focus has to be on means of attracting, retaining, developing and maintaining the human capital those individuals represent. But organizational effectiveness also depends upon making good use of their knowledge, which needs to be developed, captured and exchanged (knowledge management) in order to create organizational capital. In doing so, it should be remembered that, as stated by Daft and Weick (1984), 'individuals come and go, but organizations preserve knowledge over time'. Or, as expressed more colourfully by Fitz-enj (2000), 'organizational capital (knowledge) stays behind when the employee leaves; human capital is the intellectual asset that goes home every night with the employee'.

It is necessary to capture individual knowledge through knowledge management processes as described in Chapter 22, but it is equally important to take into account social capital considerations, that is, the ways in which knowledge is developed through interaction between people. Bontis et al (1999) point out that flows as well as stocks matter. Intellectual capital develops and changes over time and a significant part is played in these processes by people acting together. Therefore, while this chapter initially focuses on human capital theory and methods of measuring human capital, consideration is also given to the associated concepts of social and organizational capital.

HUMAN CAPITAL

Bontis *et al* (1999) define human capital as follows:

Human capital represents the human factor in the organization; the combined intelligence, skills and expertise that gives the organization its distinctive character. The human elements of the organization are those that are capable of learning, changing, innovating and providing the creative thrust which if properly motivated can ensure the long-term survival of the organization.

The term human capital was originated by Schulz (1961) who elaborated his concept in 1981 as follows: 'Consider all human abilities to be either innate or acquired. Attributes... which are valuable and can be augmented by appropriate investment will be human capital.'

But the idea of investing in human capital was first developed by Adam Smith (1776), who in the *Wealth of Nations* argued that differences between the ways of individuals with different levels of education and training reflected differences in the returns necessary to defray the costs of acquiring those skills. The return on investment in skills can therefore be compared to the returns from investing in physical capital. This comparison has its limitations, however. Firms own physical capital but not their workers, except in a slave society.

Human capital consists of the intangible resources that workers provide for their employers. Davenport (1999) comments that:

> People possess innate abilities, behaviours and personal energy and these elements make up the human capital they bring to their work. And it is they, not their employers, who own this capital and decide when, how and where they will contribute it. In other words, they can make choices. Work is a two-way exchange of value, not a one-way exploitation of an asset by its owner.

The point emphasized by Davenport, that workers as well as employers invest in human capital, is in accord with the economic theory of human capital. As expressed by Ehrenberg and Smith (1994), human capital theory 'conceptualizes workers as embodying a set of skills which can be "rented out" to employers'.

For the worker, the expected returns on human capital investments are a higher level of earnings, greater job satisfaction, better career prospects, and at one time, but less so now, a belief that security in employment is assured. In today's conditions, however, investments by workers in developing transferable skills can be attractive as means of increasing employability. The costs of such investments, as spelt out by Elliott (1991) take psychological, social and monetary forms. Psychological costs are those borne by individuals, perhaps the less able, who may find learning difficult. Social costs take the form of foregone market opportunities (ie opportunity costs – the time spent devoted to investing in human capital could have been spent in other activities). Monetary costs include both direct financial outlays and foregone market opportunities. As suggested by Elliott, the decision to acquire skills is an investment decision. Individuals will invest in human capital if they believe that the benefits to them will exceed the costs they will incur. These benefits consist of the net addition to life-long earnings that results from selling skilled rather than unskilled labour.

For the employer, the returns on investment in human capital are expected to be improvements in performance, productivity, flexibility and the capacity to innovate which should result from enlarging the skill base and increasing levels of knowledge and competence. Schuller (2000) suggests that 'The general message is persuasive: skills, knowledge and competencies are key factors in determining whether organizations and nations will prosper.' This point is also made powerfully by Reich (1991).

Human capital theory can be associated with the resource-based view of the firm as developed by Barney (1991). This proposes that sustainable competitive advantage is attained when the firm has a human resource pool that cannot be imitated or substituted by its rivals. Boxall (1996) refers to this situation as one that confers 'human capital advantage'. But he also notes (1996; 1999), that a distinction should be made between 'human capital advantage' and 'human process advantage'. The former results from employing people with competitively valuable knowledge and skills, much of it tacit. The latter, however, follows from the establishment of:

> ... difficult to imitate, highly evolved processes within the firm, such as cross-departmental cooperation and executive development. Accordingly, 'human resource advantage', the superiority of one firm's labour management over another's, can be thought of as the product of its human capital and human process advantages.

Workers as assets

The added value that people can contribute to an organization is emphasized by human capital theory. It regards people as assets and stresses that investment by organizations in people will generate worthwhile returns. The theory therefore underpins the philosophy of human resource management which, as developed in the 1980s, stated that employees should be treated as assets rather than costs.

But as Davenport (1999) maintains, the concept is limited, indeed questionable, because:

- workers should not be treated as passive assets to be bought, sold and replaced at the whim of their owners – increasingly, they actively control their own working lives;
- the notion that companies own human assets as they own machines is unacceptable in principle and inapplicable in practice; it short-changes people by placing them in the same category as plant and equipment;
- no system of 'human asset accounting' has succeeded in producing a convincing

method of attaching financial values to human resources; in any case, this demeans the more intangible added value that can be delivered to organizations by people.

Employers need to remember that workers, especially knowledge workers, may regard themselves as free agents who can choose how and where they invest their talents, time and energy. Investments by employers in training and developing people are a means of attracting and retaining human capital as well as getting better returns from those investments.

Measuring human capital

The recognized importance of achieving human capital advantage has led to an interest in the development of methods of measuring the value of that capital for the following reasons:

1. Human capital constitutes a key element of the market worth of a company and its value should therefore be included in the accounts as an indication to investors or those contemplating a merger or acquisition of the total value of a business, including its intangible as well as its tangible assets.
2. The process of identifying measures and collecting and analysing information relating to them will focus the attention of the organization on what needs to be done to find, keep, develop and make the best use of its human capital.
3. Measurements of the value of human capital can provide the basis for resource-based HR strategies which are concerned with the development of the organization's core competencies.
4. Measurements can be used to monitor progress in achieving strategic HR goals and generally to evaluate the effectiveness of HR practices.

The first, and to a certain extent the second, of these arguments were advanced in a pioneering study by Hermanson (1964). His views were popularized by Likert (1967), and in the 1960s and 1970s efforts were made to get the notion accepted by investors and businesses; to no avail. Members of the accountancy profession have generally dismissed the idea because they believe that the figures would almost certainly be based on crude assumptions and, as Schuller (2000) comments, they would involve numerical precision which would be 'wholly out of line with these assumptions'. An authoritative report by the OECD (1998) states that: 'Measures of human capital have been strongly guided by what is possible to measure, rather than by what is desirable to measure.' Allen Cook, Technical Director of the Accounting Standards Board, which sets the rules for financial accounting in the UK, has said, as reported by Outram (1998): 'We don't think you can solve problems by incorporating them in the accounts.'

According to Sackmann *et al* (1989) human resource accounting (often referred to as human asset accounting) aims to 'quantify the economic value of people to the organization' in order to provide input for managerial and financial decisions. Bontis *et al* (1999) refer to three types of human resource accounting models:

1. Cost models, which consider the historical, acquisition, replacement or opportunity cost of human assets.
2. HR value models, which combine non-monetary behavioural with monetary economic value models.
3. Monetary models which calculate discounted estimates of future earnings.

In their basic form, as indicated by Bontis *et al*, human resource accounting models attempt to calculate the contributions that human assets make to firms by capitalizing pay expenditures. A discounted cash flow of total pay is included in the asset section of the balance sheet rather than being classified as an expense.

The problem with human resource or asset accounting is that, as Bontis *et al* point out: 'All of the models suffer from subjectivity and uncertainty and lack reliability in that the measures cannot be audited with any assurance.' It is for this reason that the notion of human resource accounting is not generally accepted by accountants or financial analysts. It can also be argued that it is morally unacceptable to treat people as financial assets and, in any case, people are not 'owned' by the company.

But people in organizations do add value, and there is a case for assessing this value to provide a basis for HR planning and for monitoring the effectiveness and impact of HR policies and practices. This approach involves the assessment of the value or contribution to business success of HR practices generally, rather than simply measuring the value of human capital. The aims are to measure how efficiently organizations are using their human capital and, in the words of Mayo (1999), to assess 'the value of future earnings opportunities'.

Several consultancy and accounting firms have attempted to produce methodologies for achieving these aims. Arthur Anderson, as quoted by Outram (1998), have developed a 'human capital appraisal' instrument which looks at three key factors: fit, cost and value. 'Fit' measures whether HR management is in line with the company's overall objectives. 'Cost' measures the actual cost of HR, including recruitment, pay and the HR function itself. 'Value' assesses the worth of the output it delivers. The five areas of human capital included in this approach are recruitment, retention and retirement; rewards and performance management; career development, succession planning and training; organizational structure; and a variety of administrative and legal systems which are referred to as 'human capital enablers'.

William Mercer, as reported by Cooper (2000), have developed measures for what they regard as the critical people dimensions: structure, processes, decision-making, information flow and reward. The most popular measure is value added per employee or, at unit level, productivity. But measures relating to physical output and customer service levels are also used. The dimensions and measures provide the basis for comparing business performance, people management practices and operating environment to identify why some units in a business are consistently more successful than others.

At PricewaterhouseCoopers, as reported by Pickard (2000), a study has been carried out to quantify the value of HR. This established that there were five HR factors that were linked to differences in performance: communication from the department leader, staff turnover, training and development, the existence of openness, feedback and trust, and the quality of work.

A number of other areas for measurement and methods of doing so have been identified by Mayo (1999). He believes that value added per person is a good measure of the effectiveness of human capital, especially for making inter-firm comparisons. But he considers that the most critical indicator for the value of human capital is the level of expertise possessed by an organization. He suggests that this could be analysed under the headings of identified organizational core competencies. The other criteria he mentions are measures of satisfaction derived from employee opinion surveys and levels of attrition and absenteeism. Clearly, it is important to analyse and evaluate trends rather than simply record actuals.

Much of what has been written on this subject recently was anticipated by Boudreau (1988) who developed the concept of utility analysis (see Chapter 7). This aims to provide a decision support framework that explicitly considers the costs and benefits of HR decisions.

There is a good case for evolving methods of valuing human capital and how it is used as an aid to decision-making. This may mean identifying the key HR drivers and modelling the effect of varying them. The issue is to develop a framework within which reliable information can be collected and analysed. Quantification is desirable but not if it is based on huge, loose assumptions. It may be best to focus on readily available quantified information such as added value per employee and productivity, and measures of employee behaviour (attrition and absenteeism rates, the frequency/severity rate of accidents, and cost savings resulting from suggestion schemes or quality circles). The aim should be to keep the measurements simple, to concentrate on key areas of outcomes and behaviour, and only to measure activities if it is clear that such measurements will inform decision making.

However, the significance of the concept of human capital does not depend on the ability to quantify its value. What human capital theory can do is to provide the rationale for a 'resource capability' approach to strategic HRM as advocated by Kamoche (1996) which will be concerned with the acquisition, development and retention of human capital in order to achieve competitive advantage.

Human capital and other aspects of intellectual capital theory

Important though human capital theory may be, interest in it should not divert attention from the other aspects of intellectual capital – social and organizational capital – which are concerned with developing and embedding the knowledge possessed by the human capital of an organization. Schuller (2000) contends that 'The focus on human capital as an individual attribute may lead – arguably has already led – to a very unbalanced emphasis on the acquisition by individuals of skills and competencies which ignores the way in which such knowledge is embedded in a complex web of social relationships.' The next two sections of this chapter therefore discuss the issues relating to social and organizational capital.

SOCIAL CAPITAL

The concept of social capital has been defined by Putnam (1996) as 'the features of social life – networks, norms and trust – that enable participants to act together more effectively to pursue shared objectives'. The World Bank offers the following definition on its Web site (www.worldbank.com): 'Social capital refers to the institutions, relationships and norms that shape the quality and quantity of a society's social interactions… Social capital is not just the sum of the institutions which underpin a society – it is the glue that holds them together.'

The World Bank also notes that social capital can be perceived as a set of *horizontal associations* between people, consisting of social networks and associated norms that have an effect on community, productivity and well-being. This brings us closer to the meaning and significance of the concept of social capital as an element of intellectual capital. It should be remembered that it is individuals, not organizations, who own human capital. Therefore, as Youndt (2000) claims, since employees are free, within limits, to leave their firm, there is a significant risk that organizations may incur an intellectual capital loss 'unless individual knowledge is transferred, shared, transformed and institutionalized'.

Social capital is knowledge tied up and developed by relationships among employees, partners, customers and suppliers. It is built by the exchange of such knowledge and this requires a collaborative organizational environment in which knowledge and information can flow freely (Bontis, 1996; Coleman, 1990). Such an environment is more likely to exist in a 'boundary-less' organization where the emphasis is on lateral processes, teams and task forces that can leverage knowledge across the business. Social capital, as Schuller (2000) puts it, 'enables human capital to realize its potential'.

ORGANIZATIONAL CAPITAL

Organizational or structural capital consists of the knowledge owned by the organization rather than by individual employees. It can be described as *embedded* or *institutionalized* knowledge which may be retained with the help of information technology on readily accessible and easily extended databases. It can include explicit knowledge which has been recorded on a database or in manuals and standard operating procedures, or tacit knowledge which has been captured, exchanged and, as far as possible, codified.

Any process or procedure in an organization is constructed from the knowledge of individuals. As Davenport and Prusak (1998) comment, 'In theory this embedded knowledge is independent of those who developed it – and therefore has some organizational stability – an individual expert can disappear without bringing the process to a halt or reducing the company's stock of embedded knowledge.'

Organizational capital is created by people (human capital) but is also the outcome of social capital interactions. It belongs to the firm and can be developed by knowledge management processes which aim to obtain and record explicit and tacit knowledge.

PRACTICAL IMPLICATIONS OF INTELLECTUAL CAPITAL THEORY

Tom Cannon, the Chief Executive of the Management Charter Initiative, commented in 2000 that: 'Companies can be encouraged to grow by building on the capability of their people, thereby enhancing the human capital of the business and out of that assessment building up the capability of the organization.' Research conducted by Youndt (2000) led him to the conclusion that HR systems are fundamental in the development of intellectual capital:

HR activities do not directly increase organizational value creation, rather they help build employees' knowledge, skills and abilities (ie human capital), facilitate group interaction and knowledge sharing (ie social capital), and store knowledge in organizational systems, routines and cultures (ie organizational capital), which, in turn, drive value creation.

The need for boards to focus on the development of human capital was emphasized by Hugh Aldous, a partner in the accountants RSM Robson Rhodes, as follows in 2000:

> For business, the development of human capital needs to be a deliberate process led by the board. It is a process towards a measurable outcome, and therefore starts with an assessment of the personal development required. A major element of that assessment is matching peoples' competence and talents to the changing requirements of their job and thereby affecting their behaviour. People need to develop and maintain a capability to cope with the complexity and uncertainty which is involved in every job, from the most basic back office financial services job to the most complex pharmaceutical industry research.

The practical implications of intellectual capital theory are examined below under three headings:

1. *Human capital* issues concerning the attraction, retention, development and reward of people in order to create and maintain a skilled, committed and well-motivated work force.
2. *Social capital* considerations relating to the design and development of organizations that enhance the processes of developing, capturing and disseminating knowledge.
3. *Organizational capital* issues concerned with knowledge management.

HUMAN CAPITAL THEORY AND HR PRACTICES

Human capital theory focuses attention on resourcing, human resource development, and reward strategies and practices.

Resourcing strategies

Resourcing strategies are concerned with matching human capital resources to the strategic and operational needs of the organization and ensuring the effective utilization of those resources. The strategies contribute to the formulation of business strategy by defining future human capital requirements, identifying opportunities to make better use of human capital, and pointing out how human capital constraints may affect the implementation of the business plan, unless action is taken. These constraints could include skill shortages, problems in recruiting and retaining people, low productivity, high absenteeism, insufficient flexibility, or an employee relations climate which inhibits cooperation and commitment.

Resourcing strategies will be based on human resource planning processes which ensure that human capital needs are identified and plans made to satisfy them. 'Make or buy' decisions may have to be made. To a greater or lesser extent, organizations can concentrate on growing their own talent and promoting from within (a 'make' decision). But they may decide to buy in workers from elsewhere who already have the capabilities they need (a 'buy' decision). A policy choice needs to be made on the extent to which a 'make' or 'buy' approach is adopted.

Human resource development strategies

Human resource development strategies are business-led in that they are initiated by the strategic plans of the organization and driven by the human resource plans which define knowledge, skills and competency requirements. The strategies will address issues relating to the development of the capabilities of individuals and teams. They will also be concerned with encouraging organizational learning (see Chapter 34).

Human resource development strategies aim to attract and retain human capital as well as develop it. This is in accordance with the concept that workers are human capital investors; they will place their investable capital where it can earn the highest return. They want to develop their skills, potential and employability. Employees who undertake to do this and deliver their promises are more likely to get and to keep the sort of human capability they need. This applies to all categories of employees, not just knowledge workers.

Reward strategies

From a financial reward point of view, the implication of human capital theory is that investment in people adds to their value to the firm. Individuals expect a return on their own investment, and firms have to recognize that the increased value of their employees should be rewarded. Human capital theory encourages the use of skill-based or competence-based pay as a method of reward. It also underpins the concept of individual market worth. This indicates that individuals have their own value in the market place which they acquire and increase through investments by their employer and themselves in gaining extra expertise and competence by means of training, development and experience. The market worth of individuals may be considerably higher than the market rate of their jobs, and if they are not rewarded accordingly they may market their talents elsewhere.

But non-financial reward considerations should also be taken into account. If workers are investing their human capital they want to obtain a return not only in the form of opportunities to grow and to achieve, but also in terms of being valued by their employer. Organizations need therefore to consider how to recognize accomplishments through performance management processes and formal recognition schemes.

PRACTICAL IMPLICATIONS OF SOCIAL CAPITAL THEORY

Youndt (2000) comments that there is a strong link between social capital and value creation. This link can be strengthened, as Galbraith (1973) noted, by the creation of lateral relations such as task forces and teams (ie social capital) which facilitate information flow between interdependent departments, thereby eliminating or reducing costly information flows up and down hierarchical channels.

With regard to organization design, this means developing organizations which function by means of horizontal processes that cut across functional boundaries in de-layered structures. Ghoshal and Bartlett (1993) suggest that such an organization should be regarded as 'a portfolio of dynamic processes'. These processes will include networking and the use of inter-disciplinary project teams as means of developing, sharing and disseminating knowledge.

Social capital theory indicates that issues relating to organizational behaviour as well as structural matters need to be addressed. This means establishing organizational development programmes which will be concerned with process, not structure or systems; with the way things are done rather than what is done. Process refers to the ways in which people act and interact. It is about the roles they play on a continuing basis to develop, exchange and apply knowledge and to deal with events and situations involving other people.

Organizational development programmes can be based on action research (Lewin, 1947), survey feedback, and process consultation (Schein, 1969). They may incorporate team-building interventions and culture change programmes which aim to operationalize values relating to communication, participation, cooperation and trust.

PRACTICAL IMPLICATIONS OF ORGANIZATIONAL CAPITAL THEORY

Cannon (2000) asserts that 'The cutting edge of economic growth is knowledge'. Organizational or structural capital theory underpins the practice of knowledge management as covered in Chapter 22. Organizational capital is created by people (human capital) but is also the outcome of social capital interactions. It belongs to the firm and can be developed by knowledge management processes which aim to obtain and record explicit and tacit knowledge.

CONCLUSIONS

Intellectual capital theory focuses attention on practical issues relating to employee resourcing, development and reward, measuring the value of people, evaluating HR processes, organizational learning and knowledge management. While it may appear to support the 'hard' human resource management philosophy of treating employees as assets, it modifies what could be regarded as one of the less savoury aspects of HRM theory by emphasizing that these 'assets' are not owned by the business. In theory, people can invest in their own future and can choose how and where to make that investment. In practice, the extent to which they can do this may be restricted in many cases, but it is certainly something that knowledge workers can do, and this fact needs to be taken into account in formulating resourcing and human resource development policies.

From an organizational perspective, intellectual capital theory generates the following practical questions:

- What skills have we got?
- What skills do we need now and in the future?
- How are we going to attract, develop and retain these skills?
- How can we develop a culture and environment in which organizational and individual learning takes place which meets both our needs and the needs of our employees?
- How can we provide for both the explicit and tacit knowledge created in our organization to be captured, recorded and used effectively?

From the viewpoint of individuals, the theory emphasizes that they have the right to expect first, that they will obtain a proper return for the investment of their time and efforts in an organization in terms of the development of their skills and capabilities, and second, that they will be given opportunities to increase their employability, inside and outside the organization.

Part II

The practice of human resource management

In this part the key aspects of the roles of the HR function and HR practitioner are explored. The impact of HR is also discussed in the light of the outcomes of the considerable volume of research that has been carried out recently, and consideration is given to how the performance of the function can be evaluated. The part ends with an assessment of the role of the function in dealing with the management of people across international boundaries.

4

Role of the HR function

HR functions specialize in matters connected with the management and development of people in organizations. They may be concerned in any or all of the areas of human resource management described in Chapter 1: organization design and development, knowledge management, human resource planning, recruitment and selection, development and training, employee reward, employee relations, health and safety, welfare, HR administration, fulfilment of statutory requirements, equal opportunity issues and other matters concerned with the employment relationship.

The aim of this chapter is to review the role of the HR function by reference to:

- the overall role of the function;
- variations in practice;
- changes in the scope of the function;
- integrating the contribution of HR;
- organization;
- providing shared HR services;
- the respective roles of HR and line management;
- gaining support and commitment;
- marketing the function;
- budgeting for the function;
- outsourcing;
- the use of external consultants.

OVERALL ROLE OF THE HR FUNCTION

The overall role of the HR function is to enable the organization to achieve its objectives by taking initiatives and providing guidance and support on all matters relating to its employees. The basic aim is to ensure that management deals effectively with everything concerning the employment and development of people and the relationships that exist between management and the workforce. A further key role for the HR function is to play a major part in the creation of an environment which enables people to make the best use of their capacities and to realize their potential to the benefit of both the organization and themselves. The HR function operates as part of the full business management process and cannot be viewed in isolation. Although a support activity it must be proactive. It supports and promotes business solutions that take advantage of opportunities stemming from business issues just as it must find solutions to apparent constraints.

A new mandate for human resources

It has been stated by Ulrich (1998) that: 'The activities of HR appear to be and often are disconnected from the real work of the organization.' He believes that HR 'should not be defined by what it does but by what it delivers'. According to Ulrich, HR can deliver excellence in four ways:

● HR should become a partner with senior and line managers in strategy execution, helping to improve planning from the conference room to the marketplace.
● It should become an expert in the way work is organized and executed, delivering administrative efficiency to ensure that costs are reduced while quality is maintained.
● It should become a champion for employees, vigorously representing their concerns to senior management and at the same time working to increase employee contribution, that is, employees' commitment to the organization and their ability to deliver results.
● It should become an agent of continuous transformation, shaping processes and a culture that together improve an organization's capacity for change.

VARIATIONS IN THE ROLE OF THE HR FUNCTION

Hope-Hailey *et al* (1998) believe that HR could be regarded as a 'chameleon function' in the sense that the diversity of practice established by their research suggests that 'contextual variables dictate different roles for the function and different practices of people management'. As Sisson (1995) remarks, HR management is not a single homogeneous occupation – it involves a variety of roles and activities, which differ from one organization to another and from one level to another in the same organization. And Tyson (1987) has commented that the HR function is often 'balkanized' – not only is there a variety of roles and activities but these tend to be relatively self-centred, with little passage between them.

The HR role will vary between different organizations because of the influence of contextual variables such as:

- the values and beliefs of top management about the need for a specialist HR function and the extent to which it will make a contribution to the 'bottom line';
- the organization's business strategy and critical success factors and the degree to which top management believes that strategic goals are more likely to be attained and critical success factors given the attention they deserve if there is a specialist HR function – if HR is excluded from the 'top table' when HR business strategies are discussed then clearly this will diminish the importance attached to its role of the HR function, which could be left with relatively routine administrative duties and staffed by Storey's (1992a) so-called 'handmaidens';
- the structure of the organization, for example centralized or decentralized, homogeneous or divisionalized, hierarchical or delayered – in Chandler's (1962) phrase, structure follows strategy and although he was thinking of the business as a whole, this equally applies to the structure of HR;
- the culture of the organization generally (its norms, values and management style);
- the technology and core activities and competences of the organization, which might indicate that a key performance 'driver' is the human capital employed by their organization, namely, the skills, motivation and commitment of its employees; in these circumstances the need for internal professional advice and consultancy services is more likely to be recognized;
- the extent to which a policy of devolving the responsibility for HR matters to line managers is being applied;
- the traditional structure and power of the HR function;
- the professional and business expertise, credibility and political strengths of the head of the HR function and its key members.

CHANGES IN THE SCOPE OF THE FUNCTION

In some organizations, the most significant changes that are taking place in the work of the HR function are the marginalization of HR and the externalization of its services.

The marginalization of HR

Increasingly, key HR decisions are made by top management and many HR activities are being undertaken by line managers – one of the defining characteristics of HRM is that it is owned and driven by the line. In these circumstances, HR managers can be left with relatively routine systems maintenance functions, such as the recruitment and selection of support and manual workers and record keeping. As Sisson (1995) comments: 'If personnel specialists are not even present when key decisions are taken, this effectively means that personnel issues will almost inevitably be condemned to second-order status.'

Of course, this is by no means a universal phenomenon. Heads of HR in many organizations do get involved in strategic business issues and are the key players in the development of business-led HR strategies and in innovating the HR processes required to ensure that the organization's strategic goals are achieved. They recognize that the responsibility for managing people must be devolved to those who are directly concerned, ie line managers. They will, however, provide guidance and support wherever this is needed.

Approaches to HR management

The following four approaches to HR management have been identified by Adams (1991), each of which can be seen as representing a 'kind of scale of increasing degrees of externalization, understood as the application of market forces to the delivery of HR activities'.

1. The *in-house agency*, in which the HR department, or any of its activities such as graduate recruitment, is seen as a cost centre and the activities are cross-charged to other departments or divisions.
2. The *internal consultancy*, in which the HR department sells its services to internal customers (line managers), the implication being that managers have some freedom to go elsewhere if they are not happy with the service that is being provided.
3. The *business within a business*, in which some of the activities of the function are

formed into a quasi-independent organization which may trade not only with organizational units but also externally.

4. *External consultancy*, in which the organizational units go outside to completely independent businesses for help and advice.

The common feature of all these approaches is that the services delivered are charged for in some form of contract which may incorporate a service level agreement.

Shared services

A fairly recent development, as described later in this chapter, is the provision by the HR function of 'shared services' which are available to a number of parties.

INTEGRATING THE HR CONTRIBUTION

Two important aims of HRM are to achieve strategic integration and coherence in the development and operation of HRM policies and employment practices. Strategic integration could be described as vertical integration – the process of ensuring that HR strategies are integrated with or 'fit' business strategies. The concept of coherence could be defined as horizontal integration – the development of a mutually reinforcing and interrelated set of HR policies and practices, that is, 'bundling' or the use of 'complementarities' as described in Chapter 2.

Stratetic or vertical integration is chiefly about ensuring that the organization has the skilled, committed and well-motivated workforce it needs to achieve its business objectives. It can be attained by linking HR strategies to basic competitive strategies.

Horizontal integration is accomplished by developing a coherent – a well-knit – range of interconnected and mutually reinforcing HR policies and practices. This may be achieved by the use of shared processes, such as competence analysis, which provide a common frame of reference and performance management which is concerned with role definition, employee development and reward. Integration is also more likely to take place if shared values exist between line managers and HR specialists on how HR policies should be implemented.

Achieving integration is also about ensuring, when planning any innovation, that its implications on other aspects of HR policies and practice are fully considered and that further thought is given on how it could support those policies or practices.

The aim should be to adopt a more systematic approach by 'bundling' HRM policies and processes. As reported by Walsh (1998), a Warwick Business School study confirmed the findings of research conducted in the US which showed that bundling or the use of complementary HR practices ('complementarities') was highly effective in boosting productivity. The investigation of the working practices of 139 UK companies revealed that productivity may be up to 8 per cent higher in firms which bundled together such practices as communications, teamworking, flexibility, job security, skills training and incentive pay. The concept of bundling suggests that the more mutually supportive HR practices are, the more likely they are to deliver better results. Linking activities together can help to ensure that developments in one area can achieve improvements in others.

ORGANIZING THE HR FUNCTION

The organization and staffing of the HR function clearly depends on the size of the business, the extent to which operations are decentralized, the type of work carried out, the kind of people employed, the role assigned to the HR function and the type of services it is expected to provide.

There is no standard ratio for the number of HR specialists to the number of employees. It can vary from 1 to 80, to 1 to 1,000 or more. This ratio is affected by all the factors mentioned above and can only be decided empirically by analysing what HR services are required and then deciding on the extent to which they are provided by full-time professional staff or can be purchased from external agencies or consultants. The degree to which the organization believes that the management of human resources is the prime responsibility of line managers and team leaders affects not only the numbers of HR staff but also the nature of the guidance and support services they provide.

There are, therefore, no absolute rules for organizing the HR function, but current practice suggests that the following guidelines should be taken into account:

● The head of the function should report directly to the chief executive and should be on the board or the management committee in order to contribute to the formulation of corporate strategies and play a full part in the formulation of HR strategies (a job description for an HR Director is given on page 347).
● In a decentralized organization, subsidiary companies, divisions or operational units should be responsible for their own HR management affairs within the framework of broad strategic and policy guidelines from the centre.
● The central HR function in a decentralized organization should be slimmed down to the minimum required to develop group human resource strategies and policies. It may be concerned with resourcing throughout the group at senior management level and advising on both recruitment and career development. It

may also control remuneration and benefits policies for senior management. The centre may coordinate industrial relations negotiating if bargaining has been decentralized, especially where bargaining is related to terms and conditions such as hours of work, holidays and employee benefits. Although rates of pay may vary among subsidiaries, it is generally desirable to develop a consistent approach to benefit provision. The research conducted by Hope-Hailey *et al* (1998) identified a trend of devolving HR operations to divisions, thus reducing the significance and influence of the group HR function.

● The HR function has to be capable of delivering the level of advice and services required by the organization. Delivery may be achieved by the direct provision of services but, increasingly, businesses are outsourcing their HR services; for example, through training providers and other forms of external consultancy assistance. There is also a marked trend towards 'empowering' line managers to handle their own HR affairs. They may simply regard the HR function as a 'resource', which they use as required. This tendency underlines the significance of the internal consultancy role of HR specialists as described in Chapter 5.

● The function will be organized in accordance with the level of support and services it is required to give and the range of activities that need to be catered for. These could include resourcing, management development, training, reward management, employee relations and HR services in such areas as health and safety, welfare, HR information systems and employment matters generally. In a large department, each of these areas may be provided for separately, but they can be combined in various ways.

The organization and staffing of the HR function needs to take account of its role in formulating HR strategies and policies and intervening and innovating as required. But the function also has to provide efficient and cost-effective services in such areas as recruitment, training, pay, health and safety management and HR records. These cannot be neglected: the credibility and reputation of the function so far as line managers are concerned will be largely a function of the quality of those services to the HR department's internal customers. It is, in fact, important for members of the function to remember that line managers are their customers and deserve high levels of personal service that meet their needs.

The most important principle to bear in mind about the organization of the HR function is that it should fit the needs of the business. Against that background, there will always be a choice about the best structure to adopt, but this choice should be made on the basis of an analysis of what the organization wants in the way of HR management guidance and services. This is why there are considerable variations in HR practice.

SHARED HR SERVICES

The term 'shared services' refers to the central provision of HR services which are available to a number of parties and are therefore the same for all those who take them up. The nature of the services is determined by both the provider and the user. The customer or user defines the level of the service and decides which services to take up. Thus, 'the user is the chooser' (Ulrich, 1995). As described by Reilly (2000), administrative tasks tend to be those most commonly covered by shared services, for example:

- payroll changes;
- relocation services;
- recruitment administration;
- benefits administration (including flexible benefits and share schemes);
- company car provision;
- pensions administration;
- employee welfare support;
- training support;
- absence monitoring;
- management information.

Services can be provided through the Internet, a telephone customer help line, a consultancy pool of advisors, or 'centres of excellence' with expertise in such areas as resourcing, employee relations, reward or training. The increasing interest in shared services has been prompted by the more extensive and strategic use of HR information systems.

The organizations covered by the research conducted by Reilly on behalf of the Institute for Employment Studies (Reilly, 2000) identified one or more of the following reasons for providing shared services:

- HR will be consumer driven, more accessible, more professional;
- the quality of HR services will be improved in terms of using better processes, delivery to specification, time and budget, incorporation of good practice, the achievement of greater consistency and accuracy;
- the process can help to achieve organizational flexibility – a common service will support customers during business change;
- it can support the repositioning of HR so that it moves from a purely operational to a more strategic role, ensuring that HR is carrying out the role of 'acting as a catalyst for change... anticipating problems and making things happen' (Hutchinson and Wood, 1995).

The advantages of providing shared services include lower costs, better quality, more efficient resourcing and better customer service. But there are disadvantages which include loss of face-to-face contact, deskilling administrative jobs and, potentially, remoteness from the users.

The steps required to introduce shared services in what is often described as an 'HR service centre' are as follows (all should involve users as well as providers):

1. Identify present arrangements.
2. Obtain views from customers on the quality of existing services and what could be done to improve them (including the scope for sharing services).
3. Define the areas for shared services.
4. Define how shared services would be supplied, including who provides the service, where it is provided, and how it is provided (this will include consideration of outsourcing as discussed later in this chapter).
5. Decide on priorities.
6. Plan a programme (this could be phased and might involve pilot testing).

THE RESPECTIVE ROLES OF HR AND LINE MANAGEMENT

It has been the accepted tradition of HR management that HR specialists are there to provide support and services to line managers, not to usurp the latter's role of 'getting things done through people' – their responsibility for managing their own HR affairs. In practice, the HR function has frequently had the role of ensuring that HR policies are implemented consistently throughout the organization as well as the more recent onerous responsibility for ensuring that both the letter and the spirit of employment law are implemented consistently. The latter responsibility has often been seen as a process of ensuring that the organization does not get involved in tedious, time-wasting and often expensive employment tribunal proceedings.

Carrying out this role has often led to the HR function 'policing' line management, which can be a cause of tension and ambiguity. To avoid this result, HR specialists may have to adopt a reasonably light touch: providing advice rather than issuing dicta, except when a manager is clearly contravening the law or when his or her actions are likely to lead to an avoidable dispute or an employment tribunal case that the organization will probably lose.

It has also frequently been the case that, in spite of paying lip service to the principle that 'line managers must manage', HR departments have usurped the line managers' true role of being involved in key decisions concerning the recruitment, development and remuneration of their people, thus diminishing the managers' capacity to manage their key resource effectively. This situation has arisen most frequently in large bureaucratic organizations and/or those with a powerful centralized HR function. It still exists in some quarters, but as decentralization and devolution increase and organizations are finding that they are having to operate more flexibly, it is becoming less common.

It is necessary to reconcile what might be called the 'functional control' aspects of an HR specialist's role (achieving the consistent application of policies and acting as the guardian of the organization's values concerning people) and the role of providing services, support and, as necessary, guidance to managers without issuing commands or relieving them of their responsibilities. However, the distinction between giving advice and telling people what to do, or between providing help and taking over, can be blurred, and the relationship is one that has to be developed and nurtured with great care. The most appropriate line for HR specialists to take is that of emphasizing that they are there to help line managers achieve their objectives through their people, not to do their job for them.

In practice, however, some line managers may be only too glad to let the HR department do their people management job for them, especially the less pleasant aspects like handling discipline and grievance problems. A delicate balance has therefore to be achieved between providing help and advice when it is clearly needed and creating a 'dependency culture' which discourages managers from thinking and acting for themselves on people matters for which they are responsible. Managers will not learn about dealing with people if they are over-dependent on HR specialists. The latter therefore have to stand off sometimes and say, in effect, 'that's your problem'.

Research into HR management and the line conducted by the IPD (Hutchinson and Wood, 1995) produced the following findings:

● Most organizations reported a trend over the past five years towards greater line management responsibility for HR management without it causing any significant tension between HR and the line.

● Devolution offered positive opportunities to the HR function to become involved in strategic, proactive and internal consultancy roles because they were less involved in day-to-day operational HR activities.

● Both HR and line management were involved in operational HR activities. Line managers were more heavily involved in recruitment, selection and training decisions and in handling discipline issues and grievances. HR was still largely responsible for such matters as analysing training needs, running internal courses and pay and benefits.

- There is an underlying concern that line managers are not sufficiently competent to carry out their new roles. This may be for a number of reasons, including lack of training, pressures of work, because managers have been promoted for their technical rather than managerial skills, or because they are used to referring certain issues to the HR department.
- Some HR specialists also have difficulty in adopting their new roles because they do not have the right skills (such as an understanding of the business) or because they see devolution as a threat to their own job security.
- Other problems over devolution include uncertainty on the part of line managers about the role of the HR function, lack of commitment by line managers to performing their new roles, and achieving the right balance between providing line managers with as much freedom as possible and the need to retain core controls and direction.

The conclusion reached by the researchers was that:

If line managers are to take an effective greater responsibility for HR management activities then, from the outset, the rules and responsibilities of personnel and line managers must be clearly defined and understood. Support is needed from the personnel department in terms of providing a procedural framework, advice and guidance on all personnel management matters, and training line managers so that they have the appropriate skills and knowledge to carry out their new duties.

The research conducted by Hope-Hailey *et al* (1998) in eight British-based organizations revealed that all of them were shifting responsibility for people management down the line. In practice, this often meant that responsibility for decision-making on HR issues had been devolved to line managers, but that the HR function continued to be responsible for operational functions such as recruitment and pay systems. As Hope-Hailey *et al* commented, 'There seemed to be little indication that this move had reduced in any way the level of necessary bureaucracy associated with the implementation of personnel policies and procedures.' However, they noted that 'personnel was no longer seen as a rule maker or enforcer, but it was still regarded – in part – as an administrative function'. With reference to the activities of the HR functions in these organizations, the research established that there was 'more emphasis on achieving behavioural change through a more "nuts and bolts" systems approach rather than large scale organizational development activities'.

MARKETING THE HR FUNCTION

Top management and line managers are the internal customers whose wants and needs the HR function must identify and meet. How can this be done?

First, it is necessary to understand the needs of the business and its critical success factors – where the business is going, how it intends to get there and what are the things that are going to make the difference between success and failure.

Having ascertained the business needs, it is next necessary to find out what managers want to satisfy these needs – starting at the top. This means identifying the people issues that they believe to be important in the areas of resourcing, motivation and reward, gaining commitment, employee development and training, and employee relations. This market research is conducted partly by 'being there', listening to and, importantly, joining in discussions on business issues and establishing the people element in those issues. This is the best reason why heads of HR functions should be members of the executive board. Their role on the board is not just to defend their corners. They are there to take an active part in business discussions because only by doing so will they truly understand the issues and, by making a positive contribution, gain the respect of their colleagues. However, market research is not simply a matter of sitting on boards and committees. HR practitioners should be in the business of talking and listening to people at all levels in the organization to find out what they want.

Market research data need to be converted into marketing plans for the development of products and services to meet ascertained needs – of the business and its managers and employees. If, for example, the need is to raise the skill base or increase levels of competence, attention can be focused on such initiatives and interventions as skill-based or competence-based pay, performance management processes and continuous development programmes with an emphasis on self-development. The marketing plan should establish the costs of introducing and maintaining these initiatives and the benefits that will be obtained from them. Every effort must be made to quantify these benefits in financial terms. If the 'product' is skill-based pay then the costs of pay increases, additional training and accreditation will have to be calculated. Estimates will need to be made of the financial gains that will be achieved through increased productivity and the better use of labour through multiskilling. Any savings in cost can also be assessed by, for example, the use of better-trained employees in a just-in-time (JIT) environment to achieve a continuous flow of production to meet demand or supply requirements without delay or waste. If the 'product' is a programme for subcontracting work, the costs of procuring and employing the people required will be assessed against the savings resulting from a reduction in the size of the permanent labour force.

The next step in the marketing process is to persuade management that this is a product or service the business needs. This means spelling out its costs and benefits, covering the financial and human resources required to develop, introduce and maintain it and the impact it will make on the performance of the business. Convincing management that a product or service is worthwhile in terms of meeting business needs will be easier if the initial customer research and product development activities have been carried out thoroughly. Credibility is vital. This will be achieved if the proposal for expenditure is credible in itself, but the track record of the HR function in delivering what it proposes to do is equally important. The approach is akin to 'branding' in product planning. This identifies the product or service, spells out the benefits it provides and differentiates it from other services, thus bringing it to the attention of customers. Presentation is important through logos and distinctive brochures. Some HR departments brand products with an immediately identifiable name such as 'Gemini'.

PREPARING, JUSTIFYING AND PROTECTING THE HR BUDGET

Preparation

HR budgets are prepared like any other functional department budget in the following stages:

1. Define functional objectives and plans.
2. Forecast the activity levels required to achieve objectives and plans in the light of company budget guidelines and assumptions on future business activity levels and any targets for reducing overheads or for maintaining them at the same level.
3. Assess the resources (people and finance) required to enable the activity levels to be achieved.
4. Cost each activity area – the sum of these costs will be the total budget.

Justification

Justifying budgets means ensuring in advance that objectives and plans are generally agreed – there should be no surprises in a budget submitted to top management. A cast-iron case should then be prepared to support the forecast levels of activity in each area and, on a cost/benefit basis, to justify any special expenditures.

Protection

The best way to protect a budget is to provide in advance a rationale for each area of expenditure, which proves that it is necessary and will justify the costs involved. The worst thing that can happen is to be forced onto the defensive. If service delivery standards (service level agreements) are agreed and achieved, these will provide a further basis for protecting the budget.

OUTSOURCING HR WORK

Increasingly, HR services which have previously been regarded as a business's own responsibility are now routinely being purchased from external suppliers, ie outsourced. Managements are facing Tom Peters' (1988) challenge: 'prove it can't be subcontracted'. The formal policy of a major global corporation quoted by Wheatley (1994) reads: 'Manufacture only those items – and internally source only those support services – that directly contribute to, or help to maintain, our competitive advantage.' The Institute of Personnel and Development (1998b) has stated that 'the biggest single cause in the increase of outsourcing has been the concept of the core organization which focuses its in-house expertise on its primary function and purchases any necessary support from a range of sources in its periphery'.

The HR function is well positioned to outsource some of its activities to management consultancies and other agencies or firms who act as service providers in such fields as recruitment, executive search, training, occupational health and welfare. HR functions that have been given responsibility for other miscellaneous activities such as catering, car fleet management, facilities management and security (because there is nowhere else to put them) may gladly outsource them to specialist firms.

The case for outsourcing

There are three reasons for outsourcing:

- *Cost saving* – HR costs are reduced because the services are cheaper and the size of the function can be cut back.
- *Concentration of HR effort* – members of the function are not diverted from the key tasks which add value.
- *Obtaining expertise* – know-how and experience that is unavailable in the organization can be purchased.

Areas for outsourcing

The main areas for outsourcing as identified by the Institute of Personnel and Development (1998b) are:

- training;
- recruitment;
- health and safety monitoring and advice;
- employee welfare and counselling activities;
- childcare facilities;
- payroll management;
- specialist legal advisory services;
- occupational health and fitness services.

Problems with outsourcing

The advantages of outsourcing seem to be high, but there are problems. Surveys have shown that a very large proportion of firms that have outsourced are not satisfied with the results. One of the main problems they identified was when firms outsourced for short-term cost and headcount reductions. The problems were that some firms unthinkingly outsourced some of their core activities on an *ad hoc* basis to gain short-term advantage, while others found that they were being leveraged by their suppliers to pay higher rates. Firms may focus on a definition of the core that may have been justified at the time but did not take account of the future. Additionally, a seemingly random policy of outsourcing can lead to lower employee morale and to a 'who next' atmosphere.

Deciding to outsource

If the reasons for outsourcing are compelling, the way to minimize problems is initially to give careful consideration to the case for outsourcing. It is necessary to assess each potential area with great care in order to determine whether it can and should be outsourced and exactly what such outsourcing is intended to achieve. The questions to be answered include: Is the activity a core one or peripheral? How efficiently is it run at present? What contribution does it make to the qualitative and financial well-being of the organization? This is an opportunity to re-engineer the HR function, subjecting each activity to critical examination to establish whether the services can be provided from within or outside the organization, if at all. Outsourcing may well be worthwhile if it is certain that it can deliver a better service at a lower cost.

The decision to outsource should be based on rigorous analysis and benchmarking to establish how other organizations manage their HR activities. This will define the level of service required. The cost of providing the existing service internally should also be measured. This will be easier if an activity-based costing system is used in the organization.

Selecting service providers

Potential service providers should be required to present tenders in response to a brief. Three or four providers should be approached so that a choice can be made. The tender should set out how the brief will be met and how much it will cost. Selection should take into account the degree to which the tender meets the specification, the quality and reputation of the firm and the cost (this is an important consideration but not the only one – the level of service that will be provided is critical). References should be obtained before a contract is drawn up and agreed. The contract should be very clear about services, costs and the basis upon which it can be terminated.

Managerial and legal implications of outsourcing

Service providers need to be managed just as carefully – if not more so – than internal services. Service standards and budgets should be reviewed and agreed regularly and management information systems should be set up so that performance can be monitored. Swift corrective action should be taken if things go wrong and the contract terminated if there is a serious shortcoming.

The legal implications of outsourcing are that it will be based on a service contract and the purchaser of the services has the right to insist that the terms of the contract are fulfilled. Purchasers also have the duty to fulfil their side of the contract, for example providing agreed facilities, meeting the leasing terms set out in a car fleet management contract and paying for the services as required by the contract.

USING MANAGEMENT CONSULTANTS

Management consultants act as service providers in such fields as recruitment, executive search and training. They also provide outside help and guidance to their clients by advising on the introduction of new systems or procedures or by going through processes of analysis and diagnosis in order to produce recommendations on solutions to problems or to assist generally in the improvement of organizational performance.

Their role is to provide expertise and resources to assist in development and change.

The steps required to select and use consultants effectively

1. Define the business need – what added value consultants will provide.
2. Justify their use in terms of their expertise, objectivity and ability to bring resources to bear which might otherwise be unavailable – if the need has been established in cost–benefit terms, the use of external consultants rather than internal resources has to be justified.
3. Define clearly the objectives of the exercise in terms of the end-results.
4. Invite three or four firms or independent consultants to submit proposals.
5. Select the preferred consultants on the basis of their proposal and an interview (a 'beauty contest') – the criteria should be the degree to which the consultants understand the need, the relevance and acceptability of their proposed deliverables and programme of work, the capacity of the firm and the particular consultants to deliver, whether the consultants will be able to adapt to the culture and management style of the organization, the extent to which they are likely to be acceptable to the people with whom they will work, and the cost (a consideration, but, as for service providers, not the ultimate consideration).
6. Take up references before confirming the appointment.
7. Agree and sign a contract – this should always be in writing and should set out deliverables, timing and costs, methods of payment and arrangements for termination.
8. Agree a detailed project programme.
9. Monitor the progress of the assignment carefully without unduly interfering in the day-to-day work of the consultants, and evaluate the outcomes.

Legal implications

If there is a serious problem a consultancy assignment can be cancelled if either party has clearly failed to meet the terms of the contract (whether this is a formal contract or simply an exchange of letters). Clients can also sue consultants for professional negligence if they believe that their advice or actions have caused financial or some other form of measurable loss. Professional negligence is, however, not always easy to prove, especially in HR assignments. Consultants can always claim that their advice was perfectly good but that it has been used incorrectly by the client (this may also be difficult to prove). Suing consultants can be a messy business and should only be undertaken when it is felt that they (or their insurers) should pay for their mistakes and thus help to recoup the client's losses. It should also be remembered that independent consultants and even some small firms may not have taken out professional liability insurance. If that is the case, all the aggrieved client who sues would do is to bankrupt them, which may give the client some satisfaction but could be a somewhat pointless exercise. The latter problem can be overcome if the client only selects consultants who are insured.

5

Role of the HR practitioner

This chapter covers:

- what is expected from HR professionals;
- the activities of HR practitioners;
- how the practitioners gain support and commitment;
- the role of HR practitioners;
- models of HRM, classifying the types of roles HR specialists carry out;
- issues relating to ambiguities and conflict in the contribution of HR practitioners and the nature of professionalism in HRM;
- the factors contributing to competence in HR management.

WHAT IS EXPECTED FROM HR PROFESSIONALS

Human resource professionals:

- function as business partners;
- deliver effective people strategies;
- are committed to ethical standards;
- can apply and adapt techniques for people management and development to fit the needs of organizations and the people who work in them;

- operate as 'thinking performers';
- are skilled in the management of change;
- are personally committed to lifelong learning and Continuing Professional Development.

The focus is therefore on being businesslike, strategic and ethical, the application of professional knowledge and skills, change management and continuous development.

ACTIVITIES

The activities carried out by HR practitioners will of course vary widely according to the needs of the organization, the job they carry out and their own capabilities. In general, however, they provide services, guidance and advice.

Service provision

The basic activity carried out by HR specialists is that of providing services to internal customers. These include management, line managers, team leaders and employees. The services may be general, covering all aspects of HRM: human resource planning, recruitment and selection, employee development, employee reward, employee relations, health and safety management and welfare. Or services may be provided in only one or two of these areas by specialists. The focus may be on the needs of management (eg resourcing), or it may extend to all employees (eg health and safety).

The aims are to provide effective services that meet the needs of the business, its management and its employees and to administer them efficiently.

Guidance

To varying degrees, HR practitioners provide guidance to management. At the highest level, this will include recommendations on HR strategies that have been developed by processes of analysis and diagnosis to address strategic issues arising from business needs and human, organizational or environmental factors. At all levels, guidance may be provided on HR policies and procedures and the implications of employment legislation. In the latter area, HR practitioners are concerned with compliance – ensuring that legal requirements are met.

Providing guidance in the above areas means taking on the roles of business partner, strategist, interventionist, innovator, internal consultant and monitor as described in the next section of this chapter.

More general guidance may be given on the values the organization should adopt in managing people and the ethical considerations they should take into account. This role of acting as 'guardian' of people values is also discussed in the next section.

Guidance will also be provided to managers to ensure that consistent decisions are made on such matters as performance ratings, pay increases and disciplinary actions.

Advice

HR practitioners provide advice on such matters as job design, advertising for staff, drawing up short-lists for selection, identifying methods of satisfying training needs, the rates of pay to be offered to employees on recruitment or promotion, health and safety requirements, employee relations issues (disputes, grievances and communications) and handling people problems (discipline, capability, absenteeism, time-keeping, etc).

Advice will be given to managers and team leaders on the above issues but it will also be provided to individuals. This may deal with aspects of work and development such as the suitability of the present job, developing competence and employability, self-managed learning and career development. It may cover problems arising from work, such as physical ailments, stress, incompatibility with managers or colleagues, bullying or sexual harassment. It could extend to personal problems that affect employees at work. These activities mean that the HR practitioner can take on the roles of counsellor and mentor as well as problem solver.

GAINING SUPPORT AND COMMITMENT

HR practitioners mainly get results by exerting influence, and as Guest and Hoque (1994) note: 'By exerting influence, HR managers help to shape the framework of HR policy and practice.' Although line managers may make the day-to-day decisions, influencing skills are therefore necessary for HR specialists. But there is a constant danger of HR professionals being so overcome by the beauty and truth of their bright idea that they expect everyone else – management and employees alike – to fall for it immediately. This is not how it is. Management and employees can create blockages and barriers and their support and commitment need to be gained, which is not always easy.

Blockages and barriers within management

Managers will block or erect barriers to what the HR function believes to be progress if they are not persuaded that it will benefit both the organization and themselves at an acceptable cost (money and their time and trouble).

Blockages and barriers from employees

Employees will block or set up barriers to 'progress' or innovations if they feel they conflict with their own interests. They are likely, with reason, to be cynical about protestations that what is good for the organization will always be good for them.

Giving support from top management

The support of top management is achievable by processes of marketing the HR function and persuasion. Boards and senior managers, like anyone else, are more likely to be persuaded to take a course of action if:

- it can be demonstrated that it will meet both the needs of the organization and their own personal needs;
- the proposal realistically spells out the benefits and the costs and, as far as possible, is justified in added value terms (ie the income generated by the proposal will significantly exceed the cost of implementing it);
- there is proof that the innovation has already worked well within the organization (perhaps as a pilot scheme) or represents 'best practice' which is likely to be transferable to the organization;
- it can be shown that in some way the proposal will increase the business' competitive edge, for example enlarging the skill base or multiskilling to ensure that it can achieve competitive advantage through innovation and/or reducing time-to-market;
- it can be implemented without too much trouble, for example not taking up a lot of their time, or not meeting with strong opposition from line management, employees or trade unions (it is as well to check the likely reaction before launching a proposal);
- it will add to the reputation of the company by showing that it is a 'world class' organization, ie what it does is as good as, if not better than, the world leaders in the sector in which the business operates (a promise that publicity will be achieved through articles in professional journals, press releases and conference presentations will help);
- the proposal is brief, to the point and well argued – it should take no more than five minutes to present orally and should be summarized in writing on the proverbial one side of one sheet of paper (supplementary details can be included in appendices).

Gaining the support and commitment of line management

This can sometimes be more difficult than gaining the support of top management. Line managers can be cynical or realistic about innovation – they have seen it all before and/or they believe it won't work (sometimes with good reason). Innovations pushed down from the top can easily fail.

Gaining line management support requires providing an answer to the question 'what's in it for me?' in terms of how the innovation will help them to achieve better results without imposing unacceptable additional burdens on them. New employment practices that take up precious time and involve paperwork will be treated with particular suspicion. Many line managers, often from bitter experience, resent the bureaucracy that can surround and, indeed, engulf systems favoured by HR people, such as traditional performance appraisal schemes.

Obtaining support requires market research and networking – getting around to talk to managers about their needs and testing new ideas to obtain reactions. The aim is to build up a body of information which will indicate approaches that are likely to be most acceptable, and therefore will most probably work, or at least to suggest areas where particular efforts will need to be made to persuade and educate line management. It is also useful to form 'strategic alliances' with influential managers who are enthusiastic about the innovation and will not only lend it vocal support but will also cooperate in pilot-testing it.

On the principle that 'nothing succeeds like success', support for new HR practices can often be achieved by demonstrating that it has worked well elsewhere in the organization.

Gaining commitment will be easier if managers know that they have been consulted and that their opinions have been listened to and acted upon. It is even better to involve them as members of project teams or task forces in developing the new process or system. This is the way to achieve ownership and therefore commitment.

Gaining the support and commitment of employees

When it comes to new employment practices, employees generally react in exactly the same way as managers: they want to know 'what's in it for us?' They also want to know the hidden agenda –'Why is the company really wanting to introduce a performance management process? Will it simply be used as a means of gaining evidence for disciplinary proceedings? Or is it even going to provide the information required to select people for redundancy?' As far as possible this kind of question needs to be answered in advance.

Sounding out employee opinion can be conducted through attitude surveys or, even better, focus groups. The latter method involves getting groups of people together to discuss (to 'focus' on) various issues and propositions. A well-run focus group can generate valid information on employees' feelings about and reaction to an initiative.

Employee commitment is also more likely if they participate in the development of the new employment practice and if they know that their contributions have been welcomed and acted upon.

ROLES

As mentioned above, the activities of HR practitioners involve taking on a number of different roles. Again, the extent to which any of these roles are carried out depends on the practitioner's position in the organization, the expectations of management on the contribution HR should make, and the practitioner's own capacity to make an impact, exert influence and demonstrate that the services, guidance and advice provided add value. The main roles that can be played are described below.

The business partner role

As business partners, HR practitioners share responsibility with their line management colleagues for the success of the enterprise. As defined by Tyson (1985) and Ulrich (1998), HR specialists as business partners integrate their activities closely with top management and ensure that they serve a long-term strategic purpose, and have the capacity to identify business opportunities, to see the broad picture and to see how their HR role can help to achieve the company's business objectives.

HR practitioners in their role as business partners are aware of business strategies and the opportunities and threats facing the organization. They are capable of analysing organizational strengths and weaknesses and diagnosing the issues facing the enterprise (PEST analysis) and their human resource implications. They know about the critical success factors that will create competitive advantage and they can draw up a convincing business case for innovations that will add value.

The strategist role

As strategists, HR practitioners address major long-term issues concerning the management and development of people and the employment relationship. They are guided by the business plans of the organization but they also contribute to the formulation of the business plans. This is achieved by ensuring that top managers focus on the human resource implications of their plans. HR strategists persuade top managers that they must develop plans that make the best use of the core competences of the organization's human resources. They emphasize, in the words of Hendry and Pettigrew (1986), that people are a strategic resource for the achievement of competitive advantage.

A strategic approach to managing people as described in Chapter 2 means that HR strategists strive to achieve strategic integration and fit. Integration means that strategies are linked together to form a coherent whole. Vertical integration takes place when HR strategies are linked to and support business strategies. Horizontal integration is achieved when a range of coherent, interconnected and mutually reinforcing HR strategies are established. Strategic fit means that both the business and HR strategies meet the particular needs and circumstances of the organization.

The interventionist role

To intervene is to modify the course of events. An intervention is an action or an event in itself that is intended to achieve this purpose.

HR practitioners are well placed to observe and analyse what is happening in and to their organizations. They can take a somewhat detached, albeit empathetic, view on what is happening to organizational processes and their impact on people. Line managers may find this more difficult because of their inevitable preoccupation with operational matters. The role of HR specialists is to adopt an all-embracing, holistic approach to understanding organizational issues and their effect on people.

Following their analysis, HR professionals can produce a diagnosis of any problems and their causes and formulate proposals on what should be done about them. Interventions can be concerned with organizational processes such as interaction between departments and people, team work and structural change, for example delayering. It may be necessary to intervene with proposals on job design, team building, training, communications and involvement in anticipation of the people implications of the introduction of new technology, a business process re-engineering exercise, a change in work methods such as just-in-time (JIT) manufacturing, or the launch of total quality or improved customer service initiatives.

HR practitioners can also intervene when they believe that existing people management processes need to be improved or changed. They can observe problems of performance, productivity, competence, motivation or commitment and intervene with ideas about how these can be dealt with by, for example, performance management and reward processes. Similarly, they can identify high levels of employee turnover, a multiplicity of grievances and unfair dismissal cases or other evidence of poor morale, establish causes and then make proposals on any actions required in such areas as selection, training, pay and the provision of extra guidance and help to line managers.

A senior HR executive in Unilever, as reported by Armstrong (1989), expressed the following views about what he termed 'selective intervention':

> You intervene in different ways in different situations and it is an opportunistic business. You have to start with an overview of where the pressure points are within an organization and where you can make a useful intervention. But the opportunity to intervene can come at the most unexpected times.

But intervention should not degenerate into interference. The interventionist role has to be handled delicately. It is necessary first to establish a good business case and then to take people along progressively, helping them to understand the problem and its causes and involving them in developing solutions which they will implement, with HR guidance and help as required.

The innovation role

A proactive approach to HRM will mean that HR specialists will want to innovate – to introduce new processes and procedures which they believe will increase organizational effectiveness.

The need for innovation should be established by processes of analysis and diagnosis that identify the business need and the issues to be addressed. 'Benchmarking' can take place to identify 'best practice' as adopted by other organizations. But 'best fit' is more important than 'best practice'. In other words, the innovation should meet the particular needs of the business, which are likely to differ from those of other 'best practice' organizations. It has to be demonstrable that the innovation is appropriate, beneficial, practical in the circumstances and can be implemented without too much difficulty in the shape of opposition from those affected by it or the unjustifiable use of resources – financial and the time of those involved.

The danger, according to Marchington (1995a), is that HR people may go in for 'impression management' – aiming to make an impact on senior managers and colleagues through publicizing high profile innovations. HR specialists who aim to draw attention to themselves simply by promoting the latest flavour of the month, irrespective of its relevance or practicality, are falling into the trap which Drucker (1955), anticipating Marchington by 40 years, described as follows: 'The constant worry of all HR administrators is their inability to prove that they are making a contribution to the enterprise. Their pre-occupation is with the search for a "gimmick" which will impress their management colleagues.'

As Marchington points out, the risk is that people believe 'all can be improved by a wave of the magic wand and the slaying of a few evil characters along the way'. This facile assumption means that people can too readily devise elegant solutions which do not solve the problem because of the hazards encountered during implementation – for example, indifference or open hostility. These have to be anticipated and catered for.

The internal consultancy role

As internal consultants, HR practitioners function like external management consultants, working alongside their colleagues – their clients – in analysing problems, diagnosing issues and proposing solutions. They will be concerned with the development of HR processes or systems, for example performance management, personal development planning or new pay structures, and in 'process consulting'. The latter is concerned with process areas such as organization, team building, objective setting, quality management, customer service and, importantly, change management. Process consulting is the most challenging field for internal consultants because it requires both skill and credibility, and external consultants may seem to be more credible because of their perceived expertise and independence.

In some organizations, HR specialists may be assigned service delivery contracts in such fields as recruitment and training. HR practitioners in their roles as interventionists and innovators are ideally placed to identify needs as they arise. They do not have to wait to be asked, as do external consultants. But management consultancy requires considerable skill and this is possibly even more the case with internal as distinct from external consultancy. Internal consultants must:

- understand the strategic imperatives of the organization and its business plan, environment and culture and their advice must be embedded in this understanding;
- have well-developed analytical and diagnostic skills;
- be good project managers able to plan and conduct assignments through the stages of contact, contract (deliverables and cost), data collection, analysis, diagnosis, feedback, discussion and agreement of recommendations, and implementation;
- be able to act as 'experts' as well as helpers;
- understand the needs of their internal clients and work with them in developing solutions while at the same time preserving an appropriate degree of independence and objectivity so that they can bring their expertise to bear on the issue or problem;
- ensure that their internal clients 'own' the solution and are capable of implementing it and want to do so.

The monitoring role

As monitors of the application of HR policies and procedures and the extent to which the organization's values concerning people are concerned, HR practitioners have a delicate, even a difficult, role to play. They are not there to 'police' what line managers do but it is still necessary to ensure that the policies and procedures are implemented with a reasonable degree of consistency. This role as described by Storey (1992a) can mean that HR specialists can act as 'regulators' who are 'managers of discontent' involved in formulating and monitoring employment rules. Although the tendency is to devolve more responsibility for HR matters to line managers, they cannot be given total freedom to flout company policy or to contravene the provisions of employment, equal opportunity and health and safety legislation. A balance has to be struck between freedom and consistency or legal obligations. For example, line managers may be given authority to award pay increases within a budget, but the HR department may monitor proposals and have the right to question unusual awards or distributions of increases. When a disciplinary case arises, the HR department has the right to insist that the standard disciplinary procedure is followed.

HR practitioners may also act as the guardians of the organization's values concerning people. They point out when behaviour conflicts with those values or where proposed actions will be inconsistent with them. In a sense, their roles require them to act as the 'conscience' of management – a necessary role but not an easy one to play.

The monitoring role is particularly important with regard to employment legislation. HR practitioners have to ensure that policies and procedures comply with the legislation and that they are implemented correctly by line managers.

The reactive/proactive roles

HR practitioners can play a mainly reactive role. They do what they are told or asked to do. They respond to requests for services or advice. They provide the administrative systems required by management. This is what Storey (1992a) refers to as the non-interventionary role in which HR people merely provide a service to meet the demands of line managers.

But at a more strategic level, HR specialists take on a proactive role. They act as business partners, develop integrated HR strategies, intervene, innovate, act as internal consultants and volunteer guidance on matters concerning upholding core values, ethical principles and the achievement of consistency.

MODELS OF HR MANAGEMENT ROLES

There is, of course, a variation in HR roles which follows from the great diversity in organizations and the people who run them. There are a number of models classifying types of roles as summarized below. Although none of these is universal, they provide some insight into the different ways in which HR practitioners operate.

The Tyson and Fell (1986) models

The three management models are:

- *The clerk of works model* – in this model all authority for action is vested in line managers. HR policies are formed or created after the actions that created the need. Policies are not integral to the business and are short term and ad hoc. Authority is vested in line managers and HR activities are largely routine – employment and day-to-day administration.
- *The contracts manager model* – in this model policies are well established, often implicit, with a heavy industrial relations emphasis, possibly derived from an employers' association. The HR department will use fairly sophisticated systems, especially in the field of employee relations. The HR manager is likely to be a professional or very experienced in industrial relations. He or she will not be on the board and, although having some authority to 'police' the implementation of policies, acts mainly in an interpretative, not a creative or innovative, role.
- *The architect model* – in this model explicit HR policies exist as part of the corporate strategy. Human resource planning and development are important concepts and a long-term view is taken. Systems tend to be sophisticated. The head of the HR function is probably on the board and his or her power is derived from professionalism and perceived contribution to the business.

The 'contracts manager' model is probably less common now since the relative decline of the importance of the industrial relations aspects of the HR manager's work.

Karen Legge (1978)

Two types of HR managers are described in this model:

- *Conformist innovators* go along with their organization's ends and adjust their means to achieve them. Their expertise is used as a source of professional power to improve the position of their departments.

● *Deviant innovators* attempt to change this means/ends relationship by gaining acceptance for a different set of criteria for the evaluation of organizational success and their contribution to it.

John Storey (1992a)

Storey's model suggests a two-dimensional map: interventionary/non-interventionary and strategic/tactical as illustrated in Figure 5.1. From this he identifies four roles:

Figure 5.1 Types of personnel management
(Source: Storey, 1992a)

1. *Change masters* (interventionary/strategic), which is close to the HRM model.
2. *Advisers* (non-interventionary/strategic), who act as internal consultants, leaving much of HR practice to line managers.
3. *Regulators* (interventionary/tactical), who are 'managers of discontent' concerned with formulating and monitoring employment rules.
4. *Handmaidens* (non-interventionary/tactical) who merely provide a service to meet the demands of line managers.

Kathleen Monks (1992)

The following four models identified by Kathleen Monks' research into 97 organizations in Ireland extended those developed by Legge and Tyson and Fell:

1. *Traditional/administrative* – in this model the personnel practitioners have mainly a support role with the focus on administrative matters, record keeping and adherence to rules and regulations.
2. *Traditional/industrial relations* – personnel practitioners concentrate on industrial relations, giving their other functions lower priority.
3. *Innovative/professional* – personnel specialists are professional and expert. They aim to remove traditional practices and replace them with improved human resource planning, recruitment, human resource development and reward policies and practices.
4   *Innovative/sophisticated* – personnel specialists are on the Board, take part in integrating HR and business strategies, and are recognized as making an important contribution to organizational success. They develop and deliver sophisticated services in each of the main HR areas.

Like the other models, these simplify the complex roles that HR professionals often have to play which, in different contexts or times, may change considerably or may mean adopting varied roles to meet altering circumstances.

Paul Reilly (2000)

The different roles that practitioners can play as described by Paul Reilly are illustrated in Figure 5.2. He suggests that it is the 'strategist/integrator' who is most likely to make the longest term strategic contribution. The 'administrator/controller' is likely to make a largely tactical short-term contribution, while the 'adviser/consultant' falls between the two.

AMBIGUITIES IN THE ROLE OF HR PRACTITIONERS

HR managers, in Thurley's (1981) words, are 'specialists in ambiguity'. This arises partly because of the often equivocal nature of the attitudes of line managers to HR specialists and the relationships between them, but also because the latter are often unsure about where they stand. Ambiguity in the role of HR people can result in confusion between ideals and reality. Tyson and Fell (1986) see a contrast between the ideologies and actual realities of organizational life to which HR managers, 'as organization men or women', have to conform.

This ambiguity is reflected in the comments that have been made about the role of the personnel function. For example, Mackay and Torrington (1986) suggest that: 'Personnel management is never identified with management interests, as it becomes

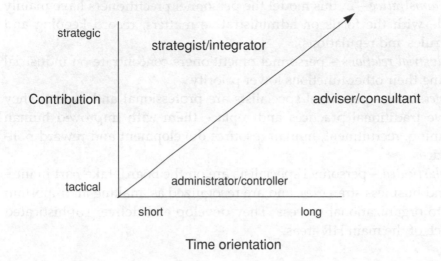

Figure 5.2 The changing role of the HR practitioner
(Source: P Reilly, *HR Shared Services and the Re-alignment of HR*, Institute for Employment Studies, Brighton, 2000)

ineffective when not able to understand and articulate the aspirations of the work force.'

In complete contrast, Tyson and Fell (1986) believe that: 'Classical personnel management has not been granted a position in decision-making circles because it has frequently not earned one. It has not been concerned with the totality of the organization but often with issues which have not only been parochial but esoteric to boot.'

The debate on HRM versus personnel management has been generated by, but has also contributed to, this ambiguity. HRM is management orientated, and sees people as a key resource to be used to further the objectives of the business. Traditional personnel management, however, has tended to be more people orientated, taking the view that if their needs are satisfied, the organization as well as its members will benefit. HR professionals can sometimes find themselves being pulled in both directions. It does not make their life any easier.

One of the questions HR practitioners have to ask themselves is: 'Who is the client – the company or the employee?' HR professionals may sometimes have to walk a fine line between serving the company that pays their salary and serving individual employees. They may be involved in counselling employees over work problems. This can only be carried out successfully if the employee trusts the HR practitioner to maintain confidentiality. But something might be revealed which is of interest to management and that places the counsellor in a dilemma – to betray or not to betray the trust? There is no pat answer to this question, but the existence of a code of professional conduct and a company ethical code can provide guidance.

CONFLICT IN THE HR CONTRIBUTION

HR specialists, as Thurley (1981) put it, often 'work against the grain'. Their values may be different from those of line managers and this is a potential cause of conflict. But conflict is inevitable in organizations, which are pluralistic societies, the members of which have different frames of reference and interests, particularly self-interest. Management may have their own priorities: 'increase shareholder value', 'keep the City happy', 'innovate', 'get the work done'. Employees might have a completely different set: 'pay me well and equitably', 'give me security', 'provide good working conditions', 'treat me fairly'. HR specialists, as noted above, may find themselves somewhere in the middle.

Conflicts in the HR contribution can arise in the following ways:

- *A clash of values* – line managers may simply regard their workers as factors of production to be used, exploited and dispensed with in accordance with organizational imperatives.
- *Different priorities* – management's priority may be to add value – make more out of less – and if this involves getting rid of people that's too bad. HR people may recognize the need to add value but not at the expense of employees.
- *Freedom versus control* – line managers may want the freedom to get on with things their own way, interpreting company policies to meet their needs, and the thrust for devolution has encouraged such feelings. But HR specialists will be concerned about the achievement of a consistent and equitable approach to managing people and implementing HR policies. They will also be concerned with the attainment of a proper degree of compliance to employment and health and safety law. They may be given the responsibility for exercising control, and conflict is likely if they use this authority too rigidly.
- *Disputes* – if unions are recognized, HR specialists may be involved in conflict during the process of resolution. Even when there are no unions, there may be conflict with individuals or groups of employees about the settlement of grievances.

As Mary Parker Follett (1924) wrote, there is the possibility that conflict can be creative if an integrative approach is used to settle it. This means clarifying priorities, policies and roles, using agreed procedures to deal with grievances and disputes, bringing differences of interpretation out into the open and achieving consensus through a solution which recognizes the interests of both parties – a win–win process. Resolving conflict by the sheer exercise of power (win–lose) will only lead to further conflict. Resolving conflict by compromise may lead to both parties being dissatisfied (lose–lose).

ETHICAL CONSIDERATIONS

HR specialists are concerned with ethical standards in two ways: their conduct as professionals and the ethical standards of their organizations.

Professional conduct

The CIPD's Code of Professional Conduct states that members must respect the following standards of conduct:

- *Accuracy* – personnel practitioners must maintain high standards of accuracy in the information and advice they provide to employers and employees.
- *Confidentiality* – personnel practitioners must respect their employer's legitimate needs for confidentiality and ensure that all personal information (including information about current, past and prospective employees) remains private.
- *Counselling* – personnel practitioners with the relevant skills must be prepared to act as counsellors to individual employees, pensioners and dependants or to refer them, where appropriate, to other professionals or helping agencies.
- *Developing others* – personnel practitioners must encourage self-development and seek to achieve the fullest possible development of employees in the service of present and future organization needs.
- *Equal opportunities* – personnel practitioners must promote fair, non-discriminatory employment practices.
- *Fair dealing* – personnel practitioners must maintain fair and reasonable standards in their treatment of individuals.
- *Self-development* – personnel practitioners must seek continuously to improve their performance and update their skills and knowledge.

Values

HR professionals are part of management. They are not there to act as surrogate representatives of the interests of employees. But this does not mean that there may not be occasions when in their professional capacity HR specialists should not speak out and oppose plans or actions which are clearly at variance with the values of the organization. And they should do their best to influence changes in those values where they feel they are necessary. They must not tolerate injustice or inequality of opportunity. If redundancies are inevitable as a result of business-led 'slimming down' or 'taking costs out of the business' processes, they must ensure that the organization takes whatever steps it can to mitigate detrimental effects by, for example, relying primarily on natural wastage and voluntary redundancy or, if people have to go involuntarily, doing whatever they can to help them find other jobs (outplacement).

HR specialists may often find themselves acting within a support function in a hard-nosed, entrepreneurial environment. But this does not mean that they can remain unconcerned about developing and helping to uphold the core values of the organization in line with their own values on how people should be managed. These may not always be reconcilable, and if this is strongly the case, the HR manager may have to make a choice on whether he or she can remain with the organization.

Ethical standards in the firm

More and more companies are, rightly, developing and publishing value statements and codes of ethics. The focus on such codes was encouraged by the Cadbury Report on corporate governance, which in 1992 recommended that companies should adopt one. The Institute of Business Ethics states that more than a third of major companies had ethics codes in 1995 compared with 18 per cent in 1987.

Ethics codes may include the guiding principles the organization follows in conducting its business and relating to its stakeholders – employees, customers, shareholders (or other providers of finance), suppliers, and society in general. A code will also summarize the ethical standards expected of employees. These may include conflicts of interest, the giving and receiving of gifts, confidentiality, environmental pollution, health and safety, equal opportunities, sexual harassment, moonlighting and political activity. More rarely, they may, as at NatWest and Lucas Aerospace, have confidential 'ethics hotlines' for employees to report and discuss concerns.

As suggested by Pickard (1995), HR practitioners can contribute to enhancing awareness of ethical issues by:

● deploying professional expertise to develop and communicate an ethics policy and field the response to it, holding training sessions to help people think through the issues and monitoring the policy;

- contributing to the formation of company strategy, especially touching on mission and values;
- setting an example through professional conduct, on issues such as fairness, equal treatment and confidentiality.

PROFESSIONALISM IN HUMAN RESOURCE MANAGEMENT

If the term is used loosely, HR specialists are professional because they display expertise in doing their work. A professional occupation such as medicine or law could, however, be defined as one that gives members of its association exclusive rights to practise their profession. A profession is not so much an occupation as a means of controlling an occupation. Human resource management is obviously not in this category.

The nature of professional work was best defined by the Hayes Committee (1972) as follows:

> Work done by the professional is usually distinguished by its reference to a framework of fundamental concepts linked with experience rather than by impromptu reaction to events or the application of laid down procedures. Such a high level of distinctive competence reflects the skilful application of specialised education, training and experience. This should be accompanied by a sense of responsibility and an acceptance of recognized standards.

A 'profession' may be identified on the basis of the following criteria:

- skills based on theoretical knowledge; the provision of training and education;
- a test of the competence of members administered by a professional body;
- a formal professional organization which has the power to regulate entry to the profession;
- a professional code of conduct.

By these standards an institution such as the UK Chartered Institute of Personnel and Development carries out all the functions of a professional body.

Another approach to the definition of a profession is to emphasize the service ethic – the professional is there to serve others. This, however, leads to confusion when applied to HR specialists. Whom do they serve? The organization and its values, or the people in the organization and their needs? (Organizational values and personal needs do not necessarily coincide.) As Tyson and Fell (1986) have commented: 'In recent years the personnel manager seems to be encouraged to make the line manager his [*sic*] client, while trying simultaneously to represent wider social standards, and to possess a sense of service to employees. This results in confusion and difficulty for the personnel executive.'

In the face of this difficulty, the question has to be asked, why bother? The answer was suggested by Watson (1977), who asserted that the adoption of a professional image by personnel managers is a strategic response by personnel to their felt lack of authority. They are in an ambiguous situation and sometimes feel they need all the help they can get to clarify and, indeed, strengthen their authority and influence.

If a profession is defined rigidly as a body of people who possess a particular area of competence, who control entry so that only members of the association can practise in that area, who unequivocally adopt the 'service ethic' and who are recognized by themselves and others as belonging to a profession, then HRM practitioners are not strictly working in a profession. This is the case even when a professional institution like the Chartered Institute of Personnel and Development exists with the objective of acting as a professional body in the full sense of the word, an aim which it does its best to fulfil.

On the basis of their research, Guest and Horwood (1981) expressed their doubts about the professional model of personnel management as follows:

> The (research) data also highlights the range of career types in personnel management. Given the diversity of personnel roles and organizational contexts, this is surely something to be welcomed. It is tempting but wrong to view personnel managers as homogeneous. Their different backgrounds and fields of operations raise doubts about the value of a professional model and of any attempt to view personnel problems as amenable to solution through a primary focus on professionalism.

However, a broader definition of professionalism as the practice of specific skills based upon a defined body of knowledge in accordance with recognized standards of behaviour would entitle the practice of HRM to be regarded as a profession.

The debate continues, but it is an academic one. What matters is that HR 'professionals' need expertise and have to use it responsibly. In other words, they should act professionally but do not have to be members of a professional association to do that. Such associations, however, have an important part to play in setting and improving professional standards.

If this definition is accepted, as it should be, then those who do practise specific HRM skills based upon a defined body of knowledge in accordance with recognized standards of behaviour can be regarded as members of a profession.

COMPETENCE IN HR MANAGEMENT

The requirements for effective HR management set out above can be summed up by the use of the language of competences. This can also be done by developing a 'competence framework' as set out in Figure 5.3, which contains seven competence areas for an HR director and gives instances of competent behaviour in each of those areas. A map of this nature can be used for the development of HR specialists.

Strategic capability	Seeks involvement in strategy formulation and contributes to the development of business strategy.	Has a clear strategic vision of how HR can support the achievement of the business strategy.	Understands the critical success factors of the business and the implications for HR strategy.	Develops and implements integrated and coherent HR strategies.
Business and cultural awareness	Understands the business' environment and the competitive pressures it faces.	Understands the key activities and processes of the business and how these affect HR strategies.	Understands the culture (values and norms) of the business as the basis for developing culture change strategies.	Adapts HR strategies to fit business and cultural imperatives.
Organizational effectiveness	Understands key factors which contribute to organizational effectiveness and acts accordingly.	Contributes to planning transformational change programmes and managing change.	Helps to develop a high-quality, skilled, committed and flexible workforce.	Facilitates team building
Internal consultancy	Analyses and diagnoses people issues and suggests practical solutions.	Adapts intervention style to fit internal client needs; acts as catalyst, facilitator or expert as required.	Uses process consultancy approaches to help resolve people problems and issues.	Coaches clients to deal with own problems; transfers skills.
Service delivery	Anticipates requirements and sets up services to meet them.	Responds promptly and efficiently to requests for help and advice.	Empowers line managers to make HR decisions but provides guidance as required.	Provides cost-effective services in each HR area.
Quality	Contributes to the development of a total quality approach throughout the organization.	Identifies internal customer requirements for HR services and responds to their needs.	Demonstrates a concern for total quality and continuous improvement in own work.	Promotes total quality and continuous improvement in HR function.
Continuous professional development	Continually develops professional knowledge and skills.	Benchmarks best HR practice and keeps in touch with new HR developments.	Demonstrates understanding of relevant HR practices.	Promotes awareness in own function.

Figure 5.3 HR competence framework

The Chartered Institute of Personnel and Development has produced the following list of the competencies required by its professional members:

Personal drive and effectiveness

The existence of a positive 'can do' mentality, anxious to find ways round obstacles and willing to exploit all the available resources to accomplish objectives.

People management and leadership

The motivation of others (whether subordinates, seniors or project team members) towards the achievement of shared goals, not through the application of formal authority but rather by personal role modelling, the establishment of professional credibility, and the creation of reciprocal trust.

Professional competence

Possession of the professional skills and technical capabilities associated with successful achievement in personnel and development.

Adding value through people

A desire not only to concentrate on tasks, but rather to select meaningful outputs which will produce added-value outcomes for the organization, or eliminate/reduce the existence of performance inhibitors, while simultaneously complying with all legal and ethical considerations.

Continuing learning

Commitment to continuous improvement and change by the application of self-managed learning techniques, supplemented where appropriate by deliberate planned exposure to external learning sources (mentoring, coaching etc).

Thinking and applied resourcefulness

Application of a systematic approach to situational analysis, development of convincing, business-focused action plans, and (where appropriate) the deployment of intuitive/creative thinking to generate innovative solutions and proactively seize opportunities.

'Customer' focus

Concern for the perceptions of the HR function's customers, including (principally) the central directorate of the organization, a willingness to solicit and act upon 'customer' feedback as one of the foundations for performance improvement.

Strategic capability

The capacity to create an achievable vision for the future, to foresee longer-term developments, to envisage options (and their probable consequences), to select sound courses of action, to rise above the day-to-day detail, and to challenge the status quo.

Influencing and interpersonal skills

The ability to transmit information to others, especially in written (report) form, both persuasively and cogently; the display of listening, comprehension and understanding skills, plus sensitivity to the emotional, attitudinal and political aspects of corporate life.

HR PROFESSIONALS AS 'THINKING PERFORMERS'

The Chartered Institute of Personnel and Development has suggested that personnel or HR professionals need to be 'thinking performers'. They have to think carefully about what they are doing in the context of their organization and within the framework of a recognized body of knowledge, and they have to perform effectively in the sense of delivering advice, guidance and services which will help the organization to achieve its strategic goals. Karen Legge (1995) made a similar point when she referred to HRM as a process of 'thinking pragmatism'.

6

The contribution of the HR function

A number of research projects as summarized later in this chapter have demonstrated that HRM practices can improve organizational performance. Typically, the ways in which this contribution has been made have included:

- developing a positive psychological contract;
- increasing motivation and commitment;
- increasing employee skills and extending the skills base;
- providing employees with extended responsibilities so that they can make full use of their skills and abilities;
- spelling out career opportunities and defining competence requirements;
- instituting processes of performance management and continuous development;
- using reward management systems to convey messages about what the organization believes to be important and what it is prepared to provide financial and non-financial rewards for;
- developing employee relations strategies which provide employees with a voice.

HR can contribute to the achievement of competitive advantage and added value and to total quality initiatives in the ways described below. The key outcomes of research into the impact of HRM are summarized at the end of this chapter.

CONTRIBUTION TO ADDED VALUE

In accounting language, added value is the difference between the income of the business arising from sales (output) and the amount spent on materials and other purchased goods and services (input). In more general terms, it is the development and use of any resource in a way which ensures that it yields a substantial and sustainable higher return on whatever has been invested in it. Added value often means the creation of more out of less, and an increasingly popular index of overall organizational performance is added value per £ of employment costs.

Added value is created by people. It is people at various levels in the organizations who create visions, define values and missions, set goals, develop strategic plans, and implement those plans in accordance with the underpinning values. Added value will be enhanced by anything that is done to obtain and develop the right sort of people, to motivate and manage them effectively, to gain their commitment to organizational values, to build and maintain stable relationships with them, to develop the right sort of organization structure, and to deploy them effectively and productively in that structure.

CONTRIBUTION TO COMPETITIVE ADVANTAGE

The concept of sustainable competitive advantage as formulated by Porter (1985) arises when a firm creates value for its customers, selects markets in which it can excel and presents a moving target to its competitors by continually improving its position. According to Porter, three of the most important factors are innovation, quality and cost leadership, but he recognizes that all these depend on the quality of an organization's human resources. The ability to gain and retain competitive advantage is crucial to a business's growth and prosperity.

Unique talents among employees, including superior performance, productivity, flexibility, innovation and the ability to deliver high levels of personal customer service, are ways in which people provide a critical ingredient in developing an organization's competitive position. People also provide the key to managing the pivotal interdependencies across functional activities and the important external relationships. It can be argued that one of the clear benefits arising from competitive advantage based on the effective management of people is that such an advantage is hard to imitate. An organization's HR strategies, policies and practices are a unique blend of processes, procedures, personalities, styles, capabilities and organizational culture. One of the keys to competitive advantage is the ability to differentiate what the business supplies to its customers from what is supplied by its competitors. Such differentiation can be achieved by having higher quality people than those competitors, by developing and nurturing the intellectual capital possessed by the business, and by functioning as a 'learning organization'.

THE IMPACT OF HRM ON BUSINESS PERFORMANCE

The outcomes of key research projects on HRM and firm performance are summarized below.

Arthur (1990, 1992, 1994)

The research conducted by Arthur collected data from 30 US steel mini-mills. He investigated the impact on labour efficiency and scrap rate of either a control strategy (enforced employee compliance through rules and procedures, little employee participation, little general training, low wages, and a high proportion of employees on bonus schemes) or a commitment strategy (shaping employee behaviours by creating psychological links between organizational and employee goals, moderate employee participation, moderate general training, high wages, and fewer employees on bonus or incentives). Comparing steel mills with a high-commitment strategy with those having a low-commitment strategy, Arthur found that the former had significantly higher levels of both productivity and quality. The average turnover rate in high-commitment mills was less than half that in firms with a low-commitment strategy.

Arthur also examined the performance effects associated with a fit between business and HR strategy. He defined fit as occurring when a cost-based business strategy was combined with a control-orientated HR strategy, and when a differentiating-based business strategy was combined with a commitment-type HR strategy. The results were not statistically significant but he did find that those mills practising a differentiation-based strategy with fit had 25 per cent higher productivity than those without fit. Thus the results did provide some modest support for the contingency hypothesis.

Huselid (1995)

Huselid conducted research into the impact of human resource management practices on company performance by analysing the responses of 968 US firms to a questionnaire. In general, he found that if firms increased their high-performance work practices, there were significant reductions in employee turnover and significant increases in productivity and profits. The three hypotheses he tested were that diminished employee turnover and increased productivity and corporate financial performance would result from:

● the use of systems of high-performance work practices;
● the development of complementarities or synergies among high performance work practices;
● the alignment of a firm's system of high performance work practices with its competitive strategy.

The main findings were that:

● turnover is determined by employee skills and organizational structures; motivation has an insignificant effect;
● productivity is determined by employee motivation;
● financial performance is determined by employee skills, motivation and organization structure;
● one standard deviation in the use of each practice reduces turnover by 1.3 per cent;
● one standard deviation increase in the use of the practices raises sales by an average of $27,044 per employee;
● one standard deviation increase in the use of the practices produces an increase in profit of $18,641 per employee.

As Huselid comments, the impact of high-performance work practices on corporate financial performance 'is in part due to their influence on employee turnover and productivity'. However, his research produced little or no evidence that internal or external fit will increase firm performance, and he concludes that the simple adoption of high-performance work practices is more important than efforts to ensure that these are internally consistent or aligned with firm competitive strategy. But he does believe that 'the theoretical arguments for internal and external fit remain compelling'.

Becker, Huselid, Pickus and Spratt (1997)

These writers summarized the outcomes of a number of research projects into the relationship between HR and company performance which they have conducted or been associated with. The focus was on the strategic impact on shareholder value of high-performance work systems. Their model of the relationship is shown in Figure 6.1.

Figure 6.1 A model of the HR–shareholder value relationship
(Source: B E Becker *et al*, HR as a source of shareholder value: research and recommendations, *Human Resource Management*, Spring, 1997)

Huselid and Becker (1996) created an index of the HRM systems in 740 firms, reflecting the degree to which the firm adopted a high-performance work system (HPWS). They found that firms with higher values on this index, other things being equal, had economically and statistically significant higher levels of firm performance. They further estimated that significant changes in the quality of a firm's HPWS system were associated with changes in market value of $15,000 to $60,000 per employee. They suggested that a properly designed and deployed HRM system represented a significant economic asset for an organization, although the research did not identify precisely *how* such a system created that value. But Becker *et al* did point out that:

> HRM systems only have a systematic impact on the bottom line when they are embedded in the management infrastructure and help the firm achieve important business priorities such as shortening product development cycle times, increasing customer service, lowering turnover among high quality employee etc.

Patterson, West, Lawthom and Nickell (1997)

Research conducted by the Institute of Work Psychology at Sheffield University on behalf of the IPD (Patterson *et al*, 1997) addressed the question of what factors most influence business performance. The study looked at the impact of employee attitudes, organizational culture, human resource management practices, and various other managerial activities. An assessment was made of the extent to which each of these factors predicted company performance as measured by productivity and profits per employee.

The results were expressed in terms of the percentage variation in performance attributable to a particular factor as follows:

- Job satisfaction explained 5 per cent of the variation between companies in change of profitability and 16 per cent of the variation in productivity;
- organizational culture explained 10 per cent of the variation in profitability and 29 per cent of the variation in productivity;
- human resource management practices explained 19 per cent of the variation in profitability and 18 per cent of the variation in productivity.

These analyses revealed very strong relationships between employee attitudes, organizational culture, HRM practices and company performance. This was particularly convincing in the case of the link between HRM practices and performance.

As the report on the research states:

> Overall these results very clearly indicate the importance of people management practices in predicting company performance... The results suggest that, if managers wish to influence the performance of their companies, the most important area they should emphasize is the management of people.

The conclusion reached by the IPD on this research was that employee commitment and a positive psychological contract are fundamental to improving performance. Two HR practices were identified as being particularly significant:

- acquisition and development of employee skills (including selection, induction and the use of appraisals);
- job design (including skill flexibility, job responsibility, variety and the use of formal teams).

Guest, Michie, Sheehan and Conway (2000)

A detailed analysis of the 1998 Workplace Employee Relations Survey found that the informal climate of employee involvement and consultation appears to have an important influence on performance. In the private sector, the use of more human resource practices also has a positive impact on performance. The links are shown in Figure 6.2:

Figure 6.2 Links between HRM practices and performance

However, the formal machinery of employee relations did not deliver business performance, although, as the researchers pointed out, it was not designed for this purpose. Employee relations practices exist primarily to protect employees' pay and employment conditions and to offer them some influence over issues in the workplace.

Two of the important conclusions reached by the researchers were that:

- business performance is associated with higher levels of job satisfaction and a positive psychological contract;
- the sophistication of personnel departments in the private sector was the most important influence on the number of HR practices adopted; in the public sector, the most important influence was the existence of an HR strategy.

Guest, Michie, Sheehan, Conway and Metochi (2000)

Research conducted by Guest *et al* (2000) as part of the Future of Work programme found a clear association between the number of HR practices adopted and the effectivness of these practices. It indicated that the effective use of a wide range of progressive HR practices is linked to superior business performance.

7

Evaluating the HR function

The potential for the HR function to play a significant role in increasing added value and achieving competitive advantage may be considerable. But how can the effectiveness of the function be measured at both the strategic level and at the level of support and service provision? Such measurements have to be made to ensure that a value-added contribution is being made and to indicate where improvements or changes in direction are needed.

APPROACHES TO EVALUATION

The research conducted by Armstrong and Long (1994) established from discussions with chief executives and other directors that the most popular basis for evaluation was their judgement related to factors such as:

- understanding of the organization – its mission, values, critical success factors, product-marketing strategies, technology or method of operation and distinctive competences;
- effectiveness of contributions to top management team decision-making on corporate/business issues;
- the extent to which innovatory, realistic and persuasive proposals were made on HR strategies, policies and programmes;

- the capacity to deliver as promised;
- the quality of the advice and services they provided, assessed mainly in subjective terms – eg, it is practical, it meets my needs, it solves my problem, they (the services) are efficient, they respond quickly to requests for help or advice;
- the ability to build and maintain stable and cooperative relationships with trade unions;
- the ability to handle difficult situations such as downsizing;
- in very general terms, the contribution they make to developing the corporate culture, their influence on management style and their abilities as facilitators and managers of change;
- their overall credibility and ability to work as a full member of the top management team.

These largely subjective evaluations were supplemented by the analysis of key employment ratios such as turnover, absenteeism, suggestions received and acted upon, health and safety statistics and the outcome of customer satisfaction surveys.

In some organizations formal surveys were made of the opinions of line managers about the services they received from the HR function, and employee attitude surveys were also used as a means of evaluation.

But this problem should not deter anyone from making a determined attempt to measure HR effectiveness, and there are a number of approaches which can be adopted as discussed below.

OVERALL METHODS OF EVALUATION

An important distinction is made by Tsui and Gomez-Mejia (1988) between:

- *process criteria* – how well things are done; and
- *output criteria* – the impact made by the process on organizational and operational performance, ie the effectiveness of the end-result.

This is broadly the old (Peter Drucker, 1967) distinction between efficiency and effectiveness – ie doing things right in terms of *what* you do (efficiency) rather than doing the right things in terms of the results you achieve (effectiveness). In terms of personnel effectiveness, it means determining the extent to which HR policies, programmes and practices and the advice and support provided by the personnel function enable line managers to achieve business objectives and meet operational requirements.

When deciding on how the HR function should be evaluated it is also necessary to distinguish between quantitative criteria such as turnover or absenteeism figures, and qualitative criteria such as line managers' opinions of the personnel function or the outcome of employee attitude surveys.

TYPES OF PERFORMANCE MEASURES

The types of performance measures that can be used to evaluate the personnel function are:

● *Money measures*, which include maximizing income, minimizing expenditure and improving rates of return.
● *Time measures* express performance against work timetables, the amount of backlog and speed of activity or response.
● *Measures of effect* include attainment of a standard, changes in behaviour (of colleagues, staff, clients or customers), physical completion of the work and the level of take-up of a service.
● *Reaction* indicates how others judge the function or its members and is therefore a less objective measure. Reaction can be measured by peer assessments, performance ratings by internal or external clients or customers or the analysis of comments and complaints.

EVALUATION CRITERIA

It has been suggested by Guest and Peccei (1994) that the effectiveness of HRM can be measured by reference to:

● *organizational effectiveness* – but it may not be possible to separate HR and organizational effectiveness, which will be affected by external events, and this approach does not provide a base for decisions about HR policy and practice;
● *specified goals* – this is a plausible method, if good measures of goal attainment can be used and if allowance is made for unanticipated events;
● *specified quantified measures* – labour costs, turnover and productivity have high credibility but may be difficult to interpret and can be affected by non-HRM factors and are insufficient on their own;
● *stakeholder perspective* – this uses the subjective views of key interest groups, eg the boards, on personnel effectiveness, and is probably the most satisfactory method.

PRACTICAL METHODS OF EVALUATION

The approaches that in practice are adopted by organizations to evaluate HR effectiveness are:

- *quantitative – macro* (organizational);
- *quantitative – micro* (specified aspects of employee behaviour or reaction);
- *quantitative/qualitative* – achievement of specified goals;
- *quantitative/qualitative* – achievement of standards set in service level agreements;
- *qualitative – macro* – an overall and largely subjective assessment of the personnel function;
- *qualitative* – client satisfaction ie 'stakeholder perspective';
- *qualitative* – employee satisfaction, also 'stakeholder perspective';
- *utility analysis*;
- *benchmarking*.

Organizational quantitative criteria

At organizational level, the quantitative criteria that can be used include:

- added value per employee;
- profit per employee;
- sales value per employee;
- costs per employee;
- added value per £ of employment costs.

Added value per £ of employment costs was used in two of the organizations covered by the Armstrong and Long (1994) research (Pilkington Optronics and Rover Group) and has the advantage of bringing together both benefits (added value) and costs (of employment).

Another reason for using quantified macro-measures, as pointed out by Tyson (1985), is that

> … the business objectives become 'sold' as part of the personnel policies. The discipline of sitting down to look at training objectives, for example in terms of sales value or added value, brings out what *can* be assessed and raises the useful question of why we are proposing this programme, if we are unable to relate it to the business.

Specific quantified criteria

Specified quantified criteria can be classified into two categories: those relating to measurable aspects of employee behaviours and those relating to the type, level and costs of the services provided by the personnel department to its clients.

Employee behaviour criteria

Employee behaviour criteria include:

- employee retention and turnover rates;
- absenteeism rate;
- ratio of suggestions received to number of employees;
- number of usable proposals from quality circles or improvement groups;
- cost savings arising from suggestions and/or quality circle recommendations;
- frequency/severity rate of accidents;
- ratio of grievances to number of employees;
- time lost through disputes;
- number of references to industrial tribunals on unfair dismissal, equal opportunity, equal pay, harassment, racial discrimination issues etc and the outcome of such references.

In some of these areas, for example employee retention and absenteeism rates, the HR function cannot be held entirely accountable. But it *is* a shared responsibility and the measures will indicate problem areas which may be related to the quality of the advice or services provided by the function.

HR department service-level criteria

The quantifiable criteria available to measure the level and value of service provision by the HR function include:

- average time to fill vacancies;
- time to respond to applicants;
- ratio of acceptance to offers made;
- cost of advertisements per reply/engagement;
- training hours/days per employee;
- time to respond to and settle grievances;
- cost of induction training per employee;
- cost of benefits per employee;

- measurable improvements in productivity as a direct result of training;
- measurable improvements in individual and organizational performance as a direct result of the operation of performance-related pay and performance management schemes;
- ratio of personnel department costs to profit, sales turnover or added value;
- personnel costs in relation to budget;
- ratio of personnel staff to employees.

The usefulness of those measures is variable, as is the practicality of collecting reliable information. Figures on training days per employee do not mean much in themselves unless there is some measure of the relevance and impact of that training. To rely on this measure would be like rewarding sales representatives on the basis of the sales volume they generate rather than the contribution their sales make to profit and fixed costs.

It is also possible that the costs of collecting and analysing some sorts of information may not be justified by the benefits that they could theoretically produce in the shape of improved performance. It is a matter of judgement to select the criteria which are likely to be the most relevant, and this will depend on the circumstances of the organization and the particular pressures to which it and its personnel function are being subjected. It may be appropriate to highlight some criteria for a period and then, if the problem has been resolved, focus attention on other areas.

Achievement of specified goals

This approach involves measuring achievements against agreed objectives – it could be the final outcome or a measure of progress towards a goal as indicated by the extent to which specified 'milestones' have been reached.

The specified objectives could be expressed in terms such as:

- all employees to have received training on the implementation of equal opportunities policies by 1 June;
- an agreement with the various trade unions to setting up single table bargaining to be reached by the end of the year;
- the competence analysis programme to be completed within 12 months;
- salary surveys to be conducted and a report on the implications on salary scales to be submitted by 1 September;
- the new performance management system to be fully operational within the next six months.

'Project' objectives set along these lines should include some indication of the standard of achievement expected, for example:

The effectiveness of the performance management system will be judged on:

(a) an evaluation of user reactions (managers and individuals);
(b) an assessment of the quality of the performance review processes;
(c) an analysis of the outputs of the system in terms of development and improvement plans;
(d) the number of upheld appeals on assessments;
(e) the impact the scheme is making on motivation, performance and commitment (as measured by a structured questionnaire to managers and individuals).

Service level agreements

A service level agreement (SLA) is an agreement between the provider of a service and the customers who use the service. It quantifies the level of service required to meet the business needs. SLAs are most commonly found in the public sector but the principles of such agreements could apply equally well in other sectors. The starting point in drawing up an SLA is to clarify precisely what the customer's needs are and which elements are most important. The aim in setting service targets is that they should be stretching but achievable – although the approach adopted by some service providers is to under-promise so that they can appear to over-achieve.

A service level agreement sets out:

● the nature of the function or service provided;
● the volumes and quality to be achieved for each of these services;
● the response times to be achieved by the provider when receiving requests for help.

For an HR function, service level standards could be drawn up for such activities as:

● response to requests for help or guidance in specific areas, eg recruitment, training, handling discipline cases and grievances and health and safety;
● the time taken to prepare job descriptions, fill vacancies or conduct a job evaluation;
● the amount of time lost through absenteeism or work-related sickness or accidents;
● the proportion of discipline and grievance issues settled at the time of the first involvement of personnel;

- the number of appeals (successful and unsuccessful) against job evaluation decisions;
- the results of evaluations by participants of training provided by the function.

Organizations that charge out the services of the personnel function to users (and this is happening increasingly in local authorities) may set standards in terms of the costs of providing recruitment, training and other services. This could take such forms as a unit charge for each person recruited, a *per capita* charge for each training day, a fixed price sum for undertaking projects such as a pay review, a daily or hourly consultancy rate for work done on an occasional basis, or a lump sum retainer fee for maintaining a general availability to provide advice or services.

To make service level agreements work as a basis for evaluation it is essential they should be agreed by both providers and customers (purchasers). They should be reasonably simple, especially to begin with (not too many headings), and it should be possible to measure performance against the standards fairly easily – an over-bureaucratic system is likely to defeat the purpose of the agreement. If these requirements can be satisfied, a service level agreement can provide a good basis for evaluation.

Subjective overall evaluation

Perhaps the most common method of evaluating the HR function is a subjective assessment by the chief executive or the board which will be related to such general factors as:

- the quality of the advice and services provided as observed or experienced directly by the evaluator;
- the degree to which members of the function are proactive rather than reactive (if that is what the management wants, which is not always the case);
- feedback from line managers obtained on a haphazard basis as to whether or not they think personnel is 'a good thing' and is 'doing a good job'.

The dangers of relying on subjective and *ad hoc* measures like these are obvious, but they are much used.

User reaction measures

Rather than relying on haphazard and highly subjective assessments, this approach involves identifying the key criteria for measuring the degree to which clients of the personnel function in the shape of directors, managers and team leaders are satisfied with the quality of advice and services they provide.

Areas in which the quality of services provided by the HR function can be assessed include:

- understanding of strategic business imperatives;
- anticipation of business and management needs;
- ability to function as a 'business partner' in the team;
- quality of advice given in terms of its relevance to the problem or issue, the clarity and conviction with which the advice is given, the practicality of the recommendations;
- the quality of the back-up advice and services offered to implement recommendations, the extent to which ultimately the proposals worked;
- speed of response to requests for advice or services;
- promptness in dealing with grievances and appeals;
- help to managers in identifying and meeting training needs;
- extent to which training and development programmes meet company/individual needs;
- delivery of advice and services that make a significant impact on improving the quality and performance of staff;
- development of programmes and processes that address short- and long-term business needs, that are 'owned' by line managers, and that produce the anticipated impact on motivation, commitment and performance.

Assessments of the contribution of the HR function in areas such as those listed above can be made by conducting surveys of client opinion.

Employee satisfaction measures

The degree to which the employee stakeholders are satisfied with personnel policies and practices as they affect them can be measured by attitude surveys that obtain opinions and perceptions of employees on:

- the extent to which they believe promotion, job evaluation, performance appraisal, performance-related pay and grievance processes and procedures operate fairly;
- the degree to which they are satisfied with pay and benefits;
- the extent to which they feel they are involved in decisions that affect them;
- how well they feel they are kept informed on matters of importance to them;
- the consistency with which personnel policies concerning pay, equal opportunity, etc are applied;

- the opportunities available to them for training and development;
- the degree to which their work makes the best use of their skills and abilities;
- the extent to which they are clear about what is expected of them;
- the support and guidance they receive from their managers and team leaders;
- their working environment from the point of view of health and safety, and the general conditions under which they work;
- the facilities (restaurant, car parking etc) with which they are provided;
- generally, the climate and management style of the organization.

Individual evaluation

The evaluation approaches listed above are directed at both the personnel function as a whole and its individual members. But it is also necessary specifically to agree the overall objectives and standards of performance expected from members of the function as a basis for assessment.

Utility analysis

Utility analysis provides a decision support framework that explicitly considers the costs and benefits of personnel decisions. The aim is to predict, explain and improve the utility or 'usefulness' of those decisions. It focuses on personnel programmes, ie sets of activities or procedures that affect personnel value.

Utility analysis as described by Boudreau (1988) requires:

- a *problem* – gap between what is desired and what is currently being achieved;
- a *set of alternatives* to address the problem;
- a *set of attributes* – the variables that describe the important characteristics of the alternatives (such as effects on productivity, costs and employee attitudes);
- a *utility function*, or a system to combine the attributes into an overall judgement of each alternative's usefulness.

Utility analysis focuses on:

- *quantity* – the effect of work behaviours over time;
- *quality* – the production of large improvements or the avoidance of large reductions in the quality of those work behaviours;
- *cost* – the minimization of the costs of developing, implementing and maintaining programmes.

These are, rightly, in line with the factors used by any other function. It is accepted that all the variables to be assessed may not be capable of being measured precisely, but uncertainty of this kind takes place in all aspects of management (eg measuring consumer preferences).

Utility analysis depends on good management information and the possible limitations of such information and the costs of collecting it should be recognized. Detailed management information will only prove useful if it serves the following purposes:

- It is likely to correct decisions that otherwise would have been incorrect.
- The corrections are important and produce large benefits.
- The cost of conducting the information does not outweigh the expected benefit of corrected decisions.

Benchmarking

The methods of measuring HR effectiveness listed above all rely on collecting and analysing internal data and opinions. But it is also desirable to 'benchmark', ie compare what the HR function is doing within the organization with what is happening elsewhere. This will involve gaining information on 'best practice' which, even if it is not transferable in total to the organization conducting the survey, should at least provide information on areas for development or improvement.

PREFERRED APPROACH

Every organization will develop its own approach to evaluating the effectiveness of the HR function and its members. There are no standard measures.

Perhaps, as Guest and Peccei (1994) suggest:

> The most sensible and the most important indicator of HRM effectiveness will be the judgements of key stakeholders... The political, stakeholder, perspective on effectiveness in organizations acknowledges that it is the interpretation placed on quantified results and the attributions of credit and blame that are derived from them that matter most in judging effectiveness. In other words, at the end of the day, it is always the qualitative interpretation by those in positions of power that matters most.

But they recognized 'the desirability of also developing clearly specified goals and quantitative indicators, together with financial criteria'.

AUDITING THE HR FUNCTION

Like any other function, the performance and contribution of HR should be audited regularly. The questions to which answers should be obtained are:

1. What strategic contribution is being made by HR to the achievement of business/corporate objectives?
2. To what extent are there well-articulated and agreed HR strategies which are aligned to the business strategy and which are integrated with one another?
3. What role does HR currently play? Is this role appropriate in the context of the organization?
4. To what extent has the responsibility for HR issues been devolved to line management?
5. How well does HR reconcile the need for devolution with the need to ensure that organizational, ethical and legal obligations and requirements are being met consistently?
6. What evidence exists that HR is being innovative in a practical and business-like way, based on an analysis of the business and people needs of the organization and benchmarking?
7. How well is HR performing by reference to quantitative measures such as added value per employee, absenteeism and attrition?
8. How well is HR performing in terms of service delivery in fields such as recruitment, training, reward management, health and safety, the management of equal opportunity and diversity, advice on employment law and legal obligations, the provision of employee assistance programmes and the maintenance and use of personnel information systems?
9. To what extent does HR express proper concern for ethical considerations, the interests of all stakeholders (employees as well as management), enhancing the quality of working life and achieving a satisfactory work/life balance?
10. What contribution has HR made to the improvement of the employee relations climate?
11. How well is HR regarded by its customers – management, line managers, employees generally, employee representatives, as measured by formal assessments or opinion surveys?
12. Is the HR function well-organized and properly staffed with qualified professionals who are actively concerned with continuous professional development?

8

International human resource management

INTERNATIONAL HUMAN RESOURCE MANAGEMENT DEFINED

International human resource management is the process of employing and developing people in international organizations which operate in Europe or globally. It means working across national boundaries to formulate and implement resourcing, development, career management and remuneration strategies, policies and practices which can be applied to an international workforce. This may include parent country nationals working for long periods as expatriates or on short-term assignments, local country nationals, or third country nationals who work for the corporation in a local country but are not parent country nationals (eg a German working in West Africa for a British-owned company).

THE CHALLENGE OF INTERNATIONAL HUMAN RESOURCE MANAGEMENT

International human resource management is likely to be more demanding than management within the boundaries of one country for four reasons. The first is likely to be managing the complexity of the workforce mix. For example, wholly owned subsidiary companies may employ both host and parent country people together with third country nationals. This may create problems with employment practices as well as remuneration. A joint venture or strategic alliance may have an even more complex workforce consisting of expatriates of the joint venture company, host country nationals, third country nationals and experts from any of the partners who are 'parachuted in' to deal with special problems or to provide consultancy services. Some of the specific problems arising in joint ventures as noted by Kanter (1989) and others include divided loyalties between the parent company and the joint venture consortium and the difficulties managers may face when trying to be both sensitive to local conditions and aware of the demands made by the consortium of their own parent company.

The second challenge is that of managing diversity – between cultures, social systems and legal requirements. International personnel managers are not in the business of controlling uniformity – if they tried, they would fail.

The third challenge of managing people globally is that of communications. Even the most sophisticated electronic communication system may not be an adequate substitute for face-to-face communications.

The final challenge is that of resourcing international operations with people of the right calibre to deal with the much more complex problems that inevitably arise. As Perkins (1997) points out, it is necessary for businesses to 'remain competitive with their employment offering in the market place, to attract and retain high quality staff with world-wide capabilities'.

CHARACTERISTICS OF INTERNATIONAL HUMAN RESOURCE MANAGEMENT

It has been suggested by Torrington (1994) that international HRM is not just about copying practices from the Americans, Japanese, Germans and so on which will not necessarily translate culturally. Neither is it simply a matter of learning the culture of every country and suitably modifying behaviour in each of them, which is an impossible ideal because of the robust and subtle nature of national cultures. He believes that international personnel management is best defined by reference to the following '7c's characteristics:

● *cosmopolitan* – people tend to be either members of a high-flying multilingual elite who are involved in high-level coordination and are constantly on the move, or expatriates who may relocate after periods of several years and can have significant problems on repatriation;

- *culture* – major differences in cultural backgrounds;
- *compensation* – special requirements for the determination of the pay and benefits of expatriates and host country nationals;
- *communication* – maintaining good communication between all parts of the organization, worldwide;
- *consultancy* – greater need to bring in expertise to deal with local needs;
- *competence* – developing a wider range of competences for people who have to work across political, cultural and organizational boundaries;
- *coordination* – devising formal and informal methods of getting the different parts of the international business to work closer together.

It has been argued by Torrington that international HRM management is in many ways simply human resource management on a larger scale, albeit more complex, more varied and involving more coordination across national boundaries. Certainly the same basic techniques of recruitment and training may be used but these have to be adapted to fit different cultures and local requirements. And the management and remuneration of expatriates can present particular difficulties.

There are no universal prescriptions for international HRM and the rest of this chapter deals only with the general considerations to be taken into account when developing approaches in the areas of employment and development strategies recruitment, employee development and the management and payment of expatriates.

THE CONTEXT OF INTERNATIONAL HUMAN RESOURCE MANAGEMENT

The world has become more competitive than ever. Firms now have to compete on the global playing field because the costs associated with the development and marketing of new products are too great to be amortized only over one market, even a large one such as the United States or Europe (Bartlett and Ghoshal, 1991). Operations are being internationalized by overseas expansion, and also by mergers and acquisitions, joint ventures and strategic partnerships. As pointed out by Schuler *et al* (1993), firms now need to manage globally, as if the world were one vast market, *and* simultaneously to manage locally, as if the world were a vast number of separate and loosely connected markets. The main contextual factors affecting international HRM are the form of organization, the extent of convergence or divergence in international HR policies, and differences between countries, especially cultural ones.

Forms of organization and governance

The intensity of global competition has, according to Perkins and Hendry (1999), 'led to organizational forms that let go the traditional loose–tight options of federated geographical firms, or the one-size fits all centre-dominant considerations'. They go on to say that:

> Governance patterns have begun to recognize that reciprocity in relationships is the key to success, with an emphasis on local commercial partnering, to combine large-scale investment, global brand recognition and multinational resource clout with insider knowledge.

The four organizational models identified by Bartlett and Ghoshal (1993) are:

1. *Decentralized federation*, in which each national unit is managed as a separate entity that seeks to optimize its performance in the local environment. This is the traditional multinational corporation.
2. *Coordinated federation*, in which the centre develops sophisticated management systems enabling it to maintain overall control, although scope is given to local management to adopt practices which recognize local market conditions.
3. *Centralized hub*, in which the focus is on the global market rather than on local markets. Such organizations are truly global rather than multinational, which is the case in those adopting a federated approach. The hub model, which is typically adopted by Japanese firms, operates through centralized decision-making and control.
4. *The transnational model*, in which the corporation develops multi-dimensional strategic capabilities directed towards competing globally, but also donates local responsiveness to market requirements.

Perkins and Hendry (1999) argue that, notwithstanding this fourfold model, international firms seem to be polarizing around two organizational approaches:

● *regionalization*, where local customer service is important;
● *'global business streams'* which involves setting up centrally controlled business segments which deal with a related range of products worldwide.

Convergence and divergence

An issue facing all international companies is the extent to which their policies should 'converge' worldwide (ie be basically the same in every location) or 'diverge' (ie be differentiated in response to local requirements). According to Sparrow (1999a), the tendency is towards convergence, although Sparrow (1999b) notes that in the field of international remuneration the trend is not universal. However, the problem with adopting a convergent approach to HR policies is that it may take insufficient account of local cultural diversity.

Cultural diversity

Hofstede (1980) has emphasized that there are a number of cultural dimensions which affect international operations. His framework has been adapted by Bento and Ferreira (1992) to produce the following cultural dualities:

● equality versus inequality;
● certainty versus uncertainty;
● controllability versus uncontrollability;
● individualism versus collectivism;
● materialistic versus personalization.

Sparrow and Hiltrop (1997) noted the following HR areas which may be affected by national culture:

● definitions of what makes an effective manager;
● giving face-to-face feedback;
● readiness to accept international assignments;
● expectations of manager–subordinate relationships;
● pay systems and differential concepts of social justice;
● approaches to organisational structuring and strategic dynamics.

Sparrow instances different approaches to managerial qualities. The Anglo-Saxon notion sees management as something separate and definable, based on general and transferable skills, especially interpersonal skills. In Germany, an entirely opposite view is adopted: value is placed on entrepreneurial skills, technical competence, functional expertise and creativity, and managers rely more on formal authority than in other European countries. In France, management is seen as an intellectually demanding task and management development systems are elitist.

Brewster (1999) comments that the 'universalistic' approach to HRM prevalent in the United States is rejected in Europe, where the basic functions of HR management are given different weights in different countries and are carried out differently. If a convergent and therefore universalistic approach is adopted by a US international firm, it might meet significant problems in getting the approach accepted in Europe. Divergences to respect cultural differences may be more appropriate if the full potential of the overseas company is to be realized.

The international balancing act

The above contextual analysis leads to the fundamental assumption made by Bartlett and Ghoshal (1991): 'Balancing the needs of co-ordination, control and autonomy and maintaining the appropriate balance are critical to the success of the multi-national enterprise.'

Ulrich (1998) suggests that to achieve this balancing act, there are six capabilities that enable firms to integrate and concentrate global activities and also separate and adopt local activities. The capabilities required to 'think globally and act locally' are:

- being able to determine core activities and non-core activities;
- achieving consistency while allowing flexibility;
- building global brand equity while honouring local customs;
- obtaining leverage (bigger is better) while achieving focus (smaller is better);
- sharing learning and creating new knowledge;
- engendering global perspective while ensuring local accountability.

HR policy and practice issues

The HR policy and practice issues arising from the context of international firms as discussed below are concerned with HR policies, employment policy, recruitment and selection practices, career planning and management development policies, and the management of expatriates. Another critical policy and practice area is that of expatriate remuneration, which is dealt with in Chapter 45.

HR POLICIES

It is necessary to consider the extent to which HR policies should be developed and controlled from corporate headquarters. This could mean that employment, employee development, career move and remuneration decisions for people in managerial, professional and technical jobs would be made at the centre. The organization would then be well placed to plan for management succession and to secure the availability of high quality staff to exploit new opportunities as well as to manage existing operations. Individuals could become more committed because they know that a systematic and worldwide approach exists for developing their potential, managing their careers and rewarding them in accordance with their contribution. But there is a possibility that this could tend to impose the corporate culture throughout the world, which could lead to local tensions.

EMPLOYMENT POLICIES

There are three possible approaches:

1. *Fill all key positions with parent country nationals.* This policy is often adopted in the early stages of internationalization or when overseas operations are being started in new countries. Parent country nationals will be qualified to transfer the organization's know-how to the overseas company or plant, but there are a number of potential problems. They might find it difficult to adjust to different conditions, cultures and methods of management. Managing the careers of expatriates is never easy. And there could be inequities between the remuneration of expatriates and local employees, who could also be frustrated by the lack of career opportunities.
2. *Appoint home country nationals.* This gets over the difficulties mentioned above but there may still be problems inherent in the relationships between the parent country managers who remain in overall control and local staff. These may arise from cultural differences, conflicting loyalties and language barriers. Furthermore, as noted by Scullion (1995), home country employees will have limited scope to gain experience outside their own country, while parent country managers will gain little hands-on international experience, thus potentially reducing the effectiveness of the organization as a global competitor.
3. *Appoint the best people regardless of nationality.* This enables the organization to develop a truly international cadre of managers, professional or technical staff, and avoids the parochial approach which might be adopted if only local nationals are appointed. But this can be a difficult strategy to implement and it does require a fair degree of centralized control.

The third, hybrid, approach is often favoured but it has to contend with the fact that some countries are insisting that their own nationals should be used wherever possible.

It is also interesting to note the findings of research conducted by Scullion (1995) who found that although 50 per cent of the companies surveyed had formal policies favouring host country nationals, in practice two-thirds of them used expatriates to manage their overseas operations.

Management development strategy

The management development strategy has to consider the extent to which a truly international perspective can be furthered throughout the global organization by means of processes identifying talent and potential, job rotation, special assignments, distance learning programmes, regional or central management training, attendance on management programmes run by international business schools and the provision of career guidance and monitoring processes from the centre.

RECRUITMENT AND SELECTION

The aim is to select the right people for the task or situation, then empower them to define what needs to be done and how to do it. When selecting international managers, Sparrow (1999a) notes that European firms suggest the following factors, in rank order:

- technical competence;
- previous achievements in the home country;
- language skills;
- motivation;
- stress resistance;
- goal-orientated personality;
- communication skills.

Sparrow adds to that list relational abilities, and adaptability and flexibility. He comments that successful achievement-orientated managers in their home country can easily fail abroad if they lack these qualities. He stresses that the need is for 'open and non-judgemental people interested in the ideas of others, capable of building relationships based on trust, and sensitive to the feelings of others'.

International managers may be judged not only by their cultural sensitivity – the ability to understand the country and adapt their behaviour as necessary – but also their capacity to lead multinational teams. This is something that can best be developed through experience, but the selection process should aim to establish the extent to which candidates can exercise leadership in situations of cultural and ethnic diversity.

When selecting people for international assignments the points to look for are:

- competency in the various factors mentioned above;

- previous experience overseas;
- any evidence that the values of the person are in accord with the values of the culture in which he or she might work; what are called 'culture adaptability assessments' can be used for this purpose;
- family circumstance – how well the person and his or her spouse/partner are likely to adapt to working overseas.

Head hunters with international connections and reputations may be used to source candidates, but global companies may concentrate on developing an international cadre of people who can manage operations centrally and also be available to carry out key roles in other countries. In addition, they may develop internal databases and tracking systems which enable them to identify suitable people for overseas appointments at lower levels.

CAREER PLANNING

Career planning and development programmes can be designed to give people the required experience and to monitor their progress. Such career planning strategies need to consider how a truly international perspective can be furthered throughout the organization by means of processes for identifying talent and potential, job rotation, special assignments, distance learning programmes, regional or central management training, attendance on management programmes run by international business schools, and the provision of career guidance and monitoring processes from the centre.

INTERNATIONAL EMPLOYEE DEVELOPMENT

International employee development is concerned with enabling home, parent and third country nationals to become more effective in their present job in an overseas location. It also aims to develop the competences required to progress either within the local organization or internationally and, overall, to ensure that the organization has the number and quality of executives it is likely to need to manage multi-country or global operations in the future.

The basic approaches and techniques used to formulate and implement international employment development strategies and programmes will broadly be along the lines described in Part VI of this book. But account will need to be taken of cultural diversity factors and the impact of different legal, political, social and value systems, and of the extent to which training should be left to local initiatives or centrally controlled.

Cultural factors

The factors which will affect how training is delivered in different countries or internationally are:

- *legal* – local legal requirements relating to the provision of training opportunities without discriminating on the basis of race, sex or religion;
- *political* – the national training and education framework, including support for youth and vocational training and further education facilities;
- *social* – national approaches to learning and training, including the relative importance attached to on-the-job and off-the-job training, the significance of further education, graduate and post-graduate qualifications;
- *value systems* – the cultural factors which influence how people learn.

Local or central?

The usual approach is to devolve responsibility for the training of local country nationals in job skills to the subsidiary or overseas establishment. But central policy guidelines on training may be issued, a consultancy service may be provided, local managers may be trained in how to train (eg coaching skills) and the effectiveness of local training arrangements may be audited from the centre.

MANAGING EXPATRIATES

The management of expatriates is probably one of the most difficult aspects of international personnel management. The research literature has suggested that the failure rate of expatriates can be high. According to Scullion (1995), British multinationals experience lower expatriate failure rates than US companies, because:

- they felt they had more effective personnel policies covering expatriates;
- closer attention was paid to the selection of expatriates;
- international experience was more highly valued;
- it was believed that British managers were more international in their outlook than US managers.

To maximize success in the difficult job of managing expatriates it is necessary to pay close attention to the following considerations: realistic previews, preparation, monitoring progress, re-entry and remuneration.

REALISTIC PREVIEWS

At interviews for candidates outside the organization, and when talking to internal staff about the possibility of an overseas assignment, it is advisable to provide a realistic preview of the job and the circumstances in which it will be carried out. At this stage it is also necessary to brief people on the opportunities they will have for career development overseas and at headquarters, their remuneration and benefits package, including details of overseas allowances, home leave, pension rights etc (see Chapter 45), how their progress will be monitored and the help that will be made available to them from the centre.

Preparation

The preparation for an overseas assignment should cover cultural familiarization – developing an understanding of the culture of the country in which the individual will work (sometimes called 'acculturization') and of methods of ensuring that he or she will be able to lead and work in multinational teams.

Monitoring progress

The progress of expatriates abroad should be reviewed regularly using performance management processes as described in Part VII. Companies such as 3M and AT&T appoint career sponsors at headquarters to keep in touch with their expatriates and to act as mentors and helpers as necessary.

Re-entry

Research conducted by Johnston (1991) found that the greatest problem met by international companies with their expatriates was re-integrating when they returned home. The main complaints made by the expatriates were lack of status, loss of autonomy, lack of career direction and lack of recognition of overseas experience. It is therefore essential to develop policies which overcome this problem.

Part III

Organizational behaviour

People perform their roles within complex systems called organizations. The study of organizational behaviour is concerned with how people within organizations act, individually or in groups, and how organizations function, in terms of their structure and processes. All managers and HR specialists are in the business of influencing behaviour in directions that will meet business needs. An understanding of organizational processes and skills in the analysis and diagnosis of patterns of organizational behaviour are therefore important. As Nadler and Tushman (1980) have said:

The manager needs to be able to understand the patterns of behaviour that are observed to predict in what direction behaviour will move (particularly in the light of managerial action), and to use this knowledge to control behaviour over the course of time. Effective managerial action requires that the manager be able to diagnose the system he or she is working in.

The purpose of this part of the book is to outline a basic set of concepts and to provide analytical tools which will enable HR specialists to diagnose organizational behaviour and to take appropriate actions. This purpose is achieved by initially (Chapter 9) providing a general analysis of the characteristics of individuals at work. The concepts of individual motivation and commitment are then explored in Chapters 10 and 11 before reviewing generally in Chapter 12 the ways in which organizations function – formal and informal structures – and how people work together in groups. The cultural factors that affect organizational behaviour are then examined in Chapter 13.

9

Characteristics of people

To manage people effectively, it is necessary to understand the factors that affect how people behave at work. This means taking into account the fundamental characteristics of people as examined in this chapter under the following headings:

- individual differences – as affected by people's abilities, intelligence, personality, background and culture, gender and race;
- attitudes – causes and manifestations;
- influences on behaviour – personality and attitudes;
- attribution theory – how we make judgements about people;
- orientation – the approaches people adopt to work;
- roles – the parts people play in carrying out their work.

INDIVIDUAL DIFFERENCES

The management of people would be much easier if everyone were the same, but they are, of course, different because of their ability, intelligence, personality, background and culture (the environment in which they were brought up), as discussed below. Gender, race and disability are additional factors to be taken into account. Importantly, the needs and wants of individuals will also differ, often fundamentally, and this affects their motivation, as described in the next chapter.

The headings under which personal characteristics can vary have been classified by Mischel (1968) as follows:

- *competencies* – abilities and skills;
- *constructs* – the conceptual framework which governs how people perceive their environment;
- *expectations* – what people have learned to expect about their own and others' behaviour;
- *values* – what people believe to be important;
- *self-regulatory plans* – the goals people set themselves and the plans they make to achieve them.

Environmental or situational variables include the type of work individuals carry out; the culture, climate and management style in the organization, the social group within which individuals work; and the 'reference groups' that individuals use for comparative purposes (eg comparing conditions of work between one category of employee and another).

Ability

Ability is the quality that makes an action possible. Abilities have been analysed by Burt (1954) and Vernon (1961). They classified them into two major groups:

- V:ed – standing for verbal, numerical, memory and reasoning abilities;
- K:m – standing for spatial and mechanical abilities, as well as perceptual (memory) and motor skills relating to physical operations such as eye/hand coordination and mental dexterity.

They also suggested that overriding these abilities there is a 'g' or general intelligence factor which accounts for most variations in performance.

Alternative classifications have been produced by

- Thurstone (1940) – spatial ability, perceptual speed, numerical ability, verbal meaning, memory, verbal fluency and inductive reasoning;
- Gagne (1977) – intellectual skills, cognitive (understanding and learning) skills, verbal and motor skills;
- Argyle (1989) – judgement, creativity and social skills.

Intelligence

Intelligence has been defined as:

- 'the capacity to solve problems, apply principles, make inferences and perceive relationships' (Argyle, 1989);
- 'the capacity for abstract thinking and reasoning with a range of different contents and media' (Toplis *et al*, 1991);
- 'the capacity to process information' (Makin *et al*, 1996);
- 'what is measured by intelligence tests' (Wright and Taylor, 1970).

The last, tautological definition is not facetious. As an operational definition, it can be related to the specific aspects of reasoning, inference, cognition (ie knowing, conceiving) and perception (ie understanding, recognition) that intelligence tests attempt to measure.

General intelligence, as noted above, consists of a number of mental abilities that enable a person to succeed at a wide variety of intellectual tasks that use the faculties of knowing and reasoning. The mathematical technique of factor analysis has been used to identify the constituents of intelligence, such as Thurstone's (1940) multiple factors listed above. But there is no general agreement among psychologists as to what these factors are or, indeed, whether there is such a thing as general intelligence.

An alternative approach to the analysis of intelligence was put forward by Guilford (1967), who distinguished five types of mental operation: thinking, remembering, divergent production (problem-solving which leads to unexpected and original solutions), convergent production (problem-solving which leads to the one, correct solution) and evaluating.

Personality

Definition

As defined by Toplis *et al* (1991), the term personality is all-embracing in terms of the individual's behaviour and the way it is organized and coordinated when he or she interacts with the environment. Personality can be described in terms of traits or types.

The trait concept of personality

Personality can be defined as the relatively stable and enduring aspects of individuals that distinguish them from other people. This is the 'trait' concept, traits being predispositions to behave in certain ways in a variety of different situations. The assumption that people are consistent in the ways they express these traits is the basis for making predictions about their future behaviour. We all attribute traits to people in an attempt to understand why they behave in the way they do. As Chell (1987) says: 'This cognitive process gives a sense of order to what might otherwise appear to be senseless uncoordinated behaviours. Traits may therefore be thought of as classification systems, used by individuals to understand other people's and their own behaviour.'

The so-called big five personality traits as defined by Deary and Matthews (1993) are:

- *neuroticism* – anxiety, depression, hostility, self-consciousness, impulsiveness, vulnerability;
- *extraversion* – warmth, gregariousness, assertiveness, activity, excitement seeking, positive emotions;
- *openness* – feelings, actions, ideas, values;
- *agreeableness* – trust, straightforwardness, altruism, compliance, modesty, tender-mindedness;
- *conscientiousness* – competence, order, dutifulness, achievement-striving, self-discipline, deliberation.

A widely used instrument for assessing traits is Cattell's (1963) 16PF test. But the trait theory of personality has been attacked by people such as Mischel (1981), Chell (1985) and Harre (1979). The main criticisms have been as follows:

- People do not necessarily express the same trait across different situations or even the same trait in the same situation. Different people may exhibit consistency in some traits and considerable variability in others.
- Classical trait theory as formulated by Cattell (1963) assumes that the manifestation of trait behaviour is independent of the situations and the persons with whom the individual is interacting – this assumption is questionable, given that trait behaviour usually manifests itself in response to specific situations.
- Trait attributions are a product of language – they are devices for speaking about people and are not generally described in terms of behaviour.

Type theories of personality

Type theory identifies a number of types of personality that can be used to categorize people and may form the basis of a personality test. The types may be linked to descriptions of various traits.

One of the most widely used type theories is that of Jung (1923). He identified four major preferences of people:

- relating to other people – extraversion or introversion;
- gathering information – sensing (dealing with facts that can be objectively verified) or intuitive (generating information through insight);
- using information – thinking (emphasizing logical analysis as the basis for decision-making) or feeling (making decisions based on internal values and beliefs);
- making decisions – perceiving (collecting all the relevant information before making a decision) or judging (resolving the issue without waiting for a large quantity of data).

This theory of personality forms the basis of personality tests such as the Myers-Briggs Types Indicator.

Eysenck (1953) produced a well-known typology. He identified three personality traits: extroversion/introversion, neuroticism and psychoticism, and classified people as stable or unstable extroverts or introverts. For example, a stable introvert is passive, careful, controlled and thoughtful, while a stable extrovert is lively, outgoing, responsive and sociable.

As Makin *et al* (1996) comment, studies using types to predict work-related behaviours are less common and may be difficult to interpret: 'In general it would be fair to say that their level of predictability is similar to that for trait measures.'

The influence of background and culture

Individual differences may be a function of people's background, which will include the environment and culture in which they have been brought up and now exist. Levinson (1978) suggested that 'individual life structure' is shaped by three types of external event:

- the socio-cultural environment;
- the roles they play and the relationships they have;
- the opportunities and constraints that enable or inhibit them to express and develop their personality.

Differences arising from gender, race or disability

It is futile, dangerous and invidious to make assumptions about inherent differences between people because of their sex, race or degree of disability. *If* there are differences in behaviour at work, these are more likely to arise from environmental and cultural factors than from differences in fundamental personal characteristics. The work environment undoubtedly influences feelings and behaviour for each of these categories. Research conducted, as cited by Arnold *et al* (1991), established that working women as a whole 'experienced more daily stress, marital dissatisfaction, and ageing worries, and were less likely to show overt anger than either housewives or men'. Ethnic minorities may find that the selection process is biased against them, promotion prospects are low and that they are subject to other overt or subtle forms of discrimination. The behaviour of disabled people can also be affected by the fact that they are not given equal opportunities. There is, of course, legislation against discrimination in each of those areas but this cannot prevent the more covert forms of prejudice.

ATTITUDES

An attitude can broadly be defined as a settled mode of thinking. Attitudes are evaluative. As described by Makin *et al* (1996), 'Any attitude contains an assessment of whether the object to which it refers is liked or disliked.' Attitudes are developed through experience but they are less stable than traits and can change as new experiences are gained or influences absorbed. Within organizations they are affected by cultural factors (values and norms), the behaviour of management (management style), policies such as those concerned with pay, recognition, promotion and the quality of working life, and the influence of the 'reference group' (the group with whom people identify).

INFLUENCES ON BEHAVIOUR AT WORK

Factors affecting behaviour

Behaviour at work is dependent on both the personal characteristics of individuals (personality and attitudes) and the situation in which they are working. These factors interact, and this theory of behaviour is sometimes called interactionism. It is because of this process of interaction and because there are so many variables in personal characteristics and situations that behaviour is difficult to analyse and predict. It is generally assumed that attitudes determine behaviour, but there is not such a direct link as most people suppose. As Arnold *et al* (1991) comment, research evidence has shown that: 'People's avowed feelings and beliefs about someone or something seemed only loosely related to how they behaved towards it.'

Behaviour will be influenced by the perceptions of individuals about the situation they are in. The term *psychological climate* has been coined by James and Sells (1981) to describe how people's perceptions of the situation give it psychological significance and meaning. They suggested that the key environmental variables are:

- role characteristics such as role ambiguity and conflict (see the last section in this chapter);
- job characteristics such as autonomy and challenge;
- leader behaviours, including goal emphasis and work facilitation;
- work group characteristics, including cooperation and friendliness;
- organizational policies that directly affect individuals, such as the reward system.

ATTRIBUTION THEORY – HOW WE MAKE JUDGEMENTS ABOUT PEOPLE

The ways in which we perceive and make judgements about people at work are explained by attribution theory, which concerns the assignment of causes to events. We make an attribution when we perceive and describe other people's actions and try to discover why they behaved in the way they did. We can also make attributions about our own behaviour. Heider (1958) has pointed out that: 'In everyday life we form ideas about other people and about social situations. We interpret other people's actions and we predict what they will do under certain circumstances.'

In attributing causes to people's actions we distinguish between what is in the person's power to achieve and the effect of environmental influence. A personal cause, whether someone does well or badly, may, for example, be the amount of effort displayed, while a situational cause may be the extreme difficulty of the task. Kelley (1967) has suggested that there are four criteria that we apply to decide whether behaviour is attributable to personal rather than external (situational) causes:

- *distinctiveness* – the behaviour can be distinguished from the behaviour of other people in similar situations;
- *consensus* – if other people agree that the behaviour is governed by some personal characteristic;
- *consistency over time* – whether the behaviour is repeated;
- *consistency over modality* (ie the manner in which things are done) – whether or not the behaviour is repeated in different situations.

Attribution theory is also concerned with the way in which people attribute success or failure to themselves. Research by Weiner (1974) and others has indicated that when people with high achievement needs have been successful, they ascribe this to internal factors such as ability and effort. High achievers tend to attribute failure to lack of effort and not lack of ability. Low achievers tend not to link success with effort but to ascribe their failures to lack of ability.

ORIENTATION TO WORK

Orientation theory examines the factors that are instrumental, ie serve as a means, in directing people's choices about work. An orientation is a central organizing principle that underlies people's attempts to make sense of their lives. In relation to work, as defined by Guest (1984): 'An orientation is a persisting tendency to seek certain goals and rewards from work which exists independently of the nature of the work and the work content.' The orientation approach stresses the role of the social environment factor as a key factor affecting motivation.

Orientation theory is primarily developed from fieldwork carried out by sociologists rather than from laboratory work conducted by psychologists. Goldthorpe *et al* (1968) studied skilled and semi-skilled workers in Luton, and, in their findings, they stressed the importance of instrumental orientation, that is, a view of work as a means to an end, a context in which to earn money to purchase goods and leisure. According to Goldthorpe, the 'affluent' worker interviewed by the research team valued work largely for extrinsic reasons.

In their research carried out with blue-collar workers in Peterborough, Blackburn and Mann (1979) found a wider range of orientations. They suggested that different ones could come into play with varying degrees of force in different situations. The fact that workers, in practice, had little choice about what they did contributed to this diversity – their orientations were affected by the choice or lack of choice presented to them and this meant that they might be forced to accept alternative orientations.

But Blackburn and Mann confirmed that pay was a key preference area, the top preferences being:

1. pay;
2. security;
3. workmates;
4. intrinsic job satisfaction;
5. autonomy.

They commented that: 'An obsession with wages clearly emerged... A concern to minimize unpleasant work was also widespread.' Surprisingly, perhaps, they also revealed that the most persistent preference of all was for outside work, 'a fairly clear desire for a combination of fresh air and freedom'.

ROLES

When faced with any situation, eg carrying out a job, people have to enact a role in order to manage that situation. This is sometimes called the 'situation-act model'. As described by Chell (1985), the model indicates that: 'The person must act within situations: situations are rule-governed and how a person behaves is often prescribed by these socially acquired rules. The person thus adopts a suitable role in order to perform effectively within the situation.'

At work, the term *role* describes the part to be played by individuals in fulfilling their job requirements. Roles therefore indicate the specific forms of behaviour required to carry out a particular task or the group of tasks contained in a *position* or job. Work role profiles primarily define the requirements in terms of the ways tasks are carried out rather than the tasks themselves. They may refer to broad aspects of behaviour, especially with regard to working with others and styles of management. A distinction can therefore be made between a *job description*, which simply lists the main tasks an individual has to carry out, and a *role profile*, which is more concerned with the behavioural aspects of the work and the outcomes the individual in the role is expected to achieve. The concept of a role emphasizes the fact that people at work are, in a sense, always acting a part; they are not simply reciting the lines but interpreting them in terms of their own perceptions of how they should behave in relation to the context in which they work, especially with regard to their interactions with other people.

The role individuals occupy at work – and elsewhere – therefore exists in relation to other people – their *role set*. These people have expectations about the individuals' role, and if they live up to these expectations they will have successfully performed the role. Performance in a role is a product of the situation individuals are in (the organizational context and the direction or influence exercised from above or elsewhere in the organization) and their own skills, competences, attitudes and personality. Situational factors are important, but the role individuals perform can both shape and reflect their personalities. Stress and inadequate performance result when roles are ambiguous, incompatible, or in conflict with one another.

Role ambiguity

When individuals are unclear about what their role is, what is expected of them, or how they are getting on, they may become insecure or lose confidence in themselves.

Role incompatibility

Stress and poor performance may be caused by roles having incompatible elements, as when there is a clash between what other people expect from the role and what individuals believe is expected of them.

Role conflict

Role conflict results when, even if roles are clearly defined and there is no incompatibility between expectations, individuals have to carry out two antagonistic roles. For example, conflict can exist between the roles of individuals at work and their roles at home.

IMPLICATIONS FOR HR SPECIALISTS

The main implications for HR specialists of the factors that affect individuals at work are as follows:

- *Individual differences* – when designing jobs, preparing training programmes, assessing and counselling staff, developing reward systems and dealing with grievances and disciplinary problems, it is necessary to remember that all people are different. What fulfils one person may not fulfil another. Abilities, aptitudes and intelligence differ widely and it is necessary to take particular care in fitting the right people into the right jobs and giving them the right training. Personalities and attitudes also differ. It is important to focus on how to manage diversity as described in Chapter 55. This should take account of individual differences, which will include any issues arising from the employment of women, people from different ethnic groups, those with disabilities and older people.
- *Personalities* should not be judged simplistically in terms of stereotyped traits. People are complex and they change, and account has to be taken of this. The problem for HR specialists and managers in general is that, while they have to accept and understand these differences and take full account of them, they have ultimately to proceed on the basis of fitting them to the requirements of the situation, which are essentially what the organization needs to achieve. There is always a limit to the extent to which an organization, which relies on collective effort to achieve its goals, can adjust itself to the specific needs of individuals. But the organization has to appreciate that the pressures it makes on people can result in stress and therefore become counter-productive.

- *Judgements about people* (attribution theory) – we all ascribe motives to other people and attempt to establish the causes of their behaviour. We must be careful, however, not to make simplistic judgements about causality (ie what has motivated someone's behaviour) – for ourselves as well as in respect of others – especially when we are assessing performance.
- *Orientation theory* – the significance of orientation theory is that it stresses the importance of the effect of environmental factors on the motivation to work.
- *Role theory* – role theory helps us to understand the need to clarify with individuals what is expected of them in behavioural terms and to ensure when designing jobs that they do not contain any incompatible elements. We must also be aware of the potential for role conflict so that steps can be taken to minimize stress.

10

Motivation

All organizations are concerned with what should be done to achieve sustained high levels of performance through people. This means giving close attention to how individuals can best be motivated through such means as incentives, rewards, leadership and, importantly, the work they do and the organization context within which they carry out that work. The aim, of course, is to develop motivation processes and a work environment that will help to ensure that individuals deliver results in accordance with the expectations of management.

Motivation theory examines the process of motivation. It explains why people at work behave in the way they do in terms of their efforts and the directions they are taking. It also describes what organizations can do to encourage people to apply their efforts and abilities in ways that will further the achievement of the organization's goals as well as satisfying their own needs.

Unfortunately, approaches to motivation are too often underpinned by simplistic assumptions about how it works. The process of motivation is much more complex than many people believe. People have different needs, establish different goals to satisfy those needs and take different actions to achieve those goals. It is wrong to assume that one approach to motivation fits all. That is why the assumptions underlying belief in the virtues of performance-related pay as a means of providing a motivational incentive are simplistic. Motivational practices are most likely to function effectively if they are based on proper understanding of what is involved. This chapter therefore:

- defines the process of motivation;
- explores in greater depth the various theories of motivation which explain and amplify the basic process;
- examines the practical implications of the motivation theories.

THE PROCESS OF MOTIVATION

What is motivation? A motive is a reason for doing something. Motivation is concerned with the factors that influence people to behave in certain ways. The three components of motivation as listed by Arnold *et al* (1991) are:

- *direction* – what a person is trying to do;
- *effort* – how hard a person is trying;
- *persistence* – how long a person keeps on trying.

Motivating other people is about getting them to move in the direction you want them to go in order to achieve a result. Motivating yourself is about setting the direction independently and then taking a course of action which will ensure that you get there. Motivation can be described as goal-directed behaviour. People are motivated when they expect that a course of action is likely to lead to the attainment of a goal and a valued reward – one that satisfies their needs.

Well-motivated people are those with clearly defined goals who take action that they expect will achieve those goals. Such people may be self-motivated, and as long as this means they are going in the right direction to achieve what they are there to achieve, then this is the best form of motivation. Most of us, however, need to be motivated to a greater or lesser degree. The organization as a whole can provide the context within which high levels of motivation can be achieved by providing incentives and rewards, satisfying work, and opportunities for learning and growth. But managers still have a major part to play in using their motivating skills to get people to give of their best, and to make good use of the motivational processes provided by the organization. To do this it is necessary to understand the process of motivation – how it works and the different types of motivation that exist.

A needs-related model of the process of motivation is shown in Figure 10.1. This suggests that motivation is initiated by the conscious or unconscious recognition of unsatisfied needs. These needs create wants, which are desires to achieve or obtain something. Goals are then established which it is believed will satisfy these needs and wants and a behaviour pathway is selected which it is expected will achieve the goal. If the goal is achieved, the need will be satisfied and the behaviour is likely to be

Figure 10.1 The process of motivation

repeated the next time a similar need emerges. If the goal is not achieved, the same action is less likely to be repeated. This process of repeating successful behaviour or actions is called reinforcement or the law of effect (Hull, 1951). It has, however, been criticised by Allport (1954) as ignoring the influence of expectations and therefore constituting 'hedonism of the past'.

TYPES OF MOTIVATION

Motivation at work can take place in two ways. First, people can motivate themselves by seeking, finding and carrying out work (or being given work) that satisfies their needs or at least leads them to expect that their goals will be achieved. Secondly, people can be motivated by management through such methods as pay, promotion, praise, etc.

There are two types of motivation as originally identified by Herzberg *et al* (1957):

● *Intrinsic motivation* – the self-generated factors that influence people to behave in a particular way or to move in a particular direction. These factors include responsibility (feeling that the work is important and having control over one's own resources), autonomy (freedom to act), scope to use and develop skills and abilities, interesting and challenging work and opportunities for advancement.
● *Extrinsic motivation* – what is done to or for people to motivate them. This includes rewards, such as increased pay, praise, or promotion, and punishments, such as disciplinary action, withholding pay, or criticism.

Extrinsic motivators can have an immediate and powerful effect, but it will not necessarily last long. The intrinsic motivators, which are concerned with the 'quality of working life' (a phrase and movement emerged from this concept), are likely to have a deeper and longer-term effect because they are inherent in individuals and not imposed from outside.

MOTIVATION THEORY

Approaches to motivation are underpinned by motivation theory. The most influential theories are classified as follows:

● *Instrumentality theory*, which states that rewards or punishments (carrots or sticks) serve as the means of ensuring that people behave or act in desired ways.
● *Content theory*, which focuses on the content of motivation. It states that motivation is essentially about taking action to satisfy needs, and identifies the main needs that influence behaviour. Needs theory was originated by Maslow (1954), and in his two-factor model, Herzberg (1957) listed needs which he termed 'satisfiers'.
● Process theory, which focuses on the psychological processes which affect motivation, by reference to expectations (Vroom, 1964), goals (Latham and Locke, 1979) and perceptions of equity (Adams, 1965).

INSTRUMENTALITY THEORY

'Instrumentality' is the belief that if we do one thing it will lead to another. In its crudest form, instrumentality theory states that people only work for money.

The theory emerged in the second half of the nineteenth century with its emphasis on the need to rationalize work and on economic outcomes. It assumes that a person will be motivated to work if rewards and penalties are tied directly to his or her performance, thus the awards are contingent upon effective performance. Instrumentality theory has its roots in Taylorism, ie the scientific management methods of Taylor (1911), who wrote: 'It is impossible, through any long period of time, to get workmen to work much harder than the average men around them unless they are assured a large and permanent increase in their pay.'

This theory is based on the principle of reinforcement and the so-called law of effect. Motivation using this approach has been, and still is, widely adopted and can be successful in some circumstances. But it is based exclusively on a system of external controls and fails to recognize a number of other human needs. It also fails to appreciate the fact that the formal control system can be seriously affected by the informal relationship existing between workers.

CONTENT (NEEDS) THEORY

The basis of this theory is the belief that an unsatisfied need creates tension and a state of disequilibrium. To restore the balance, a goal that will satisfy the need is identified, and a behaviour pathway that will lead to the achievement of the goal is selected. All behaviour is therefore motivated by unsatisfied needs.

Not all needs are equally important for a person at any one time – some may provide a much more powerful drive towards a goal than others, depending on the individual's background and present situation. Complexity is further increased because there is no simple relationship between needs and goals. The same need can be satisfied by a number of different goals and the stronger the need and the longer its duration, the broader the range of possible goals. At the same time, one goal may satisfy a number of needs – a new car provides transport as well as an opportunity to impress the neighbours.

Needs theory was developed originally by Maslow (1954), who postulated the concept of a hierarchy of needs which he believed were fundamental to the personality. Herzberg's (1957) two-factor model (see page 164) cannot strictly be classified as needs theory but he did identify a number of fundamental needs.

In addition, Alderter (1972) developed his ERG theory, which refers to the need for existence, relatedness and growth. Maslow's theory has been most influential.

Maslow's hierarchy of needs

The most famous classification of needs is the one formulated by Maslow (1954). He suggested that there are five major need categories which apply to people in general, starting from the fundamental physiological needs and leading through a hierarchy of safety, social and esteem needs to the need for self-fulfilment, the highest need of all. Maslow's hierarchy is as follows:

1. *Physiological* – the need for oxygen, food, water and sex.
2. *Safety* – the need for protection against danger and the deprivation of physiological needs.
3. *Social* – the need for love, affection and acceptance as belonging to a group.

4. *Esteem* – the need to have a stable, firmly based, high evaluation of oneself (self-esteem) and to have the respect of others (prestige). These needs may be classi-fied into two subsidiary sets: first, the desire for achievement, for adequacy, for confidence in the face of the world, and for independence and freedom, and, second, the desire for reputation or status defined as respect or esteem from other people, and manifested by recognition, attention, importance, or appreciation.
5. *Self-fulfilment (self-actualization)* – the need to develop potentialities and skills, to become what one believes one is capable of becoming.

Maslow's theory of motivation states that when a lower need is satisfied, the next highest becomes dominant and the individual's attention is turned to satisfying this higher need. The need for self-fulfilment, however, can never be satisfied. He said that 'man is a wanting animal'; only an unsatisfied need can motivate behaviour and the dominant need is the prime motivator of behaviour. Psychological development takes place as people move up the hierarchy of needs, but this is not necessarily a straightforward progression. The lower needs still exist, even if temporarily dormant as motivators, and individuals constantly return to previously satisfied needs.

One of the implications of Maslow's theory is that the higher-order needs for esteem and self-fulfilment provide the greatest impetus to motivation – they grow in strength when they are satisfied, while the lower needs decline in strength on satis-faction. But the jobs people do will not necessarily satisfy their needs, especially when they are routine or deskilled.

Maslow's needs hierarchy has an intuitive appeal and has been very influential. But it has not been verified by empirical research and it has been criticized for its apparent rigidity – different people may have different priorities and it is difficult to accept that people's needs progress steadily up the hierarchy. In fact, Maslow himself expressed doubts about the validity of a strictly ordered hierarchy.

PROCESS THEORY

In process theory, the emphasis is on the psychological processes or forces that affect motivation, as well as on basic needs. It is also known as cognitive theory because it is concerned with people's perceptions of their working environment and the ways in which they interpret and understand it. According to Guest (1992b), the process theory provides a much more relevant approach to motivation that replaces the theo-ries of Maslow and Herzberg, which, he suggests, have been shown by extensive research to be wrong.

Process or cognitive theory can certainly be more useful to managers than needs theory because it provides more realistic guidance on motivation techniques. The processes are:

- expectations (expectancy theory);
- goal achievement (goal theory);
- feelings about equity (equity theory).

Expectancy theory

The concept of expectancy was originally contained in the valency–instrumentality–expectancy (VIE) theory which was formulated by Vroom (1964). Valency stands for value, instrumentality is the belief that if we do one thing it will lead to another, and expectancy is the probability that action or effort will lead to an outcome. This concept of expectancy was defined in more detail by Vroom as follows:

> Where an individual chooses between alternatives which involve uncertain outcomes, it seems clear that his behaviour is affected not only by his preferences among these outcomes but also by the degree to which he believes these outcomes to be possible. An expectancy is defined as a momentary belief concerning the likelihood that a particular act will be followed by a particular outcome. Expectancies may be described in terms of their strength. Maximal strength is indicated by subjective certainty that the act will be followed by the outcome, while minimal (or zero) strength is indicated by subjective certainty that the act will not be followed by the outcome.

The strength of expectations may be based on past experiences (reinforcement), but individuals are frequently presented with new situations – a change in job, payment system, or working conditions imposed by management – where past experience is an adequate guide to the implications of the change. In these circumstances, motivation may be reduced.

Motivation is only likely when a clearly perceived and usable relationship exists between performance and outcome, and the outcome is seen as a means of satisfying needs. This explains why extrinsic financial motivation – for example, an incentive or bonus scheme – works only if the link between effort and reward is clear and the value of the reward is worth the effort. It also explains why intrinsic motivation arising from the work itself can be more powerful than the extrinsic motivation; intrinsic motivation outcomes are more under the control of individuals, who can place greater reliance on their past experiences to indicate the extent to which positive and advantageous results are likely to be obtained by their behaviour.

This theory was developed by Porter and Lawler (1968) into a model which follows Vroom's ideas by suggesting that there are two factors determining the effort people put into their jobs:

1. the value of the rewards to individuals in so far as they satisfy their needs for security, social esteem, autonomy, and self-actualization;
2. the probability that rewards depend on effort, as perceived by individuals – in other words, their expectations about the relationships between effort and reward.

Thus, the greater the value of a set of awards and the higher the probability that receiving each of these rewards depends upon effort, the greater the effort that will be put forth in a given situation.

But, as Porter and Lawler emphasize, mere effort is not enough. It has to be effective effort if it is to produce the desired performance. The two variables additional to effort which affect task achievement are:

●   *ability* – individual characteristics such as intelligence, manual skills, know-how;
●   *role perceptions* – what the individual wants to do or thinks he or she is required to do. These are good from the viewpoint of the organization if they correspond with what it thinks the individual ought to be doing. They are poor if the views of the individual and the organization do not coincide.

Goal theory

Goal theory as developed by Latham and Locke (1979) states that motivation and performance are higher when individuals are set specific goals, when goals are difficult but accepted, and when there is a feedback on performance. Participation in goal setting is important as a means of getting agreement to the setting of higher goals. Difficult goals must be agreed and their achievement reinforced by guidance and advice. Finally, feedback is vital in maintaining motivation, particularly towards the achievement of even higher goals.

Erez and Zidon (1984) emphasized the need for acceptance of and commitment to goals. They found that, as long as they are agreed, demanding goals lead to better performance than easy ones. Erez (1977) also emphasized the importance of feedback. As Robertson *et al* (1992) point out:

> Goals inform individuals to achieve particular levels of performance, in order for them to direct and evaluate their actions; while performance feedback allows the individual

to track how well he or she has been doing in relation to the goal, so that, if necessary, adjustments in effort, direction or possibly task strategies can be made.

Goal theory is in line with the 1960s concept of management by objectives. The latter approach, however, often failed because it was tackled bureaucratically without gaining the real support of those involved and, importantly, without ensuring that managers were aware of the significance of the processes of agreement, reinforcement and feedback, and were skilled in practising them.

Goal theory, however, plays a key part in the performance management process which was evolved from the largely discredited management-by-objectives approach. Performance management is dealt with in Part VIII.

Equity theory

Equity theory is concerned with the perceptions people have about how they are being treated as compared with others. To be dealt with equitably is to be treated fairly in comparison with another group of people (a reference group) or a relevant other person. Equity involves feelings and perceptions and is always a comparative process. It is not synonymous with equality, which means treating everyone the same, since this would be inequitable if they deserve to be treated differently.

Equity theory states, in effect, that people will be better motivated if they are treated equitably and demotivated if they are treated inequitably. It explains only one aspect of the process of motivation and job satisfaction, although it may be significant in terms of morale.

As suggested by Adams (1965), there are two forms of equity: distributive equity, which is concerned with the fairness with which people feel they are rewarded in accordance with their contribution and in comparison with others; and procedural equity, or procedural justice, which is concerned with the perceptions employees have about the fairness with which company procedures in such areas as performance appraisal, promotion and discipline are being operated.

Interpersonal factors are closely linked to feelings about procedural fairness. Five factors that contribute to perceptions of procedural fairness have been identified by Tyler and Bies (1990). These are:

1. adequate considerations of an employee's viewpoint;
2. suppression of personal bias towards the employee;
3. applying criteria consistently across employees;
4. providing early feedback to employees concerning the outcome of decisions;
5. providing employees with an adequate explanation of the decision made.

HERZBERG'S TWO-FACTOR MODEL

The two-factor model of satisfiers and dissatisfiers was developed by Herzberg *et al* (1957) following an investigation into the sources of job satisfaction and dissatisfaction of accountants and engineers. It was assumed that people have the capacity to report accurately the conditions that made them satisfied and dissatisfied with their jobs. Accordingly, the subjects were asked to tell their interviewers about the times during which they felt exceptionally good and exceptionally bad about their jobs and how long their feelings persisted. It was found that the accounts of 'good' periods most frequently concerned the content of the job, particularly achievement, recognition, advancement, responsibility, and the work itself. On the other hand, accounts of 'bad' periods most frequently concerned the context of the job. Company policy and administration, supervision, salary and working conditions more frequently appeared in these accounts than in those told about 'good' periods. The main implications of this research, according to Herzberg, are that:

> The wants of employees divide into two groups. One group revolves around the need to develop in one's occupation as a source of personal growth. The second group operates as an essential base to the first and is associated with fair treatment in compensation, supervision, working conditions and administrative practices. The fulfilment of the needs of the second group does not motivate the individual to high levels of job satisfaction and to extra performance on the job. All we can expect from satisfying this second group of needs is the prevention of dissatisfaction and poor job performance.

These groups form the two factors in Herzberg's model: one consists of the satisfiers or motivators, because they are seen to be effective in motivating the individual to superior performance and effort. The other consists of the dissatisfiers, which essentially describe the environment and serve primarily to prevent job dissatisfaction, while having little effect on positive job attitudes. The latter were named the hygiene factors in the medical use of the term, meaning preventive and environmental.

Reservations about Herzberg's theory

Herzberg's two-factor model has been strongly attacked. The research method has been criticized because no attempt was made to measure the relationship between satisfaction and performance. It has been suggested that the two-factor nature of the theory is an inevitable result of the questioning method used by the interviewers. It has also been suggested that wide and unwarranted inferences have been drawn from small and specialized samples and that there is no evidence to suggest that the satisfiers do improve productivity.

In spite of these criticisms (or perhaps because of them, as they are all from academics), the Herzberg theory continues to thrive; partly because for the layman it is easy to understand and seems to be based on 'real-life' rather than academic abstraction, and partly because it fits in well with the highly respected ideas of Maslow and McGregor in its emphasis on the positive value of the intrinsic motivating factors. It is also in accord with a fundamental belief in the dignity of labour and the Protestant ethic – that work is good in itself. As a result, Herzberg had immense influence on the job enrichment movement, which sought to design jobs in a way that will maximize the opportunities to obtain intrinsic satisfaction from work and thus improve the quality of working life. His emphasis on the distinction between intrinsic and extrinsic motivation is also important.

SUMMARY OF MOTIVATION THEORIES

The major motivation theories are summarized in Table 10.1.

THE RELATIONSHIP BETWEEN MOTIVATION AND PERFORMANCE

The basic requirements for job satisfaction may include comparatively higher pay, an equitable payment system, real opportunities for promotion, considerate and participative management, a reasonable degree of social interaction at work, interesting and varied tasks and a high degree of autonomy: control over work pace and work methods. The degree of satisfaction obtained by individuals, however, depends largely upon their own needs and expectations, and the working environment.

But research has not established any strongly positive connection between satisfaction and performance. A satisfied worker is not necessarily a high producer, and a high producer is not necessarily a satisfied worker. The claim that good performance results in satisfaction rather than vice versa has not been proved.

MOTIVATION AND MONEY

Money, in the form of pay or some other sort of remuneration, is the most obvious extrinsic reward. Money provides the carrot that most people want.

Doubts have been cast by Herzberg *et al* (1957) on the effectiveness of money because, they claimed, while the lack of it can cause dissatisfaction, its provision does

Table 10.1 Summary of motivation theories

Category	Type	Theorist(s)	Summary of theory	Implications
Instrumentality	Taylorism	Taylor	If we do one thing it leads to another. People will be motivated to work if rewards and punishments are directly related to their performance.	Basis of crude attempts to motivate people by incentives. Often used as the implied rationale for performance-related pay although this is seldom an effective motivator.
Content (needs) theory	Hierarchy of needs	Maslow	A hierarchy of five needs exist: physiological, safety, social, esteem, self-fulfilment. Needs at a higher level only emerge when a lower need is satisfied.	Focuses attention on the various needs that motivate people and the notion that a satisfied need is no longer a motivator. The concept of a hierarchy has no practical significance.
Two-factor model	Statistical dissatisfiers	Herzberg	Two groups of factors affect job satisfaction: (1) those intrinsic to the job (intrinsic motivators or satisfiers) such as achievement, recognition, the work itself, responsibility and growth; (2) those extrinsic to the job (extrinsic motivators or hygiene factors) such as pay and working conditions.	Identifies a number of fundamental needs, ie achievement, recognition, advancement, autonomy and the work itself. Strongly influences approaches to job design (job enrichment). Drew attention to the concept of intrinsic and extrinsic motivation and the fact that intrinsic motivation mainly derived from the work itself will have a longer-lasting effect. Therefore underpins the proposition that reward systems should provide for both financial and non-financial rewards.

Process/ cognitive theory	Expectancy theory	Vroom, Porter and Lawler	Motivation and performance are influenced by: (1) the perceived link between effort and performance, (2) the perceived link between performance and outcomes, and (3) the significance (valence) of the outcome to the person. Effort (motivation) depends on the likelihood that rewards will follow effort and that the reward is worthwhile.	The key theory informing approaches to rewards, ie that they must be a link between effort and reward (line of sight), the reward should be achievable and should be worthwhile.
	Goal theory	Latham and Locke	Motivation and performance will improve if people have difficult but agreed goals and receive feedback.	Provides the rationale for performance management processes, goal setting and feedback.
	Equity theory	Adams	People are better motivated if treated equitably.	Need to develop equitable reward and employment practices.

not result in lasting satisfaction. There is something in this, especially for people on fixed salaries or rates of pay who do not benefit directly from an incentive scheme. They may feel good when they get an increase; apart from the extra money, it is a highly tangible form of recognition and an effective means of helping people to feel that they are valued. But this feeling of euphoria can rapidly die away. Other dissatisfactions from Herzberg's list of hygiene factors, such as working conditions or the quality of management, can loom larger in some people's minds when they fail to get the satisfaction they need from the work itself. However, it must be re-emphasized that different people have different needs and wants and Herzberg's two-factor theory has not been validated. Some will be much more motivated by money than others. What cannot be assumed is that money motivates everyone in the same way and to the same extent. Thus it is naive to think that the introduction of a performance-related pay (PRP) scheme will miraculously transform everyone over-night into well-motivated, high-performing individuals.

Nevertheless, money provides the means to achieve a number of different ends. It is a powerful force because it is linked directly or indirectly to the satisfaction of many needs. It clearly satisfies basic needs for survival and security, if it is coming in regularly. It can also satisfy the need for self-esteem (as noted above, it is a visible mark of appreciation) and status – money can set you in a grade apart from your fellows and can buy you things they cannot to build up your prestige. Money satisfies the less desirable but still prevalent drives of acquisitiveness and cupidity.

Money may in itself have no intrinsic meaning, but it acquires significant moti-vating power because it comes to symbolize so many intangible goals. It acts as a symbol in different ways for different people, and for the same person at different times. As noted by Goldthorpe *et al* (1968) from their research into the 'affluent worker', pay is the dominant factor in the choice of employer and considerations of pay seem most powerful in binding people to their present job.

Do financial incentives motivate people? The answer is yes, for those people who are strongly motivated by money and whose expectations that they will receive a financial reward are high. But less confident employees may not respond to incen-tives that they do not expect to achieve. It can also be argued that extrinsic rewards may erode intrinsic interest – people who work just for money could find their tasks less pleasurable and may not, therefore, do them so well. What we do know is that a multiplicity of factors are involved in performance improvements and many of those factors are interdependent.

Money can therefore provide positive motivation in the right circumstances, not only because people need and want money but also because it serves as a highly tangible means of recognition. But badly designed and managed pay systems can demotivate. Another researcher in this area was Jaques (1961), who emphasized the need for such systems to be perceived as being fair and equitable. In other words, the reward should be clearly related to effort or level of responsibility and people should not receive less money than they deserve compared with their fellow workers. Jaques called this the 'felt-fair' principle.

MOTIVATION STRATEGIES

The factors that affect motivational strategies and the contribution that HR can make to achieving higher levels of motivation are summarized in Table 10.2.

Table 10.2 Motivation strategies

Factors affecting motivation strategies	The HR contribution
• The complexity of the process of motivation means that simplistic approaches based on instrumentality theory are unlikely to be successful.	• Avoid the trap of developing or supporting strategies that offer prescriptions for motivation based on a simplistic view of the process or fail to recognize individual differences.
• People are more likely to be motivated if they work in an environment in which they are valued for what they are and what they do. This means paying attention to the basic need for recognition.	• Encourage the development of performance management processes which provide opportunities to agree expectations and give positive feedback on accomplishments. • Develop reward systems which provide opportunities for both financial and non-financial rewards to recognize achievements. Bear in mind, however, that financial rewards systems are not necessarily appropriate and the lessons of expectancy, goal and equity theory need to be taken into account in designing and operating them.
• The need for work which provides people with the means to achieve their goals, a reasonable degree of autonomy, and scope for the use of skills and competencies should be recognized.	• Advise on processes for the design of jobs which take account of the factors affecting the motivation to work, providing for job enrichment in the shape of variety, decision-making responsibility and as much control as possible in carrying out the work.
• The need for the opportunity to grow by developing abilities and careers.	• Provide facilities and opportunities for learning through such means as personal development planning processes as well as more formal training. • Develop career planning processes.
• The cultural environment of the organization in the shape of its values and norms will influence the impact of any attempts to motivate people by direct or indirect means.	• Advise on the development of a culture which supports processes of valuing and rewarding employees.
• Motivation will be enhanced by leadership which sets the direction, encourages and stimulates achievement, and provides support to employees in their efforts to reach goals and improve their performance generally.	• Devise competence frameworks which focus on leadership qualities and the behaviours expected of managers and team leaders. • Ensure that leadership potential is identified through performance management and assessment centres. • Provide guidance and training to develop leadership qualities.

11

Commitment

The concept of commitment plays an important part in HRM philosophy. As Guest (1987) has indicated, HRM policies are designed to 'maximize organizational integration, employee commitment, flexibility and quality of work'. The chapter explores the meaning and significance of organizational commitment, considers certain problems about the concept and discusses how it can be developed.

THE MEANING OF COMMITMENT

Commitment refers to attachment and loyalty. As defined by Mowdray *et al* (1982), commitment consists of three components: an identification with the goals and values of the organization; a desire to belong to the organization; and a willingness to display effort on behalf of the organization.

An alternative, although closely related, definition of commitment emphasizes the importance of behaviour in creating commitment. As Salancik (1977) put it: 'Commitment is a state of being in which an individual becomes bound by his actions to beliefs that sustain his activities and his own involvement.' Three features of behaviour are important in binding individuals to acts: the visibility of the acts, the extent to which the outcomes are irrevocable, and the degree to which the person undertakes the action voluntarily. Commitment, according to Salancik, can be increased and harnessed 'to obtain support for organizational ends and interests' through such approaches as participation in decisions about actions.

THE SIGNIFICANCE OF COMMITMENT

There have been two schools of thought about commitment. One, the 'from control to commitment' school, was led by Walton (1985a, b), who saw commitment strategy as a more rewarding approach to human resource management, in contrast to the traditional control strategy. The other, 'Japanese/excellence' school, is represented by writers such as Pascale and Athos (1981) and Peters and Waterman (1982) who looked at the Japanese model and related the achievement of excellence to getting the whole-hearted commitment of the workforce to the organization.

From control to commitment

The importance of commitment was highlighted by Walton (1985a, b). His theme was that improved performance would result if the organization moved away from the traditional control-orientated approach to workforce management, which relies upon establishing order, exercising control and 'achieving efficiency in the application of the workforce'. He argued that this approach should be replaced by a commitment strategy. He suggested that workers respond best – and most creatively – not when they are tightly controlled by management, placed in narrowly defined jobs, and treated like an unwelcome necessity, but, instead, when they are given broader responsibilities, encouraged to contribute and helped to achieve satisfaction in their work.

Walton (1985a) suggested that in the new commitment-based approach:

> Jobs are designed to be broader than before, to combine planning and implementation, and to include efforts to upgrade operations, not just to maintain them. Individual responsibilities are expected to change as conditions change, and teams, not individuals, often are the organization units accountable for performance. With management hierarchies relatively flat and differences in status minimized, control and lateral coordination depend on shared goals. And expertise rather than formal position determines influence.

Put like this, a commitment strategy does not sound like a crude attempt to manipulate people to accept management's values and goals, as some have suggested. In fact, Walton does not describe it as being instrumental in this manner. His prescription is for a broad HRM approach to the ways in which people are treated, jobs are designed and organizations are managed. And he quotes a number of examples in America where unions have cooperated with management; talking about common interests and agreeing to sponsor quality-of-working programmes and employee involvement activities.

The Japanese/excellence school

Attempts made to explain the secret of Japanese business success by such writers as Ouchi (1981) and Pascale and Athos (1981) led to the theory that the best way to motivate people is to get their full commitment to the values of the organization by leadership and involvement. This might be called the 'hearts and minds' approach to motivation and, among other things, it popularized such devices as quality circles.

The baton was taken up by Peters and Waterman (1982) and their imitators later in the 1980s. This approach to excellence was summed up by Peters and Austin (1985) when they wrote:

> Trust people and treat them like adults, enthuse them by lively and imaginative leadership, develop and demonstrate an obsession for quality, make them feel they own the business, and your workforce will respond with total commitment.

PROBLEMS WITH THE CONCEPT OF COMMITMENT

A number of commentators have raised questions about the concept of commitment. These relate to three main problem areas: 1) its unitary frame of reference; 2) commitment as an inhibitor of flexibility; 3) whether high commitment does in practice result in improved organizational performance.

Unitary frame of reference

A comment frequently made about the concept of commitment is that it is too simplistic in adopting a unitary frame of reference; in other words, it assumes unrealistically that an organization consists of people with shared interests. It has been suggested by people like Cyert and March (1963), Mangham (1979) and Mintzberg (1983a) that an organization is really a coalition of interest groups where political processes are an inevitable part of everyday life. The pluralist perspective recognizes the legitimacy of different interests and values and therefore asks the question 'commitment to what?' Thus, as Coopey and Hartley (1991) put it, 'commitment is not an all-or-nothing affair (though many managers might like it to be) but a question of multiple or competing commitments for the individual'.

Legge (1989) also raises this question in her discussion of strong culture as a key requirement of HRM through 'a shared set of managerially sanctioned values'.

However, managerial values for quality, service, equal opportunity and innovation are not necessarily wrong *because* they are managerial values. But it is reasonable to believe that pursuing a value such as innovation could work against the interests of employees by, for example, resulting in redundancies. And it would be quite reasonable for any employee encouraged to behave in accordance with a value supported by management to ask 'what's in it for me?' It can also be argued that the imposition of management's values on employees without their having any part to play in discussing and agreeing them is a form of coercion.

Commitment and flexibility

It was pointed out by Coopey and Hartley (1991) that: 'The problem for a unitarist notion of organizational commitment is that it fosters a conformist approach which not only fails to reflect organizational reality, but can be narrowing and limiting for the organization'. They argue that if employees are expected and encouraged to commit themselves tightly to a single set of values and goals they will not be able to cope with the ambiguities and uncertainties that are endemic in organizational life in times of change. Conformity to 'imposed' values will inhibit creative problem solving, and high commitment to present courses of action will increase both resistance to change and the stress that invariably occurs when change takes place.

If commitment is related to tightly defined plans then this will become a real problem. To avoid it, the emphasis should be on overall strategic directions. These would be communicated to employees with the proviso that changing circumstances will require their amendment. In the meantime, however, everyone can at least be informed in general terms where the organization is heading and, more specifically, the part they are expected to play in helping the organization to get there. If they can get involved in the decision-making processes on matters that affect them (which includes management's values for performance, quality and customer service), so much the better.

Values need not necessarily be restrictive. They can be defined in ways that allow for freedom of choice within broad guidelines. In fact, the values themselves can refer to such processes as flexibility, innovation and responsiveness to change. Thus, far from inhibiting creative problem solving, they can encourage it.

The impact of high commitment

A belief in the positive value of commitment has been confidently expressed by Walton (1985a):

> Underlying all these (human resource) policies is a management philosophy, often embedded in a published statement, that acknowledges the legitimate claims of a company's multiple stakeholders – owners, employees, customers and the public. At the centre of this philosophy is a belief that eliciting employee commitment will lead to enhanced performance. The evidence shows this belief to be well founded.

However, a review by Guest (1991) of the mainly North American literature, reinforced by the limited UK research available, led him to the conclusion that: 'High organizational commitment is associated with lower labour turnover and absence, but there is no clear link to performance.'

It is probably wise not to expect too much from commitment as a means of making a direct and immediate impact on performance. It is not the same as motivation. Commitment is a wider concept and tends to be more stable over a period of time and less responsible to transitory aspects of an employee's job. It is possible to be dissatisfied with a particular feature of a job while retaining a reasonably high level of commitment to the organization as a whole.

In relating commitment to motivation it is useful to distinguish, as do Buchanan and Hucyznski (1985), three perspectives:

1. The goals towards which people aim. From this perspective, goals such as the good of the company, or effective performance at work, may provide a degree of motivation for some employees, who could be regarded as committed in so far as they feel they own the goals.
2. The process by which goals and objectives at work are selected, which is quite distinct from the way in which commitment arises within individuals.
3. The social process of motivating others to perform effectively. From this viewpoint, strategies aimed at increasing motivation also affect commitment. It may be true to say that, where commitment is present, motivation is likely to be strong, particularly if a long-term view is taken of effective performance.

It is reasonable to believe that strong commitment to work is likely to result in conscientious and self-directed application to do the job, regular attendance, nominal supervision and a high level of effort. Commitment to the organization will certainly be related to the intention to stay – in other words, loyalty to the company.

COMMITMENT AND MUTUALITY

The notion of mutuality is closely associated with the concept of commitment. Mutuality in organizations is said to exist when it is perceived generally that the interests of management and employees coincide. Management and employees are interdependent and both parties benefit from this interdependence. Mutuality means that management is concerned in the well-being of employees as well as the success of the organization, and employees are just as concerned in the success of the organization as in their own well-being. The principle of mutuality is linked to the stakeholder concept – that both management and employees as well as owners, customers and suppliers have a stake in the organization and full consideration should therefore be given to their mutual interests. Mutuality could be regarded as a unitarist concept in that it assumes that there are no underlying and inevitable differences of interest between management and workers.

The ideal of mutuality is part of the rhetoric of human resource management and Walton (1985b) emphasized the importance of mutual goals and mutual responsibility. Kochan and Dyer (1993) have suggested that the principles guiding mutual commitment firms are as follows:

1. *Strategic level:*
   ● supportive business strategies;
   ● top management value commitment;
   ● effective voice for HR in strategy making and governance.

2. *Functional (human resource policy) level:*
   ● staffing based on employment stabilization;
   ● investment in training and development;
   ● contingent compensation that reinforces cooperation, participation and contribution.

3. *Workplace level:*
   ● selection based on high standards;
   ● broad task design and teamwork;
   ● employee involvement in problem solving;
   ● climate of cooperation and trust.

Mutual commitment strategy

A mutual commitment strategy will be based on the principle of high commitment management, which was defined by Wood (1996) as being:

> … a form of management which is aimed at eliciting a commitment so that behaviour is primarily self-regulated rather than controlled by sanctions and pressures external to the individual and relations within the organization are based on high levels of trust.

A mutual commitment strategy to achieve this end will incorporate the various approaches described below. But its foundation should be a philosophy that recognizes employees as valued stakeholders in the organization. In the words of Kochan and Dyer (1993):

Staffing policies must be designed and managed in such a way that they reinforce the principle of employment security and thus promote the commitment, flexibility and loyalty of employees. This does not guarantee lifetime employment, but it does imply that the first instinct in good times and bad should be to build and protect the firm's investment in human resources, rather than to add and cut people indiscriminately in knee-jerk responses to short-term fluctuations in business conditions.

DEVELOPING A COMMITMENT STRATEGY

When developing a commitment strategy, it has first to be accepted that the interests of the organization and of its members do not necessarily coincide. It can be asserted by management that everyone will benefit from organizational success in terms of security, pay, opportunities for advancement etc. But employees and their trade unions may be difficult to convince that this is the case if they believe that the success is to be achieved by such actions as disinvestments, downsizing, cost reductions affecting pay and employment, tougher performance standards or tighter management controls. When defining values, it is important not to impose them on employees. They should be involved in their formulation and in discussing with management how they are to be upheld. This avoids what Legge (1989) refers to as a process of 'co-optation' in which management forces its own set of values down the throats of its employees. Involving employees makes sense in that they are thus much more likely to own and practise the values.

Secondly, management must not define and communicate values in such a way as to inhibit flexibility, creativity and the ability to adapt to change. Strategies have to be defined in broad terms with caveats that they will be amended if circumstances change. Values have to emphasize the need for flexibility, innovation and team-working as well as the need for performance and quality.

Thirdly, too much should not be expected from campaigns to increase commitment. Management may reduce employee turnover, increase identification with the organization and develop feelings of loyalty among its employees. They may increase job satisfaction, but there is no evidence that higher levels of job satisfaction necessarily improve performance. They may provide a context within which motivation and therefore performance will increase. But there is no guarantee that this will take place, although the chances of gaining improvements will be increased if the campaign is focused upon a specific value such as quality.

It may be naive to believe that 'hearts and minds' campaigns to win commitment will transform organizational behaviour overnight. But it is surely useful for organizations to do what they can along the lines described below to influence behaviour, to support the achievement of objectives to uphold values that are inherently worthwhile. It is good management practice to define its expectations in terms of objectives and standards of performance. It is even better management practice to discuss and agree these objectives and standards with employees.

Approaches to creating a commitment strategy

The approaches to creating a high-commitment organization as described by Beer et al (1984) and Walton (1985b) are:

- the development of career ladders and emphasis on trainability and commitment as highly valued characteristics of employees at all levels in the organization;
- a high level of functional flexibility with the abandonment of potentially rigid job descriptions;
- the reduction of hierarchies and the ending of status differentials;
- a heavy reliance on team structure for disseminating information (team briefing), structuring work (team working) and problem solving (quality circles).

Wood and Albanese (1995) added to this list:

- job design as something management consciously does in order to provide jobs which have a considerable level of intrinsic satisfaction;
- a policy of no compulsory lay-offs or redundancies and permanent employment guarantees with the possible use of temporary workers to cushion fluctuations in the demand for labour;
- new forms of assessment and payment systems and, more specifically, merit pay and profit sharing;
- a high involvement of employees in the management of quality.

Communication programmes

It seems to be strikingly obvious that commitment will only be gained if people understand what they are expected to commit to. But managements too often fail to pay sufficient attention to delivering the message in terms that recognize that the frame of reference for those who receive it is likely to be quite different from their own. Management's expectations will not necessarily coincide with those of employees: pluralism prevails. In delivering the message, the use of different and complementary channels of communication such as newsletters, briefing groups, videos, notice boards, etc is often neglected.

Education

Education is another form of communication. An educational programme is designed to increase both knowledge and understanding of, for example, total quality management. The aim will be to influence behaviour and thereby progressively change attitudes.

Training

Training is designed to develop specific competences. For example, if one of the values to be supported is flexibility, it will be necessary to extend the range of skills possessed by members of work teams through multiskilling programmes.

Commitment is enhanced if managers can gain the confidence and respect of their teams, and training to improve the quality of management should form an important part of any programme for increasing commitment. Management training can also be focused on increasing the competence of managers in specific areas of their responsibility for gaining commitment, eg performance management.

Developing ownership

A sense of belonging is enhanced if there is a feeling of 'ownership' among employees. Not just in the literal sense of owning shares (although this can help) but in the sense of believing they are genuinely accepted by management as a key part of the organization. This concept of 'ownership' extends to participating in decisions on new developments and changes in working practices that affect the individuals concerned. They should be involved in making those decisions and feel that their ideas have been listened to and that they have contributed to the outcome. They will then be more likely to accept the decision or change because it is owned by them rather than being imposed by management.

Developing job engagement

Job engagement – interest and a sense of excitement in the job – can be created by concentrating on the intrinsic motivating factors such as responsibility, achievement and recognition, and using these principles to govern the way in which jobs are designed. Job engagement is also created by the quality of leadership and the willingness of managers and team leaders to recognize that they will obtain increased motivation and commitment if they pay continuous attention to the ways in which they delegate responsibility and give their staff the scope to use their skills and abilities.

Performance management

Performance management as described in Part VIII can help to cascade corporate objectives and values throughout the organization so that consistency is achieved at all levels. Expectations of individuals are defined in terms of their own job, which they can more readily grasp and act upon than if they were asked to support some remote and, to them, irrelevant overall objectives. But individual objectives can be described in ways that support the achievement of those defined for higher levels in the organization.

Reward management

Reward management processes can make it clear that individuals will be rewarded in accordance with the extent to which they achieve objectives *and* uphold corporate values. This can reinforce the messages delivered through other channels of communication.

THE CONTRIBUTION OF HR TO DEVELOPING COMMITMENT

The HR function can play a major part in developing a high-commitment organization, as described in Chapter 2 and earlier in this chapter. The ten steps it can take are set out below.

1. Advise on methods of communicating the values and aims of management and the achievements of the organization so that employees are more likely to identify with it as one they are proud to work for.
2. Emphasize to management that commitment is a two-way process; employees cannot be expected to be committed to the organization unless management demonstrates that it is committed to them and recognizes their contribution as stakeholders.
3. Impress on management the need to develop a climate of trust by being honest with people, treating them fairly, justly and consistently, keeping its word, and showing willingness to listen to the comments and suggestions made by employees during processes of consultation and participation.
4. Develop a positive psychological contract (see Chapter 16) by treating people as stakeholders, relying on consensus and cooperation rather than control and coercion, and focusing on the provision of opportunities for learning, development and career progression.

5. Advise and assist in the establishment of partnership agreements with trade unions which emphasize unity of purpose, common approaches to working together, and the importance of giving employees a voice in matters that concern them.

6. Recommend and take part in the achievement of single status for all employees (often included in a partnership agreement) so that there is no longer an 'us and them' culture.

7. Encourage management to declare a policy of employment security and ensure that steps are taken to avoid involuntary redundancies.

8. Develop performance management processes which provide for the alignment of organizational and individual objectives.

9. Advise on means of increasing employee identification with the company through rewards related to organizational performance (profit sharing or gain-sharing) or employee share ownership schemes.

10. Develop 'job engagement' (ie identification of employees with the job they are doing) through job design processes which aim to create higher levels of job satisfaction (job enrichment).

12

How organizations function

BASIC CONSIDERATIONS

The two factors that determine how an organization functions in relation to its internal and external environment are its structure and the processes that operate within it. Organizations are also affected by the culture they develop, that is, the values and norms that affect behaviour (see Chapter 13).

Much has been written to explain how organizations function and the first part of this chapter summarizes the various theories of organization. These theories provide the background to the last three sections of the chapter which deal with organization structure, types of organizations and organizational processes.

ORGANIZATION THEORIES

The classical school

The classical or scientific management school, as represented by Fayol (1916), Taylor (1911) and Urwick (1947), believed in control, order and formality. Organizations need to minimize the opportunity for unfortunate and uncontrollable informal relations, leaving room only for the formal ones.

The bureaucratic model

The bureaucratic model of organization as described by Perrow (1980) is a way of expressing how organizations function as machines and can therefore be associated with some of the ideas generated by the classical school. It is based on the work of Max Weber (1946) who coined the term 'bureaucracy' as a label for a type of formal organization in which impersonality and rationality are developed to the highest degree. Bureaucracy, as he conceived it, was the most efficient form of organization because it is coldly logical and because personalized relationships and non-rational, emotional considerations do not get in its way.

The human relations school

The classical, and by implication, the bureaucratic model were first challenged by Barnard (1938). He emphasized the importance of the informal organization – the network of informal roles and relationships which, for better or worse, strongly influences the way the formal structure operates. He wrote: 'Formal organizations come out of and are necessary to informal organizations: but when formal organizations come into operation, they create and require informal organizations.' More recently, Child (1977) has pointed out that it is misleading to talk about a clear distinction between the formal and the informal organization. Formality and informality can be designed into structure.

Roethlisberger and Dickson (1939) reported on the Hawthorne studies – which highlighted the importance of informal groups and decent, humane leadership.

The behavioural science school

In the 1960s the focus shifted completely to the behaviour of people in organizations. Behavioural scientists such as Argyris (1957), Herzberg et al (1957), McGregor (1960) and Likert (1961) adopted a humanistic point of view which is concerned with what people can contribute and how they can best be motivated.

- *Argyris* believed that individuals should be given the opportunity to feel that they have a high degree of control over setting their own goals and over defining the paths to these goals.
- *Herzberg* suggested that improvements in organization design must centre on the individual job as the positive source of motivation. If individuals feel that the job is stretching them, they will be moved to perform it well.
- *McGregor* developed his theory of integration (theory Y) which emphasizes the importance of recognizing the needs of both the organization and the individual

and creating conditions that will reconcile these needs so that members of the organization can work together for its success and share in its rewards.

● *Likert* stated that effective organizations function by means of supportive relationships which, if fostered, will build and maintain people's sense of personal worth and importance.

The concepts of these and other behavioural scientists provided the impetus for the organization development (OD) movement as described in Chapter 18.

The systems school

Another important insight into how organizations function was provided by Miller and Rice (1967) who stated that organizations should be treated as open systems which are continually dependent upon and influenced by their environments. The basic characteristic of the enterprise as an open system is that it transforms inputs into outputs within its environment.

As Katz and Kahn (1964) wrote: 'Systems theory is basically concerned with problems of relationship, of structure and of interdependence.' As a result, there is a considerable emphasis on the concept of transactions across boundaries – between the system and its environment and between the different parts of the system. This open and dynamic approach avoided the error of the classical, bureaucratic and human relations theorists, who thought of organizations as closed systems and analysed their problems with reference to their internal structures and processes of interaction, without taking account either of external influences and the changes they impose or of the technology in the organization.

The socio-technical model

The concept of the organization as a system was extended by the Tavistock Institute researchers into the socio-technical model of organizations. The basic principle of this model is that in any system of organization, technical or task aspects are interrelated with the human or social aspects. The emphasis is on interrelationships between, on the one hand, the technical processes of transformation carried out within the organization, and, on the other, the organization of work groups and the management structures of the enterprise. This approach avoided the humanistic generalizations of the behavioural scientists without falling into the trap of treating the organization as a machine.

The contingency school

The contingency school consists of writers such as Burns and Stalker (1961), Woodward (1965) and Lawrence and Lorsch (1976) who have analysed a variety of organizations and concluded that their structures and methods of operation are a function of the circumstances in which they exist. They do not subscribe to the view that there is one best way of designing an organization or that simplistic classifications of organizations as formal or informal, bureaucratic or non-bureaucratic are helpful. They are against those who see organizations as mutually opposed social systems (what Burns and Stalker refer to as the 'Manichean world of the Hawthorne studies') that set up formal against informal organizations. They disagree with those who impose rigid principles of organization irrespective of the technology or environmental conditions.

More recent contributions to understanding how organizations function

Kotter (1995) developed the following overall framework for examining organizations:

- key organizational processes – the major information gathering, communication, decision-making, matter/energy transporting and matter/energy converting actions of the organization's employees and machines;
- external environment – an organization's 'task' environment includes suppliers, markets and competitors; the wider environment includes factors such as public attitudes, economic and political systems, laws etc;
- employees and other tangible assets – people, plant, and equipment;
- formal organizational requirements – systems designed to regulate the actions of employees (and machines);
- the social system – culture (values and norms) and relationships between employees in terms of power, affiliation and trust;
- technology – the major techniques people use while engaged in organizational processes and that are programmed into machines;
- the dominant coalition – the objectives, strategies, personal characteristics and internal relationships of those who oversee the organization as a whole and control its basic policy making.

Mintzberg (1983b) analysed organizations into five broad types or configurations:

- *simple structures*, which are dominated by the top of the organization with centralized decision making;
- *machine bureaucracy*, which is characterized by the standardization of work processes and the extensive reliance on systems;
- *professional bureaucracy*, where the standardization of skills provides the prime coordinating mechanism;
- *divisionalized structures*, in which authority is drawn down from the top and activities are grouped together into units which are then managed according to their standardized outputs;
- *adhocracies*, where power is decentralized selectively to constellations of work that are free to coordinate within and between themselves by mutual adjustments.

Drucker (1988) points out that organizations have established, through the development of new technology and the extended use of knowledge workers, 'that whole layers of management neither make decisions nor lead. Instead, their main, if not their only, function, is to serve as relays – human boosters for the faint, unfocused signals that pass for communications in the traditional pre-information organization'.

Pascale (1990) believes that the new organizational paradigm functions as follows:

- *from* the image of organizations as machines, with the emphasis on concrete strategy, structure and systems, *to* the idea of organizations as organisms, with the emphasis on the 'soft' dimensions – style, staff and shared values;
- *from* a hierarchical model, with step-by-step problem solving, *to* a network model, with parallel nodes of intelligence which surround problems until they are eliminated;
- *from* the status-driven view that managers think and workers do as they are told, *to* a view of managers as 'facilitators', with workers empowered to initiate improvements and change;
- *from* an emphasis on 'vertical tasks' within functional units, *to* an emphasis on 'horizontal tasks' and collaboration across units;
- *from* a focus on 'content' and the prescribed use of specific tools and techniques, *to* a focus on 'process' and a holistic synthesis of techniques;
- *from* the military model *to* a commitment model.

Handy (1989) describes two types of organization: the 'shamrock' and the federal.

The shamrock organization consists of three elements: 1) the core workers (the central leaf of the shamrock) – professionals, technicians and managers; 2) the contractual fringe – contract workers; and 3) the flexible labour force consisting of temporary staff.

The federal organization takes the process of decentralization one stage further by establishing every key operational, manufacturing or service provision activity as a distinct, federated unit.

ORGANIZATION STRUCTURE

Each of the members of the various schools was, in effect, commenting on the factors affecting organization structure as considered below.

Organization structure defined

All organizations have some form of more or less formalized structure which has been defined by Child (1977) as comprising 'all the tangible and regularly occurring features which help to shape their members' behaviour'. Structures incorporate a network of roles and relationships and are there to help in the process of ensuring that collective effort is explicitly organized to achieve specified ends.

Organizations vary in their complexity, but it is always necessary to divide the overall management task into a variety of activities, to allocate these activities to the different parts of the organization and to establish means of controlling, coordinating and integrating them.

The structure of an organization can be regarded as a framework for getting things done. It consists of units, functions, divisions, departments and formally constituted work teams into which activities related to particular processes, projects, products, markets, customers, geographical areas or professional disciplines are grouped together. The structure indicates who is accountable for directing, coordinating and carrying out these activities and defines management hierarchies – the 'chain of command' – thus spelling out, broadly, who is responsible to whom for what at each level in the organization.

Organization charts

Structures are usually described in the form of an organization chart. This places individuals in boxes that denote their job and their position in the hierarchy and traces the direct lines of authority (command and control) through the management hierarchies.

Organization charts are vertical in their nature and therefore misrepresent reality. They do not give any indication of the horizontal and diagonal relationships that exist within the framework between people in different units or departments, and do not recognize the fact that within any one hierarchy, commands and control information do not travel all the way down and up the structure as the chart implies. In practice, information jumps (especially computer-generated information) and managers or team leaders will interact with people at levels below those immediately beneath them.

Organization charts have their uses as means of defining – simplistically – who does what and hierarchical lines of authority. But even if backed up by organization manuals (which no one reads and which are, in any case, out of date as soon as they are produced), they cannot convey how the organization really works. They may, for example, lead to definitions of jobs – what people are expected to do – but they cannot convey the roles these people carry out in the organization; the parts they play in interacting with others and the ways in which, like actors, they interpret the parts they are given.

TYPES OF ORGANIZATION

The basic types of organization are described below.

Line and staff

The line and staff organization was the type favoured by the classical theorists. Although the term is not so much used today, except when referring to line managers, it still describes many structures. The line hierarchy in the structure consists of functions and managers who are directly concerned in achieving the primary purposes of the organization, for example manufacturing and selling or directing the organization as a whole. 'Staff' in functions such as finance, personnel and engineering provide services to the line to enable them to get on with their job.

Divisionalized organizations

The process of divisionalization, as first described by Sloan (1963) on the basis of his experience in running General Motors, involves structuring the organization into separate divisions, each concerned with discrete manufacturing, sales, distribution or service functions, or with serving a particular market. At group headquarters, functional departments may exist in such areas as finance, planning, personnel, legal and engineering to provide services to the divisions and, importantly, to exercise a degree of functional control over their activities. The amount of control exercised will depend on the extent to which the organization has decided to decentralize authority to strategic business units positioned close to the markets they serve.

Decentralized organizations

Some organizations, especially conglomerates, decentralize most of their activities and retain only a skeleton headquarters staff to deal with financial control matters, strategic planning, legal issues and sometimes, but not always, personnel issues, especially those concerned with senior management on an across the group basis (recruitment, development and remuneration).

Matrix organizations

Matrix organizations are project based. Development, design or construction projects will be controlled by project directors or managers, or, in the case of a consultancy, assignments will be conducted by project leaders. Project managers will have no permanent staff except, possibly, some administrative/secretarial support. They will draw the members of their project teams from discipline groups, each of which will be headed up by a director or manager who is responsible on a continuing basis for resourcing the group, developing and managing its members and ensuring that they are assigned as fully as possible to project teams. These individuals are assigned to a project team and they will be responsible to the team leader for delivering the required results, but they will continue to be accountable generally to the head of their discipline for their overall performance and contribution.

Flexible organizations

Flexible organizations may conform broadly to the Mintzberg (1983b) category of an adhocracy in the sense that they are capable of adapting quickly to new demands and operate fluidly. They may be organized along the lines of Handy's (1989) 'shamrock' with core workers carrying out the fundamental and continuing activities of the organization and contract workers and temporary staff being employed as required. This is also called a core–periphery organization. An organization may adopt a policy of numerical flexibility, which means that the number of employees can be quickly increased or decreased in line with changes in activity levels. The different types of flexibility as defined by Atkinson (1984) are described in Chapter 14.

The process-based organization

A process-based organization is one in which the focus is on horizontal processes that cut across organizational boundaries. Traditional organization structures consist of a range of functions operating semi-independently and each with its own, usually extended, management hierarchy. Functions acted as vertical 'chimneys' with boundaries between what they did and what happened next door. Continuity of work between functions and the coordination of activities were prejudiced. Attention was focused on vertical relationships and authority-based management – the 'command and control' structure. Horizontal processes received relatively little attention. It was, for example, not recognized that meeting the needs of customers by systems of order processing could only be carried out satisfactorily if the flow of work from sales through manufacturing to distribution was treated as a continuous process and not as three distinct parcels of activity. Another horizontal process that drew attention to the need to reconsider how organizations should be structured was total quality. This is not a top-down system. It cuts across the boundaries separating organizational units to ensure that quality is built into the organization's products and services. Business process re-engineering exercises have also demonstrated the need for businesses to integrate functionally separated tasks into unified horizontal work processes.

The result, as indicated by Ghoshal and Bartlett (1993), has been that:

> ... managers are beginning to deal with their organizations in different ways. Rather than seeing them as a hierarchy of static roles, they think of them as a portfolio of dynamic processes. They see core organizational processes that overlay and often dominate the vertical, authority-based processes of the hierarchical structure.

In a process-based organization there will still be designated functions for, say, manufacturing, sales and distribution. But the emphasis will be on how these areas work together on multi-functional projects to deal with new demands such as product/market development. Teams will jointly consider ways of responding to customer requirements. Quality and continuous improvement will be regarded as a common responsibility shared between managers and staff from each function. The overriding objective will be to maintain a smooth flow of work between functions and to achieve synergy by pooling resources from different functions in task forces or project teams.

ORGANIZATIONAL PROCESSES

The structure of an organization as described in an organization chart does not give any real indication of how it functions. To understand this, it is necessary to consider the various processes that take place within the structural framework: those of interaction and networking, communication, group behaviour, leadership, power, politics and conflict.

Group behaviour

Organizations consist of groups of people working together. Interactions take place within and between groups and the degree to which these processes are formalized varies according to the organizational context. To understand and influence organizational behaviour, it is necessary to appreciate how groups behave. In particular, this means considering the nature of:

● formal groups;
● informal groups;
● the processes that take place within groups;
● group ideology;
● group cohesion;
● the concept of a reference group and its impact on group members;
● the factors that make for group effectiveness.

Formal groups

Formal groups are set up by organizations to achieve a defined purpose. People are brought together with the necessary skills to carry out the tasks and a system exists for directing, coordinating and controlling the group's activities. The structure, composition and size of the group will depend largely on the nature of the task, although tradition, organizational culture and management style may exert considerable influence. The more routine or clearly defined the task is, the more structured the group will be. In a highly structured group the leader will have a positive role and may well adopt an authoritarian style. The role of each member of the group will be precise and a hierarchy of authority is likely to exist. The more ambiguous the task, the more difficult it will be to structure the group. The leader's role is more likely to be supportive – he or she will tend to concentrate on encouragement and coordination rather than on issuing orders. The group will operate in a more democratic way and individual roles will be fluid and less clearly defined.

Informal groups

Informal groups are set up by people in organizations who have some affinity for one another. It could be said that formal groups satisfy the needs of the organization while informal groups satisfy the needs of their members. One of the main aims of organization design and development should be to ensure, so far as possible, that the basis upon which activities are grouped together and the way in which groups are allowed or encouraged to behave satisfy both these needs. The values and norms established by informal groups can work against the organization. This was first clearly established in the Hawthorne studies, which revealed that groups could regulate their own behaviour and output levels irrespective of what management wanted. An understanding of the processes that take place within groups can, however, help to make them work for, rather than against, what the organization needs.

Group processes

As mentioned above, the way in which groups function is affected by the task and by the norms in the organization. An additional factor is size. There is a greater diversity of talent, skills and knowledge in a large group, but individuals find it more difficult to make their presence felt. According to Handy (1981), for best participation and for highest all-round involvement, the optimum size is between five and seven. But to achieve the requisite breadth of knowledge the group may have to be considerably larger, and this makes greater demands on the skills of the leader in getting participation. The main processes that take place in groups as described below are interaction, task and maintenance functions, group ideology, group cohesion, group development and identification.

Interaction

Three basic channels of communication within groups were identified by Leavitt (1951) and are illustrated in Figure 12.1.

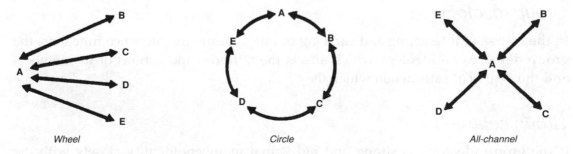

Wheel   Circle   All-channel

Figure 12.1   Channels of communication within groups

The characteristics of these different groups are as follows:

- *Wheel groups*, where the task is straightforward, work faster, need fewer messages to solve problems and make fewer errors than circle groups, but they are inflexible if the task changes.
- *Circle groups* are faster in solving complex problems than wheel groups.
- *All-channel groups* are the most flexible and function well in complex, open-ended situations.

The level of satisfaction for individuals is lowest in the circle group, fairly high in the all-channel group and mixed in the wheel group, where the leader is more satisfied than the outlying members.

Task and maintenance functions

The following functions need to be carried out in groups:

- *task* – initiating, information seeking, diagnosing, opinion-seeking, evaluating, decision-managing;
- *maintenance* – encouraging, compromising, peace-keeping, clarifying, summarizing, standard-setting.

It is the job of the group leader or leaders to ensure that these functions operate effectively. Leaderless groups can work, but only in special circumstances. A leader is almost essential – whether official or self-appointed. The style adopted by a leader affects the way the group operates. If the leader is respected, this will increase group cohesiveness and its ability to get things done. An inappropriately authoritarian style creates tension and resentment. An over-permissive style means that respect for the leader diminishes and the group does not function so effectively.

Group ideology

In the course of interacting and carrying out its task and maintenance functions, the group develops an ideology which affects the attitudes and actions of its members and the degree of satisfaction which they feel.

Group cohesion

If the group ideology is strong and individual members identify closely with the group, it will become increasingly cohesive. Group norms or implicit rules will be evolved, which define what is acceptable behaviour and what is not. The impact of group cohesion can, however, result in negative as well as positive results. Janis's (1972) study of the decision-making processes of US foreign policy groups established that a cohesive group of individuals, sharing a common fate, exerts a strong pressure towards conformity. He coined the term 'group think' to describe the exaggeration of irrational tendencies that appears to occur in groups and argued that a group setting can magnify weakness of judgement.

To be 'one of us' is not always a good thing in management circles. A sturdy spirit of independence, even a maverick tendency, may be more conducive to correct decision-making. Team-working is a good thing, but so is flexibility and independent judgement. These need not be incompatible with team membership, but could be if there is too much emphasis on cohesion and conformity within the group.

Reference group

A reference group consists of the group of people with whom an individual identifies. This means that the group's norms are accepted and if in doubt about what to do or say, reference is made to these norms or to other group members before action is taken. Most people in organizations belong to a reference group and this can significantly affect the ways in which they behave.

Impact on group members

The reference group will also affect individual behaviour. This may be through overt pressure to conform or by more subtle processes. Acceptance of group norms commonly goes through two stages – compliance and internalization. Initially, a group member complies in order not to be rejected by the group, although he or she may behave differently when away from the group. Progressively, however, the individual accepts the norm whether with the group or not – the group norm has been internalized. As noted by Chell (1987), pressure on members to conform can cause problems when:

- there is incompatibility between a member's personal goals and those of the group;
- there is no sense of pride from being a member of the group;
- the member is not fully integrated with the group;
- the price of conformity is too high.

Group development

Tuckman (1965) has identified four stages of group development:

1. *forming*, when there is anxiety, dependence on the leader and testing to find out the nature of the situation and the task, and what behaviour is acceptable;
2. *storming*, where there is conflict, emotional resistance to the demands of the task, resistance to control and even rebellion against the leader;
3. *norming*, when group cohesion is developed, norms emerge, views are exchanged openly, mutual support and cooperation increase and the group acquires a sense of its identity;
4. *performing*, when interpersonal problems are resolved, roles are flexible and functional, there are constructive attempts to complete tasks and energy is available for effective work.

Identification

Individuals will identify with their groups if they like the other members, approve of the purpose and work of the group and wish to be associated with the standing of the group in the organization. Identification will be more complex if the standing of the group is good.

Teamwork

Definition of a team

As defined by Katzenbach and Smith (1993):

> A team is a small number of people with complementary skills who are committed to a common purpose, performance goals and approach for which they hold themselves mutually accountable.

Characteristics of effective teams

The characteristics of teams as described by Katzenbach and Smith are:

●   Teams are the basic units of performance for most organizations. They meld together the skills, experiences and insights of several people.
●   Teamwork applies to the whole organization as well as specific teams. It represents 'a set of values that encourage behaviours such as listening and responding co-operatively to points of view expressed by others, giving others the benefit of

the doubt, providing support to those who need it and recognising the interests and achievements of others'.

- Teams are created and energized by significant performance challenges.
- Teams outperform individuals acting alone or in large organizational groupings, especially when performance requires multiple skills, judgements and experiences.
- Teams are flexible and responsive to changing events and demands. They can adjust their approach to new information and challenges with greater speed, accuracy and effectiveness than can individuals caught in the web of larger organizational conventions.
- High-performance teams invest much time and effort exploring, shaping and agreeing on a purpose that belongs to them, both collectively and individually. They are characterized by a deep sense of commitment to their growth and success.

Dysfunctional teams

The specification set out above is somewhat idealistic. Teams do not always work like that. They can fail to function effectively in the following ways:

- The atmosphere can be strained and over-formalized.
- Either there is too much discussion that gets nowhere or discussion is inhibited by dominant members of the team.
- Team members do not really understand what they are there to do and the objectives or standards they are expected to achieve.
- People don't listen to one another.
- Disagreements are frequent and often relate to personalities and differences of opinion rather than a reasoned discussion of alternative points of view.
- Decisions are not made jointly by team members.
- There is evidence of open personal attacks or hidden personal animosities.
- People do not feel free to express their opinions.
- Individual team members opt out or are allowed to opt out, leaving the others to do the work.
- There is little flexibility in the way in which team members operate – people tend to use a limited range of skills or specific tasks, and there is little evidence of multi-skilling.
- The team leader dominates the team; more attention is given to who takes control rather than to getting the work done.
- The team determines its own standards and norms, which may not be in accord with the standards and norms of the organization.

Team roles

The different types of roles played by team members have been defined by Belbin (1981) as follows:

- *chairmen* who control the way the team operates;
- *shapers* who specify the ways the team should work;
- *company workers* who turn proposals into practical work procedures;
- *plants* who produce ideas and strategies;
- *resource investigators* who explore the availability of resources, ideas and developments outside the team;
- *monitor-evaluators* who analyse problems and evaluate ideas;
- *team workers* who provide support to team members, improve team communications and foster team spirit;
- *completer-finishers* who maintain a sense of urgency in the team.

An alternative classification of roles has been developed by Margerison and McCann (1986). The eight roles are:

- *reporter-advisor:* gathers information and expresses it in an easily understandable form;
- *creator-innovator:* enjoys thinking up new ideas and ways of doing things;
- *explorer-promoter:* takes up ideas and promotes them to others;
- *assessor-developer:* takes ideas and makes them work in practice;
- *thruster-organizer:* gets things done, emphasizing targets, deadlines and budgets;
- *concluder-producer:* sets up plans and standard systems to ensure outputs are achieved;
- *controller-inspector:* concerned with the details and adhering to rules and regulations;
- *upholder-maintainer:* provides guidance and help in meeting standards.

According to Margerison and McCann, a balanced team needs members with preferences for each of these eight roles.

Leadership, power, politics and conflict

The main processes that affect how organizations function are leadership, power, politics and conflict.

Leadership

Leadership can be defined as the ability to persuade others willingly to behave differently. The function of team leaders is to achieve the task set for them with the help of the group. Leaders and their groups are therefore interdependent.

Leaders have two main roles. First, they must achieve the task. Secondly, they have to maintain effective relationships between themselves and the group and the individuals in it – effective in the sense that they are conducive to achieving the task. As Adair (1973) pointed out, in fulfilling their roles, leaders have to satisfy the following needs:

1. *Task needs.* The group exists to achieve a common purpose or task. The leader's role is to ensure that this purpose is fulfilled. If it is not, they will lose the confidence of the group and the result will be frustration, disenchantment, criticism and, possibly, the ultimate disintegration of the group.
2. *Group maintenance needs.* To achieve its objectives, the group needs to be held together. The leader's job is to build up and maintain team spirit and morale.
3. *Individual needs.* Individuals have their own needs, which they expect to be satisfied at work. The leader's task is to be aware of these needs so that where necessary they can take steps to harmonize them with the needs of the task and the group.

These three needs are interdependent. The leader's actions in one area affect both the others; thus successful achievement of the task is essential if the group is to be held together and its members motivated to give their best effort to the job. Action directed at meeting group or individual needs must be related to the needs of the task. It is impossible to consider individuals in isolation from the group or to consider the group without referring to the individuals within it. If any need is neglected, one of the others will suffer and the leader will be less successful.

The kind of leadership exercised will be related to the nature of the task and the people being led. It will also depend on the environment and, of course, on the actual leader. Analysing the qualities of leadership in terms of intelligence, initiative, self-assurance and so on has only limited value. The qualities required may be different in different situations. It is more useful to adopt a contingency approach and take account of the variables leaders have to deal with; especially the task, the group and their own position relative to the group.

Power

Organizations exist to get things done and in the process of doing this, people or groups exercise power. Directly or indirectly, the use of power in influencing behaviour is a pervading feature of organizations, whether it is exerted by managers, specialists, informal groups or trade union officials.

Power is the capacity to secure the dominance of one's goals or values over others. Four different types of power have been identified by French and Raven (1959):

● *reward power* – derived from the belief of individuals that compliance brings rewards; the ability to distribute rewards contributes considerably to an executive's power;
● *coercive power* – making it plain that non-compliance will bring punishment;
● *expert power* – exercised by people who are popular or admired and with whom the less powerful can identify;
● *legitimized power* – power conferred by the position in an organization held by an executive.

Politics

Power and politics are inextricably mixed, and in any organization there will inevitably be people who want to achieve their satisfaction by acquiring power, legitimately or illegitimately. Kakabadse (1983) defines politics as 'a process, that of influencing individuals and groups of people to your point of view, where you cannot rely on authority'.

Organizations consist of individuals who, while they are ostensibly there to achieve a common purpose, are, at the same time, driven by their own needs to achieve their own goals. Effective management is the process of harmonizing individual endeavour and ambition to the common good. Some individuals genuinely believe that using political means to achieve their goals will benefit the organization as well as themselves. Others rationalize this belief. Yet others unashamedly pursue their own ends.

Conflict

Conflict is inevitable in organizations because they function by means of adjustments and compromises among competitive elements in their structure and membership. Conflict also arises when there is change, because it may be seen as a threat to be challenged or resisted, or when there is frustration – this may produce an aggressive reaction; fight rather than flight. Conflict is not to be deplored. It is an inevitable result of progress and change and it can and should be used constructively.

Conflict between individuals raises fewer problems than conflict between groups. Individuals can act independently and resolve their differences. Members of groups may have to accept the norms, goals and values of their group. The individual's loyalty will usually be to his or her own group if it is in conflict with others.

Interaction and networking

Interactions between people criss-cross the organization, creating networks for getting things done and exchanging information, which is not catered for in the formal structure. 'Networking' is an increasingly important process in flexible and delayered organizations where more fluid interactions across the structure are required between individuals and teams. Individuals can often get much more done by networking than by going through formal channels. At least this means that they can canvass opinion and enlist support to promote their projects or ideas and to share their knowledge.

People also get things done in organizations by creating alliances – getting agreement on a course of action with other people and joining forces to get things done.

Communications

The communications processes used in organizations have a marked effect on how it functions, especially if they take place through the network, which can then turn into the 'grapevine'. E-mails in intranets encourage the instant flow of information (and sometimes produce information overload) but may inhibit face-to-face interactions, which are often the best ways of getting things done.

13

Organizational culture

This chapter starts with definitions of organizational culture and the associated concept of organizational climate. The notion of management style as a way of describing how managers behave within the culture of their organizations is also defined. The chapter continues with comments on the significance of the concept to organizations and how culture develops. The components of culture and methods of analysing and describing culture and the climate are then considered. The chapter concludes with a review of approaches to supporting or changing cultures.

DEFINITIONS

Organizational culture

Organizational or corporate culture is the pattern of values, norms, beliefs, attitudes and assumptions that may not have been articulated but shape the ways in which people behave and things get done. Values refer to what is believed to be important about how people and the organizations behave. Norms are the unwritten rules of behaviour.

The definition emphasizes that organizational culture is concerned with abstractions such as values and norms which pervade the whole or part of an organization.

They may not be defined, discussed or even noticed. Put another way, culture can be regarded as a 'code word for the subjective side of organizational life' (Meyerson and Martin, 1987). Nevertheless, culture can have a significant influence on people's behaviour.

The following are some other definitions of culture:

> The culture of an organization refers to the unique configuration of norms, values, beliefs and ways of behaving that characterize the manner in which groups and individuals combine to get things done.
>
> *Eldridge and Crombie (1974)*

> Culture is a system of informal rules that spells out how people are to behave most of the time.
>
> *Deal and Kennedy (1982)*

> Culture is the commonly held beliefs, attitudes and values that exist in an organization. Put more simply, culture is 'the way we do things around here'.
>
> *Furnham and Gunter (1993)*

Summing up the various definitions of culture, Furnham and Gunter (1993) list, amongst others, the following areas of agreement on the concept:

- It is difficult to define (often a pointless exercise).
- It is multi-dimensional, with many different components at different levels.
- It is not particularly dynamic, and ever changing (being relatively stable over short periods of time).
- It takes time to establish and therefore time to change a corporate culture.

Problems with the concept

Furnham and Gunter refer to a number of problems with the concept, including:

- how to categorize culture (what terminology to use);
- when and why corporate culture should be changed and how this takes place;
- what is the healthiest, most optimal or desirable culture.

They also point out that it is dangerous to treat culture as an objective entity 'as if everyone in the world would be able to observe the same phenomenon, whereas this is patently not the case'.

Organizational climate

The term organizational climate is sometimes confused with organizational culture and there has been much debate on what distinguishes the concept of climate from that of culture. In his analysis of this issue, Denison (1996) suggested that *culture* refers to the deep structure of organizations, which is rooted in the values, beliefs and assumptions held by organizational members. In contrast, *climate* refers to those aspects of the environment that are consciously perceived by organizational members. Rousseau (1988) stated that climate is a perception and is descriptive. Perceptions are sensations or realizations experienced by an individual. Descriptions are what a person reports of these sensations.

The debate about the meanings of these terms can become academic. It is easiest to regard organizational climate as how people perceive (see and feel about) the culture existing in their organization. As defined by French *et al* (1985), it is 'the relatively persistent set of perceptions held by organization members concerning the characteristics and quality of organizational culture'. They distinguish between the actual situations (ie culture) and the perception of it (climate).

THE SIGNIFICANCE OF CULTURE

As Furnham and Gunter (1993) point out:

> Culture represents the 'social glue' and generates a 'we-feeling', thus counteracting processes of differentiations which are an unavoidable part of organizational life. Organizational culture offers a shared system of meanings which is the basis for communications and mutual understanding. If these functions are not fulfilled in a satisfactory way, culture may significantly reduce the efficiency of an organization.

HOW ORGANIZATIONAL CULTURE DEVELOPS

The values and norms that are the basis of culture are formed in four ways. First, culture is formed by the leaders in the organization, especially those who have shaped it in the past. As Schein (1990) indicates, people identify with visionary leaders – how they behave and what they expect. They note what such leaders pay attention to and treat them as role models. Second, as Schein also points out, culture is formed around critical incidents – important events from which lessons are learnt about desirable or undesirable behaviour. Third, as suggested by Furnham and Gunter (1993), culture develops from the need to maintain effective working relationships among organization members, and this establishes values and expectations. Finally, culture is influenced by the organization's environment. The external environment may be relatively dynamic or unchanging.

Culture is learned over a period of time. Schein (1984) suggests that there are two ways in which this learning takes place. First, the trauma model, in which members of the organization learn to cope with some threat by the erection of defence mechanisms. Second, the positive reinforcement model, where things that seem to work become embedded and entrenched. Learning takes place as people adapt to and cope with external pressures, and as they develop successful approaches and mechanisms to handle the internal challenges, processes and technologies in their organization.

Where culture has developed over long periods of time and has become firmly embedded, it may be difficult to change quickly, if at all, unless a traumatic event occurs.

THE DIVERSITY OF CULTURE

The development process described above may result in a culture that characterizes the whole organization. But there may be different cultures within organizations. For example, the culture of an outward-looking marketing department may be substantially different from that of an internally focused manufacturing function. There may be some common organizational values or norms, but in some respects these will vary between different work environments.

THE COMPONENTS OF CULTURE

Organizational culture can be described in terms of values, norms and artefacts.

Values

Values are beliefs in what is best or good for the organization and what should or ought to happen. The 'value set' of an organization may only be recognized at top level, or it may be shared throughout the business, in which case it could be described as value driven.

The stronger the values, the more they will influence behaviour. This does not depend upon their having been articulated. Implicit values that are deeply embedded in the culture of an organization and are reinforced by the behaviour of management can be highly influential, while espoused values that are idealistic and are not reflected in managerial behaviour may have little or no effect.

Some of the most typical areas in which values can be expressed, implicitly or explicitly, are:

- performance;
- competence;
- competitiveness;
- innovation;
- quality;
- customer service;
- teamwork;
- care and consideration for people.

Values are translated into reality through *norms* and *artefacts* as described below. They may also be expressed through the media of language (organizational jargon), rituals, stories and myths.

Norms

Norms are the unwritten rules of behaviour, the 'rules of the game' that provide informal guidelines on how to behave. Norms tell people what they are supposed to be doing, saying, believing, even wearing. They are never expressed in writing – if they were, they would be policies or procedures. They are passed on by word of mouth or behaviour and can be enforced by the reactions of people if they are violated. They can exert very powerful pressure on behaviour because of these reactions – we control others by the way we react to them.

Norms refer to such aspects of behaviour as:

- how managers treat the members of their teams (management style) and how the latter relate to their managers;
- the prevailing work ethic, eg 'work hard, play hard', 'come in early, stay late', 'if you cannot finish your work during business hours you are obviously inefficient', 'look busy at all times', 'look relaxed at all times';
- status – how much importance is attached to it; the existence or lack of obvious status symbols;
- ambition – naked ambition is expected and approved of, or a more subtle approach is the norm;
- performance – exacting performance standards are general; the highest praise that can be given in the organization is to be referred to as very professional;
- power – recognized as a way of life; executed by political means, dependent on expertise and ability rather than position; concentrated at the top; shared at different levels in different parts of the organization;

- politics – rife throughout the organization and treated as normal behaviour; not accepted as overt behaviour;
- loyalty – expected, a cradle to grave approach to careers; discounted, the emphasis is on results and contribution in the short term;
- anger – openly expressed; hidden, but expressed through other, possibly political, means;
- approachability – managers are expected to be approachable and visible; everything happens behind closed doors;
- formality – a cool, formal approach is the norm; forenames are/are not used at all levels; there are unwritten but clearly understood rules about dress.

Artefacts

Artefacts are the visible and tangible aspects of an organization that people hear, see or feel. Artefacts can include such things as the working environment, the tone and language used in letters or memoranda, the manner in which people address each other at meetings or over the telephone, the welcome (or lack of welcome) given to visitors and the way in which telephonists deal with outside calls. Artefacts can be very revealing.

CLASSIFYING ORGANIZATIONAL CULTURE

There have been many attempts to classify or categorize organizational culture as a basis for the analysis of cultures in organizations and for taking action to support or change them. Most of these classifications are expressed in four dimensions and some of the best-known ones are summarized below.

Harrison

Harrison (1972) categorized what he called 'organization ideologies'. These are:

- *power-orientated* – competitive, responsive to personality rather than expertise;
- *people-orientated* – consensual, management control rejected;
- *task-orientated* – focus on competency, dynamic;
- *role-orientated* – focus on legality, legitimacy and bureaucracy.

Handy

Handy (1981) based his typology on Harrison's classification, although Handy preferred the word 'culture' to 'ideology' as culture conveyed more of the feeling of a pervasive way of life or set of norms. His four types of culture are:

- The *power culture* is one with a central power source that exercises control. There are few rules or procedures and the atmosphere is competitive, power-orientated and political.
- The *role culture* is one in which work is controlled by procedures and rules and the role, or job description, is more important than the person who fills it. Power is associated with positions, not people.
- The *task culture* is one in which the aim is to bring together the right people and let them get on with it. Influence is based more on expert power than on position or personal power. The culture is adaptable and teamwork is important.
- The *person culture* is one in which the individual is the central point. The organization exists only to serve and assist the individuals in it.

Schein

Schein (1985) identified the following four cultures:

- The *power culture* is one in which leadership resides in a few and rests on their ability and which tends to be entrepreneurial.
- The *role culture* is one in which power is balanced between the leader and the bureaucratic structure. The environment is likely to be stable and roles and rules are clearly defined.
- The *achievement culture* is one in which personal motivation and commitment are stressed and action, excitement and impact are valued.
- The *support culture* is one in which people contribute out of a sense of commitment and solidarity. Relationships are characterized by mutuality and trust.

Williams, Dobson and Walters

Williams *et al* (1989) redefined the four categories listed by Harrison and Handy as follows:

- *Power orientation* – organizations try to dominate their environment and those exercising power strive to maintain absolute control over subordinates.
- *Role orientation* emphasizes legality, legitimacy and responsibility. Hierarchy and status are important.

- *Task orientation* focuses on task accomplishment. Authority is based on appropriate knowledge and competence.
- *People orientation* – the organization exists primarily to serve the needs of its members. Individuals are expected to influence each other through example and helpfulness.

ASSESSING ORGANIZATIONAL CULTURE

A number of instruments exist for assessing organizational culture. This is not easy because culture is concerned with both subjective beliefs and unconscious assumptions (which might be difficult to measure), and with observed phenomena such as behavioural norms and artefacts. Two of the better-known instruments are summarized below.

Organizational ideology questionnaire (Harrison, 1972)

This questionnaire deals with the four orientations referred to earlier (power, role, task, self). The questionnaire is completed by ranking statements according to views on what is closest to the organization's actual position. Statements include:

- A good boss is strong, decisive and firm but fair.
- A good subordinate is compliant, hard-working and loyal.
- People who do well in the organization are shrewd and competitive, with a strong need for power.
- The basis of task assignment is the personal needs and judgements of those in authority.
- Decisions are made by people with the most knowledge and expertise about the problem.

Organizational culture inventory (Cooke and Lafferty, 1989)

This instrument assesses organizational culture under 12 headings:

1. *Humanistic-helpful* – organizations managed in a participative and person-centred way.
2. *Affiliative* – organizations that place a high priority on constructive relationships.
3. *Approval* – organizations in which conflicts are avoided and interpersonal relationships are pleasant – at least superficially.

4. *Conventional* – conservative, traditional and bureaucratically controlled organizations.
5. *Dependent* – hierarchically controlled and non-participative organizations.
6. *Avoidance* – organizations that fail to reward success but punish mistakes.
7. *Oppositional* – organizations in which confrontation prevails and negativism is rewarded.
8. *Power* – organizations structured on the basis of the authority inherent in members' positions.
9. *Competitive* – a culture in which winning is valued and members are rewarded for out-performing one another.
10. *Competence/perfectionist* – organizations in which perfectionism, persistence and hard work are valued.
11. *Achievement* – organizations that do things well and value members who set and accomplish challenging but realistic goals.
12. *Self-actualization* – organizations that value creativity, quality over quantity, and both task accomplishment and individual growth.

MEASURING ORGANIZATIONAL CLIMATE

Organizational climate measures attempts to assess organizations in terms of dimensions that are thought to capture or describe perceptions about the climate. Perceptions about climate can be measured by questionnaires such as that developed by Litwin and Stringer (1968) which covers eight categories:

1. *Structure* – feelings about constraints and freedom to act and the degree of formality or informality in the working atmosphere.
2. *Responsibility* – the feeling of being trusted to carry out important work.
3. *Risk* – the sense of riskiness and challenge in the job and in the organization; the relative emphasis on taking calculated risks or playing it safe.
4. *Warmth* – the existence of friendly and informal social groups.
5. *Support* – the perceived helpfulness of managers and co-workers; the emphasis (or lack of emphasis) on mutual support.
6. *Standards* – the perceived importance of implicit and explicit goals and performance standards; the emphasis on doing a good job; the challenge represented in personal and team goals.
7. *Conflict* – the feeling that managers and other workers want to hear different opinions; the emphasis on getting problems out into the open rather than smoothing them over or ignoring them.

8. *Identity* – the feeling that you belong to a company; that you are a valuable member of a working team.

A review of a number of questionnaires was carried out by Koys and De Cotiis (1991), which produced the following eight typical dimensions:

● *autonomy* – the perception of self-determination with respect to work procedures, goals and priorities;
● *cohesion* – the perception of togetherness or sharing within the organization setting, including the willingness of members to provide material risk;
● *trust* – the perception of freedom to communicate openly with members at higher organizational levels about sensitive or personal issues, with the expectation that the integrity of such communications will not be violated;
● *resource* – the perception of time demands with respect to task competition and performance standards;
● *support* – the perception of the degree to which superiors tolerate members' behaviour, including willingness to let members learn from their mistakes without fear of reprisal;
● *recognition* – the perception that members' contributions to the organization are acknowledged;
● *fairness* – the perception that organizational policies are non-arbitrary or capricious;
● *innovation* – the perception that change and creativity are encouraged, including risk-taking into new areas where the member has little or no prior experience.

APPROPRIATE CULTURES

It could be argued that a 'good' culture exerts a positive influence on organizational behaviour. It could help to create a 'high-performance' culture, one that will produce a high level of business performance. As described by Furnham and Gunter (1993), 'a good culture is consistent in its components and shared amongst organizational members, and it makes the organization unique, thus differentiating it from other organizations'.

However, a high-performance culture means little more than any culture that will produce a high level of business performance. The attributes of cultures vary tremendously by context. The qualities of a high-performance culture for an established retail chain, a growing service business and a consumer products company that is losing market share may be very different. Further, in addition to context differences, all cultures evolve over time. Cultures that are 'good' in one set of circumstances or period of time may be dysfunctional in different circumstances or different times.

Because culture is developed and manifests itself in different ways in different organizations, it is not possible to say that one culture is better than another, only that it is dissimilar in certain ways. There is no such thing as an ideal culture, only an appropriate culture. This means that there can be no universal prescription for managing culture, although there are certain approaches that can be helpful, as described in the next section.

SUPPORTING AND CHANGING CULTURES

While it may not be possible to define an ideal structure or to prescribe how it can be developed, it can at least be stated with confidence that embedded cultures exert considerable influence on organizational behaviour and therefore performance. If there is an appropriate and effective culture it would be desirable to take steps to support or reinforce it. If the culture is inappropriate, attempts should be made to determine what needs to be changed and to develop and implement plans for change.

Culture analysis

In either case, the first step is to analyse the existing culture. This can be done through questionnaires, surveys and discussions in focus groups or workshops. It is often helpful to involve people in analysing the outcome of surveys, getting them to produce a diagnosis of the cultural issues facing the organization and participate in the development and implementation of plans and programmes to deal with any issues. This could form part of an organizational development programme as described in Chapter 18. Groups can analyse the culture through the use of measurement instruments. Extra dimensions can be established by the use of group exercises such as 'rules of the club' (participants brainstorm the 'rules' or norms that govern behaviour) or 'shield' (participants design a shield, often quartered, which illustrates major cultural features of the organization). Joint exercises like this can lead to discussions on appropriate values, which are much more likely to be 'owned' by people if they have helped to create them rather than having them imposed from above.

While involvement is highly desirable, there will be situations when management has to carry out the analysis and determine the actions required without the initial participation of employees. But the latter should be kept informed and brought into discussion on developments as soon as possible.

Culture support and reinforcement

Culture support and reinforcement programmes aim to preserve and underpin what is good and functional about the present culture. Schein (1985) has suggested that the most powerful primary mechanisms for culture embedding and reinforcement are:

- what leaders pay attention to, measure and control;
- leaders' reactions to critical incidents and crises;
- deliberate role modelling, teaching and coaching by leaders;
- criteria for allocation of rewards and status;
- criteria for recruitment, selection, promotion and commitment.

Other means of underpinning the culture are:

- re-affirming existing values;
- operationalizing values through actions designed, for example, to implement total quality and customer care programmes, to provide financial and non-financial rewards for expected behaviour, to improve productivity, to promote and reward good teamwork, to develop a learning organization (see Chapter 34);
- using the value set as headings for reviewing individual and team performance – emphasizing that people are expected to uphold the values;
- ensuring that induction procedures cover core values and how people are expected to achieve them;
- reinforcing induction training on further training courses set up as part of a continuous development programme.

Culture change

Focus

In theory, culture change programmes start with an analysis of the existing culture. The desired culture is then defined, which leads to the identification of a 'culture gap' that needs to be filled. This analysis can identify behavioural expectations so that development and reward processes can be used to define and reinforce them. In real life, it is not quite as simple as that.

A comprehensive change programme may be a fundamental part of an organizational transformation programme as described in Chapter 18. But culture change programmes can focus on particular aspects of the culture, for example performance, commitment, quality, customer service, teamwork, organizational learning. In each case the underpinning values would need to be defined. It would probably be necessary to prioritize by deciding which areas need the most urgent attention. There is a limit to how much can be done at once except in crisis conditions.

Levers for change

Having identified what needs to be done, and the priorities, the next step is to consider what levers for change exist and how they can be used. The levers could include, as appropriate:

- *performance* – performance-related or competence-related pay schemes; performance management processes; gainsharing; leadership training, skills development;
- *commitment* – communication, participation and involvement programmes; developing a climate of cooperation and trust; clarifying the psychological contract;
- *quality* – total quality programmes;
- *customer service* – customer care programmes;
- *teamwork* – team building; team performance management; team rewards;
- *organizational learning* – taking steps to enhance intellectual capital and the organization's resource-based capability by developing a learning organization;
- *values* – gaining understanding, acceptance and commitment through involvement in defining values, performance management processes and employee development interventions.

Change management

The effectiveness of culture change programmes largely depends on the quality of change management processes. These are described in Chapter 18.

Part IV

Work and employment

This part of the handbook is concerned with the factors affecting employment in organizations. It explores the nature of work, the employment relationship and the important concept of the psychological contract.

14

The nature of work

In this chapter the nature of work is explored – what it is, the various theories about work, the organizational factors that affect it and attitudes towards work.

WHAT IS WORK?

Work is the exertion of effort and the application of knowledge and skills to achieve a purpose. Most people work to earn a living – to make money. But they also work because of the other satisfactions it brings, such as doing something worthwhile, a sense of achievement, prestige, recognition, the opportunity to use and develop abilities, the scope to exercise power, and companionship. Within organizations, the nature of the work carried out by individuals and what they feel about it are governed by the employment relationship as discussed in Chapter 15 and the psychological contract as considered in Chapter 16.

In this chapter the various theories of work are summarized in the first section. The following sections deal with the organizational factors that affect work such as the 'lean' and 'flexible' organization, changes in the pattern of working, unemployment, careers and attitudes to work.

THEORIES ABOUT WORK

The theories about work described in this section consist of labour process theory, agency theory and exchange theory. The concept of the pluralist and unitarist frame of reference is also considered.

Labour process theory

Labour process theory was originally formulated by Karl Marx (translated in 1976). His thesis was that surplus is appropriated from labour by paying it less than the value it adds to the labour process. Capitalists therefore design the labour process to secure the extraction of surplus value. The human capacity to produce is subordinated to the exploitative demands of the capitalist, which is an alien power confronting the worker who becomes a 'crippled monstrosity by furthering his skill as if in a forcing house through the suppression of a whole world of productive drives and inclinations'.

Considerably later, a version of labour process theory was set out by Braverman (1974). His view was that the application of modern management techniques, in combination with mechanization and automation, secures the real subordination of labour and de-skilling of work in the office as well as the shop-floor. He stated that the removal of all forms of control from the worker is 'the ideal towards which management tends, and in pursuit of which it uses every productive innovation shaped by science'. He saw this as essentially the application of 'Taylorism' (ie F. W Taylor's concept of scientific management, meaning the use of systematic observation and measurement, task specialism and, in effect, the reduction of workers to the level of efficiently functioning machines).

Braverman's notion of labour process theory has been criticized as being simplistic by subsequent commentators such as Littler and Salaman (1982) who argue that there are numerous determinants in the control of the labour process. And Friedman (1977) believes that Braverman's version neglects the diverse and sophisticated character of management control as it responds not only to technological advances but also to changes in the degree and intensity of worker resistance and new product and labour market conditions. Storey (1995) has commented that 'the labour process bandwagon... is now holed and patched beyond repair'.

But more recent commentators such as Newton and Findlay (1996) believe that labour process theory explains how managements have at their disposal a range of mechanisms through which control is exercised: 'Job performance and its assessment is at the heart of the labour process.' Managements, according to Newton and Findlay, are constantly seeking ways to improve the effectiveness of control mechanisms to achieve compliance. They 'try to squeeze the last drop of surplus value' out of their labour.

Agency theory

Agency or principal agent theory indicates that principals (owners and managers) have to develop ways of monitoring and controlling the activities of their agents (staff). Agency theory suggests that principals may have problems in ensuring that agents do what they are told. It is necessary to clear up ambiguities by setting objectives and monitoring performance to ensure that objectives are achieved.

Agency theory has been criticized by Gomez-Mejia and Balkin (1992) as 'managerialist'. As Armstrong (1996) wrote: 'It looks at the employment relationships purely from management's point of view and regards employees as objects to be motivated by the carrot and stick. It is a dismal theory, which suggests that people cannot be trusted.'

Exchange theory

Exchange theory sets out to explain organizational behaviour in terms of the rewards and costs incurred in the interaction between employers and employees. There are four concepts:

- *Rewards* – payoffs that satisfy needs emerging from the interactions between individuals and their organizations.
- *Costs* – fatigue, stress, anxiety, punishments and the value of rewards that people have lost because of lack of opportunity.
- *Outcomes* – rewards minus costs: if positive, the interaction yields a 'profit' and this is satisfactory as long as it exceeds the minimum level of expectation.
- *Level of comparisons* – people evaluate the outcome of an interaction against the profit they are foregoing elsewhere.

Unitary and pluralist frames of reference

One of the often expressed aims of human resource management is to increase the commitment of people to the organization by getting them to share its views and values and integrate their own work objectives with those of the organization. This concept adopts a unitary frame of reference; in other words, as expressed by Gennard and Judge (1997), organizations are assumed to be 'harmonious and integrated, all employees sharing the organisational goals and working as members of one team'.

Alternatively, the pluralist perspective as expressed by Cyert and March (1963) sees organizations as coalitions of interest groups and recognizes the legitimacy of different interests and values. Organizational development programmes, which, amongst other things, aim to increase commitment and teamwork, adopt a unitary framework. But it can be argued that this is a managerialist assumption and that the legitimate interests of the other members of a pluralist society – the stakeholders – will have their own interests, which should be respected.

ORGANIZATIONAL FACTORS AFFECTING WORK

The nature of work changes as organizations change in response to new demands and environmental pressures. Business-process engineering, downsizing and delayering all have significant effects on the type of work carried out, on feelings of security and on the career opportunities available in organizations. Three of the most important factors – the 'lean' organization, the changing role of the process worker and the flexible firm – are discussed below.

The lean organization

The term 'lean production' was popularized by Womack and Jones (1970) in *The Machine That Changed the World*. But the drive for leaner methods of working was confined initially to the car industry. In the classic case of Toyota, one of the pioneers of lean production, or more loosely, 'world class manufacturing', seven forms of waste were identified, which had to be eliminated. These were overproduction, waiting, transporting, over-processing, inventories, moving, and making defective parts or products. Lean production aims to add value by minimizing waste in terms of materials, time, space and people. Production systems associated with leanness include just-in-time, supply chain management, material resources planning and zero defects/right first time. Business process re-engineering programmes often accompany drives for leaner methods of working and total quality management approaches are used to support drives for greater levels of customer satisfaction and service.

The concept of 'leanness' has since been extended to non-manufacturing organizations. This can often be number driven and is implemented by means of a reduction in headcounts (downsizing) and a reduction in the number of levels of management and supervision (delayering). But there is no standard model of what a lean organization looks like. According to the report on the research conducted by the Institute of Personnel and Development (IPD) on lean and responsive organizations (IPD, 1998c), firms select from a menu the methods that meet their particular business needs. These include, other than delayering or the negative approach of downsizing, positive steps such as:

- team-based work organizations;
- shop-floor empowerment and problem-solving practices;
- quality built in, not inspected in;
- emphasis on horizontal business processes rather than vertical structures;
- partnership relationships with suppliers;
- cross-functional management and development teams;
- responsiveness to customer demand;
- human resource management policies aimed at high motivation and commitment and including communication programmes and participation in decision-making.

The IPD report emphasizes that qualitative change through people is a major feature of lean working but that the issue is not just that of launching change. The key requirement is to sustain it. The report also noted that HR practitioners can play a number of important roles in the process of managing change. These include that of supporter, interpreter, champion, monitor, resourcer, and anticipator of potential problems.

A question posed by Purcell, Hutchinson and Kinnie (1998) was: 'Are lean organizations usually mean organizations?' But he commented that the IPD research did not indicate that leaner methods of work have positive implications for employees. The evidence suggested that the impact on people is often negative, particularly when restructuring means downsizing and re-engineering. Employees work longer hours, stress rises, career opportunities are reduced and morale and motivation fall. He also made the point that it is clear that many initiatives fail because they do not take into account the people implications, and that the first and most significant barrier was middle management resistance.

The changing role of the process worker

A report published on a research project into process working by the Institute of Employment Studies (Giles *et al*, 1997) revealed that management structures designed in response to technological advances and competitive pressures are transforming the role of process workers.

Increasing automation and the application of new technologies to the production process mean that low-skilled manual jobs continue to disappear, and that process workers are becoming progressively less involved in manual operating tasks. Instead, they are being given more responsibility for the processes they work on, while being expected to become more customer and business oriented and, in many cases, to carry out simple engineering and maintenance tasks.

The flexible firm

The concept of the 'flexible firm' was originated by Atkinson (1984) who claimed that there is a growing trend for firms to seek various forms of structural and operational flexibility. The three kinds of flexibility areas follow:

- *Functional flexibility* is sought so that employees can be redeployed quickly and smoothly between activities and tasks. Functional flexibility may require multi-skilling – craft workers who possess and can apply a number of skills covering, for example, both mechanical and electrical engineering, or manufacturing and maintenance activities.
- *Numerical flexibility* is sought so that the number of employees can be quickly and easily increased or decreased in line with even short-term changes in the level of demand for labour.
- *Financial flexibility* provides for pay levels to reflect the state of supply and demand in the external labour market and also means the use of flexible pay systems that facilitate either functional or numerical flexibility.

The new structure in the flexible firm involves the break-up of the labour force into increasingly peripheral, and therefore numerically flexible, groups of workers clustered around a numerically stable core group that will conduct the organization's key, firm-specific activities. At the core, the focus is on functional flexibility. Shifting to the periphery, numerical flexibility becomes more important. As the market grows, the periphery expands to take up slack; as growth slows, the periphery contracts. At the core, only tasks and responsibilities change; the workers here are insulated from medium-term fluctuations in the market and can therefore enjoy job security, whereas those in the periphery are exposed to them.

CHANGING PATTERNS OF WORK

The most important developments over the past decade have been a considerable increase in the use of part-timers, a marked propensity for organizations to subcontract work and to outsource services, and a greater requirement for specialists (knowledge workers) and professionals in organizations. Teleworking has increased (working at home with a computer terminal link to the firm) and call centre work has expanded.

Projections made by Business Strategies (BSL) in 1995, as reported by Coyle (1996), indicated that in 10 years' time nearly half the workforce would be covered by 'flexible' arrangements such as temporary contracts, self-employment and part-time jobs. This will include 2.5 million people in short-term employment by 2005, a million more than in 1995. The BSL research confirmed that most part-timers and temporary workers are women, but most of those in self-employment are men. Men also account for the bulk of the new growth in temporary jobs.

Under the pressures to be competitive and to achieve 'cost leadership', organizations are not only 'downsizing' but are also engaging people on short-term contracts and make no pretence that they are there to provide careers. They want specific contributions to achieving organizational goals now and, so far as people are concerned, they may let the future take care of itself, believing that they can purchase the talent required as and when necessary. This may be short-sighted, but it is the way many businesses now operate.

When preparing and implementing human resource plans, personnel practitioners need to be aware of these factors and trends within the context of their internal and external environments. A further factor that affects the way in which the labour market operates, and therefore human resource planning decisions, is unemployment.

UNEMPLOYMENT

As Hutton (1995) commented: 'For two decades unemployment has been a grim fact of British life, bearing particularly hard on men.' High levels of unemployment are not a British phenomenon. They exist throughout Europe – France, for example, has a higher rate of youth unemployment than Britain – and indeed the world. But that is no consolation.

Economists seem unable to agree on the causes of or cures for unemployment (or anything else, it seems). The essence of the Keynesian explanation is that firms demand too little labour because individuals demand too few goods. The classical view was that unemployment was voluntary and could be cleared by natural market forces. The neo-classical theory is that there is a natural rate of unemployment, which reflects a given rate of technology, individual preferences and endowments. With flexible wages in a competitive labour market, wages adjust to clear the market and any unemployment that remains is voluntary. The latter view was that held by Milton Friedman and strongly influenced government policy in the early 1980s, but without success. There is, of course, no simple explanation of unemployment and no simple solution. All that appears to be certain is that unemployment will continue at a high level, especially if the main thrust of economic policy is to keep down the rates of inflation.

CAREER EXPECTATIONS

It is often said that the days of the life-long career are over, especially for white collar workers, and that the job security that they previously enjoyed no longer exists. Although downsizing and delayering may have increased the risk to executives and administrative staff of being made redundant, data from the Department of Education and Employment as quoted by Elliott (1996) show that in the decade between 1985 and 1995 there was very little change in the average length of job tenure. For men, it was down a fraction, for women, it was actually up a little. Burgess and Rees (1996) established that between 1975 and 1992 there was a fall of around 10 per cent in the length of time spent on a job. But they commented that: 'The data emphatically do not support the view that the dramatic changes in the labour market, technology and competition, have spelt the end of "jobs for life".'

ATTITUDES TO WORK

The IPD research into employee motivation and the psychological contract (Guest *et al*, 1996; Guest and Conway, 1997) obtained the following responses from the people they surveyed:

● Work remains a central interest in the lives of most people.
● If they won the lottery, 39 per cent would quit work, but most of the others would continue working.
● Asked to cite the three most important things they look for in a job, 70 per cent of respondents cited pay, 62 per cent wanted interesting and varied work and only 22 per cent were looking for job security.
● 35 per cent claimed that they were putting in so much effort that they could not work any harder and a further 34 per cent claimed they were working very hard.

15

The employment relationship

This chapter explores the nature of the employment relationship and the creation of a climate of trust within that relationship.

THE EMPLOYMENT RELATIONSHIP DEFINED

The term employment relationship describes the relationships that exist between employers and employees in the workplace. These may be formal, eg contracts of employment, procedural agreements. Or they may be informal, in the shape of the psychological contract, which expresses certain assumptions and expectations about what managers and employer have to offer and are willing to deliver (Kessler and Undy, 1996). They can have an individual dimension, which refers to individual contracts and expectations, or a collective dimension, which refers to relationships between management and trade unions, staff associations or members of joint consultative bodies such as works councils.

NATURE OF THE EMPLOYMENT RELATIONSHIP

The dimensions of the employment relationship as described by Kessler and Undy (1996) are shown in Figure 15.1.

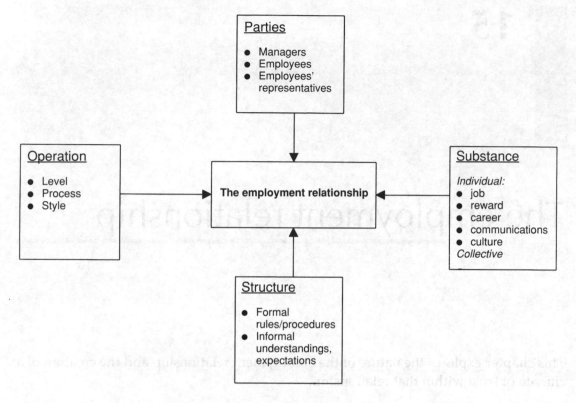

Figure 15.1 Dimensions of the employment relationship

(Source: S Kessler and R Undy, *The New Employment Relationship: Examining the psychological contract*, Institute of Personnel and Development, London, 1996)

The parties are managers, employees and employee representatives. The 'substance' incorporates the job, reward and career of individuals and the communications and culture of the organization as it affects them. It can also include collective agreements and joint employee relations machinery (works councils and the like). The formal dimensions include rules and procedures, and the informal aspect covers understanding, expectations and assumptions. Finally, the employment relationship exists at different levels in the organization (management to employees generally, and managers to individual employees and their representatives or groups of people). The operation of the relationship will also be affected by processes such as communications and consultation, and by the management style prevailing throughout the organization or adopted by individual managers.

BASIS OF THE EMPLOYMENT RELATIONSHIP

The starting point of the employment relationship is an undertaking by an employee to provide skill and effort to the employer in return for which the employer provides the employee with a salary or a wage. Initially the relationship is founded on a legal contract. This may be a written contract but the absence of such a contract does not mean that no contractual relationship exists. Employers and employees still have certain implied legal rights and obligations. The employer's obligations include the duty to pay salary or wages, to provide a safe workplace, to act in good faith towards the employee and not to act in such a way as to undermine the trust and confidence of the employment relationship. The employee has corresponding obligations, which include obedience, competence, honesty and loyalty.

An important factor to remember about the employment relationship is that, generally, it is the employer who has the power to dictate the contractual terms unless they have been fixed by collective bargaining. Individuals, except when they are much in demand, have little scope to vary the terms of the contract imposed upon them by employers.

DEFINING THE EMPLOYMENT RELATIONSHIP

Two types of contracts defining the employment relationship have been distinguished by Macneil (1985) and Rousseau and Wade-Benzoni (1994):

● *Transactional contracts* have well-described terms of exchange, which are usually expressed financially. They are of limited duration, with specified performance requirements.
● *Relational contracts* are less well defined with more abstract terms and refer to an open-ended membership of the organization. Performance requirements attached to this continuing membership are incomplete or ambiguous.

However, the employment relationships can also be expressed in terms of a *psychological contract*, which, according to Guzzo and Noonan (1994), has both transactional and relational qualities. The concept of a psychological contract expresses the view that at its most basic level the employment relationship consists of a unique combination of beliefs held by an individual and his or her employer about what they expect of one another. This concept is discussed in more detail in Chapter 16.

SIGNIFICANCE OF THE EMPLOYMENT RELATIONSHIP CONCEPT

The concept of the employment relationship is significant to personnel specialists because it governs much of what organizations need to be aware of in developing and applying HR processes, policies and procedures. These need to be considered in terms of what they will or will not contribute to furthering a productive and rewarding employment relationship between all the parties concerned.

CHANGES IN THE EMPLOYMENT RELATIONSHIP

As noted by Gallie *et al* (1998) in their analysis of the outcome of their 'employment in Britain' research programme, while there have been shifts in the ways in which people are employed: 'The evidence for a major change in the nature of the employment relationship was much less convincing.' But they did note the following characteristics of employment as revealed by the survey:

- New forms of management, often based explicitly or implicitly on HRM principles and emphasizing individual contracts rather than collective bargaining.
- There was some increase in task discretion but there was no evidence of a significant decline in managerial control; indeed, in some important respects control was intensified.
- Supervisory activity was still important.
- Integrative forms of management policy were centred on non-manual employees.
- The great majority of employees continued to attach a high level of importance to the intrinsically motivating aspects of work.
- The higher the level of skill, the more people were involved with their work.
- The raising of skill levels and the granting of increased discretion to employers are key factors in improving the quality of work experience.
- High levels of commitment to the organization can reduce absenteeism and labour turnover but there was no evidence that organizational commitment 'added anything over and above other organizational and task characteristics with regard to the quality of work performance'.

MANAGING THE EMPLOYMENT RELATIONSHIP

The dynamic and often nebulous nature of the employment relationship increases the difficulty of managing it. The problem is compounded because of the multiplicity of the factors that influence the contract: the culture of the organization; the prevailing management style; the values, espoused and practised, of top management; the existence or non-existence of a climate of trust; day-to-day interactions between employees and line managers; and the personnel policies and practices of the business.

The latter are particularly important. The nature of the employment relationship is strongly influenced by personnel actions. These cover all aspects of personnel management. But how people are treated in such areas as recruitment, performance reviews, promotion, career development, reward, involvement and participation, grievance handling, disciplinary procedures and redundancy will be particularly important. How people are required to carry out their work (including flexibility and multi-skilling), how performance expectations are expressed and communicated, how work is organized and how people are managed will also make a significant impact on the employment relationship. HR specialists can contribute to the development of a positive and productive employment relationship in the following ways:

- *during recruitment interviews* – presenting the unfavourable as well as the favourable aspects of a job in a 'realistic job preview';
- in *induction programmes* – communicating to new starters the organization's personnel policies and procedures and its core values, indicating to them the standards of performance expected in such areas as quality and customer service, and spelling out requirements for flexibility;
- by issuing and updating *employee handbooks* that reinforce the messages delivered in induction programmes;
- by encouraging the development of *performance management* processes that ensure that performance expectations are agreed and reviewed regularly;
- by encouraging the use of *personal development plans* that spell out how continuous improvement of performance can be achieved, mainly by self-managed learning;
- by using *training and management development programmes* to underpin core values and define performance expectations;
- by ensuring through *manager and team leader training* that managers and team leaders understand their role in managing the employment relationship through such processes as performance management and team leadership;
- by encouraging the maximum amount of *contact* between managers and team leaders and their team members to achieve mutual understanding of expectations and to provide a means of two-way communications;
- by adopting a general policy of *transparency* – ensuring that in all matters that

affect them, employees know what is happening, why it is happening and the impact it will make on their employment, development and prospects;

● by developing *personnel procedures* covering grievance handling, discipline, equal opportunities, promotion and redundancy and ensuring that they are implemented fairly and consistently;

● by developing and communicating *personnel policies* covering the major areas of employment, development, reward and employee relations;

● by ensuring that the *reward system* is developed and managed to achieve equity, fairness and consistency in all aspects of pay and benefits;

● generally, by advising on *employee relations procedures*, processes and issues that further good collective relationships.

These approaches to managing the employment relationship cover all aspects of people management. It is important to remember, however, that this is a continuous process. The effective management of the relationship means ensuring that values are upheld and that a transparent, consistent and fair approach is adopted in dealing with all aspects of employment.

TRUST AND THE EMPLOYMENT RELATIONSHIP

The Institute of Personnel and Development suggested in its statement *People Make the Difference* (1994) that building trust is the only basis upon which commitment can be generated. The IPD commented that: 'In too many organizations inconsistency between what is said and what is done undermines trust, generates employee cynicism and provides evidence of contradictions in management thinking.'

It has also been suggested by Herriot *et al* (1998) that trust should be regarded as social capital – the fund of goodwill in any social group that enables people within it to collaborate with one another. Thompson (1998) sees trust as a 'unique human resource capability that helps the organization fulfil its competitive advantage' – a core competency that leads to high business performance. Thus there is a business need to develop a climate of trust, as there is a business need to introduce effective pay-for-contribution processes, which are built on trust.

The meaning of trust

Trust, as defined by the Oxford English Dictionary, is a firm belief that a person may be relied on. An alternative definition has been provided by Shaw (1997) to the effect that trust is the 'belief that those on whom we depend will meet our expectations of them'. These expectations are dependent on 'our assessment of another's responsibility to meet our needs'.

A climate of trust

A high-trust organization has been described by Fox (1973) as follows:

> Organizational participants share certain ends or values; bear towards each other a diffuse sense of long-term obligations; offer each other spontaneous support without narrowly calculating the cost or anticipating any short-term reciprocation; communicate honestly and freely; are ready to repose their fortunes in each other's hands; and give each other the benefit of any doubt that may arise with respect to goodwill or motivation.

This ideal state may seldom, if ever, be attained, but it does represent a picture of an effective organization in which, as Thompson (1998) notes, trust 'is an outcome of good management'.

When do employees trust management?

Management is more likely to be trusted by employees when the latter:

- believe that the management means what it says;
- observe that management does what it says it is going to do – suiting the action to the word;
- know from experience that management, in the words of David Guest (Guest and Conway, 1998), 'delivers the deal – it keeps its word and fulfils its side of the bargain';
- feel they are treated fairly, equitable and consistently.

Developing a high-trust organization

As Thompson (1998) comments, a number of writers have generally concluded that trust is 'not something that can, or should, be directly managed'. He cites Sako (1994) who wrote that: 'Trust is a cultural norm which can rarely be created intentionally because attempts to create trust in a calculative manner would destroy the effective basis of trust.'

It may not be possible to 'manage' trust but, as Thompson argues, trust is an outcome of good management. It is created and maintained by managerial behaviour and by the development of better mutual understanding of expectations – employers of employees, and employees of employers. But Herriot *et al* (1998) point out that issues of trust are not in the end to do with managing people or processes, but are more about relationships and mutual support through change.

Clearly, the sort of behaviour that is most likely to engender trust is when management is honest with people, keeps its word (delivers the deal) and practises what it preaches. Organizations that espouse core values ('people are our greatest asset') and then proceed to ignore them will be low-trust organizations.

More specifically, trust will be developed if management acts fairly, equitably and consistently, if a policy of transparency is implemented, if intentions and the reasons for proposals or decisions are communicated both to employees generally and to individuals, if there is full involvement in developing reward processes, and if mutual expectations are agreed through performance management.

Failure to meet these criteria, wholly or in part, is perhaps the main reason why so many performance-related pay schemes have not lived up to expectations. The starting point is to understand and apply the principles of distributive and procedural justice.

Justice

To treat people justly is to deal with them fairly and equitably. Leventhal (1980), following Adams (1965), distinguished between distributive and procedural justice.

Distributive justice refers to how rewards are distributed. People will feel that they have been treated justly in this respect if they believe that rewards have been distributed in accordance with their contributions, that they receive what was promised to them and that they get what they need.

Procedural justice refers to the ways in which managerial decisions are made and personnel procedures are managed. The five factors that affect perceptions of procedural justice as identified by Tyler and Bies (1990) are:

- adequate consideration of an employee's viewpoint;
- suppression of personal bias towards an employee;
- applying criteria consistently across employees;
- providing early feedback to employees about the outcome of decisions;
- providing employees with an adequate explanation of decisions made.

Renewing trust

As suggested by Herriot *et al* (1998), if trust is lost, a four-step programme is required for its renewal:

1. admission by top management that it has paid insufficient attention in the past to employees' diverse needs;
2. a limited process of contracting whereby a particular transition to a different way of working for a group of employees is done in a form that takes individual needs into account;
3. establishing 'knowledge-based' trust, which is based not on a specific transactional deal but on a developing perception of trustworthiness;
4. achieving trust based on identification in which each party empathizes with each other's needs and therefore takes them on board themselves (although this final state is seldom reached in practice).

16

The psychological contract

The employment relationship, as described in Chapter 15, is a fundamental feature of all aspects of people management. At its most basic level, the employment relationship consists of a unique combination of beliefs held by an individual and his or her employer about what they expect of one another. This is the psychological contract, and to manage the employment relationship effectively it is necessary to understand what the psychological contract is, how it is formed and its significance.

THE PSYCHOLOGICAL CONTRACT DEFINED

Fundamentally, the psychological contract expresses the combination of beliefs held by an individual and his or her employer about what they expect of one another. It can be described as the set of reciprocal but unarticulated expectations that exist between individual employees and their employers. As defined by Schein (1965): 'The notion of a psychological contract implies that there is an unwritten set of expectations operating at all times between every member of an organization and the various managers and others in that organization.'

This definition was amplified by Rousseau and Wade-Benzoni (1994) who stated that:

Psychological contracts refer to beliefs that individuals hold regarding promises made, accepted and relied upon between themselves and another. (In the case of organizations, these parties include an employee, client, manager, and/or organization as a whole.) Because psychological contracts represent how people *interpret* promises and commitments, both parties in the same employment relationship (employer and employee) can have different views regarding specific terms.

Within organizations, as Katz and Kahn (1964) pointed out, every role is basically a set of behavioural expectations. These expectations are often implicit – they are not defined in the employment contract. Basic models of motivation such as expectancy theory (Vroom, 1964) and operant conditioning (Skinner, 1974) maintain that employees behave in ways they expect will produce positive outcomes. But they do not necessarily know what to expect. As Rousseau and Greller (1994) comment:

The ideal contract in employment would detail expectations of both employee and employer. Typical contracts, however, are incomplete due to bounded rationality, which limits individual information seeking, and to a changing organizational environment that makes it impossible to specify all conditions up front. Both employee and employer are left to fill up the blanks.

Employees may expect to be treated fairly as human beings, to be provided with work that uses their abilities, to be rewarded equitably in accordance with their contribution, to be able to display competence, to have opportunities for further growth, to know what is expected of them and to be given feedback (preferably positive) on how they are doing. Employers may expect employees to do their best on behalf of the organization – 'to put themselves out for the company' – to be fully committed to its values, to be compliant and loyal, and to enhance the image of the organization with its customers and suppliers. Sometimes these assumptions are justified – often they are not. Mutual misunderstandings can cause friction and stress and lead to recriminations and poor performance, or to a termination of the employment relationship.

To summarize in the words of Guest and Conway (1998), the psychological contract lacks many of the characteristics of the formal contract: 'It is not generally written down, it is somewhat blurred at the edges, and it cannot be enforced in a court or tribunal.' They believe that: 'The psychological contract is best seen as a metaphor; a word or phrase borrowed from another context which helps us make sense of our experience. The psychological contract is a way of interpreting the state of the employment relationship and helping to plot significant changes.'

THE SIGNIFICANCE OF THE PSYCHOLOGICAL CONTRACT

As suggested by Spindler (1994): 'A psychological contract creates emotions and attitudes which form and control behaviour.' The significance of the psychological contract was further explained by Sims (1994) as follows: 'A balanced psychological contract is necessary for a continuing, harmonious relationship between the employee and the organization. However, the violation of the psychological contract can signal to the participants that the parties no longer share (or never shared) a common set of values or goals.'

The concept highlights the fact that employee/employer expectations take the form of unarticulated assumptions. Disappointments on the part of management as well as employees may therefore be inevitable. These disappointments can, however, be alleviated if managements appreciate that one of their key roles is to manage expectations, which means clarifying what they believe employees should achieve, the competences they should possess and the values they should uphold. And this is a matter not just of articulating and stipulating these requirements but of discussing and agreeing them with individuals and teams.

The psychological contract governs the continuing development of the employment relationship, which is constantly evolving over time. But how the contract is developing and the impact it makes may not be fully understood by any of the parties involved. Spindler (1994) comments that: 'In a psychological contract the rights and obligations of the parties have not been articulated, much less agreed to. The parties do not express their expectations and, in fact, may be quite incapable of doing so.'

People who have no clear idea about what they expect may, if such unexpressed expectations have not been fulfilled, have no clear idea why they have been disappointed. But they will be aware that something does not feel right. And a company staffed by 'cheated' individuals who expect more than they get is heading for trouble.

The importance of the psychological contract was emphasized by Schein (1965) who suggested that the extent to which people work effectively and are committed to the organization depends on:

- the degree to which their own expectations of what the organization will provide to them and what they owe the organization in return match that organization's expectations of what it will give and get in return;
- the nature of *what is actually to be exchanged* (assuming there is some agreement) – money in exchange for time at work; social need satisfaction and security in exchange for hard work and loyalty; opportunities for self-actualization and challenging work in exchange for high productivity, high-quality work, and creative

effort in the service of organizational goals; or various combinations of these and other things.

THE NATURE OF THE PSYCHOLOGICAL CONTRACT

A psychological contract is a system of beliefs that may not have been articulated. It encompasses the actions employees believe are expected of them and what response they expect in return from their employer. As described by Guest *et al* (1996): 'It is concerned with assumptions, expectations, promises and mutual obligations.' It creates attitudes and emotions that form and govern behaviour. A psychological contract is implicit. It is also dynamic – it develops over time as experience accumulates, employment conditions change and employees re-evaluate their expectations.

The psychological contract may provide some indication of the answers to the two fundamental employment relationship questions that individuals pose: 'What can I reasonably expect from the organization?' and 'What should I reasonably be expected to contribute in return?' But it is unlikely that the psychological contract and therefore the employment relationship will ever be fully understood by either party.

The aspects of the employment relationship covered by the psychological contract will include, from the employee's point of view:

- how they are treated in terms of fairness, equity and consistency;
- security of employment;
- scope to demonstrate competence;
- career expectations and the opportunity to develop skills;
- involvement and influence;
- trust in the management of the organization to keep their promises.

From the employer's point of view, the psychological contract covers such aspects of the employment relationship as:

- competence;
- effort;
- compliance;
- commitment;
- loyalty.

As Guest *et al* (1996) point out:

While employees may want what they have always wanted – security, a career, fair rewards, interesting work and so on – employers no longer feel able or obliged to provide these. Instead, they have been demanding more of their employees in terms of greater input and tolerance of uncertainty and change, while providing less in return, in particular less security and more limited career prospects.

An operational model of the psychological contract

An operational model of the psychological contract as formulated by Guest *et al* (1996) suggests that the core of the contract can be measured in terms of fairness of treatment, trust, and the extent to which the explicit deal or contract is perceived to be delivered. The full model is illustrated in Figure 16.1.

Figure 16.1   A model of the psychological contract

(Source: D Guest, N Conway, R Briner and M Dickman, *The State of the Psychological Contract in Employment: Issues in people management*, Institute of Personnel and Development, London, 1996)

THE CHANGING NATURE OF THE PSYCHOLOGICAL CONTRACT

Many commentators have delivered warnings about changes to the psychological contract that are not all advantageous to employees. And the nature of the psychological contract is changing in many organizations in response to changes in their external and internal environments. This is largely because of the impact of global competition and the effect this has had on how businesses operate, including moves into 'lean' forms of operation.

As Baillie (1995) has suggested:

> For the last 50 years the psychological contract was not an issue. People knew what to expect – you turned up to work, did what was required, and the organization provided security and development. It was not a complicated relationship, and for most organizations it worked well, providing them with a loyal, committed and dependable workforce.

But the psychological contract has not been an issue because it usually did not change much. This is no longer the case because:

- business organizations are neither stable nor long-lived – uncertainty prevails, job security is no longer on offer by employers who are less anxious to maintain a stable workforce – as Mirvis and Hall (1994) point out, organizations are making continued employment explicitly contingent on the fit between people's competences and business needs;
- flexibility, adaptability and speed of response are all-important and individual roles may be subject to constant change – continuity and predictability are no longer available for employees;
- leaner organizations mean that careers may mainly develop laterally – expectations that progress will be made by promotion through the hierarchy are no longer so valid;
- leaner organizations may make greater demands on employees and are less likely to tolerate people who no longer precisely fit their requirements.

But, more positively, some organizations are realizing that steps have to be taken to increase mutuality and to provide scope for lateral career development and improvement in knowledge and skills through opportunities for learning. They recognize that because they can no longer guarantee long-term employment they have the responsibility to help people to continue to develop their careers if they have to move on. In other words they take steps to improve employability. Even those that have fully embraced the 'core–periphery' concept may recognize that they still need to obtain the commitment of their core employees and pay attention to their continuous development, although in most organizations the emphasis is likely to be on self-development.

Kissler (1994) summed up the differences between old and new employment contracts as follows:

Old	New
Relationship is pre-determined and imposed	Relationship is mutual and negotiated
You are who you work for and what you do	You are defined by multiple roles, many external to the organization
Loyalty is defined by performance	Loyalty is defined by output and quality
Leaving is treason	People and skills only needed when required
Employees who do what they are told will work until retirement	Long-term employment is unlikely; expect and prepare for multiple relationships

The following ways in which psychological contracts are changing have been suggested by Hiltrop (1995):

From	To
Imposed relationship (compliance, command and control)	Mutual relationship (commitment, participation and involvement)
Permanent employment relationship	Variable employment relationship – people and skills only obtained or retained when required
Focus on promotion	Focus on lateral career development
Finite job duties	Multiple roles
Meet job requirements	Add value
Emphasis on job security and loyalty to company	Emphasis on employability and loyalty to own career and skills
Training provided by organization	Opportunities for self-managed learning

Hiltrop suggests that a new psychological contract is emerging – one that is more situational and short term and which assumes that each party is much less dependent on the other for survival and growth. He believes that in its most naked form, the new contract could be defined as follows:

> There is no job security. The employee will be employed as long as he or she adds value to the organization, and is personally responsible for finding new ways to add value. In return, the employee has the right to demand interesting and important work, has the freedom and resources to perform it well, receives pay that reflects his or her contribution, and gets the experience and training needed to be employable here or elsewhere.

But this could hardly be called a balanced contract. To what extent do employees in general have 'the right to demand interesting and important work'? Employers still call the shots, except when dealing with the special cases of people who are much in demand and in short supply. In Britain, as Mant (1996) points out, 'people often really are regarded as merely "resources" to be acquired or divested according to short-term economic circumstances'. It is the employer who has the power to dictate contractual terms unless they have been fixed by collective bargaining. Individuals, except when they are highly sought after, have little scope to vary the terms of the contract imposed upon them by employers.

Perhaps one of the most important trends in the employment relationship as expressed by the psychological contract is that employees are now being required to bear risks that were previously carried by the organization. As Elliott (1996) notes: 'The most profound change in the labour market over the past two decades has been the massive shift in power from employee to employer. This has not only meant that workers have had their rights eroded, but also that much of the risk involved in a business has been shifted from capital to labour.'

THE STATE OF THE PSYCHOLOGICAL CONTRACT

But the dire warnings about the state of the psychological contract referred to above were not borne out by three research projects commissioned by the Institute of Personnel and Development. The research conducted by Guest *et al* (1996) established that the psychological contract (defined in terms of workers' judgements of fairness, trust and organizational delivery of 'the deal') was in better shape than many pundits suggest. A follow-up survey (Guest and Conway, 1997) found that a very high proportion of employees (90 per cent) believe that on balance they are fairly treated by their employers and 79 per cent say they trust management 'a lot' or 'somewhat' to keep its promises. Job security is not a major concern –

86 per cent feel very or fairly secure in their jobs. A majority (62 per cent) believe that management and workers are on the same side and only 18 per cent disagree. However, job satisfaction was only moderate (38 per cent express high satisfaction, but 22 per cent express low satisfaction), although commitment to the organization was high (49 per cent felt 'a lot' and 36 per cent 'some' loyalty to their organization).

A further survey (Guest and Conway, 1998) established that:

- there had been no significant changes in attitudes and behaviour since the previous survey;
- workers continue to believe that they are fairly treated – 67 per cent report fair treatment by management and 64 per cent say that they get a fair day's pay for a fair day's work;
- the number of progressive HRM practices in place is the key determinant of whether workers believe they are fairly treated, because they exert a major influence on work attitudes;
- people report that home is for relaxation, work is for challenge;
- feelings of security remain high – 88 per cent felt very or fairly secure in their jobs;
- people still expect a career – 60 per cent believe that their employer has made a career promise and of these, 65 per cent think that management has largely kept its promise (these feelings are more prevalent amongst younger workers).

The overall conclusion of the researchers in 1998 was that 'the psychological contract is very healthy'. On the whole, management is seen as fair, trustworthy and likely to keep its promises. The key influences on a healthy psychological contract are the use of progressive human resource practices, scope for direct participation at work and working in a smaller organization.

HOW PSYCHOLOGICAL CONTRACTS DEVELOP

Psychological contracts are not developed by means of a single transaction. There are many contract makers who exert influence over the whole duration of an employee's involvement with an organization. As Spindler (1994) comments:

> Every day we create relationships by means other than formal contracts... As individuals form relationships they necessarily bring their accumulated experience and developed personalities with them. In ways unknown to them, what they expect from the relationship reflects the sum total of their conscious and unconscious learning to date.

The problem with psychological contracts is that employees are often unclear about what they want from the organization or what they can contribute to it. Some employees are equally unclear about what they expect from their employees.

Because of these factors, and because a psychological contract is essentially implicit, it is likely to develop in an unplanned way with unforeseen consequences. Anything that management does or is perceived as doing that affects the interests of employees will modify the psychological contract. Similarly the actual or perceived behaviour of employees, individually or collectively, will affect an employer's concept of the contract.

DEVELOPING AND MAINTAINING A POSITIVE PSYCHOLOGICAL CONTRACT

As Guest *et al* (1996) point out: 'A positive psychological contract is worth taking seriously because it is strongly linked to higher commitment to the organization, higher employee satisfaction and better employment relations. Again this reinforces the benefits of pursuing a set of progressive HRM practices.' They also emphasize the importance of a high-involvement climate and suggest in particular that HRM practices such as the provision of opportunities for learning, training and development, focus on job security, promotion and careers, minimizing status differentials, fair reward systems and comprehensive communication and involvement processes will all contribute to a positive psychological contract.

Steps taken to manage the employment relationship as specified in Chapter 15 will also help to form a positive psychological contract. These include:

- defining expectations during recruitment and induction programmes;
- communicating and agreeing expectations as part of the continuing dialogue implicit in good performance management practices;
- adopting a policy of transparency on company policies and procedures and on management's proposals and decisions as they affect people;
- generally treating people as stakeholders, relying on consensus and cooperation rather than control and coercion.

Part V

Organization, jobs and roles

This part is concerned with the practical applications of organizational behaviour theory. It starts by looking at the processes of organizational design and development and then deals with job design and role building.

Part V

Organization, jobs and roles

17

Organization design

The management of people in organizations constantly raises questions such as 'Who does what?', 'How should activities be grouped together?', 'What lines and means of communication need to be established?', 'How should people be helped to understand their roles in relation to the objectives of the organization and the roles of their colleagues?', 'Are we doing everything that we ought to be doing and nothing that we ought not to be doing?' and 'Have we got too many unnecessary layers of management in the organization?'

These are questions involving people which must concern HR practitioners in their capacity of helping the business to make the best use of its people. HR specialists should be able to contribute to the processes of organization design or redesign as described below because of their understanding of the factors affecting organizational behaviour and because they are in a position to take an overall view of how the business is organized, which it is difficult for the heads of other functional departments to obtain.

THE PROCESS OF ORGANIZING

The process of organizing can be described as the design, development and maintenance of a system of coordinated activities in which individuals and groups of people work cooperatively under leadership towards commonly understood and accepted goals. The key word in that definition is 'system'. Organizations are systems which, as affected by their environment, have a structure which has both formal and informal elements.

The process of organizing may involve the grand design or redesign of the total structure, but most frequently it is concerned with the organization of particular functions and activities and the basis upon which the relationships between them are managed.

Organizations are not static things. Changes are constantly taking place in the business itself, in the environment in which the business operates, and in the people who work in the business. There is no such thing as an 'ideal' organization. The most that can be done is to optimize the processes involved, remembering that whatever structure evolves it will be contingent on the environmental circumstances of the organization, and one of the aims of organization is to achieve the 'best fit' between the structure and these circumstances.

An important point to bear in mind is that organizations consist of people working more or less cooperatively together. Inevitably, and especially at managerial levels, the organization may have to be adjusted to fit the particular strengths and attributes of the people available. The result may not conform to the ideal, but it is more likely to work than a structure that ignores the human element. It is always desirable to have an ideal structure in mind, but it is equally desirable to modify it to meet particular circumstances, as long as there is awareness of the potential problems that may arise. This may seem an obvious point, but it is frequently ignored by management consultants and others who adopt a doctrinaire approach to organization, often with disastrous results.

AIM

Bearing in mind the need to take an empirical and contingent approach to organizing, as suggested above, the aim of organization design could be defined as being to *optimize* the arrangements for conducting the affairs of the business. To do this it is necessary, as far as circumstances allow, to:

- clarify the overall purposes of the organization – the strategic thrusts that govern what it does and how it functions;
- define as precisely as possible the key activities required to achieve that purpose;
- group these activities logically together to avoid unnecessary overlap or duplication;

- provide for the integration of activities and the achievement of cooperative effort and teamwork in pursuit of a common purpose;
- build flexibility into the system so that organizational arrangements can adapt quickly to new situations and challenges;
- provide for the rapid communication of information throughout the organization;
- define the role and function of each organizational unit so that all concerned know how it plays its part in achieving the overall purpose;
- clarify individual roles, accountabilities and authorities;
- design jobs to make the best use of the skills and capacities of the job holders and to provide them with high levels of intrinsic motivation (job design is considered in Chapter 19);
- plan and implement organization development activities to ensure that the various processes within the organization operate in a manner that contributes to organizational effectiveness;
- set up teams and project groups as required to be responsible for specific processing, development, professional or administrative activities or for the conduct of projects.

CONDUCTING ORGANIZATION REVIEWS

Organization reviews are conducted in the following stages:

1. An *analysis*, as described below, of the existing arrangements and the factors that may affect the organization now and in the future.
2. A *diagnosis* of what needs to be done to improve the way in which the organization is structured and functions.
3. A *plan* to implement any revisions to the structure emerging from the diagnosis, possibly in phases. The plan may include longer-term considerations about the structure and the type of managers and employees who will be required to operate within it.
4. *Implementation* of the plan.

ORGANIZATION ANALYSIS

The starting point for an organization review is an analysis of the existing circumstances, structure and processes of the organization and an assessment of the strategic issues that might affect it in the future. This covers:

● The *external environment*. The economic, market and competitive factors that may affect the organization. Plans for product-market development will be significant.

● The *internal environment*. The mission, values, organization climate, management style, technology and processes of the organization as they affect the way it functions and should be structured to carry out those functions. Technological developments in such areas as cellular manufacturing may be particularly important as well as the introduction of new processes such as just-in-time or the development of an entirely new computer system.

● *Strategic issues and objectives*. As a background to the study it is necessary to identify the strategic issues facing the organization and its objectives. These may be considered under such headings as growth, competition and market position and standing. Issues concerning the availability of the required human, financial and physical resources would also have to be considered.

● *Activities*. Activity analysis establishes what work is done and what needs to be done in the organization to achieve its objectives within its environment. The analysis should cover what is and is not being done, who is doing it and where, and how much is being done. An answer is necessary to the key questions: 'Are all the activities required properly catered for?', 'Are there any unnecessary activities being carried out, ie those that do not need to be done at all or those that could be conducted more economically and efficiently by external contractors or providers?'

● *Structure*. The analysis of structure covers how activities are grouped together, the number of levels in the hierarchy, the extent to which authority is decentralized to divisions and strategic business units (SBUs), where functions such as finance, personnel and research and development are placed in the structure (eg as central functions or integrated into divisions or SBUs) and the relationships that exist between different units and functions (with particular attention being given to the way in which they communicate and cooperate with one another). Attention would be paid to such issues as the logic of the way in which activities are grouped and decentralized, the span of control managers (the number of separate functions or people they are directly responsible for), any overlap between functions or gaps leading to the neglect of certain activities, and the existence of unnecessary departments, units, functions or layers of management.

ORGANIZATION DIAGNOSIS

The diagnosis should be based on the analysis and an agreement by those concerned with what the aims of the organization should be. The present arrangements can be considered against these aims and future requirements to assess the extent to which they meet them or fall short.

It is worth repeating that there are no absolute standards against which an organization structure can be judged. There is never one right way of organizing anything and there are no absolute principles that govern organizational choice. The current fashion for delayering organizations has much to commend it, but it can go too far, leaving units and individuals adrift without any clear guidance on where they fit into the structure and how they should work with one another, and making the management task of coordinating activities more difficult.

Organization guidelines

There are no 'rules' or 'principles' of organization but there are certain guidelines that are worth bearing in mind in an organization study. These are:

- *Allocation of work.* The work that has to be done should be defined and allocated to functions, units, departments, work teams, project groups and individual positions. Related activities should be grouped together, but the emphasis should be on process rather than hierarchy, taking into account the need to manage processes that involve a number of different work units or teams.
- *Differentiation and integration.* It is necessary to differentiate between the different activities that have to be carried out, but it is equally necessary to ensure that these activities are integrated so that everyone in the organization is working towards the same goals.
- *Teamwork.* Jobs should be defined and roles described in ways that facilitate and underline the importance of teamwork. Areas where cooperation is required should be emphasized. The organization should be designed and operated across departmental or functional boundaries. Wherever possible, self-managing teams should be set up and given the maximum amount of responsibility to run their own affairs, including planning, budgeting and exercising quality control. Networking should be encouraged in the sense of people communicating openly and informally with one another as the need arises. It is recognized that these informal processes can be more productive than rigidly 'working through channels' as set out in the organization chart.
- *Flexibility.* The organization structure should be flexible enough to respond quickly to change, challenge and uncertainty. Flexibility should be enhanced by the creation of core groups and by using part-time, temporary and contract workers to handle extra demands. At top management level and elsewhere, a collegiate approach to team operation should be considered in which people

share responsibility and are expected to work with their colleagues in areas outside their primary function or skill.

- *Role clarification*. People should be clear about their roles as individuals and as members of a team. They should know what they will be held accountable for and be given every opportunity to use their abilities in achieving objectives to which they have agreed and are committed. Job/role description should define key result areas but should not act as straitjackets, restricting initiative and unduly limiting responsibility.
- *Decentralization*. Authority to make decisions should be delegated as close to the scene of action as possible. Profit centres should be set up as strategic business units which operate close to their markets and with a considerable degree of autonomy. A multiproduct or market business should develop a federal organization with each federated entity running its own affairs, although they will be linked together by the overall business strategy.
- *Delayering*. Organizations should be 'flattened' by removing superfluous layers of management and supervision in order to promote flexibility, facilitate swifter communication, increase responsiveness, enable people to be given more responsibility as individuals or teams and reduce costs.

Organization design leads into organization planning – assessing implications of structural changes on future manpower requirements and taking steps to meet those requirements.

ORGANIZATION PLANNING

Organization planning is the process of converting the analysis into the design. It determines structure, relationships, roles, human resource requirements and the lines along which changes should be implemented. There is no one best design. There is always a choice between alternatives. Logical analysis will help in the evaluation of the alternatives but the law of the situation will have to prevail. The final choice will be contingent upon the present and future circumstances of the organization. It will be strongly influenced by personal and human considerations – the inclinations of top management, the strengths and weaknesses of management generally, the availability of people to staff the new organization and the need to take account of the feelings of those who will be exposed to change. Cold logic may sometimes have to override these considerations. If it does, then it must be deliberate and the consequences must be appreciated and allowed for when planning the implementation of the new organization.

It may have to be accepted that a logical regrouping of activities cannot be introduced in the short term because no one with the experience is available to manage the new activities, or because capable individuals are so firmly entrenched in one area that to uproot them would cause serious damage to their morale and would reduce the overall effectiveness of the new organization.

The worst sin that organization designers can commit is that of imposing their own ideology on the organization. Their job is to be eclectic in their knowledge, sensitive in their analysis of the situation and deliberate in their approach to the evaluation of alternatives.

Having planned the organization and defined structures, relationships and roles, it is necessary to consider how the new organization should be implemented. It may be advisable to stage an implementation over a number of phases, especially if new people have to be found and trained.

WHO DOES THE WORK?

Organization design may be carried out by line management with or without the help of members of the personnel function acting as internal consultants, or it may be done by outside consultants. HR management should always be involved because organization design is essentially about people and the work they do. The advantage of using outside consultants is that an entirely independent and dispassionate view is obtained. They can cut through internal organizational pressures, politics and constraints and bring experience of other organizational problems they have dealt with. Sometimes, regrettably, major changes can be obtained only by outside intervention. But there is a danger of consultants suggesting theoretically ideal organizations that do not take sufficient account of the problems of making them work with existing people. They do not have to live with their solutions, as do line and personnel managers. If outside consultants are used, it is essential to involve people from within the organization so they can ensure that they are able to implement the proposals smoothly.

18

Organizational development, change and transformation

This chapter starts with a definition of the concept of organizational development which leads to a critical review of the traditional approaches to organization development (OD). Approaches to change management are then examined. These have sometimes been treated as an aspect of organizational development, but in fact they are used in any organization that is concerned with the effective introduction of changed structures, policies or practices. They therefore exist in their own right. The chapter continues with a discussion of organizational transformation principles and practice which are an extension of change management methodology into comprehensive programmes for managing fundamental changes to the culture and operations of an organization. The final section of the chapter deals with specific approaches to organizational development or change, namely: team building, culture change management, total quality management, business process re-engineering and performance management.

WHAT IS ORGANIZATIONAL DEVELOPMENT?

Organizational development is concerned with the planning and implementation of programmes designed to enhance the effectiveness with which an organization functions and responds to change. Overall, the aim is to adopt a planned and coherent approach to improving organizational effectiveness. An effective organization can be defined broadly as one that achieves its purpose by meeting the wants and needs of its stakeholders, matching its resources to opportunities, adapting flexibly to environmental changes and creating a culture that promotes commitment, creativity, shared values and mutual trust.

Organizational development is concerned with process, not structure or systems – with the way things are done rather than what is done. Process refers to the ways in which people act and interact. It is about the roles they play on a continuing basis to deal with events and situations involving other people and to adapt to changing circumstances.

Organizational development is an all-embracing term for the approaches described in this chapter to changing processes, culture and behaviour in the organization as a whole, or at least its significant sub-parts. The changes address the behaviour of groups and individuals but always within the context of the organization and what needs to be done to improve its effectiveness. These approaches consist of:

- organization development (OD);
- change management;
- team building;
- culture change or management;
- total quality management;
- business process re-engineering;
- performance management;
- organizational transformation.

ORGANIZATION DEVELOPMENT

Defined

Organization development (OD) has been defined by French and Bell (1990) as:

> A planned systematic process in which applied behavioural science principles and practices are introduced into an ongoing organization towards the goals of effecting organizational improvement, greater organizational competence, and greater organizational effectiveness. The focus is on organizations and their improvement or, to put it another way, *total systems change*. The orientation is on action – achieving desired results as a result of planned activities.

The classic and ambitious approach to OD was described by Bennis (1960) as follows: 'Organization development (OD) is a response to change, a complex educational strategy intended to change the beliefs, attitudes, values, and structure of organizations so that they can better adapt to new technologies, markets, and challenges, and the dizzying rate of change itself.'

A short history of organizational development

Origins of OD

The origin of organizational development (OD) can be traced to the work of Kurt Lewin, who developed the concept of group dynamics (the phrase was first coined in 1939). Group dynamics is concerned with the ways in which groups evolve and how people in groups behave and interact. Lewin founded the Research Centre for Group Dynamics in 1945 and out of this emerged the process of 'T-group' or sensitivity training, in which participants in an unstructured group learn from their own interaction and the evolving dynamics of the group. T-group laboratory training became one of the fundamental OD processes. Lewin also pioneered action research approaches.

The formative years of OD

During the 1950s and 1960s behavioural scientists such as Argyris, Beckhard, Bennis, Blake, McGregor, Schein, Shepart and Tannenbaum developed the concepts and approaches that together represented 'OD'. They defined the scope, purpose and philosophy of OD, methods of conducting OD 'interventions', approaches to 'process consulting' and methodologies such as action research and survey feedback.

OD – the glory years

The later 1960s and the 1970s were the days when behavioural science reigned and OD was seen, at least by behavioural scientists, as the answer to the problem of improving organizational effectiveness. Comprehensive programmes using the various approaches described below were introduced in a number of American businesses such as General Motors and Corning Glass and a few UK companies such as ICI. US research quoted by French and Bell found that positive impacts were made in between 70 and 80 per cent of the cases studied.

OD in decline

Doubt about the validity of OD as a concept was first expressed in the 1970s. Kahn (1974) wrote that: 'It is not a concept, at least not in the scientific sense of the word: it is not precisely defined; it is not reducible to specific, uniform, observable behaviour.'

A typical criticism of OD was made later by McLean (1981) who wrote that: 'There seems to be a growing awareness of the inappropriateness of some of the fundamental values, stances, models and prescriptions inherited from the 1960s. Writers are facing up to the naivete of early beliefs and theories in what might be termed a climate of sobriety and new realism.'

New approaches to improving organizational effectiveness

During the 1980s and 1990s the focus shifted from OD as a behavioural science concept to a number of other approaches. Some of these, such as organizational transformation, are not entirely dissimilar to OD. Others, such as team building, change management and culture change or management, are built on some of the basic ideas developed by writers on organization development and OD practitioners. Yet other approaches, such as total quality management, business process re-engineering and performance management, would be described as holistic processes that attempt to improve overall organizational effectiveness from a particular perspective. The tendency now is to rely more on specific interventions such as performance management, team pay or total quality management, than on all-embracing but somewhat nebulous OD programmes which were often owned by the HR department and its consultants, and not by line management.

Characteristics of the traditional approach to OD

OD concentrated on how things are done as well as what they do. It was a form of applied behavioural science that was concerned with system-wide change. The organization was considered as a total system and the emphasis was on the interrelationships, interactions and interdependencies of different aspects of how systems operate as they transform inputs and outputs and use feedback mechanisms for self-regulation. OD practitioners talked about 'the client system' – meaning that they were dealing with the total organizational system.

OD as originally conceived was based upon the following assumptions and values:

● Most individuals are driven by the need for personal growth and development as long as their environment is both supportive and challenging.

- The work team, especially at the informal level, has great significance for feelings of satisfaction and the dynamics of such teams have a powerful effect on the behaviour of their members.
- OD programmes aimed to improve the quality of working life of all members of the organization.
- Organizations can be more effective if they learn to diagnose their own strengths and weaknesses.
- But managers often do not know what is wrong and need special help in diagnosing problems, although the outside 'process consultant' ensures that decision making remains in the hands of the client.

The three main features of OD programmes were:

- They were managed, or at least strongly supported, from the top but often made use of third parties or 'change agents' to diagnose problems and to manage change by various kinds of planned activity or 'intervention'.
- The plans for organization development were based upon a systematic analysis and diagnosis of the circumstances of the organization and the changes and problems affecting it.
- They used behavioural science knowledge and aimed to improve the way the organization copes in times of change through such processes as interaction, communications, participation, planning and conflict.

The activities that may be incorporated in a traditional OD programme are summarized below.

- Action research. This is an approach developed by Lewin (1947) which takes the form of systematically collecting data from people about process issues and feeds it back in order to identify problems and their likely causes so that action can be taken cooperatively by the people involved to deal with the problem. The essential elements of action research are data collection, diagnosis, feedback, action planning, action and evaluation.
- Survey feedback. This is a variety of action research in which data are systematically collected about the system and then fed back to groups to analyse and interpret as the basis for preparing action plans. The techniques of survey feedback include the use of attitude surveys and workshops to feed back results and discuss implications.
- Interventions. The term 'intervention' in OD refers to core structured activities involving clients and consultants. The activities can take the form of action

research, survey feedback or any of those mentioned below. Argyris (1970) summed up the three primary tasks of the OD practitioner or interventionist as being to:

- generate and help clients to generate valid information that they can under-stand about their problems;
- create opportunities for clients to search effectively for solutions to their prob-lems, to make free choices;
- create conditions for internal commitment to their choices and opportunities for the continual monitoring of the action taken.

● Process consultation. As described by Schein (1969), this involves helping clients to generate and analyse information that they can understand and, following a thorough diagnosis, act upon. The information will relate to organizational processes such as inter-group relations, interpersonal relations and communica-tions. The job of the process consultant was defined by Schein as being to 'help the organization to solve its own problems by making it aware of organizational processes, of the consequences of these processes, and of the mechanisms by which they can be changed'.

● Team-building interventions as discussed later in this chapter. These deal with permanent work teams or those set up to deal with projects or to solve particular problems. Interventions are directed towards the analysis of the effectiveness of team processes such as problem solving, decision making and interpersonal rela-tionships, a diagnosis and discussion of the issues and joint consideration of the actions required to improve effectiveness.

● Inter-group conflict interventions. As developed by Blake *et al* (1964), these aim to improve inter-group relations by getting groups to share their perceptions of one another and to analyse what they have learned about themselves and the other group. The groups involved meet each other to share what they have learnt, to agree on the issues to be resolved and the actions required.

● Personal interventions. These include sensitivity training laboratories (T-groups), transactional analysis and, more recently, neuro-linguistic programming (NLP) as described in Appendix A. Another approach is behaviour modelling, which is based on Bandura's (1977) social learning theory. This states that for people to engage successfully in a behaviour they 1) must perceive a link between the behaviour and certain outcomes, 2) must desire those outcomes (this is termed 'positive valence'), and 3) must believe they can do it (termed 'self-efficacy'). Behaviours-modelling training involves getting a group to identify the problem and develop and practise the skills required by looking at videos showing what skills can be applied, role playing, practising the use of skills on the job and discussing how well they have been applied.

Use of OD

The decline of traditional OD, as described above, has been partly caused by disenchantment with the jargon used by consultants and the unfulfilled expectations of significant improvements in organizational effectiveness. There was also a reaction in the hard-nosed 1980s against the perceived softness of the messages preached by the behavioural scientists. Managements in the later 1980s and 1990s wanted more specific prescriptions which would impact on processes they believed to be important as means of improving performance, such as total quality management, business process re-engineering and performance management. The need to manage change to processes, systems or culture was still recognized as long as it was results driven, rather than activity centred. Team-building activities in the new process-based organizations were also regarded favourably as long as they were directed towards measurable improvements in the shorter term. It was also recognized that organizations were often compelled to transform themselves in the face of massive challenges and external pressures, and traditional OD approaches would not make a sufficient or speedy impact. A survey of the views of chief executives about organizational development, (IPD, 1999b) found that a large proportion of them are expecting greater team contributions, more sophisticated people management practices and processes for managing knowledge. As the IPD commented, 'HR has a pivotal role in developing the behaviours and culture to support the delivery of these strategies.'

CHANGE MANAGEMENT

The change process

Conceptually, the change process starts with an awareness of the need for change. An analysis of this situation and the factors that have created it leads to a diagnosis of their distinctive characteristics and an indication of the direction in which action needs to be taken. Possible courses of action can then be identified and evaluated and a choice made of the preferred action.

It is then necessary to decide how to get from here to there. Managing change during this transition state is a critical phase in the change process. It is here that the problems of introducing change emerge and have to be managed. These problems can include resistance to change, low stability, high levels of stress, misdirected energy, conflict and loss of momentum. Hence the need to do everything possible to anticipate reactions and likely impediments to the introduction of change.

The installation stage can also be painful. When planning change there is a tendency for people to think that it will be an entirely logical and linear process of going from A to B. It is not like that at all. As described by Pettigrew and Whipp (1991), the implementation of change is an 'iterative, cumulative and reformulation-in-use process'.

To manage change, it is first necessary to understand the types of change and why people resist change. It is important to bear in mind that while those wanting change need to be constant about ends, they have to be flexible about means. This requires them to come to an understanding of the various models of change that have been developed. In the light of an understanding of these models they will be better equipped to make use of the guidelines for change set out at the end of this section.

Types of change

There are two main types of change: strategic and operational.

Strategic change

Strategic change is concerned with organizational transformation as described in the last section of this chapter. It deals with broad, long-term and organization-wide issues. It is about moving to a future state, which has been defined generally in terms of strategic vision and scope. It will cover the purpose and mission of the organization, its corporate philosophy on such matters as growth, quality, innovation and values concerning people, the customer needs served and the technologies employed. This overall definition leads to specifications of competitive positioning and strategic goals for achieving and maintaining competitive advantage and for product-market development. These goals are supported by policies concerning marketing, sales, manufacturing, product and process development, finance and human resource management.

Strategic change takes place within the context of the external competitive, economic and social environment, and the organization's internal resources, capabilities, culture, structure and systems. Its successful implementation requires thorough analysis and understanding of these factors in the formulation and planning stages. The ultimate achievement of sustainable competitive advantage relies on the qualities defined by Pettigrew and Whipp (1991), namely: 'The capacity of the firm to identify and understand the competitive forces in play and how they change over time, linked to the competence of a business to mobilize and manage the resources necessary for the chosen competitive response through time.'

Strategic change, however, should not be treated simplistically as a linear process of getting from A to B which can be planned and executed as a logical sequence of events. Pettigrew and Whipp (1991) issued the following warning based on their research into competitiveness and managing change in the motor, financial services, insurance and publishing industries:

> The process by which strategic changes are made seldom moves directly through neat, successive stages of analysis, choice and implementation. Changes in the firm's environment persistently threaten the course and logic of strategic changes: dilemma abounds… . We conclude that one of the defining features of the process, in so far as management action is concerned, is ambiguity; seldom is there an easily isolated logic to strategic change. Instead, that process may derive its motive force from an amalgam of economic, personal and political imperatives. Their introduction through time requires that those responsible for managing that process make continual assessments, repeated choices and multiple adjustments.

Operational change

Operational change relates to new systems, procedures, structures or technology which will have an immediate effect on working arrangements within a part of the organization. But their impact on people can be more significant than broader strategic change and they have to be handled just as carefully.

Resistance to change

Why people resist change

People resist change because it is seen as a threat to familiar patterns of behaviour as well as to status and financial rewards. Joan Woodward (1968) made this point clearly:

> When we talk about resistance to change we tend to imply that management is always rational in changing its direction, and that employees are stupid, emotional or irrational in not responding in the way they should. But if an individual is going to be worse off, explicitly or implicitly, when the proposed changes have been made, any resistance is entirely rational in terms of his own best interest. The interests of the organization and the individual do not always coincide.

Specifically, the main reasons for resisting change are as follows:

● *The shock of the new* – people are suspicious of anything which they perceive will upset their established routines, methods of working or conditions of employment. They do not want to lose the security of what is familiar to them. They may not believe statements by management that the change is for their benefit as well as that of the organization; sometimes with good reason. They may feel that management has ulterior motives and, sometimes, the louder the protestations of managements, the less they will be believed.

- *Economic fears* – loss of money, threats to job security.
- *Inconvenience* – the change will make life more difficult.
- *Uncertainty* – change can be worrying because of uncertainty about its likely impact.
- *Symbolic fears* – a small change that may affect some treasured symbol, such as a separate office or a reserved parking space, may symbolize big ones, especially when employees are uncertain about how extensive the programme of change will be.
- *Threat to interpersonal relationships* – anything that disrupts the customary social relationships and standards of the group will be resisted.
- *Threat to status or skill* – the change is perceived as reducing the status of individuals or as de-skilling them.
- *Competence fears* – concern about the ability to cope with new demands or to acquire new skills.

Overcoming resistance to change

Resistance to change can be difficult to overcome even when it is not detrimental to those concerned. But the attempt must be made. The first step is to analyse the potential impact of change by considering how it will affect people in their jobs. The analysis should indicate which aspects of the proposed change may be supported generally or by specified individuals and which aspects may be resisted. So far as possible, the potentially hostile or negative reactions of people should be identified, taking into account all the possible reasons for resisting change listed above. It is necessary to try to understand the likely feelings and fears of those affected so that unnecessary worries can be relieved and, as far as possible, ambiguities can be resolved. In making this analysis, the individual introducing the change, who is sometimes called the 'change agent', should recognize that new ideas are likely to be suspect and should make ample provision for the discussion of reactions to proposals to ensure complete understanding of them.

Involvement in the change process gives people the chance to raise and resolve their concerns and make suggestions about the form of the change and how it should be introduced. The aim is to get 'ownership' – a feeling amongst people that the change is something that they are happy to live with because they have been involved in its planning and introduction – it has become *their* change.

Communications about the proposed change should be carefully prepared and worded so that unnecessary fears are allayed. All the available channels as described in Chapter 52 should be used, but face-to-face communications direct from managers to individuals or through a team briefing system are best.

Change models

The best-known change models are those developed by Lewin (1951) and Beckhard (1969). But other important contributions to an understanding of the mechanisms for change have been made by Thurley (1979), Bandura (1986) and Beer *et al* (1990).

Lewin

The basic mechanisms for managing change, according to Lewin (1951), are as follows:

- *Unfreezing* – altering the present stable equilibrium which supports existing behaviours and attitudes. This process must take account of the inherent threats that change presents to people and the need to motivate those affected to attain the natural state of equilibrium by accepting change.
- *Changing* – developing new responses based on new information.
- *Refreezing* – stabilizing the change by introducing the new responses into the personalities of those concerned.

Lewin also suggested a methodology for analysing change which he called 'field force analysis'. This involves:

- analysing the restraining or driving forces that will affect the transition to the future state; these restraining forces will include the reactions of those who see change as unnecessary or as constituting a threat;
- assessing which of the driving or restraining forces are critical;
- taking steps both to increase the critical driving forces and to decrease the critical restraining forces.

Beckhard

According to Beckhard (1969), a change programme should incorporate the following processes:

- setting goals and defining the future state or organizational conditions desired after the change;
- diagnosing the present condition in relation to these goals;
- defining the transition state activities and commitments required to meet the future state;
- developing strategies and action plans for managing this transition in the light of an analysis of the factors likely to affect the introduction of change.

Thurley

Thurley (1979) described the following five approaches to managing change:

- *Directive* – the imposition of change in crisis situations or when other methods have failed. This is done by the exercise of managerial power without consultation.
- *Bargained* – this approach recognizes that power is shared between the employer and the employed and that change requires negotiation, compromise and agreement before being implemented.
- *'Hearts and minds'* – an all-embracing thrust to change the attitudes, values and beliefs of the whole workforce. This 'normative' approach (ie one that starts from a definition of what management thinks is right or 'normal') seeks 'commitment' and 'shared vision' but does not necessarily include involvement or participation.
- *Analytical* – a theoretical approach to the change process using models of change such as those described above. It proceeds sequentially from the analysis and diagnosis of the situation, through the setting of objectives, the design of the change process, the evaluation of the results and, finally, the determination of the objectives for the next stage in the change process. This is the rational and logical approach much favoured by consultants – external and internal. But change seldom proceeds as smoothly as this model would suggest. Emotions, power politics and external pressures mean that the rational approach, although it might be the right way to start, is difficult to sustain.
- *Action-based* – this recognizes that the way managers behave in practice bears little resemblance to the analytical, theoretical model. The distinction between managerial thought and managerial action blurs in practice to the point of invisibility. What managers think is what they do. Real life therefore often results in a 'ready, aim, fire' approach to change management. This typical approach to change starts with a broad belief that some sort of problem exists, although it may not be well defined. The identification of possible solutions, often on a trial and

error basis, leads to a clarification of the nature of the problem and a shared understanding of a possible optimal solution, or at least a framework within which solutions can be discovered.

Bandura

The ways in which people change were described by Bandura (1986) as follows:

1. People make conscious choices about their behaviours.
2. The information people use to make their choices comes from their environment.
3. Their choices are based upon:
   - the things that are important to them;
   - the views they have about their own abilities to behave in certain ways;
   - the consequences they think will accrue to whatever behaviour they decide to engage in.

For those concerned in change management, the implications of this theory are that:

- the tighter the link between a particular behaviour and a particular outcome, the more likely it is that we will engage in that behaviour;
- the more desirable the outcome, the more likely it is that we will engage in behaviour that we believe will lead to it;
- the more confident we are that we can actually assume a new behaviour, the more likely we are to try it.

To change people's behaviour, therefore, we have first to change the environment within which they work, secondly, convince them that the new behaviour is something they can accomplish (training is important) and, thirdly, persuade them that it will lead to an outcome that they will value. None of these steps is easy.

Beer *et al*

Michael Beer (1990) and his colleagues suggested in a seminal *Harvard Business Review* article, 'Why change programs don't produce change', that most such programmes are guided by a theory of change that is fundamentally flawed. This theory states that changes in attitudes lead to changes in behaviour. 'According to this model, change is like a conversion experience. Once people "get religion", changes in their behaviour will surely follow.' They believe that this theory gets the change process exactly backwards:

In fact, individual behaviour is powerfully shaped by the organizational roles people play. The most effective way to change behaviour, therefore, is to put people into a new organizational context, which imposes new roles, responsibilities and relationships on them. This creates a situation that in a sense 'forces' new attitudes and behaviour on people.

They prescribe six steps to effective change, which concentrate on what they call 'task alignment' – reorganizing employees' roles, responsibilities and relationships to solve specific business problems in small units where goals and tasks can be clearly defined. The aim of following the overlapping steps is to build a self-reinforcing cycle of commitment, coordination and competence. The steps are:

1. Mobilize commitment to change through the joint analysis of problems.
2. Develop a shared vision of how to organize and manage to achieve goals such as competitiveness.
3. Foster consensus for the new vision, competence to enact it, and cohesion to move it along.
4. Spread revitalization to all departments without pushing it from the top – don't force the issue, let each department find its own way to the new organization.
5. Institutionalize revitalization through formal policies, systems and structures.
6. Monitor and adjust strategies in response to problems in the revitalization process.

Guidelines for change management

- The achievement of sustainable change requires strong commitment and visionary leadership from the top.
- Understanding is necessary of the culture of the organization and the levers for change that are most likely to be effective in that culture.
- Those concerned with managing change at all levels should have the temperament and leadership skills appropriate to the circumstances of the organization and its change strategies.
- It is important to build a working environment that is conducive to change. This means developing the firm as a 'learning organization'.
- People support what they help to create. Commitment to change is improved if those affected by change are allowed to participate as fully as possible in planning and implementing it. The aim should be to get them to 'own' the change as something they want and will be glad to live with.

- The reward system should encourage innovation and recognize success in achieving change.
- Change will always involve failure as well as success. The failures must be expected and learned from.
- Hard evidence and data on the need for change are the most powerful tools for its achievement, but establishing the need for change is easier than deciding how to satisfy it.
- It is easier to change behaviour by changing processes, structure and systems than to change attitudes or the corporate culture.
- There are always people in organizations who can act as champions of change. They will welcome the challenges and opportunities that change can provide. They are the ones to be chosen as change agents.
- Resistance to change is inevitable if the individuals concerned feel that they are going to be worse off – implicitly or explicitly. The inept management of change will produce that reaction.
- In an age of global competition, technological innovation, turbulence, disconti-nuity, even chaos, change is inevitable and necessary. The organization must do all it can to explain why change is essential and how it will affect everyone. Moreover, every effort must be made to protect the interests of those affected by change.

ORGANIZATIONAL TRANSFORMATION

Defined

Transformation, according to Webster's Dictionary, is: 'A change in the shape, structure, nature of something'. Organizational transformation is the process of ensuring that an organization can develop and implement major change programmes that will ensure that it responds strategically to new demands and continues to func-tion effectively in the dynamic environment in which it operates. Organizational transformation activities may involve radical changes to the structure, culture and processes of the organization – the way it looks at the world. This may be in response to competitive pressures, mergers, acquisitions, investments, disinvest-ments, changes in technology, product lines, markets, cost reduction exercises and decisions to downsize or outsource work. Transformational change may be forced on an organization by investors or government decisions. It may be initiated by a new chief executive and top management team with a remit to 'turn round' the business.

Transformational change means that significant and far-reaching developments are planned and implemented in corporate structures and organization-wide processes.

The change is neither incremental (bit by bit) nor transactional (concerned solely with systems and procedures). Transactional change, according to Pascale (1990), is merely concerned with the alteration of ways in which the organization does business and people interact with one another on a day-to-day basis, and 'is effective when what you want is more of what you've already got'. He advocates a 'discontinuous improvement in capability' and this he describes as transformation.

A distinction can also be made between first-order and second-order transformational development. First-order development is concerned with changes to the ways in which particular parts of the organization function. Second-order change aims to make an impact on the whole organization.

The distinction between organizational transformation and organization development

Organizational transformation programmes are business-led. They focus on what needs to be done to ensure that the business performs more effectively in adding value, especially for its owners, and achieving competitive advantage. They will be concerned with building strategic capability and improving the ways in which the business reaches its goals. This means considering what needs to be done to ensure that people work and interact well, but they are not dominated by the concepts of behavioural science, as was the case in traditional OD interventions.

Types of transformational change

The four types of transformational change as identified by Beckhard (1989) are:

- *a change in what drives the organization* – for example, a change from being production-driven to being market-driven would be transformational;
- *a fundamental change in the relationships between or among organizational parts* – for example, decentralization;
- *a major change in the ways of doing work* – for example, the introduction of new technology such as computer-integrated manufacturing;
- *a basic, cultural change in norms, values or research systems* – for example, developing a customer-focused culture.

Transformation through leadership

Transformation programmes are led from the top within the organization. They do not rely on an external 'change agent' as did traditional OD interventions, although specialist external advice might be obtained on aspects of the transformation such as strategic planning, reorganization or developing new reward processes.

The prerequisite for a successful programme is the presence of a transformational leader who, as defined by Burns (1978), motivates others to strive for higher-order goals rather than merely short-term interest. Transformational leaders go beyond dealing with day-to-day management problems; they commit people to action and focus on the development of new levels of awareness of where the future lies, and commitment to achieving that future. Burns contrasts transformational leaders with transactional leaders who operate by building up a network of interpersonal transactions in a stable situation and who enlist compliance rather than commitment through the reward system and the exercise of authority and power. Transactional leaders may be good at dealing with here-and-now problems but they will not provide the vision required to transform the future.

Managing the transition

The transition from where the organization is to where the organization wants to be is the critical part of a transformation programme. It is during the transition period of getting from here to there that change takes place. Transition management starts from a definition of the future state and a diagnosis of the present state. It is then necessary to define what has to be done to achieve the transformation. This means deciding on the new processes, systems, procedures, structures, products and markets to be developed. Having defined these, the work can be programmed and the resources required (people, money, equipment and time) can be defined. The plan for managing the transition should include provisions for involving people in the process and for communicating to them about what is happening, why it is happening and how it will affect them. Clearly the aims are to get as many people as possible committed to the change.

The transformation programme

The eight steps required to transform an organization have been summed up by Kotter (1995) as follows:

1. *Establishing a sense of urgency*
   - Examining market and competitive realities
   - Identifying and discussing crises, potential crises, or major opportunities
2. *Forming a powerful guiding coalition*
   - Assembling a group with enough power to lead the change effort
   - Encouraging the group to work together as a team

3. *Creating a vision*
    ● Creating a vision to help direct the change effort
    ● Developing strategies for achieving that vision
4. *Communicating the vision*
    ● Using every vehicle possible to communicate the new vision and strategies
    ● Teaching new behaviours by the example of the guiding coalition
5. *Empowering others to act on the vision*
    ● Getting rid of obstacles to change
    ● Changing systems or structures that seriously undermine the vision
    ● Encouraging risk taking and non-traditional ideas, activities and actions
6. *Planning for and creating short-term wins*
    ● Planning for visible performance improvement
    ● Creating those improvements
    ● Recognizing and rewarding employees involved in the improvements
7. *Consolidating improvements and producing still more change*
    ● Using increased credibility to change systems, structures and policies that don't fit the vision
    ● Hiring, promoting and developing employees who can implement the vision
    ● Reinvigorating the process with new projects, themes and change agents
8. *Institutionalizing new approaches*
    ● Articulating the connections between the new behaviours and corporate success
    ● Developing the means to ensure leadership development and succession.

The role of HR in organizational transformation

HR can and should play a key role in organizational transition and transformation programmes. It can provide help and guidance in analysis and diagnosis, highlighting the people issues that will fundamentally affect the success of the programme. HR can advise on resourcing the programme and planning and implementing the vital training, reward, communications and involvement aspects of the process. It can anticipate people problems and deal with them before they become serious. If the programme does involve restructuring and downsizing, HR can advise on how this should be done humanely and with the minimum disruption to people's lives.

DEVELOPMENT AND CHANGE PROCESSES

Team building

Team-building activities aim to improve and develop the effectiveness of a group of people who work (permanently or temporarily) together. This improvement may be defined in terms of outputs, for example the speed and quality of the decisions and actions produced by the team. It may also be defined in more nebulous terms, such as the quality of relationships or greater cooperation. The activities in team-building programmes can:

- increase awareness of the social processes that take place within teams;
- develop the interactive or interpersonal skills that enable individuals to function effectively as team members;
- increase the overall effectiveness with which teams operate in the organization.

To be effective, team-building programmes should be directly relevant to the responsibilities of the participants and be seen as relevant by all participants. They need to support business objectives, fit in with practical working arrangements and reflect the values the organization wishes to promote. Approaches such as action learning, group dynamics, group exercises, interactive skills training, interactive video, role-playing and simulation can be used. Team-building training is often based on either Belbin or Margerison and McCann classifications of team roles as listed in Chapter 12.

Outdoor learning (outdoor-based development) is another good method of providing team-building training. It can offer a closer approximation to reality than other forms of training. Participants tend to behave more normally and, paradoxically, it is precisely because the tasks are unrelated to work activities and are relatively simple that they highlight the processes involved in teamwork and provide a good basis for identifying how these processes can be improved.

Total quality management

Total quality management is an intensive, long-term effort directed at the creation and maintenance of the high standards of product quality and services expected by customers. As such, it can operate as a major influence in developing the culture and processes of the organization. The object is significantly to increase the awareness of all employees that quality is vital to the organization's success and their future. The business must be transformed into an entity that exists to deliver value to customers by satisfying their needs.

Business process re-engineering

Business process re-engineering examines processes horizontally in organizations to establish how they can be integrated more effectively and streamlined. Re-engineering exercises can provide an overall approach to developing an organization but they often promise more than they achieve and they have been criticized because they pay insufficient attention to the human element.

Performance management

Performance management as a holistic – all-embracing – process for managing performance throughout an organization is one of the most commonly used instruments for improving organizational effectiveness. It is described in Part VIII.

19

Job and role design

JOBS AND ROLES

A *job* consists of a related set of tasks that are carried out by a person to fulfil a purpose. It can be regarded as a unit in an organization structure that remains unchanged whoever is in the job. A job in this sense is a fixed entity, part of a machine that can be 'designed' like any other part of a machine. Routine or machine-controlled jobs do indeed exist in most organizations but, increasingly, the work carried out by people is not mechanistic. What is done, how it is done and the results achieved depend more and more on the capabilities and motivation of individuals and their interactions with one another and their customers or suppliers.

The rigidity inherent in the notion of a job is not in accord with the realities of organizational life for many people. A flexible approach is often required to use and develop their skills to innovate in the face of new opportunities and challenges and to respond swiftly to the new demands they face every day. The significance of teamwork and the need to be multi-skilled also suggest that an old-fashioned approach to job design may be inappropriate.

The concept of a *role* conveys these realities more than that of a *job*. Essentially, a role is the part people play in carrying out their work. A role can therefore be described in behavioural terms – given certain expectations, this is how the person needs to behave to meet them. A role profile will not spell out the tasks to be carried out but will instead indicate expectations in the form of outputs and outcomes and competency requirements in the shape of the inputs of skill and behaviours required to fulfil these expectations. The definition may be broad. It will not be prescriptive. Scope will be allowed for individuals to use their skills in accordance with their interpretation of the situation. Encouragement will be given for people both to grow in their roles and to grow their roles by developing their competencies and by extending the range of their responsibilities so that their contributions exceed expectations.

Roles are therefore more about people than jobs and this means that the extent to which a role can be 'designed' may be limited or even non-existent where flexibility and growth are important. This may apply particularly to knowledge workers.

There are, however, certain considerations that affect the ways in which roles can be developed in order to increase satisfaction with the work and to encourage growth. These considerations can also apply to jobs and this chapter therefore starts with a general review of the factors that affect job design and that are also relevant to role building. Attention is then directed to approaches to job design, which include the notions of job enlargement and job enrichment. Consideration is next given to the characteristics of team roles and what can be done to set up and maintain effective self-managed teams and high-performance work design. Finally, the focus is on roles and how they can be *built* rather than designed in today's flexible organizations on the basis of an understanding of what role holders are expected to achieve, the scope they have to go beyond these basic expectations and the capabilities they need to carry out and extend their role. This includes an examination of the concept of job enrichment.

FACTORS AFFECTING JOB DESIGN

The content of jobs is affected by the purpose of the organization or the organizational unit, the particular demands that achieving that purpose makes on the people involved, the structure of the organization, the processes and activities carried out in the organization, the technology of the organization, the changes that are taking place in that technology and the environment in which the organization operates. Job design has therefore to be considered within the context of organizational design, as described in Chapter 17, but it must also take into account the following factors:

● the process of intrinsic motivation;
● the characteristics of task structure;
● the motivating characteristics of jobs;
● the significance of the job characteristics model;
● providing intrinsic motivation.

The process of intrinsic motivation

The case for using job design techniques is based on the premise that effective performance and genuine satisfaction in work follow mainly from the intrinsic content of the job. This is related to the fundamental concept that people are motivated when they are provided with the means to achieve their goals. Work provides the means to earn money, which as an extrinsic reward satisfies basic needs and is instrumental in providing ways of satisfying higher-level needs. But work also provides intrinsic rewards, which are under the direct control of the worker.

Characteristics of task structure

Job design requires the assembly of a number of tasks into a job or a group of jobs. An individual may carry out one main task, which consists of a number of interrelated elements or functions. Or task functions may be allocated to a team working closely together in a manufacturing 'cell' or customer service unit, or strung along an assembly line. In more complex jobs, individuals may carry out a variety of connected tasks, each with a number of functions, or these tasks may be allocated to a team of workers or divided between them. In the latter case, the tasks may require a variety of skills, which have to be possessed by all members of the team (multi-skilling) in order to work flexibly.

Complexity in a job may be a reflection of the number and variety of tasks to be carried out, the different skills or competences to be used, the range and scope of the decisions that have to be made, or the difficulty of predicting the outcome of decisions.

The internal structure of each task consists of three elements: planning (deciding on the course of action, its timing and the resources required), executing (carrying out the plan), and controlling (monitoring performance and progress and taking corrective action when required). A completely integrated job includes all these elements for each of the tasks involved. The worker, or group of workers, having been given objectives in terms of output, quality and cost targets, decides on how the work is to be done, assembles the resources, performs the work, and monitors output, quality and cost standards. Responsibility in a job is measured by the amount of authority someone has to do all these things.

Motivating characteristics of jobs

The ideal arrangement from the point of view of intrinsic motivation is to provide for fully integrated jobs containing all three task elements. In practice, management and team leaders are often entirely responsible for planning and control, leaving the worker responsible for execution. To a degree, this is inevitable, but one of the aims of job design is often to extend the responsibility of workers into the functions of planning and control. This can involve empowerment – giving individuals and teams more responsibility for decision making and ensuring that they have the training, support and guidance to exercise that responsibility properly.

The job characteristics model

A useful perspective on the factors affecting job design and motivation is provided by Hackman and Oldham's (1974) job characteristics model. They suggest that the 'critical psychological states' of 'experienced meaningfulness of work, experienced responsibility for outcomes of work and knowledge of the actual outcomes of work' strongly influence motivation, job satisfaction and performance.

As Robertson *et al* (1992) point out: 'This element of the model is based on the notion of personal reward and reinforcement... Reinforcement is obtained when a person becomes aware (knowledge of results) that he or she has been responsible for (experienced responsibility) and good performance on a task that he or she cares about (experienced meaningfulness).'

Providing intrinsic motivation

Three characteristics have been distinguished by Lawler (1969) as being required in jobs if they are to be intrinsically motivating:

- *Feedback* – individuals must receive meaningful feedback about their performance, preferably by evaluating their own performance and defining the feedback. This implies that they should ideally work on a complete product, or a significant part of it that can be seen as a whole.
- *Use of abilities* – the job must be perceived by individuals as requiring them to use abilities they value in order to perform the job effectively.
- *Self-control* – individuals must feel that they have a high degree of self-control over setting their own goals and over defining the paths to these goals.

JOB DESIGN

Job design has been defined by Davis (1966) as: 'The specification of the contents, methods, and relationships of jobs in order to satisfy technological and organizational requirements as well as the social and personal requirements of the job holder'.

Job design has two aims: first, to satisfy the requirements of the organization for productivity, operational efficiency and quality of product or service, and second, to satisfy the needs of the individual for interest, challenge and accomplishment, thus providing for 'job engagement' – commitment to carrying out the job well. Clearly, these aims are interrelated and the overall objective of job design is to integrate the needs of the individual with those of the organization.

The process of job design starts, as described in Chapter 23, from an analysis of what work needs to be done – the tasks that have to be carried out if the purpose of the organization or an organizational unit is to be achieved. The job designer can then consider how the jobs can be set up to provide the maximum degree of intrinsic motivation for those who have to carry them out with a view to improving performance and productivity. Consideration has also to be given to another important aim of job design: to fulfil the social responsibilities of the organization to the people who work in it by improving the quality of working life, an aim which, as stated in Wilson's (1973) report on this subject, 'depends upon both efficiency of performance and satisfaction of the worker'. The outcome of job design may be a job description as explained in Chapter 23.

Principles of job design

Robertson and Smith (1985) suggest the following five principles of job design:

- To influence skill variety, provide opportunities for people to do several tasks and combine tasks.
- To influence task identity, combine tasks and form natural work units.
- To influence task significance, form natural work units and inform people of the importance of their work.
- To influence autonomy, give people responsibility for determining their own working systems.
- To influence feedback, establish good relationships and open feedback channels.

Turner and Lawrence (1965) identified six important characteristics, which they called 'requisite task characteristics', namely: variety, autonomy, required interactions, optional interactions, knowledge and skill, and responsibility. And Cooper (1973) outlined four conceptually distinct job dimensions: variety, discretion, contribution and goal characteristics.

An integrated view suggests that the following motivating characteristics are of prime importance in job design:

- autonomy, discretion, self-control and responsibility;
- variety;
- use of abilities;
- feedback;
- belief that the task is significant.

These are the bases of the approach used in job enrichment, as described later in this chapter.

Approaches to job design

The main job design approaches are:

- *Job rotation*, which comprises the movement of employees from one task to another to reduce monotony by increasing variety.
- *Job enlargement*, which means combining previously fragmented tasks into one job, again to increase the variety and meaning of repetitive work.
- *Job enrichment*, which goes beyond job enlargement to add greater autonomy and responsibility to a job and is based on the job characteristics approach.
- *Self-managing teams (autonomous work groups)* – these are self-regulating teams who work largely without direct supervision. The philosophy on which this technique is based is a logical extension of job enrichment but is strongly influenced by socio-technical systems theory (see Chapter 11).
- *High-performance work design*, which concentrates on setting up working groups in environments where high levels of performance are required.

Of these five approaches, it is generally recognized that, although job rotation and job enlargement have their uses in developing skills and relieving monotony, they do not go to the root of the requirements for intrinsic motivation and for meeting the various motivating characteristics of jobs as described above. These are best satisfied by using, as appropriate, job enrichment, autonomous work groups or high-performance work design.

JOB ENRICHMENT

Job enrichment aims to maximize the interest and challenge of work by providing the employee with a job that has these characteristics:

- It is a complete piece of work in the sense that the worker can identify a series of tasks or activities that end in a recognizable and definable product.

- It affords the employee as much variety, decision-making responsibility and control as possible in carrying out the work.
- It provides direct feedback through the work itself on how well the employee is doing his or her job.

Job enrichment as proposed by Herzberg (1968) is not just increasing the number or variety of tasks; nor is it the provision of opportunities for job rotation. It is claimed by supporters of job enrichment that these approaches may relieve boredom, but they do not result in positive increases in motivation.

Impact of job enrichment

The advocates of job enrichment have been so dedicated to their cause that one cannot help feeling sometimes that their enthusiasm for the philosophy of their movement has clouded their judgement of its real benefits to the organization, let alone to the individuals who are supposed to have been enriched.

There have been a number of case studies that have indicated success, although this has often been measured in subjective terms. But a study by Hulin and Blood (1968) of all relevant research on job enrichment concluded that the effects of job enrichment on job satisfaction or worker motivation are generally overstated and in some cases unfounded. They argue convincingly that many shop-floor workers are not alienated from the work environment but are alienated from the work norms and values of the middle class, especially its belief in the work-related elements of the Protestant ethic and in the virtue of striving for the attainment of responsible positions.

Fein's (1970) study of worker motivation reached essentially the same conclusion. He states:

> Workers do not look upon their work as fulfilling their existence. Their reaction to their work is the opposite of what the behaviouralists predict. It is only because workers choose not to find fulfilment in their work that they are able to function as healthy human beings. By rejecting involvement in their work which simply cannot be fulfilling, workers save their sanity.... The concepts of McGregor and Herzberg regarding workers' needs to find fulfilment through their work are sound only for those workers who choose to find fulfilment through their work.... Contrary to their postulates, the majority of workers seek fulfilment outside their work.

SELF-MANAGING TEAMS

A self-managing team or autonomous work group is allocated an overall task and given discretion over how the work is done. This provides for intrinsic motivation by giving people autonomy and the means to control their work, which will include feedback information. The basis of the autonomous work group approach to job design is socio-technical systems theory, which suggests that the best results are obtained if grouping is such that workers are primarily related to each other by way of task performance and task interdependence. As Emery (1980) has stated:

> In designing a social system to efficiently operate a modern capital-intensive plant the key problem is that of creating self-managing groups to man the interface with the technical system.

A self-managing team:

- enlarges individual jobs to include a wider range of operative skills (multi-skilling);
- decides on methods of work and the planning, scheduling and control of work;
- distributes tasks itself among its members.

The advocates of self-managing teams or autonomous work groups claim that this approach offers a more comprehensive view of organizations than the rather simplistic individual motivation theories that underpin job rotation, enlargement and enrichment. Be that as it may, the strength of this system is that it does take account of the social or group factors and the technology as well as the individual motivators.

HIGH-PERFORMANCE WORK DESIGN

High-performance work design, as described by Buchanan (1987), requires the following steps:

- Management clearly defines what it needs in the form of new technology or methods of production and the results expected from its introduction.
- Multi-skilling is encouraged – that is, job demarcation lines are eliminated as far as possible and encouragement and training are provided for employees to acquire new skills.
- Equipment that can be used flexibly is selected and is laid out to allow freedom of movement and vision.

- Self-managed teams or autonomous working groups are established, each with around a dozen members and with full 'back-to-back' responsibility for product assembly and testing, fault-finding and some maintenance.
- Managers and team leaders adopt a supportive rather than an autocratic style (this is the most difficult part of the system to introduce).
- Support systems are provided for kit-marshalling and material supply, which help the teams to function effectively as productive units.
- Management sets goals and standards for success.
- The new system is introduced with great care by means of involvement and communication programmes.
- Thorough training is carried out on the basis of an assessment of training needs.
- The payment system is specially designed with employee participation to fit their needs as well as those of management.
- Payment may be related to team performance (team pay), but with skill-based pay for individuals.
- In some cases, a 'peer performance review' process may be used which involves team members assessing one another's performance as well as the performance of the team as a whole.

ROLE BUILDING

Role building is a continuous process which is a matter between managers or team leaders and the people who report to them. It involves agreeing definitions of accountabilities, objectives and competence requirements. These may be changing significantly, and it is important to achieve mutual understanding of expectations. Roles will be developed as people develop in them – responding to opportunities and changing demands, acquiring new skills and developing competencies. This process may take place within the framework of performance management as described in Part VIII, where the performance agreement, which is updated regularly, spells out the outcomes (key result areas) and the competency requirements. It is necessary to ensure that managers, team leaders and employees generally acquire the skills necessary to define roles within the performance management framework. Ways in which role definitions can be expressed are described in Chapter 23.

Part VI

Human resource management processes

Human resource management processes are those concerned with the development of HR policies and practices that affect all aspects of HR and employment management. This part also covers another processes that affect most aspects of HRM, namely knowledge management and job, role and competence analysis.

20

HRM policies

WHAT ARE HR POLICIES?

HR policies are continuing guidelines on the approach the organization intends to adopt in managing its people. They define the philosophies and values of the organization on how people should be treated, and from these are derived the principles upon which managers are expected to act when dealing with HR matters. HR policies therefore serve as reference points when human resource management practices are being developed and when decisions are being made about people. They help to define 'the way things are done around here'. HR policies should be distinguished from procedures as discussed in Chapter 56. A policy provides generalized guidance on the approach adopted by the organization, and therefore its employees, concerning various aspects of employment. A procedure spells out precisely what action should be taken in line with the policy.

WHY HAVE HR POLICIES?

HR or employment policies help to ensure that when dealing with matters concerning people an approach in line with corporate values is adopted throughout the organization. They provide frameworks within which consistent decisions are made and promote equity in the way in which people are treated. Because they provide guidance on what managers should do in particular circumstances, they facilitate decentralization and delegation. And, while they should fit the corporate culture, they can also help to shape it.

DO POLICIES NEED TO BE FORMALIZED?

All organizations have HR policies. Some, however, exist implicitly as a philosophy of management and an attitude to employees that is expressed in the way in which HR issues are handled; for example, the introduction of new technology. The advantage of explicit policies in terms of consistency and understanding may appear to be obvious, but there are disadvantages: written policies can be inflexible, constrictive, platitudinous, or all three. To a degree, policies often have to be expressed in abstract terms and managers do not care for abstractions. But they do prefer to know where they stand – people like structure – and formalized HR policies can provide the guidelines they need.

Formalized HR policies can be used in induction, team leader and management training to help participants understand the philosophies and values of the organization and how they are expected to behave within that context.

HR POLICY AREAS

HR policies can be expressed as overall statements of the philosophy of the organization and of its values, and as guidelines in specific areas. The main points that can be included in an overall policy statement and specific policy areas are set out below.

Overall policy

The overall policy defines how the organization fulfils its social responsibilities for its employees and sets out its attitudes towards them. It is an expression of its values or beliefs about how people should be treated. Peters and Waterman (1982) wrote that if they were asked for one all-purpose bit of advice for management, one truth that they could distil from all their research on what makes an organization excellent, it would be: 'Figure out your value system. Decide what the organization stands for.' Selznick (1957) emphasized the key role of values in organizations, when he wrote: 'The formation of an institution is marked by the making of value commitments, that is, choices which fix the assumptions of policy makers as to the nature of the enterprise, its distinctive aims, methods and roles.'

The values expressed in an overall statement of HR policies may explicitly or implicitly refer to the following concepts:

- *Equity* – treating employees fairly and justly by adopting an 'even-handed' approach. This includes protecting individuals from any unfair decisions made by their managers, providing equal opportunities for employment and promotion, and operating an equitable payment system.
- *Consideration* – taking account of individual circumstances when making decisions which affect the prospects, security or self-respect of employees.
- *Quality of working life* – consciously and continually aiming to improve the quality of working life and to achieve work-life balance as a means of increasing motivation and improving results. This involves increasing the sense of satisfaction people obtain from their work by, so far as possible, reducing monotony, increasing variety and responsibility, empowerment, and avoiding placing people under too much stress.
- *Working conditions* – providing healthy, safe and, so far as practicable, pleasant working conditions.

These values are espoused by many organizations in one form or another. But to what extent are they practised when making 'business-led' decisions, which can, of course, be highly detrimental to employees if, for example, they lead to redundancy? The principle of mutuality, 'what's good for the business is good for the people in the business', sounds suspiciously like the President of General Motors saying 'what's good for General Motors is good for America'.

One of the dilemmas facing all those who formulate HR policies is: 'How can we pursue business-led policies focusing on business success *and* fulfil our obligations to employees in such terms as equity, consideration, quality of working life and working conditions?' To argue, as some do, that HR policies should be entirely business-led seems to imply that human considerations are unimportant. Organizations have obligations to all their stakeholders, not just their owners.

It may be difficult to express these policies in anything but generalized terms but employers are increasingly having to recognize that they are subject to external as well as internal pressures, which act as constraints on the extent to which they can disregard the higher standards of behaviour towards their employees that are expected of them.

Employment policies

Employment policies cover the following areas:

- *Human resource planning* – a commitment by the organization to planning ahead in order to maximize the opportunities for employees to develop their careers within the organization and to minimize the possibility of compulsory redundancy.
- *Quality of employees* – an organization may deliberately set out in its policy statement that, as an organization which is dedicated to the pursuit of excellence and professionalism in all it does, it believes in recruiting people who have the ability or potential to meet the high standards of performance that will be expected of them.
- *Promotion* – the policy would state the organization's intention to promote from within wherever this is appropriate as a means of satisfying its requirements for high-quality staff. The policy would, however, recognize that there will be occasions when the organization's present and future needs can only be met by recruitment from outside. The point could be made that a vigorous organization needs infusions of fresh blood from time to time if it is not to stagnate. In addition, the policy might state that employees will be encouraged to apply for internally advertised jobs and will not be held back from promotion by their managers, however reluctant the latter may be to lose them.
- *Employability* – a policy of increasing individual employability by providing career development and learning opportunities.
- *Work-life balance* – policies on the achievement of an appropriate balance between the work of employees and all other aspects of their lives. Such policies will be family-friendly and may include arrangements for leave, time off to deal with domestic emergencies, term-time working contracts, flexitime arrangements, scope to work at home when necessary, recognition that parents or carers may not be able to work outside their normal hours, recognition that the number of hours worked is not a criterion for assessing performance, crèches at work, and subsidized child-care.
- *Equal opportunity* – a reference should be made in the general employment policy statement to the fact that this is an equal opportunity organization.
- *Managing diversity* – how the organization manages the diverse people it employs.
- *Ethnic monitoring* – how the organization deals with monitoring the employment of ethnic minorities.
- *Age and employment* – the policy would define the approach the organization adopts to engaging, training and promoting older employees.
- *Redundancy* – the redundancy policy could state that it is the organization's intention to use its best endeavours to avoid involuntary redundancy through its redeployment and retraining procedures. However, if redundancy is unavoidable, those affected will be given fair and equitable treatment, the maximum amount of

warning, and every help that can be provided by the organization to obtain suitable alternative work.

- *Discipline* – the disciplinary policy should state that employees have the right to know what is expected of them and what could happen if they infringe the organization's rules. It would also make the point that, in handling disciplinary cases, the organization will treat employees in accordance with the principles of natural justice.
- *Grievances* – the policy should state that employees have the right to raise their grievances with their manager, to be accompanied by a representative if they so wish, and to appeal to a higher level if they feel that their grievance has not been resolved satisfactorily.
- *Sexual harassment* – the policy would express the organization's strong disapproval of sexual harassment and state the measures taken to eliminate it.
- *Bullying* – policies to prevent bullying.
- *Smoking* – the policy would define no-smoking rules.
- *Substance abuse* – how the organization treats employees with drink or drug problems.
- *AIDS* – how the organization approaches the employment of people who are HIV positive or are actually suffering from AIDS.
- *Internet* – policy on the private use of the Internet at work, and on the monitoring of Internet communications of employees.

Equal opportunity policy

The equal opportunity policy should spell out the organization's determination to give equal opportunities to all, irrespective of sex, race, creed or marital status. It could also state that the organization will use its best endeavours to provide equal opportunities to disabled people. The policy should also deal with the extent to which the organization wants to take 'affirmative action' to redress imbalances between the numbers employed according to sex or race or to differences in the levels of qualifications and skills they have achieved.

The following is an example of an equal opportunity policy statement:

The Council of the London Borough of Richmond upon Thames is an equal opportunity employer.

The Council's objective is to ensure that no job applicant or employee receives less favourable treatment, directly or indirectly, on the grounds of sex, sexual orientation, age, disability, marital status, creed/religion, colour, ethnic or national origin.

> *Where appropriate and where permissible under the relevant legislation and codes of prac-*
> *tice, employees of under-represented groups will be given positive training and encouragement*
> *to achieve equal opportunity within the Council's organization.*
>
> *The Council will implement a positive and continuing programme of action to make this*
> *policy fully effective. For example, selection criteria and all other HR procedures will be*
> *reviewed initially and regularly thereafter to ensure that individuals are appointed, promoted*
> *and treated on the basis of the relevant merits and abilities.*

Managing diversity

A policy on managing diversity recognizes that there are differences among employees and that these differences, if properly managed, will enable work to be done more efficiently and effectively. It does not focus exclusively on issues of discrimination but instead concentrates on recognizing the differences between people. As Kandola and Fullerton (1994) express it: the concept of managing diversity 'is founded on the premise that harnessing these differences will create a productive environment in which everyone will feel valued, where their talents are fully utilized, and in which organizational goals are met'.

Managing diversity is a concept that recognizes the benefits to be gained from differences. It differs from equal opportunity, which aims to legislate against discrimination, assumes that people should be assimilated into the organization and, often, relies on affirmative action.

A management of diversity policy will:

● acknowledge cultural and individual differences in the workplace;
● state that the organization values the different qualities that people bring to their jobs;
● emphasize the need to eliminate bias in such areas as selection, promotion, performance assessment, pay and learning opportunities;
● focus attention on individual differences rather than group differences.

Reward policy

The reward policy could cover such matters as:

● paying market rates;
● paying for performance;
● gainsharing – sharing in the gains (added value) or profits of the organization;
● providing an equitable pay system;
● equal pay for work of equal value, subject to overriding market considerations;

- the use of recognition schemes;
- the provision of employee benefits, including flexible benefits if appropriate;
- the importance attached to the non-financial rewards resulting from accomplishment, recognition and the opportunity to develop.

Employee development policy

The employee development policy should express the organization's commitment to the continuous development of the skills and abilities of employees in order to maximize their contribution and to give them the opportunity to enhance their skills, realize their potential, advance their careers and increase their employability both within and outside the organization.

Involvement and participation policy

The involvement and participation policy should spell out the organization's belief in involvement and participation as a means of generating the commitment of all employees to the success of the enterprise. This policy could also refer to the basis upon which the organization intends to communicate information to employees.

Employee relations policy

The employee relations policy will set out the organization's approach to the rights of employees to represent their interests to management through trade unions, staff associations or some other form of representative system. It will also cover the basis upon which the organization works with trade unions, eg emphasizing that this should be regarded as a partnership.

New technology policy

A new technology policy could be incorporated in the employment policy, but in most organizations these days the introduction of new technology is so significant that it justifies a separate policy statement. Such a statement would refer to consultation about the introduction of new technology and to the steps that would be taken by the organization to minimize the risk of compulsory redundancy.

Health and safety policy

Health and safety policies cover how the organization intends to provide healthy and safe places and systems of work.

Harassment policy

Harassment policies can:

- define harassment – sexual and bullying;
- state unequivocally that sexual harassment and bullying at work are not tolerated and are regarded as gross misconduct;
- define the role of managers in preventing harassment and dealing with complaints;
- provide a counselling service for those concerned about harassment;
- set out the procedure for dealing with harassment.

Smoking policies

Smoking policies will spell out whether or not there is a complete ban on smoking and, if not, the arrangements for restricting smoking to designated smoking areas.

FORMULATING OR REVISING POLICIES

The following steps should be taken when formulating or revising HR policies:

1. Gain understanding of the corporate culture and its shared values.
2. Analyse existing policies – written and unwritten. HR policies will exist in any organization, even if they are implicit rather than expressed formally.
3. Analyse external influences. HR policies are subject to the influence of UK employment legislation, European Community Employment Regulations, and the official codes of practice issued by bodies in the UK, such as ACAS (The Advisory, Conciliation and Arbitration Service), the EOC (Equal Opportunities Commission), the CRR (Commission on Racial Relations) or the Health and Safety Executive. The codes of practice issued by the professional institutions, especially the Chartered Institute of Personnel and Development, should also be consulted.
4. Assess any areas where new policies are needed or existing policies are inadequate.
5. Check with managers, preferably starting at the top, on their views about HR policies and where they think they could be improved.
6. Seek the views of employees about the HR policies, especially the extent to which they are inherently fair and equitable and are implemented fairly and consistently. Consider doing this through an attitude survey.

7. Seek the views of union representatives.
8. Analyse the information obtained in the first seven steps and prepare draft policies.
9. Consult, discuss and agree policies with management and union representatives.
10. Communicate the policies with guidance notes on their implementation as required (although they should be as self-explanatory as possible). Supplement this communication with training.

21

Competency-related human resource management

Competency-related human resource management is about using the concept of competency and the results of competency analysis to inform and improve the processes of recruitment and selection, employee development and employee reward. The language has dominated much of HR thinking and practice in recent years and the aim of this chapter is to define what the concept means and to summarize the ways in which it is used. (More detailed explanations of applications are given in Chapters 25 (recruitment), 26 (selection interviewing), 38 (management development) and 44 (competency-related pay)). The concept of competency has achieved this degree of prominence because it is essentially about performance. It is directly concerned with the factors contributing to high levels of individual contribution and, therefore, organizational effectiveness. As Prahalad and Hamel (1990) have stated: 'An obsession with competency building will characterize... global winners.'

Competent people at work are those who meet their performance expectations. They are capable of using their knowledge, skills and personal attributes to achieve the objectives and standards specified for their roles. Somewhat confusingly, two terms are used to describe this overall concept: competence and competency, as described below.

THE CONCEPTS OF COMPETENCY AND COMPETENCE

Competency

The concept of competency was first popularized by Boyatzis (1982). He developed it through research which established that there was no single factor but rather a range of factors that differentiated successful from less successful managers. This range of factors included personal qualities, motives, experience and behavioural characteristics under various headings. He defined competency as: 'A capacity that exists in a person that leads to behaviour that meets the job demands within the parameters of the organizational environment and that, in turn, brings about desired results.'

He suggested the following 'clusters' of competencies:

- goal and action management;
- directing subordinates;
- human resource management;
- leadership.

Since the contribution of Boyatzis to the subject, however, there have been many alternative uses of the term competency and a number of different views have been expressed about just what the concept means and how it can be applied. Lists of competencies have also proliferated. The following are some definitions of competency:

- the behavioural dimensions that affect job performance (Woodruffe, 1990);
- any individual characteristic that can be measured or counted reliably and that can be shown to differentiate significantly between effective and ineffective performance (Spencer *et al*, 1990);
- the fundamental abilities and capabilities needed to do the job well (Furnham, 1990);
- all the work-related personal attributes, knowledge, skills and values that a person draws upon to do their work well (Roberts, 1997);
- an underlying characteristic of a person that results in effective or superior performance (Mansfield, 1999).

Competencies are 'criterion validated', ie they are derived from analyses of the key aspects of behaviour, or 'soft skills' which differentiate between effective and less effective performance. Behavioural competencies include such characteristics as interpersonal skills, leadership, analytical skills and achievement orientation. The notion of competency is associated with that of emotional intelligence, as discussed at the end of the chapter.

Competence

The concept of competence was conceived in the UK as a fundamental part of the process of developing standards for National and Scottish Vocational Qualifications (NVQs/SVQs) and for the Management Charter Initiative (MCI) standards. These specify minimum standards for the achievement of set tasks and activities, expressed in ways that can be observed and assessed with a view to certification. An element of competence in NVQ language is a description of something that people in given work areas should be able to do. They are assessed on being competent or not yet competent. No attempt is made to assess the degree of competence, and the accent is more on what people should be capable of doing rather than on how they should behave in doing it.

Competence was defined by the Training Agency (1988) as being what a person who works in a given occupation should be able to do – 'actions, behaviour or outcome that the person should be able to demonstrate'. It was described as:

A wide concept which embodies the ability to transfer skills and knowledge to new situations within the occupational area. It encompasses organization and planning of work, innovation and coping with non-routine activities. It includes those qualities of personal effectiveness that are required in the workplace to deal with co-workers, managers and customers.

Competences can be defined by means of 'functional analysis', which establishes what people in particular roles have to be able to do and the standards they are expected to achieve. They can be described as work-based or occupational competences, which refer to expectations of workplace performance and the standards and outputs that people carrying out specified roles are expected to attain. They are sometimes referred to as 'hard' competences.

The concepts of competency and competence distinguished

Competency (and competencies) has become the term generally used to embrace the concepts of both competency and competence. But Charles Woodruffe (1991) believes that the word competency is being used both to refer to the ability to perform a job or part of a job competently and to the sets of behaviour the person must display in order to perform the tasks and functions of a job with competence. He therefore thinks that to avoid a potential minefield of misunderstanding and complications, the two senses of the word should be kept quite separate:

- *Competency* is a person-related concept that refers to the dimensions of behaviour lying behind competent performance.
- *Competence* is a work-related concept that refers to areas of work at which the person is competent.

Woodruffe states that areas of competence are quite specific because they are based on functional analysis, which proceeds by breaking down jobs into such areas. On the other hand, 'analysis of person-related competencies proceeds in the other direction. It starts from specific types of behaviour and groups these types under the competencies.' He points out that some of the competency lists produced by organizations mix up the two variables of aspects of the job and aspects of the person as if they were directly comparable, which is not the case.

The distinction is quite clear cut, but in practice many UK organizations adopt a hybrid approach which incorporates the use of both behavioural, people-based competencies and work-based competences. These are referred to generally as 'competencies'. But it is useful to remember that if this hybrid term is adopted it contains two aspects of competency and it is necessary to bear this in mind when analysing and defining competencies and when putting them to use. For example, in developing a competence-related pay scheme, as described in Chapter 44, it is advisable to decide whether the criteria are going to be behavioural competencies, work-based competences, or both.

Some organizations such as HSBC and ICl have abandoned the use of the term competency because of the jargon that surrounds it. Instead, they refer to capabilities, a term that simply describes what people have to be able to do and how they have to behave in order to carry out their work successfully. Capable people, like competent people, are those who do their work well, achieving their objectives and meeting the required standards of performance. Perhaps it would be preferable to avoid the jargon and use 'capability' as a term that embraces both competences and competencies.

THE CONSTITUENTS OF COMPETENCY

There are different views on the constituents of competency. Some hold that the concept of competency embodies the behaviour of individuals in carrying out their functions and the knowledge and skills that affect or underpin that behaviour. Spencer *et al* (1990) believe that competencies consist of:

- *motives* – the underlying need pattern that drives, directs and selects an individual's behaviour;
- *traits* – general dispositions to behave or respond in a certain way; for example, self-confidence, self-control, resistance to stress, 'hardiness';
- *self-concept* – the individual's attitudes or values;
- *content knowledge* of facts or procedures, either technical (how to trouble-shoot a defective computer) or interpersonal (how to give feedback);
- *cognitive and behavioural skills* – either covert (for example, deductive or inductive reasoning) or observable (for example, active listening).

Others, such as Fletcher (1991), stress that 'it is application of knowledge and not knowledge itself that is important to competent performance'.

One of the issues that exercised those responsible for developing the NVQ system, which is founded on 'competence-based standards', was the role of knowledge and understanding within these standards. Concern was expressed on how those who have been able to demonstrate effective performance 'would be able to do but not understand what they do'. Eventually the view emerged that 'underpinning knowledge and understanding' could be *inferred* from performance. Competence implies the capacity to transfer what people know and understand to different contexts, ie the various aspects of their work.

A number of people have contended that competency is only concerned with *behaviour*. Personal attributes such as knowledge, skills and 'expertise' should be considered separately as the input job holders bring to their work, which is transformed by their behaviour into outputs (immediate results) and outcomes (longer-term contributions).

TYPES OF COMPETENCIES

Competencies can be generic or specific, threshold or performance, or differentiating, as described below.

Generic and specific competencies

Competencies can be universally generic, applying to all people in an occupation, such as management, irrespective of the organization to which they belong, or their particular role. The list of competencies drawn up by the Management Charter Initiative (MCI) comes into this category. They can also be organizationally generic, applied to all staff, or they can be applied to a job family – a related group of jobs where the nature of the work is similar but carried out at different levels, or they can cover occupational categories such as managers, scientists, professional staff, sales staff or office/administrative staff.

Competencies related to individual roles (role-specific competencies) may also be defined.

Threshold and performance competencies

A distinction was made by Boyatzis (1982) between threshold and performance competencies. Threshold competencies are the basic competencies required to do the job, which do not differentiate between high and low performers. Performance competencies do make this distinction.

However, as Woodruffe (1991) comments, a problem with the distinction between threshold and performance competencies is that a good proportion of the competencies for a job are both threshold and performance. People need a certain level even to start a job, but any extra is welcome.

Differentiating competencies

Differentiating competencies define the behavioural characteristics that high performers display as distinct from those characterizing less effective people – the performance dimensions for their job. The definitions of the level of competency expected of high performers in certain areas can be used as behavioural models for discussion at the performance agreement and performance review stages of performance management.

One way of setting out the difference between high and less effective performers is to derive positive and negative indicators for each competency heading as in the following example for leadership.

Definition

Guiding, encouraging and motivating individuals and teams to achieve a desired result.

Positive indicators

- Achieves high level of performance from team.
- Defines objectives, plans and expectations clearly.
- Continually monitors performance and provides good feedback.
- Maintains effective relationships with individuals and the team as a whole.
- Develops a sense of common purpose in the team.

● Builds team morale and motivates individual members of the team effectively by recognizing their contribution while taking appropriate action to deal with poor performers.

Negative indicators

● Does not achieve high levels of performance from team.
● Fails to clarify objectives or standards of performance.
● Pays insufficient attention to the needs of individuals and the team.
● Neither monitors nor provides effective feedback on performance.
● Inconsistent in rewarding good performance or taking action to deal with poor performance.

Competencies can also be set out in the form of a scale to provide a basis for assessment as in the following example.

Personal drive

Self-confident and assertive drive to win with decisiveness and resilience:

1. Decisive even under pressure, assertive and tough-minded in arguing his/her case, very self-confident, shrugs off set-backs.
2. Will commit him/herself to definite opinions, determined to be heard, can come back strongly if attacked.
3. May reserve judgement where uncertain, but stands firm on important points, aims for compromise, fairly resilient.
4. Avoids making rapid decisions, takes an impartial coordinator role rather than pushing own ideas.
5. Doesn't pursue his/her own points, goes along with the group, allows criticisms or setbacks to deter him/her.

DESCRIBING COMPETENCIES

Descriptions of competencies may be called competency frameworks, competency maps, competency profiles or competency clusters and lists:

● *Competency frameworks* define the competency requirements that cover all the key jobs in an organization or all the jobs in a job family. The frameworks are likely to consist of 'generic competencies'.

- *Competency maps* describe the different aspects or categories of competent behaviour in an occupation against competency dimensions such as strategic capability, resource management and quality. An example of a competency map for HR specialists was given in Chapter 5.
- *Competency profiles* set out the competencies required for effective performance in a specified role. These may be set out in the form of 'differentiating competencies' as in the example given earlier in this chapter.

Typical competencies

Competency magazine in 1996 reported that the 10 most common behaviours sought by the 126 organizations they surveyed were:

- communication;
- achievement/results orientation;
- customer focus;
- teamwork;
- leadership;
- planning and organizing;
- commercial/business awareness;
- flexibility/adaptability;
- developing others;
- problem solving.

Other typical categories are analytical skills, delivery of results, drive, expertise, planning and organizing skills and strategic capabilities.

Example of a competency framework

The following is an example of a competency framework prepared for the Prince's Trust.

- *Achievement/results orientation.* The desire to get things done well and the ability to set and meet challenging goals, create own measures of excellence and constantly seek ways of improving performance.
- *Business awareness.* The capacity continually to identify and explore business opportunities, understand the business opportunities and priorities of the organization and constantly to seek methods of ensuring that the organization becomes more businesslike.

- *Communication.* The ability to communicate clearly and persuasively, orally or in writing.
- *Customer focus.* The exercise of unceasing care in looking after the interests of external and internal customers to ensure that their wants, needs and expectations are met or exceeded.
- *Developing others.* The desire and capacity to foster the development of members of his or her team, providing feedback, support, encouragement and coaching.
- *Flexibility.* The ability to adapt to and work effectively in different situations and to carry out a variety of tasks.
- *Leadership.* The capacity to inspire individuals to give of their best to achieve a desired result and to maintain effective relationships with individuals and the team as a whole.
- *Planning.* The ability to decide on courses of action, ensuring that the resources required to implement the action will be available and scheduling the programme of work required to achieve a defined end-result.
- *Problem solving.* The capacity to analyse situations, diagnose problems, identify the key issues, establish and evaluate alternative courses of action and produce a logical, practical and acceptable solution.
- *Teamwork.* The ability to work cooperatively and flexibly with other members of the team with a full understanding of the role to be played as a team member.
- *Knowledge-sharing.* The disposition to share knowledge fully and willingly with others in the interests of the organization.

USING THE CONCEPT

To cut through all the jargon it is best to treat the concept of competency quite simply as, first, a useful term for describing the sort of behaviour (the behavioural dimensions) that organizations are seeking in order to attain high levels of performance. The concept provides a common language, which helps people to focus on the key behavioural issues affecting results. Secondly, the notion of competency can be used to describe what people are expected to know and be able to do if they are to carry out their roles effectively.

The concept of competency lies at the very heart of human resource management. It is directly linked to a fundamental aim of strategic HRM – to obtain and develop highly competent people who will readily achieve their objectives and thus maximize their contribution to the attainment of the goals of the enterprise.

Integrated HR management

The language of competence and the existence of a competency framework can provide an invaluable basis for integrating key HR activities and achieving a coherent approach to the management of people. The integrated elements of HR management around the competency framework are illustrated in Figure 21.1.

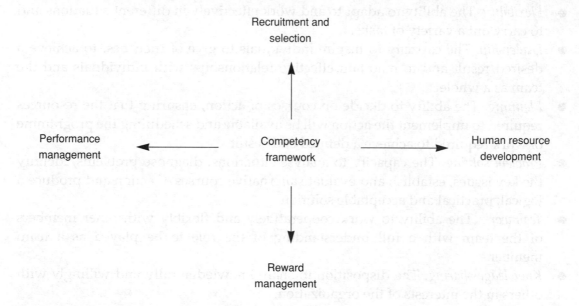

Figure 21.1 Competency-based integrated HR management

Applications in each of these areas – all linked together by the common language of competence – are summarized in the next four sections of this chapter.

Recruitment and selection

A competency approach to recruitment and selection focuses on performance rather than job content. This means defining performance criteria in terms of the competency profile for the job.

Human resource planning processes can be related to forecasts of future competency requirements and an analysis of the gaps to be filled between the likely demand for particular types of competencies and the anticipated supply of people with those competencies.

Competency-related recruitment processes are based on the identification of competencies and the preparation of competency-based people specifications. These promote a clear understanding of what the interviewer should be looking for under a number of defined headings in terms of the level of competency required. This provides a framework for structured interviews.

Assessment centres

Assessment centres use a range of assessment techniques to determine whether or not candidates are suitable for a particular job or for promotion. The focus of an assessment centre is always on behaviour, which is defined in terms of the competency dimensions that distinguish high performance. Various exercises are used to capture and stimulate the key behavioural aspects of the job, and assessors rate candidates, using a scoring system for each dimension.

Performance management

Performance management is a process for assessing and improving performance based on the agreement of objectives, competence requirements and development needs, the measurement of achievements and performance in relation to those needs and the agreement of new objectives and development plans on the basis of that measurement.

A full performance management process is concerned not only with outputs in the form of results but also with the behavioural aspects of how the role is being carried out, which determine outcomes. Assessing these indicates what may need to be done to modify that behaviour in order to improve performance.

The assessment of behaviour is best done by reference to properly researched and agreed competency dimensions, either generic competencies applying to a whole occupation, or individual job competencies.

Human resource development

An understanding of the competencies required in particular roles is the best basis for creating learning situations and plans: self-managed learning, coaching and counselling, personal development plans or more formal training events and programmes.

The NVQ/SVQ system is a means of assessing whether or not individuals have achieved defined standards of competence. NVQs are *not* training modules but they can be used as a basis for defining learning needs.

A competency framework, competency maps and competency profiles will indicate learning needs – the specific competency dimensions that need to be addressed through the provision of learning opportunities and the stimulation of self-development.

Development centres using assessment centre methodology based on competencies can help in the identification of development needs.

Reward management

One of the most recent developments in reward management practices has been the use of competence-related pay – relating grades and amounts of pay to the achievement of defined levels of competence or using competency dimensions as analytical job evaluation scheme headings (see Part X).

EMOTIONAL INTELLIGENCE

Goleman (1995) has defined emotional intelligence as: 'The capacity for recognizing our own feelings and those of others, for motivating ourselves, for managing emotions well in ourselves and in our relationships'. The concept, as explained by Goleman, is based on the belief that measures of rational thinking cannot predict success. It is not enough to have a high IQ (intelligence quotient); emotional intelligence is also required. Although the concept of emotional intelligence is associated with management development, especially the enhancement of leadership skills as discussed in Chapter 38, it refers to what are in effect a number of competencies and so it can be considered also under the heading of competency-related HR management.

Dulewicz and Higgs (1999) have produced a detailed analysis of how the emotional intelligence elements of self-awareness, emotional management, empathy, relationships, communication and personal style correspond to competencies such as sensitivity, flexibility, adaptability, resilience, impact, listening, leadership, persuasiveness, motivating others, energy, decisiveness and achievement orientation. They conclude that there are distinct associations between competency models and elements of emotional intelligence.

22

Knowledge management

Knowledge management is about storing and sharing the wisdom and understanding accumulated in an organization about its processes, techniques and operations. It treats knowledge as a key resource. There is nothing new about knowledge management. As Hansen *et al* (1999) comment, 'For hundreds of years, owners of family businesses have passed on their commercial wisdom to children, master craftsmen have painstakingly taught their trades to apprentices, and workers have exchanged ideas and know-how on the job.' But they also remark that, 'As the foundation of industrialized economies has shifted from natural resources to intellectual assets, executives have been compelled to examine the knowledge underlying their business and how that knowledge is used.'

Knowledge management is as much if not more concerned with people and how they acquire, exchange and disseminate knowledge as it is about information technology. That is why it has become an important area for HR practitioners, who are in a strong position to exert influence in this aspect of people management. Scarborough *et al* (1999) believe that they should have 'the ability to analyse the different types of knowledge deployed by the organization ... [and] to relate such knowledge to issues of organizational design, career patterns and employment security.'

The concept of knowledge management is closely associated with intellectual capital theory as described earlier in Chapter 3 in that it refers to the notions of human, social and organizational or structural capital. It is also linked to the concepts of organizational learning and the learning organization as discussed in Chapter 34. Knowledge management is considered below under the following headings:

- definition of the process of knowledge management;
- the concept of knowledge;
- types of knowledge;
- the purpose and significance of knowledge management;
- approaches to knowledge management;
- knowledge management issues;
- the contribution of HR to knowledge management.

KNOWLEDGE MANAGEMENT DEFINED

Knowledge management is 'any process or practice of creating, acquiring, capturing, sharing and using knowledge, wherever it resides, to enhance learning and performance in organizations' (Scarborough *et al*, 1999). Scarborough *et al* suggest that it focuses on the development of firm-specific knowledge and skills that are the result of organizational learning processes. Knowledge management is concerned with both stocks and flows of knowledge. Stocks included expertise and encoded knowledge in computer systems. Flows represent the ways in which knowledge is transferred from people to people or from people to a knowledge database. Knowledge management has also been defined by Tan (2000) as: 'The process of systematically and actively managing and leveraging the stores of knowledge in an organization'.

Knowledge management involves transforming knowledge resources by identifying relevant information and then disseminating it so that learning can take place. Knowledge management strategies promote the sharing of knowledge by linking people with people, and by linking them to information so that they learn from documented experiences.

Knowledge can be stored in databanks and found in presentations, reports, libraries, policy documents and manuals. It can be moved around the organization through information systems and by traditional methods such as meetings, workshops, courses, 'master classes', written publications, videos and tapes. The intranet provides an additional and very effective medium for communicating knowledge.

THE CONCEPT OF KNOWLEDGE

Blackler (1995) notes that 'Knowledge is multifaceted and complex, being both situated and abstract, implicit and explicit, distributed and individual, physical and mental, developing and static, verbal and encoded. He categorizes forms of knowledge as:

- *embedded* in technologies, rules and organizational procedures;
- *encultured* as collective understandings, stories, values and beliefs;
- *embodied* into the practical activity-based competencies and skills of key members of the organization (ie practical knowledge or 'know-how');
- *embraced* as the conceptual understanding and cognitive skills of key members (ie conceptual knowledge or 'know-how').

Nonaka (1991) suggests that knowledge is held either by individuals or collectively. In Blackler's terms, embodied or embraced knowledge is individual and embedded, and cultural knowledge is collective.

It can be argued (Scarborough and Carter, 2000) that knowledge emerges from the collective experience of work and is shared between members of a particular group or community.

It is useful to distinguish between data, information and knowledge:

- *data* consists of the basic facts – the building blocks for information and knowledge;
- *information* is data that have been processed in a way which is meaningful to individuals, it is available to anyone entitled to gain access to it; as Drucker (1988) wrote, 'information is data endowed with meaning and purpose';
- *knowledge* is information put to productive use; it is personal and often intangible and it can be elusive – the task of tying it down, encoding it and distributing it is tricky.

TYPES OF KNOWLEDGE

As argued by Nonaka (1991) and Nonaka and Takeuchi (1995), knowledge is either explicit or tacit. Explicit knowledge can be codified – it is recorded and available and is held in databases, in corporate intranets and intellectual property portfolios. Tacit knowledge exists in people's minds. It is difficult to articulate in writing and is acquired through personal experience. As suggested by Hansen *et al* (1999), it includes scientific or technological expertise, operational know-how, insights about an industry, and business judgement. The main challenge in knowledge management is how to turn tacit knowledge into explicit knowledge.

THE PURPOSE AND SIGNIFICANCE OF KNOWLEDGE MANAGEMENT

As explained by Blake (1998), the purpose of knowledge management is to capture a company's collective expertise and distribute it to 'wherever it can achieve the biggest payoff'. This is in accordance with the resource-based view of the firm which, as argued by Grant (1991), suggests that the source of competitive advantage lies within the firm (ie in its people and their knowledge), not in how it positions itself in the market. Trussler (1998) comments that 'the capability to gather, lever, and use knowledge effectively will become a major source of competitive advantage in many businesses over the next few years'. A successful company is a knowledge-creating company.

Knowledge management is about getting knowledge from those who have it to those who need it in order to improve organizational effectiveness. In the information age, knowledge rather than physical assets or financial resources is the key to competitiveness. In essence, as pointed out by Mecklenberg *et al* (1999), 'Knowledge management allows companies to capture, apply and generate value from their employees' creativity and expertise'.

APPROACHES TO KNOWLEDGE MANAGEMENT

The codification and personalization approaches

Two approaches to knowledge management have been identified by Hansen *et al* (1999):

1. *The codification strategy* – knowledge is carefully codified and stored in databases where it can be accessed and used easily by anyone in the organization. Knowledge is explicit and is codified using a 'people-to-document' approach. This strategy is therefore document driven. Knowledge is extracted from the person who developed it, made independent of that person and re-used for various purposes. It will be stored in some form of electronic repository for people to use. This allows many people to search for and retrieve codified knowl-

edge without having to contact the person who originally developed it. This strategy relies largely on information technology to manage databases and also on the use of the intranet.

2. *The personalization strategy* – knowledge is closely tied to the person who has developed it and is shared mainly through direct person-to-person contacts. This is a 'person-to-person' approach which involves sharing tacit knowledge. The exchange is achieved by creating networks and encouraging face-to-face communication between individuals and teams by means of informal conferences, workshops, brainstorming and one-to-one sessions.

Hansen *et al* state that the choice of strategy should be contingent on the organization; what it does, how it does it, and its culture. Thus consultancies such as Ernst & Young, using knowledge to deal with recurring problems, may rely mainly on codification so that recorded solutions to similar problems are easily retrievable. Strategy consultancy firms such as McKinsey or Bains, however, will rely mainly on a personalization strategy to help them to tackle the high-level strategic problems they are presented with, which demand the provision of creative, analytically rigorous advice. They need to channel individual expertise, and they find and develop people who are able to use a person-to-person knowledge-sharing approach effectively. In this sort of firm, directors or experts can be established who can be approached by consultants by telephone, e-mail or personal contact.

The research conducted by Hansen *et al* established that companies which use knowledge effectively pursue one strategy predominantly and use the second strategy to support the first. Those who try to excel at both strategies risk failing at both.

The knowledge-creating company

In the opinion of Nonaka and Takeuchi (1995), as cited by Scarborough *et al* (1999), a core competitive activity of organizations is knowledge creation – 'an organic, fluid and socially constructed process in which different knowledges are blended to produce innovative outcomes that are predicted or predictable'. Fundamental to knowledge creation is the blending of tacit and explicit knowledge through processes of socialization (tacit to tacit), externalization (tacit to explicit), internalization (explicit to tacit) and combination (explicit to explicit).

The resource-based approach

Scarborough and Carter (2000) describe knowledge management as 'the attempt by management to actively create, communicate and exploit knowledge as a resource for the organization'. They suggest that this attempt has technical, social and economic components:

- In technical terms knowledge management involves centralizing knowledge that is currently scattered across the organization and codifying tacit forms of knowledge.
- In social and political terms, knowledge management involves collectivizing knowledge so that it is no longer the exclusive property of individuals or groups.
- In economic terms, knowledge management is in response by organizations to the need to intensify their creation and exploitation of knowledge.

KNOWLEDGE MANAGEMENT ISSUES

The various approaches referred to above do not provide easy answers. The issues that need to be addressed in developing knowledge management processes are discussed below.

The pace of change

One of the main issues in knowledge management is how to keep up with the pace of change and identify what knowledge needs to be captured and shared.

Relating knowledge management strategy to business strategy

As Hansen *et al* (1999) show, it is not knowledge *per se* but the way it is applied to strategic objectives that is the critical ingredient in competitiveness. They point out that 'competitive strategy must drive knowledge management strategy', and that managements have to answer the question: 'How does knowledge that resides in the company add value for customers?' Mecklenberg *et al* (1999) argue that organizations should 'start with the business value of what they gather. If it doesn't generate value, drop it.'

Technology and people

Technology may be central to companies adopting a codification strategy but for those following a personalization strategy, IT is best used in a supportive role. As Hansen *et al* (1999) comment:

> In the codification model, managers need to implement a system that is much like a traditional library – it must contain a large cache of documents and include search engines that allow people to find and use the documents they need. In the personalization model, it's more important to have a system that allows people to find other people.

Scarborough *et al* (1999) suggest that 'technology should be viewed more as a means of communication and less as a means of storing knowledge'. Knowledge management is more about people than technology. As research by Davenport (1996) established, managers get two-thirds of their information from face-to-face or telephone conversations.

There is a limit to how much tacit knowledge can be codified. In organizations relying more on tacit than explicit knowledge, a person-to-person approach works best, and IT can only support this process; it cannot replace it.

The significance of process and social capital and culture

A preoccupation with technology may mean that too little attention is paid to the processes (social, technological and organizational) through which knowledge combines and interacts in different ways (Blackler, 1995, cited by Scarborough *et al*, 1999). The key process is the interactions between people. This constitutes the social capital of an organization, ie the 'network of relationships [that] constitute a valuable resource for the conduct of social affairs' (Nahpiet and Ghoshal, 1998). Social networks can be particularly important in ensuring that knowledge is shared. What is also required is another aspect of social capital: trust. People will not be willing to share knowledge with those whom they do not trust.

The culture of the company may inhibit knowledge sharing. The norm may be for people to keep knowledge to themselves as much as they can because 'knowledge is power'. An open culture will encourage people to share their ideas and knowledge.

Knowledge workers

Knowledge workers as defined by Drucker (1993) are individuals who have high levels of education and specialist skills combined with the ability to apply these skills to identify and solve problems. As Argyris (1991) points out: 'The nuts and bolts of management ... increasingly consists of guiding and integrating the autonomous but interconnected work of highly skilled people.' Knowledge management is about the management and motivation of knowledge workers who create knowledge and will be the key players in sharing it.

THE CONTRIBUTION OF HR TO KNOWLEDGE MANAGEMENT

HR can make an important contribution to knowledge management simply because knowledge is shared between people; it is not just a matter of capturing explicit knowledge through the use of information technology. The role of HR is to ensure that the organization has the intellectual capital it needs. The resource-based view of the firm emphasizes, in the words of Capelli and Crocker-Hefter (1996), that 'distinctive human resource practices help to create unique competencies that differentiate products and services and, in turn, drive competitiveness'.

Ten ways in which HR can contribute

The main ways in which HR can contribute to knowledge management are summarized below and described in more detail in the rest of this section.

1. Help to develop an open culture in which the values and norms emphasize the importance of sharing knowledge.
2. Promote a climate of commitment and trust.
3. Advise on the design and development of organizations which facilitate knowledge sharing through networks and communities of practice (groups of people who share common concerns about aspects of their work), and teamwork.
4. Advise on resourcing policies and provide resourcing services which ensure that valued employees who can contribute to knowledge creation and sharing are attracted and retained.
5. Advise on methods of motivating people to share knowledge and rewarding those who do so.
6. Help in the development of performance management processes which focus on the development and sharing of knowledge.
7. Develop processes of organizational and individual learning which will generate and assist in disseminating knowledge.
8. Set up and organize workshops, conferences, seminars and symposia which enable knowledge to be shared on a person-to-person basis.
9. In conjunction with IT, develop systems for capturing and, as far as possible, codifying explicit and tacit knowledge.
10. Generally, promote the cause of knowledge management with senior managers to encourage them to exert leadership and support knowledge management initiatives.

Culture development

An open culture is one in which as Schein (1985) suggests, people contribute out of a sense of commitment and solidarity. Relationships are characterized by mutuality and trust. In such a culture, organizations place a high priority on mutual support, collaboration and creativity, and on constructive relationships. There is no 'quick fix' way in which a closed culture where these priorities do not exist can be converted into an open culture. Long-established cultures are difficult to change. HR can encourage management to develop purpose and value statements which spell out that an important aim of the organization is to achieve competitive advantage by developing and effectively using unique resources of knowledge and expertise, and that to achieve the aim, sharing knowledge is core value. Such statements may be rhetoric but they can be converted into reality through the various processes described below.

Promote a climate of commitment and trust

Gaining commitment is a matter of trying to get everyone to identify with the purpose and values of the organization, which will include processes for developing and sharing knowledge. Commitment can be enhanced by developing a strategy which will include the implementation of communication, education and training programmes, initiatives to increase involvement and 'ownership', and the introduction of performance and reward processes.

Developing a high-trust organization means creating trust between management and employees as a basis for encouraging trust between individual employees or groups of employees. People are more likely to trust management if its actions are fair, equitable, consistent and transparent, and if it keeps its word.

It is difficult although not impossible to develop trust between management and employees. But it is not possible to make individual employees trust one another, and such trust is important if knowledge is to be shared. Developing a climate of trust in the organization helps, otherwise it is a matter of developing social capital in the sense of putting people into positions where they have to work together, and encouraging interaction and networking so that individuals recognize the value of sharing knowledge because it helps achieve common and accepted aims. This process can be helped by team-building activities. Trust may also be enhanced if knowledge is exchanged as a matter of course in forums, conferences etc. Dialogue occurs between people who want to connect and are given opportunities to do so in a collaborative, creative and adaptive culture.

Organization design and development

HR can contribute to effective knowledge management by advising on the design of process-based organizations in which the focus is on horizontal processes that cut across organizational boundaries. Such organizations rely largely on networking and cross-functional or inter-disciplinary project teams or task forces, and knowledge-sharing is an essential part of the operation. Attention is paid to identifying and encouraging 'communities of practice' which, as defined by Wenger and Snyder (2000), are 'groups of people informally bound together by shared expertise and a passion for joint enterprise'. They are seen as important because it is within such communities that much of the organization's tacit knowledge is created and shared.

The role definitions that emerge from organization design activities should emphasize knowledge-sharing as both an accountability (a key result area) and a competency (an expected mode of behaviour). Thus it can become an accepted part of the fabric and therefore the culture of the organization.

Organizational development activities can focus on team-building in communities with an emphasis on processes of interaction, communication and participation. The aims would be to develop a 'sharing' culture.

Resourcing

HR contributes to enhancing knowledge management processes by advising on how to attract and retain people with the required skills and abilities, including those who are likely to exhibit the behaviours needed in a knowledge-sharing culture. This means devising competency frameworks for recruitment and development purposes (see Chapter 21) which include knowledge-sharing as a key behaviour. Such a competency could be defined as 'The disposition to share knowledge fully and willingly with other members of the community'. Questions would be asked at the interview stage on the approach adopted by candidates to sharing knowledge in their present organization. Other questions along the lines of the one given below could be put to test candidates on their views:

> This organization relies to a considerable extent on achieving success through the development of new products and techniques. We believe that it is important to ensure that the knowledge generated by such developments is spread around the business as widely as possible to those who might put it to good use. What part do you think you could play as an individual in this process?

Posing this sort of question at the interview stage helps to define expectations as part of the psychological contract.

Assessment centres can also include exercises and tests designed to test the disposition and ability of individuals to share knowledge.

Retaining knowledge workers is a matter of providing a supportive workplace environment and motivating them through both tangible and intangible rewards as discussed below.

Motivation

As cited by Scarborough and Carter (2000), a study by Tampoe (1993) identified four key motivators for knowledge workers:

1. Personal growth – the opportunity for individuals to fully realize their potential.
2. Occupational autonomy – a work environment in which knowledge workers can achieve the task assigned to them.
3. Task achievement – a sense of accomplishment from producing work that is of high quality and relevance to the organization.
4. Money rewards – an income that is a just reward for their contribution to corporate success and that symbolizes their contribution to that success.

Hansen *et al* (1999) state that in their 'codification model', managers need to develop a system that encourages people to write down what they know and to get these documents into the electronics depository. They believe that real incentives – not just enticements – are required to get people to take these steps. In companies following the personalization model, rewards for sharing knowledge directly with other people may have to be different. Direct financial rewards for contributing to the codification and sharing of knowledge may often be inappropriate, but this could be a subject for discussion in a performance review as part of a performance management process.

Performance management

The promotion and development of performance management processes by HR can make an important contribution to knowledge management, by providing for behavioural expectations which are related to knowledge-sharing to be defined, and ensuring that actual behaviours are reviewed and, where appropriate, rewarded by financial or non-financial means. Performance management reviews can identify weaknesses and development needs in this aspect and initiate personal development plans which are designed to meet these needs.

One starting point for the process could be the cascading of corporate core values for knowledge-sharing to individuals, so that they understand what they are expected to do to support those core values. As mentioned earlier, knowledge-sharing can be included as an element of a competency framework, and the desired behaviour would be spelt out and reviewed. For example, positive indicators such as those listed below could be used as a basis for agreeing competency requirements and assessing the extent to which they are met. The following are examples of positive behaviour in meeting competency expectations for knowledge-sharing:

- is eager to share knowledge with colleagues;
- takes positive steps to set up group meetings to exchange relevant information and knowledge;
- builds networks which provide for knowledge sharing;
- ensures as appropriate that knowledge is captured, codified, recorded and disseminated through the intranet and/or other means of communication.

Hansen *et al* mention that at Ernst & Young, consultants are evaluated at performance reviews along five dimensions, one of which is their 'contribution to and utilization of the knowledge asset of the firm'. At Bain, partners are evaluated each year on a variety of dimensions, including how much direct help they have given colleagues.

In a 360-degree feedback process (see Chapter 32), one of the dimensions for an assessment by colleagues and direct reports could be the extent to which an individual shares knowledge.

Organizational and individual learning

Organizational learning takes place when people learn collaboratively (Hoyle, 1995). It involves accumulating, analysing and utilizing knowledge resources which contribute to the achievement of business objectives. Knowledge management approaches as described in the chapter can make a major contribution to the enhancement of learning in an organization. Practices associated with creating the right environment for sharing knowledge will in particular promote organizational learning by creating a 'rich landscape of learning and development opportunities' (Kessels, 1996).

The concept of a learning organization (see Chapter 34) is also relevant. As defined by Miller and Stewart (1999), one of the characteristics of such an organization is that 'there are well-defined processes for defining, creating, capturing, sharing and acting on knowledge'. And Garvin (1993) postulates that learning organizations 'transfer knowledge quickly and efficiently throughout the organization by means of formal training programmes linked to implementation'.

Organizational learning, however, is based on individual learning, and the significance of knowledge management and the techniques available to support it can be learnt in formal training sessions or monitoring programmes designed and facilitated by the HR function.

Workshops and conferences etc

HR can play an important part in knowledge management by setting up and facilitating workshops, conferences, seminars and forums in which members exchange information and ideas, discuss what they have learnt and agree on what use can be made of the knowledge they have acquired. Apart from their value in disseminating knowledge, such gatherings can help to develop an environment in which knowledge-sharing is accepted as a natural and continuing activity.

Working with IT

Knowledge management is neither the preserve of the IT function nor that of HR. The two functions need to work together. IT ensures that knowledge is recorded and made acceptable through means such as the intranet. HR collaborates by providing means for tacit knowledge to be collected and, where feasible, codified.

Promoting the cause

Some organizations such as ICL have appointed a 'knowledge programme director' to develop corporate knowledge assets. Others have relied upon IT or business teams. But HR can make a major contribution not only in the specific activities referred to above, but also in generally promoting the cause of knowledge management, emphasizing to senior management at every opportunity the importance of developing a culture in which the significance of knowledge management is recognized.

23

Analysing and describing jobs and roles

The analysis of jobs and roles (which incorporates skills and competence analysis) is one of the most important techniques in HR management. It provides the information required to produce job descriptions, role definitions, and personal and learning/training specifications. It is of fundamental importance in organization and job design, recruitment and selection, performance management, training management development, career management, job evaluation and the design of pay structures. Those constitute most of the key processes of HRM.

This chapter deals with the subject under the following headings:

- definitions;
- job analysis;
- role analysis;
- skills analysis;
- competence analysis;
- job descriptions;
- role profiles.

DEFINITIONS

Job analysis

Job analysis is the process of collecting, analysing and setting out information about the content of jobs in order to provide the basis for a job description and data for recruitment, training, job evaluation and performance management. Job analysis concentrates on what holders are expected to do.

Role analysis

Role analysis also collects information relating to the work people do but, essentially, it looks at the part that people play in carrying out their jobs rather than the tasks they carry out. In other words, it is concerned not so much with work content as with the broader aspects of behaviour expected of role holders in achieving the overall purpose of the role, for example, working with others, working flexibly, and the styles of management they use. In practice, the determination of the content of jobs and the roles people play is carried out by similar analytical processes although the objectives of the analysis will be somewhat different.

Some people use the term 'role analysis' to cover both the job content and behavioural aspects of the jobs. Others seem to use the terms interchangeably. But the distinction between what someone has to do and the part they play in doing it (the behavioural requirements) is worth making.

Competence analysis

Competence analysis is concerned with functional analysis to determine work-based competences and behavioural analysis to establish the behavioural dimensions that affect job performance. *Work-based or occupational competences* refer to expectations of workplace performance – what people should be capable of doing – and the standards and outputs that people carrying out specified roles are expected to attain. *Behavioural or personal competencies* are individuals' personal characteristics which they bring to their work roles.

Job description

A job description sets out the purpose of a job, where it fits in the organization structure, the context within which the job holder functions and the principal accountabilities of job holders, or the main tasks they have to carry out.

Role profile

A role profile or definition describes the part played by individuals in fulfilling their work requirements. It will spell out expectations and key result areas or accountabilities – what role holders have to achieve and what they will be held to account for (this is sometimes called an accountability statement). The role definition will also specify behavioural requirements in the form of competencies. An example of a generic role definition (ie one covering an occupation rather than a single role) is given in Figure 23.2 (on page 352).

Person specification

A person specification, also known as a job or personnel specification, sets out the education, qualifications, training, experience, personal attributes and competences a job holder requires to perform her or his job satisfactorily. Person specifications are used in recruitment and selection as described in Chapter 25.

Learning or training specification

A learning or training specification defines the knowledge and skills needed to achieve an acceptable level of performance. It is used as the basis for devising learning and development programmes (see Chapter 36). Learning specifications may be drawn up on the basis of attribute, skills and competence analyses.

JOB ANALYSIS

Job analysis produces the following information about a job:

- *overall purpose* – why the job exists and, in essence, what the job holder is expected to contribute;
- *content* – the nature and scope of the job in terms of the tasks and operations to be performed and duties to be carried out – ie the processes of converting inputs (knowledge, skills and abilities) into outputs (results);
- *accountabilities* – the results or outputs for which the job holder is accountable;
- *performance criteria* – the criteria, measures or indicators that enable an assessment to be carried out to ascertain the degree to which the job is being performed satisfactorily;
- *responsibilities* – the level of responsibility the job holder has to exercise by reference to the scope and input of the job; the amount of discretion allowed to make

decisions; the difficulty, scale, variety and complexity of the problems to be solved; the quantity and value of the resources controlled; and the type and importance of interpersonal relations;

- *organizational factors* – the reporting relationships of the job holder, ie to whom he or she reports either directly (the line manager) or functionally (on matters concerning specialist areas, such as finance or personnel management); the people reporting directly or indirectly to the job holder; and the extent to which the job holder is involved in teamwork;
- *motivating factors* – the particular features of the job that are likely to motivate or demotivate job holders if, in the latter case, nothing is done about them;
- *development factors* – promotion and career prospects and the opportunity to acquire new skills or expertise;
- *environmental factors* – working conditions, health and safety considerations, unsocial hours, mobility, and ergonomic factors relating to the design and use of equipment or work stations.

Approach to job analysis

The essence of job analysis is the application of systematic methods of the collection of information about jobs. Job analysis obtains information about the content of jobs (what employees do) and subjects this to analysis.

Job analysis is essentially about data collection and the basic steps are described below.

Data collection – basic steps

The basic steps required to collect information about jobs are as follows:

- Obtain documents such as existing organization, procedure or training manuals which give information about the job.
- Ask managers for fundamental information concerning the job, the overall purpose, the main activities carried out, the responsibilities involved and the relationships with others.
- Ask the job holders similar questions about their jobs – it is sometimes helpful to get them to keep a diary or a detailed record of work activities over a week or two.
- For certain jobs, especially those involving manual or office/administrative skills, observe job holders at work – even with managers or professional staff it is helpful, if time permits, to spend time with them.

There are a number of job analysis techniques used for data collection; these are described below.

Interviews

Information required

To obtain the full flavour of a job, it is necessary to interview job holders and check the findings with their managers or team leaders. The aim of the interview should be to obtain all the relevant facts about the job, which comprises:

● the job title of the job holder;
● the job title of the job holder's manager or team leader;
● the job titles and numbers of people reporting to the job holder (best recorded by means of an organizational chart);
● a brief description (one or two sentences) of the overall role or purpose of the job;
● a list of the main tasks or duties that the job holder has to carry out; as appropriate, these should specify the results or output expected, the resources controlled, the equipment used, the contacts made and the frequency with which the tasks are carried out.

These basic details can be supplemented by questions designed to elicit from the job holders some information about the level of their responsibilities and the demands made upon them in the job. Such questions can be difficult to phrase and answer in a meaningful way. The replies may be too vague or misleading and usually have to be checked with the job holders' managers and in subsequent interviews. But they at least give job holders an opportunity to express their feelings about the job and they can provide useful leads for development in discussion. These questions can cover such aspects of the job as:

● the amount of supervision received and the degree of discretion allowed in making decisions;
● the typical problems to be solved and the amount of guidance available when solving the problems;
● the relative difficulty of the tasks to be performed;
● the qualifications and skills required to carry out the work.

Conducting the interview

Job analysis interviews should be conducted as follows:

● Work to a logical sequence of questions that help interviewees to order their thoughts about the job.
● Probe as necessary to establish what people do – answers to questions are often vague and information may be given by means of untypical instances.

- Ensure that job holders are not allowed to get away with vague or inflated descriptions or their work – if, for example, the interview is part of a job evaluation exercise, they would not be human if they did not present the job in the best possible light.
- Sort out the wheat from the chaff: answers to questions may produce a lot of irrelevant data, which must be sifted before preparing the job description.
- Obtain a clear statement from job holders about their authority to make decisions and the amount of guidance they receive from their manager or team leader. This is not easy – if asked what decisions they are authorized to make, most people look blank because they think about their job in terms of duties and tasks rather than abstract decisions.
- Avoid asking leading questions that make the expected answer obvious.
- Allow the job holder ample opportunity to talk by creating an atmosphere of trust.

Job analysis interview checklists

It is helpful to use a checklist when conducting the interview. Elaborate checklists are not necessary; they only confuse people. The essence of the art of job analysis is 'keep it simple'. The points to be covered are:

- What is your job title?
- To whom are you responsible?
- Who reports to you? (An organization chart is helpful.)
- What is the main purpose of your job? (That is, in overall terms, what are you expected to do?)
- To achieve that purpose, what are your main interests of responsibility? (For example, principal accountabilities, key result areas or main tasks.) Describe *what* you have to do, not, in any detail, *how* you do it. Also indicate why you have to do it, ie the results you are expected to achieve by carrying out the task.
- What are the dimensions of your job, in terms such as output or sales targets, numbers of items processed, numbers of people managed, numbers of customers?
- Is there any other information you can provide about your job to amplify the above facts, such as:
  - how your job fits in with other jobs in your department or elsewhere in the company;
  - flexibility requirements in terms of having to carry out a range of different tasks;
  - how work is allocated to you and how your work is reviewed and approved;

- your decision-making authority;
- the contacts you make with others, inside and outside the company;
- the equipment, plant and tools you use;
- other features of your job such as travelling or unsocial hours or effort or stamina demands or hazards;
- the major problems you meet in carrying out your work;
- the knowledge and skills you need to do your work.

The aim is to structure the job analysis interview in line with these headings.

Checking the information

It is always advisable to check the information provided by job holders with their managers or team leaders. Different views can be held about the job and these should be reconciled. Job analysis often reveals such problems as well as various forms of organizational problems. This information can provide a useful spin-off from the job analysis process.

Advantages and disadvantages

The advantages of the interviewing method are that it is very flexible, can provide in-depth information and is easy to organize and prepare. But interviewing can be time-consuming and the results are not always easy to analyse. That is why in large analysis exercises, questionnaires are used to provide advance information about the job, thus speeding up the interviewing process or even replacing the interview altogether, although this means that much of the 'flavour' of the job – ie what it is really like – may be lost, and this flavour is needed if an understanding of the full role of the individual is to be obtained.

Questionnaires

Questionnaires covering the points included in the checklist given above can be completed by job holders and approved by the job holder's manager or team leader. They are helpful when a large number of jobs are to be covered. They can also save interviewing time by recording purely factual information and by enabling the analyst to structure questions in advance to cover areas that need to be explored in greater depth.

The advantage of questionnaires is that they can produce information quickly and cheaply for a large number of jobs. But a substantial sample is needed and the construction of a questionnaire is a skilled job that should only be carried out on the basis of some preliminary fieldwork. It is highly advisable to pilot-test questionnaires before launching into a full-scale exercise. The accuracy of the results also depends on the willingness and ability of job holders to complete questionnaires. Many people find it difficult to express themselves in writing about their work, however well they know and do it.

Checklists and inventories

A checklist for completion by job holders is similar to a questionnaire, but response requires fewer subjective judgements and tends to be of the YES or NO variety. Checklists can cover as many as 100 activities; job holders tick those tasks that are included in their jobs.

Like questionnaires, checklists need to be thoroughly prepared and a field trial is essential to ensure that the instructions for completion are adequate and that the responses make sense. Checklists can be used only where a large number of job holders exist. If the sample is below 30, the results can be erratic.

Rating scales or inventories are an improvement on the relatively crude checklist. Like the checklist, they present job holders with a list of activities. But instead of simply asking them to mark those they carry out, scales are provided for them to give a rating, typically from one to seven, according to the amount of time spent and, sometimes, the importance of the task. These scales could look like those given in Table 23.1.

There are a number of general purpose inventories available, the most widely used of which is the *Position Analysis Questionnaire* developed by McCormick *et al* (1972). This was based on studies of over 3,700 jobs, from which six major work factors were identified:

- the input of information;
- mental processes; for example, decision making;
- work input; for example, the use of machine controls;
- relationships with people;
- work environment;
- other characteristics.

Scales were devised under each heading to measure specific requirements for almost 200 job elements. Each scale describes the activity and has benchmark descriptions for each rating point, as in the example given in Table 23.2.

The *Position Analysis Questionnaire* has the advantage of being generally applicable and comprehensive and having benchmarks. However, it is time-consuming to administer and requires some specialist knowledge.

Table 23.1 Example of a job analysis rating scale

Job analysis rating scale		
Activity description	Time spent – the activity occupies:	Importance of activity
dealing with requests for information by telephone	1. hardly any time (less than 10%)	1. extremely unimportant
	2. a small proportion of the job (10–24%)	2. very unimportant
	3. rather less than half the job (25–44%)	3. not very important
	4. about half the job (45–54%)	4. fairly important
	5. a fairly large proportion of the job (55–74%)	5. important
	6. a very large proportion of the job (75–89%)	6. very important
	7. almost the whole of the job (90% or more)	7. extremely important

Observation

Observation means studying job holders at work, noting what they do, how they do it, and how much time it takes. It is appropriate for situations where a relatively small number of key jobs need to be analysed in depth, but it is time-consuming and difficult to apply in jobs that involve a high proportion of unobservable mental activities, or in highly skilled manual jobs where the actions are too speedy to observe accurately.

Self-description

Job holders can be asked to analyse their own jobs and prepare job descriptions. This saves the considerable time a job analyst can spend in interviewing or observing a job

Table 23.2 Position Analysis Questionnaire – example of benchmark scale for an element (McCormick *et al*, 1972)

	Near visual discrimination (visual discrimination of objects within arm's reach)
7	inspects precision watch parts for defect
6	proofreads newspaper articles before publishing
5	reads electric house meters
4	makes entries on sales tickets
3	observes position of knife when carving beef
2	paints house walls
1	sweeps street with push broom
0	makes no near visual discrimination

holder. But people do not always find this easy, perhaps because what they do is so much part of themselves that they find it difficult to be detached and dissect the information into its various elements. Some guidance is therefore required in most cases. If a number of job holders are involved, for example, in a job evaluation exercise, it is advisable to run special training sessions in which they practise analysing their own and other people's jobs. This method can be taken even further by getting the job holders together and, under the guidance of a job analyst, preparing their analyses and job descriptions on the spot. It is always helpful to produce a model job description to illustrate the format required.

Diaries and logs

This approach to job analysis requires job holders to analyse their own jobs by keeping diaries or logs of their activities. These can be used by the job analyst as the basic material for a job description. Job holders need guidance on how to prepare their diaries or logs. They can be asked to describe a typical day on an hour-by-hour basis, or they can record their activities in narrative form at the end of a period, usually a day. Diaries and logs are best used for managerial jobs which are fairly complex and where the job holders have the analytical skills required, as well as the ability to express themselves on paper.

Hierarchical tasks analysis

Hierarchical task analysis, as developed by Annet and Duncan (1971), breaks down jobs or areas of work into a hierarchical set of tasks, sub-tasks and plans. Tasks are defined in terms of objectives or end-products and the plan needed to achieve the objective is also analysed. The process starts with an analysis of the overall task. This is then subjected to further analysis in order to develop a hierarchy of sub-tasks, together with their outputs, and produce definitions of the sub-plans needed to achieve them.

The method involves:

- using action verbs which describe, in clear and concrete terms, what has to be done;
- defining performance standards, ie the level of performance that has to be achieved in carrying out a task or operation satisfactorily;
- listing the conditions associated with task performance, which might include environmental factors such as working in areas of high noise.

This approach is mostly used for process or manufacturing jobs, but the principles of defining outputs and performance standards, and analysing sub-tasks, are relevant when analysing any type of job.

Choice of method

In the selection of a method of job analysis, the criteria for choice are the purpose for which it will be used, its effectiveness in obtaining the data required, the degree of expertise required to conduct the analysis and the resources and amount of time available for the analysis programme. The following is a summary of the advantages or disadvantages of each method:

- *Interviewing* – this is the basic method of analysis and, as such, is the one most commonly used. It requires skill on the part of the analyst and is time consuming. Analysts need to be trained, and their effectiveness is increased by the use of a checklist.
- *Questionnaires, checklists and inventories* – these can be a useful aid in helping individuals to describe their jobs and they save interviewing time. But it may still be necessary to invest a lot of time in constructing and evaluating questionnaires, which, ideally, should be related to the particular job. They may fail to reveal the full flavour of the job. If they are over-generalized it will be too easy for job holders to provide vague or incoherent answers.
- *Observation* – the most accurate technique for analysing job content (what people actually do). But it is so time-consuming that it is seldom used except when preparing training specifications for manual or clerical jobs.

- *Self-description* – this is the quickest and most economic form of job analysis. But it relies on the often limited ability of people to describe their own jobs. It is therefore necessary to provide them with guidance in the form of questionnaires and checklists.
- *Diaries and logs* – most useful for managerial jobs but they make great demands on job holders and can be difficult to analyse.
- *Hierarchical task analysis* – this provides a helpful structure for job analysis in terms of outputs – a particularly useful feature of this approach – plans (inputs) and relationships. It can be used when analysing the data obtained by interviews or other methods.

Perhaps the most commonly used method is the interview, often supplemented with questionnaires. In a large-scale job evaluation exercise the key 'benchmark' jobs upon which the evaluation will be based may be analysed by interview, while questionnaires would be used for the other jobs.

ROLE ANALYSIS

Role analysis is an extension of job analysis and is generally conducted by means of interviews, possibly supplemented by one of the competency analysis techniques. It will concentrate on identifying the principal accountabilities (key result areas) and defining the competencies job holders require and the part they play in carrying out their work, with particular reference to how they work with other people (their relationships with their managers or team leaders, colleagues, customers, suppliers and any other people they deal with outside the organization), how they fit into the organization structure, the amount of independent action they are expected to take and how they establish their objectives and priorities.

SKILLS ANALYSIS

Skills analysis determines the skills required to achieve an acceptable standard of performance. It is mainly used for technical, craft, manual and office jobs to provide the basis for devising learning and training programmes, as discussed in Chapters 35 and 36. Skills analysis starts from a broad job analysis but goes into detail of not only what job holders have to do but also the particular abilities and skills they need to do it. The skills analysis techniques described below are mainly developed for use in manual or clerical jobs:

- job breakdown;
- manual skills analysis;
- task analysis;
- faults analysis;
- job learning analysis.

Job breakdown

The job breakdown technique analyses a job into separate operations, processes or tasks which can be broken down into manageable parts for instructional purposes.

A job breakdown analysis is recorded in a standard format of three columns:

- *The stage column* in which the different steps in the job are described – the most semi-skilled jobs can easily be broken down into their constituent parts.
- *The instruction column* in which a note is made against each step of how the task should be done. This, in effect, describes what has to be learned by the trainee.
- *The key points column* in which any special points such as quality standards or safety instructions are noted against each step so that they can be emphasized to a trainee learning the job.

Manual skills analysis

Manual skills analysis is a technique developed from work study. It isolates for instructional purposes the skills and knowledge employed by experienced workers in performing tasks that require a high degree of manual dexterity. It is used to analyse short-cycle, repetitive operations such as assembly tasks and other similar factory work.

The hand, finger and other body movements of experienced operatives are observed and recorded in great detail as they carry out their work. The analysis concentrates on the tricky parts of the job which, while presenting no difficulty to the experienced operative, have to be analysed in depth before they can be taught to trainees. Not only are the hand movements recorded in great detail, but particulars are also noted of the cues (visual and other senses) that the operative absorbs when performing the tasks. Explanatory comments are added when necessary.

Task analysis

Task analysis is a systematic analysis of the behaviour required to carry out a task with a view to identifying areas of difficulty and the appropriate training techniques and learning aids necessary for successful instruction. It can be used for all types of jobs.

The analytical approach used in task analysis is similar to those adopted in the job breakdown and manual skills analysis techniques. The results of the analysis are usually recorded in a standard format of four columns as follows:

- *task* – a brief description of each element;
- *level of importance* – the relative significance of each task to the successful performance of the whole job;
- *degree of difficulty* – the level of skill or knowledge required to perform each task;
- *training method* – the instructional techniques, practice and experience required.

Faults analysis

Faults analysis is the process of analysing the typical faults that occur when performing a task, especially the more costly faults. It is carried out when the incidence of faults is high.

A study is made of the job and, by questioning workers and team leaders, the most commonly occurring faults are identified. A faults specification is then produced, which provides trainees with information on what faults can be made, how they can be recognized, what causes them, what effect they have, who is responsible for them, what action the trainees should take when a particular fault occurs, and how a fault can be prevented from recurring.

Job learning analysis

Job learning analysis, as described by Pearn and Kandola (1993), concentrates on the inputs and process rather than the content of the job. It analyses nine learning skills that contribute to satisfactory performance. A learning skill is one used to increase other skills or knowledge and represents broad categories of job behaviour that need to be learnt. The learning skills are the following:

- *physical skills* requiring practice and repetition to get right;
- *complex procedures* or sequences of activity, which are memorized or followed with the aid of written material such as manuals;
- *non-verbal information* such as sight, sound, smell, taste and touch, which is used to check, assess or discriminate, and which usually takes practice to get right;
- *memorizing* facts or information;

- *ordering, prioritizing and planning*, which refer to the degree to which a job holder has any responsibility for and flexibility in determining the way a particular job activity is performed;
- *looking ahead* and anticipating;
- *diagnosing, analysing and problem solving*, with or without help;
- *interpreting or using written manuals* and other sources of information such as diagrams or charts;
- *adapting* to new ideas and systems.

In conducting a job learning analysis interview, the interviewer obtains information on the main aims and principal activities of the job, and then, using question cards for each of the nine learning skills, analyses each activity in more depth, recording responses and obtaining as many examples as possible under each heading.

COMPETENCE ANALYSIS

Definition

Competence analysis is concerned with functional analysis to determine work-based competences and behavioural analysis to establish the behavioural dimensions that affect job performance competencies.

Approaches to competence analysis

There are seven approaches to competence analysis. Starting with the simplest, these are:

- expert opinion;
- structured interview;
- workshops;
- functional analysis;
- critical-incident technique;
- repertory grid analysis.

Expert opinion

The basic, crudest and least satisfactory method is for an 'expert' member of the personnel department, possibly in discussion with other 'experts' from the same department, to draw up a list from their own understanding of 'what counts'.

This is unsatisfactory, because the likelihood of the competences being appropriate to the organization, realistic and measurable in the absence of detailed analysis, is fairly remote. The list tends to be bland and, because line managers and job holders have not been involved, unacceptable.

Structured interview

The structured interview method begins with a list of competences drawn up by 'experts' and proceeds by subjecting a number of job holders to a structured interview. This starts by identifying the key result areas or principal accountabilities of the role and goes on to analyse the behavioural characteristics that distinguish performers at different levels of competence.

The basic question is: 'What are the positive or negative indicators of behaviour that are conducive or non-conducive to achieving high levels of performance?' These may be analysed under such headings as:

- personal drive (achievement motivation);
- impact on results;
- analytical power;
- strategic thinking;
- creative thinking (ability to innovate);
- decisiveness;
- commercial judgement;
- team management and leadership;
- interpersonal relationships;
- ability to communicate;
- ability to adapt and cope with change and pressure;
- ability to plan and control projects;
- a disposition to share knowledge.

In each area instances that will illustrate effective behaviour will be sought.

One of the problems with this approach is that it relies too much on the ability of the expert to draw out information from interviewees. It is also undesirable to use a deductive approach, which pre-empts the analysis with a prepared list of competence headings. It is far better to do this by means of an inductive approach, which starts from specific types of behaviour and then groups them under competence headings. This can be done in a workshop by analysing positive and negative indicators to gain an understanding of the competency dimensions of an occupation or job as described below.

Workshops

Workshops bring together a group of people who have 'expert' knowledge or experience of the job – managers and job holders as appropriate – with a facilitator, usually but not necessarily a member of the personnel department or an outside consultant.

The workshop begins with an analysis of the 'core' competences of the organization – what it has to be good at doing in order to achieve success. Definitions are then agreed on the job-related competence areas – the key activities carried out by the people in the roles under consideration. These are defined in output terms, ie what has to be achieved in that particular aspect of the role. Existing role definitions can be used for this purpose.

Using the competence areas as a framework, the members of the group develop examples of effective behaviour, ie behaviour that is likely to produce the desired results. The basic question is: 'What sort of things do they do and how do they behave when they perform their role effectively?' The answers to this question are expressed in the form: 'Someone in this role will be doing it well when he/she … .' Actual examples of the type of behaviour referred to are given wherever possible. The answers are then recorded on flip charts. The group, with the aid of the facilitator, next analyses its answers and distils them into a number of competence headings which are defined in terms of the actual behaviours noted earlier. The group's words are used as far as possible so that they can 'own' the outcome. These headings form the basis for the generic competence framework or specific competence profile.

For example, one of the competency areas in a divisional personnel director's role might be human resource planning, defined as:

Prepare forecasts of human resource requirements and plans for the acquisition, retention and effective utilization of employees that ensure that the company's need for human resources is met.

The competency dimensions for this area could be expressed as: 'Someone in this role will be doing it well when he/she:

- seeks involvement in business strategy formulation;
- contributes to business planning by taking a strategic view of longer-term human resource issues that are likely to affect business strategy;
- networks with senior management colleagues to understand and respond to the human resource planning issues they raise;
- suggests practical ways to improve the use of human resources.'

The facilitator's role in the workshop is to prompt, help the group to analyse its findings and assist generally in the production of a set of competence dimensions that can be illustrated by behaviour-based examples.

Functional analysis

Functional analysis is the method used to define competence-based standards for National Vocational Qualifications. This starts by describing the key purpose of the occupation and then identifies the key *function* undertaken.

A distinction is made between *tasks*, which are the activities undertaken at work, and *functions*, which are the purposes of activities at work. The distinction is important because the analysis must focus on the outcomes of activities in order to establish expectations of workplace performance as the information required to define standards of competence.

When the units and elements of competence, as defined in Chapter 21, have been established, the next question asked is 'What are the qualities of the outcomes?' in terms of the performance criteria that an NVQ assessor can use to judge whether or not an individual's performance meets the required standards.

Functional analysis is directed towards the definition of NVQ standards; it will not result directly in the development of definitions of the behavioural dimensions of competence, especially when generic definitions are required for a whole occupational area, for example managers or team leaders.

Critical-incident technique

The critical-incident technique is a means of eliciting data about effective or less effective behaviour which is related to examples of actual events – critical incidents. The technique is used with groups of job holders and/or their managers or other 'experts' (sometimes, less effectively, with individuals) as follows:

● Explain what the technique is and what it is used for, ie 'to assess what constitutes good or poor performance by analysing events which have been observed to have a noticeably successful or unsuccessful outcome, thus providing more factual and "real" information than by simply listing tasks and guessing performance requirements.'

● Agree and list the key areas of responsibility – the principal accountabilities – in the job to be analysed. To save time, the analyst can establish these prior to the meeting but it is necessary to ensure that they are agreed provisionally by the group, which can be told that the list may well be amended in the light of the forthcoming analysis.

● Each area of the job is taken in turn and the group is asked for examples of critical incidents. If, for example, one of the job responsibilities is dealing with customers, the following request could be made:

> I want you to tell me about a particular occasion at work that involved you – or that you observed – in dealing with a customer. Think about what the circumstances were, eg who took part, what the customer asked for, what you or the other member of the staff did and what the outcome was.

● Collect information about the critical incident under the following headings:
  – what the circumstances were;
  – what the individual did;
  – the outcome of what the individual did.

This information should be recorded on a flip chart.

● Continue this process for each area of responsibility.
● Refer to the flip chart and analyse each incident by obtaining ratings of the recorded behaviour on a scale such as 1 for least effective to 5 for most effective.
● Discuss these ratings to get initial definitions of effective and ineffective performance for each of the key aspects of the job.
● Refine these definitions as necessary after the meeting – it can be difficult to get a group to produce finished definitions.
● Produce the final analysis, which can list the competences required and include performance indicators or standards of performance for each principal accountability or main task.

Repertory grid

Like the critical-incident technique, the repertory grid can be used to identify the dimensions that distinguish good from poor standards of performance. The technique is based on Kelly's (1955) personal constructs theory. Personal constructs are the ways in which we view the world. They are personal because they are highly individual and they influence the way we behave or view other people's behaviour.

The aspects of the job to which these 'constructs' or judgements apply are called 'elements'.

To elicit judgements, a group of people are asked to concentrate on certain elements, which are the tasks carried out by job holders, and develop constructs about these elements. This enables them to define the qualities that indicate the essential requirements for successful performance.

The procedure followed by the analyst is known as the 'triadic method of elicitation' (a sort of three-card trick) and involves the following steps:

1. Identify the tasks or elements of the job to be subjected to repertory grid analysis. This is done by one of the other forms of job analysis, eg interviewing.
2. List the tasks on cards.
3. Draw three cards at random from the pack and ask the members of the group to nominate which of these tasks is the odd one out from the point of view of the qualities and characteristics needed to perform it.
4. Probe to obtain more specific definitions of these qualities or characteristics in the form of expected behaviour. If, for example, a characteristic has been described as the 'ability to plan and organize', ask questions such as: 'What sort of behaviour or actions indicate that someone is planning effectively?', or 'How can we tell if someone is not organizing his or her work particularly well?'
5. Draw three more cards from the pack and repeat steps 3 and 4.
6. Repeat this process until all the cards have been analysed and there do not appear to be any more constructs to be identified.
7. List the constructs and ask the group members to rate each task on every quality, using a six- or seven-point scale.
8. Collect and analyse the scores in order to assess their relative importance. This can be done statistically as described by Markham (1987).

Like the critical-incident technique, repertory grid analysis helps people to articulate their views by reference to specific examples. An additional advantage is that the repertory grid makes it easier for them to identify the behaviour characteristics of competences required in a job by limiting the area of comparison through the triadic technique.

Although a full statistical analysis of the outcome of a repertory grid exercise is helpful, the most important results that can be obtained are the descriptions of what constitutes good or poor performance in each element of the job.

Both the repertory grid and the critical-incident techniques require a skilled analyst who can probe and draw out the descriptions of job characteristics. They are quite detailed and time-consuming but even if the full process is not followed, much of the methodology is of use in a less elaborate approach to competence analysis.

Which approach?

Techniques such as critical-incident technique and repertory grid analysis can be used effectively, but they are time-consuming and need experience to apply them effectively.

For those who have not got the time to use either of these approaches, the workshop approach as described above is probably the best. But if you have not carried out this type of analysis it is advisable to enlist the support of an external consultant who has the relevant experience. Functional analysis is used when the main objective is to develop NVQ standards.

JOB DESCRIPTIONS

Job descriptions are derived from the job analysis. They provide basic information about the job under the headings of the job title, reporting relationships, overall purpose and principal accountabilities or main tasks or duties.

The basic data may be supplemented by other information giving more details about the nature and scope of the job, the factors or criteria that indicate its level for job evaluation purposes, or the competences required, as an aid to the preparation of training programmes and for use in assessment centres. This can convert the basic job description into a full role definition if it concentrates on the behavioural aspects of the role played by job holders.

Use of job descriptions for organizational, recruitment and performance management purposes

The basic job description can be used to:

- define the place of the job in the organization and to clarify for job holders and others the contribution the job makes to achieving organizational or departmental objectives;
- provide the information required to produce person specifications for recruitment and to inform applicants about the job;
- be the basis for the contract of employment;
- provide the framework for setting objectives for performance management;
- be the basis for job evaluation and grading jobs.

Content and format

Job descriptions should not go into too much detail. What needs to be clarified is the contribution job holders are expected to make, expressed as the results to be achieved (expressed as principal accountabilities, key result areas or main tasks, activities or duties) and their positions in the organization (reporting relationships).

There are two factors to take into account when preparing this type of job description:

- *Flexibility* – operational flexibility and multi-skilling are becoming increasingly significant. It is therefore necessary to build flexibility into the job descriptions. This is achieved by concentrating on results rather than spelling out what has to be done – job descriptions should not become straitjackets by spelling out in detail the tasks to be carried out. The emphasis should be on the role job holders have to play in using their skills and competences in specified broad areas of responsibility to achieve results. The aim is to ensure that job holders who are expected to work flexibly cannot say, 'No, it's not in my job description.'
- *Teamwork* – flatter organizations rely more on good teamwork and this requirement needs to be stressed.

Format

The format of a job description for organizational, recruitment or contractual purposes comprises simply:

- the job title;
- a definition of the overall purpose or objectives of the job;
- a list of principal accountabilities, key result areas, tasks, activities or duties (what these are called does not matter too much, although the terms 'principal accountabilities' and 'key result areas' do emphasize the end results the job holder is expected to achieve).

An example of a job description is given in Figure 23.1.

Job descriptions for job evaluation purposes

For job evaluation purposes, the job description should contain the information included in an organizational description as well as a 'factor analysis' of the job by reference to the job evaluation factors or criteria used to assess relative job values (see Chapter 39). In addition, it is often helpful to include a narrative describing the nature

---

Job description – HR director

Overall purpose

To advise on HR strategies and policies and ensure that the HR function provides the support required to implement them and that 'world class' personnel processes are functioning effectively.

Principal accountabilities

1. Participate as a member of the Board in formulating corporate strategies, policies, plans and budgets and in monitoring the company's performance so as to ensure that the corporate mission and goals are achieved.

2. Advise the Chief Executive and colleagues on the HR and employee relations policies required by the company in all areas of HR management in order to uphold core values and fulfil social responsibilities.

3. Formulate and implement HR strategies that are fully integrated with business strategies and cohere over all aspects of personnel management and develop plans to implement the strategies.

4. Plan and direct human resource development, performance management and career management processes and programmes designed to improve individual and organizational effectiveness and to give employees the best opportunities to develop their abilities and careers in the company.

5. Develop reward management and remuneration (including pensions) policies, processes and procedures that attract, retain and motivate employees, are internally equitable as well as externally competitive, and operate cost-effectively.

6. Advise on employee relations and communication strategies and policies designed to maximize involvement and commitment while minimizing conflict.

7. Advise on the development of knowledge management processes.

8. Direct and control the operations of the HR function to ensure that it provides cost-effective services throughout the organization.

9. Ensure through advice and monitoring that HR policies are implemented consistently, and that the core values of the company concerning people are upheld, especially those concerned with fairness, equal opportunity and work-life balance.

Figure 23.1 Job description for an HR director

and scope of the job, as used in the Hay job evaluation system. This narrative gives general information on the environment in which the job operates. The nature of the job is described in broad terms to give evaluators an overall view of what sort of job it is. This puts flesh on the bones of a list of principal accountabilities. The scope of the job is defined wherever possible by quantifying the various aspects of the job, such as the resources controlled, the results to be achieved, budgets, the proportion of time spent on different aspects of the job, and the number of occasions over a certain period of time when decisions have to be made or actions taken.

The factor analysis attached to the job description describes the incidence of each job evaluation factor such as knowledge and skills, responsibility, decisions, complexity and contacts.

Job descriptions for training purposes

For training purposes, job descriptions should be based on the format for an organizational job description, although the details of the nature and scope of the job and the factor analysis contained in job descriptions for job evaluations contain useful additional information. The training job description and specification include an analysis of the attributes (knowledge and skills) and competences used in the job. This means that a more detailed description of the tasks the job holder has to carry out may be necessary as well as spelling out attribute and competence requirements. An example of a training specification is given in Chapter 41.

Writing a job description

Job descriptions should be based on a detailed job analysis and should be as brief and factual as possible. The headings under which the job description should be written and notes for guidance on completing each section are set out below.

Job title – the existing or proposed job title should indicate as clearly as possible the function in which the job is carried out and the level of the job within that function. The use of terms such as 'manager', 'assistant manager' or 'senior' to describe job levels should be reasonably consistent between functions with regard to gradings of the jobs.

Reporting to – the job title of the manager or supervisor to whom the job holder is directly responsible should be given under this heading. No attempt should be made to indicate here any functional relationships the job holder might have to other managers.

Reporting to job holder – the job titles of all the posts directly reporting to the job holder should be given under this heading. Again, no attempt should be made here to indicate any functional relationships that might exist between the job holder and other employees. An organization chart may be included to clarify reporting relationships.

Overall purpose – this section should describe as concisely as possible the overall purpose of the job. The aim should be to convey in one sentence a broad picture of the job which will clearly distinguish it from other jobs and establish the role of the job holders and the contribution they should make towards achieving the objectives of the company and their function or unit. No attempt should be made to describe the activities carried out under this heading, but the overall summary should lead naturally to the analysis of activities in the next section. When preparing the job description, it is often best to defer writing down the definition of overall responsibilities until the activities have been analysed and described.

Principal accountabilities or main tasks – the steps required to define principal accountabilities or main tasks are:

- Identify and produce an initial list of the main activities or tasks carried out by the job holder.
- Analyse the initial list of tasks and group them together so that no more than about 10 main activity areas remain – most jobs can be analysed into seven or eight areas and if the number is extended much beyond that, the job description will become over-complex and it will be difficult to be specific about accountabilities, key result areas or tasks.
- Define each activity as in effect a statement of accountability – an accountability statement expresses what the job holder is expected to achieve (outputs) and will therefore be held responsible (accountable) for. It may be defined as a key result area.
- Define the accountability in one sentence which should:
  - start with a verb in the active voice that provides a positive indication of what has to be done and eliminates unnecessary wording; for example: plans, prepares, produces, implements, processes, provides, schedules, completes, dispatches, maintains, liaises with, collaborates with;
  - describe the object of the verb (what is done) as succinctly as possible; for example: tests new systems, posts cash to the nominal and sales ledgers, dispatches packets to the warehouse output, schedules production, ensures that management accounts are produced, prepares marketing plans;
  - state briefly the purpose of the activity in terms of outputs or standards to be achieved; for example: tests new systems to ensure they meet agreed systems specifications; posts cash to the nominal and sales ledgers in order to provide up-to-date and accurate financial information, dispatches planned output to the warehouse so that all items are removed by carriers on the same day they are packed, schedules production in order to meet laid-down output and delivery targets, ensures that management accounts are produced that provide the required level of information to management and individual

managers on financial performance against budget and on any variances, prepares marketing plans that support the achievement of the marketing strategies of the enterprise, are realistic, and provide clear guidance on the actions to be taken by the development, production, marketing and sales departments.

Statements of accountability that emphasize the outputs required in terms of the expected results provide essential data for use in agreeing standing and short-term objectives in performance management processes as described in Chapter 30, and in defining work-based competences.

Factor analysis – when preparing job descriptions for job evaluation purposes, factor analysis techniques are used. Factor analysis is the process of taking each of the job evaluation factors, such as knowledge and skills and responsibility, and assessing the level at which they are present in the job. When writing factor analyses, reference should be made to the factor and level definitions in the job evaluation factor plan (see Chapter 41). The analysis should be backed up as far as possible with facts and examples.

An example of a job description is given in Figure 23.1.

ROLE PROFILES

Is job analysis concerned with jobs or roles or both? The terms 'job' and 'role' are often used interchangeably, but there is an important difference:

- *A job* consists of a group of finite tasks to be performed (pieces of work) and duties to be fulfilled in order to achieve an end result.
- *A role* describes the part played by people in meeting their objectives by working competently and flexibly within the context of the organization's objectives, structure and processes.

When describing a job, the traditional approach has been to concentrate on why it exists (its overall purpose) and the activities to be carried out. The implication is that these are fixed and are performed by job holders as prescribed. On the face of it, there is no room for flexibility or interpretation of how best to do the work. Jobs are the same, in fact should be the same, whoever carries them out.

The concept of a role is much wider because it is people and behaviour-orientated

– it is concerned with what people do and how they do it rather than concentrating narrowly on job content. When faced with any situation, eg carrying out a job, individuals have to enact a role in order to perform effectively within that situation. People at work are, in a sense, often acting a part; they are not simply reciting the lines but interpreting them in terms of their own perceptions of how they should behave within their work context.

Role profiles or definitions cover both the key result areas of the role and the behavioural aspects of work – the competences required to achieve acceptable levels of performance and contribution. They can stress the need for flexibility and multi-skilling, and for adapting to the different demands that are made on people in project- and team-based organizations where the emphasis is on process rather than hierarchical structure.

Preparation of role profiles

Role profiles are prepared on the basis of the job, skills and competence analysis process described above. The 'nature and scope' or 'context' section of a job description may broadly describe the role of the job holder. It may be difficult to describe a role in precise terms and it is often better to clarify roles on a face-to-face basis rather than trying to get people to express them in writing. This can be carried out as part of a performance management process (see Part VIII). The concept of a role is essentially one that describes outputs, outcomes, relationships and types of behaviours rather than precise factual statements of the tasks carried out by role holders.

Generic role profiles

Role profiles are often 'generic'; that is, they cover groups of roles that are essentially similar. Their advantage is that they can be used to define broad recruitment and learning specifications for people who carry out those roles. They provide a basis for performance management agreements and reviews where these are concerned with typical competency requirements. They can also be used in job evaluation as the point of reference for grading a role, especially in a broad-banded or job family structure (these terms are defined in Chapter 43).

Generic role profiles are prepared by means of normal job and competence analysis techniques as described earlier in this chapter. These aim to identify the common characteristics of such roles and distil them into a generalized profile. An example of a generic role profile is given in Figure 23.2.

GENERIC ROLE PROFILE FOR TEAM LEADERS

Overall purpose of role:
To lead teams in order to attain team goals and further the achievement of the organization's objectives.

Key result areas
1. Agree with team members targets and standards that support the attainment of the organization's objectives.
2. Plan with team members work schedules and resource requirements that will ensure that team targets will be reached, indeed exceeded.
3. Agree with team members performance measures and quality assurance processes that will clarify output and quality expectations.
4. Agree with team members the allocation of tasks, rotating responsibilities as appropriate to achieve flexibility and the best use of the skills and capabilities of team members.
5. Coordinate the work of the team to ensure that team goals are achieved.
6. Ensure that the team members collectively monitor the team's performance in terms of achieving output, speed of response and quality targets and standards and agree with team members any corrective action required to ensure that team goals are achieved.
7. Conduct team reviews of performance to agree improvement.

Competencies
- Builds effective team relationships, ensuring that team members are committed to the common purpose.
- Encourages self-direction amongst team members but provides guidance and clear direction as required.
- Shares information with team members.
- Trusts team members to get on with things – not continually checking.
- Treats team members fairly and consistently.
- Supports and guides team members to make the best use of their capabilities.
- Encourages self-development by example.
- Actively offers constructive feedback to team members and positively seeks and is open to constructive feedback from them.
- Contributes to the development of team members, encouraging the acquisition of additional skills and providing opportunities for them to be used effectively.
- Shares own knowledge and encourages team members to share their knowledge.

Figure 23.2 Generic role profile for team leaders

Part VII

Employee resourcing

EMPLOYEE RESOURCING DEFINED

Employee resourcing is concerned with ensuring that the organization obtains and retains the people it needs and employs them productively. It is also about those aspects of employment practice that are concerned with welcoming people to the organization and, if there is no alternative, releasing them. It is a key part of the human resource management (HRM) process.

EMPLOYEE RESOURCING AND HRM

HRM is fundamentally about matching human resources to the strategic and operational needs of the organization and ensuring the full utilization of those resources. It is concerned not only with obtaining and keeping the number and quality of staff required but also with selecting and promoting people who 'fit' the culture and the strategic requirements of the organization.

HRM places more emphasis than traditional personnel management on finding people whose attitudes and behaviour are likely to be congruent with what management believes to be appropriate and conducive to success. In the words of Townley (1989), organizations are concentrating more on 'the attitudinal and behavioural characteristics of employees'. This tendency has its dangers. Innovative and adaptive organizations need non-conformists, even mavericks, who can 'buck the system'. If managers recruit people 'in their own image' there is the risk of staffing the organization with conformist clones and of perpetuating a dysfunctional culture – one that may have been successful in the past but is no longer appropriate (nothing fails like success).

The HRM approach to resourcing therefore emphasizes that matching resources to organizational requirements does not simply mean maintaining the status quo and perpetuating a moribund culture. It can and often does mean radical changes in thinking about the competencies required in the future to achieve sustainable growth and to achieve cultural change. HRM resourcing policies address two fundamental questions:

1. *What kind of people do we need to compete effectively, now and in the foreseeable future?*
2. *What do we have to do to attract, develop and keep these people?*

Integrating business and resourcing strategies

The philosophy behind the HRM approach to resourcing is that it is people who implement the strategic plan. As Quinn Mills (1983) has put it, the process is one of 'planning with people in mind'.

The integration of business and resourcing strategies is based on an understanding of the direction in which the organization is going and of the resulting human resource needs in terms of:

● *numbers required in relation to projected activity levels;*
● *skills required on the basis of technological and product/market developments and strategies to enhance quality or reduce costs;*
● *the impact of organizational restructuring as a result of rationalization, decentralization, delayering, mergers, product or market development, or the introduction of new technology – for example, cellular manufacturing;*
● *plans for changing the culture of the organization in such areas as ability to deliver, performance standards, quality, customer service, team working and flexibility which indicate the need for people with different attitudes, beliefs and personal characteristics.*

These factors will be strongly influenced by the type of business strategies adopted by the organization and the sort of business it is in. These may be expressed in such terms as the Boston Consulting Group's classification of businesses as wild cat, star, cash cow or dog; or Miles and Snow's (1978) typology of defender, prospector and analyser organizations.

Resourcing strategies exist to provide the people and skills required to support the business strategy, but they should also contribute to the formulation of that strategy. HR directors have an obligation to point out to their colleagues the human resource opportunities and constraints that will affect the achievement of strategic plans. In mergers or acquisitions, for example, the ability of management within the company to handle the new situation and the quality of management in the new business will be important considerations.

PLAN

This part deals with the following aspects of employee resourcing:

- *human resource planning;*
- *recruitment;*
- *selection interviewing;*
- *selection testing;*
- *introduction to the organization;*
- *release from the organization.*

24

Human resource planning

THE ROLE OF HUMAN RESOURCE PLANNING

Definition

Human resource planning determines the human resources required by the organization to achieve its strategic goals. As defined by Bulla and Scott (1994) it is 'the process for ensuring that the human resource requirements of an organization are identified and plans are made for satisfying those requirements'. Human resource planning is based on the belief that people are an organization's most important strategic resource. It is generally concerned with matching resources to business needs in the longer term, although it will sometimes be concerned with shorter-term requirements. It addresses human resource needs both in quantitative and qualitative terms which means answering two basic questions:

1. How many people?
2. What sort of people?

Human resource planning also looks at broader issues relating to the ways in which people are employed and developed in order to improve organizational effectiveness. It can therefore play an important part in strategic human resource management.

Human resource planning and business planning

Conceptually, human resource planning should be an integral part of business planning. The strategic planning process should define projected changes in the scale and types of activities carried out by the organization. It should identify the core competences the organization needs to achieve its goals and therefore its skill requirements. But there are often limitations to the extent to which such plans are made or, indeed, the clarity of the plans, and this may restrict the feasibility of developing integrated human resource plans which flow from them.

In so far as there are articulated strategic business plans, human resource planning interprets them in terms of people requirements. But it may influence the business strategy by drawing attention to ways in which people could be developed and deployed more effectively to further the achievement of business goals, as well as focusing on any problems that might have to be resolved in order to ensure that the people required will be available and will be capable of making the necessary contribution. As Quinn Mills (1983) indicates, human resource planning is 'a decision-making process that combines three important activities: (1) identifying and acquiring the right number of people with the proper skills, (2) motivating them to achieve high performance, and (3) creating interactive links between business objectives and people-planning activities'. In situations where a clear business strategy does not exist, human resource planning may have to rely more on making broad assumptions about the need for people in the future, based on some form of scenario planning. Alternatively, the planning process could focus on specific areas of activity within the organization where it is possible to forecast likely future people requirements in terms of numbers and skills, for example, scientists in a product development division.

Hard and soft human resource planning

A distinction can be made between 'hard' and 'soft' human resource planning. The former is based on quantitative analysis in order to ensure that the right number of the right sort of people are available when needed. The latter, as described by Marchington and Wilkinson (1996), 'is more explicitly focused on creating and shaping the culture of the organization so that there is a clear integration between corporate goals and employee values, beliefs and behaviours'. But as they point out, the soft version becomes virtually synonymous with the whole subject of human resource management.

Human resource planning and manpower planning

Human resource planning is indeed concerned with broader issues about the employment of people than the traditional quantitative approaches of 'manpower planning'. Such approaches, as Liff (2000) comments, derive from a rational top-down view of planning in which well-tested quantitative techniques could be applied to long-term assessments of supply and demand. She notes that 'there has been a shift from reconciling numbers of employees available with predictable stable jobs, towards a greater concern with skills, their development and deployment'.

Limitations of human resource planning

Human resource planning is said to consist of three clear steps:

- forecasting future people needs (demand forecasting);
- forecasting the future availability of people (supply forecasting);
- drawing up plans to match supply to demand.

But as Casson (1978) pointed out, this conventional wisdom represents human resource planning as an 'all-embracing, policy-making activity producing, on a rolling basis, precise forecasts using technically sophisticated and highly integrated planning systems'. He suggests that it is better regarded as:

- a regular *monitoring* activity, through which human resource stocks and flows and their relationship to business needs can be better understood, assessed and controlled, problems highlighted and a base established from which to respond to unforeseen events;
- an *investigatory* activity by which the human resource implications of particular problems and change situations can be explored and the effects of alternative policies and actions investigated.

He points out that the spurious precision of quantified manpower plans 'has little value when reconciled with the complex and frequently changing nature of manpower, the business and the external environment'. The typical concept of human resource planning as a matter of forecasting the long-term demand and supply of people fails because the ability to make these estimates must be severely limited by the difficulty of predicting the influence of external events. Human resource planning today is more likely to concentrate on what skills will be needed in the future, and may do no more than provide a broad indication of the numbers required in the longer term. Such predictions will often be based on broad scenarios rather than on specific supply and demand forecasts.

The incidence of and rationale for human resource planning

Although the notion of human resource planning is well established in the HRM vocabulary, it does not seem to be commonly practised as a key HR activity. As Rothwell (1995) suggests, 'Apart from isolated examples, there has been little research evidence of increased use or of its success'. She explains the gap between theory and practice as arising from:

● the impact of change and the difficulty of predicting the future - 'the need for planning may be in inverse proportion to its feasibility';
● the 'shifting kaleidoscope' of policy priorities and strategies within organizations;
● the distrust displayed by many managers of theory or planning - they often prefer pragmatic adaptation to conceptualization;
● the lack of evidence that human resource planning works.

Be that as it may, it is difficult to reject out of hand the belief that some attempt should be made broadly to forecast future human resource requirements as a basis for planning and action. On the basis of research conducted by the Institute for Employment Studies, Reilly (1999) has suggested a number of reasons why organizations choose to engage in some form of human resource planning. These fall into the following three groups.

1. *Planning for substantive reasons*, that is, to have a practical effect by optimizing the use of resources and/or making them more flexible, acquiring and nurturing skills that take time to develop, identifying potential problems and minimizing the chances of making a bad decision.
2. *Planning because of the process benefits*, which involves understanding the present in order to confront the future, challenging assumptions and liberating thinking, making explicit decisions which can later be challenged, standing back and providing an overview, and ensuring that long-term thinking is not driven out by short-term focus.
3. *Planning for organizational reasons*, which involves communicating plans so as to obtain support/adherence to them, linking HR plans to business plans so as to influence them, (re)gaining corporate control over operating units, and coordinating and integrating organizational decision-making and actions.

The organizational context of human resource planning

Human resource planning takes place within the context of the organization. The extent to which it is used and the approach adopted will be contingent on the extent to which management recognizes that success depends on forecasting future people requirements and implementing plans to satisfy those requirements. The approach will also be affected by the degree to which it is possible to make accurate forecasts. Organizations operating in turbulent environments in which future activity levels are difficult to predict may rely on ad hoc and short-term measures to recruit and keep people. However, even these businesses may benefit from those aspects of human resource planning which are concerned with policies for attracting and retaining key staff.

The labour market context

The context for obtaining the people required will be the labour markets in which the organization is operating which are:

1. *The internal labour market* – the stocks and flows of people within the organization who can be promoted, trained, or re-deployed to meet future needs.
2. *The external labour market* – the external local, regional, national and international markets from which different sorts of people can be recruited. There are usually a number of markets, and the labour supply in these markets may vary considerably. Likely shortages will need to be identified so that steps can be taken to deal with them, for example by developing a more attractive 'employment proposition'.

As part of the human resource planning process, an organization may have to formulate 'make or buy' policy decisions. A 'make' policy means that the organization prefers to recruit people at a junior level or as trainees, and rely mainly on promotion from within and training programmes to meet future needs. A 'buy' policy means that more reliance will be placed on recruiting from outside – 'bringing fresh blood into the organization'. In practice, organizations tend to mix the two choices together to varying degrees, depending on the situation of the firm and the type of people involved. A highly entrepreneurial company operating in turbulent conditions, or one which has just started up, will probably rely almost entirely on external recruitment. When dealing with knowledge workers, there may be little choice – they tend to be much more mobile, and resourcing strategy may have to recognize that external recruitment will be the main source of supply. Management consultancies typically fall into this category. Firms which can predict people requirements fairly accurately may rely more on developing their own staff once they have been recruited.

AIMS OF HUMAN RESOURCE PLANNING

The aims of human resource planning in any organization will depend largely on its context but in general terms, the typical aims might be to:

● attract and retain the number of people required with the appropriate skills, expertise and competences;
● anticipate the problems of potential surpluses or deficits of people;
● develop a well-trained and flexible workforce, thus contributing to the organization's ability to adapt to an uncertain and changing environment;
● reduce dependence on external recruitment when key skills are in short supply by formulating retention, as well as employee development, strategies;
● improve the utilization of people by introducing more flexible systems of work.

THE PROCESS OF HUMAN RESOURCE PLANNING

The process of human resource planning as illustrated in Figure 24.1 is not necessarily a linear one, starting with the business strategy and flowing logically through to resourcing, flexibility and retention plans. It may, as Hendry (1995) suggests, be circular rather than linear, with the process starting anywhere in the cycle. For example, scenario planning may impact on resourcing strategy which in turn may influence the business strategy. Alternatively, the starting point could be demand and supply forecasts which form the basis for the resourcing strategy. The analysis of labour turnover may feed into the supply forecast, but it could also lead directly to the development of retention plans.

It cannot be assumed that there will be a well-articulated business plan as a basis for the HR plans. The business strategy may be evolutionary rather than deliberate; it may be fragmented, intuitive and incremental. Resourcing decisions may be based on scenarios that are riddled with assumptions which may or may not be correct and cannot be tested. Resourcing strategy may be equally vague or based on unproven beliefs about the future. It may contain statements about, for example, building the skills base, which are little more than rhetoric.

There is much to be said for a systematic approach to developing resourcing

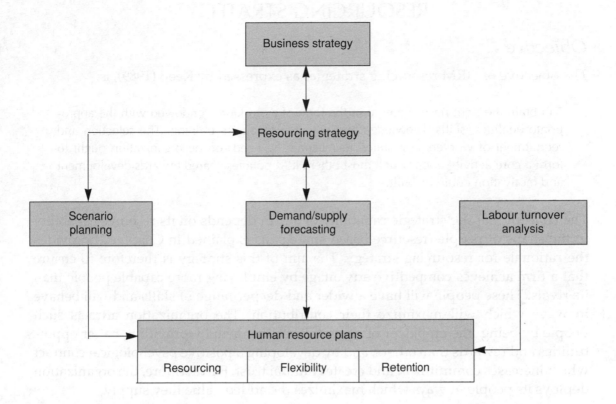

Figure 24.1 The process of HR planning

strategy, scenario planning, demand and supply forecasting and labour turnover analysis as discussed in the rest of this chapter. But, because of the factors mentioned above, there will often be reservations about the extent to which this process can be formalized. What may emerge is simply a broad statement of intent, although this could be sufficient to guide resourcing practice generally and would be better than nothing at all. The degree to which human resource planning can be carried out systematically will depend on the nature of the organization. If the future is fairly predictable, then formal planning might be appropriate. If it is not, the approach to human resource planning might have to rely on broad scenarios rather than precise forecasts.

RESOURCING STRATEGY

Objective

The objective of HRM resourcing strategies as expressed by Keep (1989), is:

> To obtain the right basic material in the form of a workforce endowed with the appropriate qualities, skills, knowledge and potential for future training. The selection and recruitment of workers best suited to meeting the needs of the organization ought to form a core activity upon which most other HRM policies geared towards development and motivation could be built.

The concept that the strategic capability of a firm depends on its resource capability in the shape of people (resource-based strategy as explained in Chapter 2) provides the rationale for resourcing strategy. The aim of this strategy is therefore to ensure that a firm achieves competitive advantage by employing more capable people than its rivals. These people will have a wider and deeper range of skills and will behave in ways which will maximize their contribution. The organization attracts such people by being 'the employer of choice'. It retains them by providing better opportunities and rewards than others, and by developing a positive psychological contract which increases commitment and creates mutual trust. Furthermore, the organization deploys its people in ways which maximizes the added value they supply.

Checklist

The resourcing strategy should attempt to provide answers to the following questions:

- In the light of the business plan, how many people are we likely to need in each of our key operational or functional areas in the short and longer term?
- What skills are we likely to need in the future?
- Will we be able to meet the needs from our existing resources?
- If not, where will we be able to find them?
- What do we need to do to develop or extend our skills base?
- What should we do about identifying people with potential and developing their abilities?
- Do we have a problem in attracting or retaining key staff? If so, what do we need to do about it?
- Is there scope to make better use of people by increasing employment flexibility?
- Is there any danger of downsizing? If so, how are we going to deal with it?

The components of resourcing strategy

These are:

- *Resourcing plans* – preparing plans for finding people from within the organization and/or for training programmes to help people learn new skills. If needs cannot be satisfied from within the organization, preparing longer-term plans for meeting them by attracting high quality candidates as the 'employer of choice'.
- *Flexibility plans* – planning for increased flexibility in the use of human resources to enable the organization to make the best use of people and adapt swiftly to changing circumstances.
- *Retention plans* – preparing plans for retaining the people the organization needs.

Resourcing strategy provides the basis for these plans within the framework of business needs. It will, however, be more strongly based if it is underpinned by a process of scenario planning.

SCENARIO PLANNING

Scenario planning is sometimes described as a formal strategic planning technique. But it can also be regarded as an informal approach to thinking about the future in broad terms, based upon an analysis of likely changes in the internal and external environment.

A scenario can be defined as 'an imagined sequence of future events' (Oxford English Dictionary). Scenario planning is simply a more or less formalized process for establishing a view about any changes that can be foreseen to the scale and type of activities in the organization and to its structure, and for identifying any external environmental changes that are likely to affect it. The aim is to obtain a better understanding of the possible situations that may have to be dealt with in the future. It is described by Reilly (1999) as follows:

> Scenario planning tries to open minds to a range of possibilities that organizations may have to confront. These possibilities are then ordered to produce a series of internally consistent pictures of alternative futures… It is an intellectual process that seeks to identify issues and examine the possible consequences of events.

The creation of a scenario involves making broad assessments of likely internal developments – the direction in which the organization is going and the likely implications this has on people requirements. The assessments may have to be made in the absence of any articulated business plan, and will thus involve questioning top management and key line managers on how they see the future, then asking them to interpret what this means in terms of their human resource needs. Assessments will also have to be made on likely changes in the external environment as they may affect the labour market.

ESTIMATING FUTURE HUMAN RESOURCE REQUIREMENTS

Scenario planning is in some situations as far as it is possible to go in estimating future people requirements. But where it is feasible and appropriate, attempts can usefully be made to produce demand and supply forecasts, and to determine what action needs to be taken if the forecasts indicate the possibility of a human resource deficit or surplus.

Demand forecasting

Demand forecasting is the process of estimating the future numbers of people required and the likely skills and competences they will need. The ideal basis of the forecast is an annual budget and longer-term business plan, translated into activity levels for each function and department or decisions on 'downsizing'. In a manufacturing company the sales budget is translated into a manufacturing plan giving the numbers and types of products to be made in each period. From this information the number of hours to be worked by each skill category to make the quota for each period can be computed.

Details are required of any plans or projects which would result in demands for additional employees or different skills: for example, setting up a new regional organization, creating a new sales department, carrying out a major project, or developing new products or services. So far as possible, plans should also be reviewed which may result in rationalization and, possibly, downsizing as a result of a cost-reduction drive, a business process re-engineering exercise, new technology leading to increased productivity, or a merger or acquisition.

The demand forecasting techniques that can be used to produce quantitative estimates of future requirements are described below.

Managerial or expert judgement

This is the most typical method of forecasting, and may be linked to some form of scenario planning. It simply requires managers or specialists to sit down, think about future workloads, and decide how many people are needed. This can be no more than guesswork unless there is reliable evidence available of forecast increases in activity levels or new demands for skills.

Ratio-trend analysis

This is carried out by studying past ratios between, say, the number of direct (production) workers and indirect (support) workers in a manufacturing plant, and forecasting future ratios, having made some allowance for changes in organization or methods. Activity-level forecasts are then used to determine, in this example, direct labour requirements, and the forecast ratio of indirects to directs would be used to calculate the number of indirect workers needed.

Work study techniques

Work study techniques can be used when it is possible to apply work measurement to calculate how long operations should take and the number of people required. Work study techniques for direct workers can be combined with ratio-trend analysis to calculate the number of indirect workers needed.

Forecasting skill and competence requirements

Forecasting skill requirements is largely a matter of managerial judgement. This judgement should, however, be exercised on the basis of a careful analysis of the impact of projected product-market developments and the introduction of new technology, either information technology or computerized manufacturing.

Supply forecasting

Supply forecasting measures the number of people likely to be available from within and outside the organization, having allowed for attrition (labour wastage and retirements), absenteeism, internal movements and promotions, and changes in hours and other conditions of work. The forecast will be based on:

- an analysis of existing human resources in terms of numbers in each occupation, skills and potential;
- forecast losses to existing resources through attrition (the analysis of labour wastage as described in the next main section of this chapter is an important

aspect of human resource planning because it provides the basis for plans to improve retention rates);
- forecast changes to existing resources through internal promotions;
- the effect of changing conditions of work and absenteeism;
- sources of supply from within the organization;
- sources of supply from outside the organization in the national and local labour markets.

Mathematical modelling techniques aided by computers can help in the preparation of supply forecasts in situations where comprehensive and reliable data on stocks and flows can be provided. As this is rarely the case, they are seldom used.

The demand and supply forecasts can then be analysed to determine whether there are any deficits or surpluses. This provides the basis for recruitment, retention and, if unavoidable, downsizing plans. Computerized planning models can be used for this purpose. It is, however, not essential to rely on a software planning package. The basic forecasting calculations can be carried out with a spreadsheet which, for each occupation where plans need to be made, sets out and calculates the number required as in the following example:

1. Number currently employed: 70
2. Annual wastage rate based on past records.   10%
3. Expected losses during the year   7
4. Balance at end-year   63
5. Number required at end-year   75
6. Number to be obtained during year (= 5 – 4)   8

LABOUR TURNOVER

The analysis of the numbers of people leaving the organization (labour turnover or wastage) provides data for use in supply forecasting, so that calculations can be made on the number of losses that may have to be replaced. More importantly, however, the analysis of the numbers of leavers and the reasons why they leave provides information which will indicate whether any action is required to improve retention rates. It can prompt further investigations to establish underlying causes and identify remedies.

In this section, consideration is given to the following aspects of labour turnover:

- its significance;
- methods of measurement;
- the reasons for turnover;
- what it costs;
- how to benchmark rates of turnover.

The significance of labour turnover

In the IRS *Employee Development Bulletin* (IRS, 2000), the point was made that 'rates of labour turnover provide a graphic illustration of the turbulence within an organization. High rates of attrition can destabilize a business and demotivate those who attempt to maintain levels of service and output against a background of vacant posts, inexperienced staff and general discontent'. Obviously, recruitment, induction and training costs all rise with an increase in labour turnover. As the CIPD (2000) has commented:

> Turnover may be a function of negative job attitudes, low job satisfaction, combined with an ability to secure employment elsewhere, ie the state of the labour market. On the other hand, turnover is a normal part of organizational functioning, and while excessively high turnover may be dysfunctional, a certain level of turnover is to be expected and can be beneficial to an organization.

Methods of measurement

There are a number of ways of measuring labour turnover as described below.

The labour turnover index

The labour turnover index (sometimes referred to as the employee or labour wastage index) is the traditional formula for measuring wastage. It has been described by the CIPD as the 'crude wastage method'. It is calculated as follows:

$$\frac{\text{Number of leavers in a specified period (usually 1 year)} \times 100}{\text{Average number of employees during the same period}}$$

This method is commonly used because it is easy to calculate and to understand. For human resource planning purposes, it is a simple matter to work out that if a company wanted to increase its workforce by 50 people from 150 to 200 but the labour turnover rate is 20 per cent (a loss of 30 people), then if this trend continues, the company would have to recruit 90 employees during the following year in order to increase and to hold the workforce at 200 in that year (50 extra employees, plus 40 to replace the 20 per cent wastage of the average 200 employees employed). It can also be used to make comparisons with other organizations that will typically adopt this method.

This wastage formula may be simple to use but it can be misleading. The main objection to the measurement of turnover in terms of the proportion of those who leave in a given period is that the figure may be inflated by the high turnover of a relatively small proportion of the workforce, especially in times of heavy recruitment. Thus, a company employing 150 people might have had an annual wastage rate of 20 per cent, meaning that 30 jobs had become vacant during the year. But this could have been spread throughout the company, covering all occupations and long- as well as short-service employees. Alternatively, it could have been restricted to a small sector of the workforce – only 20 jobs might have been affected although each of these had to be filled 10 times during the year. These are totally different situations, and unless they are understood, inaccurate forecasts would be made of future requirements and inappropriate actions would be taken to deal with the problem. The turnover index is also suspect if the average number of employees upon which the percentage is based is unrepresentative of recent trends because of considerable increases or decreases during the period in the numbers employed. When assembling and analysing labour turnover figures, it is important to obtain information on the incidence for different categories of employees, especially those who are most difficult to attract and retain such as knowledge workers or highly skilled workers.

Survival rate

A method of analysing turnover which is particularly useful for human resource planners is the survival rate: the proportion of employees engaged within a certain period, who remain with the organization after so many months or years of service. Thus, an analysis of trainees who have completed their training might show that after two years, 10 of the original cohort of 20 trainees were still with the company, a survival rate of 50 per cent.

The distribution of losses for each entry group, or cohort, can be plotted in the form of a 'survival curve' as shown in Figure 24.2. The basic shape of this curve has been found to be similar in many situations, although it has been observed that the peak of the curve may occur further along the time scale and/or may be lower when it relates to more highly skilled or trained entry cohorts. Table 24.1 shows human resource planners that unless they improve retention rates, they will have to allow for half the number of recruits in any one year to be lost over the next five years. Thus, to ensure there are 50 trained staff in five years' time, 100 people would have to be engaged this

Figure 24.2   A survival curve

Table 24.1   Survival rate analysis

Entry Cohort	Original strength	Number surviving to end of year after engagement				
		Year 1	Year 2	Year 3	Year 4	Year 5
A	40	35	28	26	22	20
B	32	25	24	19	18	17
C	48	39	33	30	25	23
D	38	32	27	24	22	19
E	42	36	30	26	23	21
TOTAL	200	167	142	125	110	100
Average survival rate	100%	83%	71%	62%	55%	50%

year. Stark figures like this can prompt action, especially when the costs of recruitment and induction are taken into account.

Half-life index

A simpler concept derived from survival rate analysis is that of the half-life index, which is defined as the time taken for a group or cohort of starters to reduce to half its original size through the wastage process (five years in the above example). Comparisons can then be made for successive entry years or between different groups of employees, in order to show where action may have to be taken to counter undesirable wastage trends.

Stability index

The stability index is considered by many to be an improvement on the turnover index. The formula is:

$$\frac{\text{Number with 1 year's service or more} \times 100}{\text{Number employed 1 year ago}}$$

This index provides an indication of the tendency for longer-service employees to remain with the company, and therefore shows the degree to which there is a continuity of employment. But this too can be misleading, because the index will not reveal the vastly different situations that exist in a company or department with a high proportion of long-serving employees in comparison with one where the majority of employees are short-service.

Length of service analysis

This disadvantage of the stability index may be partly overcome if an analysis is also made of the average length of service of people who leave, as in Table 24.2.

This analysis is still fairly crude, because it deals only with those who leave. A more refined analysis would compare for each service category the numbers leaving with the numbers employed. If, in the example shown, the total number employed with fewer than three months' service was 100 and the total with more than five years was also 100, the proportion of leavers in each category would be 28 per cent and 11 per cent respectively – more revealing figures, especially if previous periods could be analysed to reveal adverse trends.

Table 24.2 Leavers by length of service

	Leavers by length of service						Total number leaving	Average number employed	Index of labour turnover %
Occupation	Less than 3 months	3–6 months	6 months –1 year	1–2 years	3–5 years	5 or more years			
A	5	4	3	3	2	3	20	200	10
B	15	12	10	6	3	4	50	250	20
C	8	6	5	4	3	4	30	100	30
Totals	28	22	18	13	8	11	100	550	18

Choice of measurement

It is difficult to avoid using the conventional employee (labour) turnover index as the easiest and most familiar of all methods of measurement. But it needs to be supplemented with some measure of stability. An analysis of turnover or wastage as part of a human resource planning exercise requires detailed information on the length of service of leavers to identify problem areas and to provide a foundation for supply forecasts.

Analysis of reasons for turnover

An analysis of the reasons for leaving derived from exit interviews will provide useful information on which to base retention plans. Exit interviews aim to establish why people are leaving, not to persuade them to stay. The reasons for leaving can be classified under the following headings:

● more pay;
● better prospects (career move);
● more security;
● more opportunity to develop skills;
● better working conditions;
● poor relationships with manager/team leader;
● poor relationship with colleagues;
● bullying or harassment;
● personal – pregnancy, illness, moving away from area etc.

Exit interviews aim to elicit opinions on any specific reasons for dissatisfaction under any of the above non-personal headings. Some leavers will be forthcoming, others will not. It is up to the interviewer to probe skilfully and sensitively to establish reasons for dissatisfaction or unhappiness so that where those feelings are justified, something can be done about them. Judgement is required to sort out genuine complaints from unjustified or exaggerated ones. An analysis of reasons should take place and trends be noted. General issues can be addressed by reviewing employment and reward policies and practices. Issues affecting particular managers should also be tackled. This may be difficult if it is a behavioural matter, eg bullying, but if there is a build-up of information which suggests that this may be the case, the problem cannot be ignored.

However, exit interviews alone are not completely reliable, and it is desirable to gain a more comprehensive picture of the views of existing employees through attitude surveys (see Chapter 51).

The cost of labour turnover

Labour turnover can be costly. The following factors should be considered:

● leaving costs – payroll costs and personnel administration of leaver;
● direct cost of recruiting replacements (advertising, interviewing, testing etc);
● opportunity cost of time spent by HR and line managers in recruitment;
● direct cost of introducing replacements (induction course, cost of induction manuals etc);
● opportunity cost of time spent by HR and managers in introducing new starters;
● direct cost of training replacements in the necessary skills;
● opportunity cost of time spent by line managers and other staff in providing training;
● loss of the input from those leaving before they are replaced in terms of contribution, output, sales, customer satisfaction and support etc;
● loss arising from reduced input from new starters until they are fully trained.

The CIPD 2000 survey of labour turnover established that the median cost per leaver was £3,456. The median costs per person ranged from £5,206 for professional staff to £1,127. These are quite typical figures, and a calculation of the costs of labour turnover in an organization can produce alarming sums if turnover is high, especially among knowledge workers. This information can be used by HR as a powerful argument in support of changes in employment and reward policies.

Benchmarking labour turnover

Labour turnover rates provide a valuable means of benchmarking the effectiveness of HR policies and practices in organizations. They do not tell the whole story, but if turnover is significantly higher than in comparable organizations, this should stimulate action to investigate why this is the case and to do something about it.

Benchmarking can be carried out by networking with other organizations, possibly forming a 'club' to exchange information regularly. There are also a number of benchmarking agencies as listed by IRS (2000), and the European Foundation for Quality Management (EFQM) survey which uses the Internet. National sources of data include the government's Labour Force and Learning and Training at Work surveys and the annual survey of labour turnover conducted by the CIPD.

ACTION PLANNING

Action plans are derived from the broad resourcing strategies and the more detailed analysis of demand and supply factors. However, the plans often have to be short term and flexible because of the difficulty of making firm predictions about human resource requirements in times of rapid change. Plans need to be prepared in the areas of resourcing, flexibility, retention and downsizing as described below.

The resourcing plan

This concerns the need to consider approaches to obtaining people from within the organization, to recruiting them externally and to attracting high-quality candidates (becoming 'the employer of choice').

Internal resourcing

The first step is to analyse the availability of suitable people from within the organization by reference to assessments of potential and a skills database. The latter should contain a regularly updated list of employees with the sorts of skills needed by the organization. Decisions are then made on what steps should be taken to promote, redeploy and, as necessary, provide additional experience and training to eligible staff. Plans can also be made to make better use of existing employees, which may include flexibility arrangements as discussed later, or homeworking.

The recruitment plan

This will incorporate:

- the numbers and types of employees required to make up any deficits, and when they are needed;
- the likely sources of candidates – schools, colleges of further education, universities, advertising, the Internet etc;
- plans for tapping alternative sources, eg part-timers, widening the recruitment net to include, for example, more women re-entering the labour market;
- how the recruitment programme will be conducted.

Employer of choice plans

The recruitment plan should include plans for attracting good candidates by ensuring that the organization will become an 'employer of choice'. This could be achieved by such means as generally improving the image of the company as an employer and by offering:

- better remuneration packages;
- more opportunities for development, training and careers;
- enhanced future employability because of the reputation of the organization as one that employs and develops high-quality people as well as the learning opportunities it provides;
- employment conditions which address work-life balance issues by, for example, adapting working hours and arrangements and leave policies and providing child-care facilities or vouchers to meet the needs of those with domestic responsibilities;
- better facilities and scope for knowledge workers, eg research and development scientists or engineers or IT specialists;
- 'golden hellos' (sums of money paid up front to recruits);
- generous relocation payments.

Flexibility plan

The aims of the flexibility plan should be to:

- provide for greater operational flexibility;
- improve the utilization of employees' skills and capacities;
- reduce employment costs;

- help to achieve downsizing smoothly and in a way which avoids the need for compulsory redundancies;
- increase productivity.

The plan can be based on a radical look at traditional employment patterns. This means identifying the scope for using alternatives to full-time, permanent staff, which could include increasing the number of part-timers, job sharing, the expansion of home-working or teleworking, or employing more temporary workers. The two main new trends in temporary working are first, to establish permanent staffing levels to meet minimum or normal levels of demand and rely on temporary staff to cover peaks, and second, to develop a 'two-tier' workforce in order to provide greater job security for the core workers by employing a certain percentage of temporary staff at the periphery. Consideration can also be given to making more use of sub-contractors or outsourcing work, and to the introduction of more flexible working arrangements.

Use of part-time workers

The advantages of using part-time workers are as follows:

- more scope for flexing hours worked;
- better utilization of plant and equipment by, for example, the introduction of a 'twilight shift';
- lower unit labour costs because overtime levels for full-time workers are reduced;
- higher productivity on repetitive work because part-time workers can give more attention to their work during their shorter working day.

The disadvantages are:

- part-timers are generally less willing to undertake afternoon or evening work, may find it more difficult to vary their hours of work, and may be less mobile;
- rates of labour turnover may be higher among part-timers;
- part-timers may be less committed than full-time employees.

It should be remembered that The Part-time Regulations 1999 require that part-timers should not be treated less favourably than full-time workers and should be paid pro rata.

Job-sharing

Job-sharing is an arrangement whereby two employees share the work of one full-time position, dividing pay and benefits between them according to the time each works. Job-sharing can involve splitting days or weeks or, less frequently, working alternate weeks. The advantages of job-sharing include reduced employee turnover and absenteeism because it suits the needs of individuals. Greater continuity results because if one-half of the job-sharing team is ill or leaves, the sharer will continue working for at least half the time. Job-sharing also means that a wider employment pool can be tapped for those who cannot work full time but want permanent employment. The disadvantages are the administrative costs involved and the risk of responsibility being divided.

Home-working and teleworking

Home-based employees can be employed as consultants, analysts, designers, programmers or in various kinds of administrative work. The advantages of these arrangements are:

● flexibility to respond rapidly to fluctuations in demand;
● reduced overheads;
● lower employment costs if the homeworkers are self-employed (care, however, has to be taken to ensure that they are regarded as self-employed for income tax and national insurance purposes).

Teleworking involves people working at home with a terminal which is linked to the main company or networked with those of other outworkers. Its aim is to achieve greater flexibility, rapid access to skills and the retention of skilled employees who would otherwise be lost to the company. Teleworkers can be used in a number of functions such as marketing, finance and IT. The arrangement does, however, depend for its success on the involvement and education of all employees (full time and tele-workers), the careful selection and training of teleworkers, allocating adequate resources to them, and monitoring the operation of the system.

Subcontracting

Subcontracting enables:

● resources to be concentrated on core business activities;
● employment costs to be reduced;

- flexibility and productivity to be increased;
- job security for core employees to be enhanced.

The potential drawbacks include:

- the legal status of subcontractors – this has to be clarified for income tax, national insurance and employment legislation purposes;
- the degree to which subcontractors will be able to meet delivery and quality requirements – it may be more difficult to control their work;
- negative reactions from employees and trade unions who prefer work to be kept within the company.

The decision on how much work can be subcontracted is mainly an operational one, but the flexibility plan should cover the implications of subcontracting on employment levels and employee relations.

Flexible hour arrangements

Flexible hour arrangements can be included in the flexibility plan in one or more of the following ways:

- flexible daily hours – these may follow an agreed pattern day by day according to typical or expected work loads (eg flexitime systems);
- flexible weekly hours – providing for longer weekly hours to be worked at certain peak periods during the year;
- flexible daily and weekly hours – varying daily or weekly hours or a combination of both to match the input of hours to achieve the required output; such working times, unlike daily or weekly arrangements, may fluctuate between a minimum and a maximum;
- compressed working weeks in which employees work fewer than the five standard days;
- annual hours – scheduling employee hours on the basis of the number of hours to be worked, with provisions for the increase or reduction of hours in any given period, according to the demand for goods or services.

Overtime arrangements

A flexibility plan can contain proposals to reduce overtime costs through the use of flexible hours, new shift arrangements (eg twilight shifts), time off in lieu and overtime limitation agreements. The reduction of overtime is often catered for in formal productivity deals which include a quid pro quo in the form of increased pay for the elimination of overtime payments and the introduction of flexible work patterns.

Shift-working arrangements

These can be introduced or modified to meet demand requirements, reduce overtime or provide for better plant or equipment utilization.

The retention plan

Basis of the plan

Retention planning is based on a retention strategy which takes into account the particular retention issues the organization is facing, and determines ways in which these issues can be dealt with. This may mean accepting the reality, as mentioned by Capelli (2000), that the market, not the company will ultimately determine the movement of employees. Capelli believes that it may be difficult to counter the pull of the market – 'you can't shield your people from attractive opportunities and aggressive recruiters' – and suggests that 'The old goal of HR management – to minimize overall employee turnover – needs to be replaced by a new goal: to influence who leaves and when'. This, as proposed by Bevan *et al* (1997), could be based on risk analysis to quantify the seriousness of losing key people or of key posts becoming vacant.

Risk analysis

Risk analysis can be carried out as follows:

1. Identify potential risk areas – key people who may leave – and for each person or group of people:
2. Estimate the likelihood of this occurring.
3. Estimate how serious the effects of a loss would be on the business.
4. Estimate the ease with which a replacement could be made and the replacement costs.

Each of the estimates could be expressed on a scale, say: very high, high, medium, low, very low. An overview of the ratings under each heading could then indicate where action may need to be taken to retain key people or groups of people.

Analysis of reasons for leaving

Risk analysis provides specific information on areas for concern. More generally, some indication of the reasons for leaving and therefore where action needs to be taken may be provided by exit interviews, but they are fallible. More reliance can be placed on the results of attitude or opinion surveys to identify any areas of dissatisfaction. The retention plan should propose actions which focus on each of the areas in which lack of commitment and dissatisfaction can arise.

Areas for action

Depending on the outcome of the risk analysis and the overall assessment of reasons for leaving, the possible actions that can be taken are as follows:

- Uncompetitive, inequitable or unfair pay systems can be dealt with by reviewing pay levels on the basis of market surveys, introducing job evaluation or improving an existing scheme to provide for equitable grading decisions, or reviewing contingent pay schemes to ensure that they operate fairly. 'Golden handcuffs' (loyalty bonuses) may be used as an inducement to stay but as Capelli (2000) points out, there is a limit to the extent to which people can be bribed to stay if they really want to go, and golden handcuffs can be countered by the 'golden hellos' offered by aggressive recruiters.
- Design jobs to maximize skill variety, task significance, autonomy, control over their work and feedback, and ensure that they provide opportunities for learning and growth. Jobs can be 'customized' to meet the needs of particular individuals.
- Develop commitment to the work (job engagement) not only through job design but also by organizing work around projects with which people can identify more readily than with the company as a whole.
- Encourage the development of social ties within the company. In the words of Capelli, 'loyalty to companies may be disappearing but loyalty to colleagues is not'.
- Provide opportunities to learn new skills and develop careers.
- Ensure that selection and promotion procedures match the capacities of individuals to the demands of the work they have to do. Rapid turnover can result simply from poor selection or promotion decisions.
- Reduce the losses of people who cannot adjust to their new job – the 'induction crisis' – by giving them proper training and support when they join the organization.
- Take steps to improve the work-life balance by developing policies which recognize the needs of employees outside work.

- Eliminate as far as possible unpleasant working conditions or the imposition of too much stress on employees.
- Select, brief and train managers and team leaders so that they appreciate the positive contribution they can make to improving retention by the ways in which they lead their teams.

Steps such as these may contribute to the reduction of attrition, but it may be impossible to prevent key staff moving on because of the attractions offered elsewhere. Market forces may be too strong. In that case, as Capelli (2000) suggests, it may be necessary to adapt to attrition by such means as changing systems of work so that they are less dependent on scarce skills, organizing work round short-term projects, and outsourcing.

The downsizing plan

If all else fails, it may be necessary to deal with unacceptable employment costs or surplus numbers of employees by what has euphemistically come to be known as 'downsizing'. The downsizing plan should be based on the timing of reductions and forecasts of the extent to which these can be achieved by natural wastage or voluntary redundancy. The plan should set out:

- the total number of people who have to go, and when and where this needs to take place;
- arrangements for informing and consulting with employees and their trade unions;
- a forecast of the number of losses which can be taken up by natural wastage;
- any financial or other inducements to encourage voluntary redundancy;
- a forecast of the likely numbers who will volunteer to leave;
- a forecast of the balance of employees, if any, who will have to be made redundant (the plan should, of course, aim to avoid this through natural wastage and voluntary redundancy);
- the redundancy terms;
- any financial inducements to be offered to key employees whom the company wishes to retain;
- any arrangements for retraining employees and finding them work elsewhere in the organization;
- the steps to be taken to help redundant employees find new jobs by counselling, contacting other employers or offering the services of outplacement consultants;
- the arrangements for telling individual employees about the redundancies and how they are affected, and for keeping the trade unions informed.

THE CONTRIBUTION OF HR TO HUMAN RESOURCE PLANNING

Human resource planning, in the broader meaning of the term, is one of the fundamental strategic roles of the HR function. HR can make a major contribution to developing the resource capability of the firm and therefore its strategic capability by systematically reviewing the firm's strategic objectives and by ensuring that plans are made that will ensure that the human resources are available to meet those objectives. Thus HR is focusing on the acquisition and development of the human capital required by the organization.

To make this contribution, heads of HR and their colleagues in the HR function need to:

● ensure that they are aware of the strategic plans of the business and can provide advice on the human resource implications of those plans;
● point out to management the strengths and weaknesses of the human resources of the organization, and the opportunities and threats they present, so that these can be considered when developing business plans;
● be capable of scenario planning in the sense that they can identify future issues concerning the acquisition, retention and employment of people and advise on methods of addressing those issues;
● understand the extent to which quantitative assessments of the future demand for and supply of people may be feasible and useful, and know the methods that can be used to prepare such forecasts;
● understand how to analyse and cost labour turnover and to establish reasons for leaving;
● be aware of the scope to deal with future requirements by introducing various forms of flexibility;
● be capable of preparing relevant and practical resourcing plans and strategies for retaining people, based upon an understanding of the internal and external environment of the organization and the implications of analyses of labour turnover.

25

Recruitment and selection

THE RECRUITMENT AND SELECTION PROCESS

The overall aim of the recruitment and selection process should be to obtain at minimum cost the number and quality of employees required to satisfy the human resource needs of the company. The three stages of recruitment and selection are:

1. *defining requirements* – preparing job descriptions and specifications; deciding terms and conditions of employment;
2. *attracting candidates* – reviewing and evaluating alternative sources of applicants, inside and outside the company, advertising, using agencies and consultants;
3. *selecting candidates* – sifting applications, interviewing, testing, assessing candidates, assessment centres, offering employment, obtaining references; preparing contracts of employment.

This chapter covers the main features of the recruitment and selection process in the areas of obtaining and selecting candidates under the following headings:

● defining requirements;
● attracting candidates;
● advertising;

- Internet recruiting;
- outsourcing recruitment;
- educational and training establishments;
- sifting applications;
- selection methods;
- types of interviews;
- assessment centres;
- graphology;
- choice of selection methods;
- improving the effectiveness of recruitment and selection;
- references, qualifications and offers;
- final stages.

Selection interviewing and selection testing are dealt with in Chapters 26 and 27.

DEFINING REQUIREMENTS

The number and categories of people required should be specified in the recruitment programme, which is derived from the human resource plan. In addition, there will be demands for replacements or for new jobs to be filled, and these demands should be checked to ensure that they are justified. It may be particularly necessary to check on the need for a replacement or the level or type of employee that is specified. Requirements for particular positions are set out in the form of job descriptions and person specifications. These provide the basic information required to draft advertisements, brief agencies or recruitment consultants, and assess candidates. A role profile listing competence, skill, educational and experience requirements produces the job criteria against which candidates will be assessed at the interview or by means of psychological tests.

Job description

A job description sets out the basic details of the job, defining reporting relationships, the overall objective of the job, the main activities or tasks carried out and any other special requirements or features. For recruitment purposes, information may be provided on the arrangements for training and development and career opportunities. The terms and conditions for the job – pay, benefits etc – will also be included, as will special requirements such as mobility, travelling or unsocial hours.

Person specifications

A person specification, also known as a recruitment, personnel or job specification, defines the education, training, qualifications, experience and competences/competencies required by the job holder.

A person specification can be set out under the following headings:

- *competences/competencies* – what the individual needs to know and be able to do to carry out the role, including any special aptitudes or skills required;
- *qualifications and training* – the professional, technical or academic qualifications required, or the training that the candidate should have undertaken;
- *experience* – in particular, categories of work or organizations; the types of achievements and activities that would be likely to predict success;
- *specific demands* – where the role holder will be expected to achieve in specified areas, eg develop new markets, improve sales, or introduce new systems;
- *organizational fit* – the corporate culture (eg formal or informal) and the need for candidates to be able to work within it;
- *special requirements* – travelling, unsocial hours, mobility, etc;
- *meeting candidate expectations* – the extent to which the organization can meet candidates' expectations in terms of career opportunities, training, security etc.

The key parts of the specification used in structured selection interviews as described in Chapter 26 are the definitions of competences/competencies, qualifications and experience. A role definition (see Chapter 23) will set out output expectations and competency requirements for interviewing purposes (competency-based recruitment is considered in more detail below). But more information may be required to provide the complete picture for advertising and briefing candidates on terms and conditions and career prospects. An example of the key competences is given in Figure 25.1.

The biggest danger to be avoided at this stage is that of overstating the competencies and qualifications required. It is natural to go for the best, but setting an unrealistically high level for candidates increases the problems of attracting them, and results in dissatisfaction when they find their talents are not being used. Understating requirements can be equally dangerous, but it happens much less frequently. The best approach is to distinguish between essential and desirable requirements.

When the requirements have been agreed, they should be analysed under suitable headings. There are various ways of doing this. A basic approach is to set out and define the essential or desirable requirements under the key headings of competences, qualifications and training and experience. Additional information can be provided on specific demands. It is, of course, necessary to spell out separately the terms and conditions of the job.

---

1. *Work-based competences:*

   ● *Essential in:*
     – all aspects of recruitment including test administration;
     – interviewing techniques;
     – job analysis;
     – inputting data to computers;
     – administering fairly complex paperwork processes.
   ● *Desirable in:*
     – administering OPQ test;
     – job evaluation;
     – counselling techniques;
     – conducting training sessions.

2. *Behavioural competencies:*

   ● able to relate well to others and use interpersonal skills to achieve desired objectives;
   ● able to influence the behaviour and decisions of people on matters concerning recruitment and other personnel or individual issues;
   ● able to cope with change, to be flexible and to handle uncertainty;
   ● able to make sense of issues, identify and solve problems and 'think on one's feet';
   ● focus on achieving results;
   ● able to maintain appropriately directed energy and stamina, to exercise self-control and to learn new behaviours;
   ● able to communicate well, orally and on paper.

3. *Qualifications/experience:*
   ● Graduate Member of the Institute of Personnel and Development plus relevant experience in each aspect of the work.

Figure 25.1 Person specification for an HR officer

Alternatively, one of the traditional classification schemes can be used. The most familiar are the seven-point plan developed by Rodger (1952) and the fivefold grading system produced by Munro-Fraser (1954).

The seven-point plan

The seven-point plan covers:

1. *physical make-up* – health, physique, appearance, bearing and speech;
2. *attainments* – education, qualifications, experience;
3. *general intelligence* – fundamental intellectual capacity;
4. *special aptitudes* – mechanical, manual dexterity, facility in the use of words or figures;

5. *interests* – intellectual, practical, constructional, physically active, social, artistic;
6. *disposition* – acceptability, influence over others, steadiness, dependability, self-reliance;
7. *circumstances* – domestic circumstances, occupations of family.

The fivefold grading system

The fivefold grading system covers:

1. *impact on others* – physical make-up, appearance, speech and manner;
2. *acquired qualifications* – education, vocational training, work experience;
3. *innate abilities* – natural quickness of comprehension and aptitude for learning;
4. *motivation* – the kinds of goals set by the individual, his or her consistency and determination in following them up, and success in achieving them;
5. *adjustment* – emotional stability, ability to stand up to stress and ability to get on with people.

Choice of system

Of these two systems, the seven-point plan has the longer pedigree. The five-fold grading scheme is simpler, in some ways, and places more emphasis on the dynamic aspects of the applicant's career. Both can provide a good framework for interviewing, but increasingly, interviewers are using a competency-based approach.

Using a competency-based approach

A competency-based approach means that the competencies defined for a role are used as the framework for the selection process. As Roberts (1997) suggests:

> The benefit of taking a competencies approach is that people can identify and isolate the key characteristics which would be used as the basis for selection, and that those characteristics will be described in terms which both can understand and agree… . The competencies therefore become a fundamental part of the selection process.

A competencies approach can help to identify which selection techniques, such as psychological testing or assessment centres, are most likely to produce useful evidence. It provides the information required to conduct a structured interview in which questions can focus on particular competency areas to establish the extent to which candidates meet the specification as set out in competency terms.

The advantages of a competency-based approach have been summarized by Wood and Payne (1998) as follows:

● It increases the accuracy of predictions about suitability.
● It facilitates a closer match between the person's attributes and the demands of the job.
● It helps to prevent interviewers making 'snap' judgements.
● It can underpin the whole range of recruitment techniques – application forms, interviews, tests and assessment centres.

The framework can be defined in terms of work-based competences, which refer to expectations of what people have to be able to do if they are going to achieve the results required in the job. It can also include definitions of required behavioural competencies, which refer to the personal characteristics and behaviour required for successful performance in such areas as interpersonal skills, leadership, personal drive, communication skills, team membership and analytical ability.

The competencies used for recruitment and selection purposes should meet the following criteria:

● They should focus on areas in which candidates will have demonstrated their competency in their working or academic life – eg leadership, teamwork, initiative.
● They are likely to predict successful job performance, eg achievement motivation.
● They can be assessed in a targeted behavioural event interview in which, for example, if team management is a key competence area, candidates can be asked to give examples of how they have successfully built a team and got it into action.
● They can be used as criteria in an assessment centre (see below).

A competency approach along these lines can provide the most effective means of identifying suitable candidates as part of a systematic selection process.

ATTRACTING CANDIDATES

Attracting candidates is primarily a matter of identifying, evaluating and using the most appropriate sources of applicants. However, in cases where difficulties in attracting or retaining candidates are being met or anticipated, it may be necessary to carry out a preliminary study of the factors that are likely to attract or repel candidates – the strengths and weaknesses of the organization as an employer.

Analysis of recruitment strengths and weaknesses

The analysis of strengths and weaknesses should cover such matters as the national or local reputation of the organization, pay, employee benefits and working conditions, the intrinsic interest of the job, security of employment, opportunities for education and training, career prospects, and the location of the office or plant. These need to be compared with the competition in order that a list of what are, in effect, selling points can be drawn up as in a marketing exercise, in which the preferences of potential customers are compared with the features of the product in order that those aspects that are likely to provide the most appeal to the customers can be emphasized. Candidates are, in a sense, selling themselves, but they are also buying what the organization has to offer. If, in the latter sense, the labour market is a buyer's market, then the company that is selling itself to candidates must study their needs in relation to what it can provide.

The aim of the study might be to prepare a better image of the organization for use in advertisements, brochures or interviews. Or it might have the more constructive aim of showing where the organization needs to improve as an employer if it is to attract more or better candidates *and* to retain those selected. The study could make use of an attitude survey to obtain the views of existing employees. One such survey mounted by the writer in an engineering company wishing to attract science graduates established that the main concern of the graduates was that they would be able to use and develop the knowledge they had gained at university. As a result, special brochures were written for each major discipline giving technical case histories of the sort of work graduates carried out. These avoided the purple passages used in some brochures (which the survey established were distinctly off-putting to most students) and proved to be a most useful recruitment aid. Strong measures were also taken to ensure that research managers made proper use of the graduates they recruited.

Sources of candidates

First consideration should be given to internal candidates, although some organizations with powerful equal opportunity policies (often local authorities) insist that all internal candidates should apply for vacancies on the same footing as external candidates. If there are no people available within the organization the main sources of candidates, as described below, are advertising, the Internet, and outsourcing to consultants or agencies.

ADVERTISING

Advertising is the most obvious method of attracting candidates. Nevertheless, the first question to ask is whether an advertisement is really justified. This means looking at the alternative sources mentioned above and confirming, preferably on the basis of experience, that they will not do. Consideration should be given as to whether it might be better to use an agency or a selection consultant. When making the choice, refer to the three criteria of cost, speed and the likelihood of providing good candidates. The objectives of an advertisement should be to:

- *attract attention* – it must compete for the interest of potential candidates against other employers;
- *create and maintain interest* – it has to communicate in an attractive and interesting way information about the job, the company, the terms and conditions of employment and the qualifications required;
- *stimulate action* – the message needs to be conveyed in a manner that will not only focus people's eyes on the advertisement but also encourage them to read to the end, as well as prompt a sufficient number of replies from good candidates.

To achieve these aims, it is necessary to carry out the actions set out below.

Analyse the requirement, likely sources and job features

First it is necessary to establish how many jobs have to be filled and by when. Then turn to the job description and person specification to obtain information on responsibilities, qualifications and experience required.

The next step is to consider where suitable candidates are likely to come from; the companies, jobs or education establishments they are in; and the parts of the country where they can be found.

Finally, define the terms and conditions of the job (pay and benefits) and think about what about the job or the organization is likely to attract good candidates so that the most can be made of these factors in the advertisement. Consider also what might put them off, for example the location of the job, in order that objections can be anticipated. Analyse previous successes or failures to establish what does or does not work.

Decide who does what

When planning a campaign or recruiting key people, there is much to be said for using an advertising agency. An agency can provide expertise in producing eye-catching headlines and writing good copy. It can devise an attractive house style and prepare layouts that make the most of the text, the logo and any 'white space' round the advertisement. Moreover, it can advise on ways of achieving visual impact by the use of illustrations and special typographical features. Finally, an agency can advise on media, help in response analysis and take up the burden of placing advertisements.

The following steps should be taken when choosing an advertising agency:

- Check its experience in handling recruitment advertising.
- See examples of its work.
- Check with clients on the level of service provided.
- Meet the staff who will work on the advertisements.
- Check the fee structure.
- Discuss methods of working.

Write the copy

A recruitment advertisement should start with a compelling headline and then contain information on:

- the organization;
- the job;
- the person required – qualifications, experience etc;
- the pay and benefits offered;
- the location;
- the action to be taken.

The headline is all-important. The simplest and most obvious approach is to set out the job title in bold type. To gain attention, it is advisable to quote the salary (if it is worth quoting) and to put 'plus car' if a company car is provided. Salaries and cars are major attractions and should be stated clearly. Applicants are rightly suspicious of clauses such as 'salary will be commensurate with age and experience' or 'salary negotiable'. This usually means either that the salary is so low that the company is afraid to reveal it, or that salary policies are so incoherent that the company has no idea what to offer until someone tells them what he or she wants.

The name of the company should be given. Do not use box numbers – if you want to remain anonymous, use a consultant. Add any selling points, such as growth or diversification, and any other areas of interest to potential candidates, such as career prospects. The essential features of the job should be conveyed by giving a brief description of what the job holder will do and, as far as space permits, the scope and scale of activities. Create interest in the job but do not oversell it.

The qualifications and experience required should be stated as factually as possible. There is no point in overstating requirements and seldom any point in specifying exactly how much experience is wanted. This will vary from candidate to candidate, and the other details about the job and the rate of pay should provide them with enough information about the sort of experience required. Be careful about including a string of personal qualities such as drive, determination and initiative. These have no real meaning to candidates. Phrases such as 'proven track record' and 'successful experience' are equally meaningless. No one will admit to not having either of them.

The advertisement should end with information on how the candidate should apply. 'Brief but comprehensive details' is a good phrase. Candidates can be asked to write, but useful alternatives are to ask them to telephone or to come along for an informal chat at a suitable venue.

Remember that the Sex Discrimination Act 1975 makes it unlawful to discriminate in an advertisement by favouring either sex, the only exceptions being a few jobs that can be done only by one sex. Advertisements must therefore avoid sexist job titles such as 'salesman' or 'stewardess'. They must refer to a neutral title such as 'sales representative', or amplify the description to cover both sexes by stating 'steward or stewardess'. It is accepted, however, that certain job titles are unisex and therefore non-discriminatory. These include director, manager, executive and officer. It is best to avoid any reference to the sex of the candidate by using neutral or unisex titles and referring only to the 'candidate' or the 'applicant'. Otherwise you must specify 'man or woman' or 'he or she'.

The Race Relations Act 1976 has similar provisions, making unlawful an advertisement that discriminates against any particular race. As long as race is never mentioned or even implied in an advertisement, you should have no problem in keeping within the law.

Choose type of advertisement

The main types of advertisement are the following:

- Classified/run-on, in which copy is run on, with no white space in or around the advertisement and no paragraph spacing or indentation. They are cheap but suitable only for junior or routine jobs.

- Classified/semi-display, in which the headings can be set in capitals, paragraphs can be indented and white space is allowed round the advertisement. They are fairly cheap, and semi-display can be much more effective than run-on advertisements.
- Full display, which are bordered and in which any typeface and illustrations can be used. They can be expensive but obviously make the most impact for managerial, technical and professional jobs.

Plan the media

An advertising agency can advise on the choice of media (press, radio, television) and its cost. *British Rates and Data* (BRAD) can be consulted to give the costs of advertising in particular media.

The so-called 'quality papers' are best for managerial, professional and technical jobs. The popular press, especially evening papers, can be used to reach staff such as sales representatives and technicians. Local papers are obviously best for recruiting office staff and manual workers. Professional and trade journals can reach your audience directly, but results can be erratic and it may be advisable to use them to supplement a national campaign.

Avoid Saturdays and be cautious about repeating advertisements in the same medium. Diminishing returns can set in rapidly.

Evaluate the response

Measure response to provide guidance on the relative cost-effectiveness of different media. Cost per reply is the best ratio.

INTERNET RECRUITING

Internet recruiting uses the Internet to advertise or 'post' vacancies, provide information about jobs and the employer, and enable e-mail communications to take place between employers and candidates. The latter can not only apply for jobs online but can also register their CV with a range of sites and wait for e-mail from employers. Sites can contain a database that covers details of vacancies and which is constantly searched for matches with incoming CVs which have been posted by job seekers. The Internet was originally used mainly for IT jobs, but it is increasingly being used for professional and managerial jobs and to recruit graduates.

A typical approach is to advertise the vacancy on an online recruitment site. This will provide job details and information about the company together with an online application form. A job seeker returns the completed application electronically and computer software reviews the application forms for an initial match with the organisation's requirements. For example, a job offer for a business development manager in a computer firm might specify the following competencies as a basis for matching on the site against a CV, or by the employer against details provided by the candidate for each of the competence areas:

- Minimum 10 years' business and sales experience in the computer, networking or communications industry.
- Good exposure to the network consulting world, within UK.
- Formal sales training very desirable.
- Self-motivated to succeed in position.
- Ability to lead and manage small group of sales personnel.
- Strong organizational and prioritization skills.
- Ability to drive opportunities to closure.

The main types of online recruitment sites are:

- *Job sites* – these are operated by specialized firms and can contain over 100,000 vacancies with 6 or 7 million 'hits' a month. Companies pay to have their jobs listed on the sites, which are not usually linked to agencies.
- *Agency sites* – are run by established recruitment agencies. Candidates register online but may be expected to discuss their details in person before their details are forwarded to a prospective employer.
- *Media sites* – which may simply contain a copy of an advertisement appearing in the press, but may include an external description of the vacancy and the company and provide a link to the company's Web site.

The advantages of Internet recruiting are that it can reach a wider range of possible applicants, and it is quicker and cheaper than traditional methods of advertising. More details of jobs and firms can be supplied on the site, and CVs can be matched and applications submitted electronically. The disadvantages are that it may produce too many irrelevant or poor applications, and it is still not the first choice of most job seekers.

OUTSOURCING RECRUITMENT

There is much to be said for outsourcing recruitment – getting agencies or consultants to carry out at least the preliminary work of submitting suitable candidates or drawing up a short list. It costs money, but it can save a lot of time and trouble.

Using agencies

Most private agencies deal with secretarial and office staff. They are usually quick and effective but quite expensive. Agencies can charge a fee of 15 per cent or more of the first year's salary for finding someone. It can be cheaper to advertise, especially when the company is in a buyer's market. Shop around to find the agency that suits the organization's needs at a reasonable cost.

Agencies should be briefed carefully on what is wanted. They produce unsuitable candidates from time to time but the risk is reduced if they are clear about your requirements.

Using recruitment consultants

Recruitment consultants generally advertise, interview and produce a short list. They provide expertise and reduce workload. The organization can be anonymous if it wishes. Most recruitment consultants charge a fee based on a percentage of the basic salary for the job, usually ranging from 15 to 20 per cent.

The following steps should be taken when choosing a recruitment consultant:

● Check reputation with other users.
● Look at the advertisements of the various firms in order to obtain an idea of the quality of a consultancy and the type and level of jobs with which it deals.
● Check on special expertise – the large accountancy firms, for example, are obviously skilled in recruiting accountants.
● Meet the consultant who will work on the assignment to assess his or her quality.
● Compare fees, although the differences are likely to be small, and the other considerations are usually more important.

When using recruitment consultants it is necessary to:

● agree terms of reference;
● brief them on the organization, where the job fits in, why the appointment is to be made, terms and conditions and any special requirements;

- give them every assistance in defining the job and the person specification, including any special demands that will be made on the successful candidate in the shape of what he or she will be expected to achieve – they will do much better if they have comprehensive knowledge of what is required and what type of person is most likely to fit well into the organization;
- check carefully the proposed programme and the draft text of the advertisement;
- clarify the arrangements for interviewing and short-listing;
- clarify the basis upon which fees and expenses will be charged;
- ensure that arrangements are made to deal directly with the consultant who will handle the assignment.

Using executive search consultants

Use an executive search consultant, or 'head-hunter', for senior jobs where there are only a limited number of suitable people and a direct lead to them is wanted. They are not cheap. Head-hunters charge a fee of 30 to 50 per cent or so of the first year's salary, but they can be quite cost-effective.

Executive search consultants first approach their own contacts in the industry or profession concerned. The good ones have an extensive range of contacts and their own data bank. They will also have researchers who will identify suitable people who may fit the specification or can provide a lead to someone else who may be suitable. The more numerous the contacts, the better the executive search consultant.

When a number of potentially suitable and interested people have been assembled, a fairly relaxed and informal meeting takes place and the consultant forwards a short list with full reports on candidates to the client.

There are some good and some not-so-good executive search consultants. Do not use one unless a reliable recommendation is obtained.

EDUCATIONAL AND TRAINING ESTABLISHMENTS

Many jobs can, of course, be filled by school leavers. For some organizations the major source of recruits for training schemes will be universities and training establishments as well as schools. Graduate recruitment is a major annual exercise for some companies, which go to great efforts to produce glossy brochures, visit campuses on the 'milk run' and use elaborate sifting and selection procedures to vet candidates, including 'biodata' and assessment centres, as described later in this chapter, and the Internet.

SIFTING APPLICATIONS

When the vacancy or vacancies have been advertised and a fair number of replies received, the typical sequence of steps required to process and sift applications is as follows:

1. List the applications on a control sheet, setting out name, date the application was received and the actions taken (reject, hold, interview, short list, offer).
2. Send a standard acknowledgement letter to each applicant unless an instant decision can be made to interview or reject.
3. The applicant may be asked to complete and return an application form to supplement a letter or CV which may be on paper or in electronic format. This ensures that all applicants are considered on the same basis – it can be very difficult to plough through a pile of letters, often ill-written and badly organized. Even CVs may be difficult to sift, although their quality is likely to be higher if the applicant has been receiving advice from an 'outplacement' consultant, ie one who specializes in finding people jobs. However, to save time, trouble, expense and irritation, many recruiters prefer to make a decision on the initial letter plus CV, where it is quite clear that an applicant meets or does not meet the specification, rather than ask for a form. It is generally advisable for more senior jobs to ask for a CV.
4. Compare the applications with the key criteria in the job specification and sort them initially into three categories: possible, marginal and unsuitable.
5. Scrutinize the possibles again to draw up a short list for interview. This scrutiny could be carried out by the personnel or employment specialist and, preferably, the manager. The numbers on the short list should ideally be between four and eight. Fewer than four leaves relatively little choice (although such a limitation may be forced on you if an insufficient number of good applications have been received). More than eight will mean that too much time is spent on interviewing and there is a danger of diminishing returns setting in.
6. Draw up an interviewing programme. The time you should allow for the interview will vary according to the complexity of the job. For a fairly routine job, 30 minutes or so should suffice. For a more senior job, 60 minutes or more is required. It is best not to schedule too many interviews in a day – if you try to carry out more than five or six exacting interviews you will quickly run out of steam and do neither the interviewee nor your company any justice. It is advisable to leave about 15 minutes between interviews to write up notes and prepare for the next one.

7.   Invite the candidates to interview, using a standard letter where large numbers are involved. At this stage, candidates should be asked to complete an application form, if they have not already done so. There is much to be said at this stage for sending candidates some details of the organization and the job so that you do not have to spend too much time going through this information at the interview.

8.   Review the remaining possibles and marginals and decide if any are to be held in reserve. Send reserves a standard 'holding' letter and send the others a standard rejection letter. The latter should thank candidates for the interest shown and inform them briefly, but not too brusquely, that they have not been successful. A typical reject letter might read as follows:

> Since writing to you on... we have given careful consideration to your application for the above position. I regret to inform you, however, that we have decided not to ask you to attend for an interview. We should like to thank you for the interest you have shown.

Application forms

Application forms set out the information on a candidate in a standardized format. They provide a structured basis for drawing up short lists, the interview itself and for the subsequent actions in offering an appointment and in setting up personnel records. An example of a form is given in Figure 25.2.

Biodata

A highly structured method of sifting applications is provided by the use of biodata. These are items of biographical data which are criterion based (ie they relate to established criteria in such terms as qualifications and experience which indicate that individuals are likely to be suitable). These are objectively scored and, by measurements of past achievements, predict future behaviour.

The items of biodata consist of demographic details (sex, age, family circumstances), education and professional qualifications, previous employment history and work experience, positions of responsibility outside work, leisure interests and career/job motivation. These items are weighted according to their relative importance as predictors, and a range of scores is allocated to each one. The biodata questionnaire (essentially a detailed application form) obtains information on each item, which is then scored.

Biodata are most useful when a large number of applicants are received for a limited number of posts. Cut-off scores can then be determined, based on previous

APPLICATION FORM				
Surname:			First name:	
Address:				
Tel: (home)		Tel: (work)	e-mail (personal)	
Position applied for:				
Education				

Dates		Name of secondary school, college or university	Main subjects taken	Qualifications
From	To			

Specialized training received

Other qualifications and skills (including languages, keyboard skills, current driving licence etc

Employment history
(give details of all positions held since completing full-time education, start with your present or most recent position and work back)

Dates		Name of employer, address and nature of business including any service in the armed forces	Position and summary of main duties	Starting and leaving rate of pay	Reasons for leaving or wanting to leave
From	To				

Figure 25.2 Example of an application form (compressed)

Add any comments you wish to make to support your application

I confirm that the information given on this application form is correct

Signature of
applicant .... Date ....

Figure 25.2 *continued*

experience. These scores would indicate who should be accepted for the next stage of the selection process and who should be rejected, but they would allow for some possible candidates to be held until the final cut-off score can be fixed after the first batch of applicants have been screened.

Biodata criteria and predictors are selected by job and functional analysis, which produces a list of competences. The validity of these items as predictors and the weighting to be given to them are established by analysing the biodata of existing employees who are grouped into high or low performers. Weights are allocated to items according to the discriminating power of the response.

Biodata questionnaires and scoring keys are usually developed for specific jobs in an organization. Their validity compares reasonably well with other selection instruments, but they need to be developed and validated with great care and they are only applicable when large groups of applicants have to be screened.

Electronic CVs

Electronic CVs are associated with Internet recruiting. Computers can read CVs by means of high-grade, high-speed scanners using optical character recognition (OCR) software. CVs are scanned and converted into basic text format. The system's artificial intelligence reads the text and extracts key data such as personal details, skills, educational qualifications, previous employers and jobs, and relevant dates. Search criteria are created listing mandatory and preferred requirements such as qualifications, companies in which applicants have worked and jobs held. The system carries out an analysis of the CVs against these criteria, lists the candidates that satisfy all the mandatory requirements and ranks them by the number of these requirements each one meets. The recruiter can then use this ranking as a short list or can tighten the search criteria to produce a shorter list. Essentially, the computer is looking for the same key words as human recruiters, but it can carry out this task more systematically and faster, cross-referencing skills. Any recruiter knows the problem of dealing with a large number of applications and trying, often against the odds, to extract a sensible short list.

SELECTION METHODS

The main selection methods are the interview, assessment centres and tests. The various types of interviews and assessment centres are described in the next two sections of this chapter. Interviewing techniques are dealt with separately in Chapters 26 and 27. Another and much more dubious method, used by a few firms in the UK and more extensively in the rest of Europe, is graphology.

TYPES OF INTERVIEWS

Individual interviews

The individual interview is the most familiar method of selection. It involves face-to-face discussion and provides the best opportunity for the establishment of close contact – rapport – between the interviewer and the candidate. If only one interviewer is used, there is more scope for a biased or superficial decision, and this is one reason for using a second interviewer or an interviewing panel.

Interviewing panels

Two or more people gathered together to interview one candidate may be described as an interviewing panel. The most typical situation is that in which a personnel manager and line managers see the candidate at the same time. This has the advantage of enabling information to be shared and reducing overlaps. The interviewers can discuss their joint impressions of the candidate's behaviour at the interview and modify or enlarge any superficial judgements.

Selection boards

Selection boards are more formal and, usually, larger interviewing panels, convened by an official body because there are a number of parties interested in the selection decision. Their only advantage is that they enable a number of different people to have a look at the applicants and compare notes on the spot. The disadvantages are that the questions tend to be unplanned and delivered at random, the prejudices of a dominating member of the board can overwhelm the judgements of the other members, and the candidates are unable to do justice to themselves because they are seldom allowed to expand. Selection boards tend to favour the confident and articulate candidate, but in doing so they may miss the underlying weaknesses of a superficially impressive individual. They can also underestimate the qualities of those who happen to be less effective in front of a formidable board, although they would be fully competent in the less formal or less artificial situations that would face them in the job.

ASSESSMENT CENTRES

A more comprehensive approach to selection is provided by the use of assessment centres. These incorporate a range of assessment techniques and typically have the following features:

- The focus of the centre is on behaviour.
- Exercises are used to capture and simulate the key dimensions of the job. These include one-to-one role-plays and group exercises. It is assumed that performance in these simulations predicts behaviour on the job.
- Interviews and tests will be used in addition to group exercises.
- Performance is measured in several dimensions in terms of the competencies required to achieve the target level of performance in a particular job or at a particular level in the organization.
- Several candidates or participants are assessed together to allow interaction and to make the experience more open and participative.
- Several assessors or observers are used in order to increase the objectivity of assessments. Involving senior managers is desirable to ensure that they 'own' the process. Assessors must be carefully trained.

Assessment centres provide good opportunities for indicating the extent to which candidates match the culture of the organization. This will be established by observation of their behaviour in different but typical situations, and by the range of the tests and structured interviews that are part of the proceedings. Assessment centres also give candidates a better feel for the organization and its values so that they can decide for themselves whether or not they are likely to fit.

A well-conducted assessment centre can achieve a better forecast of future performance and progress than judgements made by line or even personnel managers in the normal, unskilled way.

GRAPHOLOGY

Graphology can be defined as the study of the social structure of a human being through his or her writing. Its use in selection is to draw conclusions about a candidate's personality from his or her handwriting as a basis for making predictions about future performance in a role. The use of graphology as a selection aid is extensive on the Continent but relatively uncommon in the UK – Fowler (1991a) quotes research findings that indicate that only between 0.5 and 1.0 per cent of employers use it in the UK. This very small proportion may be attributed to the suspicion the great majority of recruiters have that graphology is in some way spurious and using it as a predictor will be a waste of time and money. In an extensive review of the research literature, Fowler (1991a) established that some studies had indicated a predictive validity coefficient in the range of 0.1 to 0.3, although zero results have also been obtained. These are low figures, which achieve only a poor level of validity. Fowler's conclusion was that clues about personality characteristics may be deduced by skilled graphologists but that the use of graphology as a single or standard predictor cannot be recommended. He also suspects that, for some people, the real attraction of graphology is that it can be used without the subject's knowledge.

CHOICE OF SELECTION METHODS

There is a choice between the main selection methods. What Cook (1993) refers to as the classic trio consists of application forms, interviews and references. These can be supplemented or replaced by biodata, assessment centres and, as described in Chapter 27, psychological tests. It has been demonstrated again and again that interviews are an inefficient method of predicting success in a job. Smart (1983), for example, claims that only 94 out of 1,000 interviewees respond honestly in conventional interviews. Validity studies such as those quoted by Taylor (1998), as illustrated in Figure 25.3, produce equally dubious figures for conventional interviews and indicate that assessment centres, psychometric tests, biodata and structured interviews are more accurate methods of selection. For good and not so good reasons, organizations will retain interviews as the main method of selection where assessment centres are inappropriate. But there is a very powerful case for structuring the interview and

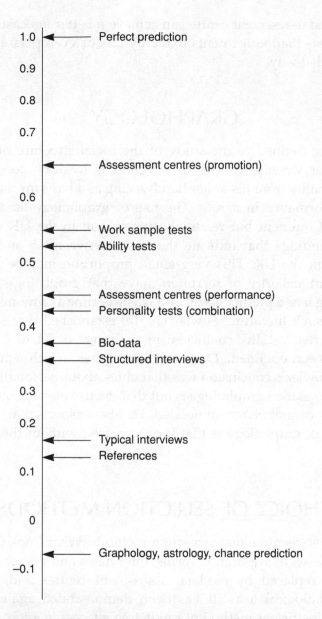

Figure 25.3 Accuracy of some methods of selection

(Reproduced with permission from Stephen Taylor (1998) *Employee Resourcing*, Institute of Personnel and Development) a strong case for supplementing it with tests. The more evidence that can be produced to help in making crucial selection decisions, the better.

IMPROVING THE EFFECTIVENESS OF RECRUITMENT AND SELECTION

An HRM approach can be adopted to recruitment, which involves taking much more care in matching people to the requirements of the organization as a whole as well as to the particular needs of the job. And these requirements will include commitment and ability to work effectively as a member of a team.

Examples of this approach in Japanese companies in the UK include the establishment of the Nissan plant in Washington and Kumatsu in Newcastle. As described by Townley (1989), both followed a conscious recruitment policy with rigorous selection procedures. Aptitude tests, personality questionnaires and group exercises were used and the initial pre-screening device was a detailed 'biodata'-type questionnaire, which enabled the qualifications and work history of candidates to be assessed and rated systematically. Subsequent testing of those who successfully completed the first stage was designed to assess individual attitudes as well as aptitude and ability. As Wickens (1987) said of the steps taken at Nissan to achieve commitment and team working: 'It is something which develops because management genuinely believes in it and acts accordingly – and recruits or promotes people who have the same belief.'

The need for a more sophisticated approach to recruitment along these lines is characteristic of HRM. The first requirement is to take great care in specifying the competences and behavioural characteristics required of employees. The second is to use a wider range of methods to identify candidates who match the specification. As noted earlier in this chapter, the predictive quality of the traditional interview is very limited. At the very least, structured interviewing techniques should be adopted as described in Chapter 26. Wherever possible, psychological tests should be used to extend the data obtained from the interview. Well-planned and administered assessment centres are the best predictors of success in a job, but they are only practical for a limited number of more complex or demanding jobs or for selecting graduates and entrants to training programmes.

REFERENCES, QUALIFICATIONS AND OFFERS

After the interviewing and testing procedure has been completed, a provisional decision to make an offer by telephone or in writing can be made. This is normally 'subject to satisfactory references' and the candidate should, of course, be told that these will be taken up. If there is more than one eligible candidate for a job it may be advisable to hold one or two people in reserve. Applicants often withdraw, especially those whose only purpose in applying for the job was to carry out a 'test marketing' operation, or to obtain a lever with which to persuade their present employers to value them more highly.

References – purpose and method

The purpose of a reference is to obtain in confidence factual information about a prospective employee and opinions about his or her character and suitability for a job.

The factual information is straightforward and essential. It is simply necessary to confirm the nature of the previous job, the period of time in employment, the reason for leaving (if relevant), the salary or rate of pay and, possibly, the attendance record.

Opinions about character and suitability are less reliable and should be treated with caution. The reason is obvious. Previous or present employers who give references tend to avoid highly detrimental remarks either out of charity or because they think anything they say or write may be construed as slanderous or libellous (references are, in fact, privileged as long as they are given without malice and are factually correct).

Personal referees are, of course, entirely useless. All they prove is that the applicant has at least one or two friends.

Written references save time, especially if they are standardized. They may take the form of an invitation to write a letter confirming the employment record and commenting on the applicant's character in general. If brief details about the job are included (these may be an extract from the advertisement – they should certainly not be an over-elaborate job description), previous employers can be asked to express their views about the suitability of the individual for the job. But this is asking a lot. Unless the job and companies are identical, how well can existing or ex-employers judge the suitability of someone they may not know particularly well for another job in a different environment?

More factual answers may be obtained if a standard form is provided for the employer to complete. The questions asked on this form could include:

- What was the period of employment?
- What was the job title?
- What work was carried out?
- What was the rate of pay or salary?

- How many days' absence over the last 12 months?
- Would you re-employ (if not, why not)?

Telephone references may be used as an alternative or in addition to written references. The great advantage of a telephone conversation is that people are more likely to give an honest opinion orally than if they have to commit themselves in writing. It may also save time to use the telephone.

Employer references are necessary to check on the facts given by the prospective employee. Opinions have to be treated with more caution. A very glowing reference may arouse suspicion, and it is worth comparing it with a reference from another employer (two employment references are desirable in any case). Poor or grudging references must create some alarm, if only because they are so infrequent. But allowance should be made for prejudice and a check should be made, by telephone if possible.

References – legal aspects

The key legal points that should be considered when asking for or giving references are:

- Once the decision has been made to make an offer, the letter should state that 'this is a provisional offer subject to references satisfactory to the company being received'.
- It has been generally held that there is no common law duty on an employer to provide references for a serving or past employee unless there is a term to that effect in the employment contract. But it has been ruled (*Spring* v *Guardian Assurance* 1994) that there might be a 'contractual duty' to provide a reference where it is 'natural practice' to require a reference from a previous employer before offering employment, and where the employee could not expect to enter that type of employment without a reference.
- If a reference contains a false or unsubstantiated statement that damages the reputation of the individual, action for damages may result.
- It is possible to succeed in a claim for damages if it can be shown that the reference provided was negligent because, if the facts had been checked, they would have been found to be groundless.
- Referees have a legal liability to the prospective employer not to give a reference that contains 'material factors' which were known to be untrue. If an employer appointed someone on the basis of a reference and found that the employee was unsuitable in respect of a material factor given in that reference, the employer can

initiate legal action alleging 'deceit'. Employers can try to protect themselves by adding the phrase 'without legal responsibility' to any references given, but this does not provide a certain defence.

Qualifications

It has been estimated by the Chartered Institute of Personnel and Development that one in eight candidates exaggerate or falsify their qualifications. If a qualification is a necessary requirement for the job, it is always worth checking with the university or college concerned, or asking the candidate to produce evidence in the shape of a certificate or diploma.

FINAL STAGES

Confirming the offer

The final stage in the selection procedure is to confirm the offer of employment after satisfactory references have been obtained, and the applicant has passed the medical examination required for pension and life assurance purposes or because a certain standard of physical fitness is required for the work. The contract of employment should also be prepared at this stage.

Contracts of employment

The basic information that should be included in a written contract of employment varies according to the level of job. Contracts of employment are dealt with in Chapter 55.

Follow-up

It is essential to follow up newly engaged employees to ensure that they have settled in and to check on how well they are doing. If there are any problems, it is much better to identify them at an early stage rather than allowing them to fester.

Following up is also important as a means of checking on the selection procedure. If by any chance a mistake has been made, it is useful to find out how it happened so that the selection procedure can be improved. Misfits can be attributed to a number of causes; for example, inadequate job description or specification, poor sourcing of candidates, weak advertising, poor interviewing techniques, inappropriate or invalidated tests, or prejudice on the part of the selector. If any of these are identified, steps can be taken to prevent their recurrence.

26

Selection interviewing

The techniques and skills of selection interviewing are described in this chapter under the following headings:

- purpose;
- advantages and disadvantages of interviews;
- nature of an interview;
- interviewing arrangements;
- preparation;
- timing;
- planning and structuring interviews;
- interviewing approaches;
- interview techniques – starting and finishing;
- interviewing techniques – asking questions;
- selection interviewing skills;
- coming to a conclusion;
- dos and don'ts of selection interviewing.

PURPOSE

The purpose of the selection interview is to obtain and assess information about a candidate which will enable a valid prediction to be made of his or her future performance in the job in comparison with the predictions made for any other candidates. Interviewing therefore involves processing and evaluating evidence about the capabilities of a candidate in relation to the person specification. Some of the evidence will be on the application form, but the aim of the interview is to supplement this data with the more detailed or specific information about experience and personal characteristics that can be obtained in a face-to-face meeting. Such a meeting also provides an opportunity for judgements by the interviewer on whether the individual will 'fit' the organization, and by both parties as to how they would get on together. Although these judgements are entirely subjective and are often biased or prejudiced, it has to be recognized that they will be made.

In particular, selection interviews aim to provide answers to these questions:

● *Can* individuals do the job – are they competent?
● *Will* individuals do the job – are they well motivated?
● *How* will individuals fit into the organization?

The interview forms a major part of the 'classic trio' of selection techniques, the other two being the application form and references. Further evidence may be obtained from psychological tests as described in Chapter 27 but, in spite of the well-publicized inadequacies of interviews as reliable means of predicting success in a job, they are still an inevitable part of a selection procedure for most people. This chapter focuses on the advantages and disadvantages of interviews, the nature of an interview and methods of carrying out effective interviews, effective in that they provide reliable and valid predictions.

ADVANTAGES AND DISADVANTAGES OF INTERVIEWS

The advantages of interviews as a method of selection are that they:

● provide opportunities for interviewers to ask probing questions about the candidate's experience and to explore the extent to which the candidate's competences match those specified for the job;
● enable interviewers to describe the job (a 'realistic job preview') and the organization in more detail, suggesting some of the terms of the psychological contract;
● provide opportunities for candidates to ask questions about the job and to clarify issues concerning training, career prospects, the organization and terms and conditions of employment;

- enable a face-to-face encounter to take place so that the interviewer can make an assessment of how the candidate would fit into the organization and what he or she would be like to work with;
- give the candidate the same opportunity to assess the organization, the interviewer and the job.

The disadvantages of interviews are that they:

- can lack validity as a means of making sound predictions of performance, and lack reliability in the sense of measuring the same things for different candidates;
- rely on the skill of the interviewer, but many people are poor at interviewing, although most think that they are good at it;
- do not necessarily assess competence in meeting the demands of the particular job;
- can lead to biased and subjective judgements by interviewers.

However, these disadvantages can be alleviated if not entirely removed, first, by using a structured approach that focuses on the competences and behaviours required for successful performance and, secondly, by training interviewers. The use of another opinion or other opinions can also help to reduce bias, especially if the same structured approach is adopted by all the interviewers.

THE NATURE OF AN INTERVIEW

An interview can be described as a conversation with a purpose. It is a conversation because candidates should be induced to talk freely with their interviewers about themselves, their experience and their careers. But the conversation has to be planned, directed and controlled to achieve the main purpose of the interview, which is to make an accurate prediction of the candidate's future performance in the job for which he or she is being considered.

However, interviews also provide a valuable opportunity for an exchange of information, which will enable both parties to make a decision: to offer or not to offer a job; to accept or not to accept the offer. It may be better for the candidates to 'de-select' themselves at this stage if they do not like what they hear about the job or the company rather than take on a disagreeable job. Interviews are often used to give the candidates a favourable impression of the organization and the job. But this must be realistic – a 'realistic job preview' will spell out any special demands that will be made on the successful applicant in terms of the standards they will be expected to achieve, the hours they may have to work, the travelling they have to do and any requirement for mobility in the UK or abroad. Clearly, if these are onerous, it will be necessary to convince good candidates that the rewards will be commensurate with the requirements. If poor candidates are put off, so much the better.

Good interviewers know what they are looking for and how to set about finding it. They have a method for recording their analyses of candidates against a set of assessment criteria, which will be spelt out in a person specification.

INTERVIEWING ARRANGEMENTS

The interviewing arrangements will depend partly on the procedure being used, which may consist of individual interviews, an interviewing panel, a selection board or some form of assessment centre, sometimes referred to as a group selection procedure. In most cases, however, the arrangements for the interviews should conform broadly to the following pattern:

- The candidate who has applied in writing or by telephone should be told where and when to come and for whom to ask. The interview time should be arranged to fit in with the time it will take to get to the company. It may be necessary to adjust times for those who cannot get away during working hours. If the company is difficult to find, a map should be sent with details of public transport. The receptionist or security guard should be told who is coming. Candidates are impressed to find that they are expected
- Applicants should have somewhere quiet and comfortable in which to wait for the interview, with reading material available and access to cloakroom facilities.
- The interviewers or interviewing panel should have been well briefed on the programme. Interviewing rooms should have been booked and arrangements made, as necessary, for welcoming candidates, for escorting them to interviews, for meals and for a conducted tour round the company.
- Comfortable private rooms should be provided for interviews with little, if any, distractions around them. Interviewers should preferably not sit behind their desks, as this creates a psychological barrier.
- During the interview or interviews, some time, but not too much, should be allowed to tell candidates about the company and the job and to discuss with them conditions of employment. Negotiations about pay and other benefits may take place after a provisional offer has been made, but it is as well to prepare the ground during the interviewing stage.
- Candidates should be told what the next step will be at the end of the interview. They may be asked at this stage if they have any objections to references being taken up.

● Follow-up studies should be carried out, comparing the performance of successful candidates in their jobs with the prediction made at the selection stage. These studies should be used to validate the selection procedure and to check on the capabilities of interviewers.

Briefing interviewers

When making arrangements for an interview it is essential that the people who are going to conduct the interview are properly briefed on the job and the procedures they should use. There is everything to be said for including training in interviewing techniques as an automatic part of the training programmes for managers and team leaders.

It is particularly important that everyone is fully aware of the provisions of the Sex, Race and Disability Discrimination Acts. It is essential that any form of prejudiced behaviour or any prejudiced judgements are eliminated completely from the interview and the ensuing discussion. Even the faintest hint of a sexist or racist remark must be totally avoided. When recording a decision following an interview it is also essential to spell out the reasons why someone was rejected, making it clear that this was absolutely on the grounds of their qualifications for the job and had nothing to do with their sex, race or disability.

Ethical considerations

Another important consideration in planning and executing a recruitment programme is to behave ethically towards candidates. They have the right to be treated with consideration and this includes acknowledging replies and informing them of the outcome of their application without undue delay.

Planning the interview programme

It is best to leave some time, say 15 minutes, between interviews to allow for comments to be made. There is a limit to how many interviews can be conducted in a day without running out of steam, and holding more than six demanding interviews of, say, one hour each in a day is unwise. Even with less demanding half-hour interviews it is preferable to limit the number to eight or so in a day.

PREPARATION

Careful preparation is essential and this means a careful study of the person specification and the candidate's application form and/or CV. It is necessary at this stage to identify those features of the applicant that do not fully match the specification so that these can be probed more deeply during the interview. It can be assumed that the candidate is only being considered because there is a reasonable match, but it is most unlikely that this match will be perfect. It is also necessary to establish if there are any gaps in the job history or items that require further explanation.

There are three fundamental questions that need to be answered at this stage:

● What are the criteria to be used in selecting the candidate – these may be classified as essential or desirable and will refer to the experience, qualifications, and competence and skill requirements as set out in the person specification.
● What more do I need to find out at the interview to ensure that the candidate meets the essential selection criteria?
● What further information do I need to obtain at the interview to ensure that I have an accurate picture of how well the candidate meets the criteria?

The preparation should include making notes of the specific questions the interviewer needs to ask to establish the relevance of the candidate's experience and the extent to which he or she has the skills, knowledge and levels of competence required. These may be quite detailed if a highly structured approach is being adopted as described below – it is essential to probe during an interview to establish what the candidate really can do and has achieved. Applicants will generally aim to make the most of themselves and this can lead to exaggerated, even false, claims about their experience and capabilities.

TIMING

The length of time allowed for an interview will be related to the seniority and complexity of the job. For relatively routine jobs, 20 to 30 minutes may suffice. For more demanding jobs, up to an hour may be necessary. Interviews should rarely, if ever, exceed an hour.

PLANNING AND STRUCTURING INTERVIEWS

The problem with interviews is that they are often inadequate as predictors of performance – an hour's interview may not cover the essential points unless it is carefully planned and, sadly, the general standard of interviewing is low. This is not simply a result of many people using poor interviewing techniques (eg they talk rather than listen). More importantly, it is a result of not carrying out a proper analysis of the competencies required, with the result that interviewers do not know the information they need to obtain from the candidate as a basis for structuring the interview.

There are a number of methods of conducting interviews. At their worst, interviewers adopt an entirely unstructured approach, which involves asking random questions that are not based on any understanding of what they are looking for. At best, they are clearly structured and related to a thorough analysis of role requirements in terms of skills and competencies.

Generally, an interview can be divided into five parts:

1. the welcome and introductory remarks;
2. the major part concerned with obtaining information about the candidate to assess against the person specification;
3. the provision of information to candidates about the organization and the job;.
4. answering questions from the candidate;
5. closing the interview with an indication of the next step.

The bulk of the time – at least 80 per cent – should be allocated to obtaining information from the candidate. The introduction and conclusion should be brief, though friendly.

The two traditional ways of planning an interview are to adopt a biographical approach or to follow the assessment headings in, for example, the seven-point plan. These approaches are sometimes classified as 'unstructured interviews' in contrast to the 'structured interview', which is generally regarded as best practice. The latter term usually has the special meaning of referring to interviews that are structured around situational-based or behavioural-based questions, focusing on one or other or both. The common element is that the questions are prepared in advance and are related to the role analysis and person specification in terms of the things candidates will be expected to do and/or the behaviour they will be expected to demonstrate. But it could be argued that a biographical or assessment heading approach is 'structured', although they may not relate so specifically to identified role requirements. A further but less common variety of structured interview is psychometric-based. All these approaches are examined below.

INTERVIEWING APPROACHES

The biographical interview

The traditional biographical interview either starts at the beginning (education) and goes on in sequence to the end (the current or last job or the most recent educational experience), or proceeds in the opposite direction, starting with the present job and going backwards to the first job and the candidate's education or training. Many interviewers prefer to go backwards with experienced candidates, spending most time on the present or recent jobs, giving progressively less attention to the earlier experience, and only touching on education lightly.

There is no one best sequence to follow but it is important to decide in advance what sequence to adopt. It is also important to get the balance right. You should concentrate most on recent experience and not dwell too much on the distant past. You should allow time not only to the candidate to talk about his or her career but also to ask probing questions as necessary. You should certainly not spend too much time at the beginning of the interview talking about the company and the job. It is highly desirable to issue that information in advance to save interview time and simply encourage the candidate to ask questions at the end of the interview (the quality of the questions can indicate something about the quality of the candidate).

This form of plan is logical but it will not produce the desired information unless interviewers are absolutely clear about what they are looking for and are prepared with questions that will elicit the data they need to make a selection decision.

Interview planned by reference to a person specification

The person specification as described in Chapter 25 provides a sound basis for a structured interview. The aim is to obtain information under each of the main headings to indicate the extent to which the candidate matches the specification. Typical headings are:

- *knowledge, skills and expertise* – what the candidate is expected to know and be able to do as a result of experience, education and training (work-based competencies), for example, technical or professional knowledge, numeracy, manual skills, and experience at the appropriate level in carrying out relevant work;
- *personal qualities* – how the candidate will be expected to behave in carrying out the job, such as working with other people, exercising leadership, influencing people, communicating (eg report writing, making presentations) achieving results, decision-making, taking the initiative, and being self-reliant (behavioural competencies);
- *qualifications* – essential academic or professional qualifications.

A 'person specification' setting out such requirements can be sent to candidates (or posted on an online recruitment site). The applicant is asked to respond with information on how they believe they match these requirements. This approach can make it much easier to sift applications.

Interviews planned by reference to assessment headings

Assessment headings such as those described in Chapter 25 can be used. They define a number of areas in which information can be generated and assessed in a broadly comparable way. But as Edenborough (1994) points out, they do not provide any clear indication of which items of the data collected are likely to predict success in a job.

Structured situational-based interviews

In a situational-based interview (sometimes described as a critical-incident interview) the focus is on a number of situations or incidents in which behaviour can be regarded as being particularly indicative of subsequent performance. A typical situation is described and candidates are asked how they would deal with it. Follow-up questions are asked to explore the response in more detail, thus gaining a better understanding of how candidates might tackle similar problems.

Situational-based questions ask candidates how they would handle a hypothetical situation that resembles one they may encounter in the job. For example, a sales assistant might be asked how he or she would respond to rudeness from a customer. Situational questions can provide some insight into how applicants might respond to particular job demands and have the advantage of being work-related. They can also provide candidates with some insight into the sort of problems they might meet in the job. But, because they are hypothetical and can necessarily only cover a limited number of areas, they cannot be relied on by themselves. They could indicate that candidates understand how they might handle one type of situation in theory but not that they would be able to handle similar or other situations in practice.

An example of part of a situation-based set of questions is given in Figure 26.1.

Structured behavioural (competency) based interviews

In a behavioural-based interview (sometimes referred to as a criterion-referenced interview) the interviewer progresses through a series of questions, each based on a criterion, which could be a behavioural competency or a competence in the form of a fundamental skill, capability or aptitude that is required to achieve an acceptable level of performance in the job. These will have been defined by job or competency

---

LISTENING

Sometimes a customer won't say directly what they want and you have to listen to the messages behind the words. Tell me about a time when you were able to help the sale along.

● Why was the customer reluctant to say what was wanted?
● How did you check that you really did understand?
● How did you show that it was OK for the customer to have the concerns shown in the hidden message?
● Did you actually do a deal that day?
● Is the customer still on your books?
● Had others experienced difficulty with that particular customer?

Figure 26.1   Part of a critical-incident interview for sales people

(*Source:* R Edenborough (1994) *Using Psychometrics*, Kogan Page)

analysis as described in Chapter 23 and will form the basis of a person specification. The aim is to collect evidence about relevant aspects of experience in using skills and competencies on the assumption that such evidence of past performance and behaviour is the best predictor of future performance and behaviour as long as the criteria are appropriate in relation to the specified demands of the job.

Behavioural-based questions ask candidates to describe how they dealt with particular situations they have come across in their past experience. In effect they are asked to indicate how they behaved in response to a problem and how well that behaviour worked. Questions are structured around the key competencies identified for the role. The definitions of these competencies should identify what is regarded as effective behaviour as a basis for evaluating answers. A list of questions can be drawn up in advance to cover the key competencies set out in the person specification. For instance, if one of these competencies is concerned with behaviour as a team member, questions such as: 'Can you tell me about any occasions when you have persuaded your fellow team members to do something which at first they didn't really want to do?' An example of a set of behavioural questions is given in Figure 26.2.

Behavioural-based interviews can provide a clear and relevant framework. But preparing for them takes time and interviewers need to be trained in the technique. A fully behavioural or criterion-referenced structure is probably most appropriate for jobs that have to be filled frequently. But even with one-off jobs, the technique of having a set of competency-referenced questions to ask, which will be applied consistently to all candidates, will improve the reliability of the prediction.

PRACTICAL CREATIVITY
The ability to originate and realize effective solutions to everyday problems

1. Tell me about a time when you used previous experience to solve a problem new to you.
2. Do you ever make things, perhaps in your spare time, out of all sorts of odds and ends? (if necessary) Tell me what you have done.
3. Tell me about a time when you got a piece of equipment or a new system to work when other people were struggling with it.
4. Have you ever found an entirely new use for a hand or power tool? Do you often do that sort of thing? Tell me more.
5. Do people come to you to help solve problems? (if so) Tell me about a problem you have solved recently.

Figure 26.2 Behavioural-based interview set

(*Source:* R Edenborough (1994) *Using Psychometrics*, Kogan Page)

Structured psychometric interviews

Another type of structured interview consists of entirely predetermined questions as in a psychometric test (see Chapter 27). There is no scope to follow through questions as in the other types of structured interviews referred to above. Responses to the questions are coded so that results can be analysed and compared. The aim is to obtain consistency between different interviews and interviewers. A typical question would be: 'Have you ever been in a situation where you have had to get someone to do something against their will?'; (*if yes*) 'Please give me a recent example.' This is a highly structured approach and, because of the research and training required, it is probably only feasible when large numbers of candidates have to be interviewed.

Choice of approach

The more the approach can be structured by the use of situational or behavioural-based questions, the better. If the criteria have been properly researched, much more insight will be obtained about candidates' capabilities by reference to analysed and specified role requirements. It is still useful, however, to review candidates' sequence of experience and the responsibilities exercised in successive jobs. It may be important, for example, to establish the extent to which the career of candidates has progressed smoothly or why there have been gaps between successive jobs. It is useful to know what responsibilities candidates have had in recent jobs and the extent to which this experience is useful and relevant. Candidates should also be given the chance to highlight their achievements. This review provides a framework within which more specific questions that refer to behavioural criteria or critical incidents can be asked. It was noted by Latham *et al* (1980) that interviews using this technique produced reasonably reliable and consistent assessments. A typical interview may include about 10 or more, depending on the job, pre-prepared behavioural event or 'situational' questions.

INTERVIEW TECHNIQUES – STARTING AND FINISHING

You should start interviews by putting candidates at their ease. You want them to provide you with information and they are not going to talk freely and openly if they are given a cool reception.

In the closing stages of the interview candidates should be asked if they have anything they wish to add in support of their application. They should also be given the opportunity to ask questions. At the end of the interview the candidate should be thanked and given information about the next stage. If some time is likely to elapse before a decision is made, the candidate should be informed accordingly so as not to be left on tenterhooks. It is normally better not to announce the final decision during the interview. It may be advisable to obtain references and, in any case, time is required to reflect on the information received.

INTERVIEWING TECHNIQUES – ASKING QUESTIONS

The interviewee should be encouraged to do most of the talking – one of the besetting sins of poor interviewers is that they talk too much. The interviewer's job is to draw the candidate out, at the same time ensuring that the information required is obtained. To this end it is desirable to ask a number of open-ended questions – questions that cannot be answered by yes or no and that promote a full response. But a good interviewer will have an armoury of other types of questions to be asked as appropriate, as described below.

Open questions

Open questions are the best ones to use to get candidates to talk – to draw them out and encourage a full response. Single-word answers are seldom illuminating. It is a good idea to begin the interview with one or two open questions, thus helping candidates to settle in.

Open questions or phrases inviting a response can be phrased as follows:

- I'd like you to tell me about the sort of work you are doing in your present job.
- What do you know about…?
- Could you give me some examples of…?
- In what ways do you think your experience fits you to do the job for which you have applied?
- How have you tackled…?
- What have been the most challenging aspects of your job?
- Please tell me about some of the interesting things you have been doing at work recently.

Open questions can give you a lot of useful information but you may not get exactly what you want, and answers can go into too much detail. For example, the question: 'What has been the main feature of your work in recent months?' may result in a one-word reply – 'marketing'. Or it may produce a lengthy explanation that takes up too much time. Replies to open questions can get bogged down in too much detail, or miss out some key points. They can come to a sudden halt or lose their way. You need to ensure that you get all the facts, keep the flow going and maintain control. Remember that you are in charge. Hence the value of probing, closed and the other types of questions which are discussed below.

Probing questions

Probing questions are used to get further details or to ensure that you are getting all the facts. You ask them when answers have been too generalized or when you suspect that there may be some more relevant information that candidates have not disclosed. A candidate may claim to have done something and it may be useful to find out more about exactly what contribution was made. Poor interviewers tend to let general and uninformative answers pass by without probing for further details, simply because they are sticking rigidly to a predetermined list of open questions. Skilled interviewers are able to flex their approach to ensure they get the facts while still keeping control to ensure that the interview is completed on time.   A candidate could say to you something like: 'I was involved in a major business process re-engineering exercise that produced significant improvements in the flow of work through the factory.' This statement conveys nothing about what the candidate actually did. You have to ask probing questions such as:

- What was your precise role in this project?
- What exactly was the contribution you made to its success?
- What knowledge and skills were you able to apply to the project?

- Were you responsible for monitoring progress?
- Did you prepare the final recommendations in full or in part? If in part, which part?

The following are some other examples of probing questions:

- You've informed me that you have had experience in…. Could you tell me more about what you did?
- Could you describe in more detail the equipment you use?

Closed questions

Closed questions aim to clarify a point of fact. The expected reply will be an explicit single word or brief sentence. In a sense, a closed question acts as a probe but produces a succinct factual statement without going into detail. When you ask a closed question you intend to find out:

- what the candidate has or has not done – 'What did you do then?'
- why something took place – 'Why did that happen?'
- when something took place – 'When did that happen?'
- how something happened – 'How did that situation arise?'
- where something happened – 'Where were you at the time?'
- who took part – 'Who else was involved?'

Hypothetical questions

Hypothetical questions as used in structured situational-based interviews to put a situation to candidates and ask them how they would respond. They can be prepared in advance to test how candidates would approach a typical problem. Such questions may be phrased: 'What do you think you would do if…?' When such questions lie well within the candidate's expertise and experience, the answers can be illuminating. But it could be unfair to ask candidates to say how they would deal with a problem without knowing more about the context in which the problem arose. It can also be argued that what candidates say they would do and what they actually do could be quite different. Hypothetical questions can produce hypothetical answers. The best data upon which judgements about candidates can be made are what they have actually done or achieved. You need to find out if they have successfully dealt with the sort of issues and problems they may be faced with if they join your organization.

Behavioural event questions

Behavioural event questions as used in behavioural-based structured interviews aim to get candidates to tell you how they would behave in situations that have been identified as critical to successful job performance. The assumption upon which such questions are based is that past behaviour in dealing with or reacting to events is the best predictor of future behaviour.

The following are some typical behavioural event questions:

● Could you give an instance when you persuaded others to take an unusual course of action?
● Could you describe an occasion when you completed a project or task in the face of great difficulties?
● Could you describe any contribution you have made as a member of a team in achieving an unusually successful result?
● Could you give an instance when you took the lead in a difficult situation in getting something worthwhile done?

Capability questions

Capability questions aim to establish what candidates know, the skills they possess and use and their competencies – what they are capable of doing. They can be open, probing or closed but they will always be focused as precisely as possible on the contents of the person specification referring to knowledge, skills and competences. Capability questions are used in behavioural-based structured interviews.

Capability questions should therefore be explicit – focused on what candidates must know and be able to do. Their purpose is to obtain from candidates evidence that shows the extent to which they meet the specification in each of its key areas. Because time is always limited, it is best to concentrate on the most important aspects of the work. And it is always best to prepare the questions in advance.

The sort of capability questions you can ask are:

● What do you know about…?
● How did you gain this knowledge?
● What are the key skills you are expected to use in your work?
● How would your present employer rate the level of skill you have reached in…?
● Could you please tell me exactly what sort and how much experience you have had in…?
● Could you tell me more about what you have actually been doing in this aspect of your work?

- Can you give me any examples of the sort of work you have done that would qualify you to do this job?
- What are the most typical problems you have to deal with?
- Would you tell me about any instances when you have had to deal with an unexpected problem or a crisis?

Questions about motivation

The degree to which candidates are motivated is a personal quality to which it is usually necessary to give special attention if it is to be properly assessed. This is best achieved by inference rather than direct questions. 'How well are you motivated?' is a leading question that will usually produce the response: 'Highly.'

You can make inferences about the level of motivation of candidates by asking questions about:

- Their career – replies to such questions as 'Why did you decide to move on from there?' can give an indication of the extent to which they have been well motivated in progressing their career.
- Achievements – not just 'What did you achieve?' but 'How did you achieve it?' and 'What difficulties did you overcome?'
- Triumphing over disadvantages – candidates who have done well in spite of an unpromising upbringing and relatively poor education may be more highly motivated than those with all the advantages that upbringing and education can bestow, but who have not made good use of these advantages.
- Spare time interests – don't accept at its face value a reply to a question about spare time interests that, for example, reveals that a candidate collects stamps. Find out if the candidate is well motivated enough to pursue the interest with determination and to achieve something in the process. Simply sticking stamps in an album is not evidence of motivation. Becoming a recognized expert on 19th-century stamps issued in Mexico is.

Continuity questions

Continuity questions aim to keep the flow going in an interview and encourage candidates to enlarge on what they have told you, within limits. Here are some examples of continuity questions:

- What happened next?
- What did you do then?

- Can we talk about your next job?
- Can we move on now to…?
- Could you tell me more about…?

It has been said that to keep the conversation going during an interview the best thing an interviewer can do is to make encouraging grunts at appropriate moments. There is more to interviewing than that, but single words or phrases like 'good', 'fine', 'that's interesting', 'carry on' can help things along.

Play-back questions

Play-back questions test your understanding of what candidates have said by putting to them a statement of what it appears they have told you, and asking them if they agree or disagree with your version. For example, you could say: 'As I understand it, you resigned from your last position because you disagreed with your boss on a number of fundamental issues – have I got that right?' The answer might simply be yes to this closed question, in which case you might probe to find out more about what happened. Or the candidate may reply 'not exactly', in which case you ask for the full story.

Career questions

As mentioned earlier, questions about the career history of candidates can provide some insight into motivation as well as establishing how they have progressed in acquiring useful and relevant knowledge, skills and experience. You can ask such questions as:

- What did you learn from that new job?
- What different skills had you to use when you were promoted?
- Why did you leave that job?
- What happened after you left that job?
- In what ways do you think this job will advance your career?

Focused work questions

These are questions designed to tell you more about particular aspects of the candidate's work history, such as:

- How many days' absence from work did you have last year?

- How many times were you late last year?
- Have you been absent from work for any medical reason not shown on your application form?
- Have you a clean driving licence? (For those whose work will involve driving.)

Questions about outside interests

You should not spend much time asking people with work experience about their outside interests or hobbies. It is seldom relevant, although, as mentioned earlier, it can give some insight into how well motivated candidates are if the depth and vigour with which the interest is pursued is explored.

Active interests and offices held at school, colleges or universities can, however, provide some insight into the attributes of candidates in the absence of any work history except, possibly, vacation jobs. If, for example, a student has been on a long back-pack trip, some information can be obtained about the student's initiative, motivation and determination if the journey has been particularly adventurous.

Unhelpful questions

There are two types of questions that are unhelpful:

- *Multiple questions* such as 'What skills do you use most frequently in your job? Are they technical skills, leadership skills, team-working skills or communicating skills?' will only confuse candidates. You will probably get a partial or misleading reply. Ask only one question at a time.
- *Leading questions* that indicate the reply you expect are also unhelpful. If you ask a question such as: 'That's what you think, isn't it?' you will get the reply: 'Yes, I do.' If you ask a question such as: 'I take it that you don't really believe that….?', you will get the reply: 'No, I don't.' Neither of these replies will get you anywhere.

Questions to be avoided

Avoid any questions that could be construed as being biased on the grounds of sex, race or disability. Don't ask:

- Who is going to look after the children? This is no concern of yours, although it is reasonable to ask if the hours of work pose any problems.
- Are you planning to have any more children?

- Would it worry you being a member of an ethnic minority here?
- With your disability, do you think you can cope with the job?

Ten useful questions

The following are 10 useful questions from which you can select any that are particularly relevant in an interview you are conducting:

- What are the most important aspects of your present job?
- What do you think have been your most notable achievements in your career to date?
- What sort of problems have you successfully solved recently in your job?
- What have you learned from your present job?
- What has been your experience in…?
- What do you know about…?
- What is your approach to handling…?
- What particularly interests you in this job and why?
- Now you have heard more about the job, would you please tell me which aspects of your experience are most relevant?
- Is there anything else about your career that hasn't come out yet in this interview but that you think I ought to hear?

SELECTION INTERVIEWING SKILLS

Establishing rapport

Establishing rapport means establishing a good relationship with candidates – getting on their wavelength, putting them at ease, encouraging them to respond and generally being friendly. This is not just a question of being 'nice' to candidates. If you achieve rapport you are more likely to get them to talk freely about both their strengths and their weaknesses.

Good rapport is created by the way in which you greet candidates, how you start the interview and how you put your questions and respond to replies. Questions should not be posed aggressively or imply that you are criticizing some aspect of the candidate's career. Some people like the idea of 'stress' interviews, but they are always counter-productive. Candidates clam up and gain a negative impression of you and the organization.

When responding to answers you should be appreciative, not critical: 'Thank you, that was very helpful; now can we go on to...?', not 'Well, that didn't show you in a good light, did it?'

Body language can also be important. If you maintain natural eye contact, avoid slumping in your seat, nod and make encouraging comments when appropriate, you will establish better rapport and get more out of the interview

Listening

If an interview is a conversation with a purpose, as it should be, listening skills are important. You need not only to hear but also to understand what candidates are saying. When interviewing, you must concentrate on what candidates are telling you. Summarizing at regular intervals forces you to listen because you have to pay attention to what they have been saying in order to get the gist of their replies. If you play back to candidates your understanding of what they have told you for them to confirm or amend, it will ensure that you have fully comprehended the messages they are delivering.

Maintaining continuity

So far as possible, link your questions to a candidate's last reply so that the interview progresses logically and a cumulative set of data is built up. You can put bridging questions to candidates such as: 'Thank you, that was an interesting summary of what you have been doing in that aspect of your work. Now, could you tell me something about your other key responsibilities?'

Keeping control

You want candidates to talk, but not too much. When preparing for the interview, you should have drawn up an agenda and you must try to stick to it. Don't cut candidates short too brutally but say something like: 'Thank you, I've got a good picture of that, now what about...?'

Focus on specifics as much as you can. If candidates ramble on a bit, ask a pointed question (a 'probe' question) that asks for an example illustrating the particular aspect of their work that you are considering.

Note taking

You won't remember everything that candidates tell you. It is useful to take notes of the key points they make, discreetly, but not surreptitiously. However, don't put candidates off by frowning or tut-tutting when you are making a negative note.

It may be helpful to ask candidates if they would mind if you take notes. They can't really object but will appreciate the fact that they have been asked.

COMING TO A CONCLUSION

It is essential not to be beguiled by a pleasant, articulate and confident interviewee who is in fact surface without substance in the shape of a good track record. Beware of the 'halo' effect that occurs when one or two good points are seized upon, leading to the neglect of negative indicators. The opposite 'horns' effect should also be avoided.

Individual candidates should be assessed against the criteria. These could be set under the headings of competence/skills, qualifications, experience, and overall suitability. Ratings can be given against each heading, for example: very acceptable, acceptable, marginally acceptable, unacceptable. The person specification should indicate which of the requirements are essential and which are only desirable. Clearly, to be considered for the job, candidates have to be acceptable or, perhaps stretching a point, marginally acceptable, in all the essential requirements. Next, compare your assessment of each of the candidates against one another. You can then make a conclusion on those preferred by reference to their assessments under each heading.

In the end, your decision between qualified candidates may well be judgemental. There may be one outstanding candidate, but quite often there are two or three. In these circumstances you have to come to a balanced view on which one is more likely to fit the job and the organization *and* have potential for a long-term career, if this is possible. Don't, however, settle for second best in desperation. It is better to try again.

Remember to make and keep notes of the reasons for your choice and why candidates have been rejected. These together with the applications should be kept for at least six months just in case your decision is challenged as being discriminatory.

DOS AND DON'TS OF SELECTION INTERVIEWING

To conclude, here is a summary of the dos and don'ts of selection interviewing:

Do

● give yourself sufficient time;
● plan the interview so you can structure it properly;

- create the right atmosphere;
- establish an easy and informal relationship – start with open questions;
- encourage the candidate to talk;
- cover the ground as planned, ensuring that you complete a prepared agenda and maintain continuity;
- analyse the candidate's career to reveal strengths, weaknesses and patterns of interest;
- ask clear, unambiguous questions;
- get examples and instances of the successful application of knowledge, skills and the effective use of capabilities;
- make judgements on the basis of the factual information you have obtained about candidates' experience and attributes in relation to the person specification;
- keep control over the content and timing of the interview.

Don't

- attempt too many interviews in a row;
- fall into the halo or horns effect trap;
- start the interview unprepared;
- plunge too quickly into demanding (probe) questions;
- ask multiple or leading questions;
- pay too much attention to isolated strengths or weaknesses;
- allow candidates to gloss over important facts;
- talk too much or allow candidates to ramble on;
- allow your prejudices to get the better of your capacity to make objective judgements.

27

Selection tests

Selection tests are used to provide more valid and reliable evidence of levels of intelligence, personality characteristics, abilities, aptitudes and attainments than can be obtained from an interview. This chapter is mainly concerned with psychological tests of intelligence or personality as defined below, but it also refers to the principal tests of ability etc that can be used.

PSYCHOLOGICAL TESTS: DEFINITION

As defined by Smith and Robertson (1986), a psychological test is:

> A carefully chosen, systematic and standardised procedure for evolving a sample of responses from candidates which can be used to assess one or more of their psychological characteristics with those of a representative sample of an appropriate population.

PURPOSE OF PSYCHOLOGICAL TESTS

Psychological tests are measuring instruments, which is why they are often referred to as psychometric tests. Psychometric literally means 'mental measurement'.

The purpose of a psychological test is to provide an objective means of measuring individual abilities or characteristics. They are used to enable selectors to gain a greater understanding of individuals so that they can predict the extent to which they will be successful in a job.

CHARACTERISTICS OF A GOOD TEST

A good test is one that provides valid data that enable reliable predictions of behaviour to be made, and therefore assist in the process of making objective and reasoned decisions when selecting people for jobs. It will be based on thorough research that has produced standardized criteria that have been derived by using the same measure to test a number of representative people to produce a set of 'norms'. The test should be capable of being objectively scored by reference to the normal or average performance of the group.

The characteristics of a good test are:

- It is a *sensitive* measuring instrument that discriminates well between subjects.
- It has been *standardized* on a representative and sizeable sample of the population for which it is intended so that any individual's score can be interpreted in relation to that of others.
- It is *reliable* in the sense that it always measures the same thing. A test aimed at measuring a particular characteristic, such as intelligence, should measure the same characteristic when applied to different people at the same or a different time, or to the same person at different times.
- It is *valid* in the sense that it measures the characteristic that the test is intended to measure. Thus, an intelligence test should measure intelligence (however defined) and not simply verbal facility. A test meant to predict success in a job or in passing examinations should produce reasonably convincing (statistically significant) predictions.

There are five types of validity:

- *Predictive validity* – the extent to which the test correctly predicts future behaviour. To establish predictive validity it is necessary to conduct extensive research over a period of time. It is also necessary to have accurate measures of performance so that the prediction can be compared with actual behaviour.
- *Concurrent validity* – the extent to which a test score differentiates individuals in relation to a criterion or standard of performance external to the test. This means comparing the test scores of high and low performances as indicated by the criteria and establishing the degree to which the test indicates who should fit into the high or low performance groups.

- *Content validity* – the extent to which the test is clearly related to the characteristics of the job or role for which it is being used as a measuring instrument.
- *Face validity* – the extent to which it is felt that the test 'looks' right, ie is measuring what it is supposed to measure.
- *Construct validity* – the extent to which the test measures a particular construct or characteristic. As Edenborough (1994) suggests, construct validity is in effect concerned with looking at the test itself. If it is meant to measure numerical reasoning, is that what it measures?

Measuring validity

A criterion-related approach is used to assess validity. This means selecting criteria against which the validity of the test can be measured. These criteria must reflect 'true' performance at work as accurately as possible. This may be difficult and Smith and Robertson (1986) emphasize that a single criterion is inadequate. Multiple criteria should be used. The extent to which criteria can be contaminated by other factors should also be considered and it should be remembered that criteria are dynamic – they will change over time.

Validity can be expressed as a coefficient of correlation in which 1.0 would equal perfect correlation between test results and subsequent behaviour, while 0.0 would equal no relationship between the test and performance. The following rule of thumb guide on whether a validity coefficient is big enough was produced by Smith (1984):

> over 0.5 excellent
> 0.40–0.49 good
> 0.30–0.39 acceptable
> less than 0.30 poor

On this basis, only ability tests, biodata and (according to Smith's figures) personality questionnaires reach acceptable levels of validity.

TYPES OF TEST

The main types of selection test as described below are intelligence, personality, ability, aptitude and attainment tests.

A distinction can be made between psychometric tests and psychometric questionnaires. As explained by Toplis *et al* (1991), a psychometric test such as one on mental ability has correct answers so that the higher the score, the better the performance. Psychometric questionnaires such as personality tests assess habitual performance and measure personality characteristics, interests, values or behaviour. With questionnaires, a high or low score signifies the extent to which a person has a certain quality and the appropriateness of the replies depends on the particular qualities required in the job to be filled.

Intelligence tests

Tests of intelligence such as Raven's Progressive Matrices measure general intelligence (termed 'g' by Spearman (1927), one of the pioneers of intelligence testing). Intelligence is defined by Toplis *et al* (1991) as 'the capacity for abstract thinking and reasoning'. The difficulty with intelligence tests is that they have to be based on a theory of what constitutes intelligence and then have to derive a series of verbal and non-verbal instruments for measuring the different factors or constituents of intelligence. But intelligence is a highly complex concept and the variety of theories about intelligence and the consequent variations in the test instruments or batteries available make the choice of an intelligence test a difficult one.

For general selection purposes, an intelligence test that can be administered to a group of candidates is the best, especially if it has been properly validated, and it is possible to relate test scores to 'norms' in such a way as to indicate how the individual taking the test compares with the rest of the population, in general or in a specific area.

Personality tests

Personality tests attempt to assess the personality of candidates in order to make predictions about their likely behaviour in a role. Personality is an all-embracing and imprecise term that refers to the behaviour of individuals and the way it is organized and coordinated when they interact with the environment. There are many different theories of personality and, consequently, many different types of personality tests. These include self-report personality questionnaires and other questionnaires that measure interests, values or work behaviour.

One of the most generally accepted ways of classifying personality is the five-factor model. As summarized by McCrae and Costa (1989), this model defines the key personality characteristics. These 'big five', as Roberts (1997) calls them, are:

- *extraversion/introversion* – gregarious, outgoing, assertive, talkative and active (extraversion); or reserved, inward-looking, diffident, quiet, restrained (introversion);
- *emotional stability* – resilient, independent, confident, relaxed; or apprehensive, dependent, under-confident, tense;

- *agreeableness* – courteous, cooperative, likeable, tolerant; or rude, uncooperative, hostile, intolerant;
- *conscientiousness* – hard-working, persevering, careful, reliable; or lazy, dilettante, careless, expedient;
- *openness to experience* – curious, imaginative, willingness to learn, broad-minded; or blinkered, unimaginative, complacent, narrow-minded.

Research cited by Roberts (1997) has indicated that these factors are valid predictors of work performance and that one factor in particular, 'conscientiousness', was very effective.

Self-report personality questionnaires are the ones most commonly used. They usually adopt a 'trait' approach, defining a trait as a fairly independent but enduring characteristic of behaviour that all people display but to differing degrees. Trait theorists identify examples of common behaviour, devise scales to measure these, and then obtain ratings on these behaviours by people who know each other well. These observations are analysed statistically, using the factor analysis technique to identify distinct traits and to indicate how associated groups of traits might be grouped loosely into 'personality types'.

'Interest' questionnaires are sometimes used to supplement personality tests. They assess the preferences of respondents for particular types of occupation and are therefore most applicable to vocational guidance, but can be helpful when selecting apprentices and trainees.

'Value' questionnaires attempt to assess beliefs about what is 'desirable or good' or what is 'undesirable or bad'. The questionnaires measure the relative prominence of such values as conformity, independence, achievement, decisiveness, orderliness and goal-orientation.

Specific work behaviour questionnaires cover behaviours such as leadership or selling.

Personality questionnaires were shown to have the low validity coefficient of 0.15 on the basis of research conducted by Schmitt *et al* (1984). But as Saville and Sik (1992) point out, this was based on a rag-bag of tests, many developed for clinical use and some using 'projective' techniques such as the Rorschach inkblots test, the interpretation of which relies on a clinician's judgement and is therefore quite out of place in a modern selection procedure. Smith's (1988) studies based on modern self-report questionnaires revealed an average validity coefficient of 0.39, which is reasonably high.

A vigorous attack was launched on personality tests by Blinkorn and Johnson (1991). They commented: 'We see precious little evidence of personality tests predicting job performance.' But Fletcher (1991) responded: 'Like any other selection procedure, they (psychometric tests) can be used well or badly. But it would be foolish to dismiss all the evidence of the value of personality assessment in selection on the basis of some misuse. Certainly the majority of applied psychologists feel the balance of the evidence supports the use of personality inventories.' Personality tests can provide interesting supplementary information about candidates that is free from the biased reactions that frequently occur in face-to-face interviews. But they have to be used with great care. The tests should have been developed by a reputable psychologist or test agency on the basis of extensive research and field testing and they must meet the specific needs of the user. Advice should be sought from a member of the British Psychological Society on what tests are likely to be appropriate.

Ability tests

Ability tests measure job-related characteristics such as number, verbal, perceptual or mechanical ability.

Aptitude tests

Aptitude tests are job-specific tests that are designed to predict the potential an individual has to perform tasks within a job. They can cover such areas as clerical aptitude, numerical aptitude, mechanical aptitude and dexterity.

Aptitude tests should be properly validated. The usual procedure is to determine the aptitudes required by means of job and skills analysis. A standard test or a test battery is then obtained from a test agency. Alternatively, a special test is devised by or for the organization. The test is then given to employees already working on the job and the results compared with a criterion, usually managers' or team leaders' ratings. If the correlation between test and criterion is sufficiently high, the test is then given to applicants. To validate the test further, a follow-up study of the job performance of the applicants selected by the test is usually carried out. This is a lengthy procedure, but without it no real confidence can be attached to the results of any aptitude test. Many do-it-yourself tests are worse than useless because they have not been properly validated.

Attainment tests

Attainment tests measure abilities or skills that have already been acquired by training or experience. A typing test is the most typical example. It is easy to find out how many words a minute a typist can type and compare that with the standard required for the job.

60   100   140

Figure 27.1 A normal curve

INTERPRETING TEST RESULTS

The two main methods of interpreting test results are the use of norms and the normal curve.

Norms

Tests can be interpreted in terms of how an individual's results compare with the scores achieved by a group on whom the task was standardized – the norm or reference group. A normative score is read from a norms table. The most common scale indicates the proportion of the reference who scored less than the individual. Thus if someone scored at the 70th percentile in a test, that person's score would be better than 65 per cent of the reference group.

The normal curve

The normal curve describes the relationship between a set of observations and measures and the frequency of their occurrence. It indicates, as illustrated in Figure 27.1, that on many things that can be measured on a scale, a few people will produce extremely high or low scores and there will be a large proportion of people in the middle.

The most important characteristic of the normal curve is that it is symmetrical – there are an equal number of cases on either side of the mean, the central axis. The normal curve is a way of expressing how scores will typically be distributed; for example, that 60 per cent of the population are likely to get scores between x and y, 15 per cent are likely to get scores below x and 15 per cent are likely to get more than y.

CHOOSING TESTS

It is essential to choose tests that meet the four criteria of sensitivity, standardization, reliability and validity. It is very difficult to achieve the standards required if an organization tries to develop its own test batteries unless it employs a qualified psychologist or obtains professional advice from a member of the British Psychological Society. This organization, with the support of the reputable test suppliers, exercises rigorous control over who can use what tests and the standard of training required and given. Particular care should be taken when selecting personality tests – there are a lot of charlatans about.

Do-it-yourself tests are always suspect unless they have been properly validated and realistic norms have been established. Generally speaking, it is best to avoid using them.

THE USE OF TESTS IN A SELECTION PROCEDURE

Tests are often used as part of a selection procedure for occupations where a large number of recruits are required, and where it is not possible to rely entirely on examination results or information about previous experience as the basis for predicting future performance. In these circumstances it is economical to develop and administer the tests, and a sufficient number of cases can be built up for the essential validation exercise. Tests usually form part of an assessment centre procedure.

Intelligence tests are particularly helpful in situations where intelligence is a key factor, but there is no other reliable method of measuring it. It may, incidentally, be as important to use an intelligence test to keep out applicants who are too intelligent for the job as to use one to guarantee a minimal level of intelligence.

Aptitude and attainment tests are most useful for jobs where specific and measurable skills are required, such as typing or computer programming. Personality tests are potentially of greatest value in jobs such as selling where 'personality' is important, and where it is not too difficult to obtain quantifiable criteria for validation purposes.

It is essential to evaluate all tests by comparing the results at the interview stage with later achievements. To be statistically significant, these evaluations should be carried out over a reasonable period of time and cover as large a number of candidates as possible.

In some situations a battery of tests may be used, including various types of intelligence, aptitude and personality tests. These may be a standard battery supplied by a test agency, or a custom-built battery may be developed. The biggest pitfall to avoid is adding extra tests just for the sake of it, without ensuring that they make a proper contribution to the success of the predictions for which the battery is being used.

The six criteria for the use of psychological tests produced by the IPD (1997b) are:

1. Everyone responsible for the application of tests including evaluation, interpretation and feedback should be trained at least to the level of competence recommended by the British Psychological Society.
2. Potential test users should satisfy themselves that it is appropriate to use tests at all before incorporating tests into their decision-making processes.
3. Users must satisfy themselves that any tests they decide to use actively measure factors which are directly relevant to the employment situation.
4. Users must satisfy themselves that all tests they use should have been rigorously developed and that claims about their reliability, validity and effectiveness are supported by statistical evidence (*The Data Protection Act 1998 is relevant here. If candidates are selected on the basis of a test they have the right to know the rationale for the selection decision.*)
5. Care must be taken to provide equality of opportunity among all individuals required to take tests.
6. The results of single tests should not be used as the sole basis for decision-making. This is particularly relevant with regard to personality tests.

28

Introduction to the organization

It is important to ensure that care is taken over introducing people to the organization through effective induction arrangements as described in this chapter.

INDUCTION DEFINED

Induction is the process of receiving and welcoming employees when they first join a company and giving them the basic information they need to settle down quickly and happily and start work. Induction has four aims:

- to smooth the preliminary stages when everything is likely to be strange and unfamiliar to the starter;
- to establish quickly a favourable attitude to the company in the mind of the new employee so that he or she is more likely to stay;
- to obtain effective output from the new employee in the shortest possible time;
- to reduce the likelihood of the employee leaving quickly.

WHY TAKING CARE ABOUT INDUCTION IS IMPORTANT

Induction is important for the reasons given below.

Reducing the cost and inconvenience of early leavers

As pointed out by Fowler (1996), employees are far more likely to resign during their first months after joining the organization. The costs can include:

- recruitment costs of replacement;
- induction costs (training etc);
- costs of temporary agency replacement;
- cost of extra supervision and error correction;
- gap between the employee's value to the company and the cost of the employee's pay and benefits.

These costs can be considerable. The cost for a professional employee could be 75 per cent of annual salary. For a support worker the cost could easily reach 50 per cent of pay. If 15 out of 100 staff paid an average of £12,500 a year leave during the year, the total cost could amount to £90,000 – 7.5 per cent of the payroll. It is worth making an effort to reduce that cost. First impressions are important, as are the impact of the first four weeks of employment. Giving more attention to induction pays off.

Increasing commitment

A committed employee is one who identifies with the organization, wants to stay with it and is prepared to work hard on behalf of the organization. The first step in achieving commitment is to present the organization as one that is worth working for and to ensure that this first impression is reinforced during the first weeks of employment.

Clarifying the psychological contract

The psychological contract, as described in Chapter 16, consists of implicit, unwritten beliefs and assumptions about how employees are expected to behave and what responses they can expect from their employer. It is concerned with norms, values and attitudes. The psychological contract provides the basis for the employment relationships, and the more this can be clarified from the outset, the better. Induction arrangements can indicate what the organization expects in terms of behavioural norms and the values that employees should uphold. Induction provides an opportunity to inform people of 'the way things are done around here' so that misapprehensions are reduced even if they cannot be eliminated.

Accelerating progress up the learning curve

New employees will be on a learning curve – they will take time to reach the required level of performance. Clearly, the length of the learning curve and rates of learning vary, but it is important to provide for it to take place in a planned and systematic manner from the first day to maximize individual contributions as quickly as possible.

Socialization

New employees are likely to settle in more quickly and enjoy working for the organization if the process of socialization takes place smoothly. The social aspects of work – relationships with colleagues – are very important for many people. The extent to which employees can directly influence the quality of socialization may often be limited, but it is a feature of introduction to the organization to which they should pay attention, as far as this is possible, during the induction arrangements described below, which are concerned with reception, documentation, initial briefing, introduction to the workplace, formal induction courses and formal and informal training activities.

RECEPTION

Most people suffer from some feelings of trepidation when they start a new job. However outwardly confident they may appear, they may well be asking themselves such questions as: What will the company be like? How will my boss behave to me? Will I get on with the other workers? Will I be able to do the job?

These questions may not be answered immediately, but at least general fears may be alleviated by ensuring that the first contacts are friendly and helpful.

The following checklist for reception is recommended by Fowler (1996):

- Ensure that the person whom the starter first meets (ie the receptionist, personnel assistant or supervisor) knows of their pending arrival and what to do next.

- Set a reporting time, which will avoid the risk of the starter turning up before the reception or office staff arrive.
- Train reception staff in the need for friendly and efficient helpfulness towards new starters.
- If the new starter has to go to another location immediately after reporting, provide a guide, unless the route to the other location is very straightforward.
- Avoid keeping the new starter waiting; steady, unhurried, guided activity is an excellent antidote to first-day nerves.

DOCUMENTATION

The new employee will be asked to hand over the P45 income tax form from the previous employer. A variety of documents may then be issued to employees, including safety rules and safety literature, a company rule book containing details of disciplinary and grievance procedures and an employee handbook as described below.

The employee handbook

An employee handbook is useful for this purpose. It need not be too glossy, but it should convey clearly and simply what new staff need to know under the following headings:

- a brief description of the company – its history, products, organization and management;
- basic conditions of employment – hours of work, holidays, pension scheme, insurance;
- pay – pay scales, when paid and how, deductions, queries;
- sickness – notification of absence, certificates, pay;
- leave of absence;
- company rules;
- disciplinary procedure;
- capability procedure;
- grievance procedure;
- promotion procedure;
- union and joint consultation arrangements;
- education and training facilities;
- health and safety arrangements;

- medical and first-aid facilities;
- restaurant and canteen facilities;
- social and welfare arrangements;
- telephone calls and correspondence;
- rules for using e-mail;
- travelling and subsistence expenses.

If the organization is not large enough to justify a printed handbook, the least that can be done is to prepare a typed summary of this information.

COMPANY INDUCTION – INITIAL BRIEFING

Company induction procedures, however, should not rely on the printed word. The member of the personnel department or other individual who is looking after new employees should run through the main points with each individual or, when larger numbers are being taken on, with groups of people. In this way, a more personal touch is provided and queries can be answered.

When the initial briefing has been completed, new employees should be taken to their place of work and introduced to their manager or team leader for the departmental induction programme. Alternatively, they may go straight to a training school and join the department later.

INTRODUCTION TO THE WORKPLACE

New starters will be concerned about who they are going to work for (their immediate manager or team leader), who they are going to work with, what work they are going to do on their first day, and the geographical layout of their place of work (location of entrances, exits, lavatories, restrooms and the canteen).

Some of this information may be provided by a member of the personnel department, or an assistant in the new employee's place of work. But the most important source of information is the immediate manager, supervisor or team leader.

The departmental induction programme should, wherever possible, start with the departmental manager, not the immediate team leader. The manager may give only a general welcome and a brief description of the work of the department before handing new employees over to their team leaders for the more detailed induction. But it is important for the manager to be involved at this stage so that he or she is not seen as a remote figure by the new employee. And at least this means that the starter will not be simply a name or a number to the manager.

The detailed induction is probably best carried out by the immediate team leader, who should have five main aims:

- to put the new employee at ease;
- to interest the employee in the job and the organization;
- to provide basic information about working arrangements;
- to indicate the standards of performance and behaviour expected from the employee;
- to tell the employee about training arrangements and how he or she can progress in the company.

The team leader should introduce new starters to their fellow team members. It is best to get one member of the team to act as a guide or 'starter's friend'. As Fowler suggests, there is much to be said for these initial guides to be people who have not been long with the organization. As relative newcomers they are likely to remember all the small points that were a source of worry to them when they started work, and so help new employees to settle in quickly.

FORMAL INDUCTION COURSES

Reason for

Formal induction courses can provide for recruits to be assembled in groups so that a number of people can be given consistent and comprehensive information at the same time, which may not be forthcoming if reliance is placed solely on supervisors. A formal course is an opportunity to deliver messages about the organization, its products and services, its mission and values, using a range of media such as videos and other visual aids that would not be available within departments. But formal induction courses cannot replace informal induction arrangements at the workplace, where the most important need – settling people well – can best be satisfied.

Arrangements

Decisions will have to be made about who attends and when. It is normal to mix people from different departments but less common to have people from widely different levels on the same course. In practice, managers and senior professional staff are often dealt with individually.

Ideally, induction courses should take place as soon as possible after starting. If there are sufficient new employees available, this could be half the first day or a half or whole day during the first week. If a lot of information is to be conveyed, supplementary half or one-day courses may be held later. However, the course may have to be delayed until sufficient numbers of new starters are available. If such delays are unavoidable, it is essential to ensure that key information is provided on the first day by personnel and the departmental supervisor. Organizations with branches or a number of different locations often hold formal induction courses at headquarters, which helps employees to feel that they are part of the total business and gives an opportunity to convey information about the role of head office.

Content

The content of formal induction courses may be selected according to the needs of the organization from the following list of subject areas:

- *information about the organization* – its products/services, structure, mission and core values;
- *learning arrangements and opportunities* – formal training, self-managed learning, personal development plans;
- *performance management processes* – how they work and the parts people play;
- *health and safety* – occupational health, prevention of injuries and accidents, protective clothing, basic safety rules;
- *conditions of service* – hours, holidays, leave, sick pay arrangements, maternity/paternity leave;
- *pay and benefits* – arrangements for paying salaries or wages, the pay structure, allowances, details of performance, competence- or skill-based pay schemes, details of profit sharing, gainsharing or share ownership arrangements, pension and life or medical insurance schemes;
- *policies, procedures and working arrangements* – equal opportunities policies, rules regarding sexual and racial harassment and bullying, disciplinary and grievance procedures, no-smoking arrangements;
- *trade unions and employee involvement* – trade union membership and recognition, consultative systems, agreements, suggestion schemes.

ON-THE-JOB INDUCTION TRAINING

Most new starters other than those on formal training schemes will learn on the job, although this may be supplemented with special off-the-job courses to develop particular skills or knowledge. On-the-job training can be haphazard, inefficient and wasteful. A planned, systematic approach is very desirable. This can incorporate:

● job or skills analysis to prepare a learning specification;
● an initial assessment of what the new starter needs to learn;
● the use of designated colleagues to act as guides and mentors – these individuals should be trained in how to carry out this role;
● coaching by team leaders or specially appointed and trained departmental trainers;
● special assignments.

These on-the-job arrangements can be supplemented by self-managed learning arrangements, by offering access to flexible learning packages and by providing advice on learning opportunities.

29

Release from the organization

GENERAL CONSIDERATIONS

The employment relationship may be ended voluntarily by some moving elsewhere. Or it may finish at the end of a career by retirement. Increasingly, however, people are having to go involuntarily. Organizations are becoming mean as well as lean. They are terminating the relationship through redundancy and they are tightening up disciplinary procedures to handle not only cases of misconduct but also those of incapability – as judged by the employer. Resourcing policies and practices concerning release from the organization have also to cover voluntary turnover and retirement.

Causes of redundancy

Redundancy, like the poor which it helps to create, has always been with us. At one time, however, it was mainly a result of adverse trading conditions, especially during times of recession. This is, of course, still a major cause of redundancy, exacerbated by the pressures of global competition and international recession. But the drive for competitive advantage has forced organizations to 'take cost out of the business' – a euphemism for getting rid of people, employment costs being the ones on which companies focus, as they are usually the largest element in their cost structures. The result has been delayering (eliminating what are deemed to be unnecessary layers of management and supervision) and 'downsizing' (another euphemism) or even 'right-sizing' (a yet more egregious euphemism).

The introduction of new technology has contributed hugely to the reduction in the number of semi-skilled or unskilled people in offices and on the shop floor. But the thrust for productivity (more from less) and added value (increasing the income derived from the expenditure on people) has led to more use of such indices as added value per £ of employment costs to measure business performance with regard to the utilization of its 'human resources' (the use of human resources in this connection implies a measure of exploitation). Business process re-engineering techniques are deployed as instruments for downsizing. Benchmarking to establish which organizations are in fact doing more with less (and if so how they do it) is another popular way of preparing the case for 'downsizing'.

Setting higher performance standards

The pressure for improved performance to meet more intense global competition explains why many organizations are setting higher standards for employees and are not retaining those who do not meet those standards. This may be done through disciplinary procedures, but performance management processes as described in the previous chapter are being used to identify under-performers. Properly administered, such processes will emphasize positive improvement and development plans but they will inevitably highlight weaknesses and, if these are not overcome, disciplinary proceedings may be invoked.

Voluntary release

Of course, people also leave organizations voluntarily to further their careers, get more money, move away from the district or because they are fed up with the way they feel they have been treated. They may also take early retirement (although this is sometimes involuntary) or volunteer for redundancy (under pressure or because they are being rewarded financially for doing so).

Managing organizational release – the role of the HR function

The HR function is usually given the task of managing organizational release and, in its involuntary form, this is perhaps the most distasteful, onerous and stressful of all the activities with which HR people get involved. In effect, the function is being asked to go into reverse. Having spent a lot of positive effort on employees' resourcing and development, it is now being placed in what appears to be an entirely negative position. HR people are indeed acting, however unwillingly, as the agents of the management who made the 'downsizing' decisions or want to 'let someone go' (there are more euphemisms in this area of management than the rest of the areas put together). Being placed in this often invidious position means that there are ethical and professional considerations to be taken into account, as discussed below.

A more positive aspect of the function's involvement in organizational release is the part HR people can play in easing retirement and analysing the reasons given by employees for leaving the organization so that action can be taken to correct organizational shortcomings.

Ethical and professional considerations

HR professionals may have no choice about taking part in a 'downsizing' exercise – that is, if they wish to remain with the organization. But they can and should make an important contribution to managing the process in order to minimize the distress and trauma that badly handled redundancies can create, or the distress and bad feeling that unfair or uncouth disciplinary practices can engender. They can press for policies and actions that will minimize, even if they cannot eliminate, involuntary redundancy. They can emphasize the need to handle redundancies sensitively, advising line managers on the approach they adopt, helping them to communicate the decision to employees, advising generally on communication within and outside the organization and laying on counselling and outplacement services. Professionally, they should ensure that there are proper redundancy procedures (including those relating to consultation) which are in line with codes of practice and legal requirements, and they must see that these practices are followed.

Similarly, a professional approach to discipline means that HR specialists should ensure that there are disciplinary procedures which conform to codes of practice and take into account legal implications. They have to communicate these procedures to line managers, provide training in how they are applied and advise on their use. Ethically, personnel professionals should do their best to see that people are treated fairly in accordance with the principles of natural justice.

Career dynamics

Career dynamics is the term used to describe how careers progress within organizations or over a working life. As long ago as 1984 Charles Handy forecast that many more people would not be working in organizations. Instead there would be an increase in the number of outworkers and subcontractors facilitated by information technology. He also predicted that there would be more requirements for specialists and professionals (knowledge workers) within organizations. In later books (eg *The Empty Raincoat*, 1994) he developed his concept of a portfolio career – people changing their careers several times during their working lives, either because they have been forced to leave their jobs or because they have seized new opportunities.

The national culture has changed too. High levels of unemployment seem set to continue, more people are working for themselves (often because they have to) and short-term contracts are becoming more common, especially in the public sector. Some commentators believe that organizations are no longer in the business of providing 'life-long careers' as they slim down, delayer and rely on a small core of workers. Clearly, this is taking place in some companies, but employees do not all necessarily see it this way. The IPD 1995 survey established that 46 per cent of their respondents viewed their current job as a long-term one in which they intended to stay. However, 16 per cent saw their present job as part of a career or profession that would probably take them to different companies and 15 per cent saw their job as one they would leave as it was not part of their career.

Organizational release activities

Against this background, organizational release activities as described in this chapter deal with redundancy, outplacement, dismissal, voluntary turnover and retirement.

REDUNDANCY

'Downsizing' is one of the most demanding areas of people management with which HR professionals can become involved. Their responsibilities, as discussed below, are to:

- plan ahead to achieve downsizing without involuntary redundancy;
- advise on and implement other methods of reducing numbers or avoiding redundancy;
- encourage voluntary redundancy if other methods fail;
- develop and apply a proper redundancy procedure;
- deal with payment arrangements for releasing employees;
- advise on methods of handling redundancies and take part as necessary to ensure that they are well managed.

HR specialists should also be involved in organizing outplacement services as described in the next section of this chapter.

Plan ahead

Planning ahead means anticipating future reductions in people needs and allowing natural wastage to take effect. A forecast is needed of the amount by which the workforce has to be reduced and the likely losses through employee turnover. Recruitment can then be frozen at the right moment to allow the surplus to be absorbed by wastage.

The problem is that forecasts are often difficult to make, and in periods of high unemployment, natural wastage rates are likely to be reduced. It is possible therefore to overestimate the extent to which they will achieve the required reduction in numbers. It is best to be pessimistic about the time it will take to absorb future losses and apply the freeze earlier rather than later.

Ideally, steps should be taken to transfer people to other, more secure jobs and retrain them where possible.

Use other methods to avoid redundancy

The other methods that can be used to avoid or at least minimize redundancy include, in order or severity:

● calling in outside work;
● withdrawing all subcontracted labour;
● reducing or preferably eliminating overtime;
● developing worksharing: two people doing one job on alternate days or splitting the day between them;
● reducing the number of part-timers, remembering that they also have employment rights;
● temporary lay-offs.

Voluntary redundancy

Asking for volunteers – with a suitable pay-off – is one way of relieving the number of compulsory redundancies. The amount needed to persuade people to go is a matter of judgement. It clearly has to be more than the statutory minimum, although one inducement for employees to leave early may be the belief that they will get another job more easily than if they hang on until the last moment. Help can be provided to place them elsewhere.

One of the disadvantages of voluntary redundancy is that the wrong people might go, ie good workers who are best able to find other work. It is sometimes necessary to go into reverse and offer them a special loyalty bonus if they agree to stay on.

Outplacement

Outplacement is the process of helping redundant employees to find other work or start new careers. It may involve counselling, which can be provided by firms who specialize in this area.

Redundancy procedure

If you are forced to resort to redundancy, the problems will be reduced if there is an established procedure to follow. This procedure should have three aims:

- to treat employees as fairly as possible;
- to reduce hardship as much as possible;
- to protect management's ability to run the business effectively.

These aims are not always compatible. Management will want to retain its key and more effective workers. Trade unions, on the other hand, may want to adopt the principle of last in, first out, irrespective of the value of each employee to the company. An example of a procedure is given in Chapter 56.

Handling redundancy

The first step is to ensure that the redundancy selection policy has been applied fairly. It is also necessary to make certain that the legal requirements for consultation have been met. The information to be presented at any consultative meetings will need to cover the reasons for the redundancy, what steps the company has taken or will take to minimize the problem and the redundancy pay arrangements. An indication should also be given of the time scale. The basis for selecting people for redundancy as set out in the redundancy policy should be confirmed.

It will then be necessary to make a general announcement if it is a large-scale redundancy or inform a unit or department if it is on a smaller scale. It is best if the announcement is made in person by an executive or manager who is known to the individuals concerned. It should let everyone know about the difficulties the organization has been facing and the steps that have been taken to overcome them. The announcement should also indicate in general how the redundancy will take place, including arrangements for individuals to be informed (as soon as possible after the general announcement), payment arrangements and, importantly, help to those affected in finding work through outplacement counselling or a 'job shop'.

If it is a fairly large redundancy, the media will have to be informed, but only after the internal announcement. A press release will need to be prepared, again indicating why the redundancy is taking place and how the company intends to tackle it.

The next step is to inform those affected. It is very important to ensure that everything possible is done to ensure that the interviews with those who are to be made redundant are handled sensitively. Managers should be given guidance and, possibly, training on how to deal with what is sometimes called (another euphemism) a 'release interview'. It may well be advisable for a member of the personnel function to be present at all interviews, although it is best for the line manager to conduct them. Advance information should be obtained on the reasons why individuals were selected and how they may react. Their personal circumstances should also be checked in case there are any special circumstances with which the interviewer should be familiar.

The interview itself should explain as gently as possible why the individual has been selected for redundancy and how it will affect him or her (payment, timing etc). Time should be allowed to describe the help that the organization will provide to find another job and to get initial reactions from the individual which may provide guidance on the next steps.

OUTPLACEMENT

Outplacement is about helping redundant employees to find alternative work. It involves assisting individuals to cope with the trauma of redundancy through counselling, helping them to redefine their career and employment objectives and then providing them with knowledgeable but sensitive guidance on how to attain those objectives.

Job shops

Help may be provided by the organization on an individual basis, but in larger-scale redundancies 'job shops' can be set up. The people who staff these scour the travel-to-work area seeking job opportunities for those who are being made redundant. This is often done by telephone. Further help may be given by matching people to suitable jobs, arranging interviews, training in CV preparation and interview techniques. Job shops are sometimes staffed by members of the personnel function (the writer successfully organized one in an aerospace firm some years ago). Alternatively, the organization may ask a firm of outplacement consultants to set up and run the job shop and provide any other counselling or training services that may be required.

Outplacement consultancy services

As described by Eggert (1991), the outplacement process usually takes place along the following lines:

- initial counselling – gaining biographical data and discussing immediate issues of concern;
- achievement list – clients write up all the achievements they can think of to do with their career;
- skills inventory – clients develop from the achievement list a personal portfolio of saleable skills;
- personal statement – clients develop a personal statement in 20 to 30 words about what is being presented to the job market;
- personal success inventory – those recent or appropriate successes that can be quantified and which support the personal profile;
- three jobs – identification of three possible types of job that can be searched for;
- psychological assessment – development of a personality profile with a psychologist;
- development and agreement of a CV (see below);
- identify job market opportunities;
- practice interview;
- plan job search campaign.

CVs

CVs provide the basic information for job searching and an outplacement consultant will guide individuals on how to write their CVs. The traditional CV uses what Eggert (1991) calls the 'tombstone' approach because it reads like an obituary. It sets out personal details and education and employment history in chronological order.

Outplacement consultants prefer what they call the 'achievement CV' which is structured on the principle of a sales brochure, providing information in simple, positive statements sequenced for the reader's convenience. The CV lists the most important areas of experience in reverse chronological order and sets out for each position a list of achievements beginning with such words as 'set up', 'developed', 'introduced', 'increased', 'reduced' and 'established'. This is designed to generate the thought in the reader's mind that 'if the individual can do it for them, he or she will be able to do it for us'. The career achievement history is followed by details of professional qualifications and education, and personal information.

Selecting an outplacement consultant

There are some highly reputable outplacement consultants around; there are also some cowboys. It is advisable only to use firms that follow a code of practice such as that produced by the IPD or the Career Development and Outplacement Association.

DISMISSAL

The legal framework

The legal framework is provided by employment statutory and case law relating to unfair dismissal. Under current UK employment legislation, an employee who has been employed for one year or more has the right not to be unfairly dismissed. Complaints by an employee that he or she has been unfairly dismissed are heard by employment tribunals.

Definition of dismissal

Legally, dismissal takes place when:

- the employer terminates the employee's contract with or without notice – a contract can be terminated as a result of a demotion or transfer as well as dismissal;
- the employee terminates the contract (resigns) with or without notice by reason of the employer's behaviour in the sense that the employer's conduct was such that the employee could not be expected to carry on – this is termed 'constructive dismissal';
- the employee is employed under a fixed-term contract of one year or more which is not renewed by the employer when it expires;
- an employee resigns while under notice following dismissal;
- an employee is unreasonably refused work after pregnancy.

Fundamental questions

The legislation lays down that employment tribunals should obtain answers to two fundamental questions when dealing with unfair dismissal cases:

1. Was there sufficient reason for the dismissal, ie was it fair or unfair?
2. Did the employer act reasonably in the circumstances?

Fair dismissal

Dismissals may be held by an employment tribunal to be fair if the principal reason was one of the following:

- incapability, which covers the employee's skill, aptitude, health and physical or mental qualities;
- misconduct;
- failure to have qualifications relevant to the job;
- a legal factor that prevents the employee from continuing work;
- redundancy – where this has taken place in accordance with a customary or agreed redundancy procedure;
- the employee broke or repudiated his or her contract by going on strike – as long as he or she was not singled out for this treatment, ie all striking employees were treated alike and no selective re-engagement took place;
- the employee was taking part in an unofficial strike or some other form of industrial action;
- some other substantial reason of a kind that would justify the dismissal of an employee holding the position that the employee held.

Unfair dismissal

Dismissals may be unfair if:

- the employer has failed to show that the principal reason was one of the admissible reasons as stated above, or if the dismissal was not reasonable in the circumstances (see below);
- a constructive dismissal has taken place;
- they are in breach of a customary or agreed redundancy procedure, and there are no valid reasons for departing from that procedure.

The onus of proof is on employers to show that they had acted reasonably in treating the reason for dismissal as sufficient. The employment tribunal is required, in considering the circumstances, to take into account the size and administrative resources of the employer's undertaking.

Reasonable in the circumstances

Even if the employer can show to a tribunal that there was good reason to dismiss the employee (ie if it clearly fell into one of the categories listed above, and the degree of incapability or misconduct was sufficient to justify dismissal), the tribunal still has to decide whether or not the employer acted in a reasonable way at the time of dismissal. The principles defining 'reasonable' behaviour on the part of an employer are as follows:

- Employees should be informed of the nature of the complaint against them.
- The employee should be given the chance to explain.
- The employee should be given the opportunity to improve, except in particularly gross cases of incapability or misconduct.
- Employees should be allowed to appeal.
- The employee should be warned of the consequences in the shape of dismissal if specified improvements do not take place.
- The employer's decision to dismiss should be based on sufficient evidence.
- The employer should take any mitigating circumstances into account.
- The employer should act in good faith.
- The offence or misbehaviour should merit the penalty of dismissal rather than some lesser penalty.

A good disciplinary procedure (see the example in Chapter 56) will include arrangements for informal and formal warnings and provisions to ensure that the other aspects of discipline are handled reasonably.

Remedies

Employment tribunals that find that a dismissal was unfair can make an order for reinstatement or re-engagement and state the terms on which this should take place. The tribunal can consider the possibility of compensation for unfair dismissal, but only after the possibility of reinstatement or re-engagement has been examined.

Approach to handling disciplinary cases

The approach should be governed by the following three principles of natural justice:

1. Individuals should know the standards of performance they are expected to achieve and the rules to which they are expected to conform.
2. They should be given a clear indication of where they are failing or what rules have been broken.
3. Except in cases of gross misconduct, they should be given an opportunity to improve before disciplinary action is taken.

There should be a disciplinary procedure which is understood and applied by all managers and team leaders. The procedure should provide for the following three-stage approach before disciplinary action is taken:

1. informal oral warnings;
2. formal oral warnings, which, in serious cases, may also be made in writing – these warnings should set out the nature of the offence and the likely consequences of further offences;
3. final written warnings, which should contain a statement that any recurrence would lead to suspension, dismissal or some other penalty.

The procedure should provide for employees to be accompanied by a colleague or employee representative at any hearing. There should also be an appeal system and a list of offences that constitute gross misconduct and may therefore lead to instant dismissal. Managers and supervisors should be told what authority they have to take disciplinary action. It is advisable to have all final warnings and actions approved by a higher authority. In cases of gross misconduct, team leaders and junior managers should be given the right to suspend, if higher authority is not immediately available, but not to dismiss. The importance of obtaining and recording the facts should be emphasized. Managers should always have a colleague with them when issuing a formal warning and should make a note to file of what was said on the spot.

VOLUNTARY LEAVERS

When people leave of their own volition, two actions may be taken: conducting exit interviews and analysing reasons for turnover as described in Chapter 24.

RETIREMENT

Retirement is a major change and should be prepared for. Retirement policies need to specify:

● when people are due to retire;
● the circumstances, if any, in which they can work on beyond their normal retirement date;
● the provision of pre-retirement training;

● the provision of advice to people about to retire.

Pre-retirement training can cover such matters as finance, insurance, State pension rights, health, working either for money or in a voluntary organization during retirement and sources of advice and help. The latter can be supplied by such charities as Help the Aged and Age Concern.

Part VIII

Performance management

Performance management processes have come to the fore in recent years as means of providing a more integrated and continuous approach to the management of performance than was provided by previous isolated and often inadequate merit rating or performance appraisal schemes. Performance management is based on the principle of management by agreement or contract rather than management by command. It emphasizes development and the initiation of self-managed learning plans as well as the integration of individual and corporate objectives. It can, in fact, play a major role in providing for an integrated and coherent range of human resource management processes which are mutually supportive and contribute as a whole to improving organizational effectiveness.

In this part, Chapter 30 covers the fundamental concepts of performance management. The practice of performance management is described in Chapter 31 and the part is completed in Chapter 32 by a review of the process of 360-degree feedback as a multi-source method of assessing performance.

30

The basis of performance management

Performance management is covered in this chapter under the following headings:

- definition;
- purpose;
- principles;
- concerns;
- scope of performance management;
- ethical considerations;
- background;
- the basic performance management processes (these are covered more comprehensively in the next chapter).

PERFORMANCE MANAGEMENT DEFINED

Performance management can be defined as a strategic and integrated approach to delivering sustained success to organizations by improving the performance of the people who work in them and by developing the capabilities of teams and individual contributors (Armstrong and Baron, 1998).

Performance management is strategic in the sense that it is concerned with the broader issues facing the business if it is to function effectively in its environment, and with the general direction in which it intends to go to achieve longer-term goals. It is integrated in four senses:

- *vertical integration* – linking or aligning business, team and individual objectives;
- *functional integration* – linking functional strategies in different parts of the business;
- *HR integration* – linking different aspects of HRM, especially organizational development, HR development and reward, to achieve a coherent approach to the management and development of people; and
- *the integration of individual needs* with those of the organization, as far as this is possible.

The meaning of performance

Performance management is, of course, about performance. But what is meant by that word? It is important to clarify what it means because if performance cannot be defined you can't measure or manage it. It has been pointed out by Bates and Holton (1995) that: 'Performance is a multi-dimensional construct, the measurement of which varies depending on a variety of factors.' They also state that it is important to determine whether the measurement objective is to assess performance outcomes or behaviour.

There are different views on what performance is. It can be regarded as simply the record of outcomes achieved. On an individual basis, it is a record of the person's accomplishments. Kane (1996) argues that performance 'is something that the person leaves behind and that exists apart from the purpose'. Bernadin *et al* (1995) are concerned that: 'Performance should be defined as the outcomes of work because they provide the strongest linkage to the strategic goals of the organization, customer satisfaction, and economic contributions.' The Oxford English Dictionary defines performance as: 'The accomplishment, execution, carrying out, working out of anything ordered or undertaken.'

This refers to outputs/outcomes (accomplishment) but also states that performance is about doing the work as well as being about the results achieved. Performance could therefore be regarded as behaviour – the way in which organizations, teams and individuals get work done. Campbell (1990) believes that: 'Performance is behaviour and should be distinguished from the outcomes because they can be contaminated by systems factors.'

A more comprehensive view of performance is achieved if it is defined as embracing both behaviour and outcomes. This is well put by Brumbach (1988):

> Performance means both behaviours and results. Behaviours emanate from the performer and transform performance from abstraction to action. Not just the instruments for results, behaviours are also outcomes in their own right – the product of mental and physical effort applied to tasks – and can be judged apart from results.

This definition of performance leads to the conclusion that when managing the performance of teams and individuals both inputs (behaviour) and outputs (results) need to be considered. This is the so-called 'mixed model' (Hartle, 1995) of performance management which covers competency levels and achievements as well as objective setting and review.

PURPOSE OF PERFORMANCE MANAGEMENT

Performance management is a means of getting better results from the organization, teams and individuals by understanding and managing performance within an agreed framework of planned goals, standards and competence requirements. It is a process for establishing shared understanding about what is to be achieved, and an approach to managing and developing people in a way that increases the probability that it *will* be achieved in the short and longer term. It is owned and driven by line management.

PRINCIPLES OF PERFORMANCE MANAGEMENT

The principles of performance management have been well summarized by IRS (1996) as follows:

- It translates corporate goals into individual, team, department and divisional goals.
- It helps to clarify corporate goals.
- It is a continuous and evolutionary process, in which performance improves over time.
- It relies on consensus and cooperation rather than control or coercion.
- It encourages self-management of individual performance.

- It requires a management style that is open and honest and encourages two-way communication between superiors and subordinates.
- It requires continuous feedback.
- Feedback loops enable the experiences and knowledge gained on the job by individuals to modify corporate objectives.
- It measures and assesses all performance against jointly agreed goals.
- It should apply to all staff; and it is not primarily concerned with linking performance to financial reward.

CONCERNS OF PERFORMANCE MANAGEMENT

Performance management is basically concerned with *performance improvement* in order to achieve organizational, team and individual effectiveness. Organizations, as stated by Lawson (1995), have 'to get the right things done successfully'.

Secondly, performance management is concerned with *employee development*. Performance improvement is not achievable unless there are effective processes of continuous development. This addresses the core competences of the organization and the capabilities of individuals and teams. Performance management should really be called performance and development management.

Thirdly, performance management is concerned with satisfying the needs and expectations of all the organization's *stakeholders* – owners, management, employees, customers, suppliers and the general public. In particular, employees are treated as partners in the enterprise whose interests are respected and who have a voice on matters that concern them, whose opinions are sought and listened to. Performance management should respect the needs of individuals and teams as well as those of the organization, recognizing that they will not always coincide.

Finally, performance management is concerned with *communication* and *involvement*. It creates a climate in which a continuing dialogue between managers and the members of their teams takes place to define expectations and share information on the organization's mission, values and objectives. This establishes mutual understanding of what is to be achieved and a framework for managing and developing people to ensure that it *will* be achieved. Performance management can contribute to the development of a high-involvement organization by getting teams and individuals to participate in defining their objectives and the means to achieve them.

ETHICAL CONSIDERATIONS

Performance management should operate in accordance with the following ethical principles as defined by Winstanley and Stuart-Smith (1996):

- *respect for the individual* – people should be treated as 'ends in themselves' and not merely as 'means to other ends';
- *mutual respect* – the parties involved in performance management processes should respect each other's needs and preoccupations;
- *procedural fairness* – the procedures incorporated in performance management should be operated fairly to limit the adverse effect on individuals;
- *transparency* – people affected by decisions emerging from the performance management process should have the opportunity to scrutinize the basis upon which decisions were made.

THE SCOPE OF PERFORMANCE MANAGEMENT

Performance management is about managing the organization. It is a natural process of management, not a system or a technique (Fowler, 1990). It is also about managing within the context of the business (its internal and external environment). This will affect how it is developed, what it sets out to do and how it operates. The context is very important, and Jones (1995) goes as far as to say 'manage context, not performance'.

Performance management concerns everyone in the business – not just managers. It rejects the cultural assumption that only managers are accountable for the performance of their teams and replaces it with the belief that responsibility is *shared* between managers and team members. In a sense, managers should regard the people who report to them as customers for the managerial contribution and services they can provide. Managers and their teams are jointly accountable for results and are jointly involved in agreeing what they need to do and how they need to do it, in monitoring performance and in taking action.

Performance management processes are part of an holistic approach to managing for performance which is the concern of everyone in the organization.

The holistic approach to performance management

Holistic means all-embracing, covering every aspect of a subject. In the case of performance management this concerns the whole organization. It takes a comprehensive view of the constituents of performance, how these contribute to desired outcomes at the organizational, departmental, team and individual levels, and what needs to be done to improve these outcomes. Performance management in its fullest sense is based on the belief that everything that people do at work at any level contributes to achieving the overall purpose of the organization. It is therefore concerned with what people do (their work), how they do it (their behaviour) and what they achieve (their results). It embraces all formal and informal measures adopted by an organization to increase corporate, team and individual effectiveness and continuously to develop knowledge, skill and competence. It is certainly not an isolated system run by the personnel department, which functions once a year (the annual appraisal) and is then forgotten. The combined impact of a number of related aspects of performance management may be expected to achieve more to improve organizational effectiveness than the various parts if they functioned separately. When designing and operating performance management it is necessary to consider the interrelationships of each process.

The concept of performance management as an integrating force

As stated by Hartle (1995), performance management 'should be integrated into the way the performance of the business is managed and it should link with other key processes such as business strategy, employee development, and total quality management'.

Vertical integration

Integration is achieved vertically with the business strategy and business plans and goals. Team and individual objectives that support the achievement of corporate goals are agreed. These take the form of interlocking objectives from the corporate level to the functional or business unit level and down to teams and the individual level. Steps need to be taken to ensure that these goals are in alignment. This can be a cascading process so that objectives flow down from the top and at each level team or individual objectives are defined in the light of higher-level goals. But it should also be a bottom-up process, individuals and teams being given the opportunity to formulate their own goals within the framework provided by the overall purpose and values of the organization. Objectives should be *agreed*, not set, and this agreement should be reached through the open dialogues that take place between managers and individuals throughout the year. In other words, this needs to be seen as a partnership in which responsibility is shared and mutual expectations are defined.

Horizontal integration

Horizontal integration means aligning performance management strategies with other HR strategies concerned with valuing, paying, involving and developing people. It can act as a powerful force in integrating these activities.

BACKGROUND TO PERFORMANCE MANAGEMENT

The concept of performance management has been one of the most important and positive developments in the sphere of human resource management in recent years. The phrase was first coined by Beer and Ruh in 1976 but it did not become recognized as a distinctive approach until the mid-1980s, growing out of the realization that a more continuous and integrated approach was needed to manage and reward performance. All too often, crudely developed and hastily implemented performance-related pay and appraisal systems were not delivering the results that, somewhat naively, people were expecting from them.

Performance management has risen like a phoenix from the old-established but somewhat discredited systems of merit rating and management by objectives. Many of the more recent developments in performance appraisal have also been absorbed into the concept of performance management, which aims to be a much wider, more comprehensive and more natural process of management. Performance appraisal has too often operated as a top-down and largely discredited bureaucratic system owned by the personnel department rather than by line managers.

THE PROCESS OF PERFORMANCE MANAGEMENT

Performance management is a continuous and flexible process that involves managers and those whom they manage acting as partners within a framework that sets out how they can best work together to achieve the required results. It focuses on future performance planning and improvement rather than on retrospective performance appraisal. It provides the basis for regular and frequent dialogues between managers and individuals or teams about performance and development needs. Performance management is mainly concerned with individual performance and development but it can also be applied to teams.

Performance management reviews provide the inputs required to create personal or team development plans, and to many people performance management is essentially a developmental process and they prefer to talk about performance and development reviews rather than performance management. Performance reviews can, however, produce data in the form of individual ratings, which may be used as the basis for performance-related pay decisions. There are, however, strong arguments against linking performance management with performance-related pay, which are set out in Chapter 31.

Performance management is a process for measuring outputs in the shape of delivered performance compared with expectations expressed as objectives. In this respect, it focuses on targets, standards and performance measures or indicators. But it is also concerned with inputs – the knowledge, skills and competencies required to produce the expected results. It is by defining these input requirements and assessing the extent to which the expected levels of performance have been achieved by using skills and competencies effectively that developmental needs are identified.

CONCLUSION

In conclusion, it must be re-emphasized that performance management is not a top-down, backward-looking form of appraising people. Neither is it just a method of generating information for pay decisions. Performance management is forward-looking and developmental. It provides a framework in which managers can *support* their team members rather than dictate to them, and its impact on results will be much more significant if it is regarded as a transformational rather than as an appraisal process.

31

Performance management processes

Performance management is concerned with improving individual and team performance. This chapter provides an overview of the key performance management activities and then deals with the main performance management processes of performance agreements, managing performance throughout the year, performance reviews, documentation, and its introduction and evaluation.

KEY ACTIVITIES

Performance management can be described as a continuous self-renewing cycle, as illustrated in Figure 31.1. The main activities are:

- *Role definition*, in which the key result areas and competence requirements are agreed.
- *The performance agreement or contract*, which defines expectations – what the individual has to achieve in the form of objectives, how performance will be measured and the competencies needed to deliver the required results. This could be described as the performance planning stage.

- *The personal development plan* (see Chapter 37), which sets out the actions people intend to take to develop themselves in order to extend their knowledge and skills, increase their levels of competence and to improve their performance in specified areas. This is the performance development stage.
- *Managing performance throughout the year*, which is the stage in which action is taken to implement the performance agreement and personal development plan as individuals carry on with their day-to-day work and their planned learning activities. It includes a continuous process of providing feedback on performance, conducting informal progress reviews, updated objectives and, where necessary, dealing with performance problems and counselling.
- *Performance review*, which is the formal evaluation stage when a review of performance over a period takes place, covering achievements, progress and problems as the basis for a revised performance agreement and personal development plan. It can also lead to performance ratings.

These activities are described in the next five sections of this chapter.

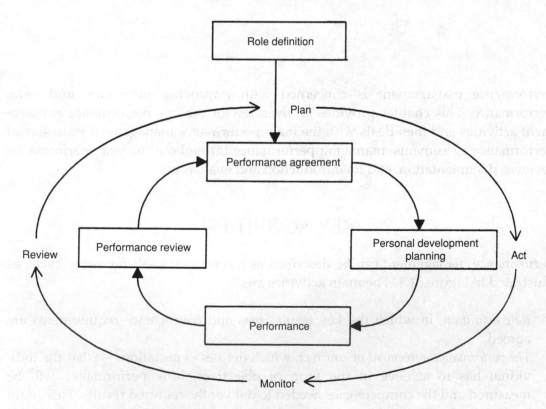

Figure 31.1 The performance management cycle

ROLE PROFILE

The role profile or definition provides the framework for performance management. It sets out:

- *The purpose of the role*, which summarizes its overall aim – what the role holder is expected to do, and provides a foundation for the performance agreement.
- The *key result* areas or principal accountabilities, which define the main output areas of the role and provide the headings against which objectives and performance standards are agreed.
- The *key competencies*, which indicate what the role holder has to be able to do and the behaviour required to perform the role effectively. They provide the basis for drawing up personal development plans and for assessing the input aspect of performance – what the individual brings to the role. This constitutes the competence profile for the role, which may refer to organizational core competencies as well as generic competence profiles developed for similar roles. It may also incorporate competencies specific to the role.

PERFORMANCE AGREEMENTS

Contents

Performance agreements, also known as performance contracts, define expectations – the results to be achieved and the competencies required to attain these results. Agreements cover the following points:

- *Objectives and standards of performance* – the results to be achieved defined in terms of targets and standards.
- *Performance measures and indicators* – to assess the extent to which objectives and standards of performance have been achieved.
- *Competency assessment* – how levels of competency will be assessed, including discussions to clarify expectations by reference to the competence profile in the role definition and agreements on the sort of evidence that will be useful in assessing competency.
- *Core values or operational requirements* – the performance agreement may also refer to the core values of the organization for quality, customer service, team working, employee development etc, which individuals are expected to uphold in carrying out their work. Certain general operational requirements may also be specified in such areas as health and safety, budgetary control, cost reduction and security.

The objectives, performance standards and performance measures aspects of performance agreements are discussed below. Competency profiling was described in Chapter 21.

Objectives

Objectives describe something that has to be accomplished – a point to be aimed at. Objectives or goals (the terms are interchangeable) define what organizations, functions, departments and individuals are expected to achieve over a period of time.

Objectives are expressed as:

- *targets* – quantifiable results to be attained, which can be measured in such terms as return on capital employed, output, throughput, sales, levels of service delivery, cost reduction, reduction of reject rates;
- *tasks/projects* – to be completed by specified dates to achieve defined results.

Objectives can be work related, referring to the results to be attained or the contribution to be made to the achievement of organizational, functional or team goals. They can also be personal, taking the form of developmental or learning objectives, which are concerned with what individuals should do to enhance their knowledge, skills and potential and to improve their performance in specified areas.

Integrating objectives

The integration of objectives is important in order to achieve a shared understanding of performance requirements throughout the organization, thus providing for everyone to make an appropriate contribution to the attainment of team, departmental and corporate goals and to upholding core values.

The integration process is not just about cascading objectives downwards. There should also be an upward flow which provides for participation in goal setting and the opportunity for individuals to contribute to the formulation of their own objectives and to the objectives of their teams, functions and, ultimately, the organization.

Characteristics of good objectives

Objectives are intended to bring about change. They should cover all the important aspects of the job (the key result areas) and not focus on one area at the expense of the others.

Objectives should be 'SMART', ie:

S = *Specific/stretching* – clear, unambiguous, straightforward, understandable and challenging.

M = *Measurable* – quantity, quality, time, money.

A = *Achievable* – challenging but within the reach of a competent and committed person.

R = *Relevant* – relevant to the objectives of the organization so that the goal of the individual is aligned to corporate goals.

T = *Time framed* – to be completed within an agreed time scale.

Defining objectives

Information on objectives can be obtained by asking these questions:

- What do you think are the most important things you do?
- What do you believe you are expected to achieve in each of these areas?
- How will you – or anyone else – know whether or not you have achieved them?

Performance standards

A performance standard can be defined as a statement of the conditions that exist when a job is being performed effectively. Performance standards are used when it is not possible to set time-based targets. Standards are sometimes described as standing or continuing objectives, because their essential nature may not change significantly from one review period to the next if the key task remains unaltered, although they may be modified if new circumstances arise.

A performance standard definition should take the form of a statement that performance will be up to standard if a desirable, specified and observable result happens. It should preferably be quantified in terms, for example, of level of service or speed of response. Where this is not possible, a more qualitative approach may have to be adopted, in which case the standard of performance definition would in effect state: 'this job or task will have been well done if… (the following things happen).' Junior or more routine jobs are likely to have a higher proportion of standing objectives to which performance standards are attached than senior and more flexible or output-orientated jobs.

Performance measures

Performance measures are agreed when setting objectives. It is necessary to define not only what is to be achieved but how those concerned will *know* that it has been achieved. Performance measures should provide evidence of whether or not the intended result has been achieved and the extent to which the job holder has produced that result. This will be the basis for generating feedback information for use not only by managers but also by individuals to monitor their own performance.

The following are guidelines for defining individual performance measures:

● Measures should relate to results, not efforts.
● The results must be within the job holder's control.
● Measures should be objective and observable.
● Data must be available for measurement.
● Existing measures should be used or adapted wherever possible.

Measures can be classified under the following headings:

● *finance* – income, economic value added, shareholder value, added value, rates of return, costs;
● *output* – units produced or processed, throughput, new accounts;
● *impact* – attainment of a standard (quality, level of service etc), changes in behaviour (internal and external customers), completion of work/project, level of take-up of a service, innovation;
● *reaction* – judgement by others, colleagues, internal and external customers;
● *time* – speed of response or turnaround, achievements compared with timetables, amount of backlog, time to market, delivery times.

Individual measures will be more meaningful if they are linked to one or other of the organizational measures described below.

The balanced scorecard

The concept of the balanced scorecard was originally developed by Kaplan and Norton (1992). They took the view that 'what you measure is what you get', and they emphasize that 'no single measure can provide a clear performance target or focus attention on the critical areas of the business. Managers want a balanced presentation of both financial and operational measures.' They therefore devised what they called the 'balanced scorecard' – a set of measures that gives managers a fast but comprehensive view of the business. Their scorecard requires managers to answer four basic questions, which means looking at the business from four related perspectives:

- how do customers see us? (customer perspective);
- what must we excel at? (internal perspective);
- can we continue to improve and create value? (innovation and learning perspective);
- how do we look at shareholders? (financial perspective).

Businesses such as NatWest and Halifax plc have modified this framework by measuring performance against four dimensions: financial results, customer service, internal processes (how well things are done) and people management. The balanced scorecard approach has then been extended to the measurement of individual performance, which is thus integrated with the organizational measures. The performance management cycle at Halifax is illustrated in Figure 31.2.

Another framework is provided by the European Foundation for Quality Management (EFQM) model as in Figure 31.3. This indicates that customer satisfaction, people (employee) satisfaction and impact in society are achieved through leadership. This drives the policy and strategy, people management, resources and processes leading to excellence in business results and can be used as a basis for measuring individual as well as organizational performance.

Figure 31.2 The performance management cycle at Halifax

Figure 31.3 The EFQM model

MANAGING PERFORMANCE THROUGHOUT THE YEAR

Perhaps one of the most important concepts of performance management is that it is a continuous process which reflects normal good management practices of setting direction, monitoring and measuring performance, and taking action accordingly. Performance management should not be imposed on managers as something 'special' they have to do. It should be treated as a natural process that all good managers follow. The sequence of performance management activities as described in this chapter does no more than provide a framework within which managers, individuals and teams work together in whatever ways best suit them to gain better understanding of what is to be done, how it is to be done and what has been achieved. This framework and the philosophy that supports it can form the basis for training newly appointed or would-be managers in this key area of their responsibilities. It can also help in improving the performance of managers who are not up to standard in this respect.

Conventional performance appraisal systems are usually built around an annual event, the formal review, which tended to dwell on the past. This was carried out at the behest of the personnel department, often perfunctorily, and then forgotten. Managers proceeded to manage without any further reference to the outcome of the review and the appraisal form was buried in the personnel record system.

A formal, often annual review is still an important part of a performance management framework but it is not the most important part. Equal, indeed more, prominence is given to the performance agreement and the continuous process of performance management.

The continuing process of performance management

Performance management should be regarded as an integral part of the continuing process of management. This is based on a philosophy that emphasizes:

- the achievement of sustained improvements in performance;
- continuous development of skills and overall competence;
- the importance of organizational learning (see Chapter 34).

Managers and individuals should be ready to define and meet development and improvement needs as they arise. Learning and work should be integrated. Everyone should be encouraged to learn from the successes, challenges and problems inherent in their everyday work.

The process of continuing assessment should be carried out by reference to agreed objectives and performance standards and to work, development and improvement plans. Progress reviews can take place informally or through an existing system of team meetings. But there should be more formal interim reviews at predetermined points in the year, eg twice yearly. For some teams or individual jobs these points could be related to 'milestones' contained in project and work plans. Deciding when such meetings should take place would be up to individual managers in consultation with their staff and would not be a laid-down part of a 'system'.

The issues that may arise in the course of managing performance throughout the year are:

- updating objectives and work plans;
- continuous learning;
- dealing with performance problems.

Updating objectives and work plans

Performance agreements and plans are working documents. New demands, new situations arise, and provision therefore needs to be made for updating or amending objectives and work and personal development plans.

This involves:

- discussing what the job holder has done and achieved;
- identifying any shortfalls in achieving objectives or meeting standards;
- establishing the reasons for any shortfalls, in particular examining changes in the circumstances in which the job is carried out, noting new pressures and demands and considering aspects of the behaviour of the individual or the manager that have contributed to the problem;
- agreeing any changes required to objectives and work plans in response to changed circumstances;
- agreeing any actions required by the individual *or* the manager to improve performance.

Any changes in duties and responsibilities should also be incorporated in the role definition as they arise. Role definitions are part of the performance management process and should be regarded as working documents.

Managing continuous learning

Performance management aims to enhance what Alan Mumford (1994) calls 'deliberate learning from experience', which means learning from the problems, challenges and successes inherent in people's day-to-day activities.

The premise is that every task individuals undertake presents them with a learning opportunity. This happens if they reflect or are helped to reflect on what they have done and how they have done it and draw conclusions as to their future behaviour if they have to carry out a similar task. Any occasion when managers issue instructions to individuals or agree with them what needs to be achieved, followed by a review of how well the task was accomplished, provides a learning opportunity.

Dealing with performance problems

The five basic steps required to handle performance problems are:

1. *Identify and agree the problem.* Analyse the feedback and, as far as possible, obtain agreement from the individual on what the shortfall has been. Feedback may be provided by managers but it should be built into the job. This takes place when individuals are aware of their targets and standards, know what performance measures will be used and either receive feedback/control information automatically or have easy access to it. They will then be in a position to measure and assess their own performance and take action. In other words, a self-regulating

feedback mechanism exists. This is a situation that managers should endeavour to create on the grounds that prevention is better than cure.

2. *Establish the reason(s) for the shortfall*. When seeking the reasons for any shortfalls the manager should not crudely be trying to attach blame. The aim should be for the manager and the individual jointly to identify the facts that have contributed to the problem. It is on the basis of this factual analysis that decisions can be made on what to do about it by the individual, the manager or the two of them working together. It is necessary first to identify any causes that are external to the job and outside the control of either the manager or the individual. Any factors that are within the control of the individual and/or the manager can then be considered. What should be determined is the extent to which the reason for the problem is because the individual:

   ● did not receive adequate support or guidance from his/her manager;
   ● did not fully understand what he/she was expected to do;
   ● could not do it – ability;
   ● did not know how to do it – skill;
   ● would not do it – attitude.

3. *Decide and agree on the action required*. Action may be taken by the individual, the manager or both parties. This could include:

   ● Changing behaviour – this is up to individuals as long as they accept that their behaviour needs to be changed; the challenge for managers is that people will not change their behaviour simply because they are told to do so.
   ● Changing attitudes – this may be more difficult to change than behaviour because attitudes are likely to be deep-rooted; it is often best to change behaviour first and encourage attitude changes thereafter.
   ● Clarifying expectations – job requirements, objectives and standards.
   ● Jointly developing abilities and skills – joint in the sense that individuals may be expected to take steps to develop themselves but managers may provide help in the form of coaching, additional experience or training. Whatever action is agreed, both parties must understand how they will know that it has succeeded. Performance measures and feedback arrangements should be agreed.

4. *Resource the action*. Provide the coaching, training, guidance, experience or facilities required to enable agreed actions to happen.

5. *Monitor and provide feedback*. Take steps to monitor performance, ensure that feedback is provided or obtained and analysed, and agree on any further actions that may be necessary. Individuals should be encouraged to monitor their own performance and take further action as required. This can be described as a 'self-managed learning process'.

PERFORMANCE REVIEWS

Performance review discussions enable a perspective to be obtained on past performance as a basis for making plans for the future. An overall view is taken of the progress made. Examples are used to illustrate that overview, and the analysis of performance concentrates not only on what has happened but also on *why* it has happened so that data are obtained for planning purposes. Obtaining a historical perspective through analysis is a necessary part of a performance review, but reaching agreement about what should be done in the future is what the discussion should be about.

Performance and development reviews provide those involved with the opportunity to reflect on past performance as a basis for making development and improvement plans. The purpose of performance and development reviews is to enable those concerned to get together so that they can engage in a dialogue about the individual's performance and development and the support provided by the manager – and such support is an essential part of performance management. They are not occasions for top-down appraisals, although some feedback will be provided. Neither are they interviews in which one person asks the questions and the other provides the answers. They should be more like free-flowing, open meetings where views are exchanged so that agreed conclusions can be reached. A performance and development review should be regarded as a conversation with a purpose, which is to reach firm and agreed conclusions about the individual's development, and, if applicable, any areas for improvement and how such improvements will be achieved.

The basis of the performance review

The performance review discussion provides the means through which the five key elements of performance management can be achieved. These are:

1. *Measurement* – assessing results against agreed targets and standards.
2. *Feedback* – giving people information on how they are doing.
3. *Positive reinforcement* – emphasizing what has been done well so that it will be done even better in the future; only making constructive criticisms, ie those that point the way to improvement.
4. *Exchange of views* – ensuring that the discussion involves a full, free and frank exchange of views about what has been achieved, what needs to be done to achieve more and what individuals think about their work, the way they are guided and managed and their aspirations. Performance and development reviews provide those involved with the opportunity to reflect on past

performance as a basis for making development and improvement plans. Obtaining historical perspective through analysis is a necessary part of the review but reaching agreement about what should be done in the future is what it is all about. The performance review should take the form of a dialogue, not a top-down interview or 'appraisal'.

5. *Agreement on action plans* to be implemented by individuals alone or by individuals with the support of their managers.

Preparation

Both parties should prepare for the meeting so that consideration should be given to the points for discussion. The manager (the reviewer) should consider how well the individual (the reviewee) has done in achieving objectives and meeting performance standards since the last review meeting and the extent to which personal development plans have been implemented. An analysis should be made of the factors that have affected performance (some could be beyond the individual's control) and the reasons for success or failure. Consideration should also be given to the feedback to be provided at the meeting, the evidence that will be used to support the feedback, any actions that might be taken to improve performance and possible objectives for the next review period.

The individual (the reviewee) should consider achievements and progress in meeting objectives and implementing personal development plans and be prepared to explain the reason for any shortfalls. More positively, thought should be given to development and training needs, any requirements for better support or guidance, aspirations for the future and possible objectives for the next review period.

Self-assessment

Preparation by the reviewee as described above is, in effect, self-assessment or self-appraisal. This is getting people to analyse and assess their own performance as the basis for discussion and action. The advantages of self-assessment are that:

- it helps to generate less inhibited and more positive discussion;
- it involves reviewees actively in the review process;
- it is likely to reduce defensive behaviour;
- it provides scope to run the review meeting as a constructive and open dialogue by reducing the top-down element of traditional performance appraisals and minimizing their unilateral nature.

But self-assessment raises a number of issues. First, individuals must have clear targets and standards against which they can assess their performance. Second, there has to be a climate of mutual trust between the reviewee and the reviewer. Reviewees must believe that reviewers will not take advantage of an honest self-assessment. Third, there is the risk that individuals, especially where there is money at stake, will overestimate their performance, leaving their reviewers in the awkward position of having to correct them. In practice, if there are no ratings for performance-related pay purposes, many people underestimate themselves. This makes life easier for reviewers who can take the opportunity to boost the confidence of the reviewee.

GUIDELINES FOR THE MEETING

Reviewing performance is *not* something that managers do to their subordinates. It *is* something that they carry out together. The meeting is essentially about:

● what individuals have learned or need to learn;
● what they believe they know and can do;
● where they have got to;
● where they are going;
● how they are going to get there;
● what help or guidance can be provided for them by the organization or their manager.

Agenda setting

Whoever sets the agenda directs the meeting. But the whole point of the review is that it should be a joint affair. Neither party should dominate. The agenda is therefore set by both the reviewer and the reviewee, ideally through their pre-meeting analyses. It can consist of the following items:

1. A review of each key element in the job (key result areas or main activities); discussing what has gone well and what has gone less well, and why.
2. A point-by-point examination of the results of the objectives, actions and personal development plans agreed at the last meeting.
3. A discussion and agreement on the performance objectives for the next period in the shape of targets and standards of performance.
4. A discussion and agreement on the reviewee's developmental objectives.

5. A discussion and agreement on the actions to be taken to ensure that the performance and developmental objectives are achieved, this will include the formulation of a personal development plan.
6. A general discussion of any other matters of concern, including the reviewee's aspirations.
7. A check that there is mutual understanding of the objectives and action plans.
8. An agreement on action plans to conclude the meeting.

An alternative approach would be to structure the discussion around forms to be completed in advance by the reviewer and the reviewee, covering the preparation points listed earlier.

Conducting a constructive review meeting

A constructive review meeting is most likely to take place if reviewers:

- encourage reviewees to do most of the talking;
- listen actively to what they say;
- allow scope for reflection and analysis;
- analyse performance, not personality – concentrate on what reviewees have done, not the sort of people they are;
- keep the whole period under review, not concentrating on isolated or recent events;
- adopt a 'no surprises' approach – performance problems should have been identified and dealt with at the time they occurred;
- recognize achievements and reinforce strengths;
- end the meeting positively with agreed action plans and an understanding of how progress in implementing them will be reviewed.

PERFORMANCE RATING

Performance appraisal schemes almost always included an overall rating of the individual's performance. Early performance management systems normally incorporated rating, especially when they were associated with performance-related pay, as was frequently the case. It is interesting to note, however, that the research conducted by Armstrong and Baron (1998) for the IPD found that 43 per cent of all the organizations with performance management did not require an overall rating.

Methods of rating

How many levels?

Englemann and Roesch (1996) accept that the number of levels in a rating scale is probably one of the most controversial issues in performance management design. The possibility is posed that the degree to which discriminatory judgements can be made will increase if there are more levels than, say, five. But the American Compensation Association (ACA) asks the question: 'How does one objectively differentiate performance at each of the five levels?' and comments that it is difficult to communicate the rationale for ratings in a way that ensures that employees understand performance expectations at different rating levels.

The first choice is between having an odd number of levels, eg three or five, or an even number, eg four or six. The argument in favour of an odd number is that this represents the normal distribution of ability, with most people being in the middle. The argument used to support an even number is that this will frustrate the tendency of managers to centralize ratings. The most typical number of levels is four or five, but some organizations favour three on the grounds that this is the limit to which accurate discrimination is possible.

There has been much debate on what constitutes the 'best' number of rating levels. Milkovich and Wigdor (1991), in their report on a research project, came to the conclusion that:

> The weight of evidence suggests the reliability of ratings drops if there are fewer than three or more rating categories. Recent work indicates that there is little to be gained from having more than five response categories. Within this range (three to five) there is no evidence that there is one best number of scale points in terms of scale quality.

Describing the levels

A rating scale format can be either behavioural, with examples of good, average and inadequate performance, or graphic, which simply presents a number of scale points along a continuum. The scale points or anchors in the latter may be defined alphabetically (a, b, c etc), numerically (1, 2, 3 etc) or by means of initials (ex for excellent etc) which purport to disguise the hierarchical nature of the scale. The scale points may be further described adjectivally; for example: excellent (A), highly acceptable (B), acceptable (C), not entirely acceptable (D) and unacceptable (E).

Some organizations just rely on verbal descriptions in order to minimize the 'putting people into boxes' problem. It is preferable to avoid the use of above average – 'above average, average, below average' – what is average? And should one really label anyone for the next 12 months as 'below average'?

The tendency is to avoid negative descriptions in the levels and to leave out an 'unsatisfactory' or 'unacceptable' level. The argument for this approach is that anyone in this category should have been dealt with at the time the performance problem emerged under the normal disciplinary procedure – action should not be delayed until the performance review.

An increasingly popular method is to have a rating scale that provides positive reinforcement at each level. This is in line with a policy of continuous improvement. The example given below emphasizes the positive and improvable nature of individual performance:

Highly effective	Frequently exceeds agreed targets and standards and consistently performs in a thoroughly proficient manner beyond normal expectations.
Effective	Achieves agreed targets and standards and meets the normal expectations of the role.
Developing	A contribution that is stronger in some aspects of the role than others, where most objectives and standards are met but in some areas further development is required to become fully effective in meeting performance expectations.
Improvable	A contribution that generally meets or almost meets the standards expected but there is clearly room for improvement in a number of definable areas.

Note that these definitions ask raters to focus on definitions that compare performance to performance expectations and avoid ratings that compare employees, such as 'average' or 'below average'.

Arguments for rating

The arguments for rating are that:

- It is not possible to have performance-related pay without an overall rating (assuming performance-related pay is wanted or needed).
- It provides a convenient means of summing up judgements so that high or low performances can easily be identified (as long as the judgements are consistent and fair).
- It can provide a basis for predicting potential on the somewhat dubious assumption that people who perform well in their existing jobs will perform well in the future in different jobs. This is dubious because past performance

is only a predictor of future performance when there is a connecting link, ie there are elements of the present job which are also important in a higher-level job.

● They let people know where they stand, at least in the mind of their manager. (But this is only desirable if the manager's opinion is honest, justified and fair, and the numbers or letters convey what is really felt and have real meaning in themselves.)

Arguments against ratings

The arguments against ratings are that:

● To sum up the total performance of a person with a single rating is a gross oversimplification of what may be a complex set of factors influencing performance, some of which, such as systems factors, may be beyond the person's control.
● Consistency between raters is difficult if not impossible to achieve.
● Ratings are likely to be based on largely subjective judgements (explicit standards against which these judgements are made are absent). They could therefore well be unfair and discriminatory.
● Managers might find it difficult to answer the question: 'What do I have to do to get a higher rating?' if there are no explicit definitions in the rating scale of the standards of performance expected of anyone in that particular role, which is most unlikely.
● Rating encourages managers to be dishonest. Either they rate everyone in the middle of a five-point range or the second point down in a four-point range (the central tendency), or they decide first on what they want a performance-related pay increase to be and rate accordingly.
● Rating can turn what may – should – have been an open, positive and constructive discussion into a top-down judgemental exercise.
● The positive developmental aspects of the review may be overshadowed by the knowledge that the end-product will be a rating that will inform a pay decision. In practice, the review and the preparation for the review may be entirely dominated by its pay implications, thus destroying its main purpose.
● To label people with a letter or a number is both demeaning and demotivating.
● Ratings convey opinions about past performance. They say nothing about the future.

These are powerful arguments supported by much of the evidence collected in the IPD research. One group personnel director, for example, said that: 'It denigrates the whole performance management process.' Some organizations that do not have performance-related pay reject ratings altogether because of the objections listed above.

The following comment on ratings was made by Englemann and Roesch (1996): 'To reduce the subjectivity of performance management systems and increase the focus on continuous improvement, organizations have tended to move away from rating categories or labels toward summary statements that are behaviour orientated and more focused on future improvements.'

And Fletcher (1993) made the point that in the UK: 'The use of ratings to compare individuals (even overall performance ratings), for so long a central element of appraisal forms and processes, is now declining.'

Some organizations recognize the problem but say: 'We've got to do it because we have PRP.' In fact, many organizations manage PRP quite effectively without ratings at the time of the performance review.

Achieving consistency

If, in spite of these objections, it is felt that the system must have ratings, then the main concern is how to achieve an acceptable degree of consistency, equity and fairness in ratings. It can be very difficult, if not impossible without very careful management, to ensure that a consistent approach is adopted by managers responsible for rating. It is almost inevitable that some people will be more generous than others, while others will be harder on their staff. Ratings can, of course, be monitored and questioned if their distribution is significantly out of line, and computer-based systems have been introduced for this purpose in some organizations. But many managers want to do the best for their staff, either because they genuinely believe that they are better or because they are trying to curry favour. It can be difficult in these circumstances to challenge them, and it could be argued that if responsibility for human resource management is being genuinely devolved to line management, it is up to them to decide how they are going to distribute their ratings.

There are six ways of attempting to achieve a degree of consistency or at least avoid what is believed to be an unacceptable distribution in ratings:

- *Forced distribution*. This requires managers to conform to a pattern, which quite often corresponds with the normal curve of distribution on the rather dubious assumption that performance levels will be distributed normally in each part of the organization. A typical distribution would be A = 5%, B = 15%, C = 60%, D = 15%, E = 5%. But managers and employees correctly resent being forced into predetermined categories and it produces win/lose situations. This approach sometimes takes the form of a quota system, which allocates the number of ratings managers are allowed to award in each category. This is also an arbitrary process and is universally resented by managers and their staff.

- *Ranking*. Staff are ranked in order of merit and then performance ratings are distributed through the rank order; for example: the top 5% get an A rating, the next 15% a B rating and so on. This is another form of forced distribution, which still depends on the objectivity and fairness of the rankings.
- *Training*. 'Consistency' workshops are run for managers to discuss how ratings can be objectively justified and test rating decisions on case study performance review data. This can build a level of common understanding about rating levels.
- *Peer reviews or moderating discussions*. Groups of managers meet to review the pattern of each other's ratings and challenge unusual decisions or distributions. This process of moderation is time-consuming but it can be a good way of achieving a reasonable degree of consistency, especially when the moderating group members share some knowledge of the performances of each other's staff as internal customers.
- *Monitoring*. The distribution of ratings is monitored by a central department. This is usually HR, which challenges any unusual patterns and identifies and questions what appear to be unwarrantable differences between departments' ratings.
- *Behaviourally anchored rating scales (BARS)*. These are designed to reduce the rating errors, which it was assumed are typical of conventional scales. They include a number of performance dimensions such as teamwork, and managers rate each dimension on a scale as in the following example:
  A Continually contributes new ideas and suggestions. Takes a leading role in group meetings but is tolerant and supportive of colleagues and respects other people's points of view. Keeps everyone informed about own activities and is well aware of what other team members are doing in support of team objectives.
  B Takes a full part in group meetings and contributes useful ideas frequently. Listens to colleagues and keeps them reasonably well informed about own activities while keeping abreast of what they are doing.
  C Delivers opinions and suggestions at group meetings from time to time but is not a major contributor to new thinking or planning activities. Generally receptive to other people's ideas and willing to change own plans to fit in. Does not always keep others properly informed or take sufficient pains to know what they are doing.
  D Tendency to comply passively with other people's suggestions. May

withdraw at group meetings but sometimes shows personal antagonism to others. Not very interested in what others are doing or in keeping them informed.

E Tendency to go own way without taking much account of the need to make a contribution to team activities. Sometimes uncooperative and unwilling to share information.

F Generally uncooperative. Goes own way, completely ignoring the wishes of other team members and taking no interest in the achievement of team objectives.

It is believed that the behavioural descriptions in such scales discourage the tendency to rate on the basis of generalized assumptions about personality traits (which were probably highly subjective) by focusing attention on specific work behaviours. But they do take a considerable amount of effort to develop properly and there is still room for making subjective judgements based on different interpretations of the definitions of levels of behaviour.

DOCUMENTATION

It is the processes of performance management as practised jointly by managers and individuals that are important, not the content of the system; and the content often seems to consist largely of documents. Performance management is about managing and improving performance. It is not about completing forms.

A case could be made for having no forms at all. The parties involved could be encouraged to record the conclusions of their discussion and their agreements on blank sheets of paper to be used as working documents during the continuing process of managing performance throughout the year.

But there is much to be said for having a format, which can help in the orderly presentation of plans and comments. And the mere existence of a form or a set of forms does demonstrate that this is a process that everyone is expected to take seriously.

Performance management forms as working documents

The main function of performance management forms is to act as working documents. They should be completed jointly by managers and individuals. The manager should never deliver a completed form to an individual and say 'What do you think?' In the past, merit ratings were sometimes not shown to the individuals concerned at all, which was a remarkable denial of the whole reason for reviewing performance.

Forms should be in continual use as reference documents on objectives and plans when reviewing progress. They should also record agreements on performance achievements and actions to be taken to improve performance or develop competence and skills. They should be dog-eared from much use – they should not be condemned to moulder away in a file.

It can be argued that for this reason the forms should be owned by the manager and the individual (both parties should have a copy) and not the HR department. Any information that the HR department needs on ratings (for performance-related pay or career planning purposes), or requests for training, would be incorporated in a separate form for their use.

Individuals can be protected against unfair assessments and ratings by providing for their manager's manager (the so-called 'grandparent') to see and comment on the completed report. These comments could be shown to individuals who should have the right to appeal through a grievance procedure if they are still unhappy about the report.

There is, however, a case for the personnel department having sight of completed review forms for quality assurance purposes, especially in the earlier days of operating performance management.

A typical set of forms used by the Peabody Trust in association with a competency framework is shown in Figure 31.4..

INTRODUCING PERFORMANCE MANAGEMENT

Performance management processes need to be introduced with great care. Too many ambitious schemes fail because this seemingly obvious requirement has been neglected.

When planning the programme of introduction the following points need to be covered:

● Where and how should performance management be introduced?
● Who should be covered?
● When should reviews take place?
● What sort of reviews should be held?
● What use should be made of pilot tests?
● What briefing arrangements should be made?

PERFORMANCE MANAGEMENT PLANNING AND REVIEW FORM

This performance management planning and review form should be completed jointly by the manager and the individual. It contains sections for planning performance and development and for reviewing outcomes. It covers three areas: (1) **what** is to be done – the expected results, (2) **how** it is to be done – the expected behaviour by reference to the Trust's generic competence framework, and (3) what further development the individual needs.

Name of manager:	Job title:	Date of review

(1) WHAT IS TO BE DONE

Key result area	Agreed results to be achieved	Joint review of results achieved
A		
B		
C		
D		
E		
F		
G		
H		
I		
J		

(2) HOW IT IS TO BE DONE

Competency area	Profile*	Joint assessment	Development need
Knowledge and skills			
Manage performance			
Manage oneself			
Manage others			
Manage relationships			
Manage communications			
Manage customer service			
Manage continuous improvement			
Manage resources			

*Indicate level of competency expected for role by reference to competence framework

Figure 31.4 Performance management and review form

(2) PERSONAL DEVELOPMENT PLAN

Key result area/competence	Development need	Method of meeting need	Target date	Review of achievement

COMMENTS

Line manager:

Senior line manager:

Individual:

Signed (line manager):	Date:
Signed (senior line manager):	Date:
Signed (individual):	Date:

Figure 31.4 *continued*

Where and how should performance management be introduced?

Performance management is usually introduced on an organization-wide basis, starting at the top. In many cases the philosophy, principles and key procedures and processes are developed centrally.

In a highly decentralized organization, separate business units may be allowed to decide for themselves whether or not they want performance management and if they do, develop it on their own.

An intermediate approach adopted by some decentralized organizations is for the centre (top management) to require all divisions and business units to introduce performance management in accordance with certain general principles, which have been discussed and agreed with local management and, preferably, staff. The business units proceed to develop their own processes, but the centre provides help as required and may monitor the introduction of performance management on each division to ensure that it is happening according to plan and in line with corporate principles and values.

The most common and best method of introduction is to set up a project team or working group for this purpose with management and staff representatives. This provides for different opinions and experiences to be considered, serves as a base for wider consultation and communications to take place and generally helps to achieve understanding and acceptance of the process. More general consultation is very desirable. As many people as possible should be brought into the discussions. Workshops and focus groups can be used to develop and discuss ideas. The aim is to get the maximum amount of 'buy-in' to the new process as possible.

Who should be covered?

Another important decision to be made at the outset is who should be covered by performance management. At one time, most schemes were restricted to managers, but performance management is now more generally being extended to all professional, administrative, technical and support staff. Some organizations also include shop-floor workers, especially high-tech firms, those that rely on production by high-performance work teams, companies with integrated pay structures and terms and conditions of employment (often high-tech and/or international firms) and companies with performance-related pay for manual workers. There is much to be said for having a universal scheme as part of a completely integrated terms and conditions of employment policy and as a means of increasing commitment by demonstrating that all employees are regarded as important.

While some organizations believe that it would be invidious to differentiate between levels so far as the essence of the approach is concerned, they might accept that different performance measures may be used.

Some organizations do distinguish between roles where quantified and regularly updated short-term objectives will be set and those where continuing performance standards are more usual. In the former case they may refer to the key result areas of the job as 'principal accountabilities'; in the latter they may use terms such as 'main tasks' or 'key activities'.

It may also be recognized that the objective setting and review process in more routine jobs may not need to be as exhaustive as for those in managerial or professional roles.

When should reviews take place?

The usual practice is to have an annual formal review with interim reviews. Some organizations require development reviews to be conducted on or about the anniversary of the day on which the employee joined the organization. This, they believe, spreads the load on managers. If there is performance pay, the pay review is carried out at a fixed time in the year and can be treated as a separate exercise (this is highly desirable if the pay review is not to contaminate the development review).

What sort of reviews should be conducted?

For the reasons given above, organizations frequently arrange for separate reviews; one that is concerned only with agreeing objectives and personal development plans and, if they have performance pay, one that is solely concerned with making pay decisions (pay reviews are discussed in Chapter 43).

Pilot tests

Pilot testing of performance management is highly desirable – bearing in mind that the usual cycle lasts 12 months and it may therefore be difficult to pilot-test the whole process.

Examples of aspects of performance management that can be tested are drawing up performance agreements, objective setting and document completion.

Prepare briefing papers

It is advisable to issue an overall description of performance management to all employees, which sets out its objectives and method of operation and the benefits it is expected to provide for the organization and its managers and employees. Some organizations have prepared elaborate and lengthy briefing documents but fairly succinct documents often suffice as long as they are written in simple language and are well produced.

It is also advisable to supplement written with oral briefings through a briefing group system, if there is one, or a special briefing programme. In a large or dispersed organization this briefing will have to be carried out by line managers and they should be issued with special briefing packs and, possibly, a list of typical questions and their answers.

MONITORING AND EVALUATING PERFORMANCE MANAGEMENT

It is important to monitor the introduction of performance management very carefully but it is equally vital to continue to monitor and evaluate it regularly, especially after its first year of operation.

The best method of monitoring and evaluation is to ask those involved – managers, individuals and teams – how it worked. As many as possible should be seen, individually and in groups, to discuss the points set out in the last section of this chapter. It is also desirable to scrutinize a sample of completed forms to check on how well and thoroughly they have been completed. The evaluation can be carried out by members of the project team and/or by the personnel function. An independent consultant or adviser can be used to conduct a special review.

Individual and group discussions can be supplemented by a special survey of reactions to performance management, which could be completed anonymously by all managers and staff. The results should be fed back to all concerned and analysed to assess the need for any amendments to the process or further training requirements.

The ultimate test, of course, is analysing organizational performance to establish the extent to which improvements can be attributed to performance management. It may be difficult to establish a direct connection but more detailed assessments with managers and staff on the impact of the process may reveal specific areas in which performance has been improved, which could be linked to an overall performance measure.

32

360-degree feedback

360-degree feedback is a relatively new feature of performance management. Although by no means common (only 11 per cent of the organizations covered by the research conducted by Armstrong and Baron (1998) for the IPD used it), interest is increasing. This chapter starts with a definition of 360-degree feedback and goes on to describe how it is used and operated and to discuss its advantages and disadvantages and methods of introduc-tion.

360-DEGREE FEEDBACK DEFINED

360-degree feedback has been defined by Ward (1995) as: 'The systematic collection and feedback of performance data on an individual or group derived from a number of the stakeholders on their performance'.

The data is usually fed back in the form of ratings against various performance dimensions. 360-degree feedback is also referred to as multi-source assessment or multi-rater feedback.

Performance data in a 360-degree feedback process can be generated for individuals (as shown in Figure 32.1) from the person to whom they report, their direct reports, their peers (who could be team members and/or colleagues in other parts of the organization) and their external and internal customers.

Figure 32.1 360-degree feedback model

The range of feedback could be extended to include other stakeholders – external customers, clients or suppliers (this is sometimes known as 540-degree feedback). A self-assessment process may also be incorporated using for comparison purposes the same criteria as the other generators of feedback.

Feedback can be initiated entirely by peers (in a team setting) or by both peers and team leaders. It can also take the form of 180-degree or upward feedback where this is given by subordinates to their managers. Feedback may be presented direct to individuals, or to their managers, or both. Expert counselling and coaching for individuals as a result of the feedback may be provided by a member of the HR department or by an outside consultant.

USE OF 360-DEGREE FEEDBACK

360-degree feedback is used for a number of purposes. Research conducted by the Ashridge Management Research Group (Handy *et al*, 1996) found that typically, 360-degree feedback forms part of a self-development or management development programme. The 45 users covered by the survey fell into the following groups:

● 71 per cent used it solely to support learning and development;

- 23 per cent used it to support a number of HR processes such as appraisal, resourcing and succession planning;
- 6 per cent used it to support pay decisions.

A 1997 survey by the Performance Management Group (unpublished) of 22 organizations using 360-degree feedback found that:

- 77 per cent either disagreed or strongly disagreed with the statement that it is 'a personal development tool and should not be used for wider HR or organizational purposes';
- 81 per cent disagreed or strongly disagreed that 'the natural use of 360-degree feedback is to provide a basis for reward'.

The research conducted by Armstrong and Baron (1998) for the IPD also found that the 51 organizations covered by the research predominantly used 360-degree feedback to help in assessing development needs, and as a basis for performance coaching. Only one-fifth of the respondents used it to determine a performance grade or pay award.

RATIONALE FOR 360-DEGREE FEEDBACK

The main rationale for 360-degree feedback has been expressed by Turnow (1993) as follows:

> 360-degree activities are usually based on two key assumptions: (1) that awareness of any discrepancy between how we see ourselves and how others see us increases self-awareness, and (2) that enhanced self-awareness is a key to maximum performance as a leader, and thus becomes a foundation block for management and leadership development programmes.

London and Beatty (1993) have suggested that the rationale for 360-degree feedback is as follows:

- 360-degree feedback can become a powerful organizational intervention to increase awareness of the importance of aligning leader behaviour, work unit results and customer expectations, as well as increasing employee participation in leadership development and work unit effectiveness.
- 360-degree feedback recognizes the complexity of management and the value of input from various sources – it is axiomatic that managers should not be assessing

behaviours they cannot observe, and the leadership behaviours of subordinates may not be known to their managers.

● 360-degree feedback calls attention to important performance dimensions which may hitherto have been neglected by the organization.

360-DEGREE FEEDBACK – METHODOLOGY

The questionnaire

360-degree feedback processes usually obtain data from questionnaires, which measure from different perspectives the behaviours of individuals against a list of competencies. In effect, they ask for an evaluation: 'how well does… do…?' The competency model may be one developed within the organization or the competency headings may be provided by the supplier of a questionnaire.

The dimensions may broadly refer to leadership, management and approaches to work. The headings used in the Performance Management Group's Orbit 360-degree questionnaire are:

● leadership;
● team player/manage people;
● self-management;
● communication;
● vision;
● organizational skills;
● decision making;
● expertise;
● drive;
● adaptability.

The leadership heading, for example, is defined as: 'Shares a clear vision and focuses on achieving it. Demonstrates commitment to the organization's mission. Provides a coherent sense of purpose and direction, both internally and externally, harnessing energy and enthusiasm of staff.'

Ratings

Ratings are given by the generators of the feedback on a scale against each heading. This may refer both to importance and performance, as in the PILAT questionnaire which asks those completing it to rate the importance of each item on a scale of 1 (not important) to 6 (essential), and performance on a scale of 1 (weak in this area) to 6 (outstanding).

Data processing

Questionnaires are normally processed with the help of software developed within the organization or, most commonly, provided by external suppliers. This enables the data collection and analysis to be completed swiftly, with the minimum of effort and in a way that facilitates graphical as well as numerical presentation.

Graphical presentation is preferable as a means of easing the process of assimilating the data. The simplest method is to produce a profile as illustrated in Figure 32.2.

Figure 32.2 360-degree feedback profile

Some of the proprietary software presents feedback data in a much more elaborate form.

Feedback

The feedback is often anonymous and may be presented to the individual (most commonly), to the individual's manager (less common) or to both the individual and the manager. Some organizations do not arrange for feedback to be anonymous. Whether or not feedback is anonymous depends on the organization's culture – the more open the culture, the more likely is the source of feedback to be revealed.

Action

The action generated by the feedback will depend on the purposes of the process, ie development, appraisal or pay. If the purpose is primarily developmental, the action may be left to individuals as part of their personal development plans, but the planning process may be shared between individuals and their managers if they both have access to the information. Even if the data only goes to the individual, it can be discussed in a performance review meeting so that joint plans can be made, and there is much to be said for adopting this approach.

DEVELOPMENT AND IMPLEMENTATION

To develop and implement 360-degree feedback the following steps need to be taken:

1. *Define objectives* – it is important to define exactly what 360-degree feedback is expected to achieve. It will be necessary to spell out the extent to which it is concerned with personal development, appraisal or pay.
2. *Decide on recipients* – who is to be at the receiving end of feedback. This may be an indication of who will eventually be covered after a pilot scheme.
3. *Decide on who will give the feedback* – the individual's manager, direct reports, team members, other colleagues, internal and external customers. A decision will also have to be made on whether HR staff or outside consultants should take part in helping managers to make use of the feedback. A further decision will need to be made on whether or not the feedback should be anonymous (it usually is).
4. *Decide on the areas of work and behaviour* on which feedback will be given – this may be in line with an existing competency model or it may take the form of a list of headings for development. Clearly, the model should fit the culture, values and type of work carried out in the organization. But it might be decided that a list of headings or questions in a software package would be acceptable, at least to start with.
5. *Decide on the method of collecting the data* – the questionnaire could be designed in-house or a consultant's or software provider's questionnaire could be adopted, with the possible option of amending it later to produce better fit.
6. *Decide on data analysis and presentation* – again, the decision is on developing the software in-house or using a package. Most organizations installing 360-degree feedback do, in fact, purchase a package from a consultancy or software house. But the aim should be to keep it as simple as possible.
7. *Plan initial implementation programme* – it is desirable to pilot the process, preferably at top level or with all the managers in a function or department. The pilot

scheme will need to be launched with communications to those involved about the purpose of 360-degree feedback, how it will work and the part they will play. The aim is to spell out the benefits and, as far as possible, allay any fears. Training in giving and receiving feedback will also be necessary.

8. *Analyse outcome of pilot scheme* – the reactions of those taking part in a pilot scheme should be analysed and necessary changes made to the process, the communication package and the training.

9. *Plan and implement full programme* – this should include briefing, communicating, training and support from HR and, possibly, the external consultants.

10. *Monitor and evaluate* – maintain a particularly close watch on the initial implementation of feedback, but monitoring should continue. This is a process that can cause anxiety and stress, or produce little practical gain in terms of development and improved performance for a lot of effort.

360-DEGREE FEEDBACK – ADVANTAGES AND DISADVANTAGES

The survey conducted by the Performance Management Group in 1997 (unpublished) revealed that respondents believed the following benefits resulted from using 360-degree feedback:

- Individuals get a broader perspective of how they are perceived by others than previously possible.
- Increased awareness of and relevance of competencies.
- Increased awareness by senior management that they too have development needs.
- More reliable feedback to senior managers about their performance.
- Gaining acceptance of the principle of multiple stakeholders as a measure of performance.
- Encouraging more open feedback – new insights.
- Reinforcing the desired competencies of the business.
- Provided a clearer picture to senior management of individual's real worth (although there tended to be some 'halo'-effect syndromes).
- Clarified to employees critical performance aspects.
- Opens up feedback and gives people a more rounded view of performance than they had previously.
- Identifying key development areas for the individual, a department and the organization as a whole.

- Identify strengths that can be used to the best advantage of the business.
- A rounded view of an individual's/team's/the organization's performance and what its strengths and weaknesses are.
- It has raised the self-awareness of people managers of how they personally impact upon others – positively and negatively.
- It is supporting a climate of continuous improvement.
- It is starting to improve the climate/morale, as measured through our employee opinion survey.
- Focused agenda for development. Forced line managers to discuss development issues.
- Perception of feedback as more valid and objective, leading to acceptance of results and actions required.

But there may be problems. These include:

- people not giving frank or honest feedback;
- people being put under stress in receiving or giving feedback;
- lack of action following feedback;
- over-reliance on technology;
- too much bureaucracy.

These can all be minimized if not avoided completely by careful design, communication, training and follow-up.

360-DEGREE FEEDBACK – CRITERIA FOR SUCCESS

360-degree feedback is most likely to be successful when:

- it has the active support of top management who themselves take part in giving and receiving feedback and encourage everyone else to do the same;
- there is commitment everywhere else to the process based on briefing, training and an understanding of the benefits to individuals as well as the organization;
- there is real determination by all concerned to use feedback data as the basis for development;
- questionnaire items fit or reflect typical and significant aspects of behaviour;
- items covered in the questionnaire can be related to actual events experienced by the individual;
- comprehensive and well-delivered communication and training programmes are followed;

- no one feels threatened by the process – this is usually often achieved by making feedback anonymous and/or getting a third-party facilitator to deliver the feedback;
- feedback questionnaires are relatively easy to complete (not unduly complex or lengthy, with clear instructions);
- bureaucracy is minimized.

Part IX

Human resource development

Human resource development (HRD) is concerned with the provision of learning, development and training opportunities in order to improve individual, team and organizational performance. HRD is essentially a business-led approach to developing people within a strategic framework.

This part considers human resource development under the following headings:

- *Strategic human resource development – definition, aims and activities.*
- *Organizational learning – the process of organizational learning and the concept of the learning organization.*
- *Individual learning and development – a review of learning theory as it affects individual learning.*
- *Training – assessing training needs and planning, conducting and evaluating training interventions and programmes to enable people to acquire the specific knowledge and skills required to carry out their roles.*
- *Personal development planning – how this contributes to individual learning.*
- *Management development – improving the performance of managers, encouraging self-development and giving them opportunities for growth; the concept of emotional intelligence and its relevance to the development of effective managers.*

● *Career management and management succession – ensuring that the organization has the people it needs to provide for growth and management succession and that individual managers are given the guidance and help they require to realize their potential. This could be regarded as an aspect of management development but is significant enough in its own right to be dealt with separately.*

33

Strategic human resource development

STRATEGIC HRD DEFINED

Strategic human resource development (strategic HRD) is concerned with the development of strategies for the provision of learning, development and training opportunities in order to improve individual, team and organizational performance. As defined by Harrison (1997), strategic HRD is 'development that arises from a clear vision about people's abilities and potential and operates within the overall strategic framework of the business'. Strategic HRD takes a broad and long-term view about how HRD policies and practices can support the achievement of business strategies. It is business-led – HRD strategies flow from business strategies, but they have a positive role in helping to ensure that the business attains its goals. It is concerned with enhancing resource capability in accordance with the belief that a firm's human resources are a major source of competitive advantage. It is therefore about developing the intellectual capital required by the organization, as well as ensuring that the right quality of people is available to meet present and future needs.

STRATEGIC HRD AIMS

Strategic HRD aims to produce a coherent and comprehensive framework for developing people. Much of the HRD process will be geared to providing an environment in which employees are encouraged to learn and develop. HRD activities may include traditional training programmes but the emphasis is much more on developing intellectual capital and promoting organizational, team and individual learning. The focus is on creating an environment in which knowledge is developed and managed systematically. Strategic HRD is also about planning approaches to the encouragement of self-development (self-managed learning) with appropriate support and guidance from within the organization.

Although strategic HRD is business-led, its policies have to take into account individual aspirations and needs. The importance of increasing employability outside as well as within the organization should be a major HRD policy consideration.

HRD AND HRM

HRD policies are closely associated with that aspect of HRM which is concerned with investing in people and developing the organization's human capital. As Keep (1989) says:

> One of the primary objectives of HRM is the creation of conditions whereby the latent potential of employees will be realized and their commitment to the causes of the organization secured. This latent potential is taken to include, not merely the capacity to acquire and utilize new skills and knowledge, but also a hitherto untapped wealth of ideas about how the organization's operations might be better ordered.

ELEMENTS OF HRD

The key elements of human resource development are:

● *Learning* – defined by Bass and Vaughan (1966) as 'a relatively permanent change in behaviour that occurs as a result of practice or experience'.
● *Education* – the development of the knowledge, values and understanding required in all aspects of life rather than the knowledge and skills relating to particular areas of activity.
● *Development* – the growth or realization of a person's ability and potential through the provision of learning and educational experiences.

● *Training* – the planned and systematic modification of behaviour through learning events, programmes and instruction which enable individuals to achieve the levels of knowledge, skill and competence needed to carry out their work effectively.

HUMAN RESOURCE DEVELOPMENT PHILOSOPHY

A human resource development philosophy could be expressed in the following terms:

We believe that:

● Human resource development makes a major contribution to the successful attainment of the organization's objectives and that investment in it benefits all the stakeholders of the organization.
● Human resource development plans and programmes should be integrated with and support the achievement of business and human resource strategies.
● Human resource development should always be performance-related – designed to achieve specified improvements in corporate, functional, team and individual performance and make a major contribution to bottom-line results.
● Everyone in the organization should be encouraged and given the opportunity to learn – to develop their skills and knowledge to the maximum of their capacity.
● Personal development processes provide the framework for individual learning.
● While we recognize the need to invest in learning and development and to provide appropriate learning opportunities and facilities, the prime responsibility for development rests with the individual, who will be given the guidance and support of his or her manager and, as necessary, members of the HR department.

34

Organizational learning and the learning organization

Organizational learning theory is concerned with how learning takes place in organizations. It focuses on collective learning but takes into account the proposition made by Argyris (1992) that organizations do not perform the actions that produce the learning; it is individual members of the organization who behave in ways that lead to it, although organizations can create conditions which facilitate such learning. The concept of organizational learning as discussed in the first section of this chapter recognizes that the way in which this takes place is affected by the context of the organization and its culture.

The concept of a learning organization, which is often associated with that of organizational learning, has been defined by Scarborough and Carter (2000) as one 'that is able to discover what is effective by reframing its own experiences and learning from that process'. The notion of the learning organization as discussed in the second part of this chapter is sometimes confused with the concept of organizational learning. However, as Harrison (1997) points out: 'Too often ... it is assumed that the terms "the learning organization" and "organizational learning" are synonymous. They are not.'

ORGANIZATIONAL LEARNING

Organizational learning is concerned with the development of new knowledge or insights that have the potential to influence behaviour (Mabey and Salaman, 1995). It takes place within the wide institutional context of inter-organizational relationships (Geppert, 1996), and 'refers broadly to an organization's acquisition of understanding, know-how, techniques and practices of any kind and by any means' (Argyris and Schon, 1996). Organizational learning theory examines how in this context individual and team learning can be translated into an organizational resource and is therefore linked to processes of knowledge management (see Chapter 22).

Organizational learning has been defined by Marsick (1994) as a process of 'co-ordinated systems change, with mechanisms built in for individuals and groups to access, build and use organizational memory, structure and culture to develop long-term organizational capacity'.

It is emphasized by Harrison (2000) that organizational learning is not simply the sum of the learning of individuals and groups across the organization. She comments that: 'Many studies (see for example Argyris and Schon, 1996) have confirmed that without effective processes and systems linking individual and organizational learning, the one has no necessary counterpart with the other'.

Outcomes of organizational learning

Organizational learning outcomes contribute to the development of a firm's resource-based capability. This is in accordance with one of the basic principles of human resource management, namely that it is necessary to invest in people in order to develop the intellectual capital required by the organization and thus increase its stock of knowledge and skills. As stated by Ehrenberg and Smith (1994), human capital theory indicates that: 'The knowledge and skills a worker has – which comes from education and training, including the training that experience brings – generate productive capital'.

Pettigrew and Whipp (1991) believe that the focus of organizational learning should be on developing 'organizational capability'. This means paying attention to the intricate and often unnoticed or hidden learning that takes place and influences what occurs within the organization. 'Hidden learning' is acquired and developed in the normal course of work by people acting as individuals and, importantly, in groups or 'communities of practice' (Wenger and Snyder, 2000).

The process of organizational learning

Organizational learning can be characterized as an intricate three-stage process consisting of knowledge acquisition, dissemination and shared implementation (Dale, 1994). Knowledge may be acquired from direct experience, the experience of others or organizational memory.

Argyris (1992) suggests that organizational learning occurs under two conditions: first, when an organization achieves what is intended, and second, when a mismatch between intentions and outcomes is identified and corrected. He distinguishes between single-loop and double-loop learning. These two types of learning have been described by West (1996) as adaptive or generative learning.

Single-loop or adaptive learning is sequential, incremental and focused on issues and opportunities that are within the scope of the organization's activities. As described by Argyris (1992), organizations where single-loop learning is the norm define the 'governing variables' – what they expect to achieve in terms of targets and standards – and then monitor and review achievements, and take corrective action as necessary, thus completing the loop. Double-loop learning occurs when the monitoring process initiates action to redefine the 'governing variables' to meet the new situation, which may be imposed by the external environment. The organization has learnt something new about what has to be achieved in the light of changed circumstances, and can then decide how this should be achieved. This learning is converted into action. The process is illustrated in Figure 34.1.

Figure 34.1 Single- and double-loop learning

Argyris believes that single-loop learning is appropriate for routine, repetitive issues – 'it helps get the everyday job done'. Double-loop learning is more relevant for complex, non-programmable issues. As Pickard (1997) points out, double-loop learning questions why the problem occurred in the first place, and tackles its root causes, rather than simply addressing its surface symptoms, as happens with single-loop learning.

A model of the learning cycle developed by the New Work Consortium (1999) is given in Figure 34.2.

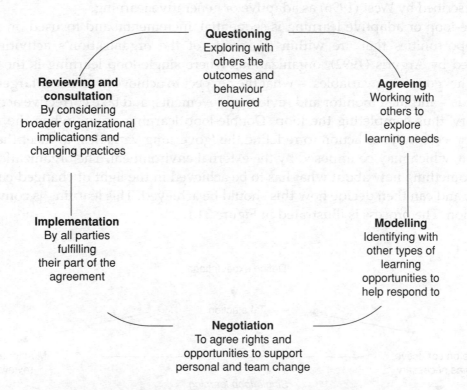

Figure 34.2 Managing learning to add value; the learning cycle

(Source: New Learning for New Work Consortium, *Managing Learning for Added Value*, IPD, 1999)

Principles of organizational learning

Harrison (1997) has defined five principles of organizational learning:

1. The need for a powerful and cohering vision of the organization to be communicated and maintained across the workforce in order to promote awareness of the need for strategic thinking at all levels.
2. The need to develop strategy in the context of a vision that is not only powerful but also open-ended and unambiguous. This will encourage a search for a wide rather than a narrow range of strategic options, will promote lateral thinking and will orient the knowledge creating activities of employees.
3. Within the framework of vision and goals, frequent dialogue, communication and conversations are major facilitators of organizational learning.
4. It is essential continuously to challenge people to re-examine what they take for granted.
5. It is essential to develop a conducive learning and innovation climate.

THE LEARNING ORGANIZATION

The philosophy underpinning the learning organization concept, as expressed by Garvin (1993), is that learning is an essential ingredient if organizations are to survive; that learning at operational, policy and strategic levels needs to be conscious, continuous and integrated; and that management is responsible for creating an emotional climate in which all staff can learn continuously.

Definition of a learning organization

Senge (1990), who first popularized the term, described a learning organization as one 'where people continually expand their capacity to create the results they truly desire, where new and expansive patterns of thinking are nurtured, where collective aspiration is set free, and where people are continually learning how to learn together'.

There have been many other definitions of a learning organization, all of which are aspirational in the vein of Senge. Pedler *et al* (1991) state that a learning organization is one 'which facilitates the learning of all its members and continually transforms itself'. Wick and Leon (1995) refer to a learning organization as one that 'continually improves by rapidly creating and refining the capabilities required for future success'.

Garvin (1993) defines a learning organization as one which is 'skilled at creating, acquiring, and transferring knowledge, and at modifying its behaviour to reflect new knowledge and insights'. He believes that learning organizations ensure that they learn from experience, develop continuous improvement programmes, use systematic problem-solving techniques, and transfer knowledge quickly and efficiently throughout the organization by means of formal training programmes linked to implementation.

As Burgoyne (1994) has pointed out, learning organizations have to be able to adapt to their context and develop their people to match the context. Many individual jobs could be learnt by processes of 'natural discovery' rather than formula learning. His definition (1988b) of a learning organization is that it channels the career and life-planning activities of individual managers in a way that allows the organization to meet its strategic needs. This is done by encouraging the identification of individual needs, organic formulation of business strategy with inputs from training departments on current skills, and continual organizational review and learning from experience. In 1999 he suggested that a learning organization 'provides a healthy environment for natural learning'.

A model of a learning organization

Kandola and Fullerton (1994) have produced a six factor model of a learning organization as follows:

1. *Shared vision* which enables the organization to identify, respond to and benefit from future opportunities.
2. *Enabling structure* which facilitates learning.
3. *Supportive culture* which encourages challenges to the status quo and the questioning of assumptions and established ways of doing things.
4. *Empowering management* – managers genuinely believe that devolved decision-making and better team-working result in improved performance.
5. *Motivated workforce* which wants to learn continuously.
6. *Enhanced learning* – processes and policies exist to encourage learning amongst all employees.

Developing a learning organization

One approach to the development of a learning organization, as advocated by Senge (1990), is to focus on collective problem-solving within an organization using team learning and a 'soft systems' approach whereby all the possible causes of a problem are considered in order to define more clearly those which can be dealt with and those which are insoluble.

Garratt (1990) believes that managers have to develop learning abilities as individuals, and work and learn as teams. He advocates the use of development activities such as job enlargement, job enrichment, monitoring, and various forms of team and project-based work.

The learning organization and knowledge management

Learning organizations are very much concerned with developing and sharing the knowledge that is critical to their strategic success. The problem is that it is hard to capture tacit knowledge in the form of the deeply embedded amalgam of wisdom and know-how that competitors are unable to copy. Methods of sharing knowledge were described in Chapter 22. One approach, as advocated by Wenger and Snyder (2000), is to encourage the development of 'communities of practice' in which people with similar concerns exchange ideas and knowledge and discuss shared problems. Wenger and Snyder claim that a community of practice could be treated as a 'learning ecology' with a life of its own in which there is scope to reflect jointly on experience so that it can be converted into learning.

Scarborough and Carter (2000) suggest that although the concepts of the learning organization and organizational learning have offered some valuable insights into the way in which knowledge and learning are fostered by management practice, they have been overshadowed, at least in terms of practitioner interest, by the explosive growth of knowledge management activity. They comment that:

> This may be attributable to the problems of translating their (knowledge management and organizational learning) broad, holistic principles into practice. Knowledge management initiatives by contrast, are often more specifically targeted and can therefore be identified more closely with business needs.

Problems with the concept of the learning organization

The notion of the learning organization remains persuasive because of its 'rationality, human attractiveness and presumed potential to aid organizational effectiveness and advancement' (Harrison, 2000). However, Scarborough et al (1999) argue that 'the dominant perspective (of the learning organization concept) is that of organization systems and design'. Little attention seems to be paid to what individuals want to learn or how they learn. The idea that individuals should be enabled to invest in their own development (a fundamental theme of human capital theory) seems to have escaped learning organization theorists, who are more inclined to focus on the imposition of learning by the organization, rather than creating a climate conducive to collaborative and self-managed learning.

Viewing organizations as learning systems is a limited notion. Argyris and Schon (1996) contend that organizations are products of visions, ideas, norms and beliefs so that their shape is much more fragile than the organization's material structure. People act as learning agents for the organization in ways that cannot easily be systematized. They are not only individual learners but also have the capacity to learn collaboratively (Hoyle, 1995). Organization learning theory analyses how this happens and leads to the belief that it is the culture and environment that are important, not the systems approach implied by the concept of the learning organization. Argyris and Schon (1996) refer to the practice-orientated and prescriptive literature of the learning organization, which is quite different from the concerns of organizational learning theorists about collaborative and informal learning processes within organizations.

The notion of a learning organization is somewhat nebulous. It incorporates miscellaneous ideas about human resource development, systematic training, action learning, organizational development and knowledge management, with an infusion of the precepts of total quality management. But they do not add up to a convincing whole. Easterby-Smith (1997) argues that attempts to create a single best-practice framework for understanding the learning organization are fundamentally flawed. Prescriptions from training specialists and management consultants abound but, as Sloman (1999) asserts, they often fail to recognize that learning is a continuous process, not a set of discrete training activities.

Burgoyne (1999), one of the earlier publicists for the idea of a learning organization, has admitted that there has been some confusion about the concept and that there have been substantial naiveties in most of the early thinking: 'The learning organization has not delivered its full potential or lived up to all our aspirations'. He also mentioned that after a decade of working with the notion of the learning organization there are distressingly few, if any, case studies of success with the idea on a large scale. He believes that the concept should be integrated with knowledge management initiatives so that different forms of knowledge can be linked, fed by organizational learning and used in adding value to goods and services. This, he states, will replace the 'soft' organizational development tools of the 1970s that were pressed hurriedly into service; 'The learning organization ran ahead of the methods available to implement it and into this vacuum were sucked traditional approaches such as teamworking, leadership and personal development.'

At least, however, the learning organization movement has helped to emphasize the importance of knowledge management as a practical proposition for promoting organizational learning. In added-value terms, this is likely to provide more benefit to organizations than pursuing the will-o'-the-wisp of the learning organization as originally conceived.

35

How people learn

The human resource development policies, strategies and practices of an organization must be driven by the business and human resource needs of the enterprise. The starting point should be the approaches adopted for the provision of learning and development opportunities, bearing in mind the distinction between learning and development made by Pedler *et al* (1989) who see learning as being concerned with an increase in knowledge or a higher degree of an existing skill, whereas development is about moving towards a different state of being or functioning. Such approaches should be based on an understanding of how people learn.

The question 'how do people learn?' is answered in this chapter by examining:

- the nature of learning;
- how learning takes place – the lessons from learning theory;
- requirements for effective learning;
- the distinction between formal and informal learning;
- the role of workplace learning;
- the notion of continuous development;
- the concept of self-managed learning.

The delivery of learning through formal training interventions and programmes is considered in the next chapter.

THE NATURE OF LEARNING

Learning has a number of key features as described in 'A declaration on learning' produced by a number of leading authorities on learning in organizations (Honey, 1998):

- Learning is complex and various, covering all sorts of things such as knowledge, skills, insights, beliefs, values, attitudes and habits.
- Learning is individual and can also be collectively generated in groups and organizations.
- Learning can be triggered by any experience – failures, successes and anything in between.
- Learning is both a process and an outcome.
- Learning may be incremental or it can be transformational.
- Learning can be conscious or unconscious.
- Learning can be both planned and unplanned.
- Learning outcomes may be desirable as well as undesirable.
- There can be no learning without change.
- Learning can be both the cause and the consequence of change.
- Learning has a moral dimension.

Learning and choice link the past to the present and create possibilities taking us from the known to the unknown. Learning for the future can give us options for sustainable development, clarity of vision and the values and the behaviour needed to achieve our purpose.

There is no one right way to learn, since a match is needed between diverse opportunities and learning style preferences. Whereas the learning process is essentially internal, making it explicit and sharing it with others adds value to the learning.

The effectiveness of how people learn can be improved. People, either singly or collectively in groups, teams and organizations, can learn to:

- analyse how they learn;
- adopt disciplines and routines to improve the way they learn;
- experiment and develop new ways of learning;
- learn from people around them;
- transfer learning to new situations.

Learning to learn is the most fundamental learning of all. When it is self-managed, learning becomes more effective and enjoyable.

HOW LEARNING TAKES PLACE

Argyris (1993) makes the point that: 'Learning is not simply having a new insight or a new idea. Learning occurs when we take effective action, when we detect and correct error. How do you know when you know something? When you can produce what it is you claim to know.'

Individuals learn for themselves and learn from other people. They learn as members of teams and by interaction with their managers, co-workers and people outside the organization. In the words of Birchall and Lyons (1995): 'For effective learning to take place at the individual level it is essential to foster an environment where individuals are encouraged to take risks and experiment, where mistakes are tolerated, but where means exist for those involved to learn from their experiences.'

To understand how people learn it is necessary to consider

- the learning process;
- the concept of the learning curve;
- the key factors of learning psychology;
- the main learning theories: reinforcement, stimulus-response, cognitive, self-efficacy;
- Kolb's learning cycle and learning styles;
- styles of learning (Honey and Mumford);
- learning to learn;
- how this learning theory can be put to good use – conditions for effective learning.

The learning process

There are three areas of learning:

- knowledge – what individuals need to know (cognitive learning);
- skill – what individuals need to be able to do;
- attitudes – what people feel about their work.

As described by Reay (1994), learning is a continuous and natural phenomenon. And the best learning is closely related to practical experience – doing things.

The learning curve

The concept of the learning curve refers to the time it takes an inexperienced person to reach the required level of performance in a job or a task. This is sometimes called the experienced worker's standard (EWS).

The standard learning curve is shown in Figure 35.1

Figure 35.1 A standard learning curve

But rates of learning vary, depending on the effectiveness of the training, the experience and natural aptitude of the learner, and the latter's interest in learning. Both the time taken to achieve the experienced worker's standard and the speed with which learning takes place at different times, which is likely to vary, affect the shape of the curve, as shown in Figure 35.2.

Learning is often stepped, with one or more plateaux while further progress is halted. This may be because learners cannot continually increase their skills or speeds of work and need a pause to consolidate what they have already learnt. The existence of steps such as those shown in Figure 35.3 can be used when planning training to provide deliberate reinforcement periods when newly acquired skills are practised in order to achieve the expected standards.

When a training module is being prepared, which describes what has to be learnt and the training required to achieve the required levels of skills and speed, it is often desirable to proceed step by step, taking one task or part of a task at a time, reinforcing it and then progressively adding other parts, consolidating at each stage. This is called the progressive parts method of training.

Key factors of learning psychology

The key factors of learning psychology as listed by Reay (1994) are:

Figure 35.2   Different rates of learning

- *Motivation or a sense of purpose* – people learn best when they see a worthwhile end-product to the process.
- *Relevance to personal interest and choice* – learning will be motivated best if it is seen as relevant by the learner.
- *Learning by doing* – the old saying is: 'I hear and forget. I see and remember. I do and understand.' Understanding is essential to effective performance and only doing can promote real understanding.
- *Freedom to make mistakes in safety* – learning by doing means that people run the risk of failure. Learning events or experiences must therefore ensure that individuals know that it is safe and permitted to fail, but trainers have to help them learn from their mistakes. As Samuel Beckett expressed it 'Try. Fail. Try again. Fail again. Fail better.'
- *Feedback* – learners need feedback on how they are doing but this is best provided by giving learners the means to evaluate their own progress, ie self-checking.
- *Freedom for learners to learn in their own time and at their own pace* – learning will be more effective if trainees can manage it themselves in accordance with their own preferences as to how it should progress.

Figure 35.3 A stepped learning curve

Learning theory

Reinforcement

Reinforcement involves commending learners when they have accomplished a task successfully, thus motivating them to extend their learning. Positive feedback and knowledge of results is an important way of ensuring that learning takes place. The concept of reinforcement has been strongly influenced by Skinner's (1974) conditioning and social engineering theories and, although they are sometimes criticized as being simplistic and manipulative, they continue to have a considerable effect on the design of training programmes.

Cybernetic and information theories

Cybernetic and information theories suggest that feedback can control people's performance in the same way that a thermostat controls a heating system. Learners react to cues of stimuli which, if they are established by means of skills analysis, can be used as the basis for training programmes. If a task can be divided into a number of small parts, each with its own cue or stimulus, the learning of each part can be accelerated by ensuring that trainees concentrate on one easily assimilated piece of learning at a time.

Cognitive theory

This describes the way in which people learn to recognize and define problems and experiment to provide solutions. If, according to this theory, people can discover things for themselves they are more likely to retain the skill or knowledge and use it when required. Cognitive theory is the basis for discovery, self-managed learning or 'do-it-yourself' processes. It provides the rationale for workshop, participative, and case study training, which help people to 'own' the solution as one they have worked out for themselves rather than something they have been forced to accept by the trainer.

Experiential learning

Experiential learning involves people reflecting on their experience in order to explain it and determine how it will be applied. Managers, team leaders and specialist trainers can help people to understand how best they can interpret and benefit from their experience.

Stimulus-response theory

This theory, as developed by Gagné (1977), relates the learning process to a number of factors, including reinforcement, namely:

- *Drive* – there must be a basic need or drive to learn.
- *Stimulus* – people must be stimulated by the learning process.
- *Response* – people must be helped by the learning process to develop appropriate responses; ie the knowledge, skills and attitudes that will lead to effective performance.
- *Reinforcement* – these responses need to be reinforced by feedback and experience until they are learnt.

Self-efficacy

The concept of self-efficacy as developed by Bandura (1977), refers to the belief of people in their capability to learn and perform a task. As Guest (1992b) has noted, a strong feeling of self-efficacy has been shown to be positively related to improvements in learning performance.

Kolb's learning cycle and learning styles

Kolb *et al* (1974) identified a learning cycle consisting of four stages as shown in Figure 35.4.

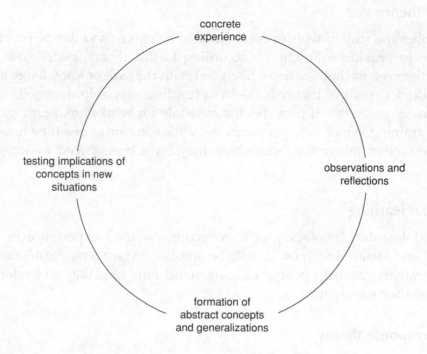

concrete
experience

observations and
reflections

formation of
abstract concepts
and generalizations

testing implications of
concepts in new
situations

Figure 35.4 The Kolb learning cycle

He defined these stages as follows:

1. *Concrete experience* – this can be planned or accidental.
2. *Reflective observation* – this involves actively thinking about the experience and its significance.
3. *Abstract conceptualization* (theorizing) – generalizing from experience in order to develop various concepts and ideas which can be applied when similar situations are encountered.
4. *Active experimentation* – testing the concepts or ideas in new situations. This gives rise to a new concrete experience and the cycle begins again.

The key to Kolb's model is that it is a simple description of how experience is translated into concepts which are then used to guide the choice of new experiences. To learn effectively, individuals must shift from being observers to participants, from direct involvement to a more objective analytical detachment. Every person has his or her own learning style and one of the most important arts that trainers have to develop is to adjust their approaches to the learning styles of trainees. Trainers must acknowledge these learning styles rather than their own preferred approach.

Kolb also defined the following learning styles of learners:

- *Accommodators* learn by trial and error, combining the concrete experience and experimentation stages of the cycle.
- *Divergers* prefer concrete to abstract learning situations and reflection to active involvement. Such individuals have great imaginative ability, and can view a complete situation from different viewpoints.
- *Convergers* prefer to experiment with ideas, considering them for their practical usefulness. Their main concern is whether the theory works in action, thus combining the abstract and experimental dimensions.
- *Assimilators* like to create their own theoretical models and assimilate a number of disparate observations into an overall integrated explanation. Thus they veer towards the reflective and abstract dimensions.

Learning styles

Another analysis of learning styles was made by Honey and Mumford (1986). They identified four styles:

- *Activists* involve themselves fully without bias in new experiences and revel in new challenges.
- *Reflectors* stand back and observe new experiences from different angles. They collect data, reflect on it and then come to a conclusion.
- *Theorists* adapt and apply their observations in the form of logical theories. They tend to be perfectionists.
- *Pragmatists* are keen to try out new ideas, approaches and concepts to see if they work.

However, none of these four learning styles is exclusive. It is quite possible that one person could be both a reflector and a theorist and someone else could be an activist/pragmatist, a reflector/pragmatist or even a theorist/pragmatist.

Learning to learn

People learn all the time and through doing so acquire knowledge, skills and insight. But they will learn more effectively if they 'learn how to learn'.

As defined by Honey (1998), the process of learning to learn is the acquisition of knowledge, skills and insights about the learning process itself. The aims, as described by Honey, are to:

- provide a basis for organizing and planning learning;
- pinpoint precisely what has been learnt and what to do better or differently as a consequence;
- share what has been learnt with other people so that they benefit;
- check on the quality of what has been learnt;
- transfer what has been learnt and apply it in different circumstances;
- improve the learning process itself so that how people learn, not just what people learn, is given constant attention.

Honey suggests that people can learn to learn by going round the stages in the learning cycle twice, as illustrated in Figure 35.5.

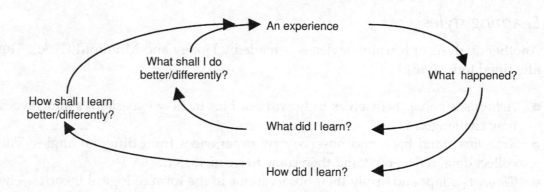

Figure 35.5   The learning to learn cycle

(Source: P Honey 'Learning to learn', presentation at IPD Annual Conference, Harrogate, 29 October 1999)

REQUIREMENTS FOR EFFECTIVE LEARNING

Learning is more likely to be effective if the following five requirements are met:

1. *The learner is motivated to learn.* This may be self-motivation or motivation as a result of the encouragement or stimulation of another person – a manager, a mentor or a trainer.

2. *The culture of the organization encourages and supports learning.* The concept of a learning organization may be somewhat nebulous but at least it emphasizes that the organization should aim to develop a culture and processes which encourage learning.
3. *Learners will benefit from guidance, encouragement, support and feedback.* All learners, even those who are largely self-motivated, will benefit if they are helped to define and satisfy their learning needs.
4. *Learning will be enhanced if note is taken of the lessons provided by learning theory.* This means paying attention to the concept of the learning curve (learning is a gradual and possibly step-by-step process) and the key factors of learning psychology as set out later in this chapter.
5. *Learning will be most effective when it satisfies the learner's needs.* People are capable of learning in many different circumstances if they expect that it will meet their needs for achievement, growth, recognition and employability.

INFORMAL LEARNING

Informal learning is experiential learning. Most learning does not take place in formal training programmes. This was the conclusion of a US Department of Labor report in 1996 which indicated that people learn 70 per cent of what they know about their job informally, through processes not structured or sponsored by the company.

Informal learning occurs in the workplace as discussed in the next section of this chapter. The characteristics of informal and formal learning as described by Davenport (1999) are summarized in Table 35.1.

The advantages of informal learning are:

● Learning efforts are relevant and focused in immediate environment.
● Understanding can be achieved in incremental steps rather than in indigestible chunks.
● Learners define how they will gain the knowledge they need – formal learning is more packaged.

The disadvantages are that:

● It may be left to chance – some people will benefit, some won't.
● It is by definition unplanned and unsystematic which means that it will not necessarily satisfy the learning needs either of the individual or the organization.
● Learners may simply pick up bad habits.

Table 35.1 Characteristics of formal and informal learning

Informal	Formal
Highly relevant to individual needs	Relevant to some, not so relevant to others
Learners learn according to need	All learners learn the same thing
May be small gap between current and target knowledge	May be valuable gaps between current and target knowledge
Learner decides how learning will occur	Trainer decides how learning will occur
Immediate applicability ('Just-in-time' learning)	Variable times, often distant
Learning readily transferable	Problems may occur in transferring learning to the workplace
Occurs in work setting	Often occurs in non-work setting

Research conducted by the Centre for Workforce Development (1998) established that informal learning is often best achieved in a team setting. The environment most likely to support informal learning in teams will be one in which the team has a reasonable degree of autonomy, the culture is open and supportive, there are diverse perspectives amongst team members which are supported by a climate of tolerance for risk-taking, and the team is competent at collective problem-solving.

WORKPLACE LEARNING

Approaches to workplace learning

Workplace learning can, as explained by Stern and Sommerlad (1999) take place in three forms. These are:

1. *The workshop as a site for learning.* In this case, learning and working are spatially separated with some form of structured learning activity occurring off or near the job. This may be in a company training centre or a 'training island' on the shop floor where the production process is reproduced for trainees.
2. *The workplace as a learning environment.* In this approach, the workplace itself becomes an environment for learning. Various on-the-job training activities take

place which are structured to different degrees. Learning is intentional and planned, aimed at training employees by supporting, structuring and monitoring their learning.

3. *Learning and working are inextricably mixed*. In this case, learning becomes an everyday part of the job and is built into routine tasks. Workers develop skills, knowledge and understanding through dealing with the challenges posed by the work. This can be described as continuous learning. As Zuboff (1988) put it: 'Learning is not something that requires time out from being engaged in productive activity; learning is the heart of productive activity.'

The continuous learning work environment provided by the third approach is regarded by some commentators as a feature of a learning organization.

Informal workshop learning could be regarded as no more than what used to be called 'the sitting by Nellie' approach in which learning was left to chance or mischance. The 'training revolution' in the 1960s when the training boards were established aimed to replace this haphazard approach by 'systematic training' as described in the next chapter. The wheel now seems to have come full circle and the perspective has shifted from training to workshop learning.

A study by Eraut *at al* (1998) established that in organizations adopting a learner-centred perspective, formal education and training provided only a small part of what was learned at work. Most of the learning described to the researchers was non-formal, neither clearly specified nor planned. It arose naturally from the challenges of work. Effective learning was, however, dependent on the employees' confidence, motivation and capability. Some formal training to develop skills (especially induction training) was usually provided, but learning from experience and other people at work predominated.

Continuous learning spectrum

The spectrum of continuous learning in the workplace from informal to formal as set out by Watkins and Marsick (1993) is:

- unanticipated experiences and encounters that result in learning as an incidental by-product, which may or may not be consciously recognized;
- new job assignments and participation in teams, or other job-related challenges that are used for learning and self-development;
- self-initiated and self-planned experiences, including the use of media and seeking out a coach or mentor;
- total quality or improvement groups/active learning designed to promote continuous learning for continuous improvement;

- planning a framework for learning associated with career planning, or personal development planning;
- the combination of less-structured with structured opportunity to learn from these experiences;
- designed programmes of mentoring, coaching or on-the-job training;
- just-in-time courses delivered in classrooms, or through self-learning packages, with or without the assistance of technology;
- formal training programmes which may lead to a qualification.

What the organization can do

It is up to the organization to assess how learning in the workplace can contribute to the achievement of business objectives by ensuring that the workforce has the necessary skills. The main concerns of management should be to:

- enhance the challenge of work itself through job design and creating the right environment for learning in the workplace;
- develop the skills of managers, supervisors and key workers in supporting and facilitating learning;
- encourage team learning and the sharing of learning which could include the development of knowledge management strategies and the creation of 'communities of practice' to capture informal learning;
- dovetail formal training in basic skills with informal learning;
- create a learning culture – one in which it is recognized that learning is important, and which is characterized by positive initiatives from management to encourage and support learning on or off the job by, for example, encouraging key workers to facilitate learning and rewarding them for their contribution to the learning processes in their places of work, or setting up open learning centres (and providing time off for attending them).

CONTINUOUS LEARNING AND DEVELOPMENT

As Harrison (1997) comments: 'In organizational life, everyday experience is the most fundamental influence on learning. This experience consists not simply of the work that people do, but of the way they interact with others in the organization, and the behaviour, attitudes and values of these others.'

It follows that when work is continuous, development can be continuous as people reflect on and learn from their experience. But this is more likely to happen if reflection and learning is encouraged and, to a reasonable degree, structured within a performance and development management framework. The IPD has commented as follows in its code of practice on continuous development: 'As far as practicable, learning and work must be integrated. This means that encouragement must be given to all employees to learn from the problems, challenges and successes inherent in their day-to-day activities.'

SELF-MANAGED LEARNING

Self-managed or self-directed learning means that individuals take responsibility for satisfying their own learning needs to improve performance, to support the achievement of career aspirations, or to enhance their employability, within and beyond their present organization. It can be based on processes that enable individuals to identify what they need to learn by reflecting on their experience and analysing what they need to know and be able to do so that they can perform better and progress their careers.

It has been argued by Knowles (1989) that all individuals may naturally be self-directed learners, even if they may need some help initially to get started. As Harrison (1997) has noted, 'no new learning will occur unless there is a stimulus to activate the learning process'.

Self-managed learning is about self-development and this will be furthered by self-assessment which leads to better self-understanding. Pedler *et al* (1989) recommended the following four-stage approach:

1. *Self-assessment* based on analysis by individuals of their work and life situation.
2. *Diagnosis* derived from the analysis of learning needs and priorities.
3. *Action planning* to identify objectives, helps and hindrances, resources required (including people) and time scales.
4. *Monitoring and review* to assess progress in achieving action plans.

Mumford (1994) suggests that self-managed learning can be carried out as follows:

- Identify the individual's learning styles.
- Review how far their learning is encouraged or restricted by their learning style.
- Review their core learning skills of observation and reflection, analysis, creativity, decision making and evaluation, and consider how to use them more effectively.
- Review the work and other experiences in which they are involved in terms of the kind of learning opportunity they offer.

- Look for potential helpers in the self-development process: managers, colleagues, trainers, or mentors (ie individuals other than the manager or a trainer who provide guidance and advice).
- Draw up learning objectives and a plan of action – a personal development plan or learning contract.
- Set aside some time each day to answer the question 'What did you learn today?'

Pedler *et al*'s concept of analysis and diagnosis and Mumford's belief in the value of reviewing work to identify learning opportunities have contributed to a better understanding of the developmental aspects of performance management. The focus is first on the real work that people do now and might do in the future and what they need to learn to do it, and on getting them to understand how this learning can be accomplished.

But it is still recognized that there has to be stimulus and there may well have to be help and guidance. And this is where performance management comes in.

Self-managed learning is based on the principle that people learn and retain more if they find things out for themselves. But they may still need to be given direction on what to look for and help in finding it. Such direction can be provided through performance management processes as described in Part VIII, in which the performance agreement can incorporate a personal learning/development plan as described in Chapter 37 but which also sets out the help the learner will receive from the manager and the organization.

The plan can be expressed in the form of a *learning agreement or contract*. This is an agreement, usually in writing, between individuals and their managers and, often, a trainer or mentor, to achieve a specified learning objective. The partners to the contract agree on how the objectives will be achieved and their respective roles. The need is to create a climate of awareness about the opportunities for learning and development and to design learning events to develop learning styles and skills.

In particular, the organization can encourage self-managed learning by ensuring that learners:

- define for themselves, with whatever guidance they may require, what they need to know to perform their job effectively;
- are given guidance on where they can get the material or information that will help them to learn;
- prepare a learning plan and programme as part of a learning contract;
- prepare a personal development plan as described in Chapter 37, setting out what they need to learn, how they should develop and the actions they need to take to achieve learning and development goals.

36

Training

DEFINITION

Training is the formal and systematic modification of behaviour through learning which occurs as a result of education, instruction, development and planned experience.

AIM

The fundamental aim of training is to help the organization achieve its purpose by adding value to its key resource – the people it employs. Training means investing in people to enable them to perform better and to empower them to make the best use of their natural abilities. The particular objectives of training are to:

● develop the skills and competences of employees and improve their performance;
● help people to grow within the organization in order that, as far as possible, its future needs for human resources can be met from within;
● reduce the learning time for employees starting in new jobs on appointment, transfer or promotion, and ensure that they become fully competent as quickly and economically as possible.

BENEFITS

Effective training can:

- minimize learning costs;
- improve individual, team and corporate performance in terms of output, quality, speed and overall productivity;
- improve operational flexibility by extending the range of skills possessed by employees (multi-skilling);
- attract high-quality employees by offering them learning and development opportunities, increasing their levels of competence and enhancing their skills, thus enabling them to obtain more job satisfaction to gain higher rewards and to progress within the organization;
- increase the commitment of employees by encouraging them to identify with the mission and objectives of the organization;
- help to mange change by increasing understanding of the reasons for change and providing people with the knowledge and skills they need to adjust to new situations;
- help to develop a positive culture in the organization, one, for example, that is orientated towards performance improvement;
- provide higher levels of service to customers.

UNDERSTANDING TRAINING

To understand how training should be developed and operated within an organization, the first requirement is to appreciate learning theory and approaches to providing learning and development opportunities in organizations as discussed in Chapter 35. It is then necessary to appreciate the following approaches to training as described in this chapter:

- training philosophy – the basis upon which training philosophies and policies should be developed;
- the process of training – how criteria for effective training, systematic training programmes and interventions can be planned, implemented and evaluated;
- identifying training needs – establishing what type of training is required and ensuring that it is relevant to the requirements of individuals and the organization;

- planning training – deciding how the longer- and shorter-term training needs of the organization and the teams and individuals working in it can be satisfied and selecting and using training techniques;
- conducting training – running training programmes for different categories of employees;
- responsibility for training – determining who plans and executes training programmes;
- evaluating training – establishing the extent to which training is achieving objectives by satisfying training needs.

TRAINING PHILOSOPHY

The training philosophy of an organization expresses the degree of importance it attaches to training. Some firms adopt a laissez-faire approach, believing that employees will find out what to do for themselves or through, in the old phrase, 'sitting by Nellie'. If this sort of firm suffers a skill shortage, it is remedied by recruiting from firms who do invest in training.

Other companies pay lip service to training and indiscriminately allocate money to it in the good times. but in the bad times these firms are the first to cut their training budgets.

Organizations with a positive training philosophy understand that they live in a world where competitive advantage is achieved by having higher-quality people than other firms employ, and that this need will not be satisfied unless they invest in developing the skills and competence of their people. They also recognize that actual or potential skills shortages can threaten their future prosperity and growth. In hard commercial terms, these firms persuade themselves that training is an investment that will pay off. They understand that it may be difficult to calculate the return on that investment but they believe that the tangible and intangible benefits of training, as described earlier in this chapter, will more than justify the cost.

It is not enough to believe in training as an act of faith. This belief must be supported by a positive and realistic philosophy of how training contributes to the bottom line. Underpinning this belief is the need to set hard objectives for training in terms of a return on investment in the same way as other investments have to demonstrate a pay-back. The areas in which such a philosophy should be developed are described below.

A strategic approach to training

Training strategy takes a long-term view of what skills, knowledge and levels of competence employees of the company need. Training philosophy emphasizes that training and development should be an integral part of the management process. Performance management requires managers to review regularly, with their teams and the individuals reporting to them, performance in relation to agreed objectives, the factors that have affected performance and the development and training needs that emerge from this analysis. The satisfaction of these needs is a joint process between managers, teams and individuals by means of coaching, counselling and relevant learning and training activities and interventions. Performance management leads to personal development plans and learning agreements or contracts.

Relevant

While some organizations do not go in for training at all, others have tended to go in for 'training for training's sake'. Although in times of recession this may be less likely, there is still the risk of organizations committing themselves to training in areas where the benefits in terms of improved performance in key activity areas have not been spelt out. Training must be relevant in that it satisfies identified and appropriate training needs.

Problem-based

Training should be problem-based in the sense that it should be planned to fill the gaps between what people can do and what they need to do, now and in the future. The problem may be a negative one in the form of a weakness that needs to be remedied. Or it may be positive because it refers to how the need to develop new skills or enhance knowledge to meet future requirements will be satisfied.

Action-orientated

Training philosophy should stress that training exists to make things happen, to get people into action, and to ensure that they can do things they are doing now better or will be able to do things that they could not do before. The objectives of any training event or programme should be defined in terms of 'deliverables' – this is what people will be able to do after training, and this is what they will achieve.

Performance-related training

A performance-related training philosophy involves relating training specifically to performance and competence requirements – for example, those following the introduction of a new product, process or system.

Continuous development

Training should not be regarded as simply the provision of short, isolated courses at various points in a person's career. Learning is a continuous process and a policy of continuous development as described in Chapter 33 should be pursued.

Training policies

Training policies are expressions of the training philosophy of the organization. They provide guidelines on the amount of training that should be given (eg everyone in managerial, professional, technical or supervisory positions should undergo at least five days' formal training every year), the proportion of turnover that should be allocated to training, the scope and aims of training schemes, and the responsibility for training.

THE PROCESS OF TRAINING

Conditions for effective training

Learning theory suggests that there are ten main conditions required for training to be effective:

1. *Individuals must be motivated to learn.* They should be aware that their present level of knowledge, skill or competence, or their existing attitude or behaviour, needs to be improved if they are to perform their work to their own and to others' satisfaction. They must, therefore, have a clear picture of the behaviour they should adopt.
2. *Standards of performance should be set for learners.* Learners must have clearly defined targets and standards which they find acceptable and can use to judge their own progress.
3. *Learners should have guidance.* They need a sense of direction and feedback on how they are doing. Self-motivated individuals may provide much of this for themselves, but the trainer should still be available to encourage and help when necessary.

4. *Learners must gain satisfaction from learning.* They are capable of learning under the most difficult circumstances if the learning is satisfying to one or more of their needs. Conversely, the best training schemes can fail if they are not seen as useful by the trainee.

5. *Learning is an active, not a passive process.* Learners need to be actively involved with their trainer, their fellow trainees and the subject matter of the training programme.

6. *Appropriate techniques should be used.* Trainers have a large repertory of training tools and materials. But they must use these with discrimination in accordance with the needs of the job, the individual and the group.

7. *Learning methods should be varied.* The use of a variety of techniques, as long as they are equally appropriate, helps learning by maintaining the interest of trainees.

8. *Time must be allowed to absorb the learning.* Learning requires time to assimilate, test and accept. This time should be provided in the training programme. Too many trainers try to cram too much into their programmes and allow insufficient scope for practice and familiarization.

9. *The learner must receive reinforcement of correct behaviour.* Learners usually need to know quickly that they are doing well. In a prolonged training programme, intermediate steps are required in which learning can be reinforced.

10. *It must be recognized that there are different levels of learning and that these need different methods and take different times.* In order of increasing complexity, the four levels are:
    - At the simplest level, learning requires direct physical responses, memorization and basic conditioning.
    - At a higher level, learning involves adapting existing knowledge or skill to a new task or environment.
    - At the next level, learning becomes a complex process when principles are identified in a range of practices or actions, when a series of isolated tasks have to be integrated or when the training deals with interpersonal skills.
    - The most complex form of learning takes place when training is concerned with the values and attitudes of people and groups. This is not only the most complex area, but also the most difficult and dangerous.

Systematic training

The concept of systematic training was originated by the Industrial Training Boards in the late 1960s. Systematic training is training which is specifically designed to meet defined needs. It is planned and provided by people who know how to train and the impact of training is carefully evaluated.

Systematic training is based on a simple four-stage model expressed as follows:

- Define training needs.
- Decide what sort of training is required to satisfy these needs.
- Use experience and trained trainers to plan and implement training.
- Follow up and evaluate training to ensure that it is effective.

The model provides a good basis for planning training programmes; but it is over-simplified – training is a more complex process than this. Another drawback to the concept of systematic training is that insufficient emphasis is placed on the responsibilities of managers and individuals for training. And under the influence of the training boards, a 'training industry' developed in the 1970s which imposed or tried to impose over-elaborate and bureaucratic routines on industry and commerce, an 'industry' which, understandably, was largely dismantled. But the essential validity of the concept of systematic training was not destroyed by the fact that it was badly implemented. What needed to be done was to develop a more realistic approach, which is described below as 'planned training'.

Planned training

Planned training, as defined by Kenney and Reid (1994), is a 'deliberate intervention aimed at achieving the learning necessary for improved job performance'. The process of planned training, as shown in Figure 36.1, consists of the following steps:

1. *Identify and define training needs* – this involves analysis of corporate, team, occupational and individual needs to acquire new skills or knowledge or to improve existing competences. The analysis covers problems to be solved as well as future demands. Decisions are made at this stage on the extent to which training is the best and most cost-effective way to solve the problem.
2. *Define the learning required* – it is necessary to specify as clearly as possible what skills and knowledge have to be learnt, what competences need to be developed and what attitudes need to be changed.
3. *Define the objectives of training* – learning objectives are set which define not only what has to be learnt but also what learners must be able to do after their training programme.
4. *Plan training programmes* – these must be developed to meet the needs and objectives by using the right combination of training techniques and locations.
5. *Decide who provides the training* – the extent to which training is provided from

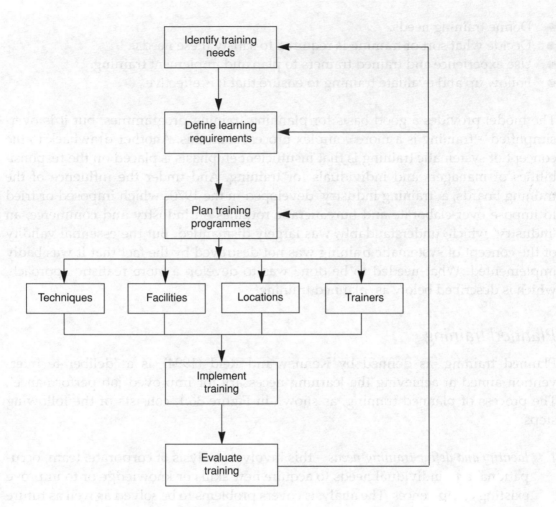

Figure 36.1 The process of planned training

within or outside the organization needs to be decided. At the same time, the division of responsibility between the training department, managers or team leaders and individuals has to be determined.

6. *Implement the training* – ensure that the most appropriate methods are used to enable trainees to acquire the skills, knowledge, levels of competence and attitudes they need.

7. *Evaluate training* – the effectiveness of training is monitored during programmes and, subsequently, the impact of training is assessed to determine the extent to which learning objectives have been achieved.

8. *Amend and extend training as necessary* – decide, on the basis of evaluation, the extent to which the planned training programme needs to be improved and how any residual learning requirements should be satisfied.

The systems approach to planned training

The training process just described will work effectively only if it is fully integrated with the systems of relationships, structures, interdependence and work in the organization. A systems approach to training has been defined by the Manpower Services Commission (1981) as the process of:

> Identifying inputs, outputs, components and sub-systems, and then seeking to identify the contribution that training can make to improving the operation by enhancing the contribution of the human components (people) as opposed to machinery and operational procedures. The systems approach is next applied to the training design, where the components are learning strategies and people, and the objectives are in terms of learning. Finally, the systems approach is applied to the interaction between training and the operation to produce a feedback which can be used to improve subsequent training.

A systems approach requires those concerned with the preparation of training plans to take account of all the factors and variables that might affect learning. In other words, the programme of training for a job in one part of the organization might be affected by events elsewhere, within or outside the company, and the design of the course must take into account these interactions.

IDENTIFYING LEARNING AND TRAINING NEEDS

Training must have a purpose and that purpose can be defined only if the learning needs of the organization and the groups and individuals within it have been systematically identified and analysed.

Training needs analysis – aims

Training needs analysis is partly concerned with defining the gap between what is happening and what should happen. This is what has to be filled by training (see Figure 36.2), ie the difference between what people know and can do and what they *should* know and be able to do.

However, it is necessary to avoid falling into the trap of adopting the 'deficiency model' approach, which implies that training is only about putting things right that

Figure 36.2 The training gap

have gone wrong. Training is much more positive than that. It is, or should be, more concerned with identifying and satisfying learning and development needs – multi-skilling, fitting people to take on extra responsibilities, increasing all-round competence and preparing people to take on higher levels of responsibility in the future.

Training needs analysis – areas

Training needs should be analysed, first, for the organization as a whole – corporate needs; second, for departments, teams, functions or occupations within the organization – group needs; and third, for individual employees – individual needs. These three areas are interconnected, as shown in Figure 36.3. The analysis of corporate needs will lead to the identification of training needs in different departments or occupations, while these in turn will indicate the training required for individual employees. The process also operates in reverse. As the needs of individual employees are analysed separately, common needs emerge which can be dealt with on a group basis. The sum of group and individual needs will help to define corporate needs, although there may be some superordinate training requirements which can be related only to the company as a whole to meet its business development needs – the whole training plan may be greater than the sum of its parts.

Sources of information

Walters (1983) identifies nine sources of information which help to identify training priorities. These are:

Figure 36.3 Training needs analysis – areas and methods

1. *Organizational goals and corporate plans* which indicate the direction in which the organization is going and, therefore, major training priorities.
2. *Human resource and succession planning* which provides information on future skill requirements and management training needs.
3. *Personnel statistics* on, for example, labour turnover, which highlight HR issues which might be addressed by training.
4. *Exit interviews* which might suggest deficiencies in training arrangements.
5. *Consultation with senior managers* which obtains opinions on training needs from key decision makers.
6. *Data on productivity, quality and performance* which show where there are any gaps between expectations and results or negative trends, and therefore suggest training needs.
7. *Departmental layout changes* which provide information about future developments and related training needs.
8. *Management requests* for training which set out perceived needs.
9. *Knowledge of financial plans* which determines whether the funds will be available for training, and may encourage fresh approaches if resources are limited.

Two other sources not directly mentioned by Walters are plans for introducing new technology or developing IT systems, and marketing plans which indicate where new skills are required to market new products or services, use different selling techniques or operate in new territories.

Methods of analysing training needs

These sources provide the basis for the detailed analysis of training needs using the methods described below.

Business and human resource plans

The training strategy of an organization should largely be determined by its business and HR strategies and plans, including plans for the introduction of new technology, from which flow human resource plans. The plans should indicate in fairly general terms the types of skills and competences that may be required in the future and the numbers of people with those skills and competences who will be needed. These broad indicators have to be translated into more specific plans which cover, for example, the outputs from training programmes of people with particular skills or a combination of skills (multi-skilling).

Job analysis

Job analysis for training purposes means examining in detail the content of jobs, the performance standards required in terms of quality and output and the knowledge, skills and competences needed to perform the job competently and thus meet the performance standards.

The techniques of job, skills and competence analysis were described in Chapter 23. For training purposes, it would be necessary to ensure that the information obtained from this analysis specifies:

- any problems faced by job holders in learning the basic skills and applying them successfully;
- any weaknesses in the performance of existing job holders arising from gaps in knowledge, lack of skill or poor motivation which needs to be rectified by training;
- any areas where competence levels are clearly not up to the standard required;
- any areas where future changes in work processes, methods or job responsibilities indicate a learning need;
- how training is carried out at present – and how effective it is.

The output of the job analysis should be a training or learning specification, as described below.

Training and learning specifications

A training or a learning specification is a product of job analysis. It breaks down the broad duties contained in the job description into the detailed tasks that must be carried out. It then sets out the characteristics or attributes that the individual should have in order to perform these tasks successfully. These characteristics are:

- *Knowledge* – what the individual needs to know. It may be professional, technical or commercial knowledge. Or it may be about the commercial, economic, or market environment; the machines to be operated; the materials or equipment to be used or the procedures to be followed; or the customers, clients, colleagues and subordinates he or she is in contact with and the factors that affect their behaviour. Or it may refer to the problems that occur and how they should be dealt with.
- *Skills* – what the individual needs to be able to do if results are to be achieved and knowledge is to be used effectively. Skills are built progressively by repeated training or other experience. They may be manual, intellectual or mental, perceptual or social.
- *Competences* – the behaviour competences needed to achieve the levels of performance required.
- *Attitudes* – the disposition to behave or to perform in a way that is in accordance with the requirements of the work.
- *Performance standards* – what the fully competent individual has to be able to achieve. A learning specification as illustrated in Figure 36.4 may be produced for trainees or new starters.

Performance reviews

Performance management processes, as described in Part VII, should be a prime source of information about individual learning and development needs. The performance management approach to learning concentrates on the preparation of performance improvement programmes and learning contracts or personal development plans, which are related to jointly determined action plans. The emphasis is on continuous development. Every contact between managers and individuals throughout the year is regarded as a learning opportunity.

LEARNING SPECIFICATION	
Role title: Product Manager	Department: Marketing

What the role holder must understand

Learning outcomes	Learning methods
• The book club market	• Coaching: Marketing Manager and Advertising Manager
• Market research availability	• Coaching: Market Research Manager
• Interpretation of marketing data	• Coaching: Operations Research Manager
• Book club fulfilment operations	• Coaching: Fulfilment Manager
• Creative department operations	• Coaching: Creative Group Leader
• Book ordering and stock control	• Coaching: Book Production Manager
• Practice of direct marketing and data based marketing	• Institute of Direct Marketing courses

What the role holder must be able to do

Learning outcomes	Learning methods
• Prepare club budget	• Coaching: Budget Accountant
• Prepare marketing plans	• Coaching: Mentor
• Conduct tests	• Coaching: Operations Research Department
• Prepare member recruitment campaigns	• Read: Product Manager's Manual
• Select advertisement lead lists and one shots	• Read: Product Manager's Manual
• Specify requirements for advertisements and leaflets	• Coaching: Club Editor and Inventory Manager
	• Coaching: Mentor, Creative Group Leader
• Analyse results of recruitment campaigns	• Read previous analyses
• Prepare marketing reports Coaching: Mentor	• Read: previous reports, observe: marketing review meetings

Notes on learning methods

• Mentoring provided by Marketing Manager and designated Senior Product Manager
• Induction programme prepared by Training and Development Manager
• Additional training courses to be planned as appropriate in project management, report writing, presentation skills, and assertiveness
• Review of progress made by Marketing Manager and Training and Development Manager
• Product Manager to manage own learning in accordance with programme

Figure 36.4 Example of a learning specification

Training surveys

Training surveys assemble all the information obtained from the other methods of analysis in order to provide a comprehensive basis for the development of a training strategy and its implementation. But it is essential to supplement that information by talking to people. The best way to start is to discuss their work requirements and problems and develop an understanding of their training needs by reference to what they tell you about work issues. People often find it difficult to articulate their training needs and can easily provide irrelevant information. But they are usually willing to talk about their work.

A training survey pays particular attention to the extent to which existing training arrangements are meeting training needs. Further information can be derived from training evaluations, as described later in this chapter.

Attitude surveys can be used to obtain the opinions of employees about the present amount and level of training provision.

PLANNING TRAINING PROGRAMMES

Every training programme needs to be designed individually, and the design will continually evolve as new learning needs emerge, or when feedback indicates that changes are required. Before consideration is given to special aspects of training programmes for managers, team leaders, craft and technical trainees, and office staff, decisions are necessary in the areas discussed below.

Objectives

It is essential to consider carefully the objectives of the training programme – ie the learning outcomes. Objectives can be defined as 'criterion behaviour', ie the standards or changes of behaviour on the job to be achieved if training is to be regarded as successful. This should be a definition of what the trainee will be able to do when he or she goes back to work on completing the course; in other words, terminal behaviour. Transfer of learning is what counts; behaviour on the job is what matters. Training objectives are best expressed as follows:

> On completing the training (or this part of the course) the trainee will be able to... (read a balance sheet, program a microcomputer, operate a word processor, work to a high degree of accuracy, etc).

Content

The content of the training programme should be determined entirely by the learning and training needs analysis and an assessment of what needs to be done to achieve the agreed training objectives.

Length

The length of the training programme obviously depends on its content. But careful consideration should be given as to how learning can be speeded up by the use of techniques such as computer-based training. Thought should also be given to where more time needs to be allowed for 'discovery learning' to take place, or for the amount of involvement required to ensure that those undergoing training have the opportunity fully to understand and 'own' the new ideas or techniques to which they have been exposed.

Where should training take place?

There are three places where training can take place: in-company, on-the-job, off-the-job; and external, off-the-job. Each has its uses, and its advantages and disadvantages as discussed below.

In-company, on-the-job

In-company, on-the-job training may consist of teaching or coaching by managers, team leaders or trainers at the desk or at the bench. It may also consist of individual or group assignments and projects and the use of mentors (see Appendix A). It is the only way to develop and practise the specific managerial, team leading, technical, selling, manual, and adminstrative skills needed by the organization. It has the advantage of actuality and immediacy. The individual works, learns and develops expertise at the same time. Theory is put into practice immediately and its relevance is obvious. Much of the learning can take place naturally as part of the performance management process and through day-to-day contacts although it will be most effective if specific learning objectives have been articulated.

The disadvantages are that the effectiveness of the learning is strongly influenced by the quality of the guidance and coaching provided on the job. Many managers and team leaders are unskilled at training and disinclined to carry it out or to encourage it. The instruction may be inadequate and the training may perpetuate bad habits. Above all, the learner may be distracted by the environment and find it difficult to acquire the basic skills quickly. To overcome this problem, it is essential to provide training to managers and team leaders on how to train and even more important, to stress that this is expected of them as a key part of their jobs and will be one of the areas in which their performance will be measured.

In-company, off-the-job

In-company, off-the-job training can take place on special courses or in training areas or centres which have been specially equipped and staffed for training. It is the best way to acquire advanced manual, office, customer service or selling skills and to learn about company procedures and products. It helps to increase the identification of the trainee with the company as a whole, and the use of systematic training techniques, special equipment and trained trainers means that the basic skills and knowledge can be acquired quickly and often economically.

The main disadvantage arises when trainees are transferred from the training course to a job to apply their knowledge and skills in practice. On a full-time manual skills course in a training centre, they will have been sheltered from the realities of the rough and tumble in most workshops, especially in batch production factories.

For managers and team leaders, the problem of transferring from the 'training situation' to 'real life' may be even more difficult. This issue of transferring learning is important in all aspects of training but it is a particular problem with management and team leader training whether in-company or provided outside. This is partly because much management training tends to deal with relatively abstract concepts like motivation and leadership and the connection between what people learn in the classroom (or out of doors) may not always be apparent. Strenuous efforts have to be made to ensure that learners perceive the reality of what they are learning and that they are expected to develop and implement action plans for putting it into practice. The concept of 'action learning', as developed by Revans (1989), is designed to mitigate this problem.

External training

External training is useful for the development of managerial, team leading, technical and social knowledge and skills, especially if the courses cover standard theory and practice which can easily be translated from the general to the particular. External training should be able to supply the quality of instruction that it might be uneconomic to provide internally. It can be used to implant highly specialized knowledge or advanced skills and has the added advantage of broadening the horizons of those taking part, not least because they will be exposed to their peers from other organizations.

The main disadvantage is that of transferring learning into practice – even more acute with external courses. However effective the training, the knowledge and skills acquired may be quickly dissipated unless they are used immediately. It may also be difficult to select relevant courses from the bewildering variety available.

Just-in-time training

Just-in-time training is training that is closely linked to the pressing and relevant needs of people by its association with immediate or imminent business activities. It is delivered as close as possible to the time when the business activity is taking place. The training will be based on an identification of the latest priorities and plans of the participants who will be briefed on the live situations in which their learning will be applied. Rapid feedback will be obtained on the effectiveness of the training and, to close the loop, the training will be amended to reflect the evaluation.

Training programme design as an art

The art of designing training programmes is to select the right blend of on-the-job and off-the-job training. There are rules for doing this. Each programme has to be considered individually. But the emphasis should always be towards putting learning into practice and, therefore, first consideration has to be given to what happens on the job – learning by doing with appropriate guidance from managers, colleagues or mentors.

Off-the-job courses, whether internal or external, should be regarded as complementary and supplementary activities that may stimulate learning or provide knowledge and skills that cannot be obtained internally. But they are always subsidiary to what individuals do and learn in their normal place of work.

Options in training delivery

As analysed by Billson (1998), the options in delivering training and their likely impact on business results are shown in Table 36.1.

TRAINING TECHNIQUES

There is a wide variety of training techniques that can be used. These can be divided into:

Table 36. 1   Options in training delivery

(Adapted from Billson, I (1998) 'How just-in-time training can support business-led competency development', *Competency*, Spring, pp 21–24)

Approach	Key features	Likely impact on delivering business results
1. external training courses	* generic subjects * not tailored	low
2. internal courses/ workshops	* some tailoring * large groups	low+
3. self-learning via multi-media packages	* tailored * practices/thinking based	medium
4. small-group coaching	* highly tailored * case study based * groups of 4–8 * short, frequent sessions	high
5. action learning	* highly tailored * focused on live business situations * short, frequent sessions	high
6. one-to-one coaching	* focused on live business situations * time-consuming, but rewarding for both parties	very high
7. just-in-time training	* highly tailored to immediate needs * small groups or individuals * use of action learning or coaching * short, frequent sessions	very high

● *On-the-job techniques*, which are practised on a day-to-day basis or as a part of a specially tailored training programme. These include demonstration, coaching, job rotation, planned experience and mentoring and other personal development activities.

● *Off-the-job techniques*, which are used in formal training courses away from the place of work. These include lectures, talks, discussions, the discovery method, case study, role-playing, simulation, group exercises, team building, distance learning, outdoor learning and workshops. They can also include personal development training such as neuro-linguistic programming (NLP).

● *On- or off-the-job techniques*, which include instruction, question and answer, action learning, assignments, projects, guided reading, computer-based training (e-learning), interactive video and video.

These techniques are described in Appendix A.

Responsibility for training?

On-the-job training can be provided by managers, team leaders, colleagues or mentors (fellow employees who are given a particular responsibility to guide, advise and generally look after trainees – see Appendix A). As mentioned earlier, it is essential to train anyone involved in on-the-job training in techniques such as coaching, instructing and mentoring.

Off-the-job training may be provided by members of the training department, external education and training establishments, or training providers – training consultants or guest speakers. Increasingly, organizations are turning to external training providers rather than maintaining their own establishment of training staff.

Line managers should also be involved as much as possible to bring reality into the classroom, to ease the transfer of learning to work (always a difficult problem) and to underline their prime responsibility for training. Anyone who provides off-the-job training must be carefully selected, briefed and monitored to ensure that they make the right contribution. Natural trainers are fairly rare and even professionals need all the guidance you can give them to ensure that they are providing relevant training.

CONDUCTING TRAINING PROGRAMMES

The only general rules for conducting training programmes are that first, the courses should continually be monitored to ensure that they are proceeding according to plan and within the agreed budget and second, all training should be evaluated after the event to check on the extent to to which it is delivering the required results. This is the job of whoever has the responsibility for employee development, who should be required to report on progress against plan at regular intervals.

There are, however, a number of considerations that affect the conduct of training for specific occupations, and those concerning managers and team leaders (these are dealt with jointly because the basic principles are similar), sales staff, skilled workers and office staff are discussed briefly below. Special approaches may also be used for particular groups of employees and these are also described below.

Management and team leader training

As the old saying goes, managers learn to manage by managing under the guidance of a good manager. The emphasis should therefore always be towards on-the-job training, by planned experience, coaching or assignments. This can be supplemented – but never replaced – by off-the-job training to extend knowledge, fill in gaps, develop skills, or modify attitudes.

Management and team leader training courses can provide:

● concentrated knowledge;
● an opportunity to acquire new skills or to develop and practise existing skills;
● a framework for analysing past experience;
● the chance to reflect on ways in which better use can be made of future experience;
● a means of getting new ideas accepted and changing attitudes through group activities not available on the job.

However, management training courses do not always (some cynics would say 'often') achieve these objectives. Following extensive research Mant (1970) noted that:

● the majority of managers do not benefit greatly from external management courses;
● managers benefit more from well-designed and well-conducted internal courses, variously termed 'in-company', 'in-plant', or 'in-house', which are linked to the job and involve problem-orientated project work;
● the organization, and not the individual, should be regarded as the main consumer of management training, the aim of which is to secure better results for the company.

Revans (1971) has taken the same standpoint in developing his concept of 'action learning' as described in Appendix A.

To get good results from external courses it is necessary to ensure that they will be relevant and well conducted and that managers are required to make practical use of what they have learnt.

Project training is one way of avoiding the problems of external courses. It provides managers and team leaders with new experiences and the opportunity to extend their knowledge over a wider range of problems and to exercise their analytical skills in solving them.

Management and team leader training should be seen as a continuous process. One of the greatest fallacies of the typical external management course is that this is sufficient. A management and team leader training programme should therefore be established as a continuing activity at all levels of management to avoid dissipation of the interest and enthusiasm that follows an isolated course, and to promote the progressive development of managerial and team leader skills as new experiences are encountered and as conditions change.

Sales training

The aim of sales training should be to equip sales representatives with the knowledge, skills, attitudes and habits required to meet or exceed their sales targets.

The first requirement is knowledge of the company and its products, customers, competitors and sales administration procedures.

Secondly, they have to acquire and develop skills: prospecting, making the approach, making presentations, handling objections, closing the sale, and handling complaints. Perhaps the most important skill to be developed, however, is analytical ability. Sales representatives must be taught how to analyse their product into its technical characteristics and, most important, its selling points – those aspects of the product that are likely to appeal to particular customers. They must also be taught how to analyse their customers from the point of view of their buying habits and the features of the product that are most likely to appeal to them. In addition, they must be able to analyse themselves – their own strengths and weaknesses.

Thirdly, training should aim to develop attitudes: of loyalty to the company and belief in its products, and of understanding and tolerance with regard to potential and existing customers. The importance of customer service must be emphasized. Sales representatives have to believe in themselves; they must be given confidence and provided with the motivation to go out and sell – a task that requires courage, determination and persistence.

The fourth requirement is to develop sound work habits: organizing time, planning activities, following up leads, maintaining records and submitting reports.

Sales training, like any other form of training, should be based on an analysis of the job and the problems sales representatives are likely to meet. The training programme should be continuous; there can never be a time in any sales representative's career when he or she would not benefit from training. Use should be made of classroom training to provide basic knowledge and an opportunity to practise skills.

But most training should be carried out on the job by sales managers or team leaders who can demonstrate sales techniques and observe and comment on the efforts of the sales representatives.

Technical and skill or craft training

Technical and skill or craft training schemes can be divided into four main types:

- *Graduate* – postgraduate training leading to a professional qualification.
- *Student* – a course of education and practical training leading to a degree or some other qualification as an engineer, scientist or technologist or technician. In the UK the courses may include 'block' release to college for periods of a number of months or the student may undergo a full degree course as the central part of the training while gaining experience before and after the course and during vacations.
- *Technician* – a course of education and training, which could last up to three or four years, leading to employment as a technician and an appropriate technician's qualification.
- *Skill or craft* – a course lasting a number of years, depending on the level of skill that has to be attained and often leading to a craft certificate or other record of achievement. At one time such training schemes were always called apprenticeships and the indenture agreement laid down a fixed period of training. But it did not specify what training should take place or indicate what standards had been achieved.

The old apprenticeship agreement has generally been replaced by the training agreement. This stipulates the basic and general training, and the skill modules that have to be completed to satisfactory standards before the training is completed satisfactorily. A skill module is based on skills analysis and defines what training is required to achieve an 'experienced worker's standard' in a particular skill or task. It sets out the exercises to be carried out and how attainments should be tested. The training may be built round National Vocational Qualification (NVQ) specifications, although specific training modules will be built into the programme linked to the competence elements incorporated in the NVQ level that is to be attained. The training agreement may also specify the part-time period of further education that has to be completed.

Phases of skill training

In the major craft industries – engineering and construction – the skill training for craft trainees or apprentices consists of the following three phases.

Basic training

In the basic training period trainees receive training in basic skills in a basic training workshop. This training should consist of a series of modules. Clearly, the standard modules should be chosen on the basis of an analysis of the skills required, and additional modules should be specially developed if necessary. A basic course for engineering craft apprentices may last a full year, by which time the apprentices should be fully equipped with all the basic skills.

Each module should have defined objectives – criterion behaviour. There should be methods of measuring behaviour after the module has been completed. The training should be given by trained instructors in a space set aside for training.

General training

In the general training period trainees are given experience in a number of different departments, processes or operations to consolidate training. If it is already decided that they are to become, say, computer numerically controlled machine tool operators in a flexible manufacturing system (FMS), they would be given an extended period of familiarization in the machine tool room. But they would also spend some time in related areas; for example, the design office, production planning and control and various fitting and assembly shops.

Technician, student and graduate trainees in engineering would also spend a general period of training 'round the shops' but would then move into the engineering, design or development departments, depending on their speciality. A production specialist, for example, would spend time in the planning, production control, work study and quality assurance departments.

During the period, graduate and student trainees should be given special projects which test their understanding of the design, development, engineering and manufacturing functions. Craft and technician trainees may return to the training school for advanced skill courses in machine operation, CADCAM (computer aided design and manufacturing) systems or any other speciality.

The biggest danger to avoid in this period of general training is that trainees aimlessly wander from shop to shop and find themselves relegated to a tedious job out of harm's way because no one wants to know about them. To avoid this danger, it is essential to have a syllabus of training in every workshop which is based on an analysis of skill requirements. There should be one trained supervisor responsible for training in each workshop and in a large department, such as a machine shop, there may be more than one full-time training supervisor. The training department should also monitor the progress of trainees carefully to ensure that they are following the syllabus and are acquiring the knowledge and skill they need. In a large organization there may be one or more full-time supervisors who spend all their time in the shops chasing shop team leaders or supervisors and checking on the progress of trainees.

The trainees themselves should know what they are expected to learn at each stage in order that they can request a move if they feel they are wasting their time or are not covering the syllabus. They should also be required to keep logbooks to record what they have done. These should be seen regularly by their training officer as a check on their progress.

Final training

In the final training period trainees settle down in the department of their choice, or the department for which they are best fitted. During this period trainees will probably be doing the same work as experienced skilled operators, technicians or technologists. The aim is to ensure that they are equipped to apply their learning in normal working conditions and at the pace and level of quality expected from a fully experienced and competent individual.

Throughout these three stages the training department has to work closely with the educationalists to ensure that, as far as possible, the theory is complementary to the practice.

The length of the period of training at each stage obviously depends on the level and complexity of the knowledge and skills that have to be acquired and on the type of apprenticeship. Traditional union agreements laid down the length of training in some cases but these have virtually disappeared. The experience of any company conducting training along the lines described above, however, has shown that if the basic training is sufficiently comprehensive and the period of experience is adequately planned and monitored, the length of time to reach a fully experienced worker's standard may be considerably less than the traditional period.

Training for other skilled crafts should follow the same pattern of basic training: familiarization with the application of different aspects of the craft, and final consolidation of knowledge and skills. The basic training period, however, may not be so elaborate and may well be carried out in a local training centre which is better equipped to provide the skilled instruction required.

Modern apprenticeships

Modern apprenticeships were launched as a government initiative in 1995. The aim was to increase the supply of young people with craft, technician and junior management skills. The key features of a modern apprenticeship are that it:

- incorporates a firm commitment to training by the employer and trainee;
- results in a level 3 NVQ or SVQ;
- provides training in personal skills;
- fits young people for a career in their chosen industry;
- is based on the achievement of standards rather than time-serving;
- allows flexibility to accommodate individual and company needs.

Training office staff

Office training is the most neglected form of training. Perhaps this is because both line and training managers often underestimate the skill content of most office work. This feeling has been intensified because of the tendency of systems analysts to de-skill office jobs.

However, inefficiency in office work can be an important factor in reducing the efficiency of the organization as a whole. A company cannot afford to neglect training in office skills and departmental procedures.

Office training should be divided into three areas: basic training, further education, and continuation training. During the basic training stage, when a trainee is being taught how to carry out his or her first job, a foundation is being laid for the employee's career. During this period, young trainees should obtain background knowledge of the company and acquire the basic knowledge and skills they need.

Office trainees should be encouraged to follow a further course of studies leading to a professional or commercial qualification or an NVQ. The course of studies should be decided by agreement between the employee, the departmental manager and the training department.

The third area is continuation training. Training and development should be a continuous process. When trainees have completed their basic training programme and, preferably, have obtained a qualification, their abilities should be developed by providing broader experience within the company and by short technical courses. The aim at this stage should be to ensure that staff with potential are not allowed to stagnate within a department and that they are prepared for greater responsibility.

MEETING THE TRAINING NEEDS OF SPECIAL GROUPS

Training needs analysis as described earlier in this chapter is often conducted entirely on an occupational basis but it is also necessary to consider the needs of special groups, especially the disabled and ethnic minorities. A separate needs analysis should be carried out which identifies the occupations they are likely to be in and any special training requirements arising from different types of disabilities or the particular ethnic group(s). Advice on approaches to training people with disabilities can be obtained from charities such as the Royal National Institute for the Blind, the Royal National Institute for the Deaf, the Royal Association for Disability and Rehabiliation and MENCAP. Ethnic groups may have to be given special training if there are any linguistic or cultural issues that need attention.

RESPONSIBILITY FOR TRAINING

As has been made clear throughout this chapter, most learning occurs on the job through coaching, planned experience and self-development. The onus is on managers and individuals to ensure that it takes place. Senior management must create a learning organization in which managers recognize that training and development are a key part of their role and one on which their performance will be assessed.

The role of a specialized training function is generally to provide advice and guidance to managers on their training responsibilities. In many organizations they are involved much less, if at all, in training delivery. Training functions are relying more and more on external providers to provide the actual training. This means that the huge training departments that used to exist in a lot of organizations have now been slimmed down considerably. Increasingly, the role of the company trainer is to act as an internal consultant.

The much smaller training function may still, however, be responsible for the following activities:

- developing training strategies that support the achievement of business strategies;
- analysing and identifying corporate and occupational training needs;
- developing proposals on how these needs should be satisfied;
- preparing plans and budgets for training activities;
- identifying external training resources, selecting external training providers, specifying what is required from them and ensuring that their delivery of training meets the specification;
- advising on external training courses for individuals or groups;
- organizing internal courses and training programmes, but often relying on outside help for the whole or part of formal training courses;
- training managers, supervisors and mentors in their training responsibilities;

- providing help and guidance to individuals in the preparation and implementation of personal development plans;
- monitoring and evaluating the effectiveness of training throughout the organization.

EVALUATING TRAINING

It is important to evaluate training in order to assess its effectiveness in producing the learning outcomes specified when the training intervention was planned and to indicate where improvements or changes are required to make the training even more effective.

It is at the planning stage that the basis upon which each category of training is to be evaluated should be determined. At the same time, it is necessary to consider how the information required to evaluate learning events should be obtained and analysed.

The process of evaluating training has been defined by Hamblin (1974) as: 'Any attempt to obtain information (feedback) on the effects of a training programme, and to assess the value of the training in the light of that information.' Evaluation leads to control, which means deciding whether or not the training was worthwhile (preferably in cost–benefit terms) and what improvements are required to make it even more cost-effective.

Evaluation is an integral feature of training. In its crudest form, it is the comparison of objectives (criterion behaviour) with outcomes (terminal behaviour) to answer the question of how far the training has achieved its purpose. The setting of objectives and the establishment of methods of measuring results are, or should be, an essential part of the planning stage of any training programme.

Levels of evaluation

Four levels of training evaluation have been suggested by Kirkpatrick (1994):

Level 1 – Reaction – at this level, evaluation measures how those who participated in the training have reacted to it. In a sense, it is a measure of immediate customer satisfaction. Kirkpatrick suggests the following guidelines for evaluating reactions:

- Determine what you want to find out.
- Design a form that will quantify reactions.
- Encourage written comments and suggestions.

- Get 100% immediate response.
- Get honest responses.
- Develop acceptable standards.
- Measure reactions against standards, and take appropriate action.
- Communicate reactions as appropriate.

Level 2 – Evaluating learning – this level obtains information on the extent to which learning objectives have been attained. It will aim to find how much knowledge was acquired, what skills were developed or improved, and, as appropriate, the extent to which attitudes have changed in the desired direction. So far as possible, the evaluation of learning should involve the use of tests before and after the programme – paper and pencil or performance tests.

Level 3 – Evaluating behaviour – this level evaluates the extent to which behaviour has changed as required when people attending the programme have returned to their jobs. The question to be answered is the extent to which knowledge, skills and attitudes have been transferred from the classroom to the workplace. Ideally, the evaluation should take place both before and after the training. Time should be allowed for the change in behaviour to take place. The evaluation needs to assess the extent to which specific learning objectives relating to changes in behaviour and the application of knowledge and skills have been achieved.

Level 4 – Evaluating results – this is the ultimate level of evaluation and provides the basis for assessing the benefits of the training against its costs. The evaluation has to be based on before and after measures and has to determine the extent to which the fundamental objectives of the training have been achieved in areas such as increasing sales, raising productivity, reducing accidents or increasing customer satisfaction. Evaluating results is obviously easier when they can be quantified. However, it is not always easy to prove the contribution to improved results made by training as distinct from other factors and as Kirkpatrick says: 'Be satisfied with evidence, because proof is usually impossible to get.'

Application of training evaluation

Like the similar levels of evaluation suggested by Hamblin in 1974 (reactions, learning, job behaviour, impact on unit and organizational performance), the levels defined by Kirkpatrick are links in the chain. Training produces reactions, which lead to learning, which leads to changes in job behaviour, which lead to results at unit and organizational level. Trainees can react favourably to a course – they can enjoy the experience – but learn little or nothing. They can learn something, but cannot, or will not, or are not, allowed to apply it. They apply it but it does no good within their own areas. It does some good in their function, but does not improve organizational effectiveness.

Evaluation can take place at any level. In the Kirkpatrick scheme it is easier to start at level one and progress up with increasing difficulty to level four. It could be argued that the only feedback from evaluation that matters is the results in terms of improved unit or organizational performance that training achieves. But if this is hard to measure, training could still be justified in terms of any actual changes in behaviour that the programme was designed to produce. This is based on the assumption that the analysis of training needs indicated that this behaviour is more than likely to deliver the desired results. Similarly, at the learning level, if a proper analysis of knowledge, skills and attitude requirements and their impact on behaviour has been conducted, it is reasonable to assume that if the knowledge etc has been acquired, behaviour is likely to change appropriately. Finally, if all else fails, reactions are important in that they provide immediate feedback on the quality of training given (including the performance of the trainer) which can point the way to corrective action.

37

Personal development planning

DEFINED

Personal development planning is carried out by individuals with guidance, encouragement and help from their managers as required. A personal development plan sets out the actions people propose to take to learn and to develop themselves. They take responsibility for formulating and implementing the plan but they may receive support from the organization and their managers in doing so.

PURPOSE

Personal development planning aims to promote learning and to provide people with the knowledge and portfolio of transferable skills that will help to progress their careers. A distinction can be made between the learning and developmental aspects of personal development plans. Pedler *et al* (1989) see learning as being concerned with an increase in knowledge or a higher degree of an existing skill, whereas development is about moving to a different state of being or functioning.

The initial purpose may be to provide what Tamkin *et al* (1995) call a 'self-organised learning framework'. But as they comment, within that framework: 'Some organisations have interpreted learning widely, encompassing all aspects of self development or included learning activities that have little to do with an individual's current job or even future career.'

Others have focused heavily on job-related skills or knowledge, or have laid a heavy emphasis on the user's future career and required experience.

At Guardian Royal Exchange, personal development planning is carried out for two reasons: 'To fit people better for their current job and because they need to improve or the job itself is changing' (Hegarty, 1995).

Royal Mail Anglia defines the purpose of the plan as being 'the identification of development and training needs which will enhance their personal contribution to the success of Royal Mail'.

At BP Chemicals it is stated in the guidance notes for staff that: 'It's all very well to say that the responsibility for development rests with the individual, but without the means to approach this in an analytical and systematic fashion, this is an empty statement. BP Chemicals is therefore encouraging everyone to produce a Personal Development Plan.'

The research conducted for the Institute of Employment Studies (IES) by Tamkin *et al* (1995) into personal development plans did not reveal in any of the 14 case study organizations that the use of such plans had been initiated as a deliberate step towards becoming a learning organization.

FOCUS

As the IES research showed, personal development plans were most commonly focused on job or career development or some mix of both. Less frequently, the emphasis was on the whole person. Tamkin *et al* comment: 'Personal development plans which focus solely on skill development for the current job will not be welcomed by many employees. Those which take a broader view of the individual and their future, may be more effective for encouraging flexibility and have a higher impact on employees.'

PERSONAL DEVELOPMENT PLANNING – THE OVERALL PROCESS

Personal development plans can be created as an outcome of a development or assessment centre. But these may make only a limited impact. The most common approach is to include personal development planning as a key part of performance and development management processes as described in Part VIII.

As described by BP Chemicals, the four stages in preparing a personal development plan are:

1. Assess current position.
2. Set goals.
3. Plan action.
4. Implement.

These are illustrated in Figure 37.1.

Figure 37.1 The process of personal development planning

These planning stages are in line with those proposed by Gannon (1995):

1. Analyse current situation and development needs.
2. Set goals under such headings as improving performance in the current job, improving or acquiring skills, extending relevant knowledge, developing specified areas of competence, moving across or upwards in the organization, preparing for changes in the current role.
3. Prepare action plan.

IDENTIFYING DEVELOPMENT NEEDS AND WANTS

Development needs and wants are identified in performance management processes by individuals, on their own or working in conjunction with their managers. This will include reviewing performance against agreed plans and assessing competence requirements and the capacity of people to achieve them. The analysis is therefore based on an understanding of what people do, what they have achieved, what knowledge and skills they have and what knowledge and skills they need. The analysis is always related to work and the capacity to carry it out effectively.

Individuals can make their own assessment of their personal development needs to get more satisfaction from their work, to advance their careers and to increase their employability.

IDENTIFYING THE MEANS OF SATISFYING NEEDS

Personal development planning emphasized that it was *not* just about identifying training needs and suitable courses to satisfy them. Training courses may form part of the development plan but a minor part; other learning activities were much more important. As Royal Mail Anglia states in its guidance notes on personal development planning:

'Development needs can be met using a wide variety of activities. Do not assume that a conventional training course is the only option. In many instances, activity more finely tuned to the specific need can be more rewarding and appropriate than a generalised training course.'

The examples of development activities listed by Royal Mail Anglia include:

- seeing what others do (best practice);
- project work;
- adopting a role model (mentor);
- involvement in other work areas;
- planned use of internal training media (interactive video programmes/learning library);
- input to policy formulation;
- increased professionalism on the job;
- involvement in the community;
- coaching others;
- training courses.

Other learning activities, which could be mentioned but are not on this list, include guided reading, special assignments, action learning and distance learning.

ACTION PLANNING

The action plan sets out what needs to be done and how it will be done under headings:

- development needs;
- outcomes expected (learning objectives);
- development activities to meet the needs;
- responsibility for development – what individuals will do and what support they will require from their manager, the HR department or other people;
- timing – when the learning activity is expected to start and be completed;
- outcome – what development activities have taken place and how effective they were.

The aims of the planning process are to be specific about what is to be achieved and how it is to be achieved, to ensure that the learning needs and actions are relevant, to indicate the time scale, to identify responsibility and, within reason, to ensure that the learning activities will stretch those concerned.

As noted by the IES research, the extent to which the development plan is structured varies. A highly structured approach will specify the competency areas to be developed as established in the performance review against each of the competency framework headings used by the organization. The action plan might also be structured under the headings of the type of development activity proposed. In a semi-structured process only broad headings would be incorporated in the documentation; for example, the development need and the means by which it will be met. A completely unstructured approach is occasionally used, in effect asking for the plan to be committed to a blank sheet of paper but with some guidelines on what should be recorded. Most of the organizations covered by the IPD research (Armstrong and Baron, 1998) adopted the middle of the road approach – some structure but not too much on the grounds that they did not want planning to degenerate into a bureaucratic form-filling exercise. The personal development plan form may be attached to the performance review form or, to emphasize its importance, it may be kept separately. The forms are usually quite simple. They may include only four columns covering:

- development objectives and outcome expected;
- action to be undertaken and when;
- support required;
- evidence to demonstrate activity has been undertaken.

RESPONSIBILITY FOR PERSONAL DEVELOPMENT PLANNING

In most applications it is emphasized that individuals are primarily responsible for progressing the plan and for ensuring that they play their part in implementing it. But it is generally recognized that, to different degrees, people will need encouragement, guidance and support. Managers are not expected to sit back and let their staff flounder. They have a role to play in helping, as necessary, in the preparation of the plan.

INTRODUCING PERSONAL DEVELOPMENT PLANNING

The introduction of personal development planning should not be undertaken lightly. It is not just a matter of designing a new back page to the performance review form and telling people to fill it up. Neither is it sufficient just to issue guidance notes and expect people to get on with it.

Managers, team leaders and individuals all need to learn about personal development planning. They should be involved in deciding how the planning process will work and what their roles will be. The benefits to them should be understood and accepted. It has to be recognized that everyone will need time and support to adjust to a culture in which they have to take much more responsibility for their own development. Importantly, all concerned should be given guidance on how to identify learning needs and on the features of the various means of satisfying those needs, and how they can make use of the facilities and opportunities that can be made available to them.

38

Management development

Management development is concerned with improving managers' performance in their present roles and preparing them for greater responsibilities in the future. In this chapter, the following aspects of management development are considered:

- its aims and impact;
- its nature as a business-led process and the elements involved in a management development processes;
- the main management development activities of analysis, assessment and strategy formulation;
- approaches to management development with an emphasis on integration, experiential and self-managed learning and personal development planning, and the use of competency-frameworks and development centres;
- the concept of emotional intelligence and its use in the development of leadership skills;
- the responsibility for management development.

AIMS OF MANAGEMENT DEVELOPMENT

Management development contributes to business success by helping the organization to grow the managers it requires to meet its present and future needs. It improves managers' performance, gives them development opportunities, and provides for management succession. Development processes may be *anticipatory* (so that managers can contribute to long-term objectives), *reactive* (intended to resolve or pre-empt performance difficulties) or *motivational* (geared to individual career aspirations). The particular aims of are to:

● ensure that managers understand what is expected of them; agreeing with them objectives against which their performance will be measured and the level of competence required in their roles;
● identify managers with potential, encouraging them to prepare and implement personal development plans and ensuring that they receive the required development, training and experience to equip them for more demanding responsibilities within their own locations and elsewhere in the organization;
● provide for management succession, creating a system to keep this under review.

IMPACT OF MANAGEMENT DEVELOPMENT

The capability of the organization to achieve its business strategies in the light of the critical success factors for the business (innovation, quality, cost, leadership, etc) depends largely on the capability of its managers as developed within the organization to meet its particular demands and circumstances. The relationships involved are illustrated in Figure 38.1 (adapted from Fonda, 1989).

Fonda (1989) emphasizes the far-reaching nature of the management capabilities required as follows:

● setting challenging ambitions;
● developing product-market strategies that sustain the competitiveness of the business;
● creating functional strategies that support strategic ambitions and product-market strategies;
● developing and effectively using systems for managing the business;
● shaping organizational culture for the future;
● structuring and restructuring the parts and the whole of the business in line with emerging priorities;
● optimizing profits by continually improving sales and service with today's customers and today's products.

Figure 38.1 The strategic impact of management development

THE NATURE AND ELEMENTS OF MANAGEMENT DEVELOPMENT

The most important thing to remember about the process of management development is that it must be business led even though it will be concerned with the development of individual performance and potential. The business has to decide what sort of managers it needs to achieve its strategic goals and the business must decide how it can best obtain and develop these managers. Even when the emphasis is on self-development, as it should be, the business must still indicate the directions in which self-development should go, possibly in the broadest of terms.

It has been suggested by Mumford (1993) that three elements have to be combined to produce an effective management development system:

● *self-development* – a recognition that individuals can learn but are unlikely to be taught, and that the initiative for development often rests with the individual;

- *organization-derived development* – the development of the systems of formal development beloved of personnel and management development specialists;
- *boss-derived development* – those actions undertaken by a senior manager with others, most frequently around real problems at work.

Mumford also makes the point that managers think in terms of activities, not learning opportunities, and therefore: 'Our main concern must be to facilitate learning through our understanding of real work in the manager's world, rather than attempting to impose separate management development processes.' He suggests that formal management development processes do not always function as effectively as we would like because: 'We have put too much emphasis on planning ahead, and not enough on enabling managers to use, understand and then build on their past experiences.'

MANAGEMENT DEVELOPMENT ACTIVITIES

The three essential management development activities are the:

- analysis of present and future management needs;
- assessment of existing and potential skills and effectiveness of managers against those needs;
- production of strategies and plans to meet those needs.

Management development also involves management succession planning and career management activities as described in Chapter 39.

Analysis of needs

The analysis of the future needs for managers is carried out through human resource planning processes (see Chapter 24).

In today's changeable, if not chaotic, conditions it may not be feasible to make precise forecasts of the number of managers required. But what can and should be done is to assess the skills and competences managers will need to meet future demands and challenges arising from competitive pressures, new product-market strategies and the introduction of new technology.

Assessment of skills and competences

The assessment of skills and competences against these needs can be carried out by performance management processes as described in Part VIII. It will be important, however, to include in these processes a means of identifying specific development needs and the agreement of development plans to meet not only current needs but anticipated future requirements.

These aspects of management development are discussed in the remaining sections of this chapter.

Management development strategy

The management development strategy will be concerned overall with what the organization intends to do about providing for its future management needs in the light of its business plans. The strategy will be concerned with the roles of the parties involved and with the approaches the organization proposes to use to develop its managers.

An example of management development benchmark statements in Figure 38.2.

The prime aim of these benchmark statements is to identify the key facets that make up management development activities. They provide personnel and line managers with a means of conducting their own evaluation and analysis of the state of management development within their organization. Each facet or 'dimension' in the statements brings together such aspects as the links between the management development plan, the assessment of skills and identification of skill gaps, and the delivery of appropriate and effective training and development.

The facets are broken down into four aspects of performance:

- commitment to management development;
- reviewing the current position of management development;
- making progress in management development;
- excellence in management development.

The underpinning assumption in the framework is the importance of bringing together the elements of a management development strategy into a more integrated whole. The various components do not have separate existences of their own.

APPROACHES TO MANAGEMENT DEVELOPMENT

Management development should be regarded as a range of related activities rather than an all-embracing programme. The use of the word 'programme' to describe the process smacks too much of a mechanistic approach. It is important to start from an understanding of how managers team, as considered below.

Management Development Strategy & Commitment	Identification of Need	Realizing Management Potential	Information Systems	Value for Money
A. There is a written, public, top level commitment to using management development, where appropriate, to develop individual managers, management teams and the organization.	A. There is a written, public, top level commitment to the consistent identification of development needs using a recognized system or process.	A. There is a written, public top level commitment to the members of staff performing management tasks who will have their contribution to the organization assessed and developed.	A. There is a written, public, top level commitment to make high quality information about management development activities available to all managers to make informed choices.	A. There is a written, public, top level commitment to achieving value for money in management development through the common identification of costs and benefits.
B. Management development activity is regularly reviewed to demonstrate its links to organizational objectives.	B. The organization regularly reviews, in terms of skills, knowledge, understanding and values, the development needs of its managers and management teams.	B. Management development activity is regularly audited to demonstrate how it provides access and opportunity to staff to realize management potential.	B. The organization regularly reviews its information on management development provision and its usefulness to decision makers.	B. An accepted, common approach exists for the audit of the costs and benefits of management development.
C. All Management development activity is driven by organizational objectives and is managed by line managers.	C. The organization bases its action on regular reviews, in terms of skills, knowledge, understanding and values, the development needs of its managers and management teams, both short and long-term.	C. The organization makes available resources to allow all managers, and others with management potential, to have their development needs identified and met.	C. Decisions on management development activity are based upon high quality information supplied to and received from line managers across the organization.	C. The organization bases its actions upon the accepted common approach to the auditing of the costs and benefits of management development.
D. Management development activity across the organization is integrated and coherent and meets declared organizational objectives.	D. The organization aligns and integrates its management skills, knowledge, understanding and values through a continuous process to meet declared organizational objectives.	D. Management development activity realizes all available managerial potential and aligns and integrates it with declared organizational objectives.	D. Information is used to optimize the quality and cost effectiveness of management development provision to deliver the staff the organization needs in the short and long term.	D. The organization obtains optimal value for money in all management development activity taking account of costs, short-term benefits to individuals and the organization to meeting declared organizational objectives.

Source: NHS Training Division

Figure 38.2 Management development benchmark statements

This does not imply that some systemization is not necessary; first, because many managers have to operate in more or less routine situations and have to be developed accordingly, and secondly, because organizations will not continue to thrive if they simply react to events. There must be an understanding of the approaches that can be used both to develop managers and also to assess existing managerial resources and how they meet the needs of the enterprise. And plans must be made for the development of those resources by selecting the best of the methods available. But this should not be seen as a 'programme' consisting of a comprehensive, highly integrated and rigidly applied range of management training and development techniques.

The management development activities required depend on the organization: its technology, its environment and its philosophy. A traditional bureaucratic/mechanistic type of organization may be inclined to adopt the programmed routine approach, complete with a wide range of courses, inventories, replacement charts, career plans and results-orientated review systems. An innovative and organic type of organization may rightly dispense with all these mechanisms. Its approach would be to provide its mangers with the opportunities, challenges and guidance they require, seizing the chance to give people extra responsibilities, and ensuring that they receive the coaching and encouragement they need. There may be no replacement charts, inventories or formal appraisal schemes, but people know how they stand, where they can go and how to get there.

How managers learn

It has often been said that managers learn to manage by managing – in other words, 'experience is the best teacher'. This is largely true, but some people learn much better than others. After all, a manager with 10 years' experience may have had no more than one year's experience repeated 10 times.

Differences in the ability to learn arise because some managers are naturally more capable or more highly motivated than others, while some will have had the benefit of the guidance and help of an effective boss who is fully aware of his or her responsibilities for developing managers. The saying quoted above could be expanded to read: 'Managers learn to manage by managing under the guidance of a good manager.' The operative word in this statement is 'good'. Some managers are better at developing people than others, and one of the aims of management development is to get all managers to recognize that developing their staff is an important part of their job. And for senior managers to say that people do not learn because they are not that way inclined, and to leave it at that, is to neglect one of their key responsibilities – to improve the performance of the organization by doing whatever is practical to improve the effectiveness and potentials of the managers.

To argue that managers learn best 'on the job' should not lead to the conclusion that managers are best left entirely to their own devices or that management development should be a haphazard process. The organization should try to evolve a philosophy of management development which ensures that consistent and deliberate interventions are made to improve managerial learning. Revans (1989) wants to take management development back into the reality of management and out of the classroom, but even he believes that deliberate attempts to foster the learning process through 'action learning' (see Appendix A) are necessary.

It is possible to distinguish between formal and informal approaches to management development, as described below.

Formal approaches to management development

The formal approaches to management development include:

- development on the job through coaching, counselling, monitoring and feedback by managers on a continuous basis associated with the use of performance management processes to identify and satisfy development needs, and with mentoring;
- development through work experience, which includes job rotation, job enlargement, taking part in project teams or task groups, 'action learning', and secondment outside the organization;
- formal training by means of internal or external courses;
- structured self-development by following self-managed learning programmes agreed as a personal development plan or learning contract with the manager or a management development adviser – these may include guidance reading or the deliberate extension of knowledge or acquisition of new skills on the job.

The formal approaches to management development are based on the identification of development needs through performance management or a development centre. The approach may be structured around a list of generic or core competences which have been defined as being appropriate for managers in the organization.

Informal approaches to management development

Informal approaches to management development make use of the learning experiences that managers meet during the course of their everyday work. Managers are learning every time they are confronted with an unusual problem, an unfamiliar task or a move to a different job. They then have to evolve new ways of dealing with the situation. They will learn if they analyse what they did to determine how and why it contributed to its success or failure. This retrospective or reflective learning will be effective if managers can apply it successfully in the future.

This is potentially the most powerful form of learning. The question is: can anything be done to help managers make the best use of their experience? This type of 'experiential' learning comes naturally to some managers. They seem to absorb, unconsciously and by some process of osmosis, the lessons from their experience, although in fact they they have probably developed a capacity for almost instantaneous analysis, which they store in their mental databank and which they can retrieve whenever necessary.

Ordinary mortals, however, either find it difficult to do this sort of analysis or do not recognize the need. This is where semi-formal approaches can be used to encourage and help managers to learn more effectively. These approaches include:

● emphasizing self-assessment and the identification of development needs by getting managers to assess their own performance against agreed objectives and analyse the factors that contributed to effective or less effective performance – this can be provided through performance management;
● getting managers to produce their own personal development plans or self-managed learning programmes;
● encouraging managers to discuss their own problems and opportunities with their bosses, colleagues or mentors in order to establish for themselves what they need to learn or be able to do.

An integrated approach to management development

An integrated approach to management development will make judicious use of both the formal and informal methods as described above. There are five governing principles:

● *The reality of management* – the approach to management development should avoid making simplistic assumptions on what managers need to know or do, based on the classical analysis of management as the processes of planning, organizing, directing and controlling. In reality managerial work is relatively disorganized and fragmented, and this is why many practising managers reject the facile solutions suggested by some formal management training programmes. As Kanter (1989) has said: 'Managerial work is undergoing such enormous and rapid change that many managers are reinventing their profession as they go.'
● *Relevance* – it is too easy to assume that all managers need to know about

such nostrums as strategic planning, economic value added, balance sheet analysis, etc. These can be useful but they may not be what managers really need. Management development processes must be related to the needs of particular managers in specific jobs and these processes may or may not include techniques such as those listed above. Those needs should include not only what managers should know now but also what they should know and be able to do in the future, if they have the potential. Thus, management development may include 'broadening programmes' aimed at giving managers an understanding of the wider, strategic issues which will be relevant at higher levels in the organization.

● *Self-development* – managers need to be encouraged to develop themselves and helped to do so. Performance management will aim to provide this guidance.

● *Experiential learning* – if learning can be described as a modification of behaviour through experience then the principal method by which managers can be equipped is by providing them with the right variety of experience, in good time in the course of their careers, and by helping them to learn from that experience – action learning is a method of achieving this.

● *Formal training* – courses can supplement but can never replace experience and they must be carefully timed and selected or designed to meet particular needs. A 'sheep dip' approach which exposes all managers to the same training course may be desirable in some circumstances, but the focus should generally be on identifying and meeting individual learning needs.

Competency-based management development

Competency-based management development uses competency frameworks, maps or profiles (see Chapter 21) as a means of identifying and expressing development needs and pointing the way to self-managed learning programmes or the provision of learning opportunities by the organization.

Competency-based management development may concentrate on a limited number of core or generic competences which the organization has decided will be an essential part of the equipment of their managers if they are going to take the organization forward in line with its strategic plans. For example:

● *strategic capability* to understand the changing business environment, opportunities for product-market development, competitive challenges and the strengths and weaknesses of their own organization in order to identify optimum strategic responses;

● *change management capability* to identify change needs, plan change programmes and persuade others to participate willingly in the implementation of change;

- *team management capability* to get diverse groups of people from different disciplines to work well together.
- *relationship management* to network effectively with others to share information and pool resources to achieve common objectives;
- *international management* to be capable of managing across international frontiers working well with people of other nationalities.

Development centres

The aim of development centres is to help participants build up an awareness of the competences their job requires and to construct their own personal development plans to improve their performance in the present job and to enhance their careers.

Like assessment centres (see Chapter 25), development centres are built around definitions of competence requirements. Unlike assessment centres, however, development centres look ahead at the competences needed in the future. The other significant difference between a development centre and an assessment centre is that in the latter case the organization 'owns' the results for selection or promotion purposes, while in the former case the results are owned by the individual as the basis for self-managed learning.

Development centres are not an event, nor a physical location. The activities of the centre offer participants the opportunity to examine and understand the competences they require now and in the future. Because 'behaviour predicts behaviour' the activities of the centre need to offer opportunities for competences to be observed in practice. Simulations of various kinds are therefore important features – these are a combination of case studies and role playing designed to obtain the maximum amount of realism. Participants are put into the position of practising behaviour in conditions very similar to those they will meet in the course of their everyday work.

An important part of the centre's activities will be feedback reviews, counselling and coaching sessions conducted by the directing staff, which will consist of full-time tutors and line managers who have been given special training in the techniques required.

The stages of a typical development centre as described by Hall and Norris (1992) are:

Prior to the centre delegates assess themselves against defined competencies.

Day 1

- Delegates test their pre-centre work with other delegates
- Individual task

- Structured self-insight
- Business simulation

Day 2

- Team roles questionnaire
- Personal profiles questionnaire
- Further counselling sessions and self-assessment procedures

Day 3

- Numerical reasoning tests
- Feedback on questionnaire
- Counselling on personal development plans
- Review of key points and findings

EMOTIONAL INTELLIGENCE AND LEADERSHIP QUALITIES

Management development should be concerned with enhancing leadership as well as extending and improving more general management skills. According to Goleman (1995), this process should take account of the concept of emotional intelligence as discussed in Chapter 21. Emotional intelligence has been defined by Goleman (1995) as being about:

- knowing what you are feeling and being able to handle those feelings without having them swamp you;
- being able to motivate yourself to get jobs done, be creative and perform at your peak;
- sensing what others are feeling and handling relationships effectively.

The possession of high levels of emotional intelligence is a necessary attribute for success as a leader.

Goleman has defined four components of emotional intelligence:

1. *Self-management* – the ability to control or redirect disruptive impulses and moods and regulate your own behaviour coupled with a propensity to pursue goals with energy and persistence. The six competencies associated with this component are

self-control, trustworthiness and integrity, initiative and adaptability, comfort with ambiguity, openness to change and a strong desire to achieve.

2. *Self-awareness* – the ability to recognize and understand your moods, emotions and drives as well as their effect on others. This is linked to three competencies: self-confidence, realistic self-assessment and emotional self-awareness.

3. *Social awareness* – the ability to understand the emotional make-up of other people, and skill in treating people according to their emotional reactions. This is linked to six competencies: empathy, expertise in building and retaining talent, organizational awareness, cross-cultural sensitivity, valuing diversity, and service to clients and customers.

4. *Social skills* – proficiency in managing relationships and building networks to get the desired result from others and reach personal goals, and the ability to find common ground and build rapport. The five competencies associated with this component are leadership, effectiveness in leading change, conflict management, influence/communication, and expertise in building and leading teams.

The steps required to develop emotional intelligence suggested by Goleman (1999) are:

- assess the requirements of jobs in terms of emotional skills;
- assess individuals to identify their level of emotional intelligence – 360-degree feedback can be a powerful source of data;
- gauge readiness – ensure that people are prepared to improve their level of emotional intelligence;
- motivate people to believe that the learning experience will benefit them;
- make change self-directed – encourage people to prepare a learning plan which fits their interests, resources and goals;
- focus on clear manageable goals – the focus must be on immediate, manageable steps, bearing in mind that cultivating a new skill is gradual, with stops and starts; the old ways will reassert themselves from time to time;
- prevent relapse – show people how they can learn lessons from the inevitable relapses;
- give performance feedback;
- encourage practice, remembering that emotional competence cannot be improved overnight;
- provide models of desired behaviours;
- encourage and reinforce – create a climate that rewards self-improvement;
- evaluate – establish sound outcome measures and then assess performance against them.

RESPONSIBILITY FOR MANAGEMENT DEVELOPMENT

Management development is not a separate activity to be handed over to a specialist and forgotten or ignored. The success of a management development programme depends upon the degree to which all levels of management are committed to it. The development of subordinates must be recognized as a natural and essential part of any manager's job. But the lead must come from the top.

The traditional view is that the organization need not concern itself with management development. The natural process of selection and the pressure of competition will ensure the survival of the fittest. Managers, in fact, are born not made. Cream rises to the top (but then so does scum).

The reaction to this was summed up in Humble's (1963) phrase, 'programmitis and crown prince'. Management development was seen in its infancy as a mechanical process using management inventories, multicoloured replacement charts, 'Cook's tours' for newly recruited graduates, detailed job rotation programmes, elaborate points schemes to appraise personal characteristics, and endless series of formal courses.

The true role of the organization in management development lies somewhere between these two extremes. On the one hand, it is not enough, in conditions of rapid growth (when they exist) and change, to leave everything to chance – to trial and error. On the other hand, elaborate management development programmes cannot successfully be imposed on the organization. As Peter Drucker wisely said many years ago (1955): 'Development is always self-development. Nothing could be more absurd than for the enterprise to assume responsibility for the development of a man. [sic]. The responsibility rests with the individual, his abilities, his efforts'.

But he went on to say:

> Every manager in a business has the opportunity to encourage individual self-development or to stifle it, to direct it to or to misdirect it. He [sic] should be specifically assigned the responsibility for helping all men working with him to focus, direct and apply their self-development efforts productively. And every company can provide systematic development challenges to its managers.

Executive ability is eventually something that individuals must develop for themselves while carrying out their normal duties. But they will do this much better if they are given encouragement, guidance and opportunities by their company and managers. In McGregor's (1960) phrase: managers are grown – they are neither born nor made. The role of the company is to provide conditions favourable to faster growth. And these conditions are very much part of the environment and organizational climate of the company and the management style of the chief executive. The latter has the ultimate responsibility for management development. As McGregor wrote:

> The job environment of the individual is the most important variable affecting his [sic] development. Unless that environment is conducive to his growth, none of the other things we do to him or for him will be effective. This is why the 'agricultural' approach to management development is preferable to the 'manufacturing' approach. The latter leads, among other things, to the unrealistic expectation that we can create and develop managers in the classroom.

It is remarkable that today some people are still reciting these well-established principles as if they had just discovered them.

Personal development plans

Managers must therefore take the main responsibility for their own development. The organization can help and the manager's boss must accept some responsibility for encouraging self-development and providing guidance as necessary. But individuals should be expected to draw up their own personal development plans (see also Chapter 37), the content of which would be based on answers to the following questions:

- What knowledge and/or skills do you intend to gain? and/or
- What levels of competence are you planning to achieve?
- What are your learning objectives? These should be set out in the form of definitions of the areas in which your performance will improve and/or what new things you will be able to do after the learning programme.
- How are you doing to achieve your objectives? What tasks, projects, exercises or reading will you do? What educational or training courses would you like to attend? The development plan should be broken down into defined phases and specific learning events should be itemized. The duration of each phase and the total length of the programme should be set out together with the costs, if any.
- What resources will you need in the form of computer-based training material, books, videos, individual coaching, mentoring etc?
- What evidence will you show to demonstrate your learning? What criteria will be used to ensure that this evidence is satisfactory?

Role of the human resource development specialist

Management development is not a separate activity to be handed over to a specialist and forgotten or ignored. The success of management development depends upon the degree to which it is recognized as an important aspect of the business strategy – a key organizational process aimed at delivering results. All levels of management must therefore be committed to it. The development of their staff must be recognized as a natural and essential part of any manager's job and one of the key criteria upon which their performance as managers will be judged. But the lead must come from the top.

However, human resource development specialists still have a number of important roles. They:

- interpret the needs of the business and advise on how management development strategies can play their part in meeting these needs;
- act as advocates of the significance of management development as a business-led activity;
- make proposals on formal and informal approaches to management development;
- develop in conjunction with line management competency frameworks which can be used as the basis for management development;
- provide guidance to managers on how to carry out their developmental activities;
- provide help and encouragement to managers in preparing and pursuing their personal development plans – including advice on acquiring an NVQ, professional or academic qualifications;
- provide the learning material managers need to achieve their learning objectives;
- act as tutors or mentors to individual managers or groups of managers as required;
- advise on the use and choice of external management education programmes;
- facilitate action learning projects;
- plan and conduct development centres as described at the end of this chapter;
- plan and conduct other formal learning events with the help of external providers as required.

39

Career management: management succession and career planning

DEFINITIONS

Career management consists of the processes of career planning and management succession.

Career planning shapes the progression of individuals within an organization in accordance with assessments of organizational needs and the performance, potential and preferences of individual members of the enterprise.

Management succession planning takes place to ensure that, as far as possible, the organization has the managers it requires to meet future business needs.

Career planning can be regarded as forming part of a career system which, as defined by Sonnenfeld *et al* (1992), 'is the set of policies and practices an organization uses to provide for its human resource requirements'. As they point out, such a system has two dimensions. First, there is the 'supply flow', which may be internal, when management jobs are filled from within, or could be external when managers are recruited from outside. Policy on the supply flow may involve 'make or buy' (career development or recruitment) decisions and the policy may specify the extent to which the supply should come from the internal or external labour market. Secondly, there is the 'assignment flow', which is concerned with the ways in which managers are assigned new tasks or roles. Career planning should be business led – development strategies should directly address the organization's business needs.

OVERALL AIMS

Career management has three overall aims:

1. To ensure that the organization's needs for management succession are satisfied.
2. To provide men and women of promise with a sequence of training and experience that will equip them for whatever level of responsibility they have the ability to reach.
3. To give individuals with potential the guidance and encouragement they need if they are to fulfil their potential and achieve a successful career with the organization in tune with their talents and aspirations.

THE PROCESS OF CAREER MANAGEMENT

The process of career management is illustrated in Figure 39.1. The key aspects of this process are discussed below.

Career dynamics and analysis

Career dynamics describes how career progression takes place – the ways in which people move through their careers either upwards through promotion or by enlarging or enriching their roles to take on greater responsibilities or make more use of their skills and capacities. Career analysis examines the characteristics of job ladders and families.

Career dynamics

Figure 39.2 illustrates the ways in which career progression proceeds in the following stages:

● expanding at the start of a career, when new skills are being acquired, knowledge

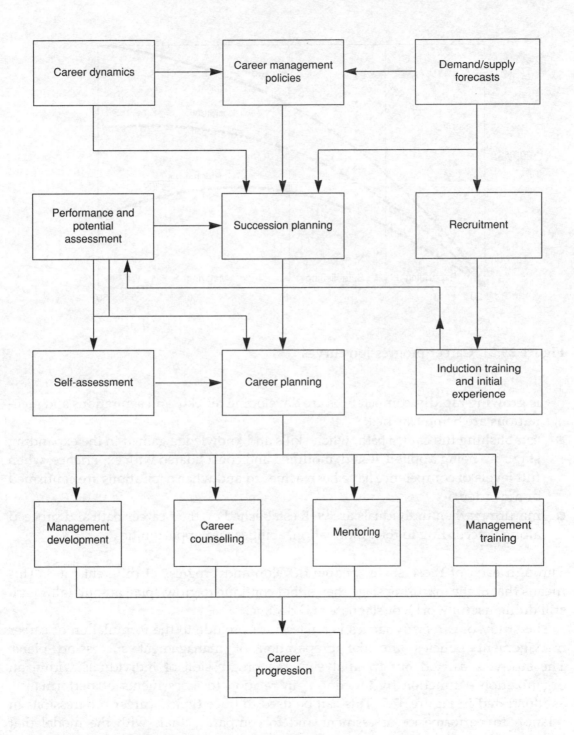

Figure 39.1 The process of career management

Figure 39.2 Career progression curves

is growing rapidly, competences are developing quickly and aspirations and inclinations are being clarified;

● establishing the career path, when skills and knowledge gained in the expanding stage are being applied, tested, modified and consolidated with experience, when full levels of competence have been achieved and when aspirations are confirmed or amended;

● maturing when individuals are well established on their career path and proceed along it according to their motivation, abilities and opportunities.

Through each of these stages people develop and progress at different rates. This means that at the maturing stage they either continue to grow, 'plateau-out' (although still doing useful work), or stagnate and decline.

The study of career dynamics is a necessary prelude to the formulation of career management policies and the preparation of management succession plans. The study is carried out by analysing the progression of individuals within an organization – function by function – in relation to assessments of performance, as illustrated in Figure 37.3. This can be used to trace typical career progressions in relation to performance assessment and to compare actuals with the model that

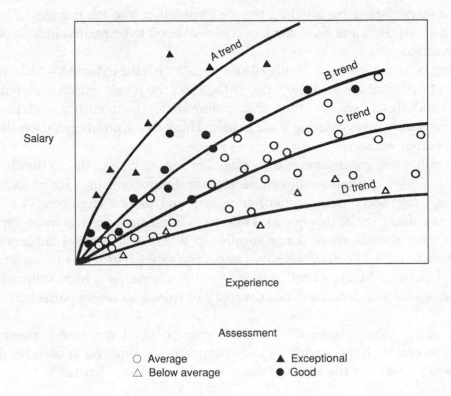

Figure 39.3 Progress analysis

can be developed from the empirically determined trend lines. An analysis of career dynamics can also point the way towards any actions required to alter career path trends for promising individuals by means of specific career management actions. Finally, the analysis reveals anomalies such as over-promotions (victims of the Peter Principle who have been promoted to the level of their own incompetence) or problems of managers who are stagnating or have gone over the hill.

Career analysis – job ladders and families

A job ladder consists of the steps individuals can take as they progress through their career in a job family. A job family consists of jobs where the nature of the work is essentially the same although there may be significant differences in the level of work undertaken. Such occupations as scientists, engineers, accountants and personnel specialists could be grouped into job families.

Job family analysis starts by dividing the job population into job families of basically similar jobs. At the same time, the jobs that will need to be treated individually should be identified.

The next step is to analyse each family of jobs to establish the extent to which work is carried out at different levels. Where this is the case, the levels within each family are analysed and described in terms that differentiate them clearly and in the language of the family, thus creating a job ladder. These descriptions can usefully be made in competency terms.

Some job families are more diverse than others and it may be useful to divide the broad family of, say, professional engineers into homogeneous groups of, for example, design engineers, development engineers and project engineers. A set of parallel ladders could then be developed. This broad family approach is more appropriate when career development it not simply up a series of parallel ladders but includes diagonal or even horizontal moves as people gain experience in a variety of roles. As Pritchard and Murlis (1992) put it: 'What is wanted is a wide staircase or scrambling net which can accommodate diversity of roles and career paths between them.'

The information gained from this analysis can be used for career planning purposes and to establish the attributes and competencies required at each level. It can also be used to evaluate the jobs and develop job family pay structures.

CAREER MANAGEMENT POLICIES

Career management policies cover the areas discussed below.

Make or buy decisions

The organization needs to decide on the extent to which it:

- makes or grows its own managers (a promotion from within policy);
- recruits or buys in deliberately from outside (bringing 'fresh blood' into the organization), which means adopting a policy that accepts a reasonable amount of wastage and even takes steps in good time to encourage people to develop their careers elsewhere if they are in danger of stagnating;
- will have to buy in talent from outside because of future shortfalls in the availability of managers, as revealed by demand and supply forecasts.

A make or buy policy may be expressed as follows: 'We plan to fill about 80 per cent of our management vacancies from within the organization. The remaining 20 per cent we expect to recruit from outside.'

Short- or long-term policies

Policies for determining the time scale for investing in careers fall into one or other of the following categories:

- *Short-term performance*. Employers who adopt, consciously or unconsciously, this policy concentrate on the 'here and now'. They recruit and train high performers who will be good at their present job and are rewarded accordingly. If they are really good, they will be promoted – there are plenty of opportunities – and the enterprise will get what it wants. Deliberately to train managers for a future that may never happen is considered a waste of time. Top managers in this type of organization may well say: 'If we can get good people to do good work, the future will take care of itself. They'll prove and mature their abilities in their present job and be ready and indeed eager to take on extra responsibilities when the occasion arises. If there's no one around at the time, then we'll buy in someone from outside – no problem!'

- *Long-term plans*. Employers who believe in long-term career planning develop highly structured approaches to career management. They go in for elaborate reviews of performance and potential, assessment centres to identify talent or confirm that it is there, 'high-flyer' schemes, and planned job moves in line with a pre-determined programme.

- *Long-term flexibility*. Employers who follow this policy appreciate that they must concentrate on getting good performance now, and that in doing so they will, to a considerable extent, be preparing people for advancement. To this extent, they adopt the same attitude as short-term employers. However, they also recognize that potential should be assessed and developed by training which is not job-specific and by deliberately broadening experience through job rotation or the redirection of career paths. This approach avoids the possible short-sightedness of the here-and-now policy and the rigidity and, often, lack of realism inherent in the structured system. In conditions of rapid development and change, how far is it actually possible to plan careers over the long term? The answer must be, to a very limited extent, except in a static organization which has implicitly recognized that it provides a 'cradle-to-grave' career for people who, in general, are willing to wait for 'Buggins' turn' – and there are fewer and fewer organizations setting out to provide 'jobs for life' nowadays.

As a generalization, the short-term system is likely to be more common in smallish, rapidly growing, 'organic' businesses where form follows function and the organization is fluid and flexible. The longer-term system is more prevalent in larger, bureaucratic, 'mechanistic' types of organization, where accurate forecasts of future needs can be made, significant changes in skill requirements are not likely to take place and there is a steady flow, according to easily assessed performance, up the promotion ladder. A longer-term flexibility approach is likely to be pursued by the majority of organizations who fall into neither of the other two categories, and this is probably the best approach in most circumstances.

Specialists or generalists

Career management policies should cover the extent to which the organization is concerned about developing better and better specialists (broadly in line with the short-term approach) or whether it attaches equal, or even more, importance to developing the appropriate number of generalists who are capable of moving into general management. Obviously, all organizations have a mix of these two categories, but it may be a matter of policy to create a dual career structure with separate career ladders for pure specialists, who would be rewarded in accordance with their technical contribution and not in line with their place in a management grade hierarchy. There is no universal law that says a top-rate specialist who is not a manager and does not want to be one, must be paid less than someone who happens to have the skills and inclinations to take him or her along the management route.

Clearly, the policy depends on the type of organization, especially its technology and the extent to which it is either a hierarchy of managers and support staff with a few specialists on the side, or a hi-tech, research-based operation where the scientist and development engineers rule.

Dealing with the 'plateaued' manager

Inevitably, the great majority of managers will eventually 'plateau-out' in their careers within an organization and this is more likely to happen in a flatter 'delayered' organization where middle management jobs have been 'stripped out' as a result of a reorganization or business process re-engineering programme. Such activities may result in redundancies, which replace the problem of coming to a dead end in an organization with another problem. Some of those who remain may be reconciled to the end of the 'rat race' but continue to work effectively. Others will become bored and frustrated, especially rising stars on the wane. These may no longer be productive and can become positively disruptive. Steps must be taken either to reshape their careers so that they still have challenging work at the same level, even if this does not involve promotion up the hierarchy. Others may have to be encouraged to start new careers elsewhere. In either of these cases the organization should provide career advice, possibly through 'outplacement' consultants who provide a counselling service.

DEMAND AND SUPPLY FORECASTS

Demand and supply forecasts are provided by the use of human resource planning techniques (see Chapter 24). Modelling can allow for sensitivity analysis of the impact of different assumptions about the future (answering 'what if' questions).

Expert systems can also be used where there is an extensive database on flows, attribute requirements (person specifications), and performance and potential assessments. Such systems can establish relationships between the opportunities and the personal attributes they demand so that careers advisers can take a set of personal attributes and identify the most appropriate available opportunities. At the career planning stage, they can also identify people with the correct abilities and skills for particular jobs and provide information on the career management programmes required to ensure that attributes and jobs are matched and careers progress at an appropriate rate. Career management systems such as ExecuGROW (Control Data) have been specially developed for this purpose.

There is a limit, however, to sophistication. There are so many variables and unpredictable changes in both supply and demand factors that it may be possible to conduct only an annual check to see what the relationship is between the numbers of managers who will definitely retire over the next four or five years and the numbers at the next level who have the potential to succeed them. If this comparison reveals a serious imbalance, then steps can be taken to reduce or even eliminate the deficit or to consider other types of deployment for those who are unlikely to progress. This comparison is represented graphically in Figure 39.4, in which the two hypothetical examples illustrate a surplus situation (a) and a deficit situation (b).

SUCCESSION PLANNING

The aim of management succession planning is to ensure that, as far as possible, suitable managers are available to fill vacancies created by promotion, retirement, death,

Figure 39.4 Demand and supply models

leaving, or transfer. It also aims to ensure that a cadre of managers is available to fill the new appointments that may be established in the future.

The information for management succession planning comes from organization reviews and demand-and-supply forecasts. The succession plans will be influenced by the career dynamics of the organization and also by the performance and potential assessments (see below), which provide information, often of limited validity, on who is ready now and in the future to fill projected vacancies. This information needs to be recorded so that decisions can be made on promotions and replacements, and training or additional experience arranged for those with potential or who are earmarked for promotion.

The records need not be elaborate. In practice, complex inventories and detailed succession charts replete with colour codes and other symbols are a waste of time, except in the largest and most bureaucratic organizations. All the information required can be recorded on a simple management succession schedule such as the one illustrated in Table 39.1.

A computerized human resource information system, as described in Chapter 57, can, with the help of competence modelling techniques, store inventories of the skills, competences and experience of individual employees together with records of their performance and potential assessments. Lists of attributes for key jobs can also be stored, and this information can be linked to the other data mentioned above to provide guidance on who is available to fill present or future vacancies and on any career plans needed to ensure that potential is realized.

Table 39.1 Management succession schedule

MANAGEMENT SUCCESSION SCHEDULE				Department		Director/Manager			
Present Managerial and Supervisory Staff						Possible successors			
			Rating		If promotable, indicate what position and when	Names (1st and 2nd choice)	Positions	When ready	
Name	Position	Age	Date due for replacement	Performance	Potential				

PERFORMANCE AND POTENTIAL ASSESSMENT

The aim of performance and potential assessment is to identify training and development needs, provide guidance on possible directions in which an individual's career might go, and indicate who has a potential for promotion. This information can be obtained from performance management processes, as described in Part VIII.

The assessment of potential can be carried out formally by managers following a performance review. They may be asked to identify managers who have a very high potential, some potential or no potential at all. They may even be asked to indicate when their managers will be ready for promotion and how far they are likely to get. The problem with this sort of assessment is that the assessors find it difficult to forecast the future for the people they are reviewing – good performance in the current job does not guarantee that individuals will be able to cope with wider responsibilities, especially if this involves moving into general management. And managers may not necessarily be aware of the qualities required for longer-term promotion. But the organization does need information on those with potential and assessors should be encouraged in their comments section at least to indicate that this is someone who is not only performing well in the present job but may perform well in higher-level jobs. This information can identify those who may be exposed to assessment or development centres which can be used to establish potential and discuss career plans. (Assessment and development centres are described in Chapters 25 and 38 respectively).

RECRUITMENT

Career management means taking into account the fact that the organization will inevitably need to recruit new managers, who will then have to prove themselves while gaining their initial experience and undergoing induction training. As soon as they have been with the company long enough to show what they can do and where they might go, their performance and potential can be assessed and they can be fed into the career management system.

CAREER PLANNING

The process of career planning

Career planning is the key process in career management. It uses all the information provided by the organization's assessments of requirements, the assessments of performance and potential and the management succession plans, and translates it in the form of individual career development programmes and general arrangements for management development, career counselling, mentoring and management training.

Career planning – the competency band approach

It is possible to define career progression in terms of the competencies required by individuals to carry out work at progressive levels of responsibility or contribution. These levels can be described as competency bands.

Competencies would be defined as the attributes and behavioural characteristics needed to perform effectively at each discrete level in a job family as described earlier in this chapter. The number of levels would vary according to the range of competencies required in a particular job family. For each band, the experience and training needed to achieve the competency level would be defined.

These definitions would provide a career map incorporating 'aiming points' for individuals, who would be made aware of the competency levels they must reach in order to achieve progress in their careers. This would help them to plan their own development, although support and guidance should be provided by their managers, HR specialists and, if they exist, management development advisers or mentors (the use of mentors is discussed in Appendix A). The provision of additional experience and training could be arranged as appropriate, but it would be important to clarify what individual employees need to do for themselves if they want to progress within the organization.

The advantage of this approach is that people are provided with aiming points and an understanding of what they need to do to reach them. One of the major causes of frustration and job dissatisfaction is the absence of this information.

A competency band career development approach can be linked to a job family pay structure, as described in Chapter 43, thus providing a fully integrated approach to career and reward management which recognizes the need to join these together. The operation of a competence band career progression system is illustrated in Figure 39.5.

Career planning is for core managers as well as high-flyers

The philosophy upon which career plans are based refers not only to advancing careers to meet organizational and individual requirements, but also the need to maximize the potential of the people in the organization in terms of productivity and satisfaction under conditions of change, when development does not necessarily

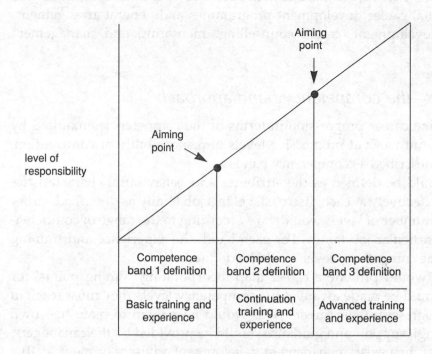

Figure 39.5 Competence band career progression system

mean promotion. An obsession with high-flyers and 'fast-tracking' may lead to a neglect of the majority of employees, who also need to be motivated, encouraged and given every opportunity to use their skills and abilities.

Career planning is for individuals as well as the organization

Career planning procedures are always based on what the organization needs. But they have to recognize that organizational needs will not be satisfied if individual needs are neglected. Career planning has to be concerned with the management of diversity.

Career plans must therefore recognize that:

- members of the organization should receive recognition as individuals with unique needs, wants, and abilities;
- individuals are more motivated by an organization that responds to their aspirations and needs;

● individuals can grow, change and seek new directions if they are given the right opportunities, encouragement and guidance.

Career planning techniques

Career planning uses all the information generated by the succession plans, performance, and potential assessments and self-assessments to develop programmes and procedures which are designed to implement career management policies, achieve succession planning objectives and generally improve motivation, commitment and performance. The procedures used are those concerned with:

● personal development planning (see Chapter 37);
● training and management development, as described in Chapters 36 and 38.
● mentoring as described in Appendix A;
● career counselling as described in the following section.

In addition, career planning procedures may cater for the rising stars by 'fast-tracking' them, that is, deliberately accelerating promotion and giving them opportunities to display and enlarge their talents. But these procedures should pay just as much, if not more, attention to those managers who are following the middle route of steady, albeit unspectacular, progression.

Career counselling

Performance management processes, as described in Chapter 31, should provide for counselling sessions between individuals and their managers. These sessions should give the former the opportunity to discuss their aspirations and the latter the chance to comment on them – helpfully – and, at a later stage, to put forward specific career development proposals to be fed into the overall career management programme.

Development centres as described in Chapter 38 can provide a valuable vehicle for career counselling and planning.

Career counselling is, however, a skilled job and the immediate boss is not always the best person to do it, although all managers should be trained in the techniques involved. Some large organizations have appointed specialists whose sole job is to provide a career counselling service to back up the efforts of line managers and to advise on what needs to be done by individuals or, more generally, by the organization as a whole. Mentoring can also be used for this purpose.

The individuals concerned may need an increased level of self-awareness, better access to information about career opportunities and improved decision-making skills.

Career prospects in flatter organizations

Flatter and leaner organization structures have resulted in significant changes in career prospects. The scope for promotion may be much more limited and development may have to proceed laterally by moving to new roles at broadly the same level rather than relying on upward career progression through an extended hierarchy. Lateral movement can, however, involve growth by offering opportunities to take on extra responsibilities such as working on inter-departmental project teams, extending experience and therefore employability and enhancing skills and competencies.

A study carried out by the Roffey Park Management Institute (Holbeche, 1994) into career development in flatter organizations estimated that about 95 per cent of UK-based organizations have undertaken delayering exercises or are about to do so. This is making a major contribution to the demise of the 'job for life' notion, and as Linda Holbeche points out, employees are having to adjust their expectations about career development within their organization and recognize that they no longer have well-defined career paths through promotion. She suggests that:

> Career management in flatter structures calls for an approach which explicitly takes into account both organizational needs and employee interests. It will encompass recruitment, personal development plans, lateral moves, international assignments, development positions, career bridges, and support for employees who want to develop.
>
> It calls for creativity in identifying ways to provide development opportunities and enhance employee loyalty.

This has also meant that the psychological contract concerning career development has to change. Holbeche (1994) states that the older version of the psychological contract would offer promotion and long-term employment with the organization, while the new contract specifies that people have responsibility for managing their own career to increase their employability but that the organization must support their efforts to become multi-skilled

To recognize the changes in career opportunities and the new psychological contract, Holbeche (1997) suggests that organizations could introduce career bands in which opportunities for lateral growth would be specified. This proposal fits the concept of broad-banded pay structures and the notion of career development pay as people move laterally through the band.

Part X

Reward management

Reward management is about how people are rewarded in accordance with their value to an organization. It is concerned with both financial and non-financial rewards, and embraces the philosophies, strategies, policies, plans and processes used by organizations to develop and maintain reward systems.

Reward management processes deal with the design, implementation and maintenance of reward systems geared to the improvement of organizational, team and individual performance. The American term 'compensation' is sometimes used as an alternative to reward but it seems to imply that work is an unpleasant necessity that employees have to be compensated for doing rather than spending their time more profitably elsewhere.

Reward management is treated in this handbook as very much part of an HRM approach to managing people. The essential features of this approach are that it:

- *supports the achievement of the business strategy;*
- *is integrated with other HRM strategies, especially those concerning human resource development;*
- *is based on a well-articulated philosophy – a set of beliefs and assumptions which are consistent with the HRM philosophies of the business and underpin the ways in which it proposes to reward its employees;*

- *recognizes that if HRM is about investing in human capital, from which a reasonable return is required, then it is proper to reward people differentially according to their contribution (ie the return on investment they generate);*
- *focuses on the development of the skills and competencies of employees in order to increase the resource-based capability of the firm (pay for competence or skill);*
- *is itself an integrated process which can operate flexibly;*
- *supports other key HRM initiatives in the fields of resourcing, development and employee relations.*

Reward management is dealt with in this part under the following headings:

- *reward management systems;*
- *job evaluation;*
- *market rate analysis;*
- *pay structures;*
- *contingent pay (a portmanteau phrase used to cover payment for performance, competence, contribution or skill schemes);*
- *rewarding special groups: directors, expatriates and sales representatives;*
- *employee benefits and pensions;*
- *managing the reward system.*

40

Reward management systems

INTRODUCTION

This chapter:

- describes the concept of a reward system in terms of its components, elements and aims;
- discusses the economic and other factors that determine pay levels;
- discusses the foundations for employee reward systems provided by reward strategies and policies;
- reviews the current and future reward management scene.

THE REWARD MANAGEMENT SYSTEM

An employee reward system consists of an organization's integrated policies, processes and practices for rewarding its employees in accordance with their contribution, skill and competence and their market worth. It is developed within the framework of the organization's reward philosophy, strategies and policies and contains arrangements in the form of processes, practices, structures and procedures which will provide and maintain appropriate types and levels of pay, benefits and other forms of reward.

COMPONENTS OF A REWARD SYSTEM

A reward system consists of financial rewards (fixed and variable pay) and employee benefits, which together comprise total remuneration. The system also incorporates non-financial rewards (recognition, praise, achievement, responsibility and personal growth) and, in many cases, performance management processes.

THE ELEMENTS OF REWARD MANAGEMENT

The elements of a reward management system are described below.

Base pay

Base or basic pay is the fixed salary or wage which constitutes the rate for the job. For manual workers it may be referred to as time or day rate. It may provide the platform for determining additional payments related to performance, competence or skill. It may also govern pension entitlements and life insurance when they are related to pay. The basic levels of pay for jobs reflect both internal and external relativities. The internal relativities may be measured by some form of job evaluation which places jobs in a hierarchy (although the trend now is to play down the notion of hierarchy in the new process-based organizations). External relativities are assessed by tracking market rates. Alternatively, levels of pay may be agreed through negotiation (collectively bargaining with trade unions) or by individual agreements. The base rate for a job is sometimes regarded as the rate for a competent or skilled person in a job. This rate may be varied in a skill-based or competence-based system according to the individual's skills or competence.

Levels of pay may be based on long-standing structures which were first created in the mists of time and have been updated since then in response to movements in market rates and inflation and through negotiations. In many organizations pay levels evolve – they are not planned or maintained systematically. Rates are fixed by managerial judgement of what is required to recruit and retain people. They may be adjusted in response to individual or collective pressures for increases or upgradings. This evolutionary and *ad hoc* process can result in a chaotic and illogical pay structure which is inequitable, leads to inconsistent and unfair pay decisions and is difficult to understand, expensive to maintain and the cause of dissatisfaction and demotivation. Pay levels are affected by economic factors as discussed later in this chapter and by negotiations with trade unions which will influence levels of pay in accordance with whatever bargaining power they possess.

Base pay may be expressed as an annual, weekly or hourly rate (time rates) and it may be adjusted to reflect increases in the cost of living or market rates by the organization unilaterally or by agreement with a trade union. Performance, skill-based or competence-related pay increases may be added to or 'consolidated' into the basic rate. Similarly, consolidated increases may be given based on time in the grade. This is a fixed incremental pay system, which is often associated with a pay spine as described in Chapter 42. But some companies pay non-consolidated performance-related cash bonuses.

Additions to base pay

Additional financial rewards may be provided which are related to performance, skill, competence or experience. Special allowances may also be paid. If such payments are not consolidated into base pay they can be described as 'variable pay'. Variable pay is sometimes defined as 'pay at risk'. For example, the pay of sales representatives on a 'commission only' basis is entirely at risk. The main types of additional pay are:

- *Individual performance-related pay* in which increases to base pay or cash bonuses are determined by performance assessment and ratings (also known as merit pay).
- *Bonuses* – rewards for successful performance, which are paid as lump sums related to the results obtained by individuals, teams or the organization.
- *Incentives* – payments linked to the achievement of previously set targets which are designed to motivate people to achieve higher levels of performance. The targets are usually quantified in such terms as output or sales.
- *Commission* – a special form of incentive in which payments to sales representatives are made on the basis of a percentage of the sales value they generate.
- *Service-related pay* – pay that increases by fixed increments on a scale or pay spine depending on service in the job. There may sometimes be scope for varying the rate of progression through the scale according to performance.
- *Skill-based pay* (sometimes called knowledge-based pay) – pay that varies according to the level of skill achieved by the individual.
- *Competence-related pay* – pay that varies according to the level of competence achieved by the individual.
- *Allowances* – these are elements of pay that are provided as a separate sum of money for such aspects of employment as overtime, shift working, call-outs and living in London or other large cities. London or large city allowances are sometimes consolidated and organizations that are simplifying their pay structure may 'buy out' the allowance and increase base pay accordingly.

- *Contribution-related pay* – pay related to the contribution of the individual performance and competence.

Total earnings

Total earnings are usually calculated as the sum of base pay and any additional payments. They constitute the amount of money paid into the bank or placed in an employee's pay packet. When explaining to individual employees how their pay package is built up, it is necessary to break the total pay down into the different components listed above and indicate how, in their case, they have combined to produce the final sum they are receiving.

Employee benefits

Employee benefits, also known as indirect pay, include pensions, sick pay, insurance cover and company cars. They comprise elements of remuneration given in addition to the various forms of cash pay and also include provisions for employees which are not strictly remuneration, such as annual holidays.

Total remuneration

Total remuneration is the value of all cash payments (total earnings) and benefits received by employees.

Non-financial rewards

These include any rewards that focus on the needs people have to varying degrees for achievement, recognition, responsibility, influence and personal growth.

Pay levels

Pay levels are the rates of pay for jobs as determined by reference to market rates, formal or informal job evaluation processes and, sometimes, collective bargaining.

Pay structures

The pay structure of an organization defines the pay levels for individual jobs. These may be grouped into grades, to each of which is attached a pay range which allows scope for pay progression related to performance, skill, competence or time. Alternatively they may be placed on a pay spine as described in Chapter 43.

The elements of a reward system and their interrelationships are illustrated in Figure 40.1.

GENERAL FACTORS DETERMINING PAY LEVELS

Pay levels for jobs and individuals are determined by a combination of the following factors:

Figure 40.1 A reward system

- *the external value of the job (external relativities)* – the market rates for jobs as influenced by economic factors operating within external labour markets as described below; these rates are assessed by means of market rate surveys;
- *the internal value of the job (internal relativities)* – the comparative value of jobs in the internal labour market as assessed by formal or informal job evaluation processes;
- *the value of the person* – the value attached to individuals as measured by formal or informal appraisal or performance management processes;
- *the contribution of the individual or team* – rewards to individuals or teams related to performance, skill or competence;
- *collective bargaining* – pay negotiations with trade unions.

ECONOMIC FACTORS AFFECTING PAY LEVELS

Labour markets

Like all other markets, the labour market has buyers (employers) and sellers (employees). It is in the external market that the economic determinants of pay levels operate. In the internal labour market pay levels and relativities may differ significantly between firms in spite of general external market pressures. These arise particularly when long-term relationships are usual, even though these are becoming less common. Pay progression related to length of service and an 'annuity' approach to pay increments (ie pay that goes up but does not come down, what economists call 'the sticky wage') may lead to higher internal rates. Pay in the internal market will also be affected by decisions on which individuals should be awarded for their particular contributions or specialized expertise, irrespective of the market rate for their job. But the relationship between internal and external rates will also depend on policy decisions within the firm on its levels of pay generally, or on the rates for specified occupations compared with 'the going rate', ie the market rate for comparable jobs. Within the external and internal labour markets the economic theories about pay are concerned with supply and demand, efficiency wage theory, human capital theory and agency theory.

Supply and demand

Classical economic competitive theory states that pay levels in labour markets are determined by supply and demand considerations. Other things being equal, if the supply of labour exceeds the demand, pay levels go down; if the demand for labour exceeds the supply, pay goes up. Pay stabilizes when demand equals supply at the 'market clearing' or 'market equilibrium wage'. This is sometimes known as the theory of equalizing differences. Classical theory, however, is based on the premises that 'other things are equal' and that a 'perfect market' for labour exists. In the real world, of course, other things are never equal and there is no such thing as a universally perfect market, that is, one in which everyone knows what the going rate is, there is free movement of labour within the market and there are no monopolistic or other forces interfering with the normal processes of supply and demand. The existence of internal markets means that individual firms exercise a good deal of discretion about how much they pay and how much attention they give to external market pressures.

Efficiency wage theory

Efficiency wage theory proposes that firms will pay more than the market rate because they believe that high levels of pay will contribute to increases in productivity by motivating superior performance, attracting better candidates, reducing labour turnover and persuading workers that they are being treated fairly. This theory is also known as 'the economy of high wages'.

Human capital theory

Human capital theory states that investment in people adds to their value to the firm. Individuals expect a return on their own investment and firms recognize that the increased value of their employees should be rewarded. Human capital theory encourages the use of skill-based or competence-related pay as a method of reward. It also underpins the concept of individual market worth which indicates that individuals have their own value in the marketplace which they acquire and increase through investments by their employer and themselves in gaining extra expertise and competence through training, development and experience. The market worth of individuals may be considerably higher than the market rate of their jobs, and if they are not rewarded accordingly they may market their talents elsewhere.

Agency theory

Agency theory, or principal agent theory, in its purest form recognizes that in most firms there is a separation between the owners (the principals) and the agents (the managers). However, the principals may not have complete control over their agents. The latter may therefore act in ways which are not fully revealed to their principals and which may not be in accordance with the wishes of those principals. This generates what economists call agency costs which arise from the difference between what might have been earned if the principals had been the managers, and the earnings achieved under the stewardship of the actual managers. To reduce these agency costs, the principals have to develop ways of monitoring and controlling the actions of their agents.

Agency theory as described above can be extended to the employment contract within firms. The employment relationship may be regarded as a contract between a principal (the employer) and an agent (the employee). The payment aspect of the contract is the method used by the principal to motivate the agent to perform work to the satisfaction of the employer. But according to this theory, the problem of ensuring that agents do what they are told remains. It is necessary to clear up ambiguities by setting objectives and monitoring performance to ensure that those objectives are achieved.

Agency theory also indicates that it is desirable to operate a system of incentives to motivate and reward acceptable behaviour. This process of 'incentive alignment' consists of paying for measurable results which are deemed to be in the best interests of the owners. Such incentive systems track outcomes in the shape of quantifiable indices of the firm's performance such as earnings per share rather than being concerned with the behaviour that led up to them. The theory is that if the incentives schemes for top managers are designed properly, those managers will out of self-interest closely monitor performance throughout the organization.

AIMS OF REWARD MANAGEMENT – THE ORGANIZATION'S REQUIREMENTS

A reward system expresses what the organization values and is prepared to pay for. It is governed by the need to reward the right things to get the right message across about what is important.

Overall aim

The overall aim of reward management is to support the attainment of the organization's strategic and shorter-term objectives by helping to ensure that it has the skilled, competent, committed and well-motivated workforce it needs.

Specific aims

From the organization's point of view, the specific aims of reward management are to:

- play a significant part in the communication of the organization's value, performance, standard and expectations;
- encourage behaviour that will contribute to the achievement of the organization's objectives and reflect the 'balanced score card' of key performance drivers – two of the basic questions to be answered when developing reward systems are: 'What sort of behaviour do we want?' and 'How can reward processes promote that behaviour?'
- underpin organizational change programmes concerned with culture, process and structure;
- support the realization of the key values of the organization in such areas as quality, customer care, teamwork, innovation, flexibility and speed of response;
- provide value for money – no reward initiative should be undertaken unless it has been established that it will add value, and no reward practice should be retained if it does not result in added value.

REWARD AIMS FROM THE EMPLOYEE'S POINT OF VIEW

From the employees' point of view the reward system should:

- treat them as stakeholders who have the right to be involved in the development of the reward policies that affect them;
- meet their expectations that they will be treated equitably, fairly and consistently in relation to the work they do and their contribution;
- be transparent – they should know what the reward policies of the organization are and how they are affected by them.

ACHIEVING THE AIMS

It is sometimes said that to achieve these aims an organization's pay practices should be 'internally equitable and externally competitive'. This is all right as far as it goes but it is not always easy to attain, and it presents a somewhat limited point of view. The first problem is that the goals of internal equity and external competitiveness are often hard to reconcile. The pressure of market forces may overcome internal equity considerations when people with scarce talents have to be recruited. On the other hand, a crude wish to be competitive may be inappropriate. As Schuster and Zingheim (1992) point out: 'The strategic view of competitive practices suggests that achieving competitive pay should be contingent upon providing a level of work quality, productivity, or performance which must justify pay levels that reflect expected reasonable goal performance.' In other words, competitive pay should be linked with competitive performance.

The aims of a reward management system are best achieved if:

- reward strategies are developed, as described later in this chapter, which are aligned to the business strategies for financial performance, market share, product/market development, quality, customer focus and organizational development (cultural and structural change);
- reward policies are formulated, as discussed later in this chapter, which enable reward philosophies and strategies to be implemented consistently but are flexed in accordance with the changing needs of the business;
- employees are valued according to their contribution, skill and competence;
- the reward system is transparent and employees are treated as stakeholders who are entitled to make representations on any area of reward that affects their interests and who will be involved in the development of reward processes;
- employee relations strategies are designed to build mutual trust and to develop a partnership approach which provides for increases in prosperity to be shared with all employees (not just the favoured few at the top);
- reward policies emphasize the need for equity and fairness while recognizing that the ideal of internal equity may not be sustainable in full because of market pressures;
- the maximum amount of responsibility is devolved to line managers to manage the reward system within their budgets and in accordance with broad policy guidelines;
- there is a constant thrust to maximize the performance leverage of any money spent on pay;
- reward initiatives are only taken if their interaction with other business and personnel policies is assessed, and an integrated approach is adopted to the development of mutually supportive processes.

REWARD STRATEGY

Reward strategy defines the intentions of the organization on how its reward policies and processes should be developed to meet business requirements. The fact that payroll costs can comprise 70 per cent or more of the total costs incurred by an organization explains the need to adopt a strategic approach to reward which ensures that added value is obtained from any investment in pay.

An effective reward strategy:

- is based on corporate values and beliefs;
- flows from the business strategy but also contributes to it;
- is driven by business needs and 'fits' the business strategy;
- aligns organizational and individual competences;
- is integrated with other personnel and developmental strategies;
- is congruent with the internal and external environment of the organization – the content of the strategy will be contingent on those environments;
- provides for the reward of results and behaviour that are consistent with key organizational goals, thus driving and supporting desired behaviour;
- is linked to business performance, adopting a competitive strategy perspective;
- is practical and implementable;
- has been evolved in consultation with key stakeholders, taking full account of their views on what they believe is best for them – unless such account is taken, reward initiatives like performance pay can fail totally.

Reward strategy should be developed as an integrated part of the total personnel strategy of the organization. The aim should be to ensure that it will support initiatives in the fields of resourcing, development and the overall goals for improving organizational performance. The strategy should also take into account the employee relations climate and the processes for negotiating pay with trade unions.

Content of reward strategy

The aspects of employee reward which may be regarded as key strategic issues include:

- competitive pay;
- achieving a more equitable and definable pay system;
- restructuring the pay system to take account of, indeed to underpin, organizational changes; for example, introducing broadbanding after a delayering exercise;
- using pay as a lever for performance improvement and culture change;
- devolution of pay decisions to line managers;
- involvement of employees in reward matters;
- developing teamwork;
- increasing levels of competence and enlarging the skill base (support to multi-skilling).

REWARD POLICY

Reward policy provides guidelines for decision making and action. It may include statements of guiding principles or common purposes. It addresses issues such as the following:

- *competitive pay* – the 'pay policy' or 'pay stance' of the organization indicates the extent to which it wants to be 'market-led', ie the relationship it wishes to maintain between its pay levels and market rates;
- *internal equity* – the policy will indicate the degree to which internal equity is a prime consideration and the circumstances in which the need to be competitive may override the principle of internal equity;
- *contingent pay* – the extent, if any, to which the firm believes that pay would vary according to performance, competence or skill;
- *variable pay* – the extent to which it is believed that contingent pay should be at risk, ie, is not consolidated;
- *individual or team reward* – the need for rewards to concentrate on individual or team performance;
- *employee benefits* – the types and levels of employee benefits to be provided and the extent to which employees can choose the benefits they want;
- *the total reward mix* – the mix of total rewards between base pay, variable pay and indirect pay (employee benefits) and the use of non-financial rewards, bearing in mind that there is always choice within a portfolio of reward practices;
- *structure* – the extent to which the organization wants a hierarchical and relatively formal (narrow-banded structure) or one which is flexible and broad-banded;
- *reward priorities* – the degree to which the organization wants to concentrate on 'piling the rewards high' for the relatively small number of key players, or recognizes the need to provide rewards which will support the steady improvement of the many (in other words, who are the people likely to exert the most leverage on overall business performance who should be rewarded accordingly?);
- *differentials* – the levels of reward at the top of the organization compared with average and minimum reward levels;
- *flexibility* – the amount of flexibility allowable in operating the reward system; the degree of consistency required in applying policies; the amount of control exercised from the centre;
- *uniformity* – the extent to which pay structures and policies should apply to the whole organization or be flexed for different levels or categories of employees;
- *devolution* – the amount of authority that will be devolved to line managers to make pay decisions;

- *control* – how much control should be exercised from the centre over the implementation of reward policies;
- *gender neutrality* – the approach that will be adopted towards eliminating gender bias in reward processes and structures so as to ensure that equal pay is provided for work of equal value;
- *partnership* – the extent to which the organization believes in sharing success with employees;
- *involvement* – how much employees will be involved in pay decisions that affect them, including the development of new approaches;
- *transparency* – how much should be published about reward policies and practices.

DEVELOPMENTS IN REWARD MANAGEMENT

The main developments in reward management as summarized by Armstrong and Brown (2001) are set out in Figure 40.2.

Old	New
• Focus on financial reward	• Focus on total reward
• Reactive pay	• Strategic pay
• Administered pay	• Business-driven pay
• Bureaucratic pay systems	• Flexible pay systems
• Stand-alone pay systems	• Integrated pay and HR processes
• Hierarchical structures	• Lateral/continuous development focus
• Pay-for-performance	• Pay-for-contribution
• Priority given to internal equity	• Market driven
• Job-centred	• People-centred
• Imposed 'best practice'	• Contingency/cultural fit
• HR control	• Devolution to the line
• Pay spines/multi-graded structures	• Broad-banded/job family structures

Figure 40.2 Developments in reward management

Focus on total reward

The total reward concept as modelled in Figure 40.3 focuses on the interlinked and cumulative impact of various forms of reward – base pay, variable pay, benefits and non-financial rewards. It hypothesizes that the aim of reward strategy should be to develop an integrated and mutually supporting range of processes which in conjunction with one another will make a much more powerful and longer-lasting impact on individual, team and organizational effectiveness.

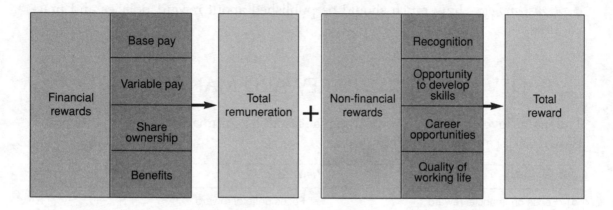

Figure 40.3   The components of total reward

Strategic reward

In the past, pay practices tended to react to business and market pressures to produce short-term panaceas. In 1990 Ed Lawler exposed the limitations of this approach when he wrote:

> The starting point for any reward system design process needs to be the strategic agenda of the organization. Thus the first step in designing the reward system for an organization is to focus on the individual and organizational behaviours that are needed in order for the organization to be successful.

Business-driven pay

Reward is no longer an isolated function, it is part of the strategic business process. This contrasts with the traditional 'salary administration' approach in which pay specialists lived an isolated life running bureaucratic systems and dealing on a day-to-day or pay review basis with immediate job grading or pay level issues.

Flexible pay systems

Increasingly, the tendency is to 'free-up' reward structures and processes, hence the development of broad banding and job families, and the relegation of job evaluation in many businesses to a support role rather than one which dominates grading and therefore pay decisions.

Integrated reward and HR processes

Pay systems and supporting processes such as job evaluation and performance appraisal used to stand alone, apart from other HR processes. They existed in their own right and had little or no contact with other HR processes. This is changing, as Armstrong commented in 2000:

> Broad banded and job-family structures are no longer treated simply as vehicles for delivering pay and are often seen as being complementary to competence and career development policies. The main aim is to provide information on development opportunities and career paths that, as part of a performance management process, can contribute to personal development planning.

In fact, organizations are often focusing initially on the business need for such policies and the processes required. Only then do they consider how reward systems can support them, frequently basing pay structures on competence frameworks and profiles.

Continuous development focus

In what was once the typical multi-graded structure the emphasis was on the hierarchy. The only way ahead was upwards through promotion or regrading. The pressure on upgrading contributed to grade drift and a reduction in the credibility of job evaluation when it was manipulated to provide the justification for a higher grade. In delayered, 'lean' organizations, the opportunities for promotion have been reduced but the scope for lateral development has expanded. Roles are more flexible and people not only grow within their roles but also grow their roles.

Pay-for-contribution

As Brown and Armstrong commented in 1999: 'The goals of performance-related pay schemes were often not clear, agreed or accepted (nor even performance-related in some cases), and even more critically, the schemes did not operate in practice as intended.' Another objection to performance-related pay was that it was solely concerned with outputs. The belief that people should be rewarded for their skill or competence (their inputs) led to the interest in competence-related pay. More recently, however, it has been recognized that people should be rewarded for both their outputs (results) and their inputs (competence): in other words, not only for what they do but how they do it. This approach is termed contribution-related pay.

Market-driven

At once time, organizations tended to give more attention to considerations of internal equity than those of external competitiveness. But now businesses such as BT, IBM and Xerox GB are recognizing that they have to compete for scarce skills in the labour market, which means that their pay levels have to be market-driven. Almost without exception, the companies covered by the CIPD research carried out in 2000 (Armstrong and Brown, 2001) had adapted market-driven pay policies, often associated with a broad-banded or job family structure.

People-centred

In 1986, Ed Lawler wrote that job evaluation tends to depersonalize people by equating them with a set of duties rather than concentrating on what people are and what they can do. He advocated a people-based rather than a job-based approach, and this has become an important aspect of the philosophy underpinning broad-banded and job family structures – that it is people not jobs that add value, and that people should be rewarded for their contribution rather than because they happen to have been given certain things to do. The focus is on roles – the part people play – rather than on jobs – the tasks they are given as prescribed in a job description.

Best fit

Reward management was governed for many years by the concept of 'best practice' – there are universal ways of doing the right thing. What is now appreciated is that 'best fit' is more important. Reward strategies and practices should be contingent on the circumstances of the organization. They should fit the needs of the business and its culture as it is now or as the organization wants it to become.

Devolution to the line

HR has traditionally controlled the implementation of pay policies and practice. Line managers have tended to do what they are told. Some shelter behind HR decisions and are glad to blame them for pay problems. Others lack the skills or inclination to spend time managing pay in their own departments. The tendency now is to devolve more responsibility for pay decisions to line managers as part of a policy of improvement which involves devolution of decision-making and responsibility.

Devolution of pay decisions is often associated with broad-banded structures because the increased flexibility of such structures means that managers who are on the spot are best equipped with the information to manage reward.

Broad-banded and job family structures

A number of the factors mentioned above have contributed to the shift away from pay spines and multi-graded structures. The most important of these have been the need to:

- achieve greater flexibility in pay management;
- reduce the bureaucracy associated with multi-grade structures and job evaluation;
- reward lateral development and continuous improvement;
- clarify career paths;
- respond to the changing nature of work;
- provide for more management involvement in pay.

These are the considerations which have led organizations to introduce broad-banded and job family structures, or a combination of the two, which are becoming the norm rather than the exception.

41

Job evaluation

Decisions on pay levels and structures provide the foundation for the reward system. These decisions are based on job evaluation as described in this chapter and market rate surveys as discussed in Chapter 42.

- job evaluation is defined;
- its nature, main features and basic methodology are discussed;
- the different types of job evaluation schemes are described;
- the considerations to be taken into account when introducing and maintaining job evaluation are considered, including equal pay for work of equal value issues.

JOB EVALUATION – DEFINITION AND PURPOSE

Job evaluation is a systematic process for establishing the relative worth of jobs within an organization. Its purpose is to:

- provide a rational basis for the design and maintenance of an equitable and defensible pay structure;
- help in the management of the relativities existing between jobs within the organization;

- enable consistent decisions to be made on grading and rates of pay;
- establish the extent to which there is comparable worth between jobs so that equal pay can be provided for work of equal value.

Job evaluation enables a framework to be designed which underpins pay decisions. It can help with internal comparisons and, to a degree, external comparisons by providing a common language for use in discussing the relative worth of jobs and people.

Research conducted by Armstrong and Baron (1998) established that 55 per cent of the 316 organizations covered by the survey had a formal job evaluation scheme. It was confirmed that the primary reason given by organizations for introducing job evaluation is to ensure a more equitable pay structure. Organizations commonly introduce job evaluation because they want to replace chaos with order, inconsistency with consistency and political judgement with rational judgement.

However, job evaluation is not a scientific and objective 'system' which, after it has been 'installed', will at a stroke remove all the problems experienced in managing internal relativities, fixing rates of pay and controlling the pay structure. This, of course, is asking far too much of job evaluation which should be regarded as a process rather than a system. This process may be systematic and it can reduce subjectivity, but it will always be more art than science and, because it relies on human judgements, it can never be fully objective.

THE KEY FEATURES OF JOB EVALUATION

Job evaluation can be regarded as:

- *A comparative process* – it deals with relationships not absolutes.
- *A judgemental process* – it requires the exercise of judgement in interpreting data on jobs and roles (job and role definitions or completed job analysis questionnaires), comparing one job with another, comparing jobs against factor level definitions and scales, and developing a grade structure from a rank order of jobs produced by job evaluation.
- *An analytical process* – job evaluation may be judgemental but it is based on informed judgements which in an analytical scheme are founded on a process of gathering facts about jobs, sorting these facts out systematically in order to break them down into various elements, and reassembling them into whatever standard format is being used.
- *A structured process* – job evaluation is structured in the sense that a framework is

provided which aims to help evaluators make consistent and reasoned judgements; this framework consists of language and criteria which are used by all evaluators, although because the criteria are always subject to interpretation, they do not guarantee that judgements will be either consistent or rational.

Jobs and people

Traditional job evaluation deliberately avoids considering the value of people. Human beings are treated as unnecessary intrusions in the pure world of job hierarchies with which job evaluation is concerned. Of course, the reason for the dogma that 'job evaluation measures the value of jobs not people' is to avoid contaminating the process of evaluation with considerations of the performance of individual job holders. And indeed it would be undesirable for job evaluators to get involved in performance assessment, which is a separate matter.

But the traditional view still implies that people have nothing to do with the value of the job they perform, and this is clearly ludicrous. It is equally misguided to make the universal assumption that people adapt to the fixed specification of their jobs rather than jobs being adapted to fit the characteristics of the people in them. In the new flexible organization, roles are created and evolve according to the strengths and limitations of the people who design and fill them. To sum up, it is people who create value, not jobs.

BASIC METHODOLOGY

The process of job evaluation begins by identifying which jobs are to be covered and the total number to be evaluated. A decision also has to be made on whether there should be one scheme for all employees or whether there should be separate schemes for different levels or categories of people. The next step is to choose one of the methods described later in this chapter. The final stages are to:

- select the representative 'benchmark' jobs which will be used as the basis for comparisons;
- decide on the factors to be used in evaluating the jobs;
- analyse the jobs and roles;
- establish the relative value of jobs by applying a process of evaluation;
- develop a pay structure – this usually means designing a grade structure and then deciding on the rates or ranges of pay in the structure through internal comparisons and 'market pricing'.

JOB EVALUATION SCHEMES

Job evaluation schemes can be divided broadly into the following types: non analytical, analytical, single factor, skill or competence based, market pricing, and the management consultants' schemes, the so-called proprietary brands.

Non-analytical schemes compare whole jobs with one another and make no attempt specifically to distinguish between the factors within the jobs that may differentiate them. Job ranking, paired comparison and job classification are usually regarded as the three main non-analytical schemes, although paired comparison is simply a statistical method of establishing rank order. Another non-analytical approach, which is not generally dignified with being called a scheme, is internal benchmarking. This may not be recognized as a proper form of job evaluation but it is, nevertheless, practised by a lot of organizations, even if they do not refer to it by that name. And once they have carried out their initial analytical job evaluation exercise, many organizations do in effect slot in jobs by internal benchmarking whenever they perceive a close affinity between the job in question and a representative benchmark job.

The *analytical schemes* are point-factor rating, as it is universally known in the United States (in the UK it is often called simply points rating or a points scheme), and factor comparison. Because of its complexity and a number of other fundamental flaws, the latter is little used in its traditional form and is therefore not dealt with in this chapter (a full description is given in Armstrong and Baron 1998). A modified form of what may be called graduated factor comparison is, however, sometimes adopted by the job evaluation 'experts' commissions by industrial tribunals to report on equal value cases.

Market pricing is used in conjunction with other internally orientated evaluation schemes to price jobs by reference to market rates.

Skill-based or competence-related schemes value people rather than jobs in terms of their attributes and competences. These are described in Chapter 42.

Management consultants' schemes – a number of management consultants such as HayGroup and Pilat (Gauge) offer 'proprietary brands'. Details are provided in Neathey (1994).

The principal features of the job ranking, job classification, internal benchmarking, point-factor and market pricing approaches are summarized below.

JOB RANKING

Job ranking is a non-analytical approach which compares whole jobs and does not attempt to assess separately different aspects of the jobs. It determines the position of jobs in a hierarchy by placing them in rank according to perceptions of their relative size.

If a graded pay structure is required (see Chapter 43), decisions are made on how the rank order should be divided into groups of jobs, the values of which are thought to be broadly comparable or at least within the same size range.

Ranking is the simplest and quickest form of job evaluation. It may be claimed that the process of assessing the value of the job as a whole to the organization is, in practice, what people do even when they go through the motions of assessing the different facets of a job in an analytical scheme. Ultimately, it can be argued, people will feel that their grading is fair by noting where their whole job is placed in relation to others.

The disadvantage of ranking, however, is that there is no rationale to defend the rank order – no defined standards for judging relative size. It is simply a matter of opinion, although it can be argued that analytical methods do no more than channel opinions into specified areas.

JOB CLASSIFICATION

Job classification is also a non-analytical method which compares whole jobs to a scale, in this case a grade definition. It is based on an initial decision on the number and characteristics of the grades into which the jobs will be placed. The grade definitions attempt to take into account discernible differences in skill, competence or responsibility and may refer to specific criteria, such as level of decisions, knowledge, equipment used and education and training required to do the work. Jobs are allotted to grades by comparing the whole job description with the grade definition.

Job classification is a simple, quick and easily implemented method of slotting jobs into an established structure. It attempts to provide some standards for judgement in the form of grade definition. Its lack of complexity and the ease with which it can be learned and used means that it is suitable for large populations and for decentralized operations in which more complex systems might be difficult to operate consistently. But it cannot cope with complex jobs with features which will not fit neatly into one grade. Like other non-analytical systems it is not being accepted for use in equal value cases and there is a danger of the descriptions becoming so generalized that they provide little help in evaluating borderline cases, especially at higher levels. Job classification also tends to be inflexible in that it is not sensitive to changes in the nature and content of jobs.

INTERNAL BENCHMARKING

Internal benchmarking is what people often do intuitively when they are deciding on the value of jobs. Evaluation by internal benchmarking simply means comparing or matching the job under review with any internal benchmark job which is believed to be properly graded and paid, and slotting the job under consideration into the same grade as the benchmark job. The comparison is usually made on a whole job basis without analysing the jobs factor by factor. However, internal benchmarking is likely to be much more accurate and acceptable if it is founded on the comparison of role definitions which indicate key result areas and the knowledge, skills and competence levels required to achieve the specified results.

Internal benchmarking is simple and quick, and it is natural in the sense that it involves comparing one job with another which, essentially, is what job evaluation is all about. It can produce reasonable results as long as it is based on the comparison of accurate job or role descriptions. But it relies on judgements which may be entirely subjective and could be hard to justify. It is also dependent on the identification of suitable benchmarks which are properly graded and paid, and such comparisons may only perpetuate existing inequities. Importantly, it would not be acceptable in equal value cases.

POINT-FACTOR RATING

Point-factor rating is an analytical method of job evaluation using job-scale comparisons.

The method is based on the breaking down of jobs into factors or key elements. It is assumed that each of the factors will contribute to job size and is a part of all the jobs to be evaluated but to different degrees. Using numerical scales, points are allocated to a job under each factor heading according to the degree to which it is present in the job. The separate factor scores are then added together to give a total score which represents job size.

The point-factor method is built on a *factor plan* which consists of:

- the choice of factors to be used in the scheme;
- the factor rating scales;
- factor weighting.

Choice of factors

A factor is a characteristic that occurs to a different degree in the jobs to be evaluated and can be used as a basis for assessing the relative value of the jobs. If, in common parlance, a job is said to be more responsible than another, and therefore worth more, responsibility is being used as a factor, however loosely responsibility is defined.

When we evaluate a job, even if there is no formal evaluation scheme, we always have some criterion in mind. It may be some generalized concept of 'responsibility', or may be more specifically related to the size of resources controlled or the contribution to end-results.

Point-factor schemes may have any number of factors, but to reduce complexity, there are normally between three and twelve. These can broadly be grouped under the three headings of:

- *Inputs* – the knowledge and skills and any other personal characteristics required to do the job. These may include such aspects as technical or professional knowledge, manual and mental skills, interpersonal skills and team-leading skills. The education, training and experience required to develop the knowledge and skills may also be regarded as a factor, as might the academic, technical or professional qualifications which indicate the level of knowledge acquired.
- *Process* – the characteristics of the work that determine the demands made by the job on job holders. These include such aspects as mental effort, problem solving, complexity, originality, creativity, judgement and initiative, team working, dealing with people (using interpersonal skills) and physical factors such as physical effort, working conditions and dangers or hazards associated with the work.
- *Outputs* – the contribution or impact the job holder can make on end-results taking into account such aspects of jobs as responsibility for output, quality, sales, profit etc, responsibility for resources such as people, assets and money, decision-making authority, and the effect of errors.

A typical list of factors would be:

- knowledge and skills (input);
- responsibility (output);
- decisions (process);
- complexity (process);
- interpersonal skills (process).

It is sometimes felt when drawing up a factor plan that a multiplicity of factors will guarantee more accurate judgements by evaluators. This is an illusion. The more factors there are, the greater the likelihood of overlap and duplication. Evaluators therefore find it difficult to make the fine distinctions required when making their judgements. And the extra work involved in using multi-factor schemes is considerable.

There are no absolute rules on what factors should be chosen although equal pay for work of equal value legislation and case law indicate that account should be taken of the demands made by a job on a worker under the headings of effort, skill and decisions.

The choice of factors and the weighting given to them will be influenced by the values of the organization or what is considered to be important when valuing the contribution of people in their roles. The selection therefore conveys a message to employees about these values and this is a good reason for involving them in the design of a tailor-made scheme.

Factor rating scales

Factor rating scales consist of definitions of the levels at which the factor can be present in any of the jobs to be evaluated. Jobs are analysed in terms of these factors and the result of this analysis is compared with the factor level definitions to establish the factor level. The maximum points score for a factor is determined by factor weighting (see below), and when this has been established, each level can be allocated a points score or a range of scores. Points progression is usually arithmetic (eg 20, 40, 60, 80, 100).

The number of levels or degrees to each factor depends on the range of jobs to be covered and the amount of sensitivity the scheme is attempting to achieve. Most schemes seem to have up to six or seven levels but there is no rule that says all factors must have the same number of levels.

When defining factor levels the aim is to produce a graduated series of definitions which will produce clear guidance on how the factor should be scored. This is difficult to achieve and can become a semantic exercise in the use of comparative adjective (big, bigger, biggest) to which no precise meaning can be attached. In some cases, however, it is possible to quantify levels in terms of outputs or the size of resources controlled. Successive levels can also be defined by reference to the use of specified skills or the need for particular qualifications, training or experience. In practice, level definitions become more meaningful to evaluators when they can relate them to benchmark jobs. What happens, in effect, is that the somewhat abstract level definition is brought to life by an example and the comparison is made from job to job as well as from job to scale.

An example of a definition of a factor and its levels is given in Figure 41.1.

COMPLEXITY

Factor definition

The variety and diversity of tasks carried out by the job holder and the range of skills used.

Level definitions

1. Highly repetitive work where the same task or group of tasks is carried out without any significant variation.
2. A fairly narrow range of tasks are carried out which tend to be closely related to one another and involve the use of a limited range of skills.
3. There is some diversity in the activities carried out although they are broadly related to one another. A fairly wide variety of skills have to be used.
4. A diverse range of broadly related tasks are carried out. A wide variety of administrative, technical or supervisory skills are used.
5. A highly diverse range of tasks are carried out, many of which are unrelated to one another. A wide variety of professional and/or managerial skills are used.
6. The work is multi-disciplinary and involves fulfilling a broad range of highly diverse responsibilities.

Figure 41.1 Examples of a definition of a factor and its levels

Factor weighting

A factor plan involves making decisions on the relative importance of the various factors – that is, their weighting for scoring purposes. It could be decided that all factors should be equally weighted but the great majority of points factor schemes do weight their factors differently.

Clearly, this is a critical decision. A factor which is overweighted in relation to its true significance as one of a number of factors could result in evaluations becoming badly skewed. For example, over-weighting a factor which refers to the number of people controlled could unduly favour managers with large numbers of easily controlled staff rather than high-powered specialists. Weighting also has equal value implications. To overweight a factor such as physical effort which mainly applies to male job holders could be seen as discriminatory.

The complete factor plan

A complete factor plan with weighted scores is illustrated in Table 41.1.

Using the factor plan

The points-factor job evaluation process involves analysing a job in terms of the factors, comparing that analysis with the factor and level definitions, allocating a

Table 41.1 A factor plan

Factor	Levels					
	1	2	3	4	5	6
knowledge and skills	20	40	60	80	100	120
responsibility	20	40	60	80	100	120
decisions	15	30	45	60	75	90
complexity	10	20	30	40	50	60
contacts	10	20	30	40	50	60

level and score for each factor, and adding up the factor scores to produce a total job evaluation score for the job as shown in Table 41.2.

This can be compared with the scores for other jobs, which produces a ranked order of jobs according to their score. If there is a graded pay structure, decisions are then made on how these jobs should be grouped into grades (this is often a matter of judgement). A separate decision is made on the pay ranges to be attached to the job grades, which will be influenced by market rate considerations and what is considered to be an appropriate range of pay in a grade and the size of the pay differentials between grades.

Advantages of point-factor schemes

The advantages of point-factor schemes are:

Table 41.2 Example of a job evaluation score

Factor	Evaluated level	Score
knowledge and skills	3	60
responsibility	4	80
decisions	4	60
complexity	5	50
contacts	3	30
total score		280

- Evaluators are forced to consider a range of factors which, as long as they are present in all the jobs and affect them in different ways, will avoid the over-simplified judgements made when using non-analytical schemes.
- Points schemes provide evaluators with defined yardsticks which should help them achieve some degree of objectivity and consistency in making their judgements.
- They at least appear to be objective, even if they are not, and this quality makes people feel that they are fair.
- They provide a rationale which helps in the design of pay structures (see Chapter 43).
- They are acceptable in equal value cases.
- They adapt well to computerization.

Disadvantages of point-factor schemes

Point schemes have these disadvantages:

- They are complex to develop, install and maintain.
- They give a somewhat spurious impression of scientific accuracy – it is still necessary to use judgement in selecting factors, defining levels within factors, deciding on weightings, and interpreting information about the jobs in relation to the definitions of factors and factor levels.
- They assume that it is possible to quantify different aspects of jobs on the same scale of values and then add them together. But skills cannot necessarily be added together in this way.
- They are based on the assumption that the factor weightings in the scheme apply equally to all jobs. But it is possible to argue that each job will have its own pattern of factor weights. In other words, not only will the levels at which factors are present in jobs vary, but within a job the relative weight to be attached to that factor will be different from its weight in other jobs.

Apart from the complexity issue, however, this list of disadvantages simply confirms what we already know about any form of job evaluation. It is not a scientific process. It cannot guarantee total objectivity or absolute accuracy in sizing jobs. It can do no more than provide a broad indication of internal relativities where jobs should be placed in a pay structure. But the analytical nature of points-factor rating will at least give a more accurate indication than non-analytical methods. If the process of using this method is carefully managed, the results are more likely to be acceptable (to be felt fair), and a sound basis for dealing with equal value issues will have been established. Additionally, and importantly, point-factor evaluation provides a good basis for designing a graded pay structure.

However, a powerful attack has been made by Lawler (1986) on point-factor evaluation for other reasons. He suggests that job evaluation was originally developed to support traditional bureaucratic management and the essential nature of point-factor schemes has not changed since they were first evolved in the early 1900s. He believes that job evaluation depersonalizes people by equating them with a set of duties rather than concentrating on what they are and what they can do. Job evaluation schemes strongly reinforce the concept of a management hierarchy and do not take account of organizations in which the emphasis is on knowledge and high technology work and where flexibility and multi-skilling is important. He proposes that the emphasis should be on people rather than jobs and the key criteria for establishing the value of people to an organization should be the levels of skill and competence they need to make an effective contribution in their roles. There is much to be said for this argument, hence the importance of new skill or competence-based approaches to job evaluation as discussed below and the increased use of 'broad-banded' pay structures or pay curves as described in Chapter 43.

SKILL-BASED EVALUATION

Skill-based evaluation grades jobs according to the level of skills or expertise required to perform them. There may be a number of skill factors, each with a rating scale or the grades may be related to NVQ levels.

This method focuses on individuals and the inputs they are capable of providing. The assumption is made that the process demands made on job holders to deliver the expected outputs can be measured by the level of inputs required. It is therefore a person rather than job-orientated approach to evaluation. Skill-based evaluation is flexible and can respond more quickly to demands for new skills, the acquisition or development of which needs to be encouraged and rewarded. It is most commonly used for technical and operational jobs in manufacturing and process industries.

The problem with this approach is that the emphasis on inputs seems to imply that skills are rewarded even when they are not delivering results. This does not make sense. Skills should only be valued if they are used productively and the analysis and evaluation process should take account of this.

Skill-based evaluation is associated with skill-based pay (see Chapter 44). Skills analysis techniques were described in Chapter 23.

COMPETENCE-BASED EVALUATION

Comptence-based evaluation measures the size of jobs by reference to the level of competence required for their successful performance. The conceptual basis for this type of job measurement is that the level of competence demanded for the effective performance of different jobs is a measure of the relative value of those jobs.

Like skill-based evaluation, competence-based measurement focuses on people. It concentrates on inputs and processes and it can be argued that it fails to assess contribution. This drawback can be tackled by incorporating performance requirements in definitions of competency levels, bearing in mind that competence is essentially the ability to apply knowledge and skills successfully, not the knowledge and skills themselves.

MARKET PRICING

Many organizations reject the idea of formal job evaluation and base their decisions on job values on 'market pricing' which involves relating internal rates of pay to market rates on the assumption that 'a job is worth what the market says it is worth', and that therefore market rate relativities should dictate internal relativities.

The problem with this approach is that the concept of a market rate is much less precise than most people think. Market rates are also volatile and unpredictable. Relying on market rate comparisons alone will not necessarily result in the provision of a sufficiently reliable or stable basis for an equitable pay structure, although market rates will, of course, influence rates of pay within the structure.

A further problem with market pricing is that it may only be possible to get market rate data for some of the jobs in the organization. It can be difficult to obtain information for unique or highly specialized jobs. It could be equally hard to determine accurately the market worth of 'individual contributors' whose value to the organization depends more on their personal level of skill and competence than on their level of responsibility in a job hierarchy. Organizations that rely on market pricing still have to make decisions on how these jobs fit into the pay structure. If they have the most common type of structure, one that groups jobs into grades, they will still have to make assumptions about the internal value of these jobs by slotting them into some form of rank order and placing them in grades. Even if they do not have a graded structure or a pay spine as described in Chapter 43, they will still need to determine internal relativities. The argument in favour of some form of systematic or analytical job evaluation process as described in this chapter is that this does at least produce a rationale for such decisions which provides for some degree of equity and consistency and, importantly, can be used to explain why decisions on job grades or values have been made.

PROS AND CONS OF FORMAL JOB-CENTRED EVALUATION

Although there are strong arguments in favour of a people rather than a job-focused approach and although market pricing recognizes the realities of the market place, many organizations prefer to adopt one of the more traditional approaches. Each of the job-centred schemes described above has its advantages and disadvantages, but before choosing between them it will be useful to summarize the arguments for and against the formal job-centred approach.

Pros

The arguments in favour of formal job evaluation are:

● A rational basis is required for making defensible decisions on job grades and rates of pay – such decisions are more likely to be accepted if the logic upon which they are based is clear.
● A consistent approach is required to the management of relativities.
● An equitable pay structure is unlikely to be achieved unless a logical method of measuring relative job size exists.
● Equal pay for work of equal value issues can ultimately only be resolved by the use of a formal and analytical method of job evaluation.
● A reasonably formal approach to job evaluation provides a strategic framework within which rational decisions can be made in response to changing organization structures and roles and to market rate pressures.
● A logical and consistent approach to measuring the relative size of jobs will not be achieved unless there is an agreed method and set of criteria for doing so which is used by all evaluators and represents the values of the organization as a whole.

Cons

The arguments against formal, traditional approaches to job evaluation are:

● No scheme has been proved to be valid in that it measures what it sets out to measure, or reliable in that it produces consistent results – an act of faith is required to believe in job evaluation.

- 'Whole-job' comparison schemes look wrong because they seem to oversimplify, but analytical systems are also suspect – apples and pears cannot be added together; the quantification of subjective judgements does not make them any more objective.
- Job evaluation relies on human judgement; its methodology may be logical and it may provide guidelines on the exercise of judgement, but these are subject to different interpretations and varying standards among assessors, and their preconceived notions ensure that subjectivity creeps in.
- Averaging a group of subjective judgements, as achieved when job evaluation panels reach a consensus view, does not make them any more objective.
- All formal evaluation schemes deteriorate as the organization changes and as evaluators become more skilled at manipulating the system; grade drift – unjustified upgradings as a result of this manipulation – occurs and the pay structure is no longer equitable.
- Job evaluation schemes can be costly to install and maintain – installation costs include not only consultancy fees, if applicable, but the inevitable increase in the pay bill after introducing job evaluation, usually at least 3 per cent.
- It is not the universal panacea that some businesses think it to be: handling its introduction can be a very delicate matter; evaluations can upset long-standing differentials and gradings and thus create more problems than they solve; the installation of job evaluation always creates expectations that everyone's pay will increase and however carefully you explain that such increases will not happen, a number of people, sometimes a lot of people, will inevitably be disappointed.

And of course, there are the convincing arguments offered by Lawler (1986) as mentioned earlier.

To sum up, job evaluation attempts to impose objectivity on a process of subjective judgement. It can never fully succeed in the task. In the last analysis, all job evaluation schemes boil down to organized rationalization.

IS JOB EVALUATION NECESSARY?

The pros for job evaluation as given above appear to be self-evident, but the cons are formidable and reading them prompts the question: 'Is job evaluation really necessary?' The answer is, of course, yes. You cannot avoid evaluating jobs. That is what you do every time you decide on what one job should be paid in relation to another. Job evaluation is therefore always necessary although it does not have to take the form of one of the traditional methods.

INTRODUCING JOB EVALUATION

Who should be covered?

Ideally, every job should be evaluated in order that comparisons can be made throughout the organization, or at least between people in comparable occupations at different levels. Some businesses, however, exclude directors and possibly senior managers on the grounds that their salary levels are largely determined on a personal basis. Senior jobs are often built round the skills of particular individuals and they can change, sometimes quite radically, when one manager leaves or is promoted and is replaced by another. Where this happens, job evaluation would clearly mean evaluating the individual, not the job.

How many schemes?

The tendency has been to have different systems for, say, managers, office staff and manual workers because of the perceived difficulty of designing a scheme which is equally applicable at all levels of responsibility, or for completely different types of work.

Increasingly, however, organizations that have harmonized and integrated their pay structures, ie that place all employees in the same pay structure, are introducing single job evaluation schemes that cover every position except, possibly, board directors.

Tailor-made scheme?

The main advantage of a specially designed scheme is clearly that it can take into account the particular values of the organization and any of the individual features of the organization, such as the need to cover different categories of employees or types of work. Special factors can be introduced at different levels and appropriate weightings can be applied. Tailor-made schemes are not necessarily less expensive to introduce than a job evaluation package because account has to be taken of the opportunity costs in the shape of the considerable amount of executive time that has to be spent in designing, developing and introducing a special scheme. This time can be reduced by getting help from management consultants, although that can be costly.

Job evaluation package

The alternative to a tailor-made scheme is a job evaluation package – a 'proprietary brand'. This will have been carefully developed and tested over time, and, at a price, is readily installed by the consultants. Some schemes are used as the basis for comparing market rates, which can provide a valuable additional source of information. A ready-made scheme is simpler to install but may not fit the organization's needs so well as one that has been specially developed.

What type of scheme?

When developing a tailor-made scheme, you have the choice between using a job-centred or people-centred approach. If you believe in the need to establish the position of jobs in a hierarchy and therefore do not want to take into account the individual characteristics of people in their different roles, a traditional job-centred approach will be appropriate. The choice is then between a job ranking or job classification system, or an analytical point-factor scheme. The natural way to evaluate jobs is to compare one whole job with another – people do this almost instinctively – but point-factor schemes are best in complex situations where it is felt that only a highly analytical approach provides an acceptable basis for evaluation, and they can provide a useful basis for designing a pay structure. Their objectivity may be suspect but their use may well be justified if it is considered that people are going to be favourably impressed both by the sheer amount of time and trouble involved in introducing the scheme, and by the apparent fairness of the process of analysis. In addition, an analytical scheme is required to avoid potential difficulties over equal pay for work of equal value claims where the leading case of *Bromley and Others v H & J Quick* (1988) established that a job evaluation scheme can only provide a defence if it is analytical in nature.

Point-factor schemes have been steadily increasing in popularity. Most organizations introducing job evaluation select this type of scheme because of its 'face validity'. People feel that it is scientific and therefore it must be all right.

People-focused skill- or competence-based schemes could be appropriate in relatively fluid organizations, especially those in the high-tech, scientific or research and development fields. Skill-based schemes may be relevant for highly skilled and multi-skilled workers. Competence-based schemes may be right for professional, scientific and technical jobs and where career development tends to be progressive rather than by means of a series of steps in a job hierarchy. Such schemes can be designed to operate analytically by referring to a range of specifically defined skills and competences.

Market pricing can be adopted by those organizations that are very much exposed to market pressures and/or cannot be bothered with a formal scheme.

DEVELOPING A POINT-FACTOR SCHEME

The majority of organizations that want to use a formal approach to job evaluation select a point-factor scheme. This section therefore describes the following steps which need to be taken when developing and introducing such a scheme:

● Inform employees and agree on how they should be involved.
● Clarify trade union attitudes, where appropriate.
● Select benchmark jobs.
● Plan the job evaluation programme.

Informing and involving employees

Employees must obviously be informed about the exercise. It affects them deeply and their help is required in analysing jobs. The objectives and potential benefits should be discussed and it should be made absolutely clear that it is the jobs that are to be evaluated and not the performance of the people carrying out the jobs. The way in which employees are consulted will depend on the organization's normal policies for consultation and negotiation.

There is much to be said for involving people in the job evaluation programme. They can assist in selecting, analysing and evaluating benchmark jobs (ie the key jobs which can be used as reference points – see below). It is becoming increasingly common to set up job evaluation panels to establish and maintain the scheme and to hear appeals.

This approach is equally desirable if a skill- or competence-based scheme is being introduced.

Trade union attitudes

If the organization is unionized, the form in which consultation and participation takes place will be strongly influenced by union attitudes. Trade unions may insist on being involved in the job evaluation programme, although they might not be prepared to commit themselves in advance to accept its findings.

Select benchmark jobs

In any exercise where there are more than 30 or 40 jobs to be evaluated, it is necessary to identify and select a sample of benchmark jobs which can be used for comparisons inside and outside the organization. The benchmark jobs should be selected to achieve a representative sample of each of the main levels of jobs in each of the principal occupations.

The size of the sample depends on the number of different jobs to be covered. It is usually difficult to produce a balanced sample unless at least 25 per cent of the distinct jobs at each level of the organization are included. The higher the proportion the better, bearing in mind the time required to analyse jobs (often as much as a day for each job).

Draw up the job evaluation programme

The steps to be taken in drawing up and implementing a job evaluation scheme are summarized in Figure 41.2.

The particular points to be covered are the following:

1. *Roles*: who is responsible for analysis, evaluation, pay comparisons and the design of the salary structure.
2. *Briefing*: of management, employees and unions on the objectives of the exercise and how they are to be achieved.
3. *Procedures*: the terms of reference, membership and methods of working of any job evaluation panel, project team or committee.
4. *Training*: the training to be given to analysts and evaluators. This is a vital part of the programme. If training is carried out thoroughly, many of the limitations of job evaluation referred to earlier can be minimized.
5. *Pay comparisons*: methods of conducting market rate surveys and the timetable for completing them.
6. *Job evaluation*: methods and procedures, including appeals, and the timetable for completing the programme.
7. *Job analysis*: the methods to be used in job analysis, the jobs to be covered and the timetable for completing the programme.
8. *Pay structure design*: the type of structure (see Chapter 43), the design methods to be used and the timetable for completing the design.
9. *Communication and negotiation*: the approach to communicating the results of the exercise to employees and for negotiating the structure with unions. It is highly desirable to produce a booklet explaining the scheme.
10. *Implementation*: the procedures for implementing the scheme, including grading or regrading jobs, deciding on how to deal with any increases, informing individual employees, drawing up maintenance procedures covering such points as evaluating or re-evaluating new or changed jobs and installing an appeal system.

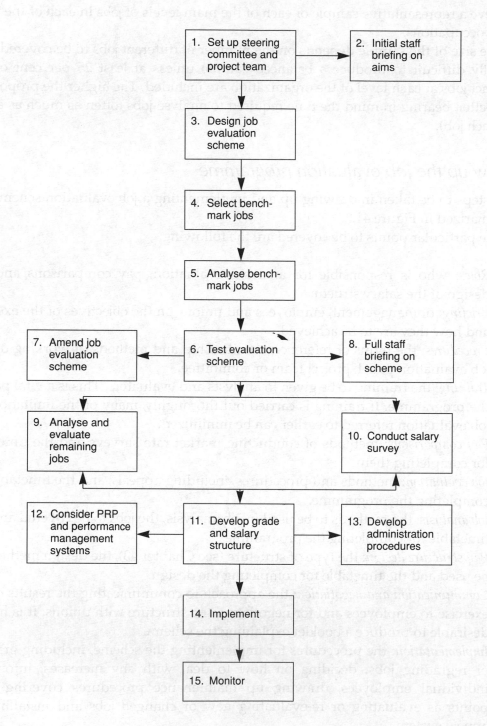

Figure 41.2 Job evaluation programme

When the programme has been drawn up, the detailed work of job analysis, pay comparisons and design of the structure can be carried out. The points to be covered when conducting a job evaluation exercise using a point-factor scheme are discussed below.

CONDUCTING THE JOB EVALUATION EXERCISE

How much time is involved?

However much the organization may want to get the scheme fully implemented, it is unwise to rush job evaluation. Even the keenest evaluation panel can grade only a limited number of jobs in a day: eight is probably a realistic average maximum. After this, the quality of evaluation tends to drop, and more time has to be spent later in checking and assessing the validity of grading. The final review of all the grades allocated to check that no inconsistencies have occurred should be done meticulously and with enough time allowed for re-evaluation if necessary. Extra time devoted at this stage will help reduce appeals to the inevitable few. Careful preparation for the communication of job grades and of the handbooks or other documents describing the scheme and its operation will also assist acceptance.

Responsibility for the exercise

Responsibility for the overall coordination of the introduction of job evaluation should be in the hands of a senior executive who can then report on progress to the board or management committee and advise it on ensuring salary policy developments.

When there is a developed personnel function, the head of personnel will take control. In larger organizations with a department specializing in pay matters, the executive in charge of this function will normally take responsibility for the introduction and maintenance of the scheme. Provided adequate training is given at the outset, job analysis is an excellent way for new personnel or other trainees to familiarize themselves with the business and the work done in its different departments. Analysts must be taught the basic skills of interviewing and the elements of a concise descriptive style for writing job descriptions.

The use of analysts either to write job descriptions or check on those written by job holders and their managers often greatly improves the quality of job descriptions submitted for evaluation.

Job evaluation panels

It is highly desirable to set up a job evaluation panel which can be involved in the design of a new scheme when a tailor-made one is to be introduced. The panel members may possibly carry out job analyses and will certainly evaluate the jobs using either their own scheme or, in conjunction with a management consultant acting in an advisory capacity, a 'proprietary brand'. The panel may continue to meet after the initial exercise to hear appeals and to conduct new evaluations or re-evaluations.

When deciding on the membership of the job evaluation panel, it is necessary to consider the extent to which different levels of employees will be included. The aim should be to set up a panel of no more than about eight members who between them have good first-hand knowledge of the jobs to be evaluated.

If trade unions are involved, they may wish to nominate an agreed number of representatives, balanced by management nominees and a mutually acceptable chair-person, preferably the head of personnel or the remuneration function who will more easily be able to act as a facilitator. When conducting evaluations the chairperson should play this role rather than acting as a decision maker. Internal or external consultants may also be used as facilitators. Panel members will need to be trained in job analysis and evaluation techniques.

Briefing for job evaluation

Thorough briefing of all members who will be affected by job evaluation is essential. This can be done at a meeting or series of meetings at which the person responsible for the introduction of the scheme outlines its aims and emphasizes the long-term benefits in terms of a fair and equitable pay structure for all concerned. A simple question-and-answer sheet given out at the meeting and covering the common, if basic, questions employees normally ask will also help remove any misgivings that may arise. Some of the most common questions are the following:

● What is job evaluation?
● Why does this company need job evaluation?
● How will it work?
● Will my performance in my job be taken into account?
● How does it affect promotion policy?
● How will the system be kept up to date?
● Does job evaluation mean that everyone whose job is in the same grade gets the same rate of pay?
● How does the publication of job grades and pay bands affect confidentiality?

- How does the system cater for additions to or alterations in jobs?
- What impact is the exercise likely to have on pay?
- What happens if individuals disagree with their grading?
- How quickly will appeals on grading be dealt with?
- How will the company go about grading new jobs created as the result of change or expansion?

It is desirable to anticipate these questions and have answers ready for them. It is particularly important to emphasize that the scheme is evaluating jobs, not people. It is even more important to defuse any expectations that job evaluation will result in massive all-round pay increases. In fact, it is advisable to play down the pay aspect of the process and stress that job evaluation is about measuring the relative size of jobs so that they can be fairly graded. The scheme itself will not determine pay levels. It only helps in the development of a framework within which fair and consistent decisions on pay can be made.

Briefing and training the job evaluation panel

Much of the success of a job evaluation panel depends on how well it is briefed and trained. The first meeting should discuss the collective responsibilities of the panel, go through the principles of job evaluation, and answer members' questions. Training should be given in job analysis and the principle of job evaluation.

If a tailor-made scheme is to be developed, the panel, with the help of the internal specialist or external consultant, will decide on the type of scheme and, if a points-factor scheme is to be used, the factor plan. If a proprietary brand is to be used, the consultants will brief the panel.

The panel should try a few practice runs before the programme of analysis and evaluation begins.

Conducting the panel meetings

The chairperson, the personnel adviser to the panel or the external consultant should act as a 'facilitator', helping the panel to understand the processes they are using and to reach consensus. Facilitators should not normally evaluate the jobs themselves – that is the function of the panel which must 'own' the final decision. But facilitators are there to provide advice on interpreting the scheme and how it is used, and they will try to achieve consensus. It is surprising how readily consensus is achieved with a well-conceived scheme, a balanced and well-trained panel and, importantly, an effective facilitator.

To begin with the panel will take some time to evaluate jobs. But as its members become familiar with how the scheme works, they will speed up. Bearing in mind that job evaluation is essentially a comparative process, consistency in judgements will more easily be achieved by comparing the evaluations for separate factors in different jobs (if a points scheme is used). Evaluating 'real' jobs will also help members to put flesh on the bones of the factor level descriptions in the scheme, which will necessarily be non-specific.

Appeals procedure

Even the most committed and highly trained job evaluation committees make mistakes. Additionally, managers may expect the people they supervise to be more highly graded as a reflection of their own or their department's status, and individuals may feel that the importance of their job has been undervalued. An appeals procedure is therefore essential.

Use of computers (computer-assisted job evaluation)

A job evaluation exercise can generate a lot of paper and take considerable time. The use of knowledge-based software systems, often referred to loosely as expert systems, can organize the analytical processes in a way which makes the best use of the databases, assists in making consistent judgements and records decisions to be added to the database. This is done by:

● defining the evaluation rules relating to the weighting of factors, the points, levels, or degrees attached to each factor, and the assessment standards which guide evaluators to the correct rating of jobs – these may take the form of benchmark jobs and/or level definitions;

● programming the computer to ask appropriate questions concerning each factor in a job to enable it to apply the evaluation rules;

● applying the rules consistently and determining the factor score for the job;

● grading the job;

● sorting the job into position in the rank order;

● storing the job information entered in the form of a factor analysis into the computer's memory so that it can be called to the screen or printed at any time.

EQUAL VALUE

Under the equal value amendment to the UK Equal Pay Act, any person can claim equal pay with any other person if he or she believes that the work is equally demanding under such factors as effort, skill and decision making. Equal value claims can be made whether or not job evaluation schemes exist, and they can cut across traditional boundaries, so that blue-collar workers can compare their jobs with those of white-collar workers and vice versa. Vulnerability to claims is highest where traditional, sex-based job segregation exists.

Claims are heard by employment tribunals, who may ask independent 'experts' appointed by ACAS (the Advisory, Conciliation and Arbitration Service) to assess equality of value between claimant and comparator. The experts carry out their evaluation by applying sets of factors to the job analysis such as knowledge, experience, judgement and decision-making, contacts, physical effort and consequence of errors.

Independent experts start with the job description to identify any areas where the content of the job is the cause of conflict. They attempt to get agreement on the facts and ask the employers to justify the differential. A precise point rating for each factor is usually considered neither necessary nor appropriate, but a general statement comparing the demands of each job under each factor heading is essential.

The existence of a job evaluation scheme which assigns values to the jobs under review can be used to prove that no discrimination is taking place only if the scheme itself is non-discriminatory. It is also desirable for it to be analytical in accordance with the ruling in *Bromley v Quick*. Job evaluation schemes can be discriminatory in the choice of factors and in the weightings attached to the factors as well as in the grading process – reflecting underlying discrimination.

The Equal Opportunities Commission has stated that job evaluation should not give a spurious objectivity to the status quo: 'a commitment to a fair job evaluation may require that some traditional assumptions are changed regarding the value attributed to work predominantly carried out by women.' It also advises that extremely high or low weightings should not be given to factors which are exclusively found in jobs performed predominantly by one sex.

42

Market rate analysis

PURPOSE

To ensure that pay levels are competitive, it is necessary to track market rates for the jobs within the business, especially those that are particularly vulnerable to market pressures because of scarcity factors. This is sometimes called benchmarking.

Job evaluation schemes can be used to determine internal relativities, but, in themselves, they cannot price jobs. To a large extent, pay levels are subject to market forces which have to be taken into account in fixing the rates for particular jobs. Some specialized jobs may not be subject to the same external pressures as others, but it is still necessary to know what effect market rates are likely to have on the pay structure as a whole before deciding on internal pay differentials which properly reflect levels of skill and responsibility. It has also to be accepted that market pressures and negotiations affect differentials within the firm.

THE CONCEPT OF THE MARKET RATE

The concept of the market rate, even in the local labour market, is an imprecise one. There is no such thing as *the* market rate, unless this is represented by a universally applied national pay scale, and such cases are now rare. There is always a range of rates paid by different employers, even for identical jobs, because of different pay policies on how they want their rates to compare with the market rates. This is particularly so in managerial jobs and other occupations where duties can vary considerably, even if the job title is the same, and where actual pay is likely to be strongly influenced by the quality and value to the business of individuals. It is therefore possible to use pay surveys only to provide a broad indication of market rates. Judgement has to be used in interpreting the results of special enquiries or the data from published surveys. And there is often plenty of scope for selecting evidence which supports whatever case is being advanced.

THE INFORMATION REQUIRED

When making market comparisons, the aim should be to:

- obtain accurate and representative data covering base pay, bonuses and benefits;
- compare like with like in terms of the type and size of the job and the type of organization – this is the process of 'job matching';
- obtain up-to-date information;
- interpret data in the light of the organization's circumstances and needs;
- present data in a way that indicates the action required.

JOB MATCHING

The aim in conducting a pay survey is to compare like with like – the process of job matching. The various methods of job matching in ascending order of accuracy are:

- *job title* – often very misleading;
- *brief (two or three lines) description of job and level of responsibility* – this provides better guidance for matching jobs but still leaves much scope for inaccuracy;
- *capsule job descriptions* which define the job and its duties in two or three hundred words, some indication being given of the size of the job in such terms as resources controlled – these can provide a better basis for job matching but may still not produce the ideal degree of accuracy;
- *full job descriptions* which provide more details about the job but demand a considerable amount of effort in making the comparisons;
- *job evaluation* can be used in support of a job description to obtain reasonably

accurate information on comparative job sizes, but it is very time consuming unless it is done through the UK surveys run on this basis by firms such as Hay and Wyatt.

PRESENTATION OF DATA

Data can be presented in two ways:

1. *Measures of central tendency*:
   - arithmetic mean (average);
   - median – the middle item in a distribution of individual items, this is the most commonly used measure because it avoids the distortions to which arithmetic averages are prone.
2. Measures of dispersion:
   - upper quartile – the value above which 25 per cent of the individual values fall;
   - lower quartile – the value below which 25 per cent of the individual values fall;
   - interquartile range – the difference between the upper and lower quartiles.

SOURCES OF INFORMATION

The following sources of information are available on market rates:

- published surveys;
- special surveys;
- club surveys;
- advertisements.

These are described below.

Published surveys

There is a wide range of published surveys which either collect general information about managerial salaries or cover the pay for specialist professional, technical or office jobs. The general surveys which are available 'over the counter' include those published by Reward, Monks Publications and Remuneration Economics. Incomes Data Services publishes a *Directory of Salary Surveys* which is a consumer's guide to all the major surveys.

When using a published survey it is necessary to check on:

- the information provided;
- the size and composition of the participants;
- the quality of the job matching information;
- the extent to which it covers the jobs for which information is required;
- the degree to which it is up to date;
- how well data are presented.

Published surveys are a quick and not too expensive way of getting information. But there may be problems in job matching and the information may be somewhat out of date.

Special surveys

Special surveys can be 'do it yourself' affairs or they can be conducted for you by management consultants. The latter method costs more but it saves a lot of time and trouble and some organizations may be more willing to respond to an enquiry from a reputable consultant.

Special surveys can be conducted as follows:

1. Decide what information is wanted.
2. Identify the 'benchmark' jobs for which comparative pay data are required. This could have been done as part of a job evaluation exercise.
3. Produce capsule job descriptions for those jobs.
4. Identify the organizations that are likely to have similar jobs.
5. Contact those organizations and invite them to participate. It is usual to say that the survey findings will be distributed to participants (this is the *quid pro quo*) and that individual organizations will not be identified.
6. Provide participants with a form to complete together with notes for guidance and capsule job descriptions.
7. Analyse the returned forms and distribute a summary of the results to participants.

Special surveys can justify the time and trouble, or expense, by producing usefully comparable data. It may, however, be difficult to get a suitable number of participants to take part, either because organizations cannot be bothered or because they are already members of a survey club or take part in a published survey.

Club surveys

Club surveys are conducted by a number of organizations who agree to exchange information on pay in accordance with a standard format and on a regular basis. They have all the advantages of special surveys plus the additional benefits of saving a considerable amount of time and providing regular information. It is well worth joining one if you can. If a suitable club does not exist, you could always try to start one, but this takes considerable effort.

Advertisements

Many organizations rely on the salary levels published in recruitment advertisements. But these can be very misleading as you will not necessarily achieve a good match and the quoted salary may not be the same as what is finally paid. However, although it is highly suspect, data from advertisements can be used to supplement other more reliable sources.

Other market intelligence

Other market intelligence can be obtained from the publications of *Incomes Data Services* and *Industrial Relations Services*. This may include useful information on trends in the 'going rate' for general, across-the-board pay increases which can be used when deciding on what sort of uplift, if any, is required to pay scales.

Using survey data

The use of market survey data as a guide on pay levels is a process based on judgement and compromise. Different sources may produce different indications of market rate levels. As a result you may have to produce what might be described as a 'derived' market rate based on an assessment of the relative reliability of the data. This would strike a reasonable balance between the competing merits of the different sources used. This is something of an intuitive process.

Once all the data available have been collected and presented in the most accessible manner possible (ie job by job for all the areas the structure is to cover), reference points can be determined for each pay range in a graded structure as described in Chapter 43. This process will take account of the place in the market the business wishes to occupy, ie its market 'stance' or 'posture'.

43

Pay structures

DEFINITION

Pay structures provide a framework for managing base pay, pay progression and, sometimes, employee benefit provision. The main types, as described later in this chapter, are traditional graded structures, broad-banded structures, job families, pay spines, structures for manual workers and individual job structures. Some organizations do not have a formal structure and instead use 'spot rates' – specific rates for individual jobs or people without any defined scope for pay progression to or beyond the rate. The majority of organizations in the UK with less than 100 employees have no formal pay structure, but simply pay individuals what they think they are worth. However, most organizations with more employees do use formal pay structures which:

- establish pay ranges or scales for jobs grouped into grades, bands or job families, generally by reference to market data and often guided by the results of job evaluation;
- provide scope for pay progression in accordance with performance, skill, competence, contribution or service through these pay ranges or scales;
- specify the basis upon which jobs and/or individuals can move between levels, grades or bands in the structure.

There may be a single, integrated pay structure covering the whole organization or, in large organizations, there may be different structures at different levels, with one structure for managerial, professional, technical, sales and administrative staff, and another for manual workers. Executive directors are often also treated separately.

RATIONALE FOR PAY STRUCTURES

Pay structures are needed to provide a logically designed framework within which equitable, fair, consistent and transparent pay policies can be implemented. They enable the organization to determine levels of pay for jobs and people, and are the basis upon which the effective management of relativities and of the processes of monitoring and controlling the implementation of pay practices can take place. The pay structure is also a medium through which the organization can communicate the pay opportunities available to employees.

CRITERIA FOR PAY STRUCTURES

Pay structures should:

- be appropriate to the characteristics and needs of the organization and its employees;
- facilitate the management of relativities and the achievement of equity, fairness and consistency in managing employee reward;
- be capable of adapting to pressures arising from market rate changes and skill shortages;
- facilitate operational flexibility and continuous development;
- provide scope as required for rewarding performance and increases in skill and competence;
- clarify reward and career opportunities;
- be constructed logically and clearly so that the basis upon which they operate can readily be communicated to employees;
- enable the organization to exercise control over the implementation of pay policies and budgets.

TYPES OF PAY STRUCTURE

Graded pay structures

Although broad-banding has come to the fore, graded pay structures remain the most typical types in the private sector. These consist of a sequence of job grades as illustrated in Figure 43.1 into which jobs of broadly equivalent value are slotted, usually on the basis of job evaluation scores. A pay range is attached to each grade. The maximum of each range is typically set at a rate between 20 per cent and 50 per cent above the minimum. For example, a '40 per cent' range could span from £20,000 to £28,000. Pay ranges are also described as a percentage of the mid-point; for example, the range could be expressed as 80 per cent to 120 per cent where the mid-point is £25,000 and the minimum and maximum are £20,000 and £30,000 respectively. The mid-point may be regarded as the rate for a fully competent individual, and aligned to market rates in accordance with company policies on the relationship between its pay levels and market rates for similar jobs (this is sometimes called the 'pay stance'). The pay range provides scope for pay progression.

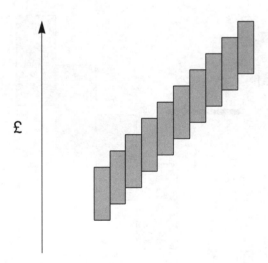

Figure 43.1   A graded pay structure

There may be ten or more grades in a structure, generally depending on the size and degree of hierarchy in the structure of the organization. Grades may be defined by job evaluation in points terms, by grade definitions, or simply by the jobs that have been slotted into the grades. Differentials between pay ranges are typically around 20 per cent, and there is usually an overlap between ranges, often of up to about 50 per cent. Ranges are often designed to be wider at more senior levels, on the assumptions that there is more scope to deliver different levels of performance at these levels and such differences should be rewarded accordingly. What are sometimes called 'mid-point management' techniques are often used to analyse and control pay progression by comparing actual pay with the mid-point. 'Compa-ratios' measure the relationship between actual and policy rates of pay as a percentage. If the two coincide, the compa-ratio is 100 per cent.

Broad-banded pay structures

Increasingly, however, broad-banded structures are replacing traditional graded structures. In such structures, the number of grades is compressed into a relatively small number of much wider 'bands' as illustrated in Figure 43.2.

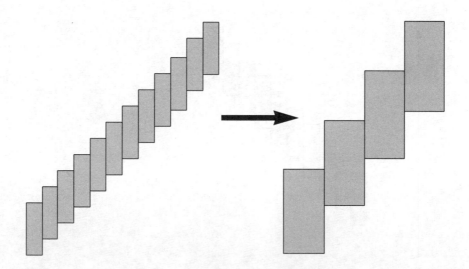

Figure 43.2 Conversion of a traditional graded structure into a broad-banded structure

In the broad bands, pay is managed more flexibly than in a conventional graded structure and increased attention is paid to market relativities. The band widths may be as much as 100 per cent, although more typically they are between 50 per cent and 80 per cent. There may be only five or six bands in the structure. The band boundaries are often, but not always, still defined by job evaluation. Roles may be placed in the bands purely by reference to market rates, or more commonly by a combination of job evaluation and market rate analysis. Bands can be described in general terms by reference to the types of role allocated to them. Reference may be made to generic roles or clusters of roles, and these can be used as benchmarks against which other roles are matched when decisions have to be made on the band into which they should be placed.

While 'zones' may be defined in a band to indicate normal progression patterns, there is much more scope in a broad-banded structure for additional 'career development pay' by moving horizontally through the band (and indeed beyond the notional band limits), on the basis of increases in the scope of activities, contribution and competence. Pay progression and career development are not simply a matter of getting promotion to a higher grade.

The aims of broad-banded pay structures are commonly:

- to achieve more flexibility in pay management;
- to fit the pay structure to a delayered organization;
- to reflect an emphasis on horizontal processes in such organizations;
- to create a strong relationship between pay and contribution and de-emphasize the status-based nature of rewards; and importantly:
- to provide a framework within which people can be rewarded for lateral development.

Broad-banded structures are more likely to be introduced in flexible organizations which do not operate with extended hierarchies and believe wholeheartedly in continuous development. Such organizations have often been through a restructuring exercise which looks at the fundamental processes of the business from a cross-functional perspective, and aims to break away from the constraints of conventional organizational boundaries and from traditional hierarchical, functional and job divisions of labour.

Job family structures

Job family structures cater for separate groups or families of jobs. Families consist of roles in a function such as research, finance or HR which are related through the activities carried out and the basic skills used, but are differentiated by the level of responsibility, skill or competence required. Each job family has its own structure of levels which may be defined in terms of accountability, skill or competence. Levels may have their own finite pay range, as in a conventional graded pay structure. The pay levels in different job families may vary to reflect market rate pressures as illustrated in Figure 43.3.

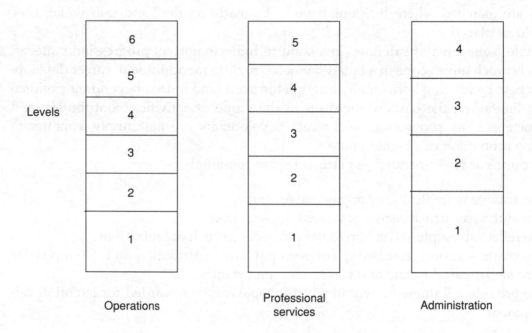

Figure 43.3   A job family structure with differing levels

Job family structures are used because it is felt that some occupations need distinct treatment from both the reward and the career development points of view. One of their perceived advantages is that career progression on the basis of increases in skill or competence can be planned, and individuals can be made aware of the development opportunities available to them in their own and other job families. They are popular in organizations which have a high proportion of professional and knowledge workers.

They may also be set up for 'market groups' where the occupations concerned are subject to particular market pressures. The market rates for such jobs are higher than those for other occupations which would be placed in the same grade on the basis of internal relativities alone. However, the creation of market groups means that there is increased risk of gender discrimination, and job families can also create barriers to lateral development across the organization.

The mixed model broad-banded job family structure

It is possible in a common broad-banded structure to cater for job families within bands. It is equally possible to use broad bands in a job family structure. Essentially, this allows for some flexibility to reward and progress the pay of individuals separately in the different families, but still maintain a common structure of bands and the ability to 'read-across' throughout the organization. This maintains an element of consistency and equity and enables lateral development across the organization to take place.

Pay spines

Pay spines consist of a series of incremental points extending from the lowest to the highest-paid jobs covered by the structure as illustrated in Figure 43.4. A pay spine increment may be standardized at, say, 3 per cent from the top to the bottom of the spine, or the increments may be wider at higher levels. Progression up the spine is based on service in the post, usually one increment per year, but if performance-related pay is introduced, individuals can be given accelerated increments. Jobs may be placed at fixed points on the spine, or ranges for different job grades may be superimposed on it.

Pay spines are found in the public sector, or in agencies and charities which have adopted a public sector approach to reward management. There has recently been a trend in some of these organizations to replace pay spines with a broad-banded or job family structure.

Individual job structures

Individual job structures simply define a separate pay range for each job. The rates for jobs and the relativities between them are often governed by market rates – job structures can often be described as 'market driven'.

Relativities between jobs can be determined by point-factor job evaluation, which may in effect convert points to pounds by the application of a formula. A broad-

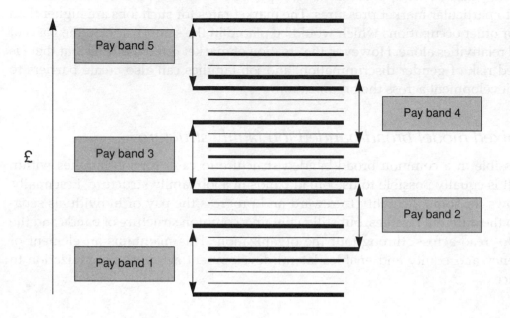

Figure 43.4 A pay spine

banded structure may incorporate 'zones' which are in effect individual job ranges in a band.

CHOICE OF STRUCTURE

The following questions need to be answered before selecting any of the above types of pay structure or modifying an existing structure:

1. What are the strengths and weaknesses of the current pay arrangements in terms of reward policies, the pay structure, methods of rewarding staff for performance, competence, skill or contribution, performance management processes, and employee benefit packages?
2. In the light of the answer to question 1, why is it believed that a new or revised structure is necessary?

3. In general, how would a new or revised structure meet the needs of the business as defined in the business strategy?
4. In particular, what should be the aims of a new or revised structure?
5. What are the characteristics of the organization which should be taken into account in order to ensure 'good fit'? These characteristics could include the type of business, its culture, the organization structure, and the type of people employed.
6. How might any pay structure developments support proposed organizational or cultural change and reinforce other HR policies and practices?
7. How ready are we to introduce a new or changed structure?
8. What issues will have to be addressed in the process of developing and introducing a new structure?

Making the choice

The choice of pay structure depends on the type of organization and the sort of people it employs as established by a diagnostic review. There is no such thing as a model structure or 'best practice' in broad-banding or job families. As the CIPD research has established (Armstrong and Brown, 2001), there is a wide diversity of approaches; every organization adopts its own type of pay structure to suit its circumstances. While the general trend in large organizations is towards flatter, broader and more flexible structures, there are a number of fast-growing technology companies which have recently introduced more grades in their pay structures as part of the professionalism of management in the organization.

Generally, however, companies and institutions with formal, hierarchical organization structures have tended to prefer conventional graded structures which permit orderly administration and make for ease in managing internal relativities. Organizations that want to achieve more flexibility but within a defined framework may opt for a broad-banded or job family structure or a mixed model. More flexibility is possible if greater freedom is given to line managers to make pay decisions in different parts of the organization. Even more flexibility can be achieved if an individual job grade or spot rate system is used. The disadvantage of the latter two approaches is that internal equity considerations may be neglected, and the danger of paying unequally for work of equal value is increased. They may also be more complex and difficult to administer.

A comparison of the features and advantages and disadvantages of the most typical structures is summarized in Table 43.1.

Table 43.1 Comparison of pay structures

	Traditional graded	Broad-banded	Job family	Mixed model	Pay spine
Features	• A sequence of job grades, 12 or more • Narrow pay ranges eg 20–40% • Progression usually linked to performance	• A series of often 5 or 6 'broad' bands • Wide pay bands – typically between 50% and 80% • Progression linked to contribution and competence	• Separate pay structures for families containing similar jobs • Progression linked to competence and/or contribution	• Either job families inserted into a broad-banded structure; or broad bands inserted into a job family structure • Progression linked to competence and/or contribution	• A series of incremental pay points covering all jobs • Grades may be superimposed • Progression linked to service
Advantages	• Clearly indicate pay relativities • Facilitate control • Easy to understand	• More flexible • Reward lateral development and growth in competence	• Clarify career paths • Facilitate pay differentiation between market groups	• Can combine the merits of broad-banded and job family structures	• Easy to manage • Pay progression not based on managerial judgement
Disadvantages	• Create hierarchical rigidity • Prone to grade drift • Inappropriate in a delayered organisation	• Create unrealistic expectations of scope for pay rises • Seem to restrict scope for promotion • Difficult to understand	• May inhibit lateral career development • May be difficult to maintain internal equity between job families	• Can incorporate the disadvantages of both broad-banded and job family structures • Can be very complex to operate and understand	• No scope for differentiating rewards according to performance • May be costly as staff drift up the spine
When	• In a large bureaucratic organization with well-defined hierarchies • When close and rigid control is required • When some but not too much scope for pay progression related to performance is wanted	• In delayered, process-based, flexible organizations • Where more flexibility in pay determination is wanted • Where the focus is on continuous improvement and lateral development	• Where there are distinct groups of jobs in families • When it is believed that career paths need to be defined more clearly in terms of competence requirements • When there are distinct market groups who need to be rewarded differentially	• When the conditions for either broad-banding and/or job families are favourable and it is felt that the advantages outweigh the disadvantages	• In a public sector or voluntary organization this is the traditional approach • Where it is believed to be impossible to measure differential levels of performance fairly and consistently

Source: M Armstrong and D Brown, *Pay: The new dimensions*, Chartered Institute of Personnel and Development, 2001

PAY STRUCTURES FOR MANUAL WORKERS

A pay structure for manual workers consists of the rates paid to employees who work on the shop-floor, in distribution, transport, public services and anywhere else where the work primarily involves manual skills and tasks. The structure will be similar to any other pay structure in that it incorporates pay differentials between jobs which reflect real and assumed differences in skill and responsibility but are influenced by pressures from the local labour market, by custom and practice and by settlements reached between management and trade unions. These pay levels are underpinned by what can be described as the 'effort bargain'.

The effort bargain

The task of management is to assess what level and type of inducements it has to offer in return for the contribution it requires from its workforce. The worker's aim is to strike a bargain about the relationship between what he or she regards as a reasonable contribution and what the employer is prepared to offer to elicit that contribution. This is termed the 'effort bargain' and is, in effect, an agreement which lays down the amount of work to be done for a rate of pay or wage rate, not just the hours to be worked. Explicitly or implicitly, all employees are in a bargaining situation with regard to pay. A system will not be accepted as effective and workable until it is recognized as fair and equitable by both parties.

Rates of pay

The basic method of paying manual workers is the time rate for the job, which is paid according to the level of the job (eg skilled, semi-skilled or unskilled) and the hours worked as described below. There may also be an incentive element which is related to some measure of performance or skill. This arrangement is described in Chapter 42.

Time rates

Time rates, also known as day rates or flat rates, are an arrangement under which workers are simply paid a predetermined rate per month, week, day or hour for the actual time worked. Pay is fixed in accordance with the level of the job or the skills regularly used and only varies with time, never with output, performance or any additional skills the workers acquire.

In some companies, what are termed high time or day rates are paid which are set at a level above the minimum rates. The high day rate may include a consolidated bonus element and is probably greater than the local labour market rate to attract and retain good quality workers. High day rates have been common in industries such as motor manufacturing where above average earnings are expected because of a history of payment by results, and where there is a high degree of machine control over output. They are appropriate in machine-paced assembly lines and in some high technology plants where multi-skilling and flexibility are important – both these requirements may be inhibited by a traditional payment-by-results scheme.

Time rates are often used when it is believed that it is undesirable or impossible to operate an incentive scheme, for example, in maintenance work. But they are being increasingly introduced in situations where a payment-by-result scheme has proved to be unsatisfactory in the sense that it creates wage drift, is costly to run, creates conflict or is not providing value for money in the shape of increased productivity. Time rates may also be adopted where there is a focus on total quality.

From the point of view of many operators, time rates are better because earnings are predictable and steady and they do not have to engage in endless arguments with industrial engineers, rate fixers and supervisors about piecework rates or work measures time allowances.

The obvious argument against time rates is that they do not provide the motivation of a direct financial incentive which clearly relates pay to performance. The point is often made that people want money and will work harder to get it. The argument is a powerful one and is supported by the many successful incentive schemes that are still in operation, although the difficulty of maintaining an effective payment-by-result scheme should never be underestimated.

Plus rates

Many structures incorporate various 'plus rates' for particular skills or demands made on employees. These may include shift rates, pay for 'unsocial working hours', overtime rates, and pay for difficult or unpleasant working conditions.

INTEGRATED PAY STRUCTURES

Integrated pay structures cover groups of employees who have traditionally been paid under separate arrangements. An integrated structure may have one grading system which includes all employees – managers, professional, technical and office staff *and* manual workers, although such structures frequently leave out senior management.

An integrated pay structure may be based on the same system of job evaluation which is applied to all employees. It will involve the harmonization to some extent of employee benefits and conditions of employment such as holidays, hours of work, sick pay and pensions, although the scale of such benefits may still be related to position in the grade hierarchy.

RATE FOR AGE SCALES

Rate for age scales provide for a specific rate of pay or a pay bracket to be linked to age for staff in certain jobs. They are relatively uncommon nowadays because of changing patterns of work. The rationale for rate for age scales used to be the learning curve principle, but that can be catered for in a graded pay structure. They are, however, still in use for employees below the age of 21 on formal training schemes extending over two or three years.

CASE STUDY: INTRODUCTION OF A BROAD-BANDED/JOB FAMILY STRUCTURE

The previous pay system

There was no overall pay system applying to each of the separate divisions of this organization. To varying degrees, each division had its own structure. It was therefore decided that a strategy for harmonizing pay should be formulated that would support the overall strategy of establishing more coherence in the direction and management of the organization. In principle, it was agreed that the pay harmonization strategy:

- should fit the culture and values of the organization;
- provide a framework within which a consistent approach to pay would take place;
- provide for a reasonable degree of flexibility in rewarding people for their contribution.

The pay harmonization probject

A project team was set up which was involved in developing a job-evaluation scheme. The factors were:

- concern for people;
- complexity of decisions and freedom to act;
- problem solving and innovation;
- communication;
- influencing and interpersonal skills;

- management of resources and process;
- planning;
- flexibility;
- capability.

The scheme was computerized using GAUGE software. A very large proportion of jobs were then evaluated. A market rate survey was also conducted. To provide for flexibility within a framework it was decided that a job family structure should be designed with 'bands', ie individual job ranges for roles, in each family. The pay range for each band was fixed at 20 per cent below and 10 per cent above an 'anchor rate'. This rate was determined by reference to both market pay levels and job evaluation scores. Internal equity was regarded as important, but it was recognized that the need to be competitive might prevail in certain instances. Progress through a zone would be related to contribution. Eight job families were identified and defined. Profiles were produced for the generic roles in each family. The pay bands were defined as follows:

Senior Manager   Responsible to a director or head of department for managing a functional and/or geographic group, including line management responsibility for other managers, and/or for managing and/or developing complex programmes.

Manager   Responsible either to a senior manager or to a director for operations delivery or the development of services delivery. May have line management responsibility for non-managers.

Executive   Responsible for developing contracts with, delivering programmes to and/or developing programmes for clients. May have supervisory responsibilities. Likely to have significant experience of target markets.

Junior Executive   Responsible for developing contacts with, delivering programmes to and/or developing programmes for clients. May have supervisory responsibilities. Likely to have less experience and/or less responsibility than operations delivery executives.

Assistant   Trainee, working alongside an executive or junior executive. Likely to have limited experience of programmes or client delivery.

Outcomes

The key components of the system are that it is owned by staff, there is a strong cultural fit and it is transparent. As the Director of Human Resources commented: 'It's getting it to fit and getting it to develop with the culture that counts. It's relatively easy to design the system, its getting it to work that matters.'

44

Contingent pay: paying for performance, competence, skill and contribution

CONTINGENT PAY DEFINED

Contingent pay consists of payments related to individual performance, contribution, competence or skill, or to team or organizational performance. In the form of payment by results, contingent pay has been a feature of shop-floor payment systems for many years.

A distinction can be made between performance – what a person achieves – and contribution – the impact made by that person on the performance of the team and the organization. The level of contribution will depend on the competence, skill and motivation of individuals, the opportunities they have to demonstrate their competence and the use they make of the guidance and leadership they receive. The term contribution-related pay refers to arrangements where payments are related to both competence and results.

There are two considerations that need to be examined before describing the rationale and criteria for contingent pay and the types of pay as mentioned above: the use of variable pay and the difference between a reward and an incentive.

Variable pay

Contingent pay can be awarded in two ways: as a consolidated increase to the basic rate of pay, or as a cash lump sum. The latter is called variable pay and it is increasingly being used to counter the argument against consolidation, which assumes that past performance will continue at the same level in the future and should therefore be rewarded with a permanent increase in pay. It is, in fact, a sort of gift that goes on giving – an annuity. But there is no basis for the confident assumption that past performance predicates future performance. The future does not necessarily resemble the past. The rationale for variable pay is that the additional pay should be re-earned every year and employees have to accept the risk that they might not re-earn it. It has always been the rule in executive pay, sales representatives' remuneration and payment-by-result schemes for manual workers. It has been less common in performance-related pay schemes, although organizations with such schemes are increasingly turning towards the use of achievement or sustained high performance bonuses, often in the form of 'spot' payments for a particular achievement.

However, competence-related and skill-based payments are usually consolidated. This is on the assumption that the achievement of certain levels of competence or skill does predict continuing performance at those, or higher, levels. Consolidation recognizes that the acquisition of competence or skill enhances the value of individuals to the organization in the longer term and, in fact, increases their market worth.

The distinction between incentives and rewards

When developing contingent pay policies and processes, it is necessary to be clear about the extent to which a scheme is designed to provide an incentive or a reward. Incentives are forward-looking while rewards are retrospective:

- *Financial incentives* aim to motivate people to achieve their objectives, improve their performance or enhance their competence or skills by focusing on specific targets and priorities.
- *Financial rewards* provide financial recognition to people for their achievements in the shape of attaining or exceeding their performance targets or reaching certain levels of competence or skill.

Financial incentives are designed to provide direct motivation – 'do this and you will get that'. A shop-floor payment-by-result scheme or a sales representative's commission system is an example of a financial incentive. An achievement bonus or a team-based lump-sum payment is an example of a financial reward. Financial rewards provide a tangible form of recognition and can therefore serve as indirect motivators, as long as people expect that further achievements will produce worthwhile rewards.

This distinction is important because it highlights the fact that schemes designed to 'incentivize' and therefore motivate people may fail to do this directly, although they could be a useful means of recognizing contribution.

THE RATIONALE FOR CONTINGENT PAY

Basic reasons

There are three basic reasons for using contingent pay:

- *Motivation*. Pay related to performance, competence or skill motivates people to achieve higher levels of performance and to increase the range and depth of their competences or skills.
- *Message*. Contingent pay delivers a general message that the organization regards performance, competence, skill and contribution as important – 'this is what we expect you to do and this is how we will reward you for doing it'. It can also deliver messages that certain values or aspects of performance are important; for example, quality, customer service, leadership and teamworking.
- *Equity*. It is right and proper that pay should be related to people's performance, contribution, competence or skill.

The first reason is probably the most popular one, but it is also the most dubious. Contingent pay can motivate but only if a number of stringent conditions are satisfied, as described later in this chapter.

Contingent pay can also deliver messages about values and expectations. It can make certain aspects of the psychological contract more explicit and it can focus attention on the things that matter. But it is not the only way of delivering such messages. There are others, namely the normal processes of management and leadership. Contingent pay can underpin and support these processes, but it cannot replace them.

Impact on the organization

Contingent pay can enable an organization to:

- establish a clear relationship between pay and performance, competence or skill;
- build on the benefits of performance management by recognizing achievement in a tangible way;

- reinforce a performance-orientated culture;
- demonstrate that the organization believes in the importance of developing skills and competences;
- reward and therefore reinforce team as well as individual effort;
- concentrate effort in priority areas, clarifying key issues;
- attract and retain people who are confident in their ability to deliver results but expect to be rewarded accordingly;
- improve pay competitiveness;
- improve employee commitment by enabling them to share in the success of the organization.

But contingent pay does not provide an easy answer to achieving these highly desirable objectives. It is hard to get it right and it often fails to deliver because the process has been misconceived, badly introduced or poorly managed.

CONTINGENT PAY STRATEGY

The basic considerations affecting the basis and content of a contingent pay strategy are summed up in Figure 44.1.

Figure 44.1 Contingent pay strategy

(Source: M Armstrong, *Employee Reward*, 2nd Edition, Institute of Personnel and Development, 1999)

CRITERIA FOR CONTINGENT PAY

The most important criterion for contingent pay is conveyed by the concept of 'line of sight' as originated by Lawler (1990). This is that individuals and teams should have a clear line of sight between what they do and what they will get for doing it. The notion of line of sight expresses the essence of expectancy theory, that motivation only takes place when people expect that they will get worthwhile rewards for their effort and contribution.

In addition to the line of sight criterion, there are six golden rules for successful contingent pay schemes:

1. Individuals and teams need to be clear about the targets and standards of performance required.
2. They must be in a position to influence the performance by changing their behaviour or decisions.
3. The rewards should be meaningful enough to make the efforts required worthwhile – and the communication of the rewards should be positively handled.
4. The incentive or bonus formula should be easy to understand.
5. The reward should follow the accomplishment as quickly as possible.

PERFORMANCE-RELATED PAY

Individual performance-related pay (PRP) relates pay progression (increases to base rate) or bonuses to the assessed performance of individuals.

Method of operation

Methods of operating PRP vary considerably but its typical main features are as follows.

- *Pay structure* – this is designed to provide scope for pay progression within pay brackets attached to job grades.
- *Pay progression and performance* – the rate and limits of progression through the pay brackets are determined by performance ratings.
- *Decelerated progression* – pay progression relating to performance is typically planned to decelerate through the grade because it is argued in line with learning curve theory that pay increases should be higher during the earlier period in a job when learning is at its highest rate.

- *Performance-related pay increases* may be added cumulatively to basic pay (ie consolidated) until either the maximum rate of pay for the grade or a limit within the grade defined in terms of a level of performance is reached. PRP increases are often relatively small. The 1998 IPD survey showed that the median increase below senior management level was 4 per cent. But this can vary considerably between organizations and between different categories of people within organizations. Alternatively, performance-related pay increases can be paid as non-consolidated lump sum bonuses (variable pay), although this is less common.
- *Pay matrix* – this determines increases on the basis of ratings and position in the pay range as illustrated in Figure 44.2.
- *Holistic approach* – increasingly, for the reasons given in Chapter 31, organizations are rejecting the mechanistic approach of relating performance pay to ratings and, therefore, the use of a pay matrix. Instead they adopt an holistic approach which involves taking an overall view of the employee's performance, competence or contribution and deciding on the level of increase or bonus which would appropriately reflect that overview. Individual pay reviews are typically held at a different time from the performance review to avoid prejudicing the developmental purpose of that review. Clearly, there is a read-across from the performance management review which will inform decisions on the appropriate increase or bonus.

Rating	Position in pay range (compa-ratio)			
	80–90%	91–100%	101–110%	111–120%
Exceptional	12	10	8	6
Very effective	10	8	6	4
Effective	6	4	3	0
Developing	4	3	0	0
Ineligible	0	0	0	0

Figure 44.2 A pay matrix

Number of PRP schemes

The 1998 IPD survey of performance-related pay schemes established that 40 per cent of 1,158 respondents had adopted performance-related pay. Contrary to the popular belief that organizations are becoming disillusioned with performance-related pay, its use is growing. Fifty-nine per cent of the respondents had introduced it during the five years prior to 1998. Twenty-three per cent of respondents who currently do not have performance pay processes had discontinued them between 1990 and 1998. This represents an annual cessation rate of 3 per cent a year, smaller than the growth experienced over the past five years.

Impact of performance-related pay

The IPD survey established that 74 per cent of respondents believed that PRP improves performance. This is a strong vote of confidence in the system. The only reservation that can be made about this information is that it represents the opinion of the respondents, who were mainly HR specialists and might be expected to be bullish about PRP. The opinion of employees in receipt of PRP was not sought.

The survey found that respondents largely believed that PRP delivered a clear message about organizational performance (67 per cent) and rewarded people in a way they think is fair (57 per cent), although 14 per cent felt that PRP had worsened perception about fairness.

In the opinion of the survey respondents, PRP schemes made their most positive impact on the behaviour of the high performers (21 per cent compared to 4 per cent of average performers and 4 per cent of poor performers). The writers of the IPD's executive summary commented that: 'These high performers may be precisely the type of employee that many employers wish to nurture and develop.' This may be so, except that it could be argued that these high performers may well be motivated by a number of other factors (eg achievement) rather than money. The survey does reveal that 41 per cent of respondents thought that there was no real change in average performance as a result of PRP, and 52 per cent believed that there was no real change in poor performers. But these are the very people whose performance should be addressed by PRP. Other methods of motivation provided by performance management have to be deployed as well as money.

Advantages of PRP

The advantages claimed for PRP can be summarized as follows:

● It motivates.

- It delivers the right message.
- It is fair to reward people according to their performance.
- It provides a tangible means of rewarding and recognizing achievements.

Disadvantages of PRP

The disadvantages of PRP, as pointed out by its many critics, are that:

- It is not a guaranteed motivator; the performance pay criteria mentioned earlier in this chapter are often difficult if not impossible to meet.
- It has to be based on some form of performance assessment, usually a rating. But it may be difficult to produce realistic performance measures. As a result, ratings may be unfair, subjective and inconsistent. If there is undue emphasis on individual performance, teamwork will suffer.
- PRP can lead to pay rising faster than performance (pay drift). In other words, it is not cost-effective.
- PRP schemes are difficult to manage well. They rely upon effective performance management processes, which many organizations will not have. And Vicky Wright (1991) has emphasized that: 'Even the most ardent supporters of performance-related pay recognize that it is extraordinarily difficult to manage well.'
- PRP can inhibit teamwork because of its individualistic nature.
- PRP can produce poor-quality performance because people are concentrating on achieving quantitative targets.
- PRP can lead to 'short-termism' – the pursuit of quick results rather than paying attention to the achievement of longer-term strategic goals.

A research project conducted by Marsden and French (1998) in the Inland Revenue found that while there was general support for the principle of performance pay, most respondents did not believe that it had improved their motivation. A majority of employees believed that it was divisive and inhibits cooperation and there was a widespread belief that line managers used it to reward their favourites. In fact, PRP in the public sector has seldom worked well, probably for these reasons coupled with considerable trade union hostility.

According to Hague (1996), other research, including that conducted by Bevan and Thompson (1991), has suggested that performance-related pay, far from rewarding performance, is demotivating staff.

These disadvantages may appear to be formidable, and the messages from much of the academic research are negative, but the fact remains that in many organizations, as shown by the 1998 IPD survey, the advantages of PRP are perceived as exceeding its disadvantages. Perhaps the most compelling reason for taking this view is that it is equitable to reward people who perform well more than those who perform badly. And even if PRP is not a powerful direct motivator, it will provide for indirect motivation because achievement will have been recognized by tangible means. It will also deliver the message that high performance is vital and will be rewarded – 'This is what we believe to be important and this is what we will pay for.' The ultimate question that many organizations have had to answer is: 'What's the alternative?' If you do not want to pay everyone in a job the same irrespective of their contribution, or if you dislike the notion of paying people for 'being there' as in a service-related incremental pay system, then you have to consider some form of contingent pay. But if you do take that route, it is essential to consider with great care the criteria for PRP.

What PRP can offer

The process of PRP can be said to be more important than the pay itself. In spite of all the criticisms, the most convincing argument for PRP is that people should be rewarded according to their contribution – the value they create.

But it is still necessary not to be starry-eyed or to believe that it is an easy option. PRP is most likely to fail if it is introduced complacently without sufficient thought on the basis of simplistic views about what it can do. Brown and Armstrong (1999) make the following points about how PRP can be made to work and its strengths and limitations.

PRP is not a universal solution

PRP cannot be endorsed universally, out-of-hand; it appears to work in some situations but not in others. It is more likely to work in high-involvement cultures and in entrepreneurial cultures in which performance can be measured readily. Situational variables (culture, management style, type of people involved, technology etc) rather than the scheme's design are important determinants of success or failure. Success is far more dependent on communications and support systems as mentioned above.

PRP is not universally successful or successful

All PRP schemes have their strengths and weaknesses, and the key issue for practising managers is not only to pick out the most appropriate pay scheme for their situation, but also to try and maximize the potential advantages and minimize the disadvantages.

Simplistic views about the power of money to motivate are unhelpful

It is a bad mistake to believe that money by itself will result in sustained motivation. It can assist in the motivation process but as Kohn (1993) correctly points out, rarely in a crude, behaviourist, Pavlov's-dog type of way. People react in widely different ways to any form of motivation. The assumption that money in the form of PRP will motivate all people equally is untenable. And it is this belief that has led governments, as well as managements, in the direction of making the naive and unjustified assumption that PRP by itself can act as a lever for change and can make a major impact on performance.

The significance of goal setting

The objective-setting and review processes associated with performance management can make as much or more impact on performance as PRP. Goal theory (see Chapter 10) indicates that objective setting is a powerful motivator in its own right. As Brown and Armstrong comment: 'Who is to say whether a pay scheme influences behaviour because of the money on offer, or because of the objectives and target achievements which have to be satisfied?'

Conclusions

The limited power of PRP to provide an incentive through financial means alone should be recognized, but that does not mean that it should be rejected out of hand. It does work as a reward process in some circumstances, and it does satisfy the basic principle that it is equitable to reward people who do well more than those who do badly. Rewards can be provided by non-financial means, but tangible recognition can be a valuable part of a total reward system as long as it is appropriate in the situation and is well-conceived and managed.

Criteria for installing and monitoring PRP

The following questions should be answered before launching PRP or deciding whether or not it should be retained:

- Will the proposed scheme, or does the existing scheme, motivate people?
- Is it possible to devise or maintain fair and consistent methods of measuring performance?
- Is there an effective performance management process in place, based on measuring and assessing performance against agreed targets and standards?

- Can managers be trained (or are managers properly trained) to rate performance fairly and consistently?
- Will rewards be fairly and consistently related to performance?
- Will there be, is there, enough money available to provide worthwhile rewards?
- Will the proposed scheme, or does the existing scheme, satisfy the other criteria for an effective performance pay system, namely, clear targets and standards, ability to track performance, ability to influence performance, clarity on the relationship between effort and reward, and does the reward follows the accomplishment fairly closely?
- Will the scheme be, or is the scheme, cost-effective?

If an organization cannot answer these questions satisfactorily, one alternative is not to use PRP as a means of adding performance-related increases to the base rate. It could be replaced with a 'variable pay' system which only awards cash bonuses as and when they are earned for notable and measurable achievements. In addition, cash bonuses could be paid for people who have achieved sustained levels of high performance as demonstrated by exceeding targets and standards over an extended period.

Other alternatives, to which a number of organizations are turning, is competence-related pay or contribution-related pay as described below.

COMPETENCE-RELATED PAY

How it works

Competence-related pay provides for pay progression to be linked to assessments of the levels of competence people have achieved. It rewards people for their ability to perform, not just their performance. Typically, the headings in a competence profile or framework are used as the basis for assessment. The level of competence expected from a fully effective individual in a role is defined and the actual levels achieved are compared with requirements.

In some schemes, people are assessed against each competence heading and an overall assessment is then made, which may be expressed on a scale such as: exceeds the level of competence required, fully competent, not yet competent but developing at the expected rate, not yet competent but developing at less than the expected rate. These assessments are then translated into a pay increase.

However, as noted by Armstrong and Brown (1998), there are many different forms of competence-related schemes and they pointed out that in many cases, 'competence is just one factor, albeit an important one, used to inform pay decisions'.

Measuring competence

The problem with competence-related pay, as Sparrow (1996) pointed out, is that of measuring levels of competence, although Brown and Armstrong (1997) have asserted that measurement and assessment are possible if a well-researched and clearly defined competence framework exists and people are trained in how to collect and assess evidence on competence levels. This is easier when hard, work-based competences are used rather than softer, behaviourally based competencies. If competence or capabilities are used they will have been defined in output terms, ie 'in this aspect of the role the person should be capable of... '. The capability will be described in terms of doing something that will produce a result. The measurement of competence therefore starts by reviewing results in each area of capability and thus assessing how effectively the competence has been used.

If this approach is adopted, competence-related pay begins to look suspiciously like performance-related pay. But if competence is not about performance, what is it about?

Differences between performance-related and competence-related pay

However, there are differences between performance and competence-related pay. These are:

● Competence-related pay is based on an agreed framework of competences or capabilities, some of which are generic (applicable to a number of roles), some specific to particular roles.
● Competence-related pay is not based on the achievement of specific results expressed in the form of targets or projects to be completed, although it can be said that it is concerned with the attainment on a continuing basis of agreed standards of performance.
● Competence-related pay looks forward in the sense that it implies that when people have reached a certain level of competence they will be able to go on using it effectively into the future; conversely, performance-related pay looks backwards – this is what you have just achieved, and this is your reward for achieving it.
● Competence-related pay is or should be based on agreed definitions of competence requirements expressed in the language of role holders and on agreements about the evidence that can be used to assess levels of competence. In

contrast, performance-related pay is often, although not always, based on managerial judgements which the individuals concerned may find difficult to accept.

Advantages and disadvantages of competence-related pay

The list of differences between competence- and performance-related pay given above summarizes a number of the advantages of the former. If the organization really believes that successful performance depends on raising levels of competence then some form of competence-related pay makes sense.

But however carefully competences are defined, there may still be problems in measuring them, and translating any measurements into an overall assessment can seem to be an arbitrary process. Competence-related pay also seems to ignore the fact that performance is about delivering results. That is why some organizations have introduced hybrid schemes in which base pay is related to competence but out-of-the-ordinary achievements are rewarded with cash bonuses. Many people think that this is the best way forward.

Conditions necessary to introduce competence-related pay

An organization should not contemplate the introduction of competence-related pay lightly. The following demanding criteria need to be met if it is to work:

- Well researched and analysed competence frameworks must be in place.
- Reliable, fair and consistent methods of assessing competence must be available.
- Managers, team leaders and employees generally should be trained in how the process operates and must be convinced that it is workable and fair.

Competence-related pay is generally more likely to be appropriate for 'knowledge workers' in organizations where the values and processes focus on flexibility, adaptability and continuous development.

SKILL-BASED PAY

Skill-based pay is a payment method in which pay progression is linked to the number, kind and depth of skills that individuals develop and use. It involves paying for the horizontal acquisition of the skills required to undertake a wider range of tasks, and/or for the vertical development of the skills needed to operate at a higher level, or the development in depth of existing skills.

Skill-based pay systems are people rather than job orientated. Individuals are paid for the skills they are capable of using (as long as those skills are necessary), not for the job they happen to be doing at the time. There may be a basic job rate for individuals with the minimum level of skills, but above that level they will be paid for what they can do themselves and as members of teams. Skill-based pay, however, is not concerned with how well people use their skills. This is the role of performance-related pay, although it is possible to add a performance pay dimension to a skill-based pay system.

The creation of National Vocational Qualifications (NVQs) as a means of defining and assessing competence levels has arisen from the need to extend skills bases and has encouraged the growth of skill-based pay schemes.

How skill-based pay operates

There are many varieties of skill-based pay, but a typical scheme for operatives is likely to have the following features:

- The scheme is based on defined skill blocks or modules – clusters or sets of skills which the organization is willing to reward with extra pay.
- The type and number of skill blocks that individuals need to learn and can learn are defined.
- The successful acquisition of the skills contained in a skills block or module results in an increment to base pay.
- The incremental skills payments will be limited to a defined hierarchy or range of skills.
- Training modules and programmes are defined for each skill block to provide the necessary 'cross-training'.
- The achievement of levels of competence by experience and training can be accredited under the NVQ system or certified by the company and/or an education and training institution.

Skill-based pay has a lot to offer organizations that are keen to extend their skills base and increase multi-skilling. It avoids many of the problems associated with performance pay but it can be expensive to introduce and operate.

CONTRIBUTION-RELATED PAY

As discussed above, it is possible to make a number of distinctions between performance-related and competence-related pay. But these can become distinctions without differences – more apparent than real. This happens when competence levels are defined and competence is assessed against those levels not just by observing behaviour but by analysing the impact of that behaviour in achieving results and meeting required standards of performance.

The distinction between them becomes even less real if the evidence of competence is based on what people have done as well as how they have done it. But if performance can be defined as being both what people achieve (outcomes) and how they achieve it (competences), then a mixed model becomes appropriate. This could be described as 'contribution-related pay'.

Contribution defined

Contribution is what people do to bring about a result. Individuals and teams contribute to the achievement of the purpose of their role. In financial terms, contribution is the difference between the sales revenue for a product and its directly attributable marginal or variable costs. It thus indicates what income a product generates towards achieving profit and covering fixed costs. In the context of performance management and pay, however, contribution is a more general concept which describes the overall part people play in generating results as the basis of the attributes they bring to their roles (skills and competences) and how they use these attributes.

Contribution-related pay defined

In accordance with the definition given above, contribution can be measured in terms of both inputs and outputs – competence and results. Contribution-related pay recognizes that performance embraces both these factors. The questions to be answered when assessing levels of pay and pay increases or bonus are:

● What impact has the person in this role made on team, departmental or organizational performance?
● What level of competence has been brought to bear in handling the demands made by the role?
● How has the contribution made to end-results been affected by the level of competence displayed and applied?

Contribution-related pay can therefore be defined as a process for making pay decisions which are based on assessments of both the outcomes of the work carried out by individuals and the levels of skill and competence which have influenced these outcomes.

How contribution-related pay works

Contribution-related pay can work effectively within a broad-banded pay structure in which movement across the bands depends on both competence and performance. It also fits well with a belief that the delivery of pay should be based on performance, competence and career progression considerations.

Paying for contribution, as suggested by Brown (1998), means paying for results plus competence and for past performance and future success as illustrated in Figure 44.3.

Figure 44.3 Paying for contribution model

Contribution-related pay therefore works by applying the mixed model of performance management – assessing inputs and outputs and coming to a conclusion on the level of pay that is appropriate for individuals in their roles, looking both at past performance and, importantly, the future.

There are two approaches. The first is to take a holistic view of what people have contributed on the basis of information about their competence and what they have delivered. This can be based on a competence framework so that behaviour can be considered analytically, although ultimately an overall view will be formed. Similarly, an overview of performance in achieving objectives or meeting standards can take place. The information from the sources is then combined and the level of contribution compared with others in similar roles in order to reach a pay review decision. The second approach involves rating both results and competence and taking both these ratings into account in deciding on pay increases. This could be done somewhat mechanistically with the help of a pay matrix as illustrated in Table 44.1.

Table 44.1 Contribution pay matrix

		Competence			
		a	b	c	d
	A	–	%	%	–
Results	B	–	3%	4%	5%
	C	2%	4%	6%	8%
	D	4%	6%	8%	10%

Paying for contribution is appropriate when it is believed that a well-rounded approach is required to make crucial pay decisions which are related to the criticality of the role now and in the future and to get the balance of factors affecting pay right in the light of organizational requirements.

TEAM-BASED PAY

Team-based pay provides rewards to teams or groups of employees carrying out similar and related work which is linked to the performance of the team. Performance may be measured in terms of outputs and/or the achievement of service delivery standards. The quality of the output and the opinion of customers about service levels are also often taken into account.

As described by Armstrong and Ryden (1996), team pay is usually paid in the form of a bonus which is shared amongst team members in proportion to their base rate of pay (much less frequently, it is shared equally). Individual team members may be eligible for competence-related or skill-based pay but not for performance-related pay.

Advantages of team pay

Team pay can:

- encourage effective team working and cooperative behaviour;

- clarify team goals and priorities;
- enhance flexible working within teams;
- encourage multi-skilling;
- provide an incentive for the team collectively to improve performance;
- encourage less effective team members to improve to meet team standards.

Disadvantages of team pay

The disadvantages of team pay are that:

- it only works in cohesive and mature teams;
- individuals may resent the fact that their own efforts are not rewarded specifically;
- peer pressure which compels individuals to conform to group norms could be undesirable.

Conditions suitable for team pay

Team pay is more likely to be appropriate when:

- teams can be readily identified and defined;
- teams are well-established;
- the work carried out by team members is interrelated – team performance depends on the collective efforts of team members;
- targets and standards of performance can be determined and agreed readily with team members;
- acceptable measurements of team performance compared with targets and standards are available;
- generally, the formula for team pay meets the criteria for performance pay.

SHOP-FLOOR INCENTIVE SCHEMES

Shop-floor incentive schemes relate the pay or part of the pay received by employees to the number of items they produce or process, the time they take to do a certain amount of work and/or some other aspect of their performance. They usually provide for pay to fluctuate with performance in the short term, but they can, as in measured daywork, provide for a long-term relationship. They are often referred to as payment-by-result schemes.

Traditionally, the ratio of base rate to incentive has been 2:1, but the current trend is to reduce the target proportion of incentive pay to one-third or one-quarter to minimize fluctuations in earnings and to control wage or earnings drift (increases in incentive-based earnings which are higher than the increases in output that generated the incentive payment – wage drift is an undesirable but common phenomenon associated with old and decaying payment-by-result schemes). A further reason for reducing the incentive element is that many organizations find it more difficult to justify highly personalized differentiated pay because it can be counter-productive in terms of the achievement of quality and teamwork.

There might also be a guaranteed or 'fall-back' rate for workers in payment-by-results schemes, which would be related to the consolidated time rate for a worker at a similar level. The main types of incentive or payment-by-results schemes are individual piecework, work-measured schemes and measured daywork.

Individual piecework

In individual or straight piecework a uniform price is paid per unit of production. Operators are therefore rewarded according to the number of 'pieces' they produce or process, so pay is directly proportional to results. Most piecework schemes provide a fall-back rate or minimum earnings level. It is common for the minimum rate to be set at 70 to 80 per cent of average earnings, although some companies set it as low as 30 per cent and others set it equal to the minimum time rate. Companies may also provide guaranteed payments for downtime due to machine failure, maintenance work or waiting for materials.

The advantages to employers of piecework is that the system is easy to operate, simple to understand and can be left to run by itself, provided there is adequate supervision to ensure that quality does not suffer. Piecework can also enable employers to estimate and control manufacturing costs effectively. But employers can find that they lose control over the level of production, which depends largely on the self-motivation of the workforce. Quality can suffer if close supervision is not exercised and the negotiation of piece rates for new work can be time consuming and fractious.

The advantages to employees are that they can predict their earnings in the short term and regulate their pace of work in accordance with the level of pay they want to attain. But it may be difficult to predict longer-term earnings if work fluctuates from week to week. The intensity of work required in this system may lead to repetitive strain injury (RSI).

Piecework has become more inappropriate as an incentive method as new technology has changed work arrangements. In larger-scale manufacturing, it has largely been replaced by work-measured schemes or some other form of incentive or bonus payment.

Work-measured schemes

In a work-measured scheme the job, or its component tasks, is timed and the incentive payment is related to performance above the standard time allowed for the job. The amount of incentive pay received depends on the difference between the actual time taken to perform the task and the standard time allowed. If a task is done in less than the standard time, then there is a time saving, which means that the operator's output will increase.

Work measurement involves working out standard values or times for a complete task, which can, however, be broken down into components to each of which standard minute values can be allocated. Work study or industrial engineers can measure the time taken for each component with the help of a stop-watch. A large number of timings will be made in each task to ensure that the variety of conditions under which an operator works are included so as to minimize distortions. Measurements may therefore be taken at different times of the day, and a number of operators may be timed on the same task to extend the range of timings and reduce the risk of errors.

The work study engineer who measures the job will be entirely objective about the stop-watch timing but a subjective assessment will also have to be made of the operator's speed, or effectiveness. This is known as the operator's effort rating. The performance of a qualified worker, if motivated, without over-exertion, is known as standard performance. Industrial engineers sometimes relate this to walking at a reasonably brisk pace, say four miles an hour. All operators who have been timed are given an effort rating relative to this standard and this is taken into account when deciding on standard times.

Measured daywork

Measured daywork schemes became popular in large batch or mass production factories in the 1950s and 1960s when it became evident that, in spite of all efforts, it was impossible to control wage drift. They provide for the pay of employees to be fixed on the understanding that they will maintain a specified level of performance, but pay does not fluctuate in the short term with their performance. The arrangement depends on work measurement to define the required level of performance and to monitor the actual level. The fundamental principles of measured daywork are that there is an incentive level of performance and that the incentive payment is guaranteed in advance, thereby putting employees under an obligation to perform at the effort level required. In contrast, a conventional work-measured incentive scheme allows employees discretion on their effort level but relates their pay directly to the results they achieve. Between these two extremes there are a variety of alternatives, including banded incentives, stepped schemes and various forms of high day rate.

Measured daywork seeks to produce an effort–reward bargain in which enhanced and stable earnings are exchanged for an incentive level of performance. Its disadvantage is that the set performance target can become an easily attainable norm and may be difficult to change, even after extensive renegotiation.

Group or team incentive schemes

Group or team incentive schemes provide for the payment of a bonus either equally or proportionately to individuals within a group or team. The bonus is related to the output achieved by the group in relation to defined targets or to the time saved on jobs – the difference between allowed time and actual time.

ORGANIZATION-WIDE SCHEMES

Bonus schemes

Organization-wide bonus schemes pay sums of money to employees, the sums being related to company or plant-wide performance. They are designed to share the company's prosperity with its employees and thus to increase their commitment to its objectives and values. Because they do not relate reward directly to individual effort they are not effective as direct motivators, although gainsharing schemes can focus directly on what needs to be done to improve performance and so get employees involved in productivity improvement or cost-reduction plans. The three main types of schemes are gainsharing, profit sharing and profit-related pay.

Gainsharing

Gainsharing is a formula-based company or factory-wide bonus plan that provides for employees to share in the financial gains resulting from increases in added value or another measure of productivity. The link between their efforts and the payout can usefully be made explicit by involving them in analysing results and identifying areas for improvement.

Profit sharing

Profit sharing is the payment to eligible employees of sums in the form of cash or shares related to the profits of the business. The amount shared may be determined by a published or unpublished formula or entirely at the discretion of management. Profit sharing differs from gainsharing in that the former is based on more than improved productivity. A number of factors outside the individual employee's control contribute to profit. Gainsharing aims to relate its payouts much more specifically to productivity and performance improvements within the control of employees. It is not possible to use profit sharing schemes as direct incentives, as for most employees the link between individual effort and the reward is so remote. But they can increase identification with the company and many managements operate profit sharing schemes because they believe that they should share the company's success with its employees.

Employee share schemes

Share ownership is most commonly provided through one or other of the following schemes:

- an *All Employee Share Ownership Plan* which allows for the issue to employees of free shares up to a maximum of £3,000, which are gifts to be held by trustees for at least three years, or 'partnership shares' which are purchased by employees by deductions from salary, up to a maximum per month of the lower of 10 per cent of pay or £125. Both types of share entitle the owners to dividends. The sums involved in giving or purchasing shares are free of income tax and National Insurance as long as the shares are held for at least five years;
- a *Savings-related Share Option Scheme* under which a company grants share options linked to savings made by the employee. A share option entitles the employee to acquire the share at a future date.

CHOICE OF APPROACH

The first choice is whether or not to have contingent pay related to performance, competence, contribution or skill. Public or voluntary sector organizations with fixed incremental systems (pay spines), where progression is solely based on service, may want to retain them because they do not depend on possibly biased judgements by managers and they are perceived as being fair – everyone gets the same. However, the fairness of such systems can be questioned. Is it fair for a poor performer to be paid more than a good performer simply for being there?

The alternative to fixed increments are either spot rates or some form of contingency pay. Spot rate systems in their purest form are rare except in smaller organizations and new businesses where the need for formal practices has not yet been recognized. Even on the shop-floor, where high day rates are paid and there is no payment-by-results scheme, there is often a factory-wide bonus scheme. Some organizations may not have a graded pay structure for staff with scope for salary progression in grades. But the so-called spot rates for jobs are usually varied by paying people what it is believed they are worth. This is a variety of contingent pay, although pay decisions in these circumstances are often arbitrary and unsystematic.

If it is decided that a more formal type of contingent pay should be adopted, the choice is between the various types of performance pay, competence-related or contribution-related pay, team pay, payment related to organizational performance and skill-based pay. The choice of approach will largely depend on factors relating to the circumstances of the organization. These include the corporate culture, the type of organization, the categories of employees who will be involved, the time scale required, and the impact it is hoped the scheme will make on individual and corporate performance.

Individual schemes are more appropriate when performance or contribution can be attributed directly to the efforts and abilities of individuals and the nature of the scheme will not prejudice teamwork. Group or team pay may be more appropriate when results depend on team rather than individual effort and roles have generally to be more flexible. New working arrangements such as just-in-time, flexible manufacturing systems and cellular manufacturing are driving the move towards more team pay systems.

In general, incentive and bonus schemes where there is a clear target-related incentive and the reward closely follows the performance are likely to make the most immediate impact on motivation. Performance-related pay, where awards are usually made some time after the event, will have a medium-term effect and will not impact so directly on motivation. Schemes relating the reward to organizational performance are also likely to have a medium-term effect and will impact on commitment and retention rather than serving as direct motivators.

The main features and disadvantages of different forms of contingent pay and the conditions when they are likely to be appropriate are summarised in Table 44.2.

Table 44.2 Comparison of contingent pay schemes

Type	Main features	Advantages	Disadvantages	When appropriate
Performance-related pay	Increases to basic pay or bonuses are related to assessment of performance	• May motivate (but this is uncertain) • Links rewards to objectives • Meets the need to be rewarded for achievement • Delivers message that good performance is important and will be rewarded	• May *not* motivate • Relies on judgements of performance which may be subjective • Prejudicial to teamwork • Focuses on outputs, not quality • Relies on good performance management processes	• For people who are likely to be motivated by money • In organizations with a performance-orientated culture • When performance can be measured objectively
Competence-related pay	Pay increases are related to the level of competence	• Focuses attention on need to achieve higher levels of competence • Encourages competence development • Can be integrated with other applications of competency-based HR management	• Assessment of competence levels may be difficult • Ignores outputs – danger of paying for competencies that will not be used • Relies on well-trained and committed line managers	• As part of an integrated approach to HRM where competencies are used across a number of activities • Where competence is a key factor where it may be inappropriate or hard to measure outputs • Where well-established competency frameworks exist
Contribution-related pay	Increases in pay or bonuses are related both to inputs (competence) and outputs (performance)	• Rewards people not only for what they do but how they do it	• As for both PRP and competence-related pay, it may be hard to measure contribution	• When it is believed that a well-rounded approach covering both inputs and outputs is appropriate
Team pay	Bonuses for team members are related to team performance	• Encourages and rewards effective team work • Provides an incentive for the team collectively to improve its performance • Reflects and supports a culture in which team work is important	• Will only work for well-defined and mature teams • Ignores individual contribution, which may be resented • May be difficult to establish suitable performance measures so that rewards properly reflect team performance	• Where there are clearly defined teams whose members are interdependent and are jointly responsible for team performance • Where fair methods of measuring team performance – preferably in relation to quantified outputs – exist • Where the culture is very much in favour of team working

45

Rewarding special groups: directors, expatriates and sales staff

Special considerations apply to the reward of directors and senior executives, expatriates and sales staff. These are examined in this chapter.

REWARDING DIRECTORS AND SENIOR EXECUTIVES

Probably no aspect of remuneration has attracted as much attention in recent years as that of the pay of directors and senior executives. The outcry over top executive reward levels led to the Cadbury Report in 1993, the Greenbury Report in 1995 and the Hampel Report in 1997, followed by the Hampel combined code on corporate governance in 1998.

The reward scene at the top

Research conducted by the TUC established that in 1999 the highest-paid directors in the top 1,000 UK companies were paid an average of 20.7 times the average pay of their employees, compared with 15.7 times in 1994. Over those five years, the average pay of directors, excluding share options, rose by 72 per cent from £239,000 to £410,000, while their employees received an average increase of 18 per cent from £17,332 to £20,485. Why has this happened? The usual reason given for this situation is that top executives have to be paid very well because of the high demand for their services globally (and pay differentials are even higher in the United States) and the need to secure their loyalty against the attractions of a competitor. This market argument has been invoked whenever high levels of executive pay have been criticized. It is protested loudly and at length that 'Unless we keep up with what other organizations are paying, our key executives will be headhunted away.'

But to what extent is this market-rate argument valid? The market for top executives in large companies is very small. It can hardly be called a market at all in the real sense of the word. And IDS (1995) has commented that:

> For many top executives, the market has become a modern mantra, invoked every time they face criticism over excessive pay rises... The market for top executives is not defined in the usual way, by the trading of commodities (executives themselves), but by comparability with similar employees in other organizations, as defined by salary surveys... When top executives talk about the market, what they actually mean is comparability. Real markets play no role at all.

And in their guidelines for remuneration committees, the Institute of Directors (not notorious for advocating limits on the pay of directors) states that 'It is important that Remuneration Committees and Boards should avoid setting remuneration packages which are generous in relation to market levels and beware of pressure always to be in the "upper quartile".' The IoD also pointed out the limitations on the extent to which market comparisons, especially international comparisons, are relevant.

Comparability studies could be biased because they select inappropriate comparators or even firms which are known to be high payers. The practice of basing comparisons on high-paying concerns is one that only a disreputable management consultant retained by a remuneration committee would indulge in.

Whether justified or not, fury about the 'gravy train' for 'fat cat' (to mix metaphors) top executives resulted in the reports, guides and regulations summarized below.

The Cadbury Report

The report of the Cadbury Committee in 1993 on the Financial Aspects of Corporate Governance made the following recommendations concerning the remuneration of directors.

- Directors' service contracts should not exceed three years without shareholder approval.
- There should be full and clear disclosure of directors' total emoluments and those of the chairman and the highest-paid UK director, including pension contributions and stock options.
- Separate figures should be given for salary and performance-related elements, and the basis upon which performance is measured should be explained.
- Executive directors' pay should be subject to the recommendations of a remuneration committee made up of non-executive directors.
- The chief executive role should be separated from that of the board chairman (as a counter to remuneration policies dominated by the chief executive).

The Cadbury Committee's report increased the amount of disclosure and led to a large number of remuneration committees being set up. But this remedy did not work. More information on pay resulted in a greater outcry, and remuneration committees consisting of non-executive directors were criticized on the assumption (not necessarily true) that such committees would be filled by 'old pals' who were also executive directors in other companies and would support higher pay because it was in their own interest.

The Greenbury Report

The 1995 Greenbury Report expressed the belief that 'UK companies mostly deal with directors' remuneration in a sensible and responsible way'. However, the report did add, 'We fully understand the concerns which shareholders, employees and the public have expressed in recent times about executive remuneration and compensation payments. There have been, in our view, mistakes and misjudgments.' The key recommendations of the report are as follows:

- the remuneration committee should consist exclusively of non-executive directors, and should determine remuneration policy and the reward packages of individual executive directors;
- the remuneration committee report should include statements on remuneration policy and the methods used to form that policy;
- listed companies should make full disclosure of named individual directors' remuneration – levels and components of pay, performance criteria and measurements, pension provision, contracts of service and compensation arrangements for early termination;
- remuneration committees must provide a remuneration package sufficient to

attract, retain and motivate directors but should avoid paying more than is necessary; they should be sensitive to wider issues, eg pay and employment conditions elsewhere in the company;

- performance-related elements should be designed to align the interests of directors and shareholders;
- any new longer-term incentive arrangement should preferably replace existing executive share option plans, or at least form part of an integrated approach which should be approved by shareholders;
- notice or service contract periods should be set at, or reduced to, a year or less. However, in some cases periods of up to two years may be acceptable;
- remuneration committees should take a robust line on the payment of compensation where performance has been unsatisfactory

The Hampel Code 1998

This code pulled together the Cadbury and Greenbury recommendations, as well giving its own views on corporate governance. The key principles for directors' remuneration it set out were that:

- levels of remuneration should be sufficient to attract and retain the directors needed to run the company successfully;
- the component parts of remuneration should link rewards to corporate and individual performance;
- companies should establish a formal and transparent procedure for developing policy on executive remuneration and for fixing remuneration packages;
- the company's annual report should contain a statement of remuneration policy and details of the remuneration of each director.

Remuneration committees

All the above reports and codes on directors' pay have emphasized the importance of having a committee with the responsibility for making decisions on the remuneration of chief executives and directors, including basic salaries, bonus and incentive schemes and targets, policy on share options, pension arrangements, car entitlement and other benefits.

The purpose of remuneration committees is to provide an independent basis for setting the salary levels and the rules covering incentives, share options, benefit entitlements and contract provisions for executive directors. Such committees are accountable to shareholders for the decisions they take, and the non-executive directors who sit on them should have no personal financial interests at stake. They should be constituted as sub-committees of company boards, and boards should elect both the chairman and the members. Greenbury recommends that remuneration committees in larger companies should consist of at least three members.

The role of the remuneration committee is to:

● set broad policy for executive remuneration as a whole as well as the remuneration packages of executive directors and, sometimes, other senior executives;
● focus on encouraging corporate performance contribution and ensure that individuals are fairly but responsibly rewarded for their individual contribution;
● comply with the appropriate codes (the Stock Exchange and Hampel);
● report and account to shareholders directly for their decisions on behalf of the board;
● ensure the relationship between boardroom remuneration and policy for employees below this level remains consistent and sensible;
● ensure proper and professional advice is obtained to assist in their deliberations.

Greenbury recommended that the remuneration committee should be supported by a senior executive of the company with suitable expertise in remuneration issues, and that it should seek external help from consultants as required. The committee should certainly obtain information on remuneration levels and practices in comparable companies from an internal or external advisor.

Directors' and executives' remuneration

The main elements of directors' and executives' remuneration are basic pay, short and long-term bonus or incentive schemes, share option and share ownership schemes, benefits and service contracts.

Decisions on the base salary of directors and senior executives are usually founded on views about the market worth of the individuals concerned. At this level the positions may not be evaluated through a formal scheme and are frequently excluded from the pay structure, although most companies will pay some attention formally or informally to internal relativities. They may, for example, suggest that directors and senior managers should be paid respectively 70 per cent and 50 per cent of the chief executive's salary.

Remuneration on joining the company is usually settled by negotiation, often subject to the approval of a remuneration committee. Reviews of base salaries are then undertaken by reference to market movements and success as measured by company performance. Decisions on base salary are important not only in themselves but also because the level agreed is likely to be the platform on which so much else rests. Bonuses are expressed as a percentage of base salary, share options may be allocated as a declared multiple of basic pay and, commonly, pension will be a proportion of final salary.

Bonus schemes

Bonus schemes provide directors and executives with cash sums based on the measures of company and, frequently, individual performance. Recent surveys have shown that about 90 per cent of participating organizations have bonus schemes for main board directors. The typical aims of an executive bonus scheme are to:

- increase executive motivation and, therefore, business performance;
- reward individual contributions;
- focus the attention of directors and executives on the company's critical success factors and on the achievement of defined objectives;
- ensure that total remuneration levels are competitive;
- enable executives to share in the prosperity of the business.

Bonus schemes may be short- or long-term. A short-term scheme rewards individual directors and executives on the basis of some measure of company and, often, individual performance. Cash payments are usually made annually, although shorter periods such as half-yearly are sometimes adopted in fast-moving businesses.

The objection to short-term bonuses (sometimes called STIs, for short-term incentives) is that they encourage 'short-termism', that is, paying more attention to immediate profits than to the longer-term growth and prosperity of the business. There has therefore been a marked shift in the direction of long-term incentives (LTIs) related to performance over three years or more. This move has the overwhelming support of the institutional investors who are the majority shareholders in many organizations. They and, increasingly, remuneration committees favour LTIs because such schemes can motivate directors to concentrate on longer-term strategic objectives and so be less influenced by the short-term negative aspects of investment decisions which should pay off in the longer term. A further perceived virtue of LTIs is that they provide a strong retention incentive (the so-called golden handcuff) because payment is not generally made until the end of the prescribed period. Longer-term incentives may be provided in the form of cash and/or shares.

At executive director level most, if not all, of the bonus is usually related to the performance of the business as a whole, on the grounds that directors are jointly accountable for that performance. Part of the bonus, however, may be related to the achievement of individual targets. Below board level there may be more emphasis on linking bonuses with the achievement of such targets. The most used performance criterion is pre-tax profit. The next most popular measure is earnings per share (profit after interest, taxation and ordinary dividends divided by the number of ordinary shares issued by the company), followed by return on capital employed and then cash flow. Profit and earnings per share are the most common criteria used by analysts and the financial press to assess company performance.

Individual targets would be linked with the key result areas of the role. To concentrate attention on these areas and to avoid complicating the scheme, it is best not to have more than three or four factors.

Performance-related bonuses are related to the achievement of a target. This may simply be the profit target in the annual budget or the longer-term plan. An alternative method of setting a target is to relate it to a minimum level of improvement compared with the previous year or, if the previous year was a poor one, the highest level reached in the previous two or three years. (This avoids setting the target at too low a figure.)

In a short-term scheme the bonus for achieving the target is typically between 20 per cent and 30 per cent of base pay, but the figure can vary considerably.

Share options

Executive share option schemes provide individual directors and executives with the right to buy a block of shares on some future date at the share price ruling when the option was granted. They are a form of long-term incentive on the assumption that executives will be motivated to perform more effectively if they can anticipate a substantial capital gain when they sell their shares at a price above that prevailing when the option was granted. When share options first became popular in the 1980s one of the attractions was that money received in this way would be subject only to capital gains tax and not income tax, although a subsequent equalization of income tax and capital gains tax diminished the advantage. The November 1995 budget provided that options granted in share schemes which on the date of grant have a market value of up to £20,000 will not be subject to income tax either on the date of grant or on the date of exercise, and any subsequent increase in the value of the shares under option will be subject only to capital gains tax. Options above that level granted since 17 July 1995 will, however, be subject to income tax.

Benefits

Employee benefits for executives may amount to over 20 per cent of the total reward package. The most important element is the pension scheme, and directors may be provided with a much higher accrual rate in a final salary scheme. This means that, typically, the maximum two-thirds pension can be achieved after 20 years' service rather than the 40 years it takes in a typical one-sixtieth scheme. Additional pensions through unapproved pension schemes (which do not attract income tax exemptions) may be provided to take the director's pension above the maximum amount permitted in an approved pension scheme (the 'cap'). Directors and executives may receive the same range of benefits as other staff but on a larger scale (a bigger car) or in the form of more generous arrangements for such benefits as medical care.

Service contracts

Three-year service contracts for directors, which have been fairly typical, attracted much adverse publicity in the middle 1990s because of the high severance payments to departing chief executives and directors, even when it was suspected or actually the case that they had been voted off the board because of inadequate performance. Following the outcry and the Greenbury Report, rolling contracts for directors are likely to be restricted to one year in most cases.

EXPATRIATE PAY

There are two basic approaches to devising expatriate pay packages: home-based pay and host-based pay, as described below.

Home-based pay

The home-based pay approach aims to ensure that the value of the expatriate's salary is the same as in the home country. The home-base salary may be a notional one for long-term assignments (ie the salary which it is assumed would be paid to expatriates were they employed in a job of equivalent level at the parent company). For shorter-term assignments it may be the actual salary of the individual. The notional or actual home-base salary is used as the foundation upon which the total remuneration package is built. This is sometimes called the 'build-up' or 'balance sheet' approach.

The policy of most organizations that employ expatriates is to ensure that they are no worse off because they have been posted abroad. In practice, various additional allowances or payments, such as hardship allowances or incentive premiums (as described in the next section of this chapter), mean that they are usually better off financially than if they had stayed at home.

The salary 'build-up' starts with the actual or notional home-base salary. To it is added a cost of living adjustment which is applied to 'spendable income' – the portion of salary which would be used at home for everyday living. It usually excludes income tax, social security, pensions and insurance, and can exclude discretionary expenditure on major purchases or holidays on the grounds that these do not constitute day-to-day living expenses. The cost of housing in the home country (mortgage payments) is a special case. It is usually treated separately, consideration being given to factors such as the housing arrangements in the host country and any income earned from renting the home property.

Spendable income varies widely, although Employment Conditions Abroad (ECA), the consultancy specializing in expatriate remuneration, says that it averages 65 per cent of salary. The cost of living adjustment is usually based on the overseas cost of living indices produced by organizations such as ECA. Thus, if the index for an overseas location were 120 (UK = 100) and the spendable income were 65 per cent of home-base salary, an individual whose notional UK salary was £30,000 would receive a cost of living allowance of £3,900.

The expatriate's salary would then consist of the actual or notional home-base salary plus the cost of living adjustment. In addition, it may be necessary to adjust salaries to take account of the host country's tax regime in order to achieve tax equalization. Moves of less than a year which might give rise to double taxation require particular attention.

Some or all of the following allowances may be added to this salary:

- 'incentive to work abroad' premium;
- hardship and location;
- housing and utilities;
- school fees;
- 'rest and recuperation' leave.

The expatriate's total home-based remuneration package would consist of this sum plus, as appropriate, pension, insurance, company car and home leave.

Total earnings expressed in the local currency may be paid entirely to the expatriates in their host country. Generally, however, the salary is split between the home and host countries. Expatriates can then pay for continuing domestic commitments such as mortgage and insurance payments and build up some capital. (The opportunity to acquire capital is often a major inducement for people to work as expatriates.)

Home-based pay ensures that expatriates will not be worse off through working abroad, and it can be developed as an attractive package. It can also be used for third-country nationals using their own country salary as a base. But it can be costly and it can create inequities between the remuneration of expatriates and that of their colleagues who are nationals of the host country. If a number of third-country nationals from different parts of the world are employed, home-based pay can create an even more complicated situation.

Host-based pay

The host-based pay approach provides expatriates with salaries and benefits such as company cars and holidays which are in line with those given to nationals of the host country in similar jobs. This method ensures equity between expatriates and host country nationals. It is adopted by companies using the so-called market rate system, which ensures that the salaries of expatriates match the market levels of pay in the host country for similar jobs.

Companies using the host-based approach commonly pay traditional allowances such as school fees, accommodation and medical insurance. They may also fund long-term benefits like social security, life assurance and pensions from home.

The host-based method is certainly equitable from the viewpoint of local nationals, and it can be less expensive than home-based pay. But it may be much less attractive as an inducement for employees to work abroad, especially in unpleasant locations, and it can be difficult to collect market rate data locally to provide a basis for setting pay levels.

SALES STAFF

There are no hard-and-fast rules governing how sales representatives should be paid. It depends on the type of company, the products or services it offers its customers, and the nature of the sales process – how sales are organized and made.

The reward mix for the sales force

The main elements of the sales reward mix as described in the rest of this section are basic salary, commission, bonus and other motivators such as incentives (rewards in kind in the form of gifts, travel vouchers, etc), competitions and non-financial rewards generally.

Basic salary

Some organizations pay basic salary only. Although salary progression is likely to be performance-related in companies like these, there are no specific commission or bonus schemes related solely to sales volume or the achievement of sales targets. This approach may be adopted when companies want to discourage 'quick sales at all costs' attitudes and actions, and encourage sales staff to build up long-term relationships with their customers, the emphasis being on customer service rather than on high-pressure selling.

Basic salary plus commission and/or bonus

While the advantages of basic salary only may be becoming more apparent in some businesses, many companies still believe that the special nature of selling and the type of person they need to attract to their sales force require some form of additional bonus or commission to be paid. This is intended to act as an incentive and as a reward and a means of recognizing achievement, but a policy decision has to be made on what percentage of total earnings should be variable or at risk. The proportion of the reward package that is represented by high-risk pay is sometimes called leverage. This is likely to be high when creative personal selling and highly developed persuasive skills are required to get customers to buy. Leverage will be lower when sales staff are mainly order-takers, when customer service is an important factor, or when sales people spend a considerable proportion of their selling day in non-selling activities. It may be even lower (or non-existent) in high-technology businesses when the sales force is involved in persuasive communication with highly trained engineers or buyers, and sales representatives must possess the technological know-how to talk to these people on equal terms. The main types of schemes are:

- *commission only* plans which provide sales representatives with payments based on a percentage of the sales turnover they generate;
- *basic salary plus commission* plans which provide for a proportion of total earnings to be paid in commission, the rest in the form of a fixed salary;
- *bonus schemes* which provide pay in addition to basic salary which is related to the achievement of defined and, preferably, agreed targets (eg sales volume or contribution to profit).

Choice of approach

The factors affecting a choice between the main methods of payment are broadly as follows:

- basic salary only when the aim is to build and maintain long-term relationships with customers through non-selling activities;

- salary plus commission where a more flexible approach is required and non-selling activities are important;
- salary plus bonus where flexibility in providing rewards for different aspects of the sales task is important and where attention needs to focus on more profitable lines and the various selling and non-selling activities which contribute to effective sales performance.

Other methods of motivation

There are other and sometimes more effective ways of motivating people besides cash, and for sales representatives they include incentives (gifts, vouchers etc, competitions, perks and non-financial rewards generally). The latter are particularly important. Good sales people are natural achievers but they should still be given the scope to use their natural talents, and even people with very high levels of achievement motivation still like their successes to be recognized. Additional training, the opportunity to take on a more challenging and potentially rewarding role, and greater responsibility, either in a managerial capacity or for handling larger accounts, can also act as motivating forces.

46

Employee benefits, pensions and allowances

EMPLOYEE BENEFITS

Definition

Employee benefits are elements of remuneration given in addition to the various forms of cash pay. They also include items that are not strictly remuneration, such as annual holidays.

Objectives

The objectives of the employee benefits policies and practices of an organization are to:

- provide an attractive and competitive total remuneration package which both attracts and retains high-quality employees;
- provide for the personal needs of employees;
- increase the commitment of employees to the organization;
- provide for some people a tax-efficient method of remuneration.

Note that these objectives do not include 'to motivate employees'. This is because the normal benefits provided by a business seldom make a direct and immediate impact on performance. They can, however, create more favourable attitudes towards the business which can improve commitment and organizational performance in the longer term.

Main types of employee benefits

Benefits can be divided into the following categories:

- *Pension schemes*: these are generally regarded as the most important employee benefit.
- *Personal security*: these are benefits which enhance the individual's personal and family security with regard to illness, health, accident or life insurance.
- *Financial assistance*: loans, house purchase schemes, relocation assistance and discounts on company goods or services.
- *Personal needs*: entitlements which recognize the interface between work and domestic needs or responsibilities, eg holidays and other forms of leave, child care, career breaks, retirement counselling, financial counselling and personal counselling in times of crisis, fitness and recreational facilities.
- *Company cars and petrol*: still a much appreciated benefit in spite of the fact that cars are now more heavily taxed.
- *Other benefits:* which improve the standard of living of employees such as subsidized meals, clothing allowances, refund of telephone costs, mobile phones (as a 'perk' rather than a necessity) and credit card facilities.
- *Intangible benefits*: characteristics of the organization which contribute to the quality of working life and make it an attractive and worthwhile place in which to be employed.

Taxation

It should be remembered that most benefits are taxable as 'benefits in kind', the notable exceptions being approved pension schemes, meals where these are generally available to employees, car parking spaces, professional subscriptions and accommodation where this is used solely for performing the duties of the job.

Choice of benefits

It cannot always be assumed that the benefits a business is prepared to provide to its employees are those that are equally attractive to all employees. A 'cafeteria' or flexible benefits or 'cafeteria' system allows employees to exercise choice over a range of options within defined financial limits.

Flexible benefit systems have not yet really been introduced to any great extent in the UK, probably because of the perceived problems of administering the system fairly and the amount of extra effort involved, although some companies are allowing their executives to take a cash payment instead of their company car. However, the use of 'flex' is increasing.

But such a system does enable businesses to:

● discover which benefits are popular and which are not, leading to the concentration of resources on those benefits welcomed by employees;
● develop mechanisms to control benefit costs;
● inform employees of the real costs of benefits which otherwise they take for granted.

Total remuneration

The concept of total remuneration is based on the principle of treating all aspects of pay and benefits provision as a whole. The cost to the business and the value to the individual of each element can be assessed with the object of adjusting the package according to organizational and individual needs. Consideration can also be given to the overall competitiveness of the total package in the market place.

OCCUPATIONAL PENSION SCHEMES

The reasons for having a worthwhile pension scheme are that it:

● demonstrates that the organization is a good employer;
● attracts and retains high-quality people by helping to maintain competitive levels of total remuneration;
● indicates that the organization is concerned about the long-term interests of its employees.

Definition

An occupational pension scheme is an arrangement under which an employer provides pensions for employees when they retire, income for the families of members who die, and deferred benefits to members who leave. A 'group scheme' is the typical scheme which provides for a number of employees.

Operation

Occupational pension schemes are administered by trusts which are supposed to be outside the employer's control. The trustees are responsible for the pension fund from which pension benefits are paid.

The pension fund is fed by contributions from employers and usually (but not always) employees. The size of the fund and its capacity to meet future commitments depend both on the size of contributions and on the income the trustees can generate. They do this by investing fund money with the help of advisers in stocks, shares and other securities, or through an insurance company. In the latter case, insurance companies offer either a *managed fund* – a pool of money managed by the insurance company for a number of clients – or a *segregated fund* which is managed for a single client.

Contributions

In a *contributory scheme* employees as well as employers make contributions to the pension fund. Pensionable earnings are total earnings from which may be excluded such payments as overtime or special bonuses. A sum equal to the State flat rate pension may also be excluded.

The level of contributions varies considerably, although in a typical contributory scheme, employees would be likely to contribute about 5 per cent of their earnings and employers would contribute approximately twice that amount.

Approved scheme

Members of an occupational scheme that has been approved by the Inland Revenue (an *approved scheme*) obtain full tax relief on their contributions. The company also recovers tax on its contributions and the income tax deductible from gains realized on UK investments. This makes a pension fund the most tax-efficient form of saving available in the UK.

Employers can establish unapproved pension schemes which provide benefits in excess of approved schemes but at the expense of the generous tax allowances for the latter type of scheme.

Retiring age and sex discrimination

Traditionally, the retiring age was 65 for men and 60 for women. However, under the

Sex Discrimination Act (1986), it is unlawful for employers to require female employees to retire at an earlier age than male employees. In its judgement on the *Barber v Guardian Royal Exchange* case on 17 May 1990 the European Court ruled that pension was 'pay' under Article 119 of the Treaty of Rome (which provided for equal pay) and that it was unlawful to discriminate between men and women with regard to pension rights. It has since been agreed that pensions would not be considered as pay prior to 17 May 1990.

Benefits statements

Every member of an occupational scheme is entitled to an annual statement setting out his or her prospective benefits.

Types of occupational pension schemes

A defined benefit or *final salary* group pension scheme offers a guaranteed pension, part of which may be surrendered for a tax-free cash sum. In its final pay or salary form, the pension is a fraction of final pensionable earnings for each year of service (typically 1/60th). To achieve the maximum two-thirds pension in a 1/60th scheme would therefore take 40 years' service. Defined benefit schemes provide employers with a predictable level of pension. But for employers, they can be costly and unpredictable because they have to contribute whatever is necessary to buy the promised benefits.

In a defined contribution or *money purchase* scheme employers fix the contributions they want to pay for employees by undertaking to pay a defined percentage of earnings irrespective of the benefits available on retirement. The retirement pension is therefore whatever annual payment can be purchased with the money accumulated in the fund for a member.

A defined contribution scheme offers the employee unpredictable benefits because these depend on the total value of the contributions invested, the investment returns achieved and the rate at which the accumulated fund can be converted into pension on retirement. For the employer, however, it offers certainty of costs.

Stakeholder pensions

In October 2001 all employers with five or more people on their payroll will be obliged to provide access to a stakeholder pension for employees who have no access to a company pension. Stakeholder pensions will be money-purchase schemes and, initially, employers do not have to make a contribution and employees are not required to take them out (although these conditions may be changed). Employers can designate a stakeholder scheme from a provider but in choosing one are required to consult with the employees concerned.

ALLOWANCES AND OTHER PAYMENTS TO EMPLOYEES

The main areas in which allowances and other special payments may be made to employees are:

- *Location allowances* – London and large town allowances may be paid because of housing and other cost-of-living differentials. Allowances are paid as an addition to basic pay although many employers in effect consolidate them by paying the local market rate which takes into account explicit or implicit location allowances and costs.
- *Subsistence allowances* – the value of subsistence allowances for accommodation and meals varies greatly between organizations. Some have set rates depending on location or the grade of employee. Others allow 'reasonable' rates without any set scale but usually, and desirably, with guidelines on acceptable hotel and meal costs.
- *Overtime payments* – most manual workers are eligible for paid overtime as well as many staff employees up to management level. Higher-paid staff may receive time off in lieu if they work longer hours. Typically organizations that make overtime payments give time and a half as an overtime premium from Monday to Saturday, with double time paid on Sundays and statutory holidays. Some firms also pay double time from around noon on Saturday. Work on major statutory holidays such as Christmas Day and Good Friday often attracts higher overtime premiums.
- *Shift payments* are made at rates which usually vary according to the shift arrangement. A premium of, say, one-third of basic pay may be given to people working nights while those on an early or late day shift may receive less, a premium, say, of one-fifth of basic pay.
- *Stand-by and call-out allowances* may be made to those who have to be available to come in to work when required. The allowance may be made as a standard payment added to basic pay. Alternatively, special payments may be made for unforeseen call-outs.

47

Managing reward systems

REWARD BUDGETS AND FORECASTS

Reward budgets and forecasts are concerned with overall payroll costs and the costs of general and individual pay increases.

Payroll budgets

A payroll budget is a statement of the planned allocation and use of human resources required to meet the objectives of the organization. It is usually a major part of the master budget. The budget is based on forecast levels of activity which determine the number of people required. The annual payroll budget is a product of the number of people to be employed and the rates at which they will be paid during the budget year. It will incorporate the cost of benefits (eg pensions contributions) and the employer's National Insurance contributions. The budget will be adjusted to take account of forecasts covering increases or decreases to employee numbers, the likely costs of general and individual pay reviews, changes to the pay structure and increases to the cost of employee benefits.

Managers in charge of budget centres will have their own payroll budget which they have to account for. This budget will incorporate forecasts of pay increases as well as the manager's assessment of the numbers of employees needed in different categories. Managers will be required to ensure that individual pay increases are made within that budget, which may, however, be flexed upwards or downwards if activity levels or the assumptions on which forecast pay increases were based change.

Review budgets

A general review budget simply incorporates the forecast costs of any across-the-board pay increases that may be granted or negotiated during the budget year. Individual performance review budgets may be expressed as the percentage increase to the payroll that can be allowed for performance, skill-based or competence-related increases. The size of the budget will be affected by the following considerations:

- the amount the organization believes it can afford to pay on the basis of budgeted revenue, profit, and payroll costs;
- the organization's policies on pay progression – the size and range of increases;
- any allowances that may need to be made for increasing individual rates of pay to remove anomalies, for example after a job evaluation exercise.

The basic budget would be set for the organization as a whole but, within that figure, departmental budgets could be flexed to reflect different needs and circumstances. Pay modelling techniques which cost alternative pay review proposals on distributions of awards can be used to prepare individual review budgets. Increasingly, organizations are replacing individual review budgets with a total payroll budgeting approach. This means that departmental heads have to fund individual increases from their payroll budget. In effect, they are expected to add value from performance pay or at least ensure that it is self-financing.

EVALUATING THE REWARD SYSTEM

The reward system should be audited regularly to assess its effectiveness, the extent to which it is adding value and its relevance to the present and future needs of the organization. This audit should include an assessment of opinions about the reward system by its key users and those who are affected by it. This leads to a diagnosis of strengths and weaknesses and an assessment of what needs to be done and why.

The operation of the reward system should be monitored continually by the personnel department through such audits and by the use of compa-ratios and attrition analysis as discussed below. In particular it is necessary to analyse data on upgradings, the effectiveness with which performance management processes are functioning and the amount paid out on pay-for-performance schemes and the impact they are making on results.

Internal relativities should also be monitored by carrying out periodic studies of the differentials that exist vertically within departments or between categories of employees. The studies should examine the differentials built into the pay structure and also analyse the differences between the average rates of pay at different levels. If it is revealed that because of changes in roles or the impact of pay reviews differentials no longer properly reflect increases in job values and/or are no longer 'felt fair', then further investigations to establish the reasons for this situation can be conducted and, if necessary, corrective action taken.

External relativities should be monitored by tracking movements in market rates by studying published data and conducting pay surveys as described in Chapter 42.

No reward innovations should take place unless a cost–benefit analysis has forecast that they will add value. The audit and monitoring processes should establish the extent to which the predicted benefits have been obtained and check on the costs against the forecast.

Compa-ratio analysis

A compa-ratio (short for comparative ratio) measures the relationship in a graded pay structure between actual and policy rates of pay as a percentage. The policy value used is the midpoint or reference point in a pay range which represents the 'target rate' for a fully competent individual in any job in the grade. This point is aligned to market rates in accordance with the organization's market stance policy.

Compa-ratios are used to define where an individual is placed in a pay range. The analysis of compa-ratios indicates what action might have to be taken to slow down or accelerate increases if compa-ratios are too high or too low compared with the policy level. This process is sometimes called 'midpoint management'.

Compa-ratios are calculated as follows:

$$\frac{\text{actual rate of pay}}{\text{mid or reference point of range}} \times 100$$

A compa-ratio of 100 per cent means that actual and policy pay are the same. Compa-ratios which are higher or lower than 100 per cent mean that, respectively, pay is above or below the policy target rate. For example, if the target (policy) rate in a range were £20,000 and the average pay of all the individuals in the grade were £18,000, the compa-ratio would be 90 per cent.

Compa-ratios establish differences between policy and practice and the reasons for such differences need to be established.

Analysing attrition

Attrition or slippage takes place when employees enter jobs at lower rates of pay than the previous incumbents. If this happens payroll costs will go down given an even flow of starters and leavers and a consistent approach to the determination of rates of pay. In theory attrition can help to finance pay increases within a range. It has been claimed that fixed incremental systems can be entirely self-financing because of attrition, but the conditions under which this can be attained are so exceptional that it probably never happens.

Attrition can be calculated by the formula: total percentage increase to payroll arising from general or individual pay increases minus total percentage increase in average rates of pay. If it can be proved that attrition is going to take place, the amount involved can be taken into account as a means of at least partly financing individual pay increases. Attrition in a pay system with regular progression through ranges and a fairly even flow of starters and leavers is typically between 2 and 3 per cent but this should not be regarded as a norm.

PAY REVIEWS

Pay reviews can be general or individual. General reviews give 'across-the-board increases' in response to market trends, increases in the cost of living or negotiated pay settlements. Individual reviews decide on any performance, skill-based or competence-related increases in pay for individual employees.

General reviews

General reviews take place when an increase is given to employees in response to general market rate movements, increases in the cost of living or union negotiations. General reviews are often combined with individual reviews but employees are usually informed of the general and individual components of any increase they receive. Alternatively, the general review may be conducted separately to enable better control to be achieved over costs and to focus employees' attention on the performance-related aspect of their remuneration.

Many organizations, however, prefer not to link pay rises explicitly to the cost of living. Their policy is to respond to movements in market rates in order to maintain their competitive position, bearing in mind that increases in market rates are affected by the cost of living. They do not want to be committed to an 'index-linked' approach, even in times of low inflation.

Individual reviews

Individual reviews determine performance-, skill- or competence-related pay increases, or special achievement or sustained good performance bonuses as additions or alternatives to base pay rate increases. They may be based on some form of performance and/or competence rating or the acquisition of additional skills.

Performance-related pay (PRP) reviews may be conducted by reference to performance ratings. Guidelines are provided to managers on the relationships between pay increases and performance rating and, frequently, the position of employees in their pay range (their compa-ratio). A PRP increase matrix may be used to indicate levels of increase, or guidelines may be given on the distribution of increases or the maximum and minimum increases that can be awarded. Line managers should work within a review or payroll budget.

As noted in Chapter 44, many organizations have rejected this mechanistic process. Instead the pay review is held at a separate time from the performance review so as not to prejudice the developmental purpose of that review. The manager makes an overall judgement of the performance of the individual. This overview will take account of the individual's competence and contribution and will be informed by the performance review, but is not linked to it by a formal rating. The overview may simply result in a recommendation that the individual should receive an average, above average or below average increase, in accordance with budget guidelines on the percentage increase or bonus that is applicable to each of these categories. A holistic approach may be adopted, which means taking into account the relationship of the individual's pay to that of his or her peers, and making adjustments if the individual's pay is below what is regarded as equitable. This may involve some form of ranking. If any special market rate adjustments are necessary, these are also included. The result is a decision on what the appropriate and equitable total rate of pay for the individual should be, and the difference between that and the present rate represents the increase. Thus the increase is holistic in that it is expressed as a move to a new level of pay on the basis of a number of criteria, rather than a percentage increase on the present level based on one criterion, ie performance.

Individual reviews usually take place on a fixed date, typically once a year, although fast-moving organizations may prefer more frequent reviews, say twice a year. The review date can be varied to suit the circumstances of the organization.

Some organizations like to hold rolling reviews for individuals based on their birthday or starting/promotion date in order to allow more attention to be given to the individual's review. But this system is more difficult to budget for and control.

CONTROL

Control over the implementation of pay policies generally and payroll costs in particular will be easier if it is based on:

- a clearly defined and understood pay structure;
- specific pay review guidelines and budgets;
- defined procedures for grading jobs and fixing rates of pay;
- clear statements of the degree of authority managers have at each level to decide on rates of pay and increases;
- an HR function which is capable of monitoring the implementation of pay policies and providing the information and guidance managers require and has the authority and resources (including computer software) to do so;
- a systematic process for monitoring the implementation of pay policies and costs against budgets.

REWARD PROCEDURES

Reward management procedures are required to achieve and monitor the implementation of reward management policies. They deal with methods of fixing pay on appointment or promotion and dealing with anomalies. They will also refer to methods of appealing against grading or pay decisions, usually through the organization's normal appeals procedure.

Procedures for grading jobs

The procedures for grading new jobs or re-grading existing ones should lay down that grading or re-grading can only take place after a proper job evaluation study. It is necessary to take action to control grade drift by insisting that this procedure is followed. Pressures to upgrade because of market forces or difficulties in recruitment or retention should be resisted. These problems should be addressed by such methods as market premiums or creating special market groups of jobs.

Fixing rates of pay on appointment

Line managers should have a major say in pay offers and some freedom to negotiate when necessary, but they should be required to take account of relevant pay policy guidelines which should set out the circumstances in which pay offers above the minimum of the range can be made. It is customary to allow a reasonable degree of freedom to make offers up to a certain point, eg the 90 per cent level in an 80 to 120 per cent pay range. Pay policies frequently allow offers to be made up to the midpoint or reference point depending on the extent to which the recruit has the necessary experience, skills and competences. Offers above the midpoint should be exceptional because they would leave relatively little room for expansion. Such offers will sometimes be made because of market pressures, but they need to be very carefully considered because of the inevitably of grade drift unless the individual is promoted fairly soon. If the current rates are too low to attract good candidates, it may be necessary to reconsider the scales or to agree on special market rate premiums. To keep the latter under control, it is advisable to require that they should only be awarded if they are authorized by the personnel department or a more senior manager. Many organizations require that all offers should be vetted and approved by a member of the personnel function and/or a higher authority.

Promotion increases

Promotion increases should be meaningful, say 10 per cent or more. They should not normally take the promoted employee above the midpoint or reference point in the pay range for his or her new job so that there is adequate scope for performance-related increases. One good reason for having reasonably wide differentials is to provide space for promotions.

Dealing with anomalies

Within any pay structure, however carefully monitored and maintained, anomalies will occur and they need to be addressed during a pay review. Correction of anomalies will require higher level increases for those who are under-paid relative to their performance and time in the job, and lower levels of increase for those who are correspondingly over-paid. It is worth noting that over-payment anomalies cannot be corrected in fixed incremental structures, and this is a major disadvantage of such systems. The cost of anomaly correction should not be huge in normal circumstances if at every review managers are encouraged to 'fine tune' their pay recommendations as suggested earlier.

In a severely anomalous situation, which may be found at the implementation stage of a new structure or at a major review, a longer-term correction programme may be necessary either to mitigate the demotivating effects of reducing relative rates of pay or to spread costs over a number of years.

As well as individual anomaly correction there may be a need to correct a historical tendency to over-pay or under-pay whole departments, divisions or functions by applying higher or lower levels of increases over a period of time. This would involve adjustments to pay review budgets and guidelines and, obviously, it would have to be handled with great care.

RESPONSIBILITY FOR REWARD

The trend is to devolve more responsibility for pay decisions to line managers, especially those concerned with individual pay reviews. But there are obvious dangers. These include inconsistency between managers' decisions, favouritism, prejudice (gender or racial) and illogical distributions of rewards. Research has shown that many managers tend not to differentiate between the performance of individual members of their staff. Ratings can be compressed, with most people clustered around the midpoint and very few staff rated as good or poor performers.

Devolving more authority to line managers may in principle be highly desirable but managers must be briefed thoroughly on their responsibilities, the organization's pay policies (including methods of progressing pay), the principles to be followed in conducting review and how they should interpret and apply pay review guidelines. The need to achieve equity and a reasonable degree of consistency across the organization should be emphasized. Managers should be given whatever training, guidance and help they need to ensure that they are capable of exercising their discretionary powers wisely. This training should cover:

● how information on market rates supplied by the personnel department should be interpreted and used;
● how data provided by the personnel department on the levels of pay and pay progression histories of individual members of staff and the distribution of pay by occupation throughout the department should be used as the basis for planning pay;
● methods of assessing performance and contribution levels;
● how to interpret any generic competence profiles to assess individual development needs and agree career pathways;

- how to assess competence requirements for specific roles (as they exist now or as they may develop), and how to counsel employees on the preparation of personal development plans;
- methods of reviewing progress in achieving these plans and in career development, and how to interpret information from these reviews when making pay decisions;
- generally, how to distribute rewards within budgets, fairly, equitably and consistently by reference to assessments of contribution, competence, progress or growth.
- the guidance available from the personnel function on how to manage pay – it should be emphasized that guidance must always be sought if line managers have any doubts as to how they should exercise their discretion.

Full devolution implies that the decisions of managers on pay increases are not reviewed and questioned as long as they keep within their budgets. However, it is usual for senior managers, personnel or pay specialists to monitor pay proposals to spot inconsistencies or what appear to be illogical recommendations, especially when the scheme is initiated or with newly appointed managers. The use of computerized personnel information systems makes it easier for managers to communicate their proposals and for the personnel department to monitor them. If the personnel department is involved, it should aim to provide support and guidance, not to act as a police force. Monitoring can be relaxed as managers prove that they are capable of making good pay decisions.

COMMUNICATING TO EMPLOYEES

Employee reward systems communicate messages to employees about the beliefs of the organization on what is felt to be important when valuing people in their roles. They deliver two messages: this is how we value your contribution; this is what we are paying for. It is therefore important to communicate to employees collectively about the reward policies and practices of the organization and individually about how those policies affect them – now and in the future. Transparency is essential.

What to communicate to employees generally

Employees generally should understand:

- the *reward policies* of the organization in setting pay levels, providing benefits and progressing pay;

- the *pay structure* – grades and pay ranges and how the structure is managed;
- the *benefits structure* – the range of benefits provided, with details of the pension scheme and other major benefits;
- *methods of grading and regrading jobs* – the job evaluation scheme and how it operates;
- *pay progression* – how pay progresses within the pay structure and how pay decisions affecting employees collectively and individually are made;
- *pay-for-performance schemes* – how individual, team and organization-wide schemes work and how employees can benefit from them;
- *pay for skill or competence* – how any skill-based or competence-based schemes work, the aims of the organization in using such schemes, and how employees can benefit from them;
- *performance management* – how performance management processes operate and the parts played by managers and employees;
- *reward developments and initiatives* – details of any changes to the reward system, the reasons for such changes, and how employees will be affected by them – the importance of doing this thoroughly cannot be over-emphasized.

What to communicate to individual employees

Individual employees should know and understand:

- their *job grade* and how it has been determined;
- the basis upon which their *present rate* of pay has been determined;
- the *pay opportunities* available to them – the scope in their grade for pay progression, the basis upon which their pay will be linked to their performance and the acquisition and effective use of skills and competences as their career develops, and what actions and behaviour are expected of them if their pay is to progress;
- *performance management* – how their performance will be reviewed and the part they play in agreeing objectives and formulating personal development and performance improvement plans;
- *the value of the employee benefits they receive* – the level of total remuneration provided for individuals by the organization, including the values of such benefits as pension and sick pay schemes;
- *appeals and grievances* – how they can appeal against grading and pay decisions or take up a grievance on any aspect of their remuneration.

Part XI

Employee relations

EMPLOYEE RELATIONS DEFINED

Employee relations consist of all those areas of human resource management that involve relationships with employees – directly and/or through collective agreements where trade unions are recognized. Employee relations are concerned with generally managing the employment relationship as considered in Chapter 15.

These relationships will be concerned with the agreement of terms and conditions of employment and with issues arising from employment. They will not necessarily be subject to collective agreements or joint regulation. Employee relations, therefore, cover a broader spectrum of the employment relationship than industrial relations, which are usually regarded as being essentially about dealings between managements and trade unions. This wider definition recognizes the move away from collectivism towards individualism in the ways in which employers relate to their employees. The move in this direction has been prompted by a growing insistence on management's prerogative supported by the philosophy of HRM, the requirement to meet competition with slimmer and more efficient organizations, a massive restructuring of industry in the 1980s, the 1980s concept of the market economy and free enterprise and by trade union legislation.

Employee relations practices include formal processes, procedures and channels of communication. It is important to remember, however, that employee relations are mainly conducted on a day-to-day informal basis by line managers and team leaders; without the framework of employment and employee relations policies but acting mainly on their own initiative.

PLAN

This part covers the broad subject of employee relations under the following headings:

● *the framework of employee relations – the conceptual framework to industrial relations. The HRM approach to employee relations developments in industrial relations and the parties involved (Chapter 48);*
● *employee relations processes, including collective bargaining (Chapter 49);*
● *negotiating and bargaining skills (Chapter 50);*
● *processes for employee involvement, participation and communications (Chapter 51).*

48

The framework of employee relations

The purpose of this chapter is to provide a general introduction to the complex subject of employee relations. It starts with a summary of the elements of employee relations and then deals with the following industrial relations concepts:

- the systems theory of industrial relations, which sees the subject as a system of regulations and rules;
- the types of regulations and rules contained in the system;
- the nature of collective bargaining and bargaining power;
- the unitarist and pluralist views about the basis of the relationship between management and trade unions in particular or employees in general;
- the reconciliation of interests;
- individualism and collectivism as approaches to employee relations;
- the voluntarist approach to industrial relations and its decline;
- human resource management (HRM) as a new paradigm for employee relations;
- the role of the employee relations function.

The chapter continues with a summary of developments in industrial relations and a review of the current industrial relations scene, followed by a summary of the 1998 Workplace Employer Relations Survey. The chapter concludes with a description of the various parties to industrial relations and the institutions, agencies and officers involved.

THE ELEMENTS OF EMPLOYEE RELATIONS

The elements of employee relations consist of:

- The formal and informal employment policies and practices of the organization.
- The development, negotiation and application of formal systems, rules and procedures for collective bargaining, handling disputes and regulating employment. These serve to determine the reward for effort and other conditions of employment, to protect the interests of both employees and their employers, and to regulate the ways in which employers treat their employees and how the latter are expected to behave at work.
- Policies and practices for employee involvement and communications.
- The informal as well as the formal processes that take place in the shape of continuous interactions between managers and team leaders or supervisors on the one hand and employee representatives and individuals on the other. These may happen within the framework of formal agreements but are often governed by custom and practice and the climate of relationships that has been built up over the years.
- The philosophies and policies of the major players in the industrial relations scene: the government of the day, management and the trade unions.
- A number of parties each with different roles. These consist of the state, management, employers' organizations, the trade unions, individual managers and supervisors, HR managers, employee representatives or shop stewards and employees.
- The legal framework.
- A number of institutions such as the Advisory, Conciliation and Arbitration Service (ACAS) and the employment tribunals.
- The bargaining structures, recognition and procedural agreements and practices which have evolved to enable the formal system to operate.

This chapter starts by concentrating on the industrial relations aspects of employee relations, which are governed by a system of rules as described below.

INDUSTRIAL RELATIONS AS A SYSTEM OF RULES

Industrial relations can be regarded as a system or web of rules regulating employment and the ways in which people behave at work. The systems theory of industrial relations, as propounded by Dunlop (1958), states that the role of the system is to produce the regulations and procedural rules that govern how much is distributed in the bargaining process and how the parties involved, or the 'actors' in the industrial relations scene, relate to one another. According to Dunlop, the output of the system takes the form of:

> The regulations and policies of the management hierarchy; the laws of any worker hierarchy; the regulations, degrees, decisions, awards or orders of governmental agencies; the rules and decisions of specialized agencies created by the management and worker hierarchies; collective bargaining arrangements and the customs and traditions of the work place.

The system is expressed in many more or less formal or informal guises: in legislation and statutory orders, in trade union regulations, in collective agreements and arbitration awards, in social conventions, in managerial decisions, and in accepted 'custom and practice'. The 'rules' may be defined and coherent, or ill-defined and incoherent. Within a plant the rules may mainly be concerned with doing no more than defining the *status quo* which both parties recognize as the norm from which deviations may be made only by agreement. In this sense, therefore, an industrial relations system is a normative system where a norm can be seen as a rule, a standard, or a pattern for action which is generally accepted or agreed as the basis upon which the parties concerned should operate.

Systems theory, however, does not sufficiently take into account the distribution of power between management and trade unions, nor the impact of the state. Neither does it adequately explain the role of the individual in industrial relations.

TYPES OF REGULATIONS AND RULES

Job regulation aims to provide a framework of minimum rights and rules. Internal regulation is concerned with procedures for dealing with grievances, redundancies or disciplinary problems and rules concerning the operation of the pay system and the rights of shop stewards. External regulation is carried out by means of employment legislation, the rules of trade unions and employers' associations, and the regulative content of procedural or substantive rules and agreements.

Procedural rules are intended to regulate conflict between the parties to collective bargaining, and when their importance is emphasized, a premium is being placed on industrial peace. *Substantive rules* settle the rights and obligations attached to jobs. It is interesting to note that in the UK, the parties to collective agreements have tended to concentrate more on procedural than on substantive rules. In the USA, where there is greater emphasis on fixed-term agreements, the tendency has been to rely more on substantive rules.

COLLECTIVE BARGAINING

The industrial relations system is regulated by the process of collective bargaining, defined by Flanders (1970) as a social process that 'continually turns disagreements into agreements in an orderly fashion'. Collective bargaining aims to establish by negotiation and discussion agreed rules and decisions on matters of mutual concern to employers and unions as well as methods of regulating the conditions governing employment.

It therefore provides a framework, often in the form of a collective agreement, within which the views of management and unions about disputed matters that could lead to industrial disorder can be considered with the aim of eliminating the causes of the disorder. Collective bargaining is a joint regulating process, dealing with the regulation of management in its relationships with work people as well as the regulation of conditions of employment. It has a political as well as an economic basis – both sides are interested in the distribution of power between them as well as the distribution of income.

Collective bargaining can be regarded as an exchange relationship in which wage–work bargains take place between employers and employees through the agency of a trade union. Traditionally, the role of trade unions as bargaining agents has been perceived as being to offset the inequalities of individual bargaining power between employers and employees in the labour market.

Collective bargaining can also be seen as a political relationship in which trade unions, as Chamberlain and Kuhn (1965) noted, share industrial sovereignty or power over those who are governed, the employees. The sovereignty is held jointly by management and union in the collective bargaining process.

Above all, collective bargaining is a power relationship that takes the form of a measure of power sharing between management and trade unions (although recently the balance of power has shifted markedly in the direction of management).

Bargaining power

The extent to which industrial sovereignty is shared by management with its trade unions (if at all) depends upon the relative bargaining powers of the two parties. Bargaining power can be defined as the ability to induce the other side to make a decision that it would otherwise not make. As Fox and Flanders (1969) commented: 'Power is the crucial variable which determines the outcome of collective bargaining.' It has been suggested by Hawkins (1979) that a crucial test of bargaining power is 'whether the cost to one side in accepting a proposal from the other is higher than the cost of not accepting it'. Singh (1989) has pointed out that bargaining power is not static but varies over time. He also notes that:

> Bargaining power is inherent in any situation where differences have to be reconciled. It is, however, not an end in itself and negotiations must not rely solely on bargaining power. One side may have enormous bargaining power, but to use it to the point where the other side feels that it is impossible to deal with such a party is to defeat the purpose of negotiations.

Atkinson (1989) asserts that:

● what creates bargaining power can be appraised in terms of subjective assessments by individuals involved in the bargaining process;
● each side can guess the bargaining preferences and bargaining power of the other side;
● there are normally a number of elements creating bargaining power.

Forms of collective bargaining

Collective bargaining takes two basic forms, as identified by Chamberlain and Kuhn (1965):

● *conjunctive bargaining*, which 'arises from the absolute requirement that some agreement – any agreement – may be reached so that the operations on which both are dependent may continue', and results in a 'working relationship in which each party agrees, explicitly or implicitly, to provide certain requisite services, to recognize certain seats of authority, and to accept certain responsibilities in respect of each other';
● *cooperative bargaining*, in which it is recognized that each party is dependent on the other and can achieve its objectives more effectively if it wins the support of the other.

A similar distinction was made by Walton and McKersie (1965), who referred to *distributive bargaining* as the 'complex system of activities instrumental to the attainment of one party's goals when they are in basic conflict with those of the other party' and to *integrative bargaining* as the 'system of activities which are not in fundamental conflict with those of the other party and which therefore can be integrated to some degree'. Such objectives are said to define 'an area of common concern, a purpose'.

THE UNITARY AND PLURALIST VIEWS

There are two basic views expressed about the basis of the relationship between management and trade unions in particular or employees in general: the unitary and the pluralist perspectives.

The unitary view is typically held by managements who see their function as that of directing and controlling the workforce to achieve economic and growth objectives. To this end, management believes that it is the rule-making authority. Management tends to view the enterprise as a unitary system with one source of authority – itself – and one focus of loyalty – the organization. It extols the virtue of teamwork, where everyone strives jointly to a common objective, everyone pulls their weight to the best of their ability, and everyone accepts their place and function gladly, following the leadership of the appointed manager or supervisor. These are admirable sentiments, but they sometimes lead to what McClelland (1963) referred to as an orgy of 'avuncular pontification' on the part of the leaders of industry. This unitary view, which is essentially autocratic and authoritarian, has sometimes been expressed in agreements as 'management's right to manage'. The philosophy of HRM with its emphasis on commitment and mutuality is based on the unitary perspective.

In contrast, the *pluralist view*, as described by Fox (1966), is that an industrial organization is a plural society, containing many related but separate interests and objectives which must be maintained in some kind of equilibrium. In place of a corporate unity reflected in a single focus of authority and loyalty, management has to accept the existence of rival sources of leadership and attachment. It has to face the fact that in Drucker's (1951) phrase, a business enterprise has a triple personality: it is at once an economic, a political and a social institution. In the first, it produces and distributes incomes. In the second, it embodies a system of government in which managers collectively exercise authority over the managed, but are also themselves involved in an intricate pattern of political relationships. Its third personality is revealed in the plant community, which evolves from below out of face-to-face relations based on shared interests, sentiments, beliefs and values among various groups of employees.

Pluralism conventionally regards the workforce as being represented by 'an opposition that does not seek to govern' (Clegg, 1976). Pluralism, as described by Cave (1994), involves 'a balance of power between two organized interests and a sufficient degree of trust within the relationship (usually) for each side to respect the other's legitimate and, on occasions, separate interests, and for both sides to refrain from pushing their interest separately to the point where it became impossible to keep the show on the road'. It has been noted by Guest (1995) that: 'The tradition of bargaining at plant or even organization level has reinforced a pluralistic concept.'

THE RECONCILIATION OF INTERESTS

The implication of the pluralistic approach to employee relations is that there has to be some process for reconciling different interests. This can be achieved through formal agreements where there are recognized trade unions or staff associations. The absence of these may indicate that management adopts a unitarist philosophy. But it is to be hoped that in these circumstances management's efforts to increase mutuality and gain commitment adopt a stakeholder or partnership approach which at least involves consultation with employees on how the joint interests of the organization and its members can best be satisfied.

The process of reconciling interests has been modelled by Gennard and Judge (1997), as shown in Figure 48.1.

INDIVIDUALISM AND COLLECTIVISM

Purcell (1987) argues that the distinction between pluralist and unitary frames of management has 'provided a powerful impetus to the debate about management style, but the mutually exclusive nature of these categories has limited further development'. Moreover, wide variations can be found within both the unitary and the pluralist approach. He therefore suggests an alternative distinction between 'individualism' – policies focusing on individual employees – and 'collectivism' – the extent to which groups of workers have an independent voice and participate in decision making with managers. He believes that companies can and do operate on both these dimensions of management style.

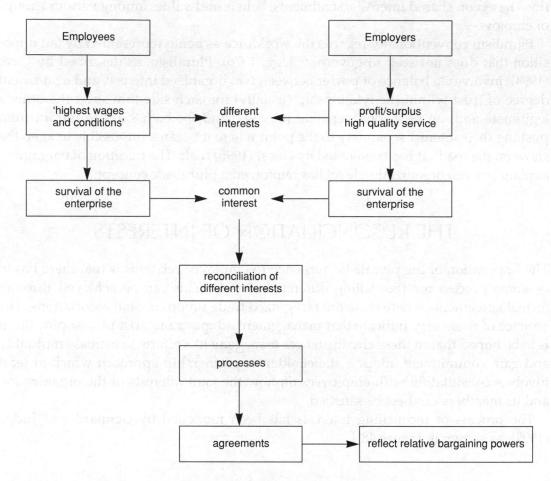

Figure 48.1 Employee relations: reconciliation of interests

VOLUNTARISM AND ITS DECLINE

The essence of the systems theory of industrial relations is that the rules are jointly agreed by the representatives of the parties to employment relations; an arrangement which, it is believed, makes for readier acceptance than if they were imposed by a third party such as the State. This concept of voluntarism was defined by Kahn-Freund (1972) as 'the policy of the law to allow the two sides by agreement and practice to develop their own norms and their own sanctions and to abstain from legal compulsion in their collective relationship'. It was, in essence, voluntarism that came under attack by government legislation from 1974 onwards, including the principle of 'immunities' for industrial action and the closed shop.

THE HRM APPROACH TO EMPLOYEE RELATIONS

The HRM model

The philosophy of HRM has been translated into the following prescriptions, which constitute the HRM model for employee relations:

- a drive for commitment – winning the 'hearts and minds' of employees to get them to identify with the organization, to exert themselves more on its behalf and to remain in it, thus ensuring a return on their training and development;
- an emphasis on mutuality – getting the message across that 'we are all in this together' and that the interests of management and employees coincide;
- the organization of complementary forms of communication, such as team briefing, alongside traditional collective bargaining – ie approaching employees directly as individuals or in groups rather than through their representatives;
- a shift from collective bargaining to individual contracts;
- the use of employee involvement techniques such as quality circles or improvement groups;
- continuous pressure on quality – total quality management;
- increased flexibility in working arrangements, including multi-skilling, to provide for the more effective use of human resources, sometimes accompanied by an agreement to provide secure employment for the 'core' workers;
- emphasis on teamwork;
- harmonization of terms and conditions for all employees.

The key contrasting dimensions of traditional industrial relations and HRM have been presented by Guest (1995) as follows:

Table 48.1 Contrasting dimensions of industrial relations and HRM

Dimension	Industrial Relations	HRM
Psychological contract	Compliance	Commitment
Behaviour references	Norms, custom and practice	Values/mission
Relations	Low trust, pluralist, collective	High trust, unitarist, individual
Organization design	Formal roles, hierarchy, division of labour, managerial control	Flexible roles, flat structure, teamwork/autonomy, self control

Guest notes that this model aims to support the achievement of the three main sources of competitive advantage identified by Porter (1980), namely, innovation, quality and cost leadership. Innovation and quality strategies require employee commitment while cost leadership strategies are believed by many managements to be achievable only without a union. 'The logic of a market-driven HRM strategy is that where high organisational commitment is sought, unions are irrelevant. Where cost advantage is the goal, unions and industrial relations systems appear to carry higher costs.'

An HRM approach is still possible if trade unions are recognized by the organization. In this case, the strategy might be to marginalize or at least side-step them by dealing direct with employees through involvement and communications processes.

THE CONTEXT OF INDUSTRIAL RELATIONS

Industrial relations are conducted within the external context of the national political and economic environment, the international context and the internal context of the organization.

The political context

The political context is formed by the government of the day. Conservative administrations from 1979 to 1997 set out to curb the power of the trade unions through legislation and succeeded to a degree. Labour administrations have not yet made any major changes to existing legislation except in the area of trade union recognition.

The economic context

The economic context over the past 15 years has been one of recessions and recovery from recessions accompanied by marked fluctuations in productivity. Unemployment also fluctuated, being particularly high in 1986 and 1993 (the peak of the two recessions). Employment in manufacturing declined by 3 million or over 40 per cent between 1979 and 1993, while employment in services rose by 1.9 million or 15 per cent in the same period. Inflation has been brought under control.

Perhaps the most significant feature of the changing economic environment from the industrial relations viewpoint has been the drastic cutbacks in manufacturing industry where unions had traditionally been strongly organized.

The European context

Employee relations in the UK are affected by European Union regulations and initiatives. A number of Articles in the original treaty of Rome referred to the promotion of improvements in working conditions and the need to develop dialogue between the two sides of industry. It seems likely that the conduct of employee relations in Britain will be increasingly affected by EU directives, such as those concerning works councils and working hours.

The organizational context

The need to 'take cost out of the business' has meant that employers have focused on the cost of labour – usually the highest and most easily reduced cost. Hence 'the lean organization' movement and large-scale redundancies, especially in manufacturing. There has been pressure for greater flexibility and increased management control of operations, which has had a direct impact on employee relations policies and union agreements.

The widespread introduction of new technology and information technology has aimed to increase productivity by achieving higher levels of efficiency and reducing labour costs. Organizations are relying more on a core of key full-time employees, leaving the peripheral work to be undertaken by subcontractors and the increasing numbers of part-timers – women *and* men. This has reduced the number of employees who wish to join unions or remain trade union members.

DEVELOPMENTS IN INDUSTRIAL RELATIONS

Developments in the practice of industrial relations since the 1950s can be divided into the following phases:

1. The traditional system existing prior to the 1970s.
2. The Donovan analysis of 1968.
3. The interventionist and employment protection measures of the 1970s.
4. The 1980s programme for curbing what were perceived by the Conservative Government to be the excesses of rampant trade unionism.

The traditional system – to 1971

Relations prior to 1971 and indeed for most of the 1970s could be described as a system of collective representation designed to contain conflict. Voluntary collective bargaining between employees and employers' associations was the central feature of the system, and this process of joint regulation was largely concerned with pay and basic conditions of employment, especially hours of work in industry, and legal abstention on the part of the state and the judiciary. During this period and, in fact, for most of the twentieth century, the British system of industrial relations was characterized by a tradition of voluntarism.

The Donovan analysis

The high incidence of disputes and strikes, the perceived power of the trade unions and some well-publicized examples of shop steward militancy (although the majority were quite amenable) contributed to the pressure for the reform of industrial relations which led to the setting up of the Donovan Commission. This concluded in 1968 that the formal system of industry-wide bargaining was breaking down. Its key findings were that at plant level, bargaining was highly fragmented and ill-organized, based on informality and custom and practice. The Commission's prescription was for a continuation of voluntarism, reinforced by organized collective bargaining arrangements locally, thus relieving trade unions and employers' associations of the 'policing role', which they so often failed to carry out. This solution involved the creation of new, orderly and systematic frameworks for collective bargaining at plant level by means of formal negotiation and procedural agreements.

Since Donovan, comprehensive policies, structures and procedures to deal with pay and conditions, shop steward facilities, discipline, health and safety, etc have been developed at plant level to a substantial extent. The support provided by Donovan to the voluntary system of industrial relations was, however, underpinned by a powerful minority note of reservation penned by Andrew Shonfield in the 1968 report of the Royal Commission. He advocated a more interventionist approach, which began to feature in government policies in the 1970s.

Interventionism in the 1970s

The received wisdom in the 1960s, as reflected in the majority Donovan report, was that industrial relations could not be controlled by legislation. But the Industrial Relations Act introduced by the Conservative Government in 1971 ignored this belief and drew heavily on Shonfield's minority report. It introduced a strongly interventionist legal framework to replace the voluntary regulation of industrial relations systems. Trade unions lost their general immunity from legal action and had to register under the Act if they wanted any rights at all. Collective agreements were to become legally binding contracts and a number of 'unfair industrial practices' were proscribed. Individual workers were given the right to belong or not belong to a trade union but no attempt was made to outlaw the closed shop. But the Act failed to make any impact, being ignored or side-stepped by both trade unions and employers, although it did introduce the important general right of employees 'not to be unfairly dismissed'.

The Labour Government of 1974 promptly repealed the 1971 Industrial Relations Act and entered into a 'social contract' with the trade unions which incorporated an agreement that the Trades Union Congress (TUC) would support the introduction of a number of positive union rights. These included a statutory recognition procedure and in effect meant that the unions expressed their commitment to legal enforcement as a means of restricting management's prerogatives.

Statutory rights were also provided for minimum notice periods, statements of terms and conditions, redundancy payments and unfair dismissal.

The 1980s – curbing the trade unions

The strike-ridden 'winter of discontent' in 1978 and the return of a Conservative Government in 1979 paved the way for the ensuing step-by-step legislation which continued throughout the 1980s and into the early 1990s.

The ethos of the Conservative Governments in the 1980s was summed up by Phelps Brown (1990) as follows:

> People are no longer seen as dependent on society and bound by reciprocal relationship to it; indeed the very notion of society is rejected. Individuals are expected to shift for themselves and those who get into difficulties are thought to have only themselves to blame. Self-reliance, acquisitive individualism, the curtailment of public expenditure, the play of market forces instead of the restraints and directives of public policy, the prerogatives of management instead of the power of the unions, centralisation of power instead of pluralism.

The legislation on trade unions followed this ethos and was guided by an ideological analysis expressed in the 1981 Green Paper on *Trade Union Immunities* as follows: 'Industrial relations cannot operate fairly and efficiently or to the benefit of the nation as a whole if either employers or employees collectively are given predominant power – that is, the capacity effectively to dictate the behaviour of others.'

The government described industrial relations as 'the fundamental cause of weakness in the British economy', with strikes and restrictive practices inhibiting the country's ability to compete in international markets. The balance of bargaining power was perceived to have moved decisively in favour of trade unions which were described as 'irresponsible, undemocratic and intimidatory', while the closed shop was described as being destructive of the rights of the individual worker.

Developments since 1990

Kessler and Bayliss (1992) commented that 'the needs of employers have increasingly been towards enterprise orientated rather than occupationally orientated trade unions'. They also noted that: 'It is clear that the significance of industrial relations in many firms has diminished. It is part of a management controlled operation – a branch of human resource management. It is no longer a high profile problem-ridden part of personnel management as it so often was in the 1970s.'

Guest (1995) noted that the industrial relations system may continue as a largely symbolic 'empty shell', insufficiently important for management to confront and eliminate, but retaining the outward appearance of health to the casual observer: 'Management sets the agenda, which is market-driven, while industrial relations issues are relatively low on the list of concerns.'

Cave's (1994) examination of 'whatever happened to industrial relations?' produced the following key points:

● In the early and mid-1980s the structure of the traditional industrial relations system still held. By 1990 it did not: 'It is now wrong to depict the UK scene as one in which traditional, union-based industrial relations is the norm: such a system covers at most 40 per cent of the economy.'
● 'The break with the voluntarist or "abstentionist" tradition is absolute – and almost certainly irreversible. The conduct of industrial relations is now tightly regulated by legislative requirements.'
● Employers have become more free to decide the basis 'on which they are to conduct their employee relations – whether with or without unions. They can largely inoculate themselves from any agreements, rules and procedures which have been drawn up outside their gates.'
● Employers have gradually adjusted their behaviour in order to take advantage of the leverage that the new legislative framework gives them. The use of injunctions, for example, has become part of the tactical armoury of employers to influence the course of disputes (hopefully to pre-empt them altogether), rather than to engage in acts of retribution against unions.
● Trade unions now have to operate within a regulatory environment that is arguably tighter than any other group in society.
● Trade unions have no legal scope to act on issues that fall outside the immediate 'bread and butter' concerns of the members' workplace.

Findings of the 1998 Workplace Employee Relations Survey (WERS)

WERS 1998 was a large-scale survey covering 3,000 workplaces. It was sponsored by the Department of Trade and Industry, ACAS, the Economic and Social Research Council and the Policy Studies Institute. Its key findings were:

- In 47 per cent of workplaces there are no union members at all – a substantial change from 36 per cent of workplaces in 1990.
- All employees are union members in 2 per cent of workplaces – down from 7 per cent in 1990.
- Nearly two-thirds of employees are union members in the 29 per cent of workplaces where management is in favour of union membership.
- There has been an 8 per cent decline since 1990 in the number of union recognition agreements (from 53 per cent to 45 per cent).
- Over half of all workplaces have no independent worker representatives.
- 70 per cent of workplace managers agreed with the statement that 'we do not introduce any changes here without first discussing it with employees' – but employees are sceptical about this claim; 40 per cent judged managers as being poor or very poor in this respect.
- The level of overt industrial conflict was low – industrial action was reported in 2 per cent of the workplaces and strikes in only 1 per cent.
- A majority of managers, workers' representatives and employees rated relations as being good or very good, though both worker representatives and employees were more circumspect – 90 per cent of managers thought relations were good or very good compared with 58 per cent of worker representatives and 54 per cent of employees.
- 'Numerical flexibility' (adjusting the size of workforces in line with requirements and demand) has increased greatly over the past five years – more use is being made of independent contractors.
- New practices comprising team working, team briefings and performance appraisals were each reported in more than half the workplaces.
- Two-thirds of workplaces are covered by formal written equal opportunity policies.
- 7 per cent of employees were very satisfied with their work, 47 per cent were satisfied, 27 per cent were neither satisfied nor dissatisfied and 19 per cent were dissatisfied.
- 71 per cent of employees were satisfied or very satisfied with three aspects of their work – job influence, sense of achievement and respect from their managers.

- One-third of employees were content with their pay but 41 per cent were dissatisfied.

Overall, the findings of the survey indicate that unionism in the workplace continues to decline, relationships in workplaces are reasonably good and job satisfaction is quite high, except with regard to pay.

The conclusion reached by Millward *et al* (2000) from their analysis of the survey is that it confirms that there has been a transformation in the structure and conduct of British industrial relations in recent years. Individual pay determination is replacing collective bargaining even in those workplaces that recognize unions or have partnership agreements. All forms of communication through employee representatives, including consultative committees, are in decline. They have been replaced with direct contacts between managers and employees and problem-solving or briefing groups. Millward *et al* come to the pessimistic conclusion that 'the prospect is for a further disintegration of what remains of joint regulation and employee voice'.

THE PARTIES TO INDUSTRIAL RELATIONS

The parties to industrial relations are:

- the trade unions;
- shop stewards or employee representatives;
- the Trades Union Congress (the TUC);
- management;
- employer's organizations;
- the Confederation of British Industry;
- various institutions, agencies and officers.

The role of each of these parties is summarized below

The trade unions

Traditionally the fundamental purpose of trade unions is to promote and protect the interests of their members. They are there to redress the balance of power between employers and employees. The basis of the employment relationship is the contract of employment. But this is not a contract between equals. Employers are almost always in a stronger position to dictate the terms of the contract than individual employees. Trade unions, as indicated by Freeman and Medoff (1984), provide workers with a 'collective voice' to make their wishes known to management and thus bring actual and desired conditions closer together. This applies not only to terms of employment such as pay, working hours and holidays, but also to the way in which individuals are treated in such aspects of employment as the redress of grievances, discipline and redundancy. Trade unions also exist to let management know that there will be, from time to time, an alternative view on key issues affecting employees. More broadly, unions may see their role as that of participating with management on decision making on matters affecting their members' interests.

Within this overall role, trade unions have had two specific roles, namely to secure, through collective bargaining, improved terms and conditions for their members, and to provide protection, support and advice to their members as individual employees.

An additional role, that of providing legal, financial and other services to their members, has come into prominence more recently.

Trade union structure

Trade unions are run by full-time central and, usually, district officials. There may be local committees of members. National officials may conduct industry-wide or major employer pay negotiations while local officials may not be involved in plant negotiations unless there is a 'failure to agree' and the second stage of a negotiating procedure is invoked. Major employers who want to introduce significant changes in agreements or working arrangements may deal direct with national officials.

The trade union movement is now dominated by the large general unions and the recently merged craft and public service unions.

Decline of the trade unions

The decline of the trade unions in the 1980s and 1990s is illustrated by the following figures:

- Total trade union membership fell from 13 million in 1979 to 8.5 million in 1992.
- The total membership as a proportion of the civilian workforce in employment (union density) fell from 53 per cent in 1979 to 37 per cent in 1990.
- The proportion of the workforce covered by collective agreements fell from 50 per cent in 1983 to 35 per cent in 1992.

The problem, as defined by Basset and Cave (1993), is that there has been 'quite simply a collapse in demand for the core product that unions have offered to their twin markets (employees and employers) – collectivism enshrined most obviously in collective bargaining'.

The reasons for this decline are not primarily disenchantment with the trade unions, or the impact of trade union legislation, or large-scale de-recognitions. The real causes are structural and economic, namely:

● a shift in the economy away from large-scale manufacturing industries (traditionally heavily unionized) to the service industries (traditionally non-unionized);
● the trend to decentralize organizations;
● a decline in the number of workplaces employing large numbers of people;
● growing numbers of women, white-collar workers, and part-time workers;
● the impact of unemployment.

The actions taken by the unions to counteract this trend have included mergers to increase their perceived power and enable them to operate more cost-effectively, recruitment drives in non-unionized sectors (not very successfully), and what used to be known as 'enterprise trade unionism'. The latter approach emphasizes the valuable role that unions can play as partners in the workplace, helping to manage change and improving productivity. This has worked in some instances, but most employers have remained unconvinced that the unions can play such a positive role.

Shop stewards

Shop stewards or employee representatives may initially be responsible for plant negotiations, probably with the advice of full-time officials. They will certainly be involved in settling disputes and resolving collective grievances and in representing individual employees with grievances or over disciplinary matters. They may be members of joint consultative committees, which could be wholly or partly composed of trade union representatives.

At one time, shop stewards were the ogres of the industrial relations scene. Undoubtedly there were cases of militant shop stewards, but where there are recognized trade unions, managements have generally recognized the value of shop stewards as points of contact and channels of communication.

The Trades Union Congress (TUC)

The TUC acts as the collective voice of the unions. Its roles are to:

- represent the British trade union movement in the UK and internationally;
- conduct research and develop policies on trade union, industrial, economic and social matters and to campaign actively for them;
- regulate relationships between unions;
- help unions in dispute;
- provide various services (eg research) to affiliated unions.

But the TUC has effectively been marginalized by successive Conservative governments and is but a shadow of its former self, especially since its interventionary role concerning union disputes over membership (the Bridlington rules) has now effectively been abolished by legislation.

International union organizations

The two main international union organizations are the European Trade Union Confederation and the International Trade Union Confederation. At present neither of these makes much impact on the UK, but this could change.

Staff associations

Staff associations may sometimes have negotiating and/or representational rights but they seldom have anything like the real power possessed by a well-organized and supported trade union. They are often suspected by employees as being no more than management's poodle. Managements have sometimes encouraged the development of staff associations as an alternative to trade unions but this strategy has not always worked. In fact, in some organizations the existence of an unsatisfactory staff association has provided an opportunity for a trade union to gain membership and recognition. Staff associations have their uses as channels of communication, and representatives can play a role in consultative processes and in representing colleagues who want to take up grievances or who are being subjected to disciplinary proceedings.

The role of management

The balance of power has undoubtedly shifted to managements who now have more choice over how they conduct relationships with their employees. But the evidence is that there has been no concerted drive by managements to de-recognize unions. As Kessler and Bayliss (1992) point out: 'If managers in large establishments and companies wanted to make changes they looked at ways of doing so within the existing arrangements and if they could produce the goods they used them. Because managers found that the unions did not stand in their way they saw no reason for getting rid of them.' They argued that management's industrial relations objectives are now generally to:

- control the work process;
- secure cost-effectiveness;
- reassert managerial authority;
- move towards a more unitary and individualistic approach.

As Storey (1992a) found in most of the cases he studied, there was a tendency for managements to adopt HRM approaches to employee relations while still coexisting with the unions. But they gave increasing weight to systems of employee involvement, in particular communication, which bypass trade unions.

Employers' organizations

Traditionally, employers' organizations have bargained collectively for their members with trade unions and have in general aimed to protect the interests of those members in their dealings with unions. Multi-employers or industry-wide bargaining, it was believed, allowed companies to compete in product markets without undercutting their competitors' employment costs and prevented the trade unions 'picking off' individual employers in a dispute.

The trend towards decentralizing bargaining to plant level has reduced the extent to which employers' organizations fulfil this traditional role, although some industries such as building and electrical contracting with large numbers of small companies in competitive markets have retained their central bargaining function, setting a floor of terms and conditions for the industry.

The Confederation of British Industry (CBI)

The CBI is a management organization which is only indirectly concerned with industrial relations. It provides a means for its members to influence economic policy and it provides advice and services to them, supported by research.

Institutions, agencies and officers

There are a number of bodies and people with a role in employee relations, as described below.

The Advisory Conciliation and Arbitration Service (ACAS)

ACAS was created by the government but functions independently. It has three main statutory duties:

- to resolve disputes;
- to provide conciliatory services for individuals in, for example, unfair dismissal cases;
- to give advice, help and information on industrial relations and employment issues.

ACAS helps to resolve disputes in three ways: collective conciliation, arbitration and mediation.

During the 1980s and early 1990s the use of ACAS's collective conciliation and arbitration services declined considerably. But the individual conciliation case load has been very heavy and the ACAS advisory work has flourished. These are aimed at encouraging non-adversarial approaches to preventing and resolving problems at work by facilitating joint working groups of employers, employees and their representatives.

The Central Arbitration Committee (CAC)

The CAC is an independent arbitration body that deals with disputes. It arbitrates at the request of one party but with the agreement of the other. It does not handle many arbitrations but it deals more frequently with claims by trade unions for disclosure of information for collective bargaining purposes.

Employment tribunals

Employment tribunals are independent judicial bodies that deal with disputes on employment matters such as unfair dismissal, equal pay, sex and race discrimination and employment protection provisions. They have a legally qualified chair and two other members, one an employer, the other a trade unionist.

The Employment Appeal Tribunal (EAT)

The EAT hears appeals from the decisions of industrial tribunals on questions of law only.

ROLE OF THE HR FUNCTION IN EMPLOYEE RELATIONS

The HR function provides guidance and training and will develop and help to introduce and maintain formal processes; but it does not do line managers' jobs for them. However, in their role as industrial relations specialists, HR practitioners may deal directly with trade unions and their representatives. They are also likely to have a measure of responsibility for maintaining participation and involvement processes and for managing employee communications. They can and should play a major part in developing employee relations strategies and policies that aim to:

- achieve satisfactory employment relationships, taking particular account of the importance of psychological contracts;
- build stable and cooperative relationships with employees which recognize that they are stakeholders in the organization and minimize conflict;
- achieve commitment through employee involvement and communications processes;
- develop mutuality – a common interest in achieving the organization's goals through the development of organizational cultures based on shared values between management and employees;
- clarify industrial relations processes with trade unions and build harmonious relationships with them on a partnership basis.

In these capacities HR practitioners can make a major contribution to the creation and maintenance of a good employee relations climate.

49

Employee relations processes

Employee relations processes consist of the approaches and methods adopted by employers to deal with employees either collectively through their trade unions or individually. They will be based on the organization's articulated or implied employee relations policies and strategies as examined in the first two sections of this chapter. The way in which they are developed and how they function will be influenced by, and will influence, the employee relations climate, the concept of which is examined in the third section of the chapter.

Industrial relations processes, ie those aspects of employee relations that are concerned with the dealings between employers and trade unions, consist of:

- approaches to recognizing or de-recognizing trade unions;
- formal methods of collective bargaining;
- partnership as an approach to employee relations;
- the informal day-to-day contacts on employment issues that take place in the workplace between management and trade union representatives or officials;
- features of the industrial relations scene such as union membership in the workplace, the check-off and strikes.

These processes are considered later in this chapter. Negotiating techniques and skills as an aspect of collective bargaining are dealt with separately in the next chapter. In addition there are the employee relations processes of involvement, participation and communication which are discussed in Chapter 51.

The outcomes of these processes are various forms of procedural and substantive agreements and employment procedures, including harmonization of terms and conditions, and the approaches used by organizations to manage with and without trade unions. These are described in the last three sections of this chapter.

EMPLOYEE RELATIONS POLICIES

Approaches to employee relations

Four approaches to employee relations policies have been identified by Industrial Relations Services (1994):

- *Adversarial:* the organization decides what it wants to do, and employees are expected to fit in. Employees only exercise power by refusing to cooperate.
- *Traditional:* a good day-to-day working relationship but management proposes and the workforce reacts through its elected representatives.
- *Partnership:* the organization involves employees in the drawing up and execution of organization policies, but retains the right to manage.
- *Power sharing:* employees are involved in both day-to-day and strategic decision making.

Adversarial approaches are much less common than in the 1960s and 1970s. The traditional approach is still the most typical but more interest is being expressed in partnership, as discussed later in this chapter. Power sharing is rare.

Nature and purpose of employee relations policies

Against the background of a preference for one of the four approaches listed above, employee relations policies express the philosophy of the organization on what sort of relationships between management and employees and their unions are wanted, and how they should be handled. A partnership policy will aim to develop and maintain a positive, productive, cooperative and trusting climate of employee relations.

When they are articulated, policies provide guidelines for action on employee relations issues and can help to ensure that these issues are dealt with consistently. They provide the basis for defining management's intentions (its employee relations strategy) on key matters such as union recognition and collective bargaining.

Policy areas

The areas covered by employee relations policies are:

- *trade union recognition* – whether trade unions should be recognized or de-recognized, which union or unions the organization would prefer to deal with, and whether or not it is desirable to recognize only one union for collective bargaining and/or employee representational purposes;
- *collective bargaining* – the extent to which it should be centralized or decentralized and the scope of areas to be covered by collective bargaining;
- *employee relations procedures* – the nature and scope of procedures for redundancy, grievance handling and discipline;
- *participation and involvement* – the extent to which the organization is prepared to give employees a voice on matters that concern them;
- *partnership* – the extent to which a partnership approach is thought to be desirable;
- *the employment relationship* – the extent to which terms and conditions of employment should be governed by collective agreements or based on individual contracts of employment (ie collectivism versus individualism);
- *harmonization* of terms and conditions of employment for staff and manual workers;
- *working arrangements* – the degree to which management has the prerogative to determine working arrangements without reference to trade unions or employees (this includes job-based or functional flexibility).

When formulating policies in these areas, organizations may be consciously or unconsciously deciding on the extent to which they want to adopt the HRM approach to employee relations. This emphasizes commitment, mutuality and forms of involvement and participation that mean that management approaches and communicates with employees directly rather than through their representatives.

Policy choices

There is, of course, no such thing as a model employee relations policy. Every organization develops its own policies. In a mature business these will be in accordance with established custom and practice, its core values and management style and the actual or perceived balance of power between management and unions. In younger organizations, or those being established on a green field site, the policies will depend on the assumptions and beliefs of management and, where relevant, the existing philosophy and policies of the parent organization. In both these cases policies will be affected by the type of people employed by the organization, its business strategies, technology, the industry or sector in which it operates, and its structure (for example, the extent to which it is centralized or decentralized).

The following four policy options for organizations on industrial relations and HRM have been described by Guest (1995):

- *The new realism – a high emphasis on HRM and industrial relations.* The aim is to integrate HRM and industrial relations. This is the policy of such organizations as Rover, Nissan and Toshiba. A review of new collaborative arrangements in the shape of single-table bargaining (IRS, 1993) found that they were almost always the result of employer initiatives, but that both employers and unions seem satisfied with them. They have facilitated greater flexibility, more multi-skilling, the removal of demarcations and improvements in quality. They can also extend consultation processes and accelerate moves towards single status.
- *Traditional collectivism – priority to industrial relations without HRM.* This involves retaining the traditional pluralist industrial relations arrangements within an eventually unchanged industrial relations system. Management may take the view in these circumstances that it is easier to continue to operate with a union, since it provides a useful, well-established channel for communication and for the handling of grievance, discipline and safety issues.
- *Individualized HRM – high priority to HRM with no industrial relations.* According to Guest, this approach is not very common, excepting North American-owned firms. It is, he believes, 'essentially piecemeal and opportunistic'.
- *The black hole – no industrial relations.* This option is becoming more prevalent in organizations in which HRM is not a policy priority for managements but where they do not see that there is a compelling reason to operate within a traditional industrial relations system. When such organizations are facing a decision on whether or not to recognize a union, they are increasingly deciding not to do so. And, as shown by Millward (1994), non-union firms are not replacing the unions with an HRM strategy. Marginson *et al* (1993) similarly found no support for a non-union HRM strategy.

Policy formulation

Employee relations policies usually evolve in the light of the circumstances of the firm, traditional practices, management's values and style and the power of trade unions to exert influence. They will change as new situations emerge and these may include competitive pressure, new management, a takeover, different views amongst employees about the value of trade unions, or new trade union policies.

Sometimes these changes will be deliberate. Management may decide that it no longer has any use for trade unions and will therefore de-recognize them. On other occasions the changes will simply emerge from the situation in which management finds itself.

The evolutionary and emergent nature of employee relations policies is the most typical case. But there is much to be said for managements occasionally to sit back and think through their policies in order to establish the extent to which they are still appropriate. This review should be based on an analysis of current policies and their relevance to the changing environment of the organization. The analysis could be extended to discussions with union representatives within the firm and local or even national officials to obtain their views. Employees could also be consulted so that their views could be obtained and acted upon, thus making it more likely that they will accept and be committed to policy changes. If there is a staff association, its role as a representative body should be reconsidered. Alternatively, the case for setting up a staff association should be reviewed. The outcome of attitude surveys designed to elicit the opinions of employees on matters of general concern to them can provide additional information on which to base policy decisions.

The result of such a review might, for example, be a decision not to make a frontal assault on the union, but simply to diminish its power by restricting the scope of collective bargaining and bypassing it and its shop stewards through more direct approaches to individual employees. As recent surveys have shown, this, rather than outright de-recognition, has been the typical policy of unionized firms. And it is probable in most of these cases that the policy evolved over time, rather than being formulated after a systematic review.

Alternatively, processes of consultation with trade unions and employees may lead to the development of a more positive policy of partnership with the trade union which recognizes the mutual advantages of working together.

Expressing policy

Most organizations seem reluctant to commit their employee relations policies to writing. And this is understandable in the light of their fluid nature and, in some cases, the reluctance of managements to admit publicly that they are anti-union.

Policies that are deeply embedded as part of the managerial philosophy and values of the organization do not need to be formalized. They will be fully understood by management and will therefore be acted upon consistently, especially when they are in effect broad expressions of the views of management rather than specific action guidelines.

The argument for having written policies is that everyone – line managers, team leaders and employees generally – will be clear about where they stand and how they are expected to act. Firms may also want to publish their employee relations policies to support a 'mutual commitment' strategy. But this presupposes the involvement of employees in formulating the policies.

EMPLOYEE RELATIONS STRATEGIES

Nature and purpose

Employee relations strategies set out how objectives such as those mentioned above are to be achieved. They define the intentions of the organization about what needs to be done and what needs to be changed in the ways in which the organization manages its relationships with employees and their trade unions. Like all other aspects of personnel or HR strategy, employee relations strategies will flow from the business strategy but will also aim to support it. For example, if the business strategy is to concentrate on achieving competitive edge through innovation and the delivery of quality to its customers, the employee relations strategy may emphasize processes of involvement and participation, including the implementation of programmes for continuous improvement and total quality management. If, however, the strategy for competitive advantage, or even survival, is cost reduction, the employee relations strategy may concentrate on how this can be achieved by maximizing cooperation with the unions and employees and by minimizing detrimental effects on those employees and disruption to the organization.

Employee relations strategies should be distinguished from employee relations policies. Strategies are dynamic. They provide a sense of direction, and give an answer to the question 'how are we going to get from here to there?' Employee relations policies are more about the here and now. They express 'the way things are done around here' as far as dealing with unions and employees is concerned. Of course they will evolve but this may not be a result of a strategic choice. It is when a deliberate decision is made to change policies that a strategy for achieving this change has to be formulated. Thus if the policy is to increase commitment, the strategy could consider how this might be achieved by involvement and participation processes.

Strategic directions

The intentions expressed by employee relations strategies may direct the organization towards any of the following:

● changing forms of recognition, including single union recognition, or de-recognition;

- changes in the form and content of procedural agreements;
- new bargaining structures, including decentralization or single-table bargaining;
- the achievement of increased levels of commitment through involvement or participation;
- deliberately bypassing trade union representatives to communicate directly with employees;
- increasing the extent to which management controls operations in such areas as flexibility;
- generally improving the employee relations climate in order to produce more harmonious and cooperative relationships;
- developing a 'partnership' with trade unions, recognizing that employees are stakeholders and that it is to the advantage of both parties to work together (this could be described as a unitarist strategy aiming at increasing mutual commitment).

Formulating strategies

Like other business and HR strategies, those concerned with employee relations can, in Mintzberg's (1987) words, 'emerge in response to an evolving situation'. But it is still useful to spend time deliberately formulating strategies and the aim should be to create a shared agenda which will communicate a common perspective on what needs to be done. This can be expressed in writing but it can also be clarified through involvement and communication processes.

EMPLOYEE RELATIONS CLIMATE

The employee relations climate of an organization represents the perceptions of management, employees and their representatives about the ways in which employee relations are conducted and how the various parties (managers, employees and trade unions) behave when dealing with one another. An employee relations climate can be good, bad or indifferent according to perceptions about the extent to which:

- management and employees trust one another;
- management treats employees fairly and with consideration;
- management is open about its actions and intentions – employee relations policies and procedures are transparent;
- harmonious relationships are generally maintained on a day-to-day basis, which results in willing cooperation rather than grudging submission;

- conflict, when it does arise, is resolved without resort to industrial action and resolution is achieved by integrative processes which result in a 'win–win' solution;
- employees are generally committed to the interests of the organization and, equally, management treats them as stakeholders whose interests should be protected as far as possible.

Improving the climate

Improvements to the climate can be attained by developing fair employee relations policies and procedures and implementing them consistently. Line managers and team leaders who are largely responsible for the day-to-day conduct of employee relations need to be educated and trained on the approaches they should adopt. Transparency should be achieved by communicating policies to employees, and commitment increased by involvement and participation processes. Problems that need to be resolved can be identified by simply talking to employees, their representatives and their trade union officials. Importantly, as discussed below, the organization can address its obligations to the employees as stakeholders and take steps to build trust.

An ethical approach

Businesses aim to achieve prosperity, growth and survival. Ideally, success should benefit all the stakeholders in the organization – owners, management, employees, customers and suppliers. But the single-minded pursuit of business objectives can act to the detriment of employees' well-being and security. There may be a tension between accomplishing business purposes and the social and ethical obligations of an organization to its employees. But the chances of attaining a good climate of employee relations are slight if no attempt is made to recognize and act on an organization's duties to its members.

An ethical approach will be based on high-commitment and high-involvement policies. The commitment will be mutual and the arrangements for involvement will be genuine, ie management will be prepared not only to listen but to act on the views expressed by employees or at least, if it cannot take action, the reasons why will be explained. It will also be transparent and, although the concept of a 'job for life' may no longer be valid in many organizations, at least an attempt will be made to maintain 'full employment' policies.

Building trust

The Institute of Personnel and Development's (IPD) statement *People Make the Difference* (1994) makes the point that much has been done in recent years to introduce a sense of reality into employee relations. But, according to the IPD, 'Managers should not kid themselves that acquiescence is the same thing as enthusiastic involvement. The pace of life and changing work patterns in the future will put a strain on the best of relationships between employees and managers.'

The IPD suggests that employee relations policies aimed at building trust should be based on the principles that employees cannot just be treated as a factor of production and that organizations must translate their values concerning employee relations into specific and practical action. In too many organizations, inconsistency between what is said and what is done undermines trust, generates employee cynicism and provides evidence of contradictions in management thinking.

UNION RECOGNITION AND DE-RECOGNITION

Recognition

An employer fully recognizes a union for the purposes of collective bargaining when pay and conditions of employment are jointly agreed between management and trade unions. Partial recognition takes place when employers restrict trade unions to representing their members on issues arising from employment. An independent trade union can apply to the CAC for recognition, which will agree where either a majority of the workers already belong to the union, or when the union wins majority support for recognition by at least 40 per cent of those entitled to vote in a secret ballot.

De-recognition

De-recognition is far more widely spread than is generally assumed, as a study by Gall (1993) showed. Once largely restricted to national newspapers, ports and shipping, it is slowly spreading to other industrial sectors. The 1998 Workplace Employee Relations Survey (WERS) established that there had been an 8 per cent decline since 1999 in union recognition agreements.

Single union recognition

The existence of a number of unions within one organization was frequently criticized in the 1980s because of the supposed increase in the complexity of bargaining arrangements and the danger of inter-union demarcation disputes (who does what). The answer to this problem was thought to be single union representation through single union deals. These had a number of characteristics that were considered to be advantageous to management.

Single-union deals have the following typical features:

● a single union representing all employees, with constraints put on the role of union full-time officials;
● flexible working practices – agreement to the flexible use of labour across traditional demarcation lines;
● single status for all employees – the harmonization of terms and conditions between manual and non-manual employees;
● an expressed commitment by the organization to involvement and the disclosure of information in the form of an open communications system and, often, a works council;
● the resolution of disputes by means of devices such as pendulum arbitration, a commitment to continuity of production and a 'no-strike' provision.

Single-union deals have generally been concluded on green field sites, often by Japanese firms such as Nissan, Sanyo, Matshushsita and Toyota. A 'beauty contest' may be held by the employer to select a union from a number of contenders. Thus, the initiative is taken by the employer, who can lay down radical terms for the agreement.

Factors influencing recognition or de-recognition

Employers are in a strong position now to choose whether they recognize a union or not, which union they want to recognize and the terms on which they would grant recognition, for example a single union and a no-strike agreement.

When setting up on green field sites employers may refuse to recognize unions. Alternatively they hold 'beauty contests', as mentioned above, to select the union they prefer to work with, which will be prepared to reach an agreement in line with what management wants.

An organization deciding whether or not to recognize a union will take some or all of the following factors into account:

● the perceived value or lack of value of having a process for regulating collective bargaining;
● if there is an existing union, the extent to which management has freedom to manage; for example, to change working arrangements and introduce flexible working or multi-skilling;

- the history of relationships with the union;
- the proportion of employees who are union members and the degree to which they believe they need the protection their union provides; a decision on de-recognition has to weigh the extent to which its perceived advantages outweigh the disadvantages of upsetting the *status quo*;
- any preferences as to a particular union, because of its reputation or the extent to which it is believed a satisfactory relationship can be maintained.

In considering recognition arrangements employers may also consider entering into a 'single union deal' as described above.

COLLECTIVE BARGAINING ARRANGEMENTS

Collective bargaining arrangements are those set up by agreements between managements, employers' associations, or joint employer negotiating bodies and trade unions to determine specified terms and conditions of employment for groups of employees. Collective bargaining processes are usually governed by procedural agreements and result in substantive agreements and agreed employee relations procedures.

The considerations to be taken into account in developing and managing collective bargaining arrangements are:

- collective agreements;
- the level at which bargaining should take place;
- single-table bargaining where a number of unions are recognized in one workplace;
- dispute resolution.

Collective agreements

Collective agreements can be classified as procedural agreements or substantive agreements. The former provide the framework for collective bargaining, and the latter are the outcome of collective bargaining. Two forms of collective procedural agreements have become prominent: partnership agreements and new-style agreements.

Procedural agreements

Procedural agreements set out the respective responsibilities and duties of managers and unions, the steps through which the parties make joint decisions, and the procedure to be followed if the parties fail to agree. Their purpose is to regulate the behaviour of the parties to the agreement, but they are not legally enforceable, and the degree to which they are followed depends on the goodwill of both parties or the balance of power between them. Procedural agreements are seldom broken and, if so, never lightly. The basic presumption of collective bargaining is that both parties will honour agreements that have been made freely between them. An attempt to make collective agreements legally enforceable in the 1971 Industrial Relations Act failed because employers generally did not seek to enforce its provisions.

A typical procedure agreement contains the following sections:

- a preamble defining the objectives of the agreement;
- a statement that the union is recognized as a representative body with negotiating rights;
- a statement of general principles, which may include a commitment to use the procedure (a no-strike clause) and/or a status quo clause which restricts the ability of management to introduce changes outside negotiated or customary practice;
- a statement of the facilities granted to unions, including the rights of shop stewards and the right to hold meetings;
- provision for joint negotiating committees (in some agreements);
- the negotiating or disputes procedure;
- provision for terminating the agreement.

The scope and content of such agreements can, however, vary widely. Some organizations have limited recognition to the provision of representational rights only, others have taken an entirely different line in concluding single-union deals which, when they first emerged in the 1980s, were sometimes dubbed 'new style agreements', or referred to as the 'new realism'.

An agreement may incorporate or have attached to it employee relations procedures such as those concerned with grievances, discipline and redundancy. In addition, agreements are sometimes reached on health and safety procedures.

Substantive agreements

Substantive agreements set out agreed terms and conditions of employment, covering pay and working hours and other aspects such as holidays, overtime regulations, flexibility arrangements and allowances. Again, they are not legally enforceable. A substantive agreement may detail the operational rules for a payment-by-results scheme which could include arrangements for timing or re-timing and for payments during waiting time or on new, untimed, work.

Partnership agreements

A partnership agreement is one in which both parties (management and the trade union) agree to work together to their mutual advantage and to achieve a climate of more cooperative and therefore less adversarial industrial relations. A partnership agreement may include undertakings from both sides; for example, management may offer job security linked to productivity, more involvement and better communications, and the union may agree to new forms of work organization or work practices which might, for example, require more flexibility on the part of employees.

Five key values for partnership have been set down by Roscow and Casner-Lotto (1997):

1. Mutual trust and respect.
2. A joint vision for the future and the means to achieve it.
3. Continuous exchange of information.
4. Recognition of the central role of collective bargaining.
5. Devolved decision-making.

Their research in the United States indicated that if these matters were addressed successfully by management and unions, then companies could expect productivity gains, quality improvements, a better-motivated and committed workforce and lower absenteeism and turnover rates.

The Department of Trade and Industry and Department for Education and Employment report on Partnerships at Work (1997) concludes that partnership is central to the strategy of successful organizations. A growing understanding that organizations must focus on customer needs has brought with it the desire to engage the attitudes and commitment of all employees in order to effectively meet those needs, says the report. The five main themes or 'paths' identified by the report are:

1. Shared goals – 'understanding the business we are in'.
2. Shared culture – 'agreed values binding us together'.
3. Shared learning – 'continuously improving ourselves'.
4. Shared effort – 'one business driven by flexible teams'.
5. Shared information – 'effective communication throughout the enterprise'.

New-style agreements

As described by Farnham (2000), a major feature of new-style agreements is that their negotiating and disputes procedures are based on the mutually accepted 'rights' of the parties expressed in the recognition agreement. The intention is to resolve any differences of interests on substantive issues between the parties by regulations, with pendulum arbitration providing a resolution of those issues where differences exist. New-style agreements will typically include provision for single-union recognition, single status, labour flexibility, company council and a no-strike clause to the effect that issues should be resolved without resource to industrial action.

Bargaining levels

There has been a pronounced trend away from multi-employer bargaining, especially in the private sector. This has arisen because of decentralization and a reluctance on the part of central management to get involved.

Single-table bargaining

Single-table bargaining brings together all the unions in an organization as a single bargaining unit. The reasons organizations advance for wanting a 'single-table deal' are:

- a concern that existing multi-unit bargaining arrangements not only are inefficient in terms of time and management resources but are also a potential source of conflict;
- the desire to achieve major changes in working practices, which it is believed can be achieved only through single-table bargaining;
- a belief in the necessity of introducing harmonized or single-status conditions.

Marginson and Sisson (1990), however, identified a number of critical issues which need to be resolved if single-table bargaining is to be introduced successfully. These comprise:

- the commitment of management to the concept;
- the need to maintain levels of negotiation which are specific to particular groups below the single-bargaining table;
- the need to allay the fears of managers that they will not be able to react flexibly to changes in the demand for specific groups of workers;

- the willingness of management to discuss a wider range of issues with union representatives – this is because single-table bargaining adds to existing arrangements a top tier in which matters affecting all employees, such as training, development, working time and fringe benefits can be discussed;
- the need to persuade representatives from the various unions to forget their previous rivalries, sink their differences and work together (not always easy);
- the need to allay the fears of trade unions that they may lose representation rights and members, and of shop stewards that they will lose the ability to represent members effectively.

These are formidable requirements to satisfy, and however desirable single-table bargaining may be, it will never be easy to introduce or to operate.

Dispute resolution

The aim of collective bargaining is, of course, to reach agreement, preferably to the satisfaction of both parties. Negotiating procedures, as described in the next section of this chapter, provide for various stages of 'failure to agree' and often include a clause providing for some form of dispute resolution in the event of the procedure being exhausted. The processes of dispute resolution are conciliation, arbitration and mediation.

Conciliation

Conciliation is the process of reconciling disagreeing parties. It is carried out by a third party, often an ACAS (Advisory, Conciliation and Arbitration Service) conciliation officer, who acts in effect as a go-between, attempting to get the employer and trade union representatives to agree on terms. Conciliators can only help the parties to come to an agreement. They do not make recommendations on what that agreement should be. That is the role of an arbitrator.

The incentives to seek conciliation are the hope that the conciliator can rebuild bridges and the belief that a determined, if last-minute, search for agreement is better than confrontation, even if both parties have to compromise.

Arbitration

Arbitration is the process of settling disputes by getting a third party, the arbitrator, to review and discuss the negotiating stances of the disagreeing parties and make a recommendation on the terms of settlement which is binding on both parties. The arbitrator is impartial and the role is often undertaken by ACAS officials, although industrial relations academics are sometimes asked to act in this capacity. Arbitration is the means of last resort for reaching a settlement where disputes cannot be resolved in any other way.

Procedure agreements may provide for either side unilaterally to invoke arbitration, in which case the decision of the arbitrator is not binding on both parties. The process of arbitration in its fullest sense, however, only takes place at the request of both parties who agree in advance to accept the arbitrator's findings. ACAS will only act as an arbitrator if the consent of both parties is obtained, conciliation is considered, any agreed procedures have been used to the full and a failure to agree has been recorded.

The number of arbitration cases referred to ACAS declined significantly during the 1980s and 1990s. The decline in arbitration is attributed by Kessler and Bayliss (1992) to management dominance, which has meant that arbitration was seen as pointless because managements were confident that their final offer would be accepted. In the prevailing climate, unions, if dissatisfied and denied arbitration, would in most cases be unwilling to take industrial action.

Pendulum arbitration

Pendulum or final offer arbitration increases the rigidity of the arbitration process by allowing an arbitrator no choice but to recommend either the union's or the employer's final offer – there is no middle ground. The aim of pendulum arbitration is to get the parties to avoid adopting extreme positions. As defined by Millward (1994), the features of pendulum arbitration are that the procedure has to be written and agreed by management and the union or unions, and it has to provide for arbitration that is independent, is equally accessible to both parties, is binding on both parties, and involves finding wholly in favour of one party or the other.

The adoption of pendulum arbitration can be viewed as a concession by management, since it means giving up the power to impose a settlement on employees. But the evidence from the Workplace Industrial Relations Survey (1990) is that the full version of pendulum arbitration as defined above was extremely rare.

Mediation

Mediation is a watered-down form of arbitration, although it is stronger than conciliation. It takes place when a third party (often ACAS) helps the employer and the union by making recommendations which, however, they are not bound to accept.

INFORMAL EMPLOYEE RELATIONS PROCESSES

The formal processes of union recognition, collective bargaining and dispute resolution described earlier in this chapter provide the framework for industrial relations in so far as this is concerned with agreeing terms and conditions of employment and working arrangements and settling disputes. But within or outside that framework, informal employee relations processes are taking place continuously.

Informal employee relationships take place whenever a line manager or team leader is handling an issue in contact with a shop steward, an employee representative, an individual employee or a group of employees. The issue may concern methods of work, allocation of work and overtime, working conditions, health and safety, achieving output and quality targets and standards, discipline or pay (especially if a payment-by-results scheme is in operation, which can generate continuous arguments about times, standards, re-timings, payments for waiting time or when carrying out new tasks, and fluctuations or reductions in earnings because of alleged managerial inefficiency).

Line managers and supervisors handle day-to-day grievances arising from any of these issues and are expected to resolve them to the satisfaction of all parties without involving a formal grievance procedure. The thrust for devolving responsibility to line managers for personnel matters has increased the onus on them to handle employee relations effectively. A good team leader will establish a working relationship with the shop steward representing his or her staff which will enable issues arising on the shop-floor or with individual employees to be settled amicably before they become a problem.

Creating and maintaining a good employee relations climate in an organization may be the ultimate responsibility of top management, advised by personnel specialists. But the climate will be strongly influenced by the behaviour of line managers and team leaders. The personnel function can help to improve the effectiveness of this behaviour by identifying and defining the competences required, advising on the selection of supervisors, ensuring that they are properly trained, encouraging the development of performance management processes that provide for the assessment of the level of competence achieved by line managers and team leaders in handling employee relations, or by providing unobtrusive help and guidance as required.

OTHER FEATURES OF THE INDUSTRIAL RELATIONS SCENE

There are four features of the industrial relations scene which are important, besides the formal and informal processes discussed above. These features are harmonization, union membership arrangements within the organization, the 'check-off' system, and strikes and other forms of industrial action (which should more realistically be called industrial inaction if it involves a 'go slow' or 'work to rule').

Harmonization

Harmonization is the process of introducing the same conditions of employment for all employees. It is distinguished by Roberts (1990) from single status and staff status as follows:

- Single status is the removal of differences in basic conditions of employment to give all employees equal status. Some organizations take this further by putting all employees into the same pay and grading structure.
- Staff status is a process whereby manual and craft employees gradually receive staff terms and conditions of employment, usually upon reaching some qualifying standard, for example length of service.
- Harmonization means the reduction of differences in the pay structure and other employment conditions between categories of employee, usually manual and staff employees. The essence of harmonization is the adoption of a common approach and criteria to pay and conditions for all employees. It differs from staff status in that, in the process of harmonization, some staff employees may have to accept some of the conditions of employment of manual workers.

According to Duncan (1989), the pressure towards harmonization has arisen for the following reasons:

- *New technology* – status differentials can obstruct efficient labour utilization, and concessions on harmonization are invariably given in exchange for an agreement on flexibility. Moreover, technology, by de-skilling many white-collar jobs and enhancing the skills of former blue-collar workers, has made differential treatment harder to defend.
- *Legislation* – equal pay, the banning of sex and racial discrimination, and employment protection legislation have extended to manual workers rights that were previously the preserve of staff. The concept of equal value has been a major challenge to differentiation between staff and manual workers.
- *Improving productivity* by the more flexible use of labour.
- *Simplifying personnel administration* and thereby reducing costs.
- *Changing employee attitudes* and so improving commitment, motivation and morale.

In Roberts' view, questions of morality are probably of least importance.

Union membership within organizations

The closed shop, which enforced union membership within organizations, has been made illegal. But many managers prefer that all their employees should be in the union because on the whole it makes their life easier to have one channel of representation to deal with industrial relations issues and also because it prevents conflict between members and non-members of the union.

The 'check-off' system

The 'check-off' is a system that involves management in deducting the subscriptions of trade union members on behalf of the union. It is popular with unions because it helps to maintain membership and provides a reasonably well guaranteed source of income. Managements have generally been willing to cooperate as a gesture of good faith to their trade union. They may support a check-off system because it enables them to find out how many employees are union members. Employers also know that they can exert pressure in the face of industrial action by threatening to end the check-off. However, the Trade Union and Employment Rights Act 1993 provides that if an employer is lawfully to make check-off deductions from a worker's pay, there must be prior written consent from the worker and renewed consent at least every three years. This three-year renewal provision can inhibit the maintenance of the system.

Strikes

Strikes are the most politically charged of all the features of industrial relations. The Conservative Government in the 1980s believed that 'strikes are too often a weapon of first rather than last resort'. However, those involved in negotiation – as well as trade unions – have recognized that a strike is a legitimate last resort if all else fails. It is a factor in the balance of power between the parties in a negotiation and has to be taken into account by both parties.

Unlike other Western European countries, there is no legal right in Britain for workers or their unions to take strike action. What has been built up through common law is a system of legal liability that suspends union liability for civil wrongs or 'torts' as long as industrial action falls within the legal definition of a trade dispute and takes place 'in contemplation of furtherance of a trade dispute'.

The Conservative Government's 1980s and 1990s legislation has limited this legal immunity to situations where a properly conducted ballot has been conducted by the union authorizing or endorsing the action and where the action is between an employer and their direct employees, with all secondary or sympathy action being unlawful. Immunity is also removed if industrial action is taken to impose or enforce a closed shop or where the action is unofficial and is not repudiated in writing by the union. The impact of this law is to deter the calling of strikes without careful consideration of where the line of legal immunity is now drawn and of the likely result of a secret ballot. But the secret ballot can in effect legitimize strike action.

The number of strikes and the proportion of days lost through strike action have diminished significantly in the UK since the 1970s. This reduction has been caused more by economic pressures than by the legislation. Unions have had to choose between taking strike action, which could lead to closure, or survival on the terms dictated by employers with fewer jobs. In addition, unions in manufacturing found that their members who remained in jobs did well out of local productivity bargaining and threatened strike action.

MANAGING WITH TRADE UNIONS

Ideally, managements and trade unions learn to live together, often on a give and take basis, the presumption being that neither would benefit from a climate of hostility or by generating constant confrontation. It would be assumed in this ideal situation that mutual advantage would come from acting in accordance with the spirit as well as the letter of agreed joint regulatory procedures. However, both parties would probably adopt a realistic pluralist viewpoint, recognizing the inevitability of differences of opinion, even disputes, but believing that with goodwill on both sides they could be settled without recourse to industrial action.

Of course, the reality in the 1960s and 1970s was often different. In certain businesses, for example in the motor and shipbuilding industries, hostility and confrontation were rife. And newspaper proprietors tended to let their unions walk all over them in the interests of peace and profit.

Times have changed. As noted earlier, trade union power has diminished and managements have tended to seize the initiative. They may be content to live with trade unions but they give industrial relations lower priority. They may feel that it is easier to continue to operate with a union because it provides a useful, well-established channel for communication and for the handling of grievance, discipline and safety issues. In the absence of a union, management would need to develop its own alternatives, which would be costly and difficult to operate effectively. The trade union and the shop stewards remain a useful lubricant. Alternatively, as Smith and

Morton (1993) suggest, the management perspective may be that it is safer to marginalize the unions than formally to de-recognize them and risk provoking a confrontation: 'Better to let them wither on the vine than receive a reviving fertilizer'. However, the alternative view was advanced by Purcell (1979) who argued that management will have greater success in achieving its objectives by working with trade unions, in particular by encouraging union membership and participation in union affairs. More recently, The Industrial Participation 1995 report *(Towards Industrial Partnership)* recognized the high degree of common interests shared by employers and unions, and stressed the need to accept the legitimacy of representative institutions, although it did not seek to deny differences of opinions and goals.

The pattern varies considerably but there is general agreement based on studies such as the Workplace Industrial Relations Survey (1990) that employers have been able to assert their prerogative – 'management must manage' – in the workplace. They seem generally to have regained control over how they organize work, especially with regard to the flexible use of labour and multi-skilling. The 'status quo' clause, typical of many agreements in the engineering industry, whereby management could not change working arrangements without union agreement, has virtually disappeared.

Four types of industrial relations management have been identified by Purcell and Sisson (1983):

● *Traditionalists* have unitary beliefs and are anti-union with forceful management.
● *Sophisticated paternalists* are essentially unitary but they do not take it for granted that their employees accept the organization's objectives or automatically legitimize management decision making. They spend considerable time and resources in ensuring that their employees adopt the right approach.
● *Sophisticated moderns* are either constitutionalists, where the limits of collective bargaining are codified in an agreement but management is free to take decisions on matters that are not the subject of such an agreement, or consultors, who accept collective bargaining but do not want to codify everything in a collective agreement, and instead aim to minimize the amount of joint regulation and emphasize joint consultation with 'problems' having to be solved rather than 'disputes' settled.
● *Standard moderns* are pragmatic or opportunist. Trade unions are recognized, but industrial relations are seen as primarily fire-fighting and are assumed to be non-problematic unless events prove otherwise. This is by far the most typical approach.

But working with unions can mean adopting a more positive partnership approach, in the words of John Monks (1994) 'finding the common ground on issues that are best tackled through joint action'. Where collective agreements are being made, a cooperative or integrative bargaining philosophy can be adopted, based on perceptions about the mutual interdependence of management and employees and the recognition by both parties that this is a means to achieve more for themselves.

MANAGING WITHOUT TRADE UNIONS

Most organizations do, in fact, manage without trade unions as the 1998 Workplace Employee Relations Survey found. Millward *et al* (1992) established from the third Workplace Industrial Relations Survey that the characteristics of union-free employee relations were as follows:

- Employee relations were generally seen by managers as better in the non-union sector than in the union sector.
- Strikes were almost unheard of.
- Labour turnover was high but absenteeism was no worse.
- Pay levels were generally set unilaterally by management.
- The dispersion of pay was higher, it was more market related and there was more performance-related pay. There was also a greater incidence of low pay.
- In general, no alternative methods of employee representation existed as a substitute for trade union representation.
- Employee relations were generally conducted with a much higher degree of informality than in the union sector. In a quarter of non-union workplaces there were no grievance procedures and about a fifth had no formal disciplinary procedures.
- Managers generally felt unconstrained in the way in which they organized work.
- There was more flexibility in the use of labour than in the union sector, which included the greater use of freelance and temporary workers.
- Employees in the non-union sector are two and a half times as likely to be dismissed as those in unionized firms and the incidence of compulsory redundancies is higher.

The survey concluded that many of the differences between unionized and non-unionized workplaces could be explained by the generally smaller size of the non-union firms and the fact that many such workplaces were independent, rather than being part of a larger enterprise.

Another characteristic not mentioned by the survey is the use by non-unionized firms of personal contracts as an alternative to collective bargaining. In theory, employees are free to negotiate such contracts, but as an Anglia Polytechnic

University (1995) study found, little bargaining activity takes place in the 500 work-places they surveyed. The conclusion was that the personal contract 'reflects inherent inequality of bargaining power' and this suggests that there is a continuing role for trade unions.

This does not paint a very satisfactory picture of employee relations from the workers' point of view, but it is probably typical of smaller, independent firms. Some of the latter may be what Marchington (1995) describes as the traditional sweatshop employer. The pressure on the firm could be to control costs and increase flexibility and responsiveness to customer demands. These are objectives which management may feel could only be achieved without union interference.

Some larger organizations, for example IBM and Marks & Spencer, manage without unions by, in effect, adopting a 'union substitution' policy. This offers a complete employment package, which can be seen by employees as an attractive alternative to trade union membership. The package is likely to include highly competitive pay with harmonized employment conditions, recruitment tests designed to select people who match organizational norms, a focus on employee communications and information sharing, induction programmes that aim to get employees to accept the organization's ethos, an emphasis on training and career development and a commitment to providing secure and satisfying work. Such busi-nesses may broadly adhere to the HRM model (although they would not describe it as such, and this is the approach they used before HRM was invented).

HRM techniques for increasing commitment through involvement and communi-cation processes provide a route that some organizations without unions follow in order to maintain a satisfactory employee relations climate. But it is not easy. Unless HRM fits the core values of the organization and is in accord with its management style, and unless a coherent and integrated approach is adopted to introducing HRM processes, it is unlikely to succeed.

50

Negotiating and bargaining

Collective bargaining requires the exercise of negotiating skills. Bargaining skills are also necessary during the process of negotiating collective substantive agreements on terms and conditions of employment. Negotiating skills are required in many other aspects of personnel and development, including, for example, agreeing individual contracts of employment and outsourcing contracts, but this chapter concentrates on those used in collective bargaining. This chapter covers the nature and process of negotiation and bargaining, bargaining conventions, the stages of negotiation and, in summary, the skills required.

THE NATURE OF NEGOTIATING AND BARGAINING

To negotiate is to converse with a view to finding terms of agreement. To bargain is to go through the steps required to come to terms on a transaction. Collective bargaining is essentially a process of negotiation – of conferring and, it is hoped, reaching agreement without resorting to force (although hard words may be exchanged on the way).

Within this negotiating process bargaining takes place. This means coming to terms on a settlement, which in a pay negotiation may be somewhere between the union's opening demand of, say, 6 per cent increase and the employer's first response of, say, 3 per cent. The point at which a settlement is achieved between these figures will depend on the relative bargaining power of the two parties, the realism of the offer or response, the level of bargaining skills the parties can deploy and the sheer determination of either party to press its point or not to concede (this may be a function of bargaining power).

NEGOTIATIONS

Negotiations take place when two parties meet to reach an agreement. This can be a convergent process (in commercial terms this is sometimes referred to as a 'willing buyer – willing seller' situation) where both parties are equally keen to reach a win–win agreement. Clearly, if this can be achieved rather than a win–lose outcome, the future relationships between the parties are more likely to be harmonious. Certainly, the primary aim of any negotiator should be to proceed on this basis.

But some negotiations can be described as 'divergent' in which one or both of the parties aim to win as much as they can from the other while giving away as little as possible. In these circumstances, negotiating can be a war game. It is a battle in the sense that the bargainers are pitting their wits against each other while also bringing in the heavy artillery in the shape of sanctions or threatened sanctions. As with other battles, the negotiation process can produce a pyrrhic victory in which both sides, including the apparent winner, retire to mourn their losses and lick their wounds. It is a game in the sense that both sides are trying to win, but there are various conventions or rules that the parties tacitly adopt or recognize, although they may break them in the heat of the battle.

Negotiations can normally be broken down into four stages:

1. preparing for negotiation: setting objectives, defining strategy and assembling data;
2. opening;
3. bargaining;
4. closing.

Before analysing these stages in detail it may be helpful to consider the process of bargaining and list the typical conventions that operate when bargaining takes place.

The process of bargaining

The process of bargaining consists of three distinct, though related, functions. First, bargainers state their bargaining position to their opposite numbers. Second, they probe weaknesses in the bargaining position of their opposite numbers and try to convince them that they must move, by stages if this is inevitable, from their present position to a position closer to what the bargainer wants. Third, they adjust or confirm their original estimate of their own bargaining position in the light of information gleaned and reactions from their opposite numbers, in order that, if the time comes to put an estimate of bargaining position to the test, the ground chosen will be as favourable as possible.

The essence of the bargaining process was described by Peters (1968):

> In skilful hands the bargaining position performs a double function. It conceals and it reveals. The bargaining position is used to indicate – to unfold gradually, step by step – the maximum expectation of the negotiator, while at the same time concealing, for as long as necessary, his minimum expectation. By indirect means, such as the manner and timing of the changes in your bargaining position, you, as a negotiator, try to convince the other side that your maximum expectation is really your minimum breaking-off point. Since you have taken an appropriate bargaining position at the start of negotiations, each change in your position should give ever-clearer indications of your maximum expectation. Also, each change should be designed to encourage or pressure the other side to reciprocate with as much information as you give them.

Bargaining conventions

There are certain conventions in collective bargaining which most experienced and responsible negotiators understand and accept, although they are never stated and, indeed, may be broken in the heat of the moment, or by a tyro in the bargaining game. These conventions help to create an atmosphere of trust and understanding which is essential to the maintenance of the type of stable bargaining relationship that benefits both sides. Some of the most generally accepted conventions are listed below:

● Whatever happens during the bargaining, both parties are using the bargaining process in the hope of coming to a settlement.
● While it is preferable to conduct negotiations in a civilized and friendly manner, attacks, hard words, threats, and (controlled) losses of temper are sometimes used by negotiators to underline determination to get their way and to shake their opponent's confidence and self-possession – but these should be treated by both sides as legitimate tactics and should not be allowed to shake the basic belief in each other's integrity or desire to settle without taking drastic action.
● Off-the-record discussions are mutually beneficial as a means of probing attitudes and intentions and smoothing the way to a settlement, but they should not be referred to specifically in formal bargaining sessions unless both sides agree in advance.

- Each side should normally be prepared to move from its original position.
- It is normal, although not inevitable, for the negotiation to proceed by alternate offers and counter-offers from each side which lead steadily towards a settlement.
- Concessions, once made, cannot be withdrawn.
- Firm offers must not be withdrawn, although it is legitimate to make and withdraw conditional offers.
- Third parties should not be brought in until both parties are agreed that no further progress would be made without them.
- The final agreement should mean exactly what it says – there should be no trickery, and the terms agreed should be implemented without amendment.
- So far as possible, the final settlement should be framed in such a way as to reduce the extent to which the other party obviously loses face or credibility.

Preparing for negotiation

Negotiations take place in an atmosphere of uncertainty. Neither side knows how strong the other side's bargaining position is or what it really wants and will be prepared to accept. They do not know how much the other party will be prepared to concede or the strength of its convictions.

In a typical pay negotiation unions or representative bodies making the claim will define three things:

- the target they would like to achieve;
- the minimum they will accept;
- the opening claim which they believe will be most likely to help achieve the target.

Employers define three related things:

- the target settlement they would like to achieve;
- the maximum they would be prepared to concede;
- the opening offer they will make which would provide them with sufficient room to manoeuvre in reaching their target.

The difference between the union's claim and the employer's offer is the negotiating range. If your maximum exceeds their minimum, this will indicate the settlement range. This is illustrated in Figure 50.1. In this example the chance of settlement without too much trouble is fairly high. It is when your maximum is less than their minimum, as in Figure 50.2, that the trouble starts. Over a period of time a negotiation where a settlement range exists proceeds in the way demonstrated in Figure 50.3.

Figure 50.1 Negotiating range within a settlement range

Objectives

The objectives in the form of a target settlement and initial and minimum/maximum offers and agreements will be conditioned by:

● the perceptions of both parties about the relative strengths of their cases;
● the relative power of the two parties;
● the amount of room for negotiation the parties want to allow;
● the employer's ability to pay;
● the going rate elsewhere;
● the rate of inflation – although employers are reluctant to concede that it is their job to protect their employees from inflation, the cost of living is often one of the chief arguments advanced by a union for an increase.

Strategy

Negotiating strategy should clearly be designed to achieve the target settlement, with the maximum the negotiator is prepared to concede being the fall-back position. Two decisions are required:

Figure 50.2 Negotiating range with a negotiating gap

1. The stages to follow in moving from, in the union's case, the opening claim to the final agreement, and in the employer's case from the initial to the closing offer. This is dependent on the amount of room for negotiating that has been allowed.
2. The negotiating package the employer wants to use in reply to whatever package the union has put forward. The employer's aim should be to provide scope for trading concessions during the course of negotiations. From their viewpoint, there is also much to be said for having in reserve various conditions which they can ask the unions to accept in return for any concessions they may be prepared to make. Employers might, for example, ask for an extended period before the next settlement in return for an increase in their offer.

Preparation steps

Negotiators must prepare carefully for negotiations so that they do not, in Aneurin Bevan's phrase, 'go naked to the conference table'. The following steps should be taken:

● List the arguments to be used in supporting your case.

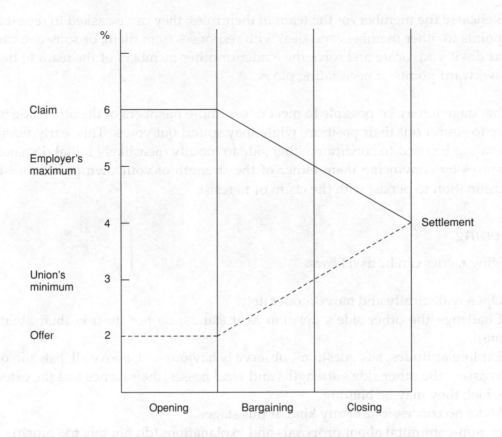

Figure 50.3 Stages of a negotiation

- List the likely arguments or counter-arguments that the other party is likely to use.
- List the counter-arguments to the arguments of the other side.
- Obtain the data you need to support your case.
- Select the negotiating team – this should never have fewer than two members, and for major negotiations should have three or more: one to take the lead and do most of the talking, one to take notes and feed the negotiator with any supporting information required, and the others to observe opposite numbers and play a specific part in negotiations in accordance with their brief.
- Brief the members of the negotiating team on their roles and the negotiating strategy and tactics that are to be adopted – if appropriate, prepared statements or arguments should be issued at this stage to be used as required by the strategic plan.

- Rehearse the members of the team in their roles; they can be asked to repeat their points to other members and deal with responses from them; or someone can act as devil's advocate and force the leader or other members of the team to handle awkward points or negotiating ploys.

At this stage it may be possible to meet one or more members of the other side informally to sound out their position, while they sound out yours. This 'early warning' system can be used to condition either side to modify their likely initial demands or responses by convincing them either of the strength of your own position or their determination to persist with the claim or to resist.

Opening

Opening tactics can be as follows:

- Open realistically and move moderately.
- Challenge the other side's position as it stands; do not destroy their ability to move.
- Explore attitudes, ask questions, observe behaviour and, above all, listen in order to assess the other side's strengths and weaknesses, their tactics and the extent to which they may be bluffing.
- Make no concessions of any kind at this stage.
- Be non-committal about proposals and explanations (do not talk too much).

Bargaining

After the opening moves, the main bargaining phase takes place in which the gap is narrowed between the initial positions and the parties attempt to persuade each other that their case is strong enough to force the other side to close at a less advantageous point than they had planned. The following tactics can be employed:

- Always make conditional proposals: 'If you will do this, then I will consider doing that' – the words to remember are: if … then… .
- Never make one-sided concessions: always trade off against a concession from the other party: 'If I concede x, then I expect you to concede y'.
- Negotiate on the whole package: negotiations should not allow the other side to pick off item by item.
- Keep the issues open to extract the maximum benefit from potential trade-offs.

Closing

When and how negotiators should close is a matter of judgement, and depends on an assessment of the strength of the other side's case and their determination to see it through. There are various closing techniques:

● making a concession from the package, preferably a minor one which is traded off against an agreement to settle – the concession can be offered more positively than in the bargaining stage: 'If you will agree to settle at x, then I will concede y';

● doing a deal: splitting the difference, or bringing in something new, such as extending the settlement time scale, agreeing to back-payments, phasing increases, or making a joint declaration of intent to do something in the future (eg introducing a productivity plan);

● summarizing what has happened to date, emphasizing the concessions that have been made and the extent to which movement has been made and stating that the final position has been reached;

● applying pressure through a threat of the dire consequences which will follow if a 'final' claim is not agreed or a 'final' offer is not accepted;

● giving the other side a choice between two courses of action.

Employers should not make a final offer unless they mean it. If it is not really their final offer and the union calls their bluff they may have to make further concessions and their credibility will be undermined. Each party will, of course, attempt to force the other side into revealing the extent to which they have reached their final position. But negotiators should not allow themselves to be pressurized. If negotiators want to avoid committing themselves and thus devaluing the word 'final', they should state as positively as they can that this is as far as they are prepared to go. But bargaining conventions accept that further moves may still be made on a *quid pro quo* basis from this 'final position'.

NEGOTIATING AND BARGAINING SKILLS

Negotiating skills

The main negotiating skills are:

● *analytical ability* – the capacity to assess the key factors which will affect the negotiating stance and tactics of both sides, and to use this assessment to ensure that all the facts and argument that can be used to support the negotiator's case or prejudice the other party's case are marshalled;

- *empathy* – the ability to put oneself in the other party's shoes to understand not only what they are hoping to achieve but also why they have these expectations and the extent to which they are determined to fulfil them;
- *planning ability* – to develop and implement negotiating strategies and tactics but to be prepared to be flexible about the tactics in the light of developments during negotiations;
- *interactive skills* – the capacity to relate well with other people, to be persuasive without being domineering, to make a point without using it as an opportunity to make the other side lose face, to show respect to the other side's arguments and points if they are valid while questioning them if they are dubious, to respond quickly to changing moods and reactions so that the opportunity can be seized to make progress towards consensus (and the achievement of consensus is the ultimate aim);
- *communicating skills* – the ability to convey information and arguments clearly, positively and logically while also being prepared to listen to the other side and to respond appropriately.

Bargaining skills

The basic bargaining skills are:

- the ability to sense the extent to which the other side wants or indeed expects to achieve its claims or sustain its offer;
- the reciprocal ability not to give real wants away (bargaining, as was mentioned earlier, is about concealing as well as revealing) – in the market place it is always easier for sellers to drive a hard bargain with buyers who have revealed somehow that they covet the article;
- flexible realism – the capacity to make realistic moves during the bargaining process to reduce the claim or increase the offer which will demonstrate that the bargainer is seeking a reasonable settlement and is prepared to respond appropriately to movements made by the other side;
- respect – the ability to demonstrate to the other party that the negotiator respects their views and takes them seriously even if he or she disagrees with them;
- sensitivity – the ability to sense changes in moods and directions or weaknesses in arguments and respond quickly to press home a point.

Acquiring the skills

Negotiating and bargaining skills are developed through experience. To a certain extent they can be taught in the classroom through role plays and simulations but these can never replace the reality of sitting down with the other side and discussing claims and counter-offers, making points, handling confrontation and working out and applying the tactics required to reach a satisfactory settlement. It is useful to be aware of the need to apply the skills listed above but they only become meaningful during actual negotiation.

The best way to learn is by being a subsidiary member of a team with the scope to observe and comment on the tactics, approaches and skills used by both sides and, increasingly, to make planned contributions. A good team leader will nurse the tyro negotiator and will review the nature of each negotiating session to assess what went right or wrong, and why. This is how the writer learnt his negotiating skills and it served him in good stead when faced with the task of leading negotiating teams at plant, local and national level in the stimulating, exciting but sometimes frustrating process of negotiation.

51

Involvement and participation

The decline in the significance of trade unions referred to in Chapter 48 has meant that in many organizations more attention has been paid to forms of involvement and participation other than collective bargaining. This interest has been enhanced by the HRM rhetoric advocating the development of mutual commitment, empowerment and direct communication. Tom Peters (1988) has suggested that employers should 'involve everyone in everything' with the result that 'productivity gains of several hundred per cent should ensue'.

In this chapter:

● Involvement and participation are defined and distinguished, as far as the latter is possible – there are a number of different definitions;
● The forms and levels of employee involvement and participation processes and the reasons for introducing them are identified.
● The main involvement processes of attitude surveys, quality circles and suggestion schemes are described (communication methods such as team briefing are discussed in the next chapter).
● The main participation methods of joint consultative committees, works councils (especially European Works Councils) and worker directors are examined.
● The incidence of involvement and participation processes and the benefits they provide are assessed.
● Approaches to introducing involvement and participation are considered.

DEFINITIONS

The terms 'involvement' and 'participation' are sometimes used synonymously to cover all forms of individual and representative information, consultation and participation, summarized in the phrase, 'giving employees a voice'. Collective bargaining may be excluded from this definition. They can refer to any processes in organizations which are introduced by management to convey information to employees on business initiatives, decisions and results. Used interchangeably, they can also cover procedures, mechanisms and processes which are set up by management unilaterally or in agreement with trade unions, thus enabling employees through their union(s) or another representative body to exert influence on and to share in decision-taking on matters affecting their interests.

The CIPD in its code for Employee Involvement and Participation, for example, uses 'participation' to cover both involvement and participation. Many commentators, however, distinguish between employee involvement and participation, although there are many different interpretations of what they mean, as set out below.

Employee involvement

As defined by Marchington and Goodman (1992), employee involvement consists of 'those practices which are initiated principally by management, and are designed to increase employee information about, and commitment to, the organization'. They suggest that the phrase is 'redolent of employer initiative'. The employer gives employees the opportunity to become involved in their work and their organization 'beyond simple performance of the wage/work bargain'.

According to Brian Stevens, Director of the Involvement and Participation Society (1990), 'Involvement assumes a recognition that employees have a great untapped potential but that managers retain the right to manage.'

Marchington and Goodman (1992) suggest that employee involvement differs from collective bargaining and industrial democracy, 'both of which are explicitly forms of power sharing and joint decision-making between management and employees – via their representative'. They believe that 'involvement has perhaps a less specific, milder and more general connotation than participation'.

Participation

Participation is defined by Guest and Fatchett (1974) as 'any process through which a person or group of persons determines (that is, intentionally affects) what another person or group of persons will do'. Stevens (1990) believes that 'participation is about employees playing a greater part in the decision-making process'. Marchington *et al* use the term participation to cover 'employee influence which may be exercised through bargaining and negotiation over a wide range of issues associated with the organization and conduct of work and the terms and conditions of employment'.

Industrial democracy

The term 'industrial democracy' was much used in the late 1970s to refer to forms of power sharing in industry, with trade unions having a significant influence over how it might operate. The aim of industrial democracy is to increase the rights of employees or their representatives to participate in decision making, often by appointing 'worker directors' onto boards. This was the era of the Bullock Committee (The Committee of Inquiry on Industrial Democracy) which reported in 1977 on *how* rather than *whether* employees (through their trade unions) should be represented on the boards of directors of private companies. The Bullock report was totally rejected and industrial democracy is not much discussed in the UK nowadays.

The distinction between employee involvement and participation

To summarize, *employee involvement* is a process usually initiated by management to increase the information given to employees and thus enhance their commitment. Involvement processes tend to treat employees as individuals, that is, they address them directly, face to face, rather than through their representatives.

In contrast, *participation* refers to collective rather than individual processes which enable employees through their representatives to influence decision making. The term participation can be extended to forms of financial participation such as profit sharing.

AIMS OF EMPLOYEE INVOLVEMENT AND PARTICIPATION

The CIPD in its *Code on Employee Involvement and Participation in the United Kingdom* (1993c) states that the involvement of, and participation by, employees in any organization, should aim to:

- generate commitment of all employees to the success of the organization;
- enable the organization better to meet the needs of its customers and adapt to changing market requirements, and hence to maximize its future prospects and the prospects of those who work in it;

- help the organization to improve performance and productivity and adopt new methods of working to match new technology, drawing on the resources of knowledge and practical skills of all its employees;
- improve the satisfaction employees get from their work;
- provide all employees with the opportunity to influence and be involved in decisions which are likely to affect their interests.

In 1988 the CBI made a statement to the effect that the CBI believes that employee involvement:

- is a range of processes designed to engage the support, understanding and optimum contribution of all employees in an organization and their commitment to its objectives;
- assists an organization to give the best possible service to customers and clients in the most cost-effective way;
- entails providing employees with the opportunity to influence and where appropriate take part in decision making on matters which affect them;
- is an intrinsic part of good management practice and is therefore not confined to relationships with employee representatives;
- can only be developed voluntarily in ways suited to the activities, structure and history of an organization.

As Kessler and Bayliss (1992) comment, the CBI's approach is individualistic and unitary, and some employers would regard their involvement policies as having failed if employees still attached importance to collective action through trade unions.

As Beardwell (1998) points out, the issue is how employees can be given a 'voice'. He suggests that the key question is: 'what is the most appropriate expression of employee perspectives within my organization?' He also comments that managements over the last ten years have moved away from the concept of 'mutuality' and are more concerned with achieving unity through partnership, but this approach understates the role of the employee voice.

FORMS OF EMPLOYEE INVOLVEMENT AND PARTICIPATION

Marchington (1995a) has identified five forms of employee involvement and participation:

Downward communications

Downward communications (team briefing and meetings) take place from managers to employees in order to inform and 'educate' staff so that they accept management plans. They were the most popular form of employee involvement in the UK in the early 1990s.

Upward problem solving

Upward problem solving is designed to tap into employee knowledge and opinion, either at an individual level or in small groups. The aims are to increase the stock of ideas in an organization, to encourage cooperative relationships at work, and to legitimize change. Attitude surveys, quality circles, suggestion schemes are discussed below and, possibly, total quality management/customer care committees come into this category.

Task participation

Task participation and job redesign processes engage employees in extending the range and type of tasks they undertake. Approaches to job design such as horizontal job redesign (extending the range of tasks undertaken at the same level) job enrichment, vertical role integration (taking greater responsibility for supervisory duties) and team working (where the team organizes its own work so that it becomes 'self-managed') may be used.

Consultation and representative participation

Consultation and representative participation enables employees to take part through their representatives in management decision-making. One of the aims of management in encouraging this form of participation is to use it as a safety valve – an alternative to formal disputes – by means of which more deep-seated employee grievances can be addressed. Joint consultation has been introduced by management in some businesses to hinder trade union recognition or, it is said, even to undermine their activities. This type of participation takes place in the form of joint consultative committees as described later in this chapter. The appointment of worker directors also falls into this category.

Financial involvement/participation

Financial involvement or participation takes the form of such schemes as profit sharing and employee share ownership. Gain sharing is also used by some companies as a means of involvement. Information on company performance is provided to employees as part of the scheme and they are encouraged to discuss with their managers or team leaders the reasons for success or failure and methods of improving performance. The aim of such schemes is to educate employees and gain their commitment.

VARIETIES OF EMPLOYEE INVOLVEMENT AND PARTICIPATION

Employee involvement and participation can vary according to the level at which it takes place, the degree to which decision making is shared, and the extent to which the mechanisms are formal or informal.

Levels

Involvement and participation takes various forms at different levels in an enterprise as defined by the Industrial Society (1974). These levels are described below.

The *job level* involves team leaders and their teams, and the processes include the communication of information about work and interchange of ideas about how the work should be done. These processes are essentially informal.

The *management level* can involve sharing information and decision making about issues which affect the way in which work is planned and carried out, and working arrangements and conditions. There are limits. Management as a whole, and individual managers, must retain authority to do what their function requires. Involvement does not imply anarchy. But it does require some degree of willingness on the part of management to share its decision-making powers. At this level, involvement and participation may become more formalized, through consultative committees, briefing groups or works councils involving management and employees or their representatives.

At the *policy-making level*, where the direction in which the business is going is determined, total participation would imply sharing the power to make key decisions. This is not much practised in the UK, although there may be processes for communicating information on proposed plans (which would almost certainly not reveal proposals for acquisitions or disinvestments or anything else where commercial security is vital) and discussing the implications of those plans.

At the *ownership level*, participation implies a share in the equity, which is not meaningful unless the workers have sufficient control through voting rights to determine the composition of the board. This is not a feature of the British employee relations scene.

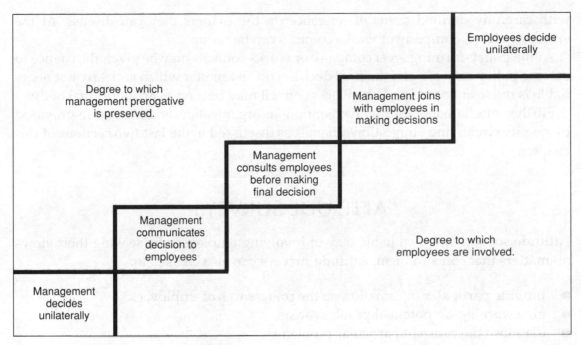

Figure 51.1 Scale of participation

The degree to which decision making is shared

At the one end of the scale, management makes decisions unilaterally; at the other end, in theory, but never in practice except in a worker's cooperative (almost non-existent in the UK), workers decide unilaterally. Between these extremes there is a range of intermediate points which can be expressed (Figure 51.1) as a scale.

The point on this scale at which participation should or can take place at any level in an organization depends on the attitudes, willingness and enthusiasm of both management and employees. Management may be reluctant to give up too much of its authority except under pressure from the unions (which is unlikely today), or from European Community directives on worker consultation.

Mechanisms for involvement and participation

At the job level, involvement and participation should be as informal as possible. Teams may be called together on an *ad hoc* basis to consider a particular problem, but formal committees should be avoided. Team briefing (see Chapter 52) can be used to provide for informal two-way communications.

At the next higher level, more formality may be appropriate in larger organizations. There is scope for the use of consultative committees or departmental councils with carefully defined terms of reference on the matters they can discuss. At the enterprise level, company or works councils can be set up.

At the policy-forming level company or works councils may be given the chance to discuss policy issues, but if the final decision on any matter which is clearly not negotiable is made at board level, the works council may be seen as an ineffectual body.

Further mechanisms for involvement on an organization-wide basis are provided by quality circles and suggestion schemes as discussed in the last two sections of this chapter.

ATTITUDE SURVEYS

Attitude surveys are a valuable way of involving employees by seeking their views on matters that concern them. Attitude surveys can also be used to:

- provide particular information on the preferences of employees;
- give warning on potential problem areas;
- diagnose the cause of particular problems;
- compare morale in different parts of the organization;
- obtain views about processes such as job evaluation, pay determination and performance management in order to assess their effectiveness and the degree to which employees feel they are fair;
- obtain views about personnel policies and how they operate in such areas as equal opportunity, employee development, involvement and health and safety;
- evaluate training;
- assess how organizational and other policy changes have been received to observe the effects of policies and actions over a period of time;
- provide a basis for additional communication and involvement, especially if the survey includes, as it should, discussions with employees on their attitudes and what actions they would like management to take.

Approach

The approach is first to identify the individual's needs and then to assess the extent to which these needs are being met. This means first asking people how they feel about various things for any job they might do, not just their present job. Thus, against the heading of 'good wages', they would be asked to indicate how they feel by ticking the appropriate heading – absolutely top priority, very important, fairly important, and not very important. Secondly, the questionnaire would ask them to express their feelings about different aspects of their present job, for example, indicating against 'pay' whether their feelings about it are very good, good, neither good nor bad, bad, or very bad. An example is given in Appendix B.

Methods of conducting attitude surveys

There are four methods of conducting attitude surveys:

1. *By the use of structured questionnaires* issued to all or a sample of employees. The questionnaires may be standardized ones, such as the Brayfield and Rothe Index of Job Satisfaction, or they may be developed specially for the organization. The advantage of using standardized questionnaires is that they have been thoroughly tested and in many cases norms are available against which results can be compared. Additional questions specially relevant to the company can be added to the standard list. A tailor-made questionnaire can be used to highlight particular issues, but it may be advisable to obtain professional help from an experienced psychologist, who can carry out the skilled work of drafting and pilot-testing the questionnaire and interpreting the results. Questionnaires have the advantage of being relatively cheap to administer and analyse, especially when there are large numbers involved.

2. *By the use of interviews.* These may be 'open-ended' or depth interviews in which the discussion is allowed to range quite freely. Or they may be semi-structured in that there is a checklist of points to be covered, although the aim of the interviewer should be to allow discussion to flow around the points so that the frank and open views of the individual are obtained. Alternatively, and more rarely, interviews can be highly structured so that they become no more than the spoken application of a questionnaire. Individual interviews are to be preferred because they are more likely to be revealing. But they are expensive and time consuming and not so easy to analyse. Discussions through 'focus groups' (ie groups of employees convened to focus their attention on particular issues) are a quicker way of reaching a large number of people, but the results are not so easy to quantify and some people may have difficulty in expressing their views in public.

3. *By a combination of questionnaire and interview.* This is the ideal approach because it combines the quantitative data from the questionnaire with the qualitative data from the interviews. It is always advisable to accompany questionnaires with some depth interviews, even if time permits only a limited sample. An alternative approach is to administer the questionnaire to a group of people and then discuss the reactions to each question with the group. This ensures that a quantified analysis is possible but enables the group, or at least some members of it, to express their feelings more fully.

4. *By the use of focus groups.* A focus group is a representative sample of employees whose attitudes and opinions are sought on issues concerning the organization and their work. The essential features of a focus group are that it is structured, informed, constructive and confidential.

Assessing results

It is an interesting fact that when people are asked directly if they are satisfied with their job, most of them (70 to 90 per cent) will say they are. This is regardless of the work being done and often in spite of strongly held grievances. The probable reason for this phenomenon is that while most people are willing to admit to having grievances – in fact, if invited to complain, they will complain – they may be reluctant to admit, even to themselves, to being dissatisfied with a job which they have no immediate intention of leaving. Many employees have become reconciled to their work, even if they do not like some aspects of it, and have no real desire to do anything else. So they are, in a sense, satisfied enough to continue, even if they have complaints. Finally, many people are satisfied with their job overall, although they grumble about many aspects of it.

Overall measures of satisfaction do not, therefore, always reveal anything interesting. It is more important to look at particular aspects of satisfaction or dissatisfaction to decide whether or not anything needs to be done. In these circumstances, the questionnaire will indicate only a line to be followed up. It will not provide the answers. Hence the advantage of individual meetings or focus group discussions to explore in depth any issue raised.

QUALITY CIRCLES

It can be argued that one of the greatest failings which result from the 'top-down' type of management prevailing in the UK and many other Western countries is that it ignores the knowledge that exists at the other levels in the organization. Quality circles, sometimes called improvement groups, can be used to overcome this problem. They are often associated with a total quality/continuous improvement programme.

Quality circles are small groups of volunteers who are engaged in related work and who meet regularly to discuss and propose ways of improving working methods or arrangements under a trained leader.

Aims

The aims of quality circles are to:

- give those doing the job more scope to use their experience and know-how;
- provide opportunities to tap the knowledge of employees, who may know more about work problems which are hidden from more remote managers and team leaders;
- improve productivity and quality;
- improve employee relations;
- win commitment to the organization.

Essential features

The essential features of quality circles are that they:

- consist of volunteers;
- have a trained leader, usually but not always a team leader;
- hold regular meetings which are strictly limited in duration – often one hour;
- have five to ten members;
- usually select which problems to tackle but may be steered away from problems which are clearly beyond their scope or are already being dealt with;
- use systematic analytical techniques or brainstorming methods in which they have been trained to define and solve problems;
- present their results to management;
- implement accepted proposals.

Prerequisites for success

The first pre-requisite is that top management believes in the value of quality circles and is committed to their success. Middle management and team leaders must also be involved in their introduction. They are the people who are most likely to have reservations about quality circles because they can see them as a threat to their authority and reputation. Without management support, quality circles 'wither on the vine', as they often do.

Trade unions should also be informed of the plan to introduce quality circles. Some unions are hostile because they feel that quality circles can reduce their influence and power, and that management is deliberately introducing them for this purpose.

The introduction and maintenance of a quality circle needs a 'facilitator' who trains, encourages and guides quality circle members, ensures that they are given the resources they need, and sets up presentation sessions. The facilitator is often a line manager rather than a personnel specialist or a trainer. This vital role also involves encouraging the circles and ensuring that top management backing continues by keeping them informed of the benefits provided by quality circles – publicity on their achievements is important. The facilitator can also deal with any problems quality circles meet in getting information or in dealing with management.

Training is an important part of the quality circles. Team leaders need an initial two- to three-day training course in the analytical techniques they will use and in team building and presentation skills. They also need refresher training from time to time. Team leaders, with the help of facilitators, also train the members of their team. This training effort is a valuable spin-off from a quality circle programme. Instruction in leadership, problem solving and analytical skills is a useful way of developing existing or potential team leaders. Membership of a quality circle is also a means of developing skills as well as getting more involved.

These requirements are demanding and although the essential concept of quality circles is valid they too often fail to survive after an initial spurt. But they can be replaced by more informal and *ad hoc* improvement groups or by regular team meetings held by team leaders (or organized by the team itself in a self-managed team) in which work problems and areas for innovation and improvement are discussed and agreed.

SUGGESTION SCHEMES

Suggestion schemes can provide a valuable means for employees to participate in improving the efficiency of the company. Properly organized, they can help to reduce the feelings of frustration endemic in all concerns where people think they have good ideas but cannot get them considered because there are no recognized channels of communication. Normally, only those ideas outside the usual scope of employees' duties are considered, and this should be made clear, as well as the categories of those eligible for the scheme – senior managers are often excluded.

The basis of a successful suggestion scheme should be an established procedure for submitting and evaluating ideas, with tangible recognition for those which have merit and an effective system for explaining to employees without discouraging them that their ideas cannot be accepted.

The most common arrangement is to use suggestion boxes with, possibly, a special form for entering a suggestion. Alternatively, or additionally, employees can be given the name of an individual or a committee to whom suggestions should be submitted. Managers and team leaders must be stimulated to encourage their staff to submit suggestions, and publicity in the shape of posters, leaflets and articles in the company magazine should be used to promote the scheme. The publicity should give prominence to the successful suggestions and how they are being implemented.

One person should be made responsible for administering the scheme. He or she should have the authority to reject facetious suggestions, but should be given clear guidance on the routing of suggestions by subject matter to departments or individuals for their comments. The administrator deals with all communications and, if necessary, may go back to the individual who submitted the suggestion to get more details of, for example, the savings in cost or improvements in output that should result from the idea.

It is desirable to have a suggestion committee consisting of management and employee representatives to review suggestions in the light of the comments of any specialist functions or executives who have evaluated them. This committee should be given the final power to accept or reject suggestions but could, if necessary, call for additional information or opinion before making its decision. The committee could also decide on the size of any award within established guidelines, such as proportion of savings during the first year. There should be a standard procedure for recording the decisions of the committee and informing those who made suggestions of the outcome – with reasons for rejection if appropriate.

JOINT CONSULTATION

Joint consultation is the most familiar method of participation although, as noted later in this chapter, it is in decline. It is essentially a means for management and employees to get together in consultative committees to discuss and determine matters affecting their joint or respective interests.

Aims of joint consultation

The aim of joint consultation is to provide a means of jointly examining and discussing problems which concern both management and employees. It should mean that mutually acceptable solutions can be sought through the exchange of views and information. Joint consultation allows management to inform employees of proposed changes which affect them and employees to express their views about those changes. It also provides a means for employees to contribute their own views on such matters as how work is organized (for example, flexibility), working conditions, the operation of personnel policies and procedures and health and safety. As noted earlier, joint consultation can act as a safety valve, relieving the pressure from grievances which, if not settled by some process of discussion, could escalate to a dispute.

Topics for joint consultation

Joint consultation does not mean power sharing, involving employees in strategic policy decisions on such matters as investments and disinvestments, product-market development plans and mergers or takeovers. These would only be the subject of joint decision making in the rare circumstances in which full participation at board level takes place.

The WIRS3 reported that 30 per cent of consultative committees were also concerned with negotiation. The majority of such committees, however, concentrate on non-negotiable matters such as working methods and organization, health and safety, working conditions and arrangements, employee facilities (restaurants, car parking, welfare etc) and works rules. Managements may upgrade consultation to cover important topics such as new products and investment plans so that negotiation becomes less meaningful or necessary. They may see consultation as simply another form of downward communication.

Joint consultation may be perceived as being meaningless or of marginal importance by either or both parties and in these circumstances will of course be ineffective. But, as Kessler and Bayliss (1992) note: 'Where trade unionism is strong and well-developed, consultation may be seen as a valuable adjunct to collective bargaining. Here the two processes are kept separate, although the representatives of each committee will be largely the same people.'

An argument which can be advanced for separating consultation and negotiation in a unionized plant is that this recognizes the distinction between cooperative or integrative bargaining and conjunctive or distributive bargaining referred to in Chapter 48. Cooperative bargaining recognizes the interdependence of management and employees and can take place in consultative committees without the power-plays and stress that frequently accompany pay negotiations.

Membership of joint consultative committees.

Depending on the degree to which the organization is unionized (if at all) joint consultative committees can be formed exclusively of trade union representatives nominated by union members, or consist of a mix of nominated trade union representatives and other non-union employees (the latter being elected) or be entirely composed of elected representatives who might or might not be trade union members.

Consultative committees often exclude managers or team leaders and, if they are left out, this can be contentious because they may well feel that they are being bypassed.

Structure

There may be one consultative committee or works council covering the whole organization but larger companies often have separate committees for each major division or unit.

Constitution

The constitution of a consultative committee normally covers the following points:

- objectives;
- terms of reference;
- composition;
- election procedures;
- arrangements for chairing and holding meetings (in some organizations the chair is held by management and employee representatives alternately).

WORKS COUNCILS

Works councils covering the whole organization often have broadly the same functions as company-wide consultative committees – only the name is different. But some works councils have wider membership, including managers, team leaders and professional, technical and office staff, thus covering everyone in the company. And as a result of the EU directive, European Works Councils are becoming significant for any UK company operating in Europe.

The aim of the Directive is 'to improve the right to information and to consultation of employees in Community-scale undertakings and Community-scale groups of undertakings'. The Directive states that it is necessary 'if economic activities are to develop in a harmonious fashion'. The subjects for discussion at a European Works Council include the general economic and financial situation of the business, and specific matters with a major impact on employees, such as relocations, closures, mergers, collective dismissals and the introduction of new technology. A Council must be set up in organizations with 1,000 employees or more and it is required to be an employee-only body and it must comprise three to 30 employees elected or appointed by employee representatives or, in their absence, the whole workforce.

WORKER DIRECTORS

The concept of worker directors on the board came to the fore in the 1970s as part of the campaign for industrial democracy. The idea was that employee representatives could get closer to the point at which strategic decisions are made. But the Bullock Committee's recommendations on this subject were totally rejected.

Experience with worker directors is very rare in the private sector and it has been argued that the few schemes which were introduced were used, as Marchington (1995) comments, 'to strengthen or reassert management control rather than to redistribute that control'.

Worker directors were appointed in public sector organizations – British Steel and the Post Office. But studies on how they functioned quoted by Marchington found that management representatives tended to conduct any sensitive or confidential business away from the board, while union members found themselves in the difficult position of attempting to defend member interests yet contributing to management decisions which may have negative implications for the workforce. For these reasons and because of the continuing hostility of managements to worker directors it seems unlikely that they will ever become a common feature of the employee relations scene.

INCIDENCE OF INVOLVEMENT AND PARTICIPATION

The WIRS 3, as analysed by Millward (1994), established that 84 per cent of the establishments covered by the survey had some form of communication channel between management and employees. The most popular form was the management chain of communication (59 per cent). The least popular channel was a consultative committee (18 per cent). The highest growth area was regular meetings with junior management (from 30 per cent in 1984 to 44 per cent in 1990).

In private manufacturing the WIRS 3 showed a marked decline in the percentage of workplaces with joint consultative committees (from 36 per cent in 1980 to 23 per cent in 1990). WIRS 3 concluded that the fall in the number of committees was primarily due to the changing composition of workplaces. It was not due to a tendency for workplaces to abandon committees, but to a fall in the number of larger more unionized workplaces which were more likely to have committees.

REQUIREMENTS FOR SUCCESSFUL EMPLOYEE INVOLVEMENT AND PARTICIPATION

According to the Department of Employment (1994), the overall success of employee involvement depends fundamentally on:

- building trust;
- eliminating status differentials;
- committing the organization to vigorous training and development;
- breaking down barriers to change the organization's culture.

It is generally accepted that the 10 basic requirements for success are:

1. The objectives of participation must be defined, discussed and agreed by all concerned.
2. The objectives must be related to tangible and significant aspects of the job, the process of management or the formulation of policies that affect the interests of employees. They must not relate to peripheral matters such as welfare or social amenities.
3. Management must believe in and must be seen to believe in involving employees. Actions speak louder than words and management must demonstrate that it will put into effect the joint decisions made during discussions.
4. The unions must believe in participation as a genuine means of advancing the interests of their members and not simply as a way of getting more power. They should show by their actions that they are prepared to support unpopular decisions to which they have been a party.
5. Joint consultation machinery should be in line with any existing systems of negotiation and representation. It should not be supported by management as a possible way of reducing the powers of the union. If this naive approach is taken, it will fail – it always does. Joint consultation should be regarded as a process of integrative bargaining complementary to the distributive bargaining that takes place in joint negotiating committees.
6. If management does introduce joint consultation in a non-union environment, it should be prepared to widen the terms of reference as much as possible to cover issues concerning company employment policies and plans and working arrangements and conditions (eg, health and safety matters). It is rare, however, for such committees or councils to be involved in negotiations on terms and conditions of employment.

7. Consultative committees should always relate to a defined working unit, should never meet unless there is something specific to discuss, and should always conclude their meetings with agreed points which are implemented quickly.
8. Employee and management representatives should be properly briefed and trained and have all the information they require.
9. Managers and team leaders should be kept in the picture and, as appropriate, involved in the consultation process – it is clearly highly undesirable for them to feel that they have been left out.
10. Consultation should take place before decisions are made.

PLANNING FOR INVOLVEMENT AND PARTICIPATION

The form of involvement and participation appropriate for an organization depends upon the attitudes and relative strengths of management and unions, its past experience of negotiation and consultation, and the current climate of employee relations. It is essential to take into account the requirements for successful participation listed earlier in this chapter and to plan its introduction or development in the following stages:

● Analyse and evaluate the existing systems of involvement, consultation, communication and other formal and informal means of participation.
● Identify the influences within and without the company which affect the climate of employee relations and suggest the most appropriate form in which participation should take place.
● Develop a plan for improving or extending employee involvement in whatever form is appropriate to the organization.
● Discuss the plan in depth with management, team leaders, work people and unions – the introduction of improved participation should itself be a participative process.
● Brief and train those concerned with employee involvement in their duties and how they should be carried out.
● Introduce new schemes on a pilot-scheme basis – do not expect immediate results and be prepared to modify them in the light of experience.
● Keep the whole process under continuous review as it develops to ensure that it is operating effectively.

52

Communications

Organizations function by means of the collective action of people, yet each individual is capable of taking independent action which may not be in line with policy or instructions, or may not be reported properly to other people who ought to know about it. Good communications are required to achieve coordinated results.

Organizations are subject to the influence of continuous change which affects the work employees do, their well-being and their security. Change can be managed only by ensuring that the reasons for and the implications of change are communicated to those affected in terms which they can understand and accept.

Individuals are motivated by the extrinsic reward system and the intrinsic rewards coming from the work itself. But the degree to which they are motivated depends upon the amount of responsibility and scope for achievement provided by their job, and upon their expectations that the rewards they will get will be the ones they want, and will follow from the efforts they make. Feelings about work and the associated rewards depend very much on the effectiveness of communications from their managers or team leaders and within the company.

Above all, good two-way communications are required so that management can keep employees informed of the policies and plans affecting them, and employees can react promptly with their views about management's proposals and actions. Change cannot be managed properly without an understanding of the feelings of those affected by it, and an efficient system of communications is needed to understand and influence these feelings.

But the extent to which good communications create satisfactory relationships rather than simply reducing unsatisfactory ones, can be exaggerated. A feature of management practices during the twentieth century is the way in which different management theories become fashionable or influential for a while and then decline in favour. Among these has been the 'good communications' theory of management. This approach to dealing with management problems is based upon the following assumptions:

- The needs and aims of both employees and management are, in the long run, the same in any organization. Managers' and employees' ideas and objectives can all be fitted together to form a single conceptual framework.
- Any differences in opinion between management and employees are due to misunderstandings which have arisen because communications are not good enough.
- The solution to industrial strife is to improve communications.

This theory is attractive and has some validity. Its weakness is that the assumptions are too sweeping, particularly the belief that the ultimate objectives of management and workers are necessarily identical. The good communications theory, like paternalism, seems to imply that a company can develop loyalty by keeping people informed and treating them well. But people working in organizations have other and, to them, more important loyalties elsewhere – and why not?

The existence of different loyalties and points of view in an organization does not mean that communication is unimportant. If anything the need for a good communications system becomes even greater when differences and conflict exist. But it can only alleviate those differences and pave the way to better cooperation. It cannot solve them.

It is therefore necessary to bear in mind that the group with which we identify – the reference group – influences our attitudes and feelings. 'Management' and the 'the union' as well as our family, our ethnic background, our political party and our religious beliefs (if any) constitute a reference group and colour our reactions to information. What each group 'hears' depends on its own interests. Shared experiences and common frames of reference have much more influence than exhortations from management. Employees may feel they have nothing to do with them because it conflicts with what they already believe.

However, although there may be limitations on the extent to which communication strategies can enhance mutuality and commitment, there is no doubt that it is essential for managements to keep people informed on matters that affect them and to provide channels for them to express their views. This is particularly necessary when new employment initiatives are taking place and effective change management is very much about communicating management's intentions to people and making sure that they understand how they will be affected.

COMMUNICATION AREAS AND OBJECTIVES

The main communication areas and their associated objectives are set out in Table 52.1.

Employee relations are mainly affected by managerial and internal communications, although external communications are an additional channel of information. The strategy for managerial communications is concerned with planning and control procedures, management information systems and techniques of delegating and giving instructions. These matters are outside the scope of this book, except in so far as the procedures and skills can be developed by training programmes.

COMMUNICATIONS STRATEGY

The strategy for internal communications should be based on analyses of:

● what management wants to say;
● what employees want to hear;
● the problems being met in conveying or receiving information.

These analyses can be used to indicate the systems of communication that need to be developed and the education and training programmes required to make them work. They should also provide guidance on how communications should be managed and timed. Bad management and poor timing are frequently the fundamental causes of ineffective communication.

What management wants to say

What management wants to say depends upon an assessment of what employees need to know, which, in turn, is affected by what they want to hear.

Management usually aims to achieve three things: first, to get employees to understand and accept what management proposes to do in areas that affect them; second, to obtain the commitment of employees to the objectives, plans and values of the organization; and, third, to help employees to appreciate more clearly the contribution they can make to organizational success and how it will benefit them.

Table 52.1 Communication areas and objectives

	Communication Area	Objectives
I. MANAGERIAL	1. the communication downwards and sideways of corporate or functional objectives, policies plans and budgets to those who have to implement them.	to ensure that managers and supervisors receive clear, accurate and prompt information on what they are expected to achieve to further the company's objectives.
	2. the communication downwards of direct instructions from a manager to a subordinate on what the latter has to do.	to ensure that the instructions are clear and precise and provide the necessary motivation to get people into action.
	3. the communication upwards and sideways of proposals, suggestions and comments on corporate or functional objectives, policies and budgets from those who have to implement them.	to ensure that managers and supervisors have adequate scope to influence corporate and functional decisions on matters about which they have specific expertise and knowledge.
	4. the communication upwards and sideways of management information on performance and results.	to enable management to monitor and control performance in order that, as necessary, opportunities can be exploited or swift corrective action taken.
II. INTERNAL RELATIONS	5. the communication downwards of information on company plans, policies or performance.	to ensure that (i) employees are kept informed of matters that affect them, especially changes to working conditions, and factors influencing their prosperity and security; (ii) employees are encouraged to identify themselves more completely with the company.
	6. the communication upwards of the comments and reactions of employees to what is proposed will happen or what is actually happening in matters that affect them.	to ensure that employees are given an opportunity to voice their suggestions and fears and that the company is in a position to amend its plans in the light of these comments.
III. EXTERNAL RELATIONS	7. the receipt and analysis of information from outside which affects the company's interests.	to ensure that the company is fully aware of all the information on legislation and on marketing, commercial, financial and technological matters that affect its interests.
	8. the presentation of information about the company and its products to the government, customers and the public at large.	to exert influence in the interests of the company, to present a good image of the company, and to persuade customers to buy its products or services.

Communications from management should be about values, plans, intentions and proposals (with the opportunity for discussion with and feedback from employees) as well as about achievements and results. Exhortations should not be used: no one listens to them. It is better to concentrate on specific requirements rather than resorting to general appeals for abstract things such as improved quality or productivity. The requirements should be phrased in a way which emphasizes how all concerned will actually work together and the mutual benefits that should result.

What employees want to hear

Clearly, employees want to hear about and to comment upon the matters that affect their interests. These will include changes in working methods and conditions, changes in the arrangements for overtime and shift working, company plans which may affect pay or security, and changes in terms and conditions of employment. It is management's job to understand what employees want to hear and plan its communications strategy accordingly. Understanding can be obtained by conducting 'focus groups' discussions which bring together groups of employees to focus on particular issues that concern them, by means of attitude surveys, by asking employee representatives, by informally listening to what employees say, and by analysing grievances to see if improved communications could modify them.

Analysing communication problems

Specific examples of employee relations problems where communication failures have been the cause or a contributory factor should be analysed to determine exactly what went wrong and what needs to be done to put it right. The problems may be any of those listed earlier in this chapter, including lack of appropriate channels of communication, lack of appreciation of the need to communicate, and lack of skill in overcoming the many formidable barriers to communication. Problems with channels of communication can be dealt with by introducing new or improved communications systems. Lack of skill is a matter for education and training.

COMMUNICATION SYSTEMS

Communication systems can be divided into those using an intranet, those using the written word such as magazines, newsletters, bulletins and notice-boards, and those using oral methods such as meetings, briefing groups and public address systems. The aim should be to make judicious use of a number of channels to make sure that the message gets across.

Communications through an intranet system

Organizations are increasingly relying on an internal e-mail system (the intranet) to communicate information, especially in workplaces where all or most of the employees have direct or indirect access to a computer. The advantage of intranet communications is that they can be transmitted swiftly to a wide audience. They can also be used for two-way communications – employees can be invited to respond to questions or surveys.

Magazines

Glossy magazines or house journals are an obvious way to keep employees informed about the company and are often used for public relations purposes as well. They can extol and explain the achievements of the company and may thus help to increase identification and even loyalty. If employees are encouraged to contribute (although this is difficult), the magazine can become more human. The biggest danger of this sort of magazine is that it becomes a public relations exercise which is seen by employees as having little relevance to their everyday affairs.

Newsletters

Newsletters aim to appear more frequently and to angle their contents more to the immediate concerns of employees than the glossier form of house magazine. To be effective, they should include articles specifically aimed at explaining what management is planning to do and how this affects everyone. They can also include more chatty 'human interest' material about the doings of employees to capture the attention of readers. Correspondence columns can provide an avenue for the expression of employees' views and replies from management, but no attempt should be made to censor letters (except those that are purely abusive) or to pull punches in reply. Anonymous letters should be published if the writer gives his name to the editor.

The key factor in the success of a newsletter or any form of house magazine is the editor, who should be someone who knows the company and its employees and can be trusted by everyone to be frank and fair. Professional expertise is obviously desirable but it is not the first consideration, as long as the editor can write reasonably well and has access to expert help in putting the paper together. It is often a good idea to have an editorial board consisting of management and employee representatives to advise and assist the editor.

Organizations often publish a newsletter in addition to a house magazine, treating the latter mainly as a public relations exercise and relying on the newsletter as the prime means of communicating with employees.

Bulletins

Bulletins can be used to give immediate information to employees which cannot wait for the next issue of a newsletter; or they can be a substitute for a formal publication if the company does not feel that the expense is justified. Bulletins are useful only if they are distributed quickly and are seen by all interested employees. They can simply be posted on notice-boards or, more effectively, given to individual employees and used as a starting point for a briefing session if they contain information of sufficient interest to merit a face-to-face discussion.

Notice-boards

Notice-boards are an obvious but frequently misused medium for communications. The biggest danger is allowing boards to be cluttered up with uninteresting or out-of-date material. It is essential to control what goes on to the boards and to appoint responsible people to service them by removing out-of-date or unauthorized notices.

A more impressive show can be made of notices and other material if an information centre is set up in the restaurant or some other suitable place where the information can be displayed in a more attractive and compelling manner than on a typical notice-board.

Employee involvement

Employee involvement through such means as consultative committees provides a channel for two-way communication. Sometimes, however, they are not particularly effective, either because their thunder has been stolen by union negotiation committees, or because their proceedings are over-formalized and restricted and fail to address the real issues. It is essential to disseminate the information revealed at committees around the offices and works, but it is impossible to rely on committee members to do this. Minutes can be posted on notice-boards, but they are seldom read, usually because they contain too much redundant material.

Videos

Specially made videos can be a cost-effective method of getting across personal messages (eg from the chief executive) or information about how the company is doing. They can, however, be regarded by employees as too impersonal and/or too slick to have any real meaning.

Team briefing

The concept of team briefing (previously called briefing groups), as originally developed by the Industrial Society, is a device to overcome the restricted nature of joint consultative committees by involving everyone in an organization, level by level, in face-to-face meetings to present, receive and discuss information. Team briefing aims to overcome the gaps and inadequacies of casual briefings by injecting some order into the system.

Team briefing should operate as follows:

1. *Organization*
    - cover all levels in an organization;
    - fewest possible steps between the top and bottom;
    - between 4 and 18 in each group;
    - run by the immediate leader of each group at each level (who must be properly trained and briefed).
2. *Subjects*
    - policies – explanations of new or changed policies;
    - plans – as they affect the organization as a whole and the immediate group;
    - progress – how the organization and the group are getting on;
    - people – new appointments, points about personnel matters (pay, security, procedures).
3. *Sequence* – the briefing groups should work to a brief prepared by the board on key issues. This briefing is written up and cascaded down the organization. The briefing group meetings should, however, allow for discussion of the brief, and the system should cater for any reactions or comments to be fed back to the top. This provides for two-way communication.
4. *Timing and duration:*
    - a minimum of once a month for those in charge of others and once every two months for every individual in the organization – but meet only if there is something to say;
    - duration not longer than 20–30 minutes.

The merit of team briefing is that it enables face-to-face communications to be planned and, to a reasonable degree, formalized. It is easy, however, for it to start on a wave of enthusiasm and then to wither away because of lack of sufficient drive and enthusiasm from the top downward, inadequately trained and motivated managers and team leaders, reluctance of management to allow subjects of real importance to be discussed throughout the system, and insufficient feedback upwards through each level.

A team briefing system must be led and controlled effectively from the top, but it does require a senior manager with specific responsibility to advise on the subject matter and the preparation of briefs (it is important to have well-prepared material to ensure that briefing is carried out consistently and thoroughly at each level), to train managers and team leaders, and to monitor the system by checking on the effectiveness and frequency of meetings.

Part XII

Health, safety and welfare

This part deals with the services provided by the HR department in order to help the organization meet its legal and social responsibilities to ensure a healthy and safe place of work, to help employees cope with their personal problems, to help elderly and retired employees and, in some cases, to make recreational facilities available.

53

Health and safety

Health and safety policies and programmes are concerned with protecting employees – and other people affected by what the company produces and does – against the hazards arising from their employment or their links with the company.

Occupational health programmes deal with the prevention of ill-health arising from working conditions. They consist of two elements:

- *occupational medicine*, which is a specialized branch of preventive medicine concerned with the diagnosis and prevention of health hazards at work and dealing with any ill-health or stress that has occurred in spite of preventive actions;
- *occupational hygiene*, which is the province of the chemist and the engineer or ergonomist engaged in the measurement and control of environmental hazards.

Safety programmes deal with the prevention of accidents and with minimizing the resulting loss and damage to persons and property. They relate more to systems of work than the working environment, but both health and safety programmes are concerned with protection against hazards, and their aims and methods are clearly inter-linked.

MANAGING HEALTH AND SAFETY AT WORK

It is estimated by the Health and Safety Executive (HSE) that in the UK about 500 people are killed at work every year and several hundred thousand more are injured or suffer ill-health. It is also estimated that, apart from the pain and misery caused to those directly or indirectly concerned, the total cost to British employers of work-related injury and illness exceeds £4 billion a year.

The achievement of a healthy and safe place of work and the elimination to the maximum extent possible of hazards to health and safety are the responsibility of everyone employed in an organization, as well as those working there under contract. But the onus is on management to achieve and indeed go beyond the high standard in health and safety matters required by the legislation – the Health and Safety at Work etc. Act in 1974 and the various regulations laid down in the Codes of Practice.

The importance of healthy and safe policies and practices is, sadly, often under-estimated by those concerned with managing businesses and by individual managers within those businesses. But it cannot be emphasized too strongly that the prevention of accidents and elimination of health and safety hazards are a prime responsibility of management and managers in order to minimize suffering and loss.

THE IMPORTANCE OF HEALTH AND SAFETY IN THE WORKPLACE

The achievement of the highest standards of health and safety in the workplace is important because the elimination, or at least minimization, of health and safety hazards and risks is the moral as well as the legal responsibility of employers – this is the over-riding reason. Close and continuous attention to health and safety is important because ill-health and injuries inflicted by the system of work or working conditions cause suffering and loss to individuals and their dependants. In addition, accidents and absences through ill-health or injuries result in losses and damage for the organization. This 'business' reason is very much less significant than the 'human' reasons given above but it is still a consideration, albeit a tangential one.

As described in this chapter, managing health and safety at work is a matter of:

- developing health and safety policies;
- conducting risk assessments which identify hazards and assess the risks attached to them;

- carrying out health and safety audits and inspections;
- implementing occupational health programmes;
- managing stress;
- preventing accidents;
- measuring health and safety performance;
- communicating the need for good health and safety practices;
- training in good health and safety practices;
- organizing health and safety.

HEALTH AND SAFETY POLICIES

Written health and safety policies are required to demonstrate that top management is concerned about the protection of the organization's employees from hazards at work and to indicate how this protection will be provided. They are, therefore, first, a declaration of intent, second, a definition of the means by which that intent will be realized, and third, a statement of the guidelines that should be followed by everyone concerned – which means all employees – in implementing the policy.

The policy statement should consist of three parts:

- the general policy statement;
- the description of the organization for health and safety;
- details of arrangements for implementing the policy.

The general policy statement

The general policy statement should be a declaration of the intention of the employer to safeguard the health and safety of employees. It should emphasize four fundamental points:

- that the safety of employees and the public is of paramount importance;
- that safety takes precedence over expediency;
- that every effort will be made to involve all managers, team leaders and employees in the development and implementation of health and safety procedures;
- that health and safety legislation will be complied with in the spirit as well as the letter of the law.

Organization

This section of the policy statement should describe the health and safety organization of the company through which high standards are set and achieved by people at all levels in the organization.

This statement should underline the ultimate responsibility of top management for the health and safety performance of the organization. It should then indicate how key management personnel are held accountable for performance in their areas. The role of safety representatives and safety committees should be defined, and the duties of specialists such as the safety adviser and the medical officer should be summarized.

CONDUCTING RISK ASSESSMENTS

What is a risk assessment?

Risk assessments are concerned with the identification of hazards and the analysis of the risks attached to them.

A *hazard* is anything that can cause harm (eg. working on roofs, lifting heavy objects, chemicals, electricity etc). A *risk* is the chance, large or small, of harm actually being done by the hazard. Risk assessments are concerned with looking for hazards and estimating the level of risk associated with them. As suggested by Holt and Andrews (1993), risk can be calculated by multiplying a severity estimate by a probability estimate. That is, risk = severity × probability.

The purpose of risk assessments is, of course, to initiate preventive action. They enable control measures to be devised on the basis of an understanding of the relative importance of risks. Risk assessments must be recorded if there are five or more employees.

There are two types of risk assessment. The first is *quantitative risk assessment*, which produces an objective probability estimate based upon risk information that is immediately applicable to the circumstances in which the risk occurs. The second is *qualitative risk assessment*, which is more subjective and is based on judgement backed by generalized data. Quantitative risk assessment is preferable if the specific data are available. Qualitative risk assessment may be acceptable if there are little or no specific data as long as it is made systematically on the basis of an analysis of working conditions and hazards and informed judgement of the likelihood of harm actually being done.

Looking for hazards

The following, as suggested by the HSE and others, are typical activities where accidents happen or there are high risks:

- receipt of raw materials, eg lifting, carrying;
- stacking and storage, eg falling materials;
- movement of people and materials, eg falls, collisions;
- processing of raw materials, eg exposure to toxic substances;
- maintenance of buildings, eg roof work, gutter cleaning;
- maintenance of plant and machinery, eg lifting tackle, installation of equipment;
- using electricity, eg using hand tools, extension leads;
- operating machines, eg operating without sufficient clearance, or at an unsafe speed; not using safety devices;
- failure to wear protective equipment, eg hats, boots, clothing;
- distribution of finished jobs, eg movement of vehicles;
- dealing with emergencies, eg spillages, fires, explosions;
- health hazards arising from the use of equipment or methods of working, eg VDUs, repetitive strain injuries from badly designed work stations or working practices.

The HSE suggests that most accidents are caused by a few key activities. It advises that assessors should concentrate initially on those that could cause serious harm. Operations such as roof work, maintenance and transport movement cause far more deaths and injuries each year than many mainstream activities.

When carrying out a risk assessment it is also necessary to consider who might be harmed, eg employees, visitors (including cleaners and contractors and the public when calling in to buy products or enlist services).

Hazards should be ranked according to their potential severity as a basis for producing one side of the risk equation. A simple three-point scale can be used such as 'low', 'moderate' and 'high'. A more complex severity rating scale has been proposed by Holt and Andrews (1993), as follows:

1. *Catastrophic* – imminent danger exists, hazard capable of causing death and illness on a wide scale.
2. *Critical* – hazard can result in serious illness, severe injury, property and equipment damage.
3. *Marginal* – hazard can cause illness, injury, or equipment damage, but the results would not be expected to be serious.

4.   *Negligible* – hazard will not result in serious injury or illness; remote possibility of damage beyond minor first-aid case.

Assessing the risk

When the hazards have been identified it is necessary to assess how high the risks are. The HSE suggests that this involves answering three questions:

● What is the worst result?
● How likely is it to happen?
● How many people could be hurt if things go wrong?

A probability rating system can be used such as the one recommended by Holt and Andrews:

1.   *Probable* – likely to occur immediately or shortly.
2.   *Reasonably probable* – probably will occur in time.
3.   *Remote* – may occur in time.
4.   *Extremely remote* – unlikely to occur.

Taking action

Risk assessment should lead to action. The type of action can be ranked in order of potential effectiveness in the form of a 'safety precedence sequence' as proposed by Holt and Andrews:

● *Hazard elimination* – use of alternatives, design improvements, change of process.
● *Substitution* – for example, replacement of a chemical with one which is less risky.
● *Use of barriers* – removing the hazard from the worker or removing the worker from the hazard.
● *Use of procedures* – limitation of exposure, dilution of exposure, safe systems of work (these depend on human response).
● *Use of warning systems* – signs, instructions, labels (these also depend on human response).
● *Use of personal protective clothing* – this depends on human response and is used as a side measure only when all other options have been exhausted.

Monitoring and evaluation

Risk assessment is not completed when action has been initiated. It is essential to monitor the hazard and evaluate the effectiveness of the action in eliminating it or at least reducing it to an acceptable level.

HEALTH AND SAFETY AUDITS

What is a health and safety audit?

Risk assessments identify specific hazards and quantify the risks attached to them. Health and safety audits provide for a much more comprehensive review of all aspects of health and safety policies, and procedures and practices programmes. As defined by Saunders (1992):

> A safety audit will examine the whole organisation in order to test whether it is meeting its safety aims and objectives. It will examine hierarchies, safety planning processes, decision-making, delegation, policy-making and implementation as well as all areas of safety programme planning.

Who carries out a health and safety audit?

Safety audits can be conducted by safety advisers and/or personnel specialists but the more managers, employees and trade union representatives are involved, the better. Audits are often carried out under the auspices of a health and safety committee with its members taking an active part in conducting them.

Managers can also be held responsible for conducting audits within their departments and, even better, individual members of these departments can be trained to carry out audits in particular areas. The conduct of an audit will be facilitated if check lists are prepared and a simple form used to record results.

Some organizations also use outside agencies such as the British Safety Institute to conduct independent audits.

What is covered by a health and safety audit?

A health and safety audit should cover:

Policies

● Do health and safety policies meet legal requirements?

- Are senior managers committed to health and safety?
- How committed are other managers, team leaders and supervisors to health and safety?
- Is there a health and safety committee? If not, why not?
- How effective is the committee in getting things done?

Procedures:

How effectively do the procedures:

- support the implementation of health and safety policies?
- communicate the need for good health and safety practices?
- provide for systematic risk assessments?
- ensure that accidents are investigated thoroughly?
- record data on health and safety which are used to evaluate performance and initiate action?
- ensure that health and safety considerations are given proper weight when designing systems of work or manufacturing and operational processes (including the design of equipment and work stations, the specification for the product or service, and the use of materials)?
- provide safety training, especially induction training and training when jobs or working methods are changed?

Safety practices

- To what extent do health and safety practices in all areas of the organization conform to the general requirements of the Health and Safety at Work Act and the specific requirements of the various regulations and codes of practice?
- What risk assessments have been carried out? What were the findings? What actions were taken?
- What is the health and safety performance of the organization as shown by the performance indicators? Is the trend positive or negative? If the latter, what is being done about it?
- How thoroughly are accidents investigated? What steps have been taken to prevent their recurrence?
- What is the evidence that managers and supervisors are really concerned about health and safety?

What should be done with the audit?

The audit should cover the questions above but its purpose is to generate action. Those conducting the audit will have to assess priorities and costs and draw up action programmes for approval by the Board.

SAFETY INSPECTIONS

Safety inspections are designed to examine a specific area of the organization – operational department or manufacturing process – in order to locate and define any faults in the system, equipment, plant or machines, or any operational errors that might be the source of accidents. Safety inspections should be carried out on a regular and systematic basis by line managers and supervisors with the advice and help of health and safety advisers. The steps to be taken in carrying out safety inspections are as follows:

- Allocate the responsibility for conducting the inspection.
- Define the points to be covered in the form of a checklist.
- Divide the department or plant into areas and list the points to which attention needs to be given in each area.
- Define the frequency with which inspections should be carried out – daily in critical areas.
- Use the check lists as the basis for the inspection.
- Carry out sample or spot checks on a random basis.
- Carry out special investigations as necessary to deal with special problems such as operating machinery without guards to increase throughput.
- Set up a reporting system (a form should be used for recording the results of inspections).
- Set up a system for monitoring that safety inspections are being conducted properly and on schedule and that corrective action has been taken where necessary.

OCCUPATIONAL HEALTH PROGRAMMES

The Health and Safety Executive reported in 1998 that almost 20 million working days a year are lost because of work-related illness. Two million people say they suffer from an illness they believe was caused by their work. Muscular disorders, including repetitive strain injury and back pain, are by far the most commonly reported illnesses with 1.2 million affected, and the numbers are rising. The next biggest problem is stress, which 500,000 people say is so bad that it is making them ill. These are large and disturbing figures and they show that high priority must be given to creating and maintaining programmes for the improvement of occupational health.

The control of occupational health and hygiene problems can be achieved by:

● eliminating the hazard at source through design and process engineering;
● isolating hazardous processes and substances so that workers do not come into contact with them;
● changing the processes or substances used, to promote better protection or eliminate the risk;
● providing protective equipment, but only if changes to the design, process or specification cannot completely remove the hazard;
● training workers to avoid risk;
● maintaining plant and equipment to eliminate the possibility of harmful emissions, controlling the use of toxic substances and eliminating radiation hazards;
● good housekeeping to keep premises and machinery clean and free from toxic substances;
● regular inspections to ensure that potential health risks are identified in good time;
● pre-employment medical examinations and regular checks on those exposed to risk;
● ensuring that ergonomic considerations (ie, those concerning the design and use of equipment, machines, processes and workstations) are taken into account in design specifications, establishing work routines and training – this is particularly important as a means of minimizing the incidence of repetitive strain injury (RSI);
● maintaining preventive medicine programmes which develop health standards for each job and involve regular audits of potential health hazards and regular examinations for anyone at risk.

Particular attention needs to be exercised on the control of noise, fatigue and stress. Control of stress should be regarded as a major part of any occupational health programme.

MANAGING STRESS

There are four main reasons why organizations should take account of stress and do something about it:

1. They have the social responsibility to provide a good quality of working life.
2. Excessive stress causes illness.
3. Stress can result in inability to cope with the demands of the job, which, of course, creates more stress.
4. Excessive stress can reduce employee effectiveness and therefore organizational performance.

The ways in which stress can be managed by an organization include:

- *job design* – clarifying roles, reducing the danger of role ambiguity and conflict and giving people more autonomy within a defined structure to manage their responsibilities;
- *targets and performance standards* – setting reasonable and achievable targets which may stretch people but do not place impossible burdens on them;
- *placement* – taking care to place people in jobs that are within their capabilities;
- *career development* – planning careers and promoting staff in accordance with their capabilities, taking care not to over- or under-promote;
- *performance management processes*, which allow a dialogue to take place between managers and individuals about the latter's work, problems and ambitions;
- *counselling* – giving individuals the opportunity to talk about their problems with a member of the personnel department or the company medical officer, or through an employee assistance programme;
- *management training* in performance review and counselling techniques and in what managers can do to alleviate their own stress and reduce it in others;
- *work–life balance policies* which take account of the pressures on employees who have responsibilities as parents, partners or carers, and which can include such provisions as special leave and flexible working hours.

ACCIDENT PREVENTION

The prevention of accidents is achieved by:

- identifying the causes of accidents and the conditions under which they are most likely to occur;

- taking account of safety factors at the design stage – building safety into the system;
- designing safety equipment and protective devices and providing protective clothing;
- carrying out regular risk assessments audits, inspections and checks and taking action to eliminate risks;
- investigating all accidents resulting in damage to establish the cause and to initiate corrective action;
- maintaining good records and statistics in order to identify problem areas and unsatisfactory trends;
- conducting a continuous programme of education and training on safe working habits and methods of avoiding accidents;
- leadership and motivation – encouraging methods of leadership and motivation that do not place excessive demands on people.

MEASURING HEALTH AND SAFETY PERFORMANCE

The saying that 'if you can't measure it you can't manage it' is totally applicable to health and safety. It is essential to know what is happening, and it is even more essential to measure trends as a means of identifying in good time where actions are necessary.

The most common measures are:

- *The frequency rate:*

$$\frac{\text{Number of injuries} \times 100,000}{\text{Number of hours worked}}$$

- *The incidence rate:*

$$\frac{\text{Number of injuries} \times 1,000}{\text{Average number employed during the period}}$$

- *The severity rate* – the days lost through accidents or occupation health problems per 1,000,000 hours worked.

  Some organizations adopt a 'total loss control' approach which covers the cost of accidents to the business under such headings as pay to people off work, damage to plant or equipment and loss of production. A cost severity rate can then be calculated, which is the total cost of accidents per 1,000,000 hours worked.

COMMUNICATING THE NEED FOR BETTER HEALTH AND SAFETY PRACTICES

As Holt and Andrews (1993) observe, various forms of propaganda selling the health and safety message have been used for many years, although: 'They are now widely felt to be of little value in measurable terms in changing behaviour and influencing attitudes to health and safety issues.' But they believe that it is still necessary to deliver the message that health and safety is important as long as this supplements rather than replaces other initiatives. They suggest that the following steps can be taken to increase the effectiveness of safety messages:

- *Avoid negatives* – successful safety propaganda should contain positive messages, not warnings of the unpleasant consequences of actions.
- *Expose correctly* – address the message to the right people at the point of danger.
- *Use attention-getting techniques carefully* – lurid images may only be remembered for what they are, not for the message they are trying to convey.
- *Maximize comprehension* – messages should be simple and specific.
- *Messages must be believable* – they should address real issues and be perceived as being delivered by people (ie. managers) who believe in what they say and are doing something about it.
- *Messages must point the way to action* – the most effective messages call for positive actions that can be achieved by the receivers and will offer them a tangible benefit.

Approaches to briefing staff on the importance of health and safety

Advice to a group of staff on the importance of health and safety in the workplace must be based on a thorough understanding of the organization's health and safety policies and procedures and an appreciation of the particular factors affecting the health and safety of the group of people concerned. The latter can be based on information provided by risk assessments, safety audits and accident reports. But the advice must be positive – why health and safety is important and how accidents can be prevented. The advice should not be over-weighted by awful warnings.

The points to be made include:

- a review of the health and safety policies of the organization with explanations of the reasoning behind them and a positive statement of management's belief that health and safety is a major consideration because (1) it directly affects the well-being of all concerned; and (2) it can, and does, minimize suffering and loss;
- a review of the procedures used by the organization for the business as a whole and in the particular area to assess risks and audit safety position;
- an explanation of the roles of the members of the group in carrying out their work safely and giving full consideration to the safety of others;
- a reiteration of the statement that one of the core values of the organization is the maintenance of safe systems of work and the promotion of safe working practices.

HEALTH AND SAFETY TRAINING

Health and safety training is a key part of the preventative programme. It should start as part of the induction course. It should also take place following a transfer to a new job or a change in working methods. Safety training spells out the rules and provides information on potential hazards and how to avoid them. Further refresher training should be provided and special courses laid on to deal with new aspects of health and safety or areas in which safety problems have emerged.

ORGANIZING HEALTH AND SAFETY

Health and safety concerns everyone in an establishment although the main responsibility lies with management in general and individual managers in particular. The specific roles are summarized below:

- *Management* develops and implements health and safety policies and ensures that procedures for carrying out risk assessments, safety audits and inspections are implemented. Importantly, management has the duty of monitoring and evaluating health and safety performance and taking corrective action as necessary.
- *Managers* can exert the greater influence on health and safety. They are in immediate control and it is up to them to keep a constant watch for unsafe conditions or practices and to take immediate action. They are also directly responsible for ensuring that employees are conscious of health and safety hazards and do not take risks.

- *Employees* should be aware of what constitutes safe working practices as they affect them and their fellow workers. While management and managers have the duty to communicate and train, individuals also have the duty to take account of what they have heard and learned in the ways they carry out their work.
- *Health and safety advisers* advise on policies and procedures and on healthy and safe methods of working. They conduct risk assessments and safety audits and investigations into accidents in conjunction with managers and health and safety representatives, maintain statistics and report on trends and necessary actions.
- *Medical advisers* have two functions: preventive and clinical. The preventive function is most important, especially on occupational health matters. The clinical function is to deal with industrial accidents and diseases and to advise on the steps necessary to recover from injury or illness arising from work. They do not usurp the role of the family doctor in non-work-related illnesses.
- *Safety committees* consisting of health and safety representatives advise on health and safety policies and procedures, help in conducting risk assessments and safety audits, and make suggestions on improving health and safety performance.

54

Welfare services

Welfare services may be provided for matters concerning employees which are not immediately connected with their jobs although they may be connected generally with their place of work. These matters will include individual services relating to employees' welfare such as private help with counselling on personal problems, assistance with problems of health or sickness and special services for retired employees. Group services may include the provision of social and sporting activities and restaurants. Child-care facilities may be provided for individual employees but on a collective basis.

WHY PROVIDE WELFARE SERVICES?

There are arguments against the provision of welfare services. They imply do-gooding and the personnel management fraternity has spent many years trying to shake off its association with what it, and others, like to think of as at best peripheral and at worst redundant welfare activities. Welfare is provided by the state services – why should industrial, commercial or public sector organizations duplicate what is already there? The private affairs of employees and their out-of-work interests should not be the concern of their employers. It is selfish to maintain large playing fields and erect huge sports pavilions if they are going to be used by a minute proportion of staff for a very limited period of time – the space and facilities could be better used by the community. The argument that the provision of employee welfare services increases the loyalty and motivation of employees has long been exploded. If such services are used at all, they are taken for granted. Gratitude, even if it exists, is not a motivating factor.

The case against employee welfare services is formidable; the last point is particularly telling and there is some truth in each of the others – although there are limitations to their validity. State welfare services are, in theory, available to all, but the ability of social workers to give individual advice, especially on problems arising from work, is limited in terms of both time and knowledge. It is all too easy for people to fall into the cracks existing in the decaying edifice of the welfare state.

The case for providing employee services rests mainly on the abstract grounds of the social responsibility of organizations for those who work in them. This is not paternalism in the Victorian sense – turkeys at Christmas – nor in the traditional Japanese sense, where the worker's whole life centres on the employer. Rather, it is simply the realization that in exchange for offering their services, employees are entitled to rather more than their pay, benefits and healthy and safe systems of work. They are also entitled to consideration as human beings, especially when it is remembered that many of their personal problems arise in the context of work and are best dealt with there. People's worries and the resulting stress may well arise from work and their concerns about security, money, health, and relationships with others. But they also bring their personal problems to work; and many of these cannot be solved without reference to the situation there – they may require time off to deal with sick children or partners, or care for relatives, or advice on how to solve their problems and so minimize interference with their work.

The argument for employee welfare services at work was well put by Martin (1967):

> Staff spend at least half their waking time at work or in getting to it or leaving it. They know they contribute to the organization when they are reasonably free from worry, and they feel, perhaps inarticulately, that when they are in trouble they are due to get something back from the organization. People are entitled to be treated as full human beings with personal needs, hopes and anxieties; they are employed as people; they bring themselves to work, not just their hands, and they cannot readily leave their troubles at home.

The social argument for employee welfare services is the most compelling one, but there is also an economic argument. Increases in morale or loyalty may not result in commensurate or, indeed, in any increases in productivity, but undue anxiety can result in reduced effectiveness. Even if welfare services cannot increase individual productivity, they can help to minimize decreases. Herzberg's two-factor model, in effect, placed welfare among the hygiene factors, but he did not underestimate the importance of 'hygiene' as a means of eliminating or at least reducing causes of anxiety or dissatisfaction.

A further practical argument in favour of employee welfare services is that a reputation for showing concern helps to improve the image of the firm as a good employer and thus assists in recruitment. Welfare may not directly increase productivity, but it may increase commitment and help in the retention of key employees.

A strong case for employee welfare services therefore exists, and the real question is not 'Why welfare?' but 'What sort of welfare?' This question needs to be answered in general terms before discussing the type of welfare services that can be provided and how they should be organized.

WHAT SORT OF WELFARE SERVICES?

Welfare services fall into two categories:

- individual or personal services in connection with sickness, bereavement, domestic problems, employment problems, and elderly and retired employees;
- group services, which consist of sports and social activities, clubs for retired staff and benevolent organizations.

Principles of personal casework

Individual services require personal casework, and the most important principle to adopt is that this work should aim to help individuals to help themselves. The employer, manager or personnel specialist should not try to stand between individuals and their problems by taking them out of their hands. Emergency action may sometimes have to be taken on behalf of individuals, but, if so, it should be taken in such a way that they can later cope with their own difficulties. Welfare action must start on the basis that disengagement will take place at the earliest possible moment when individuals can, figuratively, stand on their own two feet. This does not mean that follow-up action is unnecessary, but it is only to check that things are going according to plan, not to provide additional help unless something is seriously wrong.

Personal services should be provided when a need is established, and a welfare need exists where it is clear that help is required, that it cannot be given more effectively from another source, and that the individual is likely to benefit from the services that can be offered.

In an organizational setting, an essential element in personal casework services is confidentiality. There is no point in offering help or advice to people if they think that their personal problems are going to be revealed to others, possibly to the detriment of their future careers. This is the argument for having specialized welfare officers in organizations large enough to be able to afford them. They can be detached in a way that line managers and even personnel managers cannot be.

Principles for providing group services

Group services, such as sports or social clubs, should not be laid on because they are 'good for morale'. There is no evidence that they are. They are costly and should be provided only if there is a real need and demand for them, arising from a very strong community spirit in a company or lack of local facilities. In the latter case, the facilities should be shared in an agreed and controlled way with the local community.

INDIVIDUAL SERVICES

Sickness

These services aim to provide help and advice to employees absent from work for long periods because of illness. The practical reason for providing them is that they should help to speed the return of the employee to work, although it is not part of the employee services function to check up on possible malingerers. The social reason is to provide employees with support and counsel where a need exists. In this context, a need exists where employees cannot help themselves without support and where such aid is not forthcoming from the state medical or welfare services or the employees' own families.

Needs can be established by keeping in touch with an absent employee. This should be not done by rushing round as soon as anyone has been absent for more than, say, 10 days or has exhausted sickness benefit from work. It is generally better to write to sick absentees, expressing general concern and good wishes for a speedy recovery and reminding them that the firm can provide help if they wish, or simply asking them if they would like someone to visit them – with a stamped, addressed envelope for their reply. Such letters should preferably be sent by the employee's line manager.

There will be some cases where the employee is reluctant to request help or a visit, and the company may have to decide whether a visit should be made to establish if help is required. This will be a matter of judgement based on the known facts about employees and their circumstances.

Visits can be made by the line manager, a personnel officer, or a specialized full- or part-time sick visitor. Some organizations use retired employees for this purpose. Alternatively, arrangements can be made for a colleague to pay the visit. The aims of the visit should be, first, to show employees that their firm and colleagues are concerned about their welfare; second, to alleviate any loneliness they may feel; and, third, to provide practical advice or help. The latter may consist of putting them in touch with suitable organizations or ensuring that such organizations are informed and take action. Or more immediate help may be provided to deal with pressing domestic problems.

Bereavement

Bereavement is a time when many people need all the help and advice they can get. The state welfare services may not be able to assist and families are often non-existent or unhelpful. Established welfare organizations in industry, commerce or the public sector attach a lot of importance to this service. The advice may often be no more than putting the bereaved employee or the widow or widower of an employee in touch with the right organizations, but it is often extended to help with funeral arrangements and dealing with will and probate matters.

Domestic problems

Domestic problems seem the least likely area for employee welfare services. Why should the company intervene, even when asked, in purely private matters? If, for example, employees get into debt, that is surely their own affair. What business is it of the company?

These are fair questions. But employers who have any real interest in the well-being of staff cannot ignore appeals for help. The assistance should not consist of bailing people out of debt whenever they get into trouble, or acting as an amateur marriage guidance or family casework officer. But, in accordance with the basic principle of personnel casework already mentioned, employees can be counselled on how to help themselves or where to go for expert advice. A counselling service could be provided by company staff or through an employee assistance programme (see page 842). It can do an immense amount of good simply by providing an opportunity for employees to talk through their problems with a disinterested person. The help can be provided either through internal counselling services or by means of employee assistance programmes as described later in this chapter.

There is indeed a limit to how much can or should be done in the way of allowing employees to pour out their troubles but, used with discretion, it is a valuable service.

Employment problems

Employment problems should normally be solved by discussion between the individual and his or her manager or team leader, or through the company's grievance procedure. There may be times, however, when employees have problems over interpersonal relations, or feelings of inadequacy, about which they want to talk to a third party. Such counselling talks, as a means of relieving feelings and helping people to work through their problems for themselves, can do a lot of good, but extreme caution must be displayed by any company officials who are involved. They must not cut across line management authority, but, at the same time, they must preserve the confidentiality of the discussion. It is a delicate business, and where it affects relationships between individuals and their managers, it is one in which the giving of advice can be dangerous. The most that can be done is to provide a counselling service which gives employees an opportunity to talk about their problems and allows the counsellor to suggest actions the employee can take to put things right. Counsellors must not comment on the actions of anyone else who is involved. They can comment only on what the employee who seeks their help is doing or might do.

Elderly and retired employees

Employee services for elderly employees are primarily a matter of preparing them for retirement and dealing with any problems they have in coping with their work. Preparation for retirement is a valuable service that many firms offer. This may be limited to advising on the classes and facilities local authorities provide for people prior to retirement, or when they have retired, or it may be extended to running special pre-retirement courses held during working hours.

Some companies have made special provision for elderly employees by setting aside jobs or work areas for them. This has its dangers. Treating employees as special cases ahead of their time may make them over-aware of their condition or too dependent on the services provided for them. There is much to be said for treating elderly employees as normal workers, even though the health and safety services may take particular care to ensure that the age of the worker does not increase the danger of accident or industrial disease.

Retired employees, particularly those with long service, deserve the continuing interest of their former employer. The interest need not be oppressive, but continuing sick visiting can be carried out, and social occasions can be provided for them.

GROUP WELFARE SERVICES

Group employee services mainly consist of restaurants, sports and social clubs, and nursery facilities, although some companies still support various benevolent societies which provide additional help and finance in times of need.

Company restaurant facilities are obviously desirable in any reasonably sized establishment where there is relatively little choice of facilities in the vicinity. Alternatively, luncheon vouchers can be provided.

A massive investment in sports facilities is usually of doubtful value unless there is nothing else in the neighbourhood and, in accordance with the principles mentioned earlier, the company is prepared to share its facilities with the local community. In a large company in a large town, it is very difficult to develop feelings of loyalty towards the company teams or to encourage people to use the sports club. Why should they support an obscure side when their loyalties have always been directed to the local club? Why should they travel miles when they have perfectly adequate facilities near at hand? Such clubs are usually supported by small cliques who have little or no influence over the feelings of other employees, who leave the enthusiasts to get on with whatever they are doing.

The same argument applies to social clubs, especially those run by paternalistic companies. It is different when they arise spontaneously from the needs of employees. If they want to club together, then the company should say good luck to them and provide them with a reasonable amount of support. The subsidy, however, should not be complete. The clubs should generate their own funds as well as their own enthusiasm. Facilities can be provided within the firm's premises if they are needed and readily available. An investment in special facilities should be made only if there is a real likelihood of their being used regularly by a large proportion of employees. This is an area where prior consultation, before setting up the facility, and self-government, when it has been established, are essential.

Child care or nursery facilities (creches) have obvious value as a means of attracting and retaining parents who would not otherwise be able to work on a full or part-time basis.

PROVISION OF EMPLOYEE WELFARE SERVICES

It seems obvious that the personnel department should provide employee welfare services. Inevitably, personnel staff will be dealing with cases and providing advice because they are in constant contact with employees and may be seen to be disinterested. It is to be hoped that they will also have some expertise in counselling.

Increasingly, however, it is being recognized that employee welfare is the responsibility of line management and supervision. If the latter take on their proper role as team leaders rather than their traditional autocratic and directive role, they should be close enough to each member of their team to be aware of any personal problems affecting their work. They should be trained in identifying symptoms and at least be able to refer people for counselling if it is clear that they need more help than the team leader can provide.

Employee welfare services can be provided for either internally by means of a counselling service or externally through an agency which runs employee assistance programmes (EAPs).

INTERNAL COUNSELLING SERVICES

Internal counselling services can be provided by full-time staff or volunteers who may work on a part-time basis. No specific academic qualifications are required for this work, but those carrying it out should be carefully assessed for suitable and relevant experience and they should have undergone extended training in counselling methods.

EMPLOYEE ASSISTANCE PROGRAMMES

Employee assistance programmes (EAPs) originated in the US in the 1960s. The idea was slow to catch on in the UK, but it is now becoming more accepted.

There are a number of external agencies which provide EAP services. They offer, on a contractual basis, a 24-hour phone service giving employees and their families access to counselling on a range of problems including stress, alcohol and drug abuse, marital breakdown and financial and legal problems. Most services identify the problem and arrange for a relevant specialist to phone back, although face-to-face counselling may also be offered, either at local offices or at surgeries on company premises. In addition, employers may refer employees direct to the service. Where long-term treatment relating to alcohol and drug problems or psychological problems is needed, employees are referred to state services.

Confidentiality is guaranteed by all EAPs to users, although employers are usually provided with a periodic statistical report on take-up of the service, which may be broken down by sex, seniority, department or type of problem. Advocates of the programmes argue that the anonymity they offer makes them particularly suitable for use in this country since it helps overcome the traditional British reluctance to discuss personal matters. Larger EAP providers offer clients the option of reports on average statistics based on work for comparable companies. Additional services include workplace seminars on problems identified as particularly prevalent, training of managers and personnel staff and related literature. The service may be charged for at a per capita rate or according to take-up, which can be as much as 25 per cent of the workforce.

Part XIII

Employment and HR services

This handbook emphasizes the importance of strategic considerations in formulating HR policies and planning HR programmes to achieve defined objectives. The fact remains, however, that much of human resource management is about managing the employment relationship and dealing with the problems that will always arise when people work together, as considered in Chapter 54.

This also includes the various employment policies and procedures and approaches needed to ensure that both employees and the organization feel that their needs are being satisfied, as discussed in Chapter 55.

Organizations also need to maintain a comprehensive HR information system, not only to maintain employee records but also, and importantly, to build a computerized database which will assist in strategic decision taking. This is covered in Chapter 57.

Part XIII

Employment and HR services

55

Employment practices

Employment practices should be concerned with fundamental aspects of the employment relationship as expressed in the organization's HR policies and procedures. They should take account of the requirements of relevant UK and European legislation and case law, which it is beyond the scope of the handbook to cover in detail. Recent Acts and Regulations which are important include those concerning the minimum wage, working time and part-time workers. The last of these is especially significant because it requires that part-time workers should be entitled to the same terms and conditions as full-time workers, including pro rata pay.

Note should also be taken of the UK Human Rights Act (1998) which gave further effect to rights and freedoms guaranteed under the European Convention on Human Rights. However, the rights are essentially civil and political rather than economic or social rights, and they only apply to a narrow range of employment. Moreover, they are not directly enforceable against an employer unless it is an 'obvious' public authority. It has, however, been held by the European Court of Human Rights that statutory rights should not be unlawfully dismissed or discriminated against as they can be regarded as 'civil rights'. Provisions inserted into the Employment Rights Act must be interpreted by employment tribunals in a way that is compatible with the European Convention right to freedom of expression. This could apply to whistle-blowing.

Employment practices need to be established in the following areas as described in this chapter:

- terms and conditions and contracts of employment;
- mobility clauses;
- transfer practices (including transfer between undertakings);
- promotion practices;
- attendance management;
- equal opportunity and ethnic monitoring;
- managing diversity;
- data protection;
- age and employment;
- sexual harassment;
- smoking;
- bullying;
- substance abuse at work;
- AIDS;
- dress codes;
- use of e-mails.

Administrative procedures for dealing with the legal requirements for maternity leave and pay and sick pay will also have to be developed.

TERMS AND CONDITIONS AND CONTRACTS OF EMPLOYMENT

Terms and conditions of employment which apply generally or to groups of employees need to be defined in the areas included in the contract of employment as described below.

Individual contracts of employment must satisfy the provisions of contracts of employment legislation. They include a statement of the capacity in which the person is employed and the name or job title of the individual to whom he or she is responsible. They also include details of pay, allowances, hours, holidays, leave and pension arrangements and refer to relevant company policies, procedures and rules. Increasing use is being made of fixed-term contracts.

The basic information that should be included in a written contract of employment varies according to the level of job, but the following check list sets out the typical headings:

- job title;
- duties, preferably including a flexibility clause such as: 'The employee will perform such duties and will be responsible to such person, as the company may from time to time require', and, in certain cases: 'The employee will work at different locations as required by the company.'
- the date when continuous employment starts and basis for calculating service;
- the rate of pay, allowances, overtime and shift rates, method and timing of payment;
- hours of work including lunch break and overtime and shift arrangements;
- holiday arrangements:
    - days paid holiday per year;
    - calculation of holiday pay;
    - qualifying period;
    - accrual of holidays and holiday pay;
    - details of holiday year;
    - dates when holidays can be taken;
    - maximum holiday that can be taken at any one time;
    - carry-over of holiday entitlement;
    - public holidays.
- sickness:
    - pay for time lost;
    - duration of sickness payments;
    - deductions of National Insurance benefits;
    - termination due to continued illness;
    - notification of illness (medical certificate);
- length of notice due to and from employee;
- grievance procedure (or reference to it);
- disciplinary procedure (or reference to it);
- works rules (or reference to them);
- arrangements for terminating employment;
- arrangements for union membership (if applicable);
- special terms relating to rights to patents and designs, confidential information and restraints on trade after termination of employment;
- employer's right to vary terms of the contract subject to proper notification being given.

MOBILITY CLAUSES

Case law has established that employers can invoke mobility clauses which specify that the employee must work in any location as required by the employer as long as that discretion is exercised reasonably and not in such a way as to prevent the employee being able to carry out his or her part of the contract. A mobility clause could, however, be held to discriminate against women, who may not be in a position to move (*Meade-Hill and another vs British Council*, 1995). The acid test is whether or not the employer acts reasonably.

TRANSFER PRACTICES

Flexibility and redeployment in response to changing or seasonal demands for labour is a necessary feature of any large enterprise. The clumsy handling of transfers by management, however, can do as much long-lasting harm to the climate of employee relations as ill-considered managerial actions in any other sphere of personnel practice.

Management may be compelled to move people in the interests of production. But in making the move, managers should be aware of the fears of those affected in order that they can be alleviated as much as possible.

The basic fear will be of change itself – a fear of the unknown and of the disruption of a well-established situation: work, pay, environment, colleagues and workmates, and travelling arrangements. There will be immediate fears that the new work will make additional and unpalatable demands for extra skill or effort. There will be concern about loss of earnings because new jobs have to be tackled or because of different pay scales or bonus systems. Loss of overtime opportunities or the danger of shift or night work may also arouse concern.

Transfer policies should establish the circumstances when employees can be transferred and the arrangements for pay, resettlement and retraining. If the transfer is at the company's request and to suit the convenience of the company, it is normal to pay the employee's present rate or the rate for the new job, whichever is higher. This policy is easiest to apply in temporary transfers. It may have to be modified in the case of long-term or permanent transfers to eliminate the possibility of a multi-tiered pay structure emerging in the new location, which must cause serious dissatisfaction among those already employed there.

When transfers are made to avoid redundancy in the present location, the rate for the job in the new department should be paid. Employees affected in this way would, of course, be given the choice between being made redundant or accepting a lower-paid job.

The policies should also provide guidelines on how requests from employees for transfer should be treated. The normal approach should be to give a sympathetic hearing to such requests from long-serving employees, especially if the transfer is wanted for health or family reasons. But the transferred employees would have to accept the rate for the job in their new department.

The procedures for handling transfers may have to include joint consultation or discussions with workers' representatives on any major transfer programme. If regular transfers take place because of seasonal changes, it is best to establish a standard procedure for making transfers which would be managed by department supervisors, but they should be made aware of company policies and procedures and the need to treat the human problems involved with care and consideration.

The Transfer of Undertakings (Protection of Employment) Regulations 1981 (TUPE) provided that, following a business transfer arising from a merger or acquisition, all employees working in the business to be transferred automatically transfer into the employment of the merged business or the business making the acquisition. Following the transfer, they retain their existing terms and conditions of employment except for pensions. Employers have to give information about the business transfer to a recognized trade union.

PROMOTION PRACTICES

The aims of the promotion procedures of a company should be, first, to enable management to obtain the best talent available within the company to fill more senior posts and, second, to provide employees with the opportunity to advance their careers within the company, in accordance with the opportunities available (taking into account equal opportunity policies) and their own abilities.

In any organization where there are frequent promotional moves and where promotion arrangements cause problems, it is advisable to have a promotion policy and procedure which is known to both management and employees and this procedure should take full account of equal opportunity policies (it is often incorporated in equal opportunity policy statements). The basic points that should be included in such a procedure are:

● Promotion vacancies should be notified to the personnel department.
● Vacancies should be advertised internally.
● Departmental managers should not be allowed to refuse promotions within a reasonable time unless the individual has been in the department for less than, say, one year, or the department has recently suffered heavy losses through promotions or transfers.

- Promotion opportunities should be open to all, irrespective of race, creed, sex or marital status.

ATTENDANCE MANAGEMENT

Attendance management is the process of minimizing lateness and absenteeism. The traditional method was to require hourly paid wage earners to clock on, and to deduce pay for lateness or unauthorized absence. There is now an increasing tendency to harmonize conditions of employment by granting full staff terms and conditions to manual workers, which includes payment when absent from work. Some 'single-status' organizations require all employees to clock on; others have abolished clocking on altogether. Whether or not harmonization has taken place or clocking on is in operation, it is still necessary to control lateness and absenteeism.

Timekeeping

The best approach to the control of timekeeping is to give team leaders the responsibility for maintaining control overall. They keep the records (which might be computerized) and take whatever action is required if the trust bestowed on employees is abused. In serious cases this could mean pay deductions and, ultimately, more stringent disciplinary action. But it is the responsibility of the team leader to exercise leadership and develop the team spirit which will minimize such actions.

Causes of absence

The causes of absence have been analysed by Huczynski and Fitzpatrick (1989) under three headings: job situation factors, personal factors and attendance factors.

Job situation factors

Job situation factors include:

- Job scope – a high degree of task repetitiveness is associated with absenteeism although job dissatisfaction itself is a contributory rather than a primary cause of absence.
- Stress – it is estimated that 40 million working days are lost each year in

the UK through stress. This can be attributed to workload, poor working conditions, shift work, role ambiguity or conflict, relationships and organizational climate.

- Frequent job transfers increase absenteeism.
- Management style — the quality of management, especially immediate supervisors, affects the level of absenteeism.
- Physical working conditions.
- Work group size — the larger the organization, the higher the absence rate.

Personal factors

- Employee values – for some workers, doing less work for the same reward improves the deal made with the employer (the effort-reward bargain). The following positive outcomes of absence have been shown by research to be particularly important to employees: break from routine, leisure time, dealing with personal business and a break from co-workers.
- Age – younger employees are more frequently absent than older ones.
- Sex – women are more prone to sickness absence than men.
- Personality – some people are absence-prone (studies have noted that between 5 and 10 per cent of workers account for about half of the total absence, while a few are never absent at all).

Attendance factors

Attendance factors include:

- Reward systems — as pay increases, attendance improves.
- Sick pay schemes may increase absenteeism.
- Work group norms can exert pressure for or against attendance.

Control of absenteeism

Absenteeism can be disruptive and costly. It needs to be controlled. The steps required to achieve effective absence control are:
- *commitment* on the part of management to reduce the cost of absenteeism;
- *trust* – the control of absenteeism is also best carried out on the basis that employees are to be trusted – companies that are operating on this basis provide sickness benefit for all workers and rely upon the commitment and motivation of their employees (which they work hard at achieving) to minimize abuse, but they

reserve the right to review sickness benefit if the level of sickness absence is unacceptable;

- *information* – sadly, a trusting approach will not necessarily work and hard, accurate information on absence is required – this can be provided by computerized systems;
- *a documented attendance policy* which spells out the organization's views on absenteeism and the rules for sick pay;
- *regular training for managers and team leaders* which ensures that they are aware of their responsibilities for controlling absenteeism and indicates the actions they can take;
- *getting managers to conduct return-to-work interviews* to welcome employees back and, if appropriate, enquire about the cause of absence and what can be done by the employee or the manager to reduce future occurrences;
- *communications* which inform employees why absence control is important;
- *counselling* for employees at return-to-work interviews which provides advice on any attendance problems they may have and creates trust;
- *disciplinary procedure* – this must be operated fairly and consistently.

EQUAL OPPORTUNITY

Equal opportunity policies were considered in Chapter 20. To get them into action the following are the key steps as set out in the Chartered Institute of Personnel and Development's code of conduct:

1. *The recruitment process*:
   - have accurate, up-to-date job descriptions which are not sex biased;
   - avoid over-inflated job criteria in person specifications;
   - check that job requirements are really necessary to the job and are not a reflection of traditional biased practices;
   - guard against sex/race stereotyping in advertisements and recruitment literature.
2. *The interview – to reduce interview bias*:
   - provide training to all who conduct selection interviews;
   - ensure that only trained interviewers conduct preliminary interviews;
   - avoid discriminatory questions, although interviews can discuss with applicants any domestic or personal circumstances which might have an adverse effect on job performance as long as this is done without making assumptions based on the sex of the applicant.

3. *Training*:
   - check that women and men have equal opportunities to participate in training and development programmes;
   - take late entrants into training schemes;
   - ensure that selection criteria for training do not discriminate against women;
   - consider using positive training provisions for women and ethnic minorities.
4. *Promotion*:
   - improve performance review procedures to minimize bias;
   - avoid perpetuating the effects of past discriminatory practices in selection for promotion;
   - do not presume that women or minorities do not want promotion.

ETHNIC MONITORING

The Commission for Racial Equality's (CRE) guide on ethnic monitoring recommends that analyses of the workforce should be conducted in sufficient detail to show whether there is an under-representation in more skilled jobs and grades, as well as whether there are general concentrations of ethnic minority employees in certain jobs, levels or departments in the organization. The Chartered Institute of Personnel and Development Equal Opportunities Code states that the most important processes to monitor are recruitment and selection since these are easily influenced by prejudice or indirect discrimination. But the proportion of ethnic minorities at different levels in the organization should also be checked regularly.

The CRE has suggested that ethnic monitoring should collect employment information under the following ethnic classifications:

- white;
- black-Caribbean;
- black-African;
- black-other;
- Indian;
- Pakistani;
- Bangladeshi;
- Chinese;
- other (those describing themselves in this category should be invited to provide further information).

The results of ethnic monitoring should be used to establish whether:

- in comparison with the workforce as a whole, or in comparison with the local labour market, ethnic minority workers are significantly under- or over-represented in any area;
- representative numbers of ethnic minorities apply for and are accepted for jobs;
- higher or lower proportions of employees from ethnic minorities leave the organization;
- there are any disparities in the proportion of members of ethnic minorities.

If necessary, positive affirmative action, as recommended by the CRE, can be taken along the following lines:

- job advertisements designed to reach members of under-represented groups;
- the use of employment agencies and careers offices in areas where these groups are concentrated;
- recruitment and training for school leavers designed to reach members of these groups;
- encouragement of employees from these groups to apply for promotion or transfer opportunities;
- training for promotion or skill training for employees of these groups who lack particular expertise but show potential.

MANAGING DIVERSITY

As described by Kandola and Fullerton (1994):

> The basic concept of managing diversity accepts that the workforce consists of a diverse population of people. The diversity consists of visible and non-visible differences which will include factors such as sex, age, background, race, disability, personality and work-style. It is founded on the premise that harnessing these differences will create a productive environment in which everybody feels valued, where their talents are being fully utilized and in which organizational goals are met.

Managing diversity is about ensuring that all people maximize their potential and their contribution to the organization. It means valuing diversity, that is, valuing the differences between people and the different qualities they bring to their jobs which can lead to the development of a more rewarding and productive environment.

The International Distillers and Vintners statement on managing diversity as quoted by Kandola and Fullerton explains that:

> Managing diversity is about managing people who are not like you, and who do not necessarily aspire to be like you. It is about having management skill to allow their different perspectives and views to improve the quality of your decisions.

Kandola and Fullerton also quote the following 10 most successful initiatives adopted by organizations who are pursuing diversity policies:

1. introducing equal rights and benefits for part-time workers (compared with full-time workers);
2. allowing flexibility in uniform/dress requirements;
3. allowing time off for caring for dependants beyond that required by law, eg extended maternity/paternity leave;
4. benefits provided for employees' partners are equally available to same-sex and different-sex partners;
5. buying specialized equipment, eg braille keyboards;
6. employing helpers/signers for those who need them;
7. training trainers in equal opportunities;
8. eliminating age criteria from selection decisions;
9. providing assistance with child care;
10. allowing staff to take career breaks.

THE DATA PROTECTION ACT

The Data Protection Act (1998) is built round the eight data protection principles included in the 1984 Data Protection Act. The most important of these is that data should be accessible to the individuals concerned, who may, where appropriate, correct or erase them. The 1998 Act covers manually maintained records (eg filing systems) as well as records held on a computer database. It also places restrictions on the processing of sensitive data, which includes data on racial or ethnic origin, political opinions, religious beliefs, trade union membership, physical or mental health, sex life, and the commission or alleged commission of any offence. Under the Act, employees must give explicit consent to the processing of personal data, especially sensitive data.

AGE AND EMPLOYMENT

Recruitment, employment and training practices should take into account the following key facts about age and age discrimination as listed by the Chartered Institute of Personnel and Development:

- Age is a poor predictor of job performance.
- It is misleading to equate physical and mental ability with age.
- More of the population than ever before are living active, healthy lives as they get older.
- Age is rarely a genuine employment requirement.
- Society's attitudes may encourage compliance with outmoded personnel practices regarding recruitment, promotion, training, redundancy and retirement.
- Reduced self-confidence, self-esteem and motivation, together with loss or reduction of financial independence for individuals and their dependants, are some of the harmful effects of age discrimination.

SEXUAL HARASSMENT

Sadly, sexual harassment has always been a feature of life at work. Perhaps it is not always quite so blatant today as it has been in the past, but it is still there, in more or less subtle forms, and it is just as unpleasant.

Persons subject to harassment can take legal action but, of course, it must be the policy of the company to make it clear that it will not be tolerated.

Problems of dealing with harassment

The first problem always met in stamping out sexual harassment is that it can be difficult to make a clear-cut case. An accusation of harassment can be hard to prove unless there are witnesses. And those who indulge in this practice usually take care to carry it out on a one-to-one basis. In this situation, it may be a case of one person's word against another's. The harasser, almost inevitably a man, resorts to two defences: one, that it did not take place ('it was all in her mind'); and two, that if anything did take place, it was provoked by the behaviour of the female. In these situations, whoever deals with the case has to exercise judgement and attempt, difficult though it may be, to remove any prejudice in favour of the word of the man, the woman, the boss or the subordinate.

The second problem is that victims of sexual harassment are often unwilling to take action and in practice seldom do so. This is because of the actual or perceived difficulty of proving their case. But they may also feel that they will not get a fair hearing and are worried about the effect making such accusations will have on how they are treated by their boss or their colleagues in future – whether or not they will have substantiated their accusation.

The third and possibly the most deep-rooted and difficult problem of all is that sexual harassment can be part of the culture of the organization – a way of life, a 'norm', practised at all levels.

Solutions

There are no easy solutions to these problems. It may be very hard to eradicate sexual harassment completely. But an effort must be made to deal with it and the following approaches should be considered:

1. Issue a clear statement by the chief executive that sexual harassment will not be tolerated. The absolute requirement to treat all people equally, irrespective of sex, role, creed, sexual orientation or disability, should be one of the funda-mental values of the organization. This should be reinforced by the explicit condemnation of harassment as a direct and unacceptable contravention of that value.
2. Back up the value statement with a policy directive on sexual harassment which spells out in more detail how the company deplores it, why it is not acceptable and what people who believe they are being subjected to harassment can do about it.
3. Reinforce the value and policy statements by behaviour at senior level which demonstrates that they are not simply words but that these exhortations have meaning.
4. Ensure that the company's policy on harassment is stated clearly in induction courses and is conveyed to everyone in the form of a strong reminder on promo-tion.
5. Make arrangements for employees subjected to sexual harassment to be able to seek advice, support and counselling in total confidence without any obligation to take a complaint further. A counsellor can be designated to provide advice and assistance covering such functions as:
   - offering guidance on handling sexual harassment problems;
   - assisting in resolving problems informally by seeking, with the consent of the complainant, a confidential and voluntary interview with the person complained against in order to pursue a solution without resource to the formal disciplinary or grievance procedure;
   - assisting in submitting a grievance if the employee wishes to complain formally;

- securing an undertaking, where appropriate, by the person who is the subject of the complaint to stop the behaviour which has caused offence;
- counselling the parties as to their future conduct where a problem has been resolved without recourse to formal procedures.

6. Create a special procedure for hearing complaints about sexual harassment – the normal grievance procedure may not be suitable because the sexual harasser could be the employee's line manager. The procedure should provide for employees to bring their complaint to someone of their own sex, should they so choose.

7. Handle investigations of complaints with sensitivity and due respect for the rights of both the complainant and the accused. Ensure that hearings are conducted fairly, both parties being given an equal opportunity to put their case. The principles of natural justice mentioned earlier in this chapter should prevail. Care should be taken to ensure that the careers and reputations of neither party are unjustly affected.

8. Where sexual harassment has taken place, crack down on it. It should be stated in the policy that it is regarded as gross industrial misconduct and, if it is proved, makes the individual liable to instant dismissal. Less severe penalties may be reserved for minor cases but there should always be a warning that repetition will result in dismissal.

9. Ensure that everyone is aware that the organization does take action when required to punish those who indulge in sexual harassment.

10. Provide training to managers and team leaders to ensure that the policy is properly implemented and to make them aware of their direct responsibility to prevent harassment taking place and to take action if it does.

SMOKING

Smoking policies at work are designed to provide employees with a healthy and efficient workplace and to avoid conflict. A smoking policy should be developed in consultation with employees and may involve the use of an opinion survey. Most smokers agree to the right of non-smokers to work in air free from tobacco smoke. Smoking policies can involve a total ban on all smoking except, usually, in a smoking-permitted area away from the workplace. Remember that smokers do have some rights and that a ban in all areas may be oppressive. Sometimes, by agreement, there is a partial ban with separate working areas for those who wish to smoke. Kitchens and lifts are always non-smoking areas and rest rooms generally are.

It is sometimes appropriate to introduce smoking bans in stages, starting by restricting smoking in meeting rooms, corridors and canteens before extending the restriction to other communal and work areas.

SUBSTANCE ABUSE AT WORK

Substance abuse is the use of alcohol, drugs or other substances which cause difficulties at work such as absenteeism, low performance standards and interpersonal problems, for example, unpredictable reactions to criticism, paranoia, irritability, avoiding colleagues, borrowing money or physical or verbal abuse of colleagues. A policy on how to deal with incidents of substance abuse is necessary because:

- many employers have some employees with a drink problem and possibly a drug problem;
- substance abuse may be a result of work pressures, for which employers must take some responsibility;
- employers are required to maintain a safe and healthy work environment.

The Chartered Institute of Personnel and Development has produced guidelines for a substance-abuse policy which suggest that the following issues are the ones most likely to be covered:

- an assurance that employees identified as having abuse problems will be offered advice and other necessary assistance;
- any reasonable absence from work necessary to receive treatment will be granted under the organization's sickness scheme provided that there is full cooperation from the employee;
- an opportunity to discuss the matter once it has become evident or suspected that work performance is being affected by substance-related problems;
- the right to be accompanied at any discussion by a friend or employee representative;
- the right to full confidentiality;
- the provision of agencies to whom an employee can be referred for help or a commitment to provide the same expertise where employers operate their own treatment or counselling services;
- the safeguarding of all employment rights during any reasonable period of treatment, including the right, if proven capable, of returning to the same job or to suitable alternative employment;

- the links between substance-abuse policy and the disciplinary procedure;
- the policy to deal with subsequent recurrences (recurrences will be given due consideration and evaluated on their merits);
- the procedure for monitoring, evaluating and reviewing the policy;
- the designation of responsibilities for ensuring that the policy is carried out, and the selection of the person primarily responsible for its implementation;
- a commitment to an employee education programme, and a training programme for designated staff to provide them with the skills and knowledge necessary to carry out their duties under the policy.

BULLYING

Bullying is a form of harassment and can be very unpleasant. It is perhaps one of the most difficult aspects of employee relationship to control – it can be hard to prove that bullying has taken place and employees may be very reluctant to complain about a bullying boss, simply because he or she is a bully. But this does not mean that the organization should ignore the problem. A policy should be published which states that bullying constitutes unacceptable behaviour and indicating that those who indulge in the practice can face severe disciplinary action. It should be announced that anyone who is being bullied has the right to discuss the problem with someone in the HR department or lodge a complaint, and in such discussions employees should also have the right to be accompanied by a representative.

AIDS

There are no logical reasons why AIDS should be treated differently from any other disease that employees may be carrying, many of which are contagious and some of which are fatal. However, AIDS is a frightening and threatening disease which has received enormous publicity, not all of which has been accurate. Because of this fact it is necessary to develop a company policy, which might include the following points:

- The risks of infection through workplace contact are negligible.
- Where the occupation does involve blood contact as in laboratories, hospitals and doctors' surgeries, the special precautions advised by the Health and Safety Commission will be implemented.
- Employees who know that they are infected with HIV will not be obliged to disclose the fact to the company, but if they do, the fact will remain completely confidential.

- There will be no discrimination against anyone with, or at risk of acquiring, AIDS.
- Employees infected by HIV or suffering from AIDS will be treated no differently from anyone else suffering from a serious illness.

DRESS CODES

An employer can require employees to conform to a dress code as long as it is reasonable 'in accordance with the law'. In a recent European Court of Human Rights case (Kara v United Kingdom) affecting a British worker, it was held that:

> employers may require their employees to conform to certain requirements which are reasonably related to the type of work being undertaken, eg. safety helmets, hygienic covering uniforms. This may also involve requiring employees, who come into contact with the public or other organizations, to conform to a dress code which may be regarded as enhancing the employer's public image and facilitating its external contacts.

An Employment Appeals Tribunal case held in the UK (Boychack v Symons Holdings) ruled that it was within an employer's discretion to instruct an employee not to wear something that could be expected to be off-putting to other employees or to customers. If a company wants to impose a dress code it is best to spell it out as part of the terms and conditions of employment, for example in an employees' handbook.

E-MAILS

Increasingly, companies are cracking down on staff using e-mails at work for private purposes (eg online shopping), surfing the Internet, or sending pornographic e-mails through the company's intranet. Employers are concerned about the waste of time and money and the undesirability of pornographic or defamatory material being distributed round the office. They are often, therefore, introducing policies which state that the sending of offensive e-mails is prohibited and that the senders of such messages are subject to normal disciplinary procedures. They may also prohibit any browsing or downloading of material not related to the business, although this can be difficult to enforce. Some companies have always believed that reasonable use of the telephone is acceptable, and that policy may be extended to e-mails.

If it is decided that employees' e-mails should be monitored to check on excessive or unacceptable use, then this should be included in an e-mail policy which would therefore be part of the contractual arrangements. A policy statement could be included to the effect that: 'The company reserves the right to access and monitor all e-mail messages created, sent, received or stored on the company's system.'

The legal position needs to be considered. The Lawful Business Practice Regulations (2000) permit access to e-mails by employers as long as they have taken reasonable steps to inform the parties concerned. However, the Code of Practice issued by the Data Protection Commission suggests that employers should not check sites accessed by employees, but should clarify what can or cannot be downloaded. The Code also suggests that the term 'pornography' is not sufficiently precise, and the Commissioner does not believe that there needs to be a ban on downloading unsuitable material even if other employees find it offensive, and that employers should simply deal with cases as they arise. Many employers may find it difficult to accept this suggestion, but 'proportionality' is required in dealing with any problems, ie there may be situations when a dismissal for 'gross misconduct' is inappropriate, and employers should be aware that downloading unsuitable material can be done innocently.

56

Human resource management procedures

Human resource management procedures set out the ways in which certain actions concerning people should be carried out by the management or individual managers. In effect they constitute a formalized approach to dealing with specific matters of policy and practice. They should be distinguished from HR policies as described in Chapter 20. These describe the approach the organization adopts to various aspects of people management and define key aspects of the employment relationship. They serve as guidelines on people management practices but do not necessarily lay down precisely the steps that should be taken in particular situations. Procedures are more exacting. They state what *must* be done as well as spelling out how to do it. It is desirable to have the key HRM procedures written down to ensure that HR policies are applied consistently and in accordance with both legal requirements and ethical considerations. The existence of a written and well-publicized procedure ensures that everyone knows precisely what steps need to be taken when dealing with certain significant and possibly recurring employment issues.

The introduction or development of HR procedures should be carried out in consultation with employees and, where appropriate, their representatives. It is essential to brief everyone on how the procedures operate and they should be published either in an employee handbook or as a separate document. Line managers may need special training on how they should apply the procedures and the HR department should provide guidance wherever necessary. HR will normally have the responsibility of ensuring that procedures are followed consistently.

The main areas where procedures are required are those concerned with handling grievances and disciplinary, capability and redundancy issues.

GRIEVANCE PROCEDURE

Grievance procedures spell out the policy on handling grievances and the approach to dealing with them. An example of a grievance procedure is given below.

Grievance procedure

POLICY

It is the policy of the company that employees should:

- be given a fair hearing by their immediate supervisor or manager concerning any grievances they may wish to raise;
- have the right to appeal to a more senior manager against a decision made by their immediate supervisor or manager;
- have the right to be accompanied by a fellow employee of their own choice, when raising a grievance or appealing against a decision.

The aim of the procedure is to settle the grievance as nearly as possible to its point of origin.

PROCEDURE

The main stages through which a grievance may be raised are as follows:

1. The employee raises the matter with his or her immediate team leader or manager and may be accompanied by a fellow employee of his or her own choice.
2. If the employee is not satisfied with the decision, the employee requests a meeting with a member of management who is more senior than the team leader or manager who initially heard the grievance. This meeting takes place

---

within five working days of the request and is attended by the manager, the manager responsible for personnel, the employee appealing against the decision, and, if desired, his or her representative. The manager responsible for personnel records the result of the meeting in writing and issues copies to all concerned.

3.   If the employee is still not satisfied with the decision, he or she may appeal to the appropriate director. The meeting to hear this appeal is held within five working days of the request and is attended by the director, the manager responsible for personnel, the employee making the appeal, and, if desired, his or her representative. The manager responsible for personnel records the result of this meeting in writing and issues copies to all concerned.

DISCIPLINARY PROCEDURE

Disciplinary procedures set out the stages through which any disciplinary action should proceed. An example is given below.

Disciplinary procedure (part 1)

POLICY

It is the policy of the company that if disciplinary action has to be taken against employees it should:

● be undertaken only in cases where good reason and clear evidence exist;
● be appropriate to the nature of the offence that has been committed;
● be demonstrably fair and consistent with previous action in similar circumstances;
● take place only when employees are aware of the standards that are expected of them or the rules with which they are required to conform;
● allow employees the right to be represented by a representative or colleague during any formal proceedings;
● allow employees the right to know exactly what charges are being made against them and to respond to those charges;

- allow employees the right of appeal against any disciplinary action.

RULES

The company is responsible for ensuring that up-to-date rules are published and available to all employees.

PROCEDURE

The procedure is carried out in the following stages:

1. *Informal warning.* A verbal or informal warning is given to the employee in the first instance or instances of minor offences. The warning is administered by the employee's immediate team leader or manager.
2. *Formal warning.* A written formal warning is given to the employee in the first instance of more serious offences or after repeated instances of minor offences. The warning is administered by the employee's immediate team leader or manager – it states the exact nature of the offence and indicates any future disciplinary action which will be taken against the employee if the offence is repeated within a specified time limit. A copy of the written warning is placed in the employee's personnel record file but is destroyed 12 months after the date on which it was given, if the intervening service has been satisfactory. The employee is required to read and sign the formal warning and has the right to appeal to higher management if he or she thinks the warning is unjustified. The HR manager should be asked to advise on the text of the written warning.
3. *Further disciplinary action.* If, despite previous warnings, an employee still fails to reach the required standards in a reasonable period of time, it may become necessary to consider further disciplinary action. The action taken may be up to three days' suspension without pay, or dismissal. In either case the departmental manager should discuss the matter with the personnel manager before taking action. Staff below the rank of departmental manager may only recommend disciplinary action to higher management, except when their manager is not present (for example, on night-shift), when they may suspend the employee for up to one day pending an inquiry on the following day. Disciplinary action should not be confirmed until the appeal procedure has been carried out.

Disciplinary procedure (part 2)
SUMMARY DISMISSAL

An employee may be summarily dismissed (ie given instant dismissal without notice) only in the event of gross misconduct, as defined in company rules. Only departmental managers and above can recommend summary dismissal, and the action should not be finalized until the case has been discussed with the HR manager and the appeal procedure has been carried out. To enable this review to take place, employees should be suspended pending further investigation, which must take place within 24 hours.

APPEALS

In all circumstances, an employee may appeal against suspension, dismissal with notice, or summary dismissal. The appeal is conducted by a member of management who is more senior than the manager who initially administered the disciplinary action. The HR manager should also be present at the hearing. If he or she wishes, the employee may be represented at the appeal by a fellow employee of his or her own choice. Appeal against summary dismissal or suspension should be heard immediately. Appeals against dismissal with notice should be held within two days. No disciplinary action that is subject to appeal is confirmed until the outcome of the appeal.

If an appeal against dismissal (but not suspension) is rejected at this level, the employee has the right to appeal to the chief executive. The head of HR and, if required, the employee's representative should be present at this appeal.

CAPABILITY PROCEDURE

Some organizations deal with matters of capability under a disciplinary procedure, but there is a good case to be made for dealing with poor performance issues separately, leaving the disciplinary procedure to be invoked for situations such as poor timekeeping. An example of a capability procedure follows.

Capability procedure

POLICY

The company aims to ensure that performance expectations and standards are defined, performance is monitored and employees are given appropriate feedback, training and support to meet these standards.

Procedure

1. If a manager/team leader believes that an employee's performance is not up to standard an informal discussion will be held with the employee to try to establish the reason and to agree the actions required to improve performance by the employee and/or the manager/team leader. If, however:
    (a) it is agreed that the established standards are not reasonably attainable, they will be reviewed;
    (b) it is established that the performance problems are related to the employee's personal life, the necessary counselling/support will be provided;
    (c) it is decided that the poor performance emanates from a change in the organizations' standards, those standards will be explained to the employee and help will be offered to obtain conformity with the standards;
    (d) it is apparent that the poor performance constitutes misconduct, the disciplinary procedure will be invoked.
2. Should the employee show no (or insufficient) improvement over a defined period (weeks/months), a formal interview will be arranged with the employee (together with a representative if so desired). The aims of this interview will be to:
    (a) explain clearly the shortfall between the employee's performance and the required standard;
    (b) identify the cause(s) of the unsatisfactory performance and to determine what – if any – remedial treatment (eg training, retraining, support, etc) can be given;
    (c) obtain the employee's commitment to reaching that standard;
    (d) set a reasonable period for the employee to reach the standard and agree on a monitoring system during that period; and
    (e) tell the employee what will happen if that standard is not met.
    The outcome of this interview will be recorded in writing and a copy will be given to the employee.

3. At the end of the review period a further formal interview will be held, at which time:
    (a) if the required improvement has been made, the employee will be told of this and encouraged to maintain the improvement;
    (b) if some improvement has been made but the standard has not yet been met, the review period will be extended;
    (c) if there has been no discernible improvement this will be indicated to the employee and consideration will be given to whether there are alternative vacancies that the employee would be competent to fill; if there are, the employee will be given the option of accepting such a vacancy or being dismissed;
    (d) if such vacancies are available, the employee will be given full details of them in writing before being required to make a decision;
    (e) in the absence of suitable alternative work, the employee will be informed and invited to give his or her views on this before the final decision is taken, to take disciplinary action, including dismissal.
4. Employees may appeal against their dismissal. The appeal must be made within three working days.

REDUNDANCY PROCEDURE

Redundancy procedures aim to meet statutory, ethical and practical considerations when dealing with this painful process. An example of a procedure is given below.

Redundancy procedure (part 1)

DEFINITION

Redundancy is defined as the situation in which management decides that an employee or employees are surplus to requirements in a particular occupation and cannot be offered suitable alternative work.

Employees may be surplus to requirements because changes in the economic circumstances of the company mean that fewer employees are required, or because changes in methods of working mean that a job no longer exists in its previous form. An employee who is given notice because he or she is unsuitable or inefficient is not regarded as redundant and would be dealt with in accordance with the usual disciplinary or capability procedure.

OBJECTIVES

The objectives of the procedure are to ensure that:

- employees who may be affected by the discontinuance of their work are given fair and equitable treatment;
- the minimum disruption is caused to employees and the company;
- as far as possible, changes are effected with the understanding and agreement of the unions and employees concerned.

PRINCIPLES

The principles governing the procedure are as follows:

- The trade unions concerned will be informed as soon as possible of the possibility of redundancy.
- Every attempt will be made to:
  - absorb redundancy by the natural wastage of employees;
  - find suitable alternative employment within the company for employees who might be affected, and provide training if this is necessary;
  - give individuals reasonable warning of pending redundancy in addition to the statutory period of notice.
- If alternative employment in the company is not available and more than one individual is affected, the factors to be taken into consideration in deciding who should be made redundant will include:
  - length of service with the company;
  - age (especially those who could be retired early);
  - value to the company;
  - opportunities for alternative employment elsewhere.
- The first three of these factors should normally be regarded as the most important; other things being equal, however, length of service should be the determining factor.
- The company will make every endeavour to help employees find alternative work if that is necessary.

Redundancy procedure (part 2)

PROCEDURE

The procedure for dealing with employees who are surplus to requirements is set out below.

Review of employee requirements

Management will continuously keep under review possible future developments which might affect the number of employees required, and will prepare overall plans for dealing with possible redundancies.

Measures to avoid redundancies

If the likelihood of redundancy is foreseen, the company will inform the union(s), explaining the reasons, and in consultation with the union(s) will give consideration to taking appropriate measures to prevent redundancy.

Departmental managers will be warned by the management of future developments that might affect them in order that detailed plans can be made for running down staff, retraining, or transfers.

Departmental managers will be expected to keep under review the work situation in their departments in order that contingency plans can be prepared and the manager responsible for personnel warned of any likely surpluses.

Consultation on redundancies

If all measures to avoid redundancy fail, the company will consult the union(s) at the earliest opportunity in order to reach agreement.

Selection of redundant employees

In the event of impending redundancy, the individuals who might be surplus to requirements should be selected by the departmental manager with the advice of the manager responsible for personnel on the principles that should be adopted.

The manager responsible for personnel should explore the possibilities of transferring affected staff to alternative work.

The manager responsible for personnel should inform management of proposed action (either redundancy or transfer) to obtain approval.

The union(s) will be informed of the numbers affected but not of individual names.

The departmental manager and the HR manager responsible for personnel will jointly interview the employees affected either to offer a transfer or, if a suitable alternative is not available, to inform them they will be redundant. At this interview, full information should be available to give to the employee on, as appropriate:

- the reasons for being surplus;
- the alternative jobs that are available;
- the date when the employee will become surplus (that is, the period of notice);
- the entitlement to redundancy pay;
- the employee's right to appeal to an appropriate director;
- the help the company will provide.

Redundancy procedure (part 3)

An appropriate director will hear any appeals with the manager responsible for personnel.

The manager responsible for personnel will ensure that all the required administrative arrangements are made.

If the union(s) have any points to raise about the selection of employees or the actions taken by the company, these should be discussed in the first place with the manager responsible for personnel. If the results of these discussions are unsatisfactory, a meeting will be arranged with an appropriate director.

Alternative work within the company

If an employee is offered and accepts suitable alternative work within the company, it will take effect without a break from the previous employment and will be confirmed in writing. If the offer is refused, the employee may forfeit his or her redundancy payment. Employees will receive appropriate training and will be entitled to a four-week trial period to see if the work is suitable. This trial period may be extended by mutual agreement to provide additional training. During this period, employees are free to terminate their employment and if they do, would be treated as if they had been made redundant on the day the old job ended. They would then receive any redundancy pay to which they are entitled.

Alternative employment

Employees for whom no suitable work is available in the company will be given reasonable opportunities to look for alternative employment.

57

Computerized human resource information systems

WHAT DO COMPUTERS DO?

Computers:

- provide information to line managers to assist in the devolution to them of increased responsibility for people management;
- match CVs to person specifications for short-listing purposes;
- link with Internet recruitment.

BENEFITS OF A COMPUTERIZED HUMAN RESOURCE INFORMATION SYSTEM

A human resource information system can:

- enable the function to provide better services to line management;
- provide a conduit to link personnel policies and processes throughout the organization, thus facilitating the development of an integrated and coherent approach to personnel management;

- provide essential data for strategic personnel decision taking, enabling personnel people to access and analyse information quickly to put their ideas and plans to the test – it helps in the identification of the benefits of personnel strategies in terms that the business can recognize as adding value, not just cutting costs;
- reduce the workload of the HR function, eliminating low-value tasks while still enabling the function to provide efficient administrative services.

These benefits will only be achieved in full if a strategic and corporate view is taken of HR information requirements. If the system is simply used to automate certain aspects of HR administration such as record keeping it will not realize its full potential.

HR INFORMATION STRATEGY

The HR strategy of an organization in relation to HR information is concerned first with the use of computerized information for strategic decision making, second with the range of applications which should be included in the system and finally with the provision to line managers of the facility to have direct access to any personnel data they need to manage their own teams in a devolved organization.

Strategic decision taking

The strategic areas involving computerized information and the knowledge gained from analysing that information include macro concerns about organization, human resource requirements, the utilization of human resources, employee development and organizational health.

Specifically the information may focus on areas such as:

- organization development – how the structure may need to adapt to future needs and how IT can enable structural change, for example, high performance team structures;
- human resource plans, especially those concerned with 'mapping' future competence requirements and enlarging the skills base;
- determination of future development and training needs;
- determination of the performance and personality characteristics of the people who will be successful in the organization;
- assessment of the 'health' of the organization measured by attitude surveys and turnover and absence statistics, leading to the development of motivation, retention and absence control strategies;

- analysis of productivity levels as the basis for productivity improvement programmes;
- analysis of the scope for cutting down the number of employees – taking unnecessary costs out of the business.

Range of applications

There is an immense range of applications to choose from, starting from basic employee records and extending to highly sophisticated 'expert' systems which focus on fundamental HR decision areas.

THE FUNCTIONS OF A COMPUTERIZED HR SYSTEM

The basic functions of a computerized HR system are to:

- hold personal details about individual employees including career history, skills and qualifications, leave and absence records;
- hold details about employees' jobs, including grade, pay and benefits, hours, locations, job description or role definition;
- produce reports summarizing different aspects of this information.

The additional 'functionality' that a system can incorporate comprises:

- the recording and analysis of absence, attendance and labour turnover, which includes making comparisons between different occupations and locations and producing data on trends;
- recruitment and training administration;
- job evaluation;
- sophisticated modelling tools for such activities as human resource planning and reward management, which enable the system to be used to support strategic decision-making;
- linkages to the Internet (for example as part of an Internet recruitment system) or to the internal intranet.

Systems may be completely integrated with payroll, or more commonly they maintain a direct link. Some systems are entirely stand-alone. There may be one comprehensive software package to cover all applications, or specialized software for such functions as attendance management or job evaluation may be used.

RATING OF SYSTEM FEATURES

Research conducted by the IPD and the Institute for Employment Studies (IPD, 1999a) established that the systems features rated highly by organizations were:

- employee records;
- payroll;
- sick pay and maternity pay calculations;
- equal opportunity monitoring;
- production of standard letters and contracts;
- absence recording and monitoring;
- annual leave records;
- enquiries;
- attendance recording;
- disciplinary recording.

The features that were not so highly rated were:

- psychometric testing;
- IiP evaluation;
- shift or roster planning;
- organization charting;
- succession planning;
- 'what-if' modelling;
- jobs/skills matching;
- workforce planning;
- training needs analysis;
- appraisal records;
- salary modelling.

AN EFFECTIVE SYSTEM

The IPD guide on using computerized personnel systems (1999a) states that an effective system will have the following features:

- meets business needs;
- user-friendliness;
- good reporting facilities;

- flexibility;
- value for money;
- good supplier support;
- reliability.

PROBLEMS AND HOW TO DEAL WITH THEM

The 1999 IPD guide lists a number of typical problems and suggests how they can be dealt with. The problems and their solutions are set out in Table 57.1.

Table 57.1 Computer system problems and solutions

Problem	Solution
Poor data quality	Pay particular attention to getting accurate data into the system by training and monitoring
Lack of understanding of the system by users	Provide 'contextual training' covering: ● data sources (who provides the data and in what form) ● why different pieces of data are collected ● links to other systems
Inadequate coding of data producing unhelpful reports	Take care in setting up coding structures and train users in how to use codes
Lack of clarity about responsibilities for generating information on how the system can be used to generate useful information	Ensure that care is taken in specifying responsibilities and spelling out how information can be used supported by training and continuing guidance (a 'help line' to a systems or networks manager is a good idea)
Inadequate reporting capability – this is an aspect of systems that causes most dissatisfaction	● Define report specifications carefully in advance ● Take care in designing report layouts and contents on the basis of surveys of user needs ● Check views about the quality of reports and amend them as necessary
Line managers resent having to contribute or maintain information	● Minimize form filling ● Ensure that managers can access the system easily, possibly via the intranet ● Advise managers on how they can use the system to their benefit

Involving line managers

With the universal availability of personal computers (PCs) and the development of distributed data processing in local area networks (LANS) and the wide area networks (WANS), it is possible for data for use by line managers to be downloaded from the centre (a mainframe, minicomputer or UNIX system). Managers can also maintain their own data and manipulate the figures by the use of spreadsheets, for example, considering alternative ways of distributing their budget for a payroll increase among their staff. All this will, of course, be subjected to intensive security so that information goes only to authorized people and some data may be on a 'read only' basis.

The strategy for extending the system to line managers will clearly be entirely dependent on the organization's policies for devolving personnel decisions to them. But if this is the policy, its implementation will be much more likely to take place if the information required by line managers is made available.

DEVELOPING AN INFORMATION SYSTEM

Overall approach

The following are the typical stages in the development of an HR information system.

- Establish the current and future needs of the business and how these impinge on HR, and the implications for information systems.
- Define what outputs are required from the system in the form of information and reports.
- Prepare a high-level statement of requirement.
- Identify the options available to meet the HR business requirements.
- Prepare a recommendation on how to proceed for executive approval and buy-in. This must be supported both by a financial evaluation and by an analysis of the benefits to the business and any associated changes in business practices. A transition plan will be required which sets out the sequence of activities that would allow the organization to move swiftly and efficiently to any new system with the minimum of disruption.

Preferred characteristics of an information system

The preferred characteristics of an information system are:

- direct input of data at source;
- systems that can be used by the 'occasional user', not just a dedicated expert;
- systems able to deal with administrative processes, not simply a management information system;
- systems that provide the information needed by line managers in an easily understood format.

The range of applications will be defined by the information strategy. It will be vital to ensure that the hardware is appropriate to the organizational requirements in that PCs and terminals are provided where needed and are linked together in a network as required.

It is equally essential to ensure that the system is designed in such a way as to hold all the base data needed to provide management information. The system should be user-friendly, bearing in mind that the task which demands most time in using a system is data entry and that the enquiry system for obtaining information must be as easy to learn and use as possible.

The detailed points to be considered when developing a system are:

- the choice of hardware;
- the choice of software;
- database management;
- the degree to which the system is integrated with the payroll;
- the development programme.

Choice of hardware

There may be no choice of hardware – some systems are still linked to a mainframe computer. But the number of networked PC systems using either mini or microcomputers is increasing, either because this is happening generally within organizations or because of the special advantages of having a distributed and easily accessible system for a personnel application. The number of UNIX systems is still small but is growing as manufacturers promote this approach (UNIX is a shared multitasking operating system developed initially for minicomputers but now being used more for workstations which fall somewhere between microcomputers and minicomputers).

Database management

The system should be founded on a database – a self-describing collection of integrated personnel records. Particular attention has to be paid to the database management system (DBMS), the program or set of programs that develops and uses the database and database applications. Careful attention has also to be given to the design of database forms: data entry forms which are custom developed, video displays used to enter and change data, queries using standard query language (SQL) and report forms which are the hard copy output of database data. The base data is likely to be of much better quality if it is used in such day-to-day processes as recruitment, training administration and job evaluation.

Integration

Although many organizations have separated the payroll and purely personnel applications (the former usually being controlled by the accounts department), there is a lot to be said for having an integrated system. This makes economic use of one comprehensive database and facilitates such processes as flexible payment (cafeteria) systems.

Software

There is a massive and almost bewildering choice of software packages for application programs to provide information and generate reports. The software houses are constantly innovating and developing their products and between them provide something for everyone. However, if the organization has its own systems analysis and programming resources there are advantages in developing tailor-made software. But great care will need to be taken to debug the system, especially if a distributed system involving line managers is being created.

The development programme

The 10 steps required to develop and implement an information system are:

1. Determine objectives – are they to save administrative costs, speed up processing, provide advanced decision support, or a combination of any of these?
2. Prepare a business case for the system, setting out the benefits and the costs.
3. Carry out a feasibility study to consider applications and their likely costs and benefits. This study could be carried out in-house or with the help of outside consultants or software houses who provide a consultancy service. The feasibility study will broadly analyse and define user requirements and ensure that all concerned are aware of what is being planned, how they will benefit from it and

the contribution they will be expected to make to the development and application of the system. The information the system will be required to store and process and the uses to which the information will be put should be specified. Account should be taken of the provisions of the Data Protection Act (1998) as described in Chapter 55.

4. Prepare a requirements specification which will set out in detail what the system is expected to do and how the company would like to use it. This specification can be used to brief hardware and software suppliers before selecting the system.

5. Select the system in the form of the hardware and the software required. This may involve decisions on the extent to which existing hardware or systems (eg payroll systems) will be used. The need and scope for networking, that is, linking users by means of terminals, will also need to be considered.

6. Plan the implementation programme to ensure that the objectives will be achieved within a given time scale and in line with the cost budget.

7. Involve users to ensure that everyone who will benefit from the system (line managers as well as members of the personnel department) can contribute their ideas and thus feel that it is their system rather than one imposed upon them.

8. Control the project against the implementation programme to ensure that it delivers what is required, on time and within the budget. As the IPD guide on implementing computerized personnel systems (1997) emphasizes, it is essential to ensure that the selection and implementation of a system is a managed process. This means selecting an individual to act as project manager with the responsibility for dealing with all the steps listed above.

9. Provide training to all users to ensure that they can operate and get the most out of the system.

10. Monitor performance to ensure that the system lives up to expectations.

EXAMPLES OF APPLICATIONS

Personal records

These can include personal details, job details, employment contracts, pay details, performance appraisal, contacts and addresses and employee transactional data. The latter includes all the special items of information a company may need for its employees including qualifications, special skills and competences, training, absence, medical history and discipline.

Human resource planning

An information system can be used to model the effects on groups of people within the organization of change over time in the numbers and structure of each group and movements into, through and out of each group. Such a model looks at the organization, using a staffing system consisting of grades and flows. The user has considerable freedom in defining the number and type of flows required whether into, through, or out of each level of the system, ie:

- flows in – recruitment, transfers in;
- flows out – transfers out, retirement, resignation (uncontrolled losses), early retirement (controlled losses).

Employee turnover monitoring and control

Computer models can monitor and help in the control of employee turnover. They can therefore provide a critical input to other areas of human resource decision making such as policies on recruitment, promotion, redeployment, training and career planning.

Employee scheduling

An information system can be used to provide an integral system for matching the numbers of employees to business needs. The process of scheduling human resources to meet output in processing targets is becoming increasingly complex with the availability of more flexible ways of deploying people. They include multi-skilling (employees who are capable of carrying out different tasks and are not subject to trade-union-imposed constraints in doing so), the use of contract workers, the use of outworkers (people working at home or in another centre, a process which is facilitated by computer networking and electronic mailing), twilight shifts, more part-timers, job sharing etc.

Human resource planning is an interactive process which is always using output from one part of the process to influence another part of the process. Thus, assessments of the demand and supply of people, scheduling policies and possibilities, and the scope for flexing workloads and the use of people all influence the human resource supply policies adopted by the organization.

Employee profiling

Profiling is a particular aspect of employee scheduling concerned with the matching of staff to workloads and ensuring that the right number of people are available to meet fluctuations in activity levels over time. Profiling techniques are used where there are measurable volumes of work that can be costed and forecast with reasonable accuracy. Profiling can be linked with employee budgeting control in the sense that the use of people is both constrained and influenced by the cash budget and performance and employee establishment targets.

Profiling models can be used to:

- monitor and analyse employee utilization;
- test the effects of moving some activities to different times of the year and analyse their predicted impact on the employment profile;
- monitor movements in expenditure on pay and other employee benefits and carry out sensitivity tests on the impact of different pay assumptions;
- forecast future employee requirements;
- synchronize the recruitment of permanent and temporary employees with forecast workloads;
- flex employee budgets on the basis of revised activity level forecasts;
- control employee budgets.

Skills inventories and audits

Many organizations need to store detailed information about the skills, competences and experience of the individuals they employ. A separate skills inventory can be linked to a personnel database in order that any individual changes in experience or additional training can be fed through automatically to it.

Periodical audits can be carried out by the information system of the skills and competences available in the organization. These can be compared with estimates of current and future requirements to identify areas where recruitment or training action is required.

Competency modelling

Competency modelling brings together organization planning and performance management data to establish the skills or competencies required to do particular jobs. This assists in appointment, promotion and training decisions. Competency analysis looks both at what tasks have to be carried out and the competencies required. Profiles can then be developed by the computer and matched to assessments of current job holders or job applicants.

Recruitment

A recruitment system can carry out the following tasks:

- storage of applicants' details;
- retrieval and amendment of those details;
- matching CVs to person specifications for short-listing purposes;
- link with Internet recruiting processes;
- letter writing (linking the system to word-processing facilities) – acknowledgements, invitations to interview, offers and rejections;
- management reports, analysis of response by media and monitoring recruitment costs.

Computerized recruitment control packages not only automate recruitment correspondence (coupling the system with word processors) but also enable users to determine instantly who has applied for which post, track progress in recruiting for a specific post and match and process internal candidates.

The database can be used in more advanced applications to assist in establishing selection profiles with the standards against which potential job holders can be assessed in order that the right people can be appointed to or promoted into jobs.

Reward management

The system can be used for pay modelling and to carry out a number of reward administration activities. It can also be used in job evaluation as described on page 889.

Pay models provide the answers to 'what if?' questions such as, 'How much would it cost if we gave x per cent to this part of the company, y per cent to another part of the company, and implemented the following special package across these job functions?'

A system can also:

- analyse and report on average pay or pay distributions by job, grade, age or length of service;
- calculate compa-ratios to show how average pay in a range differs from the target pay;
- calculate the effects of attrition;
- assist in job evaluation;
- forecast future payroll costs on the basis of assumptions about numbers, promotions and pay levels;
- administer pay reviews, producing review forms, analysing proposals against the budgets and calculating the cost of performance-related pay awards in accor-

dance with different assumptions about amounts and the distribution of awards within a budget;

- provide information to line managers which will guide them to their pay decisions;
- generate instructions to adjust pay as well as letters to individuals informing them of their increases.

Performance management

An information system can help to operate performance management, generating forms, analysing and reporting on the result of performance reviews showing the distribution of people with different degrees of potential or performing at different levels, and highlighting individuals with particular skills or special promise. This system can be linked to others to provide an integrated basis for creating and implementing human resource management policies.

Training administration (computer-managed learning)

A system can be used for training administration by:

- storing competence-based training modules on the database, which enables trainers to select an appropriate module or mix of modules to meet a specified learning need;
- analysing the training recommendations contained in performance review reports to identify collective and individual training needs;
- identifying suitable training courses to meet training needs;
- making arrangements for off-the-job courses;
- informing employees about the arrangements for courses;
- handling correspondence about training courses;
- storing data on standard or individually tailored induction, continuation or development training programmes, including syllabi, routings, responsibilities for giving training, test procedures and progress reporting;
- generating instructions and notes for guidance for all concerned with providing or undergoing on-the-job training programmes;
- storing progress reports and monitoring achievements against training objectives;
- producing reports summarizing current and projected training activities and calculating the output of training programmes – this can be linked to human resource planning models including those designed to determine the input of trainees required for training schemes;
- recording and monitoring training expenditure against budget.

Computers can also be used as training aids (see Appendix A).

Career management

A system can help in the implementation of career management policies and procedures which embrace both career planning and management development. The system does this by analysing the progression of individuals and comparing the results of that analysis, first, with assessments of organizational requirements as generated by the human resource planning models and, second, with the outputs of the performance management system.

Absence control

Absence control can be carried out with the help of computerized time recording and attendance systems which:

● record clocking-on or -out time and the hours actually worked;
● enable employees to record the time spent on particular jobs;
● get employees to explain the reason for late arrival, early departure, or any other absence;
● can be linked to the payroll system for pay and bonus calculation purposes and to a flexible working hours system;
● provide team leaders with a statement showing the length and reasons for absence.

Advanced systems link information obtained from clocking-on or -out direct to a screen in team leaders' offices so that they can have instant information on how many people are at work and on the incidence of lateness.

Equal opportunity monitoring

The system can store records of the ethnic composition of the workforce. This information can be analysed to produce data on the distribution of ethnic minorities by occupation, job grade, age, service and location. The analysis could show the overall proportion of ethnic minority employees compared with the proportion in each job grade. Similar statistics can be produced for men and women. The analysis can be extended to cover career progression, splitting the results of the overall analysis into comparisons of the rate at which women and men of different ethnic groups progress.

Expert systems

Knowledge-based software or expert systems are computer programs which contain knowledge about particular fields of human activity and experience, which, through linkages and rules built into the system design, can help solve human resource management problems. Unlike a database system which stores, sorts, manipulates, and presents bits of information – ie data – expert systems store, sort, manipulate and present managers with ready-to-use knowledge of management practice, written in a language that management understands, as opposed to computerese.

Expert systems are developed through a process of knowledge engineering which starts from a knowledge base containing facts and a body of expertise ('heuristics', or rules of thumb) about the use of those facts. These 'rules' enable decisions to be made on the basis of factual information presented to the computer. Thus, a fact may be information on employee turnover during the last three years, and the rule of thumb may be the method by which turnover could be predicted over the next three years. These facts and rules are processed by what is termed the 'inference engine', which solves problems or makes predictions, and the results of this process are presented to the user in the 'user interface'.

An expert system can produce a list of suitable candidates for promotion by using information from the database. If more information were required, it would ask the user to answer questions. It would also respond to users' questions about why particular candidates had been identified, by giving details of qualifications, performance appraisal results and so on.

What can loosely be described as expert systems are also used in job evaluation applications where they make use of a database of job analyses and evaluations in order to make consistent judgements about evaluation scores. This is done by:

- defining the evaluation rules;
- programming the computer to ask appropriate questions concerning each factor in a job to enable it to apply the evaluation rules – this involves the analysis of structured questionnaires which have been specially designed to facilitate the systematic collection and analysis of data;
- applying the rules consistently and determining the factor score for the job;
- grading and ranking jobs;
- storing the information in the computer's memory so that it can be called to the screen or printed at any time.

AUDITING THE SYSTEM

As suggested by Robinson (1999), regular audit of the system should be carried out to obtain answers to these questions:

- Is the system being used efficiently and effectively?
- Are there any barriers to the effective use of the system?
- Does the technology enable managers or merely dictate to them?
- Are there any aspects of the system which are causing dissatisfaction in the HR department, with senior management or line managers?
- Are there any problems with data inaccuracy?
- Are reports accurate, helpful and used for decision-making?
- What is the functionality of the system? That is, what does the system do, and how well does it do it? What additional functions might be useful?
- How effective are the systems links, the use of data in different applications?

Appendix A

Training techniques

The training techniques analysed in this appendix are classified into three groups according to where they are generally used:

1. *on-the-job techniques* – demonstration, coaching, mentoring, job rotation/planned experience;
2. *on-the-job or off-the-job techniques* – action learning, job (skill) instruction, question and answer, assignments, projects, guided reading, computer-based training, video, interactive video, multimedia training;
3. *off-the-job techniques* – lecture, talk, discussion, case study, role-playing, simulation, group exercises, group dynamics, T-groups, inter-active skills training, assertiveness training, neuro-linguistic programming, distance learning, outdoor learning.

ON-THE-JOB TRAINING TECHNIQUES

Demonstration

Demonstration is the technique of telling or showing trainees how to do a job and then allowing them to get on with it. It is the most commonly used – and abused – training method. It is direct and the trainee is actively engaged. Reinforcement or feedback can be good, if the supervisor, trainer, or colleague (that well-known character, Nellie, by whom the trainee sits) does it properly by clearly defining what results have been achieved and how they can be improved. But demonstration in its typically crude form does not provide a structured learning system where trainees understand the sequence of training they are following and can proceed by deliberate steps along the learning curve. This is more likely to happen if job (skill) instruction techniques are used, as described later.

Coaching

Coaching is a person-to-person technique designed to develop individual skills, knowledge and attitudes.

Coaching is most effective if it can take place informally as part of the normal process of management or team leadership. This type of coaching consists of:

- helping people to become aware of how well they are doing and what they need to learn;
- controlled delegation;
- using whatever situations arise as learning opportunities;
- providing guidance on how to carry out specific tasks as necessary, but always on the basis of helping individuals to learn rather than force-feeding them with instructions on what to do and how to do it.

Mentoring

Mentoring is the process of using specially selected and trained individuals to provide guidance and advice which will help to develop the careers of the 'protégés' allocated to them.

Mentoring is aimed at complementing learning on the job, which must always be the best way of acquiring the particular skills and knowledge the job holder needs. Mentoring also complements formal training by providing those who benefit from it with individual guidance from experienced managers who are 'wise in the ways of the organization'.

Mentors provide for the person or persons allocated to them (their 'protégés'):

- advice in drawing up self-development programmes or learning contracts;
- general help with learning programmes;
- guidance on how to acquire the necessary knowledge and skills to do a new job;
- advice on dealing with any administrative, technical or people problems individuals meet, especially in the early stages of their careers;

- information on 'the way things are done around here' – the corporate culture and its manifestations in the shape of core values and organizational behaviour (management style);
- coaching in specific skills;
- help in tackling projects – not by doing it for protégés but by pointing them in the right direction, that is – helping people to help themselves;
- a parental figure with whom protégés can discuss their aspirations and concerns and who will lend a sympathetic ear to their problems.

There are no standard mentoring procedures. Typically, however, a mentor is allocated one or more protégés and given a very general brief to carry out the functions described above.

Job rotation/planned experience

Job rotation aims to broaden experience by moving people from job to job or department to department. It can be an inefficient and frustrating method of acquiring additional knowledge and skills unless it is carefully planned and controlled. What has sometimes been referred to as the 'Cook's tour' method of moving trainees from department to department has incurred much justified criticism because of the time wasted by them in locations where no one knew what to do with them or cared.

It is better to use the term 'planned sequence of experience' rather than 'job rotation' to emphasize that the experience should be programmed to satisfy a learning specification for acquiring knowledge and skills in different departments and occupations. Success in using this method depends on designing a programme which sets down what trainees are expected to learn in each department or job in which they gain experience. There must also be a suitable person available to see that trainees are given the right experience or opportunity to learn, and arrangements must be made to check progress. A good way of stimulating trainees to find out for themselves is to provide them with a list of questions to answer. It is essential, however, to follow up each segment of experience to check what has been learnt and, if necessary, modify the programme.

ON- OR OFF-THE-JOB TECHNIQUES

Action learning

Action learning, as developed by Revans (1971), is a method of helping managers develop their talents by exposing them to real problems. They are required to analyse them, formulate recommendations, and then, instead of being satisfied with a report, take action. It accords with the belief that managers learn best by doing rather than being taught.

The concept of action learning is based on six assumptions:

1. Experienced managers have a huge curiosity to know how other managers work.
2. We learn not as much when are are motivated to learn, as when we are motivated to learn something.
3. Learning about oneself is threatening and is resisted if it tends to change one's self-image. However, it is possible to reduce the external threat to a level which no longer acts as a total barrier to learning about oneself.
4. People learn only when they do something, and they learn more the more responsible they feel the task to be.
5. Learning is deepest when it involves the whole person – mind, values, body, emotions.
6. The learner knows better than anyone else what he or she has learned. Nobody else has much chance of knowing.

A typical action learning programme brings together a group, or 'set', of four or five managers to solve the problem. They help and learn from each other, but an external consultant, or 'set adviser', sits in with them regularly. The project may last several months, and the set meets frequently, possibly one day a week. The adviser helps the members of the set to learn from one another and clarifies the process of action learning. This process involves change embedded in the web of relationships called 'the client system'. The web comprises at least three separate networks; the power network, the information network, and the motivational network (this is what Revans means by 'who can, who knows, and who cares'). The forces for change are already there within the client system and it is the adviser's role to point out the dynamics of this system as the work of diagnosis and implementation proceeds.

The group or set has to manage the project like any other project, deciding on objectives, planning resources, initiating action and monitoring progress. But all the time, with the help of their adviser, they are learning about the management processes involved as they actually happen.

Job instruction

Job instruction techniques should be based on skills analysis and learning theory as discussed in Chapters 23 and 35. The sequence of instruction should follow four stages:

1. preparation;
2. presentation – explanation and demonstration;
3. practice and testing;
4. follow-up.

Preparation for each instruction period means that the trainer must have a plan for presenting the subject matter and using appropriate teaching methods, visual aids and demonstration aids. It also means preparing trainees for the instruction that is to follow. They should want to learn. They must perceive that the learning will be relevant and useful to them personally. They should be encouraged to take pride in their job and to appreciate the satisfaction that comes from skilled performance.

Presentation should consist of a combination of telling and showing – explanation and demonstration.

Explanation should be as simple and direct as possible: the trainer explains briefly the ground to be covered and what to look for. He or she makes the maximum use of films, charts, diagrams, and other visual aids. The aim should be to reach first things first and then proceed from the known to the unknown, the simple to the complex, the concrete to the abstract, the general to the particular, the observation to reasoning, and the whole to the parts and back to the whole again.

Demonstration is an essential stage in instruction, especially when the skill to be learned is mainly a doing skill. Demonstration takes place in three stages:

1. The complete operation is shown at normal speed to show the trainee how the task should be carried out eventually.
2. The operation is demonstrated slowly and in correct sequence, element by element, to indicate clearly what is done and the order in which each task is carried out.
3. The operation is demonstrated again slowly, at least two or three times, to stress the how, when and why of successive movements.

Practice consists of the learner's imitating the instructor and then constantly repeating the operation under guidance. The aim is to reach the target level of performance for each element of the total task, but the instructor must constantly strive to develop coordinated and integrated performance; that is, the smooth combination of the separate elements of the task into a whole job pattern.

Follow-up continues during the training period for all the time required by the learner to reach a level of performance equal to that of the normal experienced worker in terms of quality, speed, and attention to safety. During the follow-up stage, the learner will continue to need help with particularly difficult tasks or to overcome temporary set-backs which result in a deterioration of performance. The instructor may have to repeat the presentation for the elements and supervise practice more closely until the trainee regains confidence or masters the task.

Assignments

Assignments are specific tasks or investigations which trainees do at the request of their trainer or manager. The assignment may be used as a test at the end of a training session, and, as long as it is realistic, it should help to transfer learning to the work situation. The trainer may still have to provide some guidance to trainees to ensure that the latter do not lose confidence if they meet difficulties in completing the task.

Assignments may also be given by managers to their staff as a means of extending their experience. They should be linked to a coaching programme in order that the lessons from the assignment are fully absorbed.

Projects

Projects are broader studies or tasks which trainees are asked to complete, often with only very generalized guidelines from their trainer or manager. They encourage initiative in seeking and analysing information, in originating ideas, and in preparing and presenting the results of the project. For apprentices, especially students and graduates, the project can be a practical exercise in which the trainees are required to design, manufacture, and test a piece of equipment. Projects for managers may consist of an investigation into a company policy issue or an operating problem.

Like assignments, projects give trainees or managers an opportunity to test their learning and extend their experience, although the scope of the study is likely to be wider, and the project is often carried out by a group of people.

Guided reading

Knowledge can be increased by giving trainees books, hand-outs, or company literature and asking them to read and comment on them. Guided reading may take place before a course when the members are asked to read 'pre-course' literature. They seldom do. Or it may be given during a training course and used as reinforcement. The beautiful hand-outs that lecturers prepare are often allowed to gather dust when the course is over. They can be far more effective if they are distributed at appropriate points during or immediately after the lecture and those attending are required to discuss specific questions arising from them.

Reading as part of a development programme may be a valuable way of gaining knowledge as long as the material is seen by the trainee as relevant and there is follow-up to ensure that learning has taken place. The best way is to ask trainees to read a handbook or one or two chapters from a longer test and then come back to the trainer or their manager to discuss the relevance of the material and how they can use their knowledge.

Computer-based training or e-learning

Computer-based training (CBT) or e-learning is a form of individualized learning and, as such, is a manifestation of educational technology. It uses the power of the computer to assist in the constant need to train and retrain people in new processes and procedures. It also plays an important part in 'distance learning' in the fields of occupational training and higher education for institutions such as the Open University.

CBT starts with the process of instructional systems design (ISD). Each individual lesson is planned on the basis of careful analysis, sequencing and testing. CBT enables instructors to build into their sessions the adaptability that a truly interactive process of learning should provide. Using a computer, the author can devise an interactive sequence in which the responses the students make will determine their route through the training unit or programme – a route which will be unique to them.

Most CBT systems get trainees to study text on a visual display unit (VDU). They respond to problems which appear on the screen by typing an answer on a keyboard. More advanced systems use interactive video. The Internet or an intranet can also be used.

Computers can be used for training in the following ways:

1. To simulate actual situations in order that trainees can 'learn by doing'. For example, technicians can be trained in troubleshooting and repairing electronic circuitry by looking at circuit diagrams displayed on the screen and using a light pen to measure voltage at different points in the circuit.
2. To provide diagrammatic and pictorial displays in colour and to allow interaction between the trainee and the information presented on the screen.
3. To provide a database for information which learners can access through a computer terminal.
4. To measure the performances of trainees against predefined criteria.
5. To provide tests or exercises for trainees. The technique of adaptive testing uses a program containing a large number of items designed to test trainees' comprehension of certain principles. But it is not necessary for them to work through all of them or even to satisfy them sequentially in order to demonstrate their

understanding. Their responses to a limited number of questions will show whether or not they have grasped the appropriate concepts. The process of testing can thus be speeded up considerably and prove less frustrating for the trainee.

Video

While the printed word is often limited as a medium, the ability of video to present information visually is an obvious aid to training where there is a shortage of good trainers to get the message across. They are most effective if they are backed up by a trainer's guide which ensures that the passive nature of screen-watching is followed up by active learning.

With the help of cameras, video can provide instant feedback when training is taking place in such interactive skills as interviewing, counselling, selling, running meetings, and instructing.

Interactive video

Interactive video is based on the fusion of two powerful training technologies – computer-based training and video – combined such that the sum is greater than the parts.

Computer-based training (CBT) is individualized and interactive. It is able to accommodate each trainee's needs and pace with the software. Video is effective when realistic sound and pictures are essential and a moving camera angle can compensate for the flatness of the screen, helping to portray three-dimensional reality. But video is limited as a training medium. It cannot be individualized. Watching video is a passive activity and the sequence of instruction is always linear.

Interactive video offers the trainer the best of both worlds. It is individualistic, interactive, and random-access, like CBT, but interactive video can also present, like video, realistic still or moving pictures without sound. It is expensive, but its benefits are considerable in a number of different applications, such as:

- Distance learning – where trainees are widely scattered.
- When trainees have learning difficulties – many people, especially those without much formal education, find it difficult to absorb information from large blocks of text. As long as the interactive video programme is carefully constructed on the basis of a thorough task and skills analysis, and is designed to meet the requirements of learning theory, it will be an effective way of helping people to take in and use complex instructions.
- Where there is a scarce training resource – this might include skilled trainers or

the real equipment that a trainee must operate, such as a robot system or an aircraft.

● Where interpersonal skills are important – interactive video is much better than print or CBT in improving interpersonal skills such as interviewing, dealing with customers, counselling, or handling people problems.

● When training time is at a premium – interactive video can cut the time required to achieve learning objectives.

Multimedia training

Multimedia training uses a variety of media including audio, video, text, graphics, photography and animation which are combined together to create an interactive programme that is delivered on a PC. A multimedia programme will therefore be rich in presentation, making use of a variety of learning approaches which reinforce one another. Trainees receive rapid feedback and can work at their own speed, thus enhancing concentration and information retention. Multimedia training is well suited to procedural-driven or process training where simulations, drills and practice are part of the educational requirement. It is also appropriate for the 'soft skills' of managing people and handling interpersonal relations where scenarios and role plays can be used to practise and develop the skills required.

OFF-THE-JOB TRAINING TECHNIQUES

Lecture

A lecture is a talk with little or no participation except a question-and-answer session at the end. It is used to transfer information to an audience with controlled content and timing. When the audience is large, there may be no alternative to a 'straight lecture' if there is no scope to break it up into discussion groups.

The effectiveness of a lecture depends on the ability of the speaker to present material with the judicious use of visual aids. But there are several limits on the amount an inert audience can absorb. However effective the speaker, it is unlikely that more than 20 per cent of what was said will be remembered at the end of the day. And after a while, all will be forgotten unless the listeners have put some of their learning into practice. For maximum effectiveness, the lecture must never be longer than 30 or 40 minutes; it must not contain too much information (if the speaker can convey three new ideas which more than one-half of the audience understands and remembers, the lecture will have been successful); it must reinforce learning with appropriate visual aids (but not too many); and it must clearly indicate the action that should be taken to make use of the material.

Talk

A talk is a less formal lecture for a small group or not more than 20 people, with plenty of time for discussion. The encouragement of participation and interest means that more learning is likely to be retained than in a lecture, but the discussion may be dominated by the more articulate and confident members of the group unless carefully controlled.

Discussion

The objectives of using discussion techniques are to:

- get the audience to participate actively in learning;
- give people an opportunity of learning from the experience of others;
- help people to gain understanding of other points of view;
- develop powers of self-expression.

The aim of the trainer should be to guide the group's thinking. He or she may, therefore, be more concerned with shaping attitudes than imparting new knowledge. The trainer has unobtrusively to stimulate people to talk, guide the discussion along predetermined lines (there must be a plan and an ultimate objective), and provide interim summaries and a final summary.

The following techniques should be used to get active participation:

- Ask for contributions by direct questions.
- Use open-ended questions which will stimulate thought.
- Check understanding; make sure that everyone is following the argument.
- Encourage participation by providing support rather than criticism.
- Prevent domination by individual members of the group by bringing in other people and asking cross-reference questions.
- Avoid dominating the group yourself. The leader's job is to guide the discussion, maintain control and summarize from time to time. If necessary, 'reflect' opinions expressed by individuals back to the group to make sure they find the answer for themselves. The leader's job is to help them reach a conclusion, not to do it for them.
- Maintain control – ensure that the discussion is progressing along the right lines towards a firm conclusion.

Case study

A case study is a history or description of an event or a set of circumstances which is analysed by trainees in order to diagnose the causes of a problem and work out how to solve it. Case studies are mainly used in courses for managers and team leaders because they are based on the belief that managerial competence and understanding can best be achieved through the study and discussion of real events.

Case studies should aim to promote enquiry, the exchange of ideas, and the analysis of experience in order that the trainees can discover underlying principles which the case study is designed to illustrate. They are not light relief. Nor are they a means of lightening the load on the instructor. Trainers have to work hard to define the learning points that must come out of each case, and they must work even harder to ensure that these points do emerge.

The danger of case studies is that they are often perceived by trainees to be irrelevant to their needs, even if based on fact. Consequently, the analysis is superficial and the situation is unrealistic. It is the trainer's job to avoid these dangers by ensuring that the participants are not allowed to get away with half-baked comments. Trainers have to challenge assumptions and force people to justify their reasoning. Above all, they have to seize every chance to draw out the principles they want to illustrate from the discussion and to get the group to see how these are relevant to their own working situation.

Role-playing

In role-playing, the participants act out a situation by assuming the roles of the characters involved. The situation will be one in which there is interaction between two people or within a group. It should be specially prepared with briefs written for each participant explaining the situation and, broadly, their role in it. Alternatively, role-playing could emerge naturally from a case study when the trainees are asked to test their solution by playing the parts of those concerned.

Role-playing is used to give managers, team leaders or sales representatives practice in dealing with face-to-face situations such as interviewing, conducting a performance review meeting, counselling, coaching, dealing with a grievance, selling, leading a group or running a meeting. It develops interactive skills and gives people insight into the way in which people behave and feel.

The technique of 'role reversal', in which a pair playing, say, a manager and a team leader run through the case and then exchange roles and repeat it, gives extra insight into the feelings involved and the skills required.

Role-playing enables trainees to get expert advice and constructive criticism from the trainer and their colleagues in a protected training situation. It can help to increase confidence as well as developing skills in handling people. The main difficulties are either that trainees are embarrassed or that they do not take the exercise seriously and overplay their parts.

Simulation

Simulation is a training technique which combines case studies and role playing to obtain the maximum amount of realism in classroom training. The aim is to facilitate the transfer of what has been learned off the job to on-the-job behaviour by reproducing, in the training room, situations which are as close as possible to real life. Trainees are thus given the opportunity to practise behaviour in conditions identical to or at least very similar to those they will meet when they complete the course.

Group exercises

In a group exercise the trainees examine problems and develop solutions to them as a group. The problem may be a case study or it could be a problem entirely unrelated to everyday work. The aims of an exercise of this kind are to give members practice in working together and to obtain insight into the way in which groups behave in tackling problems and arriving at decisions.

Group exercises can be used as part of a team-building programme and to develop interactive skills. They can be combined with other techniques such as the discovery method to enable participants to work out for themselves the techniques and skills they need to use.

Group dynamics

Group dynamics training is largely based on the work of Kurt Lewin and the Research Centre for Group Dynamics at MIT in 1946. It has three interconnected and often overlapping aims: first, to improve the effectiveness with which groups operate (team building), second, to increase self-understanding and awareness of social processes and, third, to develop interactive skills which will enable people to function more effectively in groups. Group training can also help in modifying individual attitudes and values.

Group dynamics programmes may emphasize one of these aims more than the others, and they come in a number of forms. The basic variety is 'T-group' or 'sensitivity' training as described below, but this approach can be modified for use in courses primarily designed to improve interactive skills. There are also various packaged group dynamics courses, of which the best known are Blake's Managerial Grid and Coverdale Training.

T-group training

'T-group' stands for 'training group', which is not a very helpful description. It is also referred to as 'sensitivity training', 'group dynamics', and 'group relations training'. T-group training has three aims:

1. to increase sensitivity – the ability to perceive accurately how others are reacting to one's behaviour;
2. to increase diagnostic ability – the ability to perceive accurately the state of relationships between others;
3. to increase action skill – the ability to carry out skilfully the behaviour required by the situation.

In a T-group, trainers explain the aims of the programme and may encourage discussion and contribute their own reactions. But they do not take a strong lead, and the group is largely left to its own devices to develop a structure that takes account of the goals of both the members of the group and the trainer, and provides a climate in which the group are sufficiently trusting of one another to discuss their own behaviour. They do this by giving feedback or expressing their reactions to one another. Members may not always accept comments about themselves, but as the T-group develops they will increasingly understand how some aspects of their behaviour are hidden from them, and they will, therefore, be well on the way to an increase in sensitivity, diagnostic ability, and action skill.

The design of a T-group 'laboratory' may include short inputs from trainers to clarify problems of group behaviour, intergroup exercises to extend T-group learning to problems of representation, negotiation, and conflict management, and application groups in which members get together to decide how they can best transfer what they have learned to their actual job behaviour. As much opportunity as possible is given to members to test out and develop their own behaviour (interactive) skills – seeking or giving information, enlisting support, persuading, and commanding.

T-group laboratories in their purest form are unlikely ever to become a major part of company training programmes, but the group dynamics approach has valid uses in the modified forms described below.

Interactive skills training

Interactive skills training is defined by Rackham *et al* (1967) as 'any form of training which aims to increase the effectiveness of an individual's interaction with others'. It has the following features:

- It is based on the assumption that the primary limitation on managerial effectiveness lies not within each job boundary, but on the interface between jobs.
- There are no preconceived rules about how people should interact. It is assumed that the way interaction happens is dependent upon the situation and the people in it – this is what has to be analysed and used as a basis for the programme.
- The training takes place through groups, enabling people to practise interactive skills – such skills can only be acquired through practice.
- Participants have to receive controlled and systematic feedback on their performance – this is achieved by using specially developed techniques of behaviour analysis.

A typical interactive skills programme consists of three stages:

1. The diagnostic stage in which the groups undertake a wide range of activities. These are designed to provide reliable behaviour samples which the trainer records and analyses.
2. The formal feedback stage, in which the trainer gives groups and individuals feedback on their interactive performance during the diagnostic phase.
3. The practise, monitoring, feedback stage, in which the group undertakes further activities to develop and practise new behaviour patterns and receives feedback from the trainer to gauge the success of attempts at behaviour change.

Assertiveness training

Assertiveness training is designed to help people to become more effective by expressing their opinions, beliefs, wants and feelings in direct, honest and appropriate ways. It is mainly about interpersonal skills and relies largely on role plays and simulations. Self-report questionnaires (ie questionnaires completed by the trainee) may be used to help people to understand their behaviour in situations where it is necessary to be assertive – fighting their corner and standing up for their rights in such a way that they do not violate other people's rights.

Workshops

A workshop is a specially assembled group of people who, with the help of a facilitator, jointly examine organization issues and/or review their effectiveness as a team in order to develop agreed courses of action to which they will be fully committed.

Neuro-linguistic programming

The basis of neuro-linguistic programming (NLP) is that each person's concept of reality is actually their subjective interpretation, because the mind is a filtering mechanism. People learn to programme their reactions to others and develop unconscious strategies for interacting with them. NLP helps people to identify these strategies so that they can choose and control what would otherwise be automatic responses and behaviour. NLP involves thinking of the outcome required in a situation and identifying the personal resources needed to bring about that outcome. These resources are then rehearsed so that positive outcomes can be achieved in new situations.

Distance learning

Distance learning enables trainees to learn, often in their own time and at home, from instructional material prepared and sometimes presented elsewhere.

The most familiar method of distance learning is the correspondence course. This is normally conducted by post and thus suffers from a time lag between the student's sending in work and receiving it back marked by the tutor. These delays could be protracted, which is a disadvantage when what is really required to enable learning to take place is a dialogue between pupil and teacher. Success in taking a correspondence course relies on the tenacity of the student as well as the quality of instruction and the speed with which correspondence is turned round.

In the UK, the Open University provides a highly developed form of distance learning with some elements of the correspondence course, but a lot is added to this basic approach by the use of television, radio, and video as well as highly sophisticated teaching texts which often rely on the discovery method or a form of programmed learning. Computer-based training techniques are also used, and there is the opportunity to be exposed directly to the Open University tutors at summer schools.

Outdoor learning

Outdoor learning involves exposing individuals to various 'Outward Bound' type activities: sailing, mountain walking, rock climbing, canoeing, caving etc. It means placing participants, operating in teams, under pressure to carry out physical activities which are completely unfamiliar to them. The rationale is that these tests are paradigms of the sort of challenges people have to meet at work, but their unfamiliar nature means that they can learn more about how they act under pressure as team leaders or team members. Outdoor learning involves a facilitator helping participants to learn individually and collectively from their experiences.

Appendix B

Example of an attitude survey

Purpose

The purpose of this survey is to obtain your opinion on the existing pay arrangements and the performance appraisal process in XYZ Ltd. Your views and those of all the other staff of the company who are being asked to complete this questionnaire will provide a valuable input to the work currently being carried out to devise new approaches to pay and performance appraisal. Feedback on the overall results of the survey will be provided to all staff.

Confidentiality

Your answers to the questionnaire will be completely confidential. No individual will be identified and no one in the company will see the forms, which will be analysed by an independent research firm. You are being asked to identify your function but that is simply to make comparisons; the forms will not be analysed on an individual basis.

Completing and forwarding the survey form

Please complete the form and send it by 1st July in the attached envelope which is addressed to the firm which will be carrying out the analysis.

How to complete the questionnaire

The questionnaire will take about 15 minutes to complete. Please indicate your views about the statements overleaf by placing a ring around the number which most closely matches your opinion. For example:

	Strongly agree	Inclined to agree	Neither agree nor disagree	Inclined to disagree	Strongly disagree
I like my job	(1)	2	3	4	5

Function/department

Please circle one of the following:

1. corporate office;

2. marketing;

3. manufacturing;

4. finance;

5. IT;

6. HR;

7. customer service;

8. marketing, development, fundraising, PR, HR.

	QUESTIONNAIRE					
	I believe that:	_Strongly agree_	_Inclined to agree_	_Neither agree nor disagree_	_Inclined to disagree_	_Strongly disagree_
1	My pay adequately rewards me for my contribution	1	2	3	4	5
2	The pay system is clear and easy to understand	1	2	3	4	5
3	It is right for staff to be rewarded according to their contribution	1	2	3	4	5
4	The basis upon which my pay is determined is fair	1	2	3	4	5
5	Highly competent staff should be paid more than less competent staff	1	2	3	4	5
6	Rates of pay in the Company are not consistent with levels of responsibility	1	2	3	4	5
7	My rate of pay compares favourably with rates paid outside the Company	1	2	3	4	5
8	My pay does not reflect my performance	1	2	3	4	5
9	The current pay system encourages better performance	1	2	3	4	5
10	The pay system badly needs to be reviewed	1	2	3	4	5
11	I am clear about the standards of performance I am expected to achieve	1	2	3	4	5
12	I do not understand the competence levels I am expected to reach	1	2	3	4	5
13	The performance appraisal scheme is helpful	1	2	3	4	5
14	I receive good feedback from my manager on my performance	1	2	3	4	5
15	My manager is not really interested in carrying out my appraisal	1	2	3	4	5
16	I am motivated by my performance review meeting	1	2	3	4	5
17	The process of setting objectives and reviewing achievements is fair	1	2	3	4	5
18	The assessment of my performance by my manager is objective and fair	1	2	3	4	5
19	Performance appraisal does not help me to improve my performance	1	2	3	4	5
20	Performance appraisal clearly indicates any further training I might need	1	2	3	4	5

References

Advisory, Conciliation and Arbitration Service (ACAS) (1982) *Developments in Harmonization: Discussion paper no 1*, London

ACAS (1991) *Effective Organizations: The people factor*, ACAS advisory booklet no 6, ACAS, London

Adair, J (1973) *The Action-Centred Leader*, McGraw-Hill, London

Adams, J S (1965) Injustice in social exchange, in *Advances in Experimental Psychology*, vol 2, ed L Berkowitz, Academic Press, New York

Adams, K (1991) Externalisation vs specialisation: what is happening to personnel? *Human Resource Management Journal*, **14**, pp 40–54

Akinnusi, D K (1991) Personnel management in Africa: a comparative analysis of Ghana, Kenya and Nigeria, in *International Human Resource Management*, ed C Brewster and S Tyson, Pitman, London

Alderfer, C (1972) *Existence, Relatedness and Growth*, Free Press, New York

Aldous, H (2000) Education and business: partners in building human capital, in *Human Capital and Corporate Regulation*, ed A Carey and N Sleigh-Johnson, Institute of Chartered Accountants, London

Allport, G (1954) The historical background of modern social psychology, in *Theoretical Models and Personality*, ed G Lindzey, Addison-Wesley, Cambridge, Mass

Allport, G (1960) The open system in personality theory, *Journal of Abnormal and Social Psychology*, **61**, pp 301–11

Anglia Polytechnic University (1995) *Collectivism or Individualism in Employee Contracts*, Employment Relations, Research and Development Centre, Chelmsford

Annet, J and Duncan, K (1971) *Task Analysis*, HMSO, London

Argyle, M (1989) *The Social Psychology of Work*, Penguin, Harmondsworth

Argyris, C (1957) *Personality and Organization*, Harper & Row, New York

Argyris, C (1970) *Intervention Theory and Method*, Addison-Wesley, Reading, Mass

Argyris, C (1991) Teaching smart people how to learn, *Harvard Business Review*, May–June, pp 54–62

Argyris, C (1992) *On Organizational Learning*, Blackwell, Cambridge, Mass

Argyris, C (1993) *Knowledge for Action: A guide to overcoming barriers to organizational change*, Jossey Bass, San Francisco

Argyris, C and Schon, D A (1996) *Organizational Learning: A theory of action perspective*, Addison-Wesley, Reading, Mass

Armstrong, M (1996) *A Handbook of Personnel Management Practice*, 6th edn, Kogan Page, London

Armstrong, M (1987) Human resource management: a case of the emperor's new clothes, *Personnel Management*, August, pp 30–5

Armstrong, M (1989) *Personnel and the Bottom Line*, Institute of Personnel Management, London

Armstrong, M (1999) *Employee Reward*, 2nd edn, Institute of Personnel and Development, London

Armstrong, M (2000a) Feel the width, *People Management*, 3 February, pp 34–38

Armstrong, M (2000b) The name has changed but has the game remained the same? *Employee Relations*, **22** (6), pp 576–89

Armstrong, M (2000c) *Team Rewards*, Chartered Institute of Personnel and Development, London

Armstrong, M and Baron, A (1995) *The Job Evaluation Handbook*, Institute of Personnel and Development, London

Armstrong, M and Baron, A (1998) *Performance Management: The new realities*, Institute of Personnel and Development, London

Armstrong, M and Brown, D (1998) Relating competencies to pay: The UK experience, *Compensation & Benefits Review*, May/June, pp 28–39

Armstrong, M and Brown, D (2001) *Pay: The new dimensions*, Chartered Institute of Personnel and Development, London

Armstrong, M and Long, P (1994) *The Reality of Strategic HRM*, Institute of Personnel and Development, London

Armstrong, M and Murlis, H (1998) *Reward Management*, 4th edn, Kogan Page, London

Arnold, J, Robertson, I T and Cooper, C L (1991) *Work Psychology*, Pitman, London

Arthur, J (1990) *Industrial Relations and Business Strategies in American Steel Minimills*, unpublished PhD dissertation, Cornell University

Arthur, J (1992) The link between business strategy and industrial relations systems in American steel mills, *Industrial and Labor Relations Review*, **45**(3), pp 488–506

Arthur, J (1994) Effects of human resource systems on manufacturing performance and turnover, *Academy of Management Review*, **37**(4), pp 670–87

Atkinson, G (1989) *The Effective Negotiator*, Negotiating Systems Publications, Newbury

Atkinson, J (1984) Manpower strategies for flexible organizations, *Personnel Management*, August, pp 28–31

Atkinson, J and Meager, N (1986) *Changing Patterns of Work*, IMS/OECD, London

Bailey, T (1993) *Discretionary Authority and the Organization of Work: Employee participation and work reform since Hawthorne*, Working Paper, Columbia University, New York

Baillie, J (1995) *The Changing Nature of Work and the Psychological Contract*, IPD, London (unpublished)

Bales, R F (1950) *Interaction Process Analysis*, Addison-Wesley, Reading, Mass

Bandura, A (1977) *Social Learning Theory*, Prentice-Hall, Englewood Cliffs, NJ

Bandura, A (1982) Self-efficacy mechanism in human agency, *American Psychologist*, **37**, pp 122–47

Bandura, A (1986) *Social Boundaries of Thought and Action*, Prentice-Hall, Englewood Cliffs, NJ

Barnard, C (1938) *The Functions of an Executive*, Harvard University Press, Cambridge, Mass

Barney, J (1991) Firm resources and sustained competitive advantage, *Journal of Management*, 17, pp 99–120

Bartlett, C A and Ghoshal, S (1989) *Managing Across Borders: The transnational solution*, Harvard Business School Press, Boston, Mass

Bartlett, C A and Ghoshal, S (1991) *Managing Across Borders: The transnational solution*, London Business School, London

Bartlett, C A and Ghoshal, S (1993) Beyond the M-form: toward a management theory of the firm, *Strategic Management Journal*, **14**, pp 23–46

Bass, B M and Vaughan, J A (1966) *Training in Industry: The management of learning*, Tavistock, London

Basset, P and Cave, A (1993) *All for One: The future of trade unions*, Fabian Society, London

Bates, R A and Holton, E F (1995) Computerised performance monitoring: a review of human resource issues, *Human Resource Management Review*, Winter, pp 267–88

Beard, D (1993) Learning to change organizations, *Personnel Management*, January, pp 32–35

Beardwell, I (1998) Voices on, *People Management*, 28 May, pp 32–36

Becker, B E *et al* (1997) HR as a source of shareholder value: research and recommendations, *Human Resource Management*, Spring, **36**(1), pp 39–47

Beckhard, R (1969) *Organization Development: Strategy and models*, Addison-Wesley, Reading, Mass

Beckhard, R (1989) A model for the executive management of transformational change, in *Human Resource Strategies*, ed G Salaman, Sage, London

Beer, M (1981) Performance appraisal: dilemmas and possibilities, *Organization Dynamics*, Winter, pp 24–36

Beer, M (1984) Reward systems, in *Managing Human Assets*, M Beer, B Spector, P R Lawrence, D Quinn Mills and R Walton, Free Press, New York

Beer, M, Eisenstat, R and Spector, B (1990) Why change programs don't produce change, *Harvard Business Review*, November–December, pp 158–66

Beer, M and Ruh, R A (1976) Employee growth through performance management, *Harvard Business Review*, July–August, pp 59–66

Beer, M and Spector, B (1985) Corporate transformations in human resource management, in *HRM Trends and Challenges*, ed R Walton and P Lawrence, Harvard University Press, Boston, Mass

Beer, M, Spector, B, Lawrence, P, Quinn Mills, D and Walton, R (1984) *Managing Human Assets*, Free Press, New York

Belbin, M (1981) *Management Teams: Why they succeed or fail*, Heinemann, London

Bell, W and Hanson, C (1987) *Profit Sharing and Profitability*, Kogan Page, London

Bennis, W (1960) *Organizational Development*, Addison-Wesley, Reading, Mass

Bennis, W and Nanus, B (1985) *Leaders*, Harper & Row, New York

Bento, R and Ferreira, L (1992) Incentive pay and organizational culture, in *Performance Measurement, Evaluation and Incentives*, ed W Bruns, Harvard Business School Press, Boston, Mass

Berlet, K and Cravens, D (1991) *Performance Pay as a Competitive Weapon*, Wiley, New York

Bernadin, H K, Kane, J S, Ross, S, Spina, J D and Johnson, D L (1995) Performance appraisal design, development and implementation, in *Handbook of Human Resource Management*, ed G R Ferris, S D Rosen and D J Barnum, Blackwell, Cambridge, Mass

Berridge, J (1992) Human resource management in Britain, *Employee Relations*, **14**(5), pp 62–85

Bevan, S, Barber, l and Robinson, D (1997) *Keeping the Best: A practical guide to retaining key employees*, Institute for Employment Studies, Brighton

Bevan, S and Thompson, M (1991) Performance management at the crossroads, *Personnel Management*, November, pp 36–39

Billson, I (1998) How just-in-time training can support business-led competency development, *Competency*, Spring, pp 21–24

Birchall, D and Lyons, L (1995) *Creating Tomorrow's Organisation*, Pitman, London

Blackburn, R M and Mann, R (1979) *The Working Class in the Labour Market*, Macmillan, London

Blackler, F (1995) Knowledge, knowledge work and organisations, *Organisation Studies*, **16**(6), pp 16–36

Blake, P (1998) The knowledge management explosion, *Information Today*, **15**(1), pp 12–13

Blake, R and Mouton, J (1964) *The Managerial Grid*, Gulf Publishing, Houston

Blake, R, Shepart, H and Mouton, J (1964) Breakthrough in organizational development, *Harvard Business Review*, **42**, pp 237–58

Blinkorn, S and Johnson, C (1991) Study shows personality tests are 'useless' for predicting performance, *Personnel Management Plus*, 18 September, p 3

Blyton, P and Turnbull, P (eds) (1992) *Reassessing Human Resource Management*, Sage, London

Bontis, N (1996) There's a price on your head: managing intellectual capital strategically, *Business Quarterly*, Summer, pp 4–47

Bontis, N (1998) Intellectual capital: an exploratory study that develops measures and models, *Management Decision*, **36**(2), pp 63–76

Bontis, N, Dragonetti, N C, Jaconsen, K and Roos, G (1999) The knowledge toolbox: a review of the tools available to measure and manage intangible resources, *European Management Journal*, **17**(4), pp 391–402

Boudreau, J W (1988) Utility analysis, in *Human Resource Management: Evolving roles and responsibilities*, ed L Dyer, Bureau of National Affairs, Washington, DC

Bower, J L (1982) Business policy in the 1980s, *Academy of Management Review*, **7**(4), pp 630–38

Bowles, M L and Coates, G (1993) Image and substance: the management of performance as rhetoric or reality? *Personnel Review*, **22**(2), pp 3–21

Boxall, P F (1992) Strategic HRM: a beginning, a new theoretical direction, *Human Resource Management Journal*, **2**(3), pp 61–79

Boxall, P F (1993) The significance of human resource management: a reconsideration of the evidence, *International Journal of Human Resource Management*, **4**(3), pp 645–65

Boxall, P (1994) Placing HR strategy at the heart of the business, *Personnel Management*, July, pp 32–35

Boxall, P (1996) The strategic HRM debate and the resource-based view of the firm, *Human Resource Management Journal*, **6**(3), pp 59–75

Boxall, P (1999) Human resource strategy and competitive advantage: a longitudinal study of engineering consultancies, *Journal of Management Studies*, **36**(4), pp 443–63

Boyatzis, R (1982) *The Competent Manager*, Wiley, New York

Boyett, J H and Conn, H P (1995) *Maximum Performance Management*, Glenbridge, Oxford

Braverman, H (1974) *Labour and Monopoly Capital*, Monthly Review Press, New York

Brayfield, A H and Crockett, W H (1955) Employee attitudes and employee performance, *Psychological Bulletin*, **52**, pp 346–424

Brewster, C (1993) Developing a 'European' model of human resource management, *International Journal of Human Resource Management*, **4**(4), pp 765–84

Brewster, C (1999) Strategic human resource management: the value of different paradigms, in *Strategic Human Resource Management*, ed R S Schuler and S E Jackson, Blackwell, Oxford

Brewster, C and Holt Larsen, H (1992) Human resource management in Europe: evidence from ten countries, *International Journal of Human Resource Management*, **3**(3), pp 409–34

Brewster, C and Lloyd, J (1994) The changing face of union negotiations, *Human Resources*, Summer, pp 148–52

Brown, D (1998) Presentation to the Compensation Forum meeting, February

Brown, J A C (1954) *The Social Psychology of Industry*, Penguin Books, Harmondsworth

Brown, W B D (1962) *Piecework Abandoned: The effect of wage incentive systems on managerial authority*, Heinemann, London

Brown, D and Armstrong, M (1997) Terms of endearment, *People Management*, 11 September, pp 36–38

Brown, D and Armstrong, M (1999) *Paying for Contribution*, Kogan Page, London

Brumbach, G B (1988) Some ideas, issues and predictions about performance management, *Public Personnel Management*, Winter, pp 387–402

Buchanan, D (1987) Job enrichment is dead: long live high performance work design! *Personnel Management*, May, pp 40–43

Buchanan, D and Huczynski, A (1985) *Organizational Behaviour*, Prentice-Hall, Englewood Cliffs, NJ

Bulla, D N and Scott, P M (1994) Manpower requirements forecasting: a case example, in *Human Resource Forecasting and Modelling*, ed D Ward, T P Bechet and R Tripp, Human Resource Planning Society, New York

Burdett, J O (1991) What is empowerment anyway? *Journal of European Industrial Training*, **15**(6), pp 23–30

Burgess, S and Rees, H (1996) Job tenure in Britain, *Economic Journal*, March, pp 334–44

Burgoyne, J (1988a) *Competency Approaches to Management Development*, Centre for the Study of Management Learning, University of Lancaster

Burgoyne, J (1988b) Management development for the individual and the organization, *Personnel Management*, June, pp 40–44

Burgoyne, J (1994) As reported in *Personnel Management Plus*, May, p 7

Burgoyne, J (1999) Design of the times, *People Management*, 3 June, pp 39–44

Burns, J M (1978) *Leadership*, Harper & Row, New York

Burns, T and Stalker, G (1961) *The Management of Innovation*, Tavistock, London

Burt, C (1954) The differentiation of intellectual ability, *British Journal of Educational Psychology*, **24**

Campbell, J P (1990) Modelling the performance prediction problem in industrial and organizational psychology, in *Handbook of Industrial and Organizational Psychology*, ed M P Dunnette and L M Hugh, Blackwell, Cambridge, Mass

Cannell, M and Wood, S (1992) *Incentive Pay: Impact and evolution*, Institute of Personnel Management, London

Cannon, T (2000) Knowledge entrepreneurs and the responsible corporation, in *Human Capital and Corporate Regulation*, ed A Carey and N Sleigh-Johnson, Institute of Chartered Accountants, London, pp 18–20

Capelli, P (2000) A market-driven approach to retaining talent, *Harvard Business Review*, January–February, pp 103–11

Cappelli, P and Crocker-Hefter, A (1996) *Organizational Dynamics*, Winter, pp 7–22

Capelli, P and Singh, H (1992) Integrating strategic human resources and strategic management, in *Research Frontiers in Industrial Relations and Human Resources*, ed D Lewin, O Mitchell and P Scheller, Industrial Relations Research Association Series, Industrial Relations Research Association, Madison, Wis

Cardy, R L and Dobbins, G H (1994) *Performance Appraisal: Alternative perspectives*, South-Western Publishing, Cincinnati, Ohio

Carlton, I and Sloman, M (1992) Performance appraisal in practice, *Human Resource Management Journal*, **2**(3), Spring, pp 80–94

Casson, J (1978) *Re-evaluating Company Manpower Planning in the Light of Some Practical Experiences*, Institute of Manpower Studies, Brighton

Cattell, R B (1963) *The Sixteen Personality Factor Questionnaire*, Institute for Personality and Ability Training, Ill

Cave, A (1994) *Organizational Change in the Workplace*, Kogan Page, London

Confederation of British Industry (CBI)/HAY Management Consultants (1996) *Trends in Pay and Benefits Systems*, CBI, London

CBI/Wyatt (1993) *Variable Pay*, CBI, London

Centre for Workforce Development (1998) *The Teaching Firm: Where productive work and learning converge*, Centre for Workforce Development, Newton, Mass

Chadwick, C and Cappelli, P (1998) Alternatives to generic strategy typologies in human resource management, in *Research in Personnel and Human Resource Management*, ed P Wright, L Dyer, J Boudreau and G Milkovichl, JAI, Greenwich, Conn

Chamberlain, N W and Kuhn, J (1965) *Collective Bargaining*, McGraw-Hill, New York

Chandler, A D (1962) *Strategy and Structure*, MIT Press, Cambridge, Mass

Chartered Institute of Personnel and Development (CIPD) (2000) *Report on Labour Turnover Survey*, CIPD, London

Chell, E (1985) *Participation and Organisation*, Macmillan, London

Chell, E (1987) *The Psychology of Behaviour in Organisations*, Macmillan, London

Child, J (1977) *Organization: A guide to problems and practice*, Harper & Row, London

Clegg, I I (1976) *The System of Industrial Relations in Great Britain*, Blackwell, Oxford

Coleman, J S (1990) *Foundations of Social Theory*, Harvard University Press, Cambridge, Mass

Collard, R (1992) Total quality: the role of human resources, in *Strategies for Human Resource Management*, ed M Armstrong, Kogan Page, London

Collard, R (1993) *Total Quality: Success through people*, IPM, London

Cook, M (1993) *Personnel Selection and Productivity*, Wiley, Chichester

Cooke, R and Lafferty, J (1989) *Organizational Culture Inventory*, Human Synergistic, Plymouth, MD

Cooper, C (2000) In for the count, *People Management*, 12 October, pp 28–33

Cooper, R (1973) Task characteristics and intrinsic motivation, *Human Relations*, August, pp 387–408

Coopers & Lybrand (1985) *A Challenge to Complacency: Changing attitudes to training*, Manpower Services Commission, Sheffield

Coopey, J and Hartley, J (1991) Reconsidering the case for organizational commitment, *Human Resource Management Journal*, **3**, Spring, pp 18–31

Coyle, D (1996) Flexible jobs seen as future face of labour, *The Independent*, 8 March, p 4

Cross, M (1991) Monitoring multiskilling: the way to guarantee long-term change, *Personnel Management*, March, pp 44–49

Cyert, R M and March, J G (1963) *A Behavioural Theory of the Firm*, Prentice-Hall, Englewood Cliffs, NJ

Dale, M (1994) Learning organizations, in *Managing Learning*, ed C Mabey and P Iles, Routledge, London

Daft, R L and Weick, K E (1984) Towards a model of organisations as interpretation systems, *Academy of Management Review*, **9**, pp 284–95

Daniels, A C (1987) What is PM?, *Performance Management*, July, pp 8–12

Davenport, T H (1996) Why re-engineering failed: the fad that forgot people, *Fast Company*, Premier issue, pp 70–74

Davenport, T O (1999) *Human Capital*, Jossey Bass, San Francisco

Davenport, T H and Prusak, L (1998) *Working Knowledge: How organizations manage what they know*, Harvard Business School Press, Boston, Mass

Davis, L E (1966) The design of jobs, *Industrial Relations*, **6**

Deal, T and Kennedy, A (1982) *Corporate Cultures*, Addison-Wesley, Reading, Mass

Deary, I J and Matthews, G (1993) Personality traits are alive and well, *The Psychologist*, **6**, pp 299–311

Delaney, J T and Huselid, M A (1996) The impact of human resource management practices on perceptions of organizational performance, *Academy of Management Journal*, **39**(4), pp 949–69

Delery, J E and Doty, H D (1996) Modes of theorizing in strategic human resource management: tests of universality, contingency and configurational performance predictions, *International Journal of Human Resource Management*, **6**, pp 656–70

Deming, W E (1982) *Quality, Productivity and Competitive Position*, MIT Centre for Advanced Engineering Study, Cambridge, Mass

Deming, W E (1986) *Out of the Crisis*, MIT Centre for Advanced Engineering Study, Cambridge, Mass

Denison, D R (1996) What *is* the difference between organizational culture and organizational climate? A native's point of view on a decade of paradigm wars, *Academy of Management Review*, July, pp 619–54

Department of Employment (1994) *People and Companies: Employee involvement in Britain*, HMSO, London

Departments of Trade and Industry and Education and Employment (1997) *Partnerships at Work*, London

Digman, L A (1990) *Strategic Management: Concepts, decisions, cases*, Irwin, Georgetown, Ontario

Drucker, P (1951) *The New Society*, Heinemann, London

Drucker, P (1955) *The Practice of Management*, Heinemann, London

Drucker, P (1967) *The Effective Executive*, Heinemann, London

Drucker, P (1988) The coming of the new organization, *Harvard Business Review*, January–February, pp 45–53

Drucker, P (1993) *Post-Capitalist Society*, Butterworth-Heinemann, Oxford

Drucker, P (1995) The information executives truly need, *Harvard Business Review*, January–February, pp 54–62

Dulewicz, V (1989) Assessment centres as the route to competence, *Personnel Management*, November, pp 56–59

Dulewicz, V and Higgs, M (1999) The seven dimensions of emotional intelligence, *People Management*, 28 October, p 53

Duncan, C (1989) Pay and payment systems, in *A Handbook of Industrial Relations Practice*, ed B Towers, Kogan Page, London

Dunlop, J T (1958) *Industrial Relations Systems*, Holt, New York

Dyer, L and Holder, G W (1998) Strategic human resource management and planning, in *Human Resource Management: Evolving roles and responsibilities*, ed L Dyer, Bureau of National Affairs, Washington, DC

Dyer, L and Reeves, T (1995) Human resource strategies and firm performance: what do we know and where do we need to go? *International Journal of Human Resource Management*, **6**(3), September, pp 656–70

Eagleton, T (1983) *Literary Theory*, Blackwell, Oxford

Easterby-Smith, M (1997) Disciplines of organizational learning: contributions and critiques, *Human Relations*, **50**(9), pp 1085–1113

Edenborough, R (1994) *Using Psychometrics*, Kogan Page, London

Edvinson, L and Malone, M S (1997) *Intellectual Capital: Realizing your company's true value by finding its hidden brainpower*, Harper Business, New York

Edwards, M R and Ewen, A T (1996) *360-degree Feedback*, American Management Association, New York

Edwards, M R, Ewen, A T and O'Neal, S (1994) Using multi-source assessment to pay people not jobs, *ACA Journal*, Summer, pp 6–17

Egan, G (1990) *The Skilled Helper: A systematic approach to effective helping*, Brooks Cole, London

Egan, G (1995) A clear path to peak performance, *People Management*, 18 May, pp 34–37

Eggert, M (1991) *Outplacement: A guide to management and delivery*, Institute of Personnel Management, London

Ehrenberg, R G and Smith, R S (1994) *Modern Labor Economics*, HarperCollins, New York

Eldridge, J and Crombie, A (1974) *The Sociology of Organizations*, Allen & Unwin, London

Elliot, L (1996) Dealing with the dirty end of jobs for life, *The Guardian*, 23 April, p 14

Elliott, R F (1991) *Labor Economics*, McGraw-Hill, Maidenhead

Emery, F F (1980) Designing socio-technical systems for greenfield sites, *Journal of Occupational Behaviour*, **1**(1), pp 19–27

Engelmann, C H and Roesch, C H (1996) *Managing Individual Performance*, American Compensation Association, Scottsdale, Ariz

Eraut, M J *et al* (1998) Development of knowledge and skills in employment, *Economic and Social Research Council*, London

Erez, M (1977) Feedback: a necessary condition for the goal-setting performance relationship, *Journal of Occupational Psychology*, **62**(5), pp 624–27

Erez, M and Zidon, I (1984) Effect of good acceptance on the relationship of goal difficulty on performance, *Journal of Applied Psychology*, **69**(1), pp 69–78

Eysenck, H J (1953) *The Structure of Human Personality*, Methuen, London

Farnham, D (2000) *Employee Relations in Context*, 2nd edn, Institute of Personnel and Development, London

Fayol, H (1916) *Administration Industrielle et General*, tr C Storrs as *General and Industrial Management*, Pitman, London, 1949

Fein, M (1970) *Approaches to Motivation*, Lawrence Erlbaum, Hillsdale, NJ

Fernie, S, Metcalf, D and Woodland, S (1994) *What Has Human Resource Management Achieved in the Workplace?* Employment Policy Institute, London

Fiedler, F (1967) *A Theory of Leadership Effectiveness*, McGraw-Hill, New York

Fitz-enj, J (2000) *The ROI of Human Capital*, American Management Association, New York

Flanders, A (1970) *Management and Unions: The theory and reform of industrial relations*, Faber and Faber, London

Fletcher, C (1984) What's new in performance appraisal, *Personnel Management*, February, pp 20–22

Fletcher, C (1991) Study shows personality tests are 'useless' for predicting performance, *Personnel Management Plus*, p 3

Fletcher, C (1993) *Appraisal: Routes to improved performance*, Institute of Personnel Management, London

Fletcher, C and Williams, R (1992) The route to performance management, *Personnel Management*, October, pp 42–47

Fletcher, S (1991) *NVQs, Standards and Competence*, Kogan Page, London

Fletcher, S (1992) *Competence-Based Assessment Techniques*, Kogan Page, London

Follett, M P (1924) *Creative Experience*, Longmans Green, New York

Fombrun, C J, Tichy, N M and Devanna, M A (1984) *Strategic Human Resource Management*, Wiley, New York

Fonda, N (1989) Management development: the missing link in sustained business performance, *Personnel Management*, December, pp 50–53

Fowler, A (1987) When chief executives discover HRM, *Personnel Management*, January, p 3

Fowler, A (1990) Performance Management: the MBO of the 90s, *Personnel Management*, July, pp 47–51

Fowler, A (1991a) An even-handed approach to graphology, *Personnel Management*, March, pp 40–43

Fowler, A (1991b) How to conduct interviews effectively, *Personnel Management Plus*, August, pp 20–21

Fowler, A (1993) Implement a customer care scheme, *Personnel Management Plus*, January, pp 23–24

Fowler, A (1994) How to obtain an Investors in People Award, *Personnel Management Plus*, June, pp 31–32

Fowler, A (1996) *Induction*, 3rd edn, Institute of Personnel and Development, London

Fox, A (1966) Industrial sociology and industrial relations, *Royal Commission on Trade Unions and Employers Associations Research Paper no 3*, HMSO, London

Fox, A (1973) *Beyond Contract*, Faber and Faber, London

Fox, A and Flanders, A (1969) Collective bargaining: from Donovan to Durkheim, in *Management and Unions*, ed A Flanders, Faber and Faber, London

Freeman, R and Medoff, J (1984) *What do Unions do?* Basic Books, New York

French, J R and Raven, B (1959) The basis of social power, in *Studies in Social Power*, ed D Cartwright, Institute for Social Research, Ann Arbor, Mich

French, W L and Bell, C H (1990/1994) *Organization Development*, Prentice-Hall, Englewood Cliffs, NJ

French, W L, Kast, F E and Rosenzweig, J E (1985) *Understanding Human Behaviour in Organizations*, Harper & Row, New York

Friedman, A (1977) *Industry and Labour: Class structure and monopoly capitalism*, Macmillan, London

Furnham, A (1990) A question of competency, *Personnel Management*, June, p 37

Furnham, A and Gunter, B (1993) *Corporate Assessment*, Routledge, London

Gagné, R M (1977) *The Conditions of Learning*, 3rd edn, Rinehart and Winston, New York

Galbraith, J R (1973) *Organizational Design*, Addison-Wesley, Reading, Mass

Gall, G (1993) *New Trade Union Recognition Agreements in Britain*, University of Stirling Gallie, D, White, M, Cheng, Y and Tomlinson, M (1998) *Restructuring the Employment Relationship*, Clarendon Press, Oxford

Gallie, D, White, M, Cheng, Y and Tomlinson, M (1998) *Restructuring the Employment Relationship*, Clarendon Press, Oxford

Gannon, M (1995) Personal development planning, in *The Performance Management Handbook*, ed M Walters, Institute of Personnel and Development, London

Garratt, R (1990) *Creating a Learning Organization*, Institute of Directors, London

Garvin, D A (1993) Building a learning organization, *Harvard Business Review*, July–August, pp 78–91

Gennard, J and Judge, G (1997) *Employee Relations*, Institute of Personnel and Development, London

Gennard, J and Kelly, J (1994) Human resource management: the views of personnel directors, *Human Resource Management Journal*, 5(1), pp 15--32

Geppert, M (1996) Paths of managerial learning in the East German context, *Organization Studies*, **17**(2), pp 249–68

Ghoshal, S and Bartlett, C A (1993) Changing the role of top management: beyond structure to process, *Harvard Business Review*, January-February, pp 86–96

Gilbert, D and Abosch, K S (1996) *Improving Organizational Effectiveness Through Broadbanding*, American Compensation Association, Scottsdale, Ariz

Giles, E and Williams, R (1991) Can the personnel department survive quality management? *Personnel Management*, April, pp 28–33

Giles, L, Kodz, J and Evans, C (1997) *Productive Skills for Process Operatives*, Institute of Employment Studies, IES Report 336

Glaze, T (1989) Cadbury's dictionary of competence, *Personnel Management*, July, pp 44–48

Gluckman, M (1964) *Closed Systems and Open Minds*, Oliver and Boyd, London

Goldthorpe, J H, Lockwood, D C, Bechofer, F and Platt, J (1968) *The Affluent Worker: Industrial attitudes and behaviour*, Cambridge University Press, Cambridge

Goleman, D (1995) *Emotional Intelligence*, Bantam, New York

Goleman, D (1999) *Emotional Intelligence*, Presentation at IPD Conference, October

Gomez-Mejia, L R and Balkin, D B (1992) *Compensation, Organisational Strategy, and Firm Performance*, Southwestern Publishing, Cincinnati

Goold, M and Campbell, A (1986) *Strategies and Styles: The role of the centre in managing diversified corporations*, Blackwell, Oxford

Gospel, H (1992) *Markets, Firms and the Management of Labour*, Cambridge University Press, Cambridge

Grant, R M (1991) The resource-based theory of competitive advantage: implications for strategy formulation, *California Management Review*, **33**(3), pp 114–35

Gratton, L (1999) People processes as a source of competitive advantage, in *Strategic Human Resource Management*, ed L Gratton, V H Hailey, P Stiles and C Truss, Oxford University Press, Oxford

Gratton, L *et al* (1999) *Strategic Human Resource Management*, Oxford University Press, Oxford

Gratton, L and Hailey, V H (1999) The rhetoric and reality of new careers, in *Strategic Human Resource Management*, ed L Gratton, V H Hailey, P Stiles and C Truss, Oxford University Press, Oxford

Grint, K (1993) What's wrong with performance appraisal? A critique and a suggestion, *Human Resource Management Journal*, Spring, pp 61–77

Gross, S E (1995) *Compensation for Teams*, Hay, New York

Guest, D E (1984) What's new in motivation, *Personnel Management*, May, pp 30–33

Guest, D E (1987) Human resource management and industrial relations, *Journal of Management Studies*, **14**(5), pp 503–21

Guest, D E (1989a) Human resource management: its implications for industrial relations, in *New Perspectives on Human Resource Management*, ed J Storey, Routledge, London

Guest, D E (1989b) Personnel and HRM: can you tell the difference? *Personnel Management*, January, pp 48–51

Guest, D E (1990) Human resource management and the American dream, *Journal of Management Studies*, **27**(4), pp 378–97

Guest, D E (1991) Personnel management: the end of orthodoxy, *British Journal of Industrial Relations*, **29**(2), pp 149–76

Guest, D E (1992a) Human resource management in the UK, in *The Handbook of Human Resource Management*, ed B Towers, Blackwell, Oxford

Guest, D E (1992b) Motivation after Herzberg, unpublished paper delivered at the Compensation Forum, London

Guest, D E (1993) Current perspectives on human resource management in the United Kingdom, in *Current Trends in Human Resource Management in Europe*, ed C Brewster, Kogan Page, London

Guest, D E (1995) Human resource management: trade unions and industrial relations, in *Human Resource Management: A Critical Text*, ed J Storey, Routledge, London

Guest, D E (1997) Human resource management and performance: a review of the research agenda, *International Journal of Human Resource Management*, **8**(3), pp 263–76

Guest, D E (1999a) Human resource management: the workers' verdict, *Human Resource Management Journal*, **9**(2), pp 5–25

Guest, D (1999b) Do people strategies really enhance business success and if so, why don't more people use them? Presentation at the Annual Conference of the Institute of Personnel and Development, October

Guest, D E and Conway, N (1997) *Employee Motivation and the Psychological Contract*, Institute of Personnel and Development, London

Guest, D E and Conway, N (1998) *Fairness at Work and the Psychological Contract*, Institute of Personnel and Development, London

Guest, D E *et al* (1996) *The State of the Psychological Contract in Employment*, Institute of Personnel and Development, London

Guest, D E and Fatchett, D (1974) *Worker Participation: Industrial control and performance*, Institute of Personnel Management, London

Guest, D E and Hoque, K (1994) Yes, personnel management does make the difference, *Personnel Management*, November, pp 40–44

Guest, D E and Hoque, K (1995) An assessment and further analysis of the 1990 Workshop Industrial Relations Survey, in *The Contribution of Personnel Management to Organizational Performance*, ed D E Guest *et al*, IPD, London

Guest, D E and Horwood, R (1981) Characteristics of the successful personnel manager, *Personnel Management*, May, pp 18–23

Guest, D E, Michie, J, Sheehan, M and Conway, N (2000) *Employment Relations, HRM and business performance*, Institute of Personnel and Development, London

Guest, D, Michie, J, Sheehan, S and Metochi, M (2000) *Effective People Management: Initial findings of The Future of Work survey*, Chartered Institute of Personnel and Development, London

Guest, D E and Peccei, R (1994) The nature and causes of effective human resource management, *British Journal of Industrial Relations*, June, pp 219–42

Guilford, J P (1967) *The Nature of Human Intelligence*, McGraw-Hill, New York

Gunnigle, P and Moore, S (1994) Linking business strategy and human resource management: issues and implications, *Personnel Review*, **23**(1), pp 63–83

Guzzo, R A and Noonan, K A (1994) Human resource practices as communication and the psychological contract, *Human Resource Management*, Fall

Hackman, J R and Oldham, G R (1974) Motivation through the design of work: test of a theory, *Organizational Behaviour and Human Performance*, **16**(2), pp 250–79

Hague, H (1996) The end for merit pay? *Personnel Today*, 4 June, pp 28–29

Hall, P and Norris, P (1992) Development centres: making the learning organization happen, *Human Resources*, Autumn, pp 126–28

Hall, R (1992) The strategic analysis of intangible resources, *Strategic Management Journal*, 13, pp 135–44

Hall, R (1996) Supply Change Management: the challenge for the 21st century, Paper presented to the CIPS Conference at Durham University Business School, 9 May

Halpin, A and Winer, B A (1957) *Factorial Study of the Leader Behaviour Description*, Ohio State University

Hamblin, A C (1974) *Evaluation and Control of Training*, McGraw-Hill, Maidenhead

Hamel, G and Prahalad, C K (1989) Strategic intent, *Harvard Business Review*, May-June, pp 63–76

Handy, C (1981) *Understanding Organizations*, Penguin, Harmondsworth

Handy, C (1984) *The Future of Work*, Blackwell, Oxford

Handy, C (1989) *The Age of Unreason*, Business Books, London

Handy, C (1994) *The Empty Raincoat*, Hutchinson, London

Handy, L, Devine, M and Heath, L (1996) *360-degree Feedback: Unguided missile or powerful weapon?* Ashridge Management Group, Berkhamsted

Hansen, M T, Nohria, N and Tierney, T (1999) What's your strategy for managing knowledge? *Harvard Business Review*, March–April, pp 106–16

Harre, R (1979) *Social Being*, Blackwell, Oxford

Harrison, R (1972) Understanding your organization's character, *Harvard Business Review*, **5**, pp 119–28

Harrison, R (1992) *Employee Development*, 1st edn, Institute of Personnel Management, London

Harrison, R (1997) *Employee Development*, 2nd edn, Institute of Personnel and Development, London

Hartle, F (1995) *Transforming the Performance Management Process*, Kogan Page, London

Harvey-Jones, J (1989) *Making it Happen*, Collins, Glasgow

Hawkins, K A (1979) *A Handbook of Industrial Relations Practice*, Kogan Page, London

Hayes Committee on Personnel Management (1972) *Training for the Management of Human Resources*, Department of Employment, HMSO, London

Hegarty, S (1995) Self service, *Personnel Today*, 6 June, pp 25–26

Heider, F (1958) *The Psychology of Interpersonal Relationships*, Wiley, New York

Heinrich, H W (1959) *Industrial Accident Prevention*, McGraw-Hill, New York

Hendry, C (1995) *Human Resource Management: A strategic approach to employment*, Butterworth-Heinemann, Oxford

Hendry, C and Pettigrew, A (1986) The practice of strategic human resource management, *Personnel Review*, **15**, pp 2–8

Hendry, C and Pettigrew, A (1990) Human resource management: an agenda for the 1990s, *International Journal of Human Resource Management*, **1**(3), pp 17–43

Hermanson, R (1964) *Accounting for Human Assets*, Bureau of Business and Economic Research, Michigan State University, Occasional Paper, November

Herriot, P, Hirsh, W and Riley, P (1998) *Trust and Transition: Managing the employment relationship*, Wiley, Chichester

Herzberg, F (1968) One more time: how do you motivate employees?, *Harvard Business Review*, January-February, pp 109–20

Herzberg, F W, Mausner, B and Snyderman, B (1957) *The Motivation to Work*, Wiley, New York

Heskett, J (1986) *Managing in the Service Economy*, Harvard Business School Press, Boston, Mass

Hiltrop, J M (1995) The changing psychological contract: the human resource challenge of the 1990s, *European Management Journal*, **13**(3), September, pp 286–94

Hofstede, G (1980) *Cultural Consequences: International differences in work-related values*, Sage, Beverley Hills, Calif

Holbeche, L (1994/1995) *Career Development in Flatter Structures*, Roffey Park Management Institute, Horsham

Holbeche, L (1997) *Career Development: The impact of flatter structures on careers*, Butterworth-Heinemann, Oxford

Holbeche, L (1998) *Motivating People in Lean Organizations*, Butterworth-Heinemann, Oxford

Holt, A and Andrews, H (1993) *Principles of Health and Safety at Work*, IOSH, London

Honey, P (1998) The debate starts here, *People Management*, 1 October, pp 28–29

Honey, P and Mumford, A (1986) *The Manual of Learning Styles*, Peter Honey, Maidenhead

Hope-Hailey, V, Gratton, L, McGovern, P, Stiles, P and Truss, C (1998) A chameleon function? HRM in the '90s, *Human Resource Management Journal*, **7**(3), pp 5–18

Hoyle, E (1995) The school as a learning organisation, Paper delivered at the AERA Conference, San Francisco, April

Huczynski, A and Fitzpatrick, M J (1989) *Managing Employee Absence for a Competitive Edge*, Pitman, London

Hulin, C L and Blood, M R (1968) Job enlargement, individual differences and worker responses, *Psychological Bulletin*, **69**(1)

Hull, C (1951) *Essentials of Behaviour*, Yale University Press, New Haven, Conn

Humble, J (1963) Programmitis and crown princes, *The Manager*, December

Humble, J (1970) *Management by Objectives in Action*, McGraw-Hill, Maidenhead

Hunter, J E and Hunter, R F (1984) Validity and utility of alternative predictors of job performance, *Psychological Bulletin*, **96**(1)

Huselid, M A (1995) The impact of human resource management: an agenda for the 1990s, *International Journal of Human Resource Management*, **1**(1), pp 17–43

Huselid, M A and Becker, B E (1996) Methodological issues in cross-sectional and panel estimates of the human resource-firm performance link, *Industrial Relations*, **35**(3), pp 400–22

Hutchinson, S and Wood, S (1995) *Personnel and the Line: Developing the employment relationship*, IPD, London

Hutton, W (1995) *The State We're In*, Cape, London

IBM/Towers Perrin (1992) *Priorities for Competitive Advantage*, Towers Perrin, New York

Ichniowski, C, Shaw, K and Prennushi, G (1997) The effects of human resource management practices on productivity: a study of steel finishing lines, *American Economic Review*, June

Incomes Data Services (IDS) (1997) *IDS Study no 626, Performance Management*, May, Incomes Data Services, London

IDS (1993) Managers, teams and reward, *IDS Management Pay Review*, August, pp 20–23

IDS (1995) Executive benefits, *Management Pay Review* no 174, August

Industrial Participation Association (1995) *Towards Industrial Partnership*, IPA, London

Industrial Society (1974) *Practical Policies for Participation*, Industrial Society, London

Institute of Personnel and Development (IPD) (1993a) *Code of Professional Conduct*, IPD, London

IPD (1993b) *Quality: People management matters*, IPD, London

IPD (1993c) *Code on Employee Involvement and Participation*, IPD, London

IPD (1994) *People Make the Difference*, IPD, London

IPD (1995) *The Development of the New Psychological Contract* (unpublished)

IPD (1997a) *The IPD Guide on Implementing Computerised Personnel Systems*, IPD, London

IPD (1997b) *IPD Key Facts on Psychological Testing*, IPD, London

IPD (1998a) *IPD 1998 Performance Pay Survey: Executive summary*, IPD, London

IPD (1998b) *The IPD Guide to Outsourcing*, IPD, London

IPD (1988c) *Getting Fit and Staying Fit: Developing lean and responsive organisations*, IPD, London

IPD (1999a) *The IPD Guide on Using Your Computerised Personnel Effectively*, IPD, London

IPD (1999b) *Organisational Development – Whose Responsibility?*, IPD, London

IPD (1999c) *IPD Key Facts on References*, IPD, London

Institute of Personnel Management (IPM) (1992a) *Performance Management in the UK: An analysis of the issues*, IPM, London

IPM (1992b) *Statement on Counselling in the Workplace*, IPM, London

Inland Revenue Service (IRS) (1991) 20 years of industrial relations, *IRS Employment Trends* no 500, IRS, p 2

IRS (1993) Multi-employer bargaining, *IRS Employment Trends* no 544, IRS, pp 6–8

IRS (1994a) Management development, *IRS Employee Development Bulletin* no 54, June, IRS, pp 10–12

IRS (1994b) Where are the unions going, *IRS Employment Trends* no 556, IRS, pp 14–16

IRS (1996) Using human resources to achieve strategic objectives, *IRS Management Review*, **1** (2), July

IRS (1998) Pay prospects survey, *Pay and Benefits Bulletin* no 459 November, pp 10–13

IRS (2000) *IRS Employee Development Bulletin*, November, IRS, pp 8–12

Ishikawa, K (1976) *Guide to Quality Control*, Asian Productivity Organization, Tokyo

Jackson, L (1989) Transforming management performance: a competency approach, Presentation at the Institute of Personnel Management annual conference, October (unpublished)

James, R and Sells, S B (1981) Psychological climate: theoretical perspectives and empirical research, in *Towards a Psychology of Situations: An interactional perspective*, ed D Magnusson, Erlbaum, Hillsdale, NJ

Janis, I (1972) *Victims of Groupthink*, Houghton Mifflin, Boston, Mass

Jaques, E (1961) *Equitable Payment*, Heinemann, London

Johnson, G and Scholes, K (1993) *Exploring Corporate Strategy*, Prentice-Hall, Hemel Hempstead

Johnston, J (1991) An empirical study of repatriation of managers in UK multi-nationals, *Human Resource Management Journal*, **1**(4), pp 102–8

Jones, P, Palmer, J, Whitehead, D and Needham, P (1995) Prisms of performance, *Ashridge Journal*, April, pp 10–14

Jones, T W (1995) Performance management in a changing context, *Human Resource Management*, Fall, pp 425–42

Jung, C (1923) *Psychological Types*, Routledge and Kegan Paul, London

Juran, J N (1979) *Quality Control Handbook*, McGraw-Hill, New York

Kahn, R (1974) *Organizational Stress*, Wiley, New York

Kahn-Freund, O (1972) *Labour and the Law*, Stevens, London

Kakabadse, A (1983) *The Politics of Management*, Gower, Aldershot

Kalleberg, A L and Loscocco, K A (1983) Aging, values and rewards: explaining age differences in job satisfaction, *American Sociological Review*, **48**, pp 323–36

Kamoche, K (1996) Strategic human resource management within a resource capability view of the firm, *Journal of Management Studies*, **33**(2), pp 213–33

Kandola, R and Fullerton, J (1994) *Managing the Mosaic: Diversity in action*, Institute of Personnel and Development, London

Kane, J S (1996) The conceptualisation and representation of total performance effectiveness, *Human Resource Management Review*, Summer, pp 123–45

Kanter, R M (1984) *The Change Masters*, Allen & Unwin, London

Kanter, R M (1989) *When Giants Learn to Dance*, Simon & Schuster, London

Kaplan, R S and Norton, D P (1992) The balanced scorecard: measures that drive performance, *Harvard Business Review*, January–February, pp 71–79

Katz, D and Kahn, R (1964) *The Social Psychology of Organizations*, Wiley, New York

Katzenbach, J and Smith, D (1993) *The Magic of Teams*, Harvard Business School Press, Boston, Mass

Kay, J (1993) *Functions of Corporate Success*, Oxford University Press, Oxford

Keenoy, T (1990a) HRM: a case of the wolf in sheep's clothing, *Personnel Review*, **19**(2), pp 3–9

Keenoy, T (1990b) HRM: rhetoric, reality and contradiction, *International Journal of Human Resource Management*, **1**(3), pp 363–84

Keenoy, T (1997) HRMism and the images of re-presentation, *Journal of Management Studies*, **4**(5), pp 825–41

Keenoy, T and Anthony, P (1992) HRM: metaphor, meaning and morality, in *Reassessing Human Resource Management*, ed P Blyton and P Turnbull, Sage, London

Keep, E (1989) Corporate training strategies, in *New Perspectives on Human Resource Management*, ed J Storey, Blackwell, Oxford

Kelley, H H (1967) Attribution theory in social psychology, in *Nebraska Symposium on Motivation*, ed D Levine, University of Nebraska Press, Lincoln, Neb

Kelly, G (1955) *The Psychology of Personal Constructs*, Norton, New York

Kenney, J and Reid, M (1994) *Training Interventions*, 4th edn, Institute of Personnel and Development, London

Kessels, J (1996) Knowledge productivity and the corporate curriculum, in *Knowledge Management: Organisation, competence and methodology: proceedings of the Fourth International ISMICK Symposium*, ed J F Scjhreinmakers, Rotterdam, October

Kessler, S and Bayliss, F (1992) *Contemporary British Industrial Relations*, Macmillan, London

Kessler, S and Undy, R (1996) *The New Employment Relationship: Examining the psychological contract*, Institute of Personnel and Development, London

Kirkpatrick, D L (1994) *Evaluating Training Programs*, Berret-Koehler, San Francisco

Kissler, G D (1994) The new employment contract, *Human Resource Management*, Fall, **33**(3), pp 335–52

Knowles, M S (1989) Everything you wanted to know from Malcolm Knowles, *Training*, August, pp 8–10

Kochan, T A and Dyer, L (1993) Managing transformational change: the role of human resource professionals, *International Journal of Human Resource Management*, **4**(3), pp 569–90

Kohn, A (1993) Why incentive plans cannot work, *Harvard Business Review*, September-October, pp 54–63

Kolb, D A, Rubin, I M and McIntyre, J M (1974) *Organizational Psychology: An experimental approach*, Prentice-Hall, Englewood Cliffs, NJ

Kotter, J (1990) What leaders really do, *Harvard Business Review*, May-June, pp 103–11

Kotter, J J (1995) *A 20% Solution: Using rapid re-design to build tomorrow's organization today*, Wiley, New York

Koys, D and De Cotiis, T (1991) Inductive measures of organizational climate, *Human Relations*, **44**, pp 265–85

Landy, F and Farr, J (1980) Performance ratings, *Psychological Bulletin*, **87**, pp 72–107

Latham, G and Locke, R (1979) Goal setting: a motivational technique that works, *Organizational Dynamics*, Autumn, pp 68–80

Latham, G P, Saari, L M, Pursell, E D and Campion, M A (1980) The situational interview, *Journal of Applied Psychology*, **65**, pp 442–47

Lawler, E E (1969) Job design and employee motivation, *Personnel Psychology*, **22**, pp 426–35

Lawler, E E (1986) What's wrong with point-factor job evaluation, *Compensation and Benefits Review*, March–April, pp 20–28

Lawler, E E (1990) *Strategic Pay*, Jossey Bass, San Francisco

Lawrence, P R and Lorsch, J W (1969) *Developing Organizations*, Addison-Wesley, Reading, Mass

Lawrence, P R and Lorsch, J W (1976) *Organization and Environment*, Harvard University Press, Cambridge, Mass

Lawson, P (1995) Performance management: an overview, in *The Performance Handbook*, ed M Walters, Institute of Personnel and Development, London

Leavitt, H J (1951) Some effects of certain communication patterns on group performance, *Journal of Abnormal Psychology*, **14**(3), pp 457–81

Legge, K (1978) *Power, Innovation and Problem Solving in Personnel Management*, McGraw-Hill, Maidenhead

Legge, K (1987) Women in personnel management: uphill climb or downhill slide? in *Women in a Man's World*, ed A Spencer and D Podmore, Tavistock Publications, London

Legge, K (1989) Human resource management: a critical analysis, in *New Perspectives in Human Resource Management*, ed J Storey, Routledge, London

Legge, K (1995) *Human Resource Management: Rhetorics and realities*, Macmillan, London

Legge, K (1998) The morality of HRM, in *Experiencing Human Resource Management*, ed C Mabey, D Skinner and T Clark, Sage, London

Lengnick-Hall, C A and Lengnick-Hall, M L (1990) *Interactive Human Resource Management and Strategic Planning*, Quorum Books, Westport

Leventhal, G S (1980) What should be done with equity theory? in *Social Exchange: Advances in theory and research*, ed G K Gergen, M S Greenberg and R H Willis, Plenum, New York

Levinson, D (1978) *The Seasons of Man's Life*, Knopf, New York

Levitt, T (1983) *The Marketing Imagination*, Free Press, New York

Lewin, K (1947) Frontiers in group dynamics, *Human Relations*, **1**(1), pp 5–42

Lewin, K (1951) *Field Theory in Social Science*, Harper & Row, New York

Liff, S (2000) Manpower or HR planning: what's in a name? in *Personnel Management*, 3rd edn, ed S Bach and K Sisson, Blackwell, Oxford

Likert, R (1961) *New Patterns of Management*, Harper & Row, New York

Likert, R (1967) *The Human Organization*, McGraw-Hill, New York

Littler, C and Salaman, G (1982) Bravermania and beyond: recent theories of the labour process, *Sociology*, **16**(2), pp 215–69

Litwin, G H and Stringer, R A (1968) *Motivation and Organizational Climate*, Harvard University Press, Boston, Mass

Locke, E A (1984) Effect of self-efficacy, goals and task strategies on task performance, *Journal of Applied Psychology*, **69**(2), pp 241–51

London, M and Beatty, R W (1993) 360-degree feedback as competitive advantage, *Human Resource Management*, Summer–Fall, pp 353–72

Lorenz, K (1966) *On Aggression*, Methuen, London

Lowry, P (1990) as reported in *Personnel Management Plus*, December, p 7

Lupton, T (1975) Best fit in the design of organizations, *Personnel Review*, **4**(1), pp 15–22

Luthans, F and Kreitner, R (1975) *Organizational Behaviour Modification*, Scott-Foresman, Glenview, Ill

Mabey, C and Salaman, G (1995) *Strategic Human Resource Management*, Blackwell Business, Oxford

Mabey, C, Skinner, D and Clark, T (1998) *Experiencing Human Resource Management*, Sage, London

McCartan, P (1998) Fairness at work: developing labour-management partnerships, Presentation at IPD National Conference, Harrogate

McClelland, G (1963) *British Journal of Industrial Relations*, June, p 278

McCormick, E J, Jeanneret, P R and Mecham, R C (1972) A study of job characteristics and job dimensions based on the Position Analysis Questionnaire (PAQ), *Journal of Applied Psychology*, **56**, pp 347–68

McCrae, R and Costa, P (1989) More reasons to adopt the five factor model, *American Psychologist*, **44**, pp 451–52

MacDuffie, J P (1995) Human resource bundles and manufacturing performance, *Industrial Relations Review*, **48**(2), pp 199–221

McGregor, D (1957) An uneasy look at performance appraisal, *Harvard Business Review*, May-June, pp 89–94

McGregor, D (1960) *The Human Side of Enterprise*, McGraw-Hill, New York

Mackay, L and Torrington, D (1986) *The Changing Nature of Personnel Management*, Institute of Personnel Management, London

MacLachlan, R (1994) Robust research – or just headline-seeking analysis? *Personnel Management Plus*, June, p 9

McLean, A (1981) Organization development: a case of the Emperor's new clothes? *Personnel Review*, **4**(1), pp 38–46

Macneil, R (1985) Relational contract: what we do and do not know, *Wisconsin Law Review*, pp 483–525

Maier, N (1958) *The Appraisal Interview*, Wiley, New York

Makin, P, Cooper, C and Cox, C (1996) *Organizations and the Psychological Contract*, BPS Books, Leicester

Mangham, L L (1979) *The Politics of Organizational Change*, Associated Business Press, London

Manpower Services Commission (1981) *Glossary of Training Terms*, 3rd edn, HMSO, London

Mansfield, R (1999) What is 'competence' all about? *Competency*, **6**(3), pp 24–28

Mant, A (1970) *The Experienced Manager*, British Institute of Management, London

Mant, A (1996) The psychological contract, Presentation at IPD National Conference, October

Marchington, M (1985) *Joint Consultation Revisited*, Glasgow University, Glasgow

Marchington, M (1995a) Fairy tales and magic wands: new employment practices in perspective, *Employee Relations*, Spring, pp 51–66

Marchington, M (1995b) Employee relations, in *Strategic Prospects for HRM*, ed S Tyson, Institute of Personnel and Development, London

Marchingon, M and Goodman, J (1992) *New Developments in Employee Involvement*, Employment Department, Sheffield

Marchington, M and Wilkinson, A (1996) *Core Personnel and Development*, Institute of Personnel and Development, London

Margerison, C (1976) A constructive approach to appraisal, *Personnel Management*, July, pp 30–33

Margerison, C and McCann, R (1986) The Margerison/McCann team management resource: theory and application, *International Journal of Manpower*, **7**(2), pp 1–32

Marginson, P and Sisson, K (1990) Single table talk, *Personnel management*, May, pp 46–49

Marginson, P, Armstrong, P, Edwards, P and Purcell, J (1993) The control of industrial relations in large companies: an initial analysis of the Second Company Level Industrial Relations Survey, *Warwick Papers in Industrial Relations* no 45, University of Warwick, Coventry

Markham, C (1987) *Practical Consulting*, Institute of Chartered Accountants, London

Marsden, D and French, S (1998) *What a Performance: Performance-related pay in the public services*, Centre for Economic Performance, London

Marsh, A (1981) *Employee Relations Policy and Decision Making*, Gower, Aldershot

Marsick, V J (1994) Trends in managerial invention: creating a learning map, *Management Learning*, **21**(1), pp 11–33

Martin, A O (1967) *Welfare at Work*, Batsford, London

Marx, K (tr 1976) *Capital*, Penguin, Harmondsworth

Maslow, A (1954) *Motivation and Personality*, Harper & Row, New York

Mayo, A (1992) A framework for career management, *Personnel Management*, February, pp 36–39

Mayo, A (1999) Making human capital meaningful, *Knowledge Management Review*, January–February, pp 26–29

Mayo, A and Lank, E (1994) *The Power of Learning: A guide to gaining competitive advantage*, Institute of Personnel and Development, London

Mayo, E (1933) *Human Problems of an Industrial Civilisation*, Macmillan, London

Mecklenberg, S, Deering, A and Sharp, D (1999) Knowledge management: a secret engine of corporate growth, *Executive Agenda*, **2**, pp 5–15

Meyerson, D and Martin, J (1987) Cultural Studies and integration of three different views, *Journal of Management Studies*, **24**(6), pp 623–47.

Miles, R E and Snow, C C (1978) *Organizational Strategy, Structure and Process*, McGraw-Hill, New York

Miller, E and Rice, A (1967) *Systems of Organization*, Tavistock, London

Miller, P (1987) Strategic industrial relations and human resource management: distinction, definition and recognition, *Journal of Management Studies*, **24**, pp 101–9

Miller, P (1989) Strategic human resource management: what it is and what it isn't, *Personnel Management*, February, pp 46–51

Miller, P (1991) Strategic human resource management: an assessment of progress, *Human Resource Management Journal*, **1**(4), pp 23–39

Miller, R and Stewart, J (1999) Opened university, *People Management*, **5**(12), pp 42–46

Millward, N (1994) *The New Industrial Relations?* Policy Studies Institute, Poole

Millward, N, Bryn, A and Forth, J (2000) *All Change At Work?* Routledge, London

Millward, N et al (1992) *Workplace Industrial Relations in Transition*, Dartmouth Publishing, Hants

Mintzberg, H (1973) *The Nature of Managerial Work*, Harper & Row, New York

Mintzberg, H (1978) Patterns in strategy formation, *Management Science*, May, pp 934–48

Mintzberg, H (1981) Organization design: fashion or fit, *Harvard Business Review*, January-February, pp 103–16

Mintzberg, H (1983a) *Power In and Around Organizations*, Prentice-Hall, Englewood Cliffs, NJ

Mintzberg, H (1983b) *Structure in Fives*, Prentice-Hall, Englewood Cliffs, NJ

Mintzberg, H (1987) Crafting strategy, *Harvard Business Review*, July-August, pp 66–74

Mintzberg, H, Quinn, J B and James, R M (1988) *The Strategy Process: Concepts, contexts and cases*, Prentice-Hall, Englewood Cliffs, NJ

Mirvis, P and Hall, D (1994) Psychological success and the boundaryless career, *Journal of Organisational Behaviour*, **15**, pp 361–80

Mischel, W (1968) *Personality and Assessment*, Wiley, New York

Mischel, W (1981) *Introduction to Personality*, Holt, Rinehart and Winston, New York

Monks, J (1994) The union response to HRM: fraud or opportunity? *Personnel Management*, September, pp 42–47

Monks, K (1992) Models of personnel management: a means of understanding the diversity of personnel practices, *Human Resource Management Journal*, **3**(2), pp 29–41

Mowdray, R, Porter, L and Steers, R (1982) *Employee–Organization Linkages: The psychology of commitment, absenteeism and turnover*, Academic Press, London

Mullen, B and Cooper, C (1994) The relation between group cohesiveness and performance: an integration, *Psychological Bulletin*, **115**, pp 210–27

Mumford, A (1993) How managers can become developers, *Personnel Management*, June, pp 42–45

Mumford, A (1994) *Management Development: Strategies for action*, Institute of Personnel Management, London

Munro Fraser, J (1954) *A Handbook of Employment Interviewing*, Macdonald & Evans, London

Murlis, H and Fitt, D (1991) Job evaluation in a changing world, *Personnel Management*, May, pp 39–43

Murphy, J (1991) Developing performance through competency frameworks, from Proceedings of the annual Hay Management Consultants Conference (unpublished)

Nadler, D A and Tushman, M L (1980) A congruence model for diagnosing organizational behaviour, in *Resource Book in Macro-Organizational Behaviour*, ed R H Miles, Goodyear, Santa Monica, Calif

Nahpiet, J and Goshal, S (1998) Social capital, intellectual capital and the organizational advantage, *Academy of Management Review*, **23**(2), pp 242–66

Neathey, F (1994) *Job Evaluation in the 1990s*, Industrial Relations Services, London

New Learning for New Work Consortium (1999) *Managing Learning for Added Value*, Institute of Personnel and Development, London

Newcomb, T M (1966) On the definition of attitudes, in *Attitudes*, ed M Jahoda and N Warren, Penguin, Harmondsworth

Newton, T and Findlay, P (1996) Playing God?: the performance of appraisal, *Human Resource Management Journal*, **6**(3), pp 42–56

Nonaka, I (1991) The knowledge-creating company, *Harvard Business Review*, November–December, pp 96–104

Nonaka, I (1994) A dynamic theory of organisational knowledge creation, *Organisation Science*, **5**, pp 14–37

Nonaka, I and Takeuchi, H (1995) *The Knowledge-Creating Company*, Oxford University Press, New York

Noon, M (1992) HRM: a map, model or theory? in *Reassessing Human Resource Management*, ed P Blyton and P Turnbull, Sage, London

Opsahl, R and Dunnette, M (1966) The role of financial compensation in industrial motivation, *Psychological Bulletin*, **66**, pp 94–118

Organization for Economic Cooperation and Development (OECD) (1998) *Human Capital Investment: An international comparison*, OECD, Paris

Ouchi, W G (1981) *Theory Z*, Addison-Wesley, Reading, Mass

Outram, R (1998) Mental arithmetic, *Human Resources*, October, pp 77–79

Partridge, B (1989) The problem of supervision, in *Personnel Management in Britain*, ed K Sisson, Blackwell, Oxford

Pascale, R (1990) *Managing on the Edge*, Viking, London

Pascale, R and Athos, A (1981) *The Art of Japanese Management*, Simon & Schuster, New York

Patterson, M G, West, M A, Lawthom, R and Nickell, S (1997) *Impact of People Management Practices on Performance*, Institute of Personnel and Development, London

Pearce, J A and Robinson, R B (1988) *Strategic Management: Strategy formulation and implementation*, Irwin, Georgetown, Ontario

Pearn, K and Kandola, R (1993) *Job Analysis*, Institute of Personnel Management, London

Pedler, M, Boydell, T and Burgoyne, J (1989) Towards the learning company, *Management Education and Development*, **20**(1), pp 1–8

Pedler, M and Burgoyne, J (1994) *A Manager's Guide to Self Development*, McGraw-Hill, Maidenhead

Pedler, M, Burgoyne, J and Boydell, T (1991) *The Learning Company: A strategy for sustainable development*, McGraw-Hill, London

Perkins, S J (1997) *Internationalization: The people dimension*, Kogan Page, London

Perkins, S and Hendry, C (1999) *The IPD Guide on International Reward and Recognition*, Institute of Personnel and Development, London

Perrow, C (1970) *Organizational Analysis: A sociological view*, Tavistock, London

Perrow, C (1980) The short and glorious history of organizational theory, in *Resource Book in Macro-Organizational Behaviour*, ed R H Miles, Goodyear, Santa Monica, Calif

Personnel Standards Lead Body (1993) *A Perspective on Personnel*, Personnel Standards Lead Body, London

Peters, J (1968) *Strategies and Tactics in Labour Negotiations*, McGraw-Hill, New York

Peters, T (1988) *Thriving on Chaos*, Macmillan, London

Peters, T and Austin, N (1985) *A Passion for Excellence*, Collins, Glasgow

Peters, T and Waterman, R (1982) *In Search of Excellence*, Harper & Row, New York

Pettigrew, A and Whipp, R (1991) *Managing Change for Competitive Success*, Blackwell, Oxford

Pfeffer, G (1998) *The Human Equation*, Harvard Business School Press, Boston, Mass

Pfeffer, J (1994) *Competitive Advantage Through People*, Harvard Business School Press, Boston, Mass

Pfeffer, J and Cohen, Y (1984) Determinants of internal labour markets in organizations, *Administrative Science Quarterly*, **29**, pp 550–72

Pfeffer, J and Salancik, G R (1978) *The External Control of Organizations: A resource dependence perspective*, Harper & Row, New York

Phelps Brown, H (1990) The counter revolution of our time, *Industrial Relations*, **29**(1), pp 306–20

Pickard, J (1995) Prepare to make a moral judgement, *People Management*, 4 May, pp 22–25, 27

Pickard, J (1997) A yearning for learning, *People Management*, **3**(5), pp 34–35

Pickard, J (2000) When PwC stands for prize winning concept, *People Management*, 12 October, p 31

Pil, F K and MacDuffie, J P (1996) The adoption of high-involvement work practices, *Industrial Relations*, **35**(3), pp 423–55

Porter, L W (1961) A study of perceived need satisfaction in bottom and middle management jobs, *Journal of Applied Psychology*, **45**, pp 1–10

Porter, L W and Lawler, E E (1968) *Managerial Attitudes and Performance*, Irwin-Dorsey, Holmewood, Ill

Porter, L W, Steers, R, Mowday, R and Boulian, P (1974) Organizational commitment, job satisfaction and turnover amongst psychiatric technicians, *Journal of Applied Psychology*, **59**, pp 603–9

Porter, M (1980) *Competitive Strategy*, Free Press, New York

Porter, M (1985) *Competitive Advantage: Creating and sustaining superior performance*, Free Press, New York

Prahalad, C K and Hamel, G (1990) The core competences of the corporation, *Harvard Business Review*, May–June, pp 79–91

Pritchard, D and Murlis, H (1992) *Jobs, Roles and People*, Brearley, London

Purcell, J (1979) A strategy for management control in industrial relations, in *The Control of Work*, ed J Purcell and R Smith, Macmillan, London

Purcell, J (1987) Mapping management styles in employee relations, *Journal of Management Studies*, September, pp 78–91

Purcell, J (1989) The impact of corporate strategy on human resource management, in *New Perspectives on Human Resource Management*, ed J Storey, Routledge, London

Purcell, J (1993) The challenge of human resource management for industrial relations research and practice, *International Journal of Human Resource Management*, **4**(3), pp 511–27

Purcell, J (1994) Personnel earns a place on the board, *Personnel Management*, February, pp 26–29

Purcell, J (1999) Best practice or best fit: chimera or cul-de-sac, *Human Resource Management Journal*, **9**(3), pp 26–41

Purcell, J, Hutchinson, S and Kinnie, N (1998) *The Lean Organisation*, Institute of Personnel and Development, London

Purcell, J and Sisson, K (1983) Strategies and practice in the management of industrial relations, in *Industrial Relations in Britain*, ed G Bain, Blackwell, Oxford

Putnam, R (1996) Who killed civic America? *Prospect*, March, pp 66–72

Quinn Mills, D (1983) Planning with people in mind, *Harvard Business Review*, November–December, pp 97–105

Rackham, N, Honey, P and Colbert, M (1967) *Developing Interactive Skills*, Wellens, Northampton

Reay, D G (1994) *Understanding How People Learn*, Kogan Page, London

Recruitment Development Report (1991) New ways of managing your human resources: a survey of top employers, *Industrial Relations Review*, March

Reich, R (1991) *The Work of Nations: Preparing Ourselves for 21st Century Capitalism*, Simon & Schuster, London

Reilly, P (1999) *The Human Resource Planning Audit*, Cambridge Strategy Publications, Cambridge

Reilly, P (2000) *HR Shared Services and the Re-alignment of HR*, Institute for Employment Studies, Brighton

Revans, R W (1971) *Developing Effective Managers*, Longman, Harlow

Revans, R W (1989) *Action Learning*, Blond & Briggs, London

Richardson, R and Thompson, M (1999) *The Impact of People Management Practices on Business Performance: A literature review*, Institute of Personnel and Development, London

Richardson, W (1993) The visionary leader, *Administrator*, September, pp 3–7

Roberts, C (1990) *Harmonization: Whys and wherefores*, Institute of Personnel Management, London

Roberts, G (1997) *Recruitment and Selection: A competency approach*, Institute of Personnel and Development, London

Robertson, I T and Cooper, C L (1983) *Human Behaviour in Organizations*, Macdonald & Evans, Plymouth

Robertson, I T and Smith, M (1985) *Motivation and Job Design*, Institute of Personnel Management, London

Robertson, I T, Smith, M and Cooper, D (1992) *Motivation*, Institute of Personnel Management, London

Robinson, D (1999) *The Human Resource Information System Audit*, Cambridge Strategy Publications, Cambridge

Rodger, A (1952) *The Seven-Point Plan*, National Institute of Industrial Psychology, London

Roethlisberger, F and Dickson, W (1939) *Management and the Worker*, Harvard University Press, Cambridge, Mass

Rosow, J and Casner-Lotto, J (1998) *People, Partnership and Profits: The new labor-management agenda*, Work in America Institute, New York

Rothwell, S (1995) Human resource planning, in *Human Resource Management: A critical text*, ed J Storey, Routledge, London

Rousseau, D M (1988) The construction of climate in organizational research, in *International Review of Industrial and Organizational Psychology*, ed L C Cooper and I Robertson, Wiley, Chichester

Rousseau, D M and Greller, M M (1994) Human resource practices: administrative contract makers, *Human Resource Management*, **33**(3), pp 385–401

Rousseau, D M and Wade-Benzoni, K A (1994) Linking strategy and human resource practices: how employee and customer contracts are created, *Human Resource Management*, **33**(3), pp 463–89

Royal Commission on Trades Unions and Employers Associations (1968) *Report of the Royal Commission on Trades Unions and Employers Associations*, HMSO, London

Sackmann, S, Flamholz, E and Bullen, M (1989) Home asset accounting, *Journal of Accounting Literature*, **5**, pp 235–64

Sako, M (1994) The informational requirement of trust in supplier relations: evidence from Japan, the UK and the USA, unpublished

Salancik, G R (1977) Commitment and the control of organizational behaviour and belief, in *New Directions in Organizational Behaviour*, ed B M Staw and G R Salancik, St Clair, Chicago

Saunders, R (1992) *The Safety Audit*, Pitman, London

Saville, P and Sik, G (1992) Personality questionnaires: current issues and controversies, *Human Resources Management Yearbook*, A P Services, London, pp 28–32

Scarborough, H and Carter, C (2000) *Investigating Knowledge Management*, Chartered Institute of Personnel and Development, London

Scarborough, H, Swan, J and Preston, J (1999) *Knowledge Management: A literature review*, Institute of Personnel and Development, London

Schaffer, R (1991) Demand better results – and get them, *Harvard Business Review*, March-April, pp 142–49

Schein, E H (1965) *Organizational Psychology*, Prentice-Hall, Englewood Cliffs, NJ

Schein, E H (1969) *Process Consultation: Its role in organizational development*, Addison-Wesley, Reading, Mass

Schein, E H (1977) *Career Dynamics*, Addison-Wesley, Reading, Mass

Schein, E H (1984) Coming to a new awareness of culture, *Sloan Management Review*, Winter, pp 1–15

Schein, E H (1985) *Organization Culture and Leadership*, Jossey Bass, New York

Schein, E H (1990) *Organizational Culture*, American Psychologist, **45**, pp 109–19

Schmitt, N, Gooding, R Z, Noe, R A and Kirsch, M (1984) Meta-analysis of validity studies published between 1964 and 1982 and the investigation of study characteristics, *Personnel Psychology*, **37**(3), pp 407–22

Schuler, R S (1992) Strategic human resource management: linking people with the strategic needs of the business, *Organizational Dynamics*, **21**(1), pp 18–32

Schuler, R S, Dowling, P J and De Cieri, H (1993) An integrative framework of strategic international human resource management, *International Journal of Human Resource Management*, December, pp 717–64

Schuler, R S and Jackson, S E (1987) Linking competitive strategies with human resource management practices, *Academy of Management Executive*, **9**(3), pp 207–19

Schuller, T (2000) Social and human capital: the search for appropriate technomethodology, *Policy Studies*, **21**(1), pp 25–35

Schultz, T W (1961) Investment in human capital, *American Economic Review*, **51**, March, pp 1–17

Schultz, T W (1981) *Investing in People: The economics of population quality*, University of California Press, Berkeley, Calif

Schumacher, E F (1973) *Small is Beautiful*, Blond and Briggs, London

Schumacher, E F (1976/1977) Structuring work, *Industrial Participation*, Winter, pp 4–7

Schuster, J R and Zingheim, P K (1992) *The New Pay*, Lexington, New York

Scott, A (1994) *Willing Slaves? British workers under human resource management*, Cambridge University Press, Cambridge

Scullion, H (1989) International HRM, in *New Perspectives on Human Resource Management: A critical text*, ed J Storey, Routledge, London

Scullion, H (1991) Why companies prefer to use expatriates, *Personnel Management*, November, pp 32–33

Selznick, P (1957) *Leadership and Administration*, Row, Evanston, Ill

Senge, P (1990) *The Fifth Discipline: The art and practice of the learning organization*, Doubleday, London

Shaw, R B (1997) *Trust in the Balance*, Jossey Bass, San Francisco

Sheard, A (1992) Learning to improve performance, *Personnel Management*, November, pp 40–45

Sheehy, G (1976) *Passages: Predictable crises of adult life*, Dutton, New York

Silverman, D (1970) *The Theory of Organizations: A sociological framework*, Heinemann, London

Sims, R R (1994) Human resource management's role in clarifying the new psychological contract, *Human Resource Management*, **33**(3), Fall, pp 373–82

Singh, R (1989) Negotiations, in *A Handbook of Industrial Relations Practice*, ed B Towers, Kogan Page, London

Sisson, K (1990) Introducing the Human Resource Management Journal, *Human Resource Management Journal*, **1**(1), pp 1–11

Sisson, K (1995) Human resource management and the personnel function, in *Human Resource Management: A critical text*, ed J Storey, Routledge, London

Skinner, B F (1974) *About Behaviourism*, Knpf, New York

Sloan, A P (1963) *My Years With General Motors*, Doubleday, New York

Sloman, M (1999) Seize the day, *People Management*, 20 May, p 31

Smart, D (1983) *Selection Interviewing*, Wiley, New York

Smith, A (1776) *The Wealth of Nations*, John Murray, Edinburgh (Clarendon, Oxford, 1976)

Smith, J M and Robertson, I T (1986) *The Theory and Practice of Systematic Staff Selection*, Macmillan, London

Smith, M (1984) *Survey Item Blank*, MCB Publications, Bradford

Smith, M (1988) Calculating the sterling values of selection, *Guidance and Assessment Review*, **4**(1), pp 6–8

Smith, P and Morton, G (1993) Union exclusion and decollectivisation of industrial relations in contemporary Britain, *British Journal of Industrial Relations*, **31**(1), pp 97–114

Sonnenfeld, J A, Peiperl, M A and Kotter, J P (1992) Strategic determinants of managerial labour markets: a career systems view, in *Human Resource Strategies*, ed G Salaman, Sage, London

Sparrow, P R (1996) Too true to be good, *People Management*, December, pp 22–27

Sparrow, P R (1999a) International reward system: to converge or not to converge, in *International HRM: Contemporary issues in Europe*, ed C Brewster and H Harris, Routledge, London

Sparrow, P R (1999b) *The IPD Guide on International Recruitment, Selection and Assessment*, Institute of Personnel and Development, London

Sparrow, P R and Hiltrop, J-M (1997) Redefining the field of human resource management: a battle between national mindsets and forces of business transition? *Human Resource Management*, **36**(2), pp 201–19

Spearman, C (1927) *The Abilities of Man*, Macmillan, New York

Spencer, L, McClelland, D and Spencer, S (1990) *Competency Assessment Methods*, Hay/McBer Research, Boston

Spindler, G S (1994) Psychological contracts in the workplace: a lawyer's view, *Human Resource Management*, **33**(3), pp 325–33

Stacey, R D (1993) Strategy as order emerging from chaos, *Long Range Planning*, **26**(1), pp 10–17

Stern, E and Sommerlad, E (1999) *Workplace Learning, Culture and Performance*, Institute of Personnel and Development, London

Stevens, B (1990) Quoted at conference of the Institute of Personnel Management, Harrogate

Storey, J (1985) The means of management control, *Sociology*, **19**(2), pp 193–212

Storey, J (1987) Developments in the management of human resources: an interim report, *Warwick Papers on Industrial Relations* no 17, University of Warwick

Storey, J (1989) From personnel management to human resource management, in *New Perspectives on Human Resource Management*, ed J Storey, Routledge, London

Storey, J (1992a) *New Developments in the Management of Human Resources*, Blackwell, Oxford

Storey, J (1992b) HRM in action: the truth is out at last, *Personnel Management*, April, pp 28–31

Storey, J (1993) The take-up of human resource management by mainstream companies: key lessons from research, *International Journal of Human Resource Management*, 4(3), pp 529–57

Storey, J (1995) Human resource management: still marching on or marching out? in *Human Resource Management: A critical text*, ed J Storey, Routledge, London

Storey, J and Sisson, K (1990) Limits to transformation: human resource management in the British context, *Industrial Relations Journal*, 21(1), pp 60–65

Strauss, G and Sayles, L R (1972) *Personnel: The human problems of management*, Prentice-Hall, Englewood Cliffs, NJ

Tamkin, P, Barber, L and Hirsh, W (1995) *Personal Development Plans: Case studies of practice*, Institute for Employment Studies, Brighton

Tampoe, M (1993) Motivating knowledge workers: the challenge for the 1990s, *Long-range Planning*, 26(2), pp 37–44

Tan, J (2000) Knowledge management: just more buzzwords? *British Journal of Administrative Management*, March–April, pp 10–11

Tannenbaum, S I, Beard, R L and Sales, E (1992) Team building and its influence on team effectiveness: an examination of conceptual and empirical developments, in *Issues, Theory and Research in Industrial/Organizational Psychology*, ed K Kelley, North Holland, London

Taylor, F W (1911) *Principles of Scientific Management*, New York, Harper

Taylor, S (1998) *Employee Resourcing*, Institute of Personnel and Development, London

Thompson, M (1998) Trust and reward, in *Trust, Motivation and Commitment: A reader*, ed S Perkins and St J Sandringham, Strategic Remuneration Research Centre, Farringdon, London

Thurley, K (1979) *Supervision: A reappraisal*, Heinemann, London

Thurley, K (1981) Personnel management: a case for urgent treatment, *Personnel Management*, August, pp 24–29

Thurstone, L L (1940) Current issues in factor analysis, *Psychological Bulletin*, 30, pp 26–38

Toplis, J, Dulewicz, V and Fletcher, C (1991) *Psychological Testing*, Institute of Personnel Management, London

Torrington, D P (1989) Human resource management and the personnel function, in *New Perspectives on Human Resource Management*, ed J Storey, Routledge, London

Torrington, D P (1994) *International Personnel Management*, Prentice-Hall, Hemel Hempstead

Torrington, D P and Cooper, C L (1977) The management of stress in organisations and the personnel initiative, *Personnel Review*, Summer, pp 48–54

Torrington, D and Hall, L (1991) *Personnel Management: A new approach*, Prentice-Hall, Englewood Cliffs, NJ

Townley, B (1989) Selection and appraisal: reconstructing social relations? in *New Perspectives on Human Resource Management*, ed J Storey, Routledge, London

Trades Union Congress (1992) *The Quality Challenge*, TUC, London

Training Agency (TA) (1988) *Competence and Assessment*, Standards Methodology Unit, Sheffield

TA (1988–90) *The Development of Assessable Standards of Occupational Competence*, Training Agency, Sheffield

Trist, E L, Higgin, J W, Murray, H and Pollack, A B (1963) *Organizational Choice*, Tavistock, London

Truss, C (1999) Soft and hard models of HRM, in *Strategic Human Resource Management*, ed L Gratton, V H Hailey, P Stiles and C Truss, Oxford University Press, Oxford

Trussler, S (1998) The rules of the game, *Journal of Business Strategy*, **19**(1), pp 16–19

Tsui, A S and Gomez-Mejia, L R (1988) Evaluating human resource effectiveness, in *Human Resource Management: Evolving roles and responsibilities*, ed L Dyer, Bureau of National Affairs, Washington, DC

Tuckman, B (1965) Development sequences in small groups, *Psychological Bulletin*, **63**

Turner, A N and Lawrence, P R (1965) *Industrial Jobs and the Worker: An investigation of response to task attributes*, Harvard University Graduate School of Business Administration, Boston, Mass

Turnow, W W (1993) Introduction to special issue on 360-degree feedback, *Human Resource Management*, Spring, pp 311–16

Tyler, T R and Bies, R J (1990) Beyond formal procedures: the interpersonal context of procedural justice, in *Applied Social Psychology and Organizational Settings*, ed J S Carrol, Lawrence Erlbaum, Hillsdale, NJ

Tyson, S (1985) Is this the very model of a modern personnel manager? *Personnel Management*, **26**, pp 35–39

Tyson, S (1987) The management of the personnel function, *Journal of Management Studies*, September, pp 523–32

Tyson, S (1997) Human resource strategy: a process for managing the contribution of HRM to organizational performance, *International Journal of Human Resource Management*, **8**(3), pp 277–90

Tyson, S and Fell, A (1986) *Evaluating the Personnel Function*, Hutchinson, London

Tyson, S and Witcher, M (1994) Getting in gear: post-recession HR management, *Personnel Management*, August, pp 20–23

Ulrich, D (1995) Shared services: from vogue to value, *Human Resource Planning*, **18**(3), pp 12–23

Ulrich, D (1998) A new mandate for human resources, *Harvard Business Review*, January–February, pp 124–34

Ulrich, D and Black, J S (1999) Worldly wise, *People Management*, 28 October, pp 42–46

Ulrich, D and Lake, D (1990) *Organizational Capability: Competing from the inside out*, John Wiley, New York

Urwick, L F (1947) *Dynamic Administration*, Pitman, London

US Department of Labor (1993) *High Performance Work Practices and Work Performance*, US Government Printing Office, Washington, DC

Vernon, P E (1961) *The Structure of Human Abilities*, Methuen, London

Vroom, V (1964) *Work and Motivation*, Wiley, New York

Walker, J W (1992) *Human Resource Strategy*, McGraw-Hill, New York

Walsh, J (1998) HRM's full complement works better, *People Management*, 23 July, p 14

Walters, B (1983) Identifying training needs, in *A Handbook of Techniques and Strategies in Personnel Management*, ed D Guest and T Kenny, Institute of Personnel Management, London.

Walton, R E (1969) *Interpersonal Peacemaking: Confrontations and third party peacemaking*, Addison-Wesley, Reading, Mass

Walton, R E (1985a) From control to commitment in the workplace, *Harvard Business Review*, **63**, pp 76–84

Walton, R E (1985b) Towards a strategy of eliciting employee commitment based on principles of mutuality, in *HRM Trends and Challenges*, ed R E Walton and P R Lawrence, Harvard Business School Press, Boston, Mass

Walton, R E and McKersie, R B (1965) *Behavioural Theory of Labour Negotiations*, McGraw-Hill, New York

Ward, P (1995) A 360-degree turn for the better, *People Management*, February, pp 20–22

Ware, J and Barnes, L (1991) Managing interpersonal conflict, in *Managing People and Organizations*, ed J Gabarro, Harvard Business School Publications, Boston, Mass

Waterman, R (1988) *The Renewal Factor*, Bantam, New York

Watkins, K and Marsick, V (1993) *Sculpting the Learning Organization*, Falmer, London

Watson, A (1977) *The Personnel Managers*, Routledge and Kegan Paul, London

Weber, M (1946) *From Max Weber*, ed H H Gerth and C W Mills, Oxford University Press, Oxford

Wedderburn, Lord (1989) Freedom of association and philosophies of labour law, *Industrial Law Journal*, **18**, p 28

Weiner, B (1974) *Achievement Motivation and Attribution Theory*, General Learning Press, New Jersey

Welch, J (1991) Quoted in *Managing People and Organizations*, ed J Gabarro, Harvard Business School Publications, Boston, Mass

Wenger, E and Snyder, W M (2000) Communities of practice: the organizational frontier, *Harvard Business Review*, January–February, pp 33–41

West, M A and Slater, J A (1995) Teamwork: myths, reality and research, *Occupational Psychologist*, April, pp 24–29

West, P (1996) The learning organization: losing the luggage in transit? *Journal of European Industrial Training*, **18**(11), pp 30–38

Wheatley, M (1994) Is nothing sacred? *Human Resources*, Spring, pp 8–12

Whipp, R (1992) HRM: competition and strategy, in *Reassessing Human Resource Management*, ed P Blyton and P Turnbull, Sage, London

Whitehead, M (1998) Employee happiness levels impact on the bottom line, *People Management*, 10 December, p 14

Whittington, R (1993) *What Is Strategy – and Does It Matter?* Routledge, London

Wick, C W and Leon, L S (1995) Creating a learning organisation: from ideas to action, *Human Resource Management*, Summer, pp 299–311

Wickens, P (1987) *The Road to Nissan*, Macmillan, London

Williams, A, Dobson, P and Walters, M (1989) *Changing Culture: New organizational approaches*, IPA, London

Williams, S (1991) Strategy and objectives, in *The Handbook of Performance Management*, ed F Neale, Institute of Personnel Management, London

Williamson, E E and Ouchi, W C (1983) The markets and hierarchical programmes of research, origins, implications and prospects, in *Power, Efficiency and Institutions*, ed A Francis, J Turk and P Willmar, Heinemann, London

Willmott, H (1993) Strength is ignorance, slavery is freedom: managing culture in modern organizations, *Journal of Management Studies*, **29**(6), pp 515–52

Wilson, N A B (1973) *On the Quality of Working Life*, HMSO, London

Winstanley, D and Stuart-Smith K (1996) Policing performance: the ethics of performance management, *Personnel Review*, Summer, pp 66–84

Womack, J and Jones, D (1970) *The Machine That Changed the World*, Rawson, New York

Wood, R and Payne, T (1998) *Competency-based Recruitment and Selection*, Wiley, Chichester

Wood, S (1996) High commitment management and organization in the UK, *International Journal of Human Resource Management*, February, pp 41–58

Wood, S and Albanese, M (1995) Can we speak of a high commitment management on the shop floor? *Journal of Management Studies*, March, pp 215–47

Woodruffe, C (1990) *Assessment Centres*, Institute of Personnel Management, London

Woodruffe, C (1991) Competent by any other name, *Personnel Management*, September, pp 30–33

Woodward, J (1965) *Industrial Organization*, Oxford University Press, Oxford

Woodward, J (1968) Resistance to change, *Management International Review*, **8**

Wooldridge, B and Floyd, S W (1990) The strategy process, middle management involvement and organizational performance, *Strategic Management Journal*, **11**, pp 231–41

Wooldridge, E (1989) The Donovan analysis: does it still stand? *Personnel Management*, June, pp 38–42

Workplace Employee Relations Survey: Summary (1998) Stationery Office, London

Workplace Industrial Relations Survey (1990) Stationery Office, London

Wright, D S and Taylor, A (1970) *Introducing Psychology*, Penguin, Harmondsworth

Wright, P M and Snell, S A (1998) Towards a unifying framework for exploring fit and flexibility in strategic human resource management, *Academy of Management Review*, **23**(4), pp 756–72

Wright, V (1991) Performance-related pay, in *The Handbook of Performance Management*, ed F Neale, Institute of Personnel Management, London

Wright, V and Brading, L (1992) A balanced performance, *Total Quality Magazine*, October, pp 275–78

Youndt, M A (2000) Human resource considerations and value creation: the mediating role of intellectual capital, Paper delivered at National Conference of US Academy of Management, Toronto, August

Zuboff, S (1988) *In the Age of the Smart Machine*, Basic Books, New Yorks

Subject index

Author index